Greenhill Books

A HISTORY
OF THE
PENINSULAR
WAR

A HISTORY OF
THE PENINSULAR WAR

Volume I: 1807–1809
From the Treaty of Fontainebleau to the
Battle of Corunna

Volume II: January to September 1809
From the Battle of Corunna to the End of the Talavera
Campaign

Volume III: September 1809 to December 1810
Ocaña, Cadiz, Bussaco, Torres Vedras

Volume IV: December 1810 to December 1811
Masséna's Retreat, Fuentes de Oñoro, Albuera,
Tarragona

Volume V: October 1811 to August 1812
Valencia, Ciudad Rodrigo, Badajoz, Salamanca, Madrid

Volume VI: September 1, 1812 to
August 5, 1813
The Siege of Burgos, The Retreat from Burgos, The
Campaign of Vittoria, The Battles of the Pyrenees

Volume VII: August 1813 to April 14, 1814
The Capture of St. Sebastian, Wellington's Invasion of
France, Battles of the Nivelle, The Nive, Orthez and
Toulouse

A HISTORY
OF THE
PENINSULAR
WAR

General Joseph Palafox
From the Portrait by Goya in the Prado Gallery.

Walker & Cockerell Ph. Sc.

A HISTORY
OF THE
PENINSULAR
WAR

Volume II: January – September 1809
From the Battle of Corunna to the End
of the Talavera Campaign

SIR CHARLES OMAN

Greenhill Books, London
Stackpole Books, Pennsylvania

Greenhill Books

This edition of *A History of the Peninsular War*, volume II
first published 1995 by
Greenhill Books, Lionel Leventhal Limited, Park House,
1 Russell Gardens, London NW11 9NN
and
Stackpole Books, 5067 Ritter Road, Mechanicsburg,
PA 17055, USA

British Library Cataloguing in Publication Data
Oman, Sir Charles
History of the Peninsular War. – Vol. II: January – September
1809: From the Battle of Corunna to the End of the Talavera
Campaign. – New ed
I. Title
940.27
ISBN 1-85367-215-7

Library of Congress Cataloging in Publication Data
Oman, Charles William Chadwick, Sir, 1860–1946.
A history of the Peninsular War / by Charles Oman
720 p. 22 cm.
Includes index.
Contents: v. I. From the Treaty of
Fontainebleau to the Battle of
Corunna... [etc.]
1. Peninsular War, 1807–1814. I. Title.
DC231.05 1995
946'.06—dc20
95-15735

PUBLISHING HISTORY
A History of the Peninsular War, volume II, was first published
in 1903 (Oxford), and is reproduced now exactly as the original
edition, complete and unabridged, with the addition of an
Introduction by Col. John R. Elting (USA, Ret). The original
maps have been re-presented by John Richards, in the
interests of clarity.

Printed and bound in Great Britain.

A HISTORY
OF THE
PENINSULAR
WAR

PREFACE

THE second volume of this work has swelled to an even greater bulk than its predecessor. Its size must be attributed to two main causes: the first is the fact that a much greater number of original sources, both printed and unprinted, are available for the campaigns of 1809 than for those of 1808. The second is that the war in its second year had lost the character of comparative unity which it had possessed in its first. Napoleon, on quitting Spain in January, left behind him as a legacy to his brother a comprehensive plan for the conquest of the whole Peninsula. But that plan was, from the first, impracticable: and when it had miscarried, the fighting in every region of the theatre of war became local and isolated. Neither the harassed and distracted French King at Madrid, nor the impotent Spanish Junta at Seville, knew how to combine and co-ordinate the operations of their various armies into a single logical scheme. Ere long, six or seven campaigns were taking place simultaneously in different corners of the Peninsula, each of which was practically independent of the others. Every French and Spanish general fought for his own hand, with little care for what his colleagues were doing: their only unanimity was that all alike kept urging on their central governments the plea that their own particular section of the war was more critical and important than any other. If we look at the month of May, 1809, we find that the following six disconnected series of operations were all in progress at once, and that each has to be treated as a separate unit, rather than as a part of one great general scheme of strategy—(1) Soult's campaign against Wellesley in Northern Portugal, (2) Ney's invasion of the Asturias, (3) Victor's and Cuesta's movements in Estremadura, (4) Sebastiani's demonstrations against Venegas in La Mancha, (5) Suchet's contest with Blake in Aragon, (6) St. Cyr's attempt to subdue Catalonia. When a war has broken up into so many fractions, it becomes not only hard to follow but very lengthy to narrate. Fortunately for the historian and the student, a certain amount of unity is restored in July, mainly owing to the fact that the master-mind of Wellesley has been brought to bear upon the situation. When the British general attempted to combine with the Spanish armies of Estremadura and La Mancha for a common march upon Madrid, the whole of the hostile forces in the Peninsula [with the exception of those in Aragon and Catalonia] were once more drawn into a single scheme of operations. Hence the Talavera campaign is the central fact in the annals of the Peninsular War for the year 1809. I trust that it will not be considered that I have devoted a disproportionate amount of space to the setting forth and discussion of the various problems which it involved.

The details of the battle of Talavera itself have engaged my special attention. I thought it worth while to go very carefully over the battlefield, which fortunately remains much as it was in 1809. A walk around it explained many difficulties, but suggested certain others, which I have done my best to solve.

In several other chapters of this volume I dis-

covered that a personal inspection of localities produced
most valuable results.   At Oporto, for example, I
found Wellesley's passage of the Douro assuming
a new aspect when studied on the spot.   Not one
of the historians who have dealt with it has taken the
trouble to mention that the crossing was effected at
a point where the Douro runs between lofty and precipitous cliffs, towering nearly 200 feet above the
water's edge!   Yet this simple fact explains how it
came to pass that the passage was effected at all—
the French, on the plateau above the river, could not
see what was going on at the bottom of the deeply
sunk gorge, which lies in a 'dead angle' to any
observer who has not come forward to the very edge
of the cliff.   I have inserted a photograph of the spot,
which will explain the situation at a glance.   From
Napier's narrative and plan I am driven to conclude
that he had either never seen the ground, or had forgotten its aspect after the lapse of years.

A search in the Madrid *Deposito de la Guerra*
produced a few important documents for the Talavera
campaign, and was made most pleasant by the
extreme courtesy of the officers in charge.   It is
curious to find that our London Record Office
contains a good many Spanish dispatches which do
not survive at Madrid.   This results from the laudable
zeal with which Mr. Frere, when acting as British
minister at Seville, sent home copies of every Spanish
document, printed or unprinted, on which he could
lay his hands.   Once or twice he thus preserved
invaluable 'morning states' of the Peninsular armies,
which it would otherwise have been impossible to
recover.   Among our other representatives in Spain
Captain Carroll was the only one who possessed to a

similar degree this admirable habit of collecting original documents and statistics. His copious 'enclosures' to Lord Castlereagh are of the greatest use for the comprehension of the war in the Asturias and Galicia.

Neither Napier nor any other historian of the Peninsular War has gone into the question of Beresford's reorganization of the Portuguese army. Comparing English and Portuguese documents, I have succeeded in working it out, and trust that Chapter III of Section XIII, and Appendix No. V, may suffice to demonstrate Beresford's very real services to the allied cause.

It is my pleasant duty to acknowledge much kind help that I have received from correspondents on both sides of the sea, who have come to my aid in determining points of difficulty. Of those in England I must make particular notice of Colonel F. A. Whinyates, R.A., a specialist in all matters connected with the British artillery. I owe to him my Appendix No. XI, which he was good enough to draw up, as well as the loan of several unpublished diaries of officers of his own arm, from which I have extracted some useful and interesting facts. I must also express my obligation to Mr. E. Mayne, for information relating to Sir Robert Wilson's Loyal Lusitanian Legion, of which his relative, Colonel W. Mayne, was in 1809 the second-in-command. The excerpts which he was kind enough to collect for me have proved of great service, and could not have been procured from any other quarter. Nor must I omit to thank two other correspondents, Colonel Willoughby Verner and the Rev. Alexander Craufurd, for their notes concerning the celebrated 'Light Division,' in which the one is interested as the historian of the old 95th, and the other as the grandson of Robert Craufurd, of famous memory.

Of helpers from beyond the Channel I must make special mention of Commandant Balagny, the author of *Napoléon en Espagne*, who has supplied me with a great number of official documents from Paris, and in especial with a quantity of statistics, many of them hitherto unpublished, which serve to fix the strength and the losses of various French corps in 1809. I also owe to him my Appendix VI (iii), a most interesting *résumé* of the material in the French archives relating to the strange 'Oporto conspiracy' of Captain Argenton and his confederates. This obscure chapter of the history of the Peninsular War is, I think, brought out in its true proportions by the juxtaposition of the English and French documents. It is clear that Soult's conduct was far more sinister than Napier will allow, and also that the plot to depose the Marshal was the work of a handful of military intriguers, not of the great body of highly-placed conspirators in whose existence the mendacious Argenton has induced some historians to believe.

At Madrid General Arteche placed at my disposal, with the most bountiful liberality, his immense stores of knowledge, which I had learnt to appreciate long before, as a conscientious student of his *Guerra de la Independencia*. He pointed out to me many new sources, which had escaped my notice, and was good enough to throw light on many problems which had been vexing me. For his genial kindness I cannot too strongly express my obligation.

Of the officers at the Madrid *Deposito de la Guerra*, whose courtesy I have mentioned above, I must give special thanks to Captain Emilio Figueras, from whom (just as these pages are going to press) I have received some additional figures relating to the Army of Estremadura in 1809.

Finally, as in my first volume, I must make special acknowledgement of the assistance of two helpers in Oxford—the indefatigable compiler of the Index, and Mr. C. E. Doble, whose corrections and suggestions have been as valuable in 1903 as in 1902.

C. OMAN.

ALL SOULS COLLEGE,
June 20, 1903.

CONTENTS

SECTION IX

AFTER CORUNNA (JAN.–FEB. 1809)

SECTION X

THE AUTUMN AND WINTER CAMPAIGN IN CATALONIA

SECTION XI

THE SECOND SIEGE OF SARAGOSSA (DEC. 1808–FEB. 1809)

SECTION XII

THE SPRING CAMPAIGN IN LA MANCHA AND ESTREMADURA

SECTION XIII

SOULT'S INVASION OF PORTUGAL

CONTENTS

APPENDICES

MAPS AND PLANS

ILLUSTRATIONS

ERRATA IN VOL. II

The following facts I discovered in Madrid and Lisbon when it was too late to correct the chapters in which the mis-statements occur.

(1) Page 82, note 2. I have found from a Madrid document that part, though not the whole, of the Regiment of Baza was present at Valls. One battalion was left behind with Wimpffen : one marched with Reding : about 800 men therefore must be added to my estimate of the Spanish infantry.

(2) Page 318, note 2. I found in Lisbon that the regiments which marched with Beresford to Lamego were not (as I had supposed) nos. 7 and 19, but nos. 2 and 14, with the 4th cazadores. Those which joined from the direction of Almeida were two battalions of no. 11 (1st of Almeida) and one of no. 9.

(3) Page 366. A dispatch of Beresford at Lisbon clears up my doubts as to Silveira's culpability. Beresford complains that the latter lost a whole day by marching from Amarante to Villa Pouca without orders ; the dispatch directing him to take the path by Mondim thus reached him only when he had gone many miles on the wrong road. The time lost could never be made up.

SECTION IX
AFTER CORUNNA

CHAPTER I

THE CONSEQUENCES OF MOORE'S DIVERSION: RALLY OF
THE SPANISH ARMIES: BATTLE OF UCLES

WITH the departure of Napoleon from Madrid on December 21,
the offensive action of the French army in central Spain came to
a stand. The Emperor had taken away with him the field army,
which had been destined to deliver those blows at Lisbon and
Seville that were to end the war. The troops which he had left
behind him in the neighbourhood of Madrid were inadequate in
numbers for any further advance, and were forced to adopt
a defensive attitude. The only regions in which the invaders
continued to pursue an active policy were Aragon and Catalonia,
from which, on account of their remoteness, the Emperor had
not withdrawn any troops for his great encircling movement
against Sir John Moore. In both those provinces important
operations began on the very day on which Bonaparte set out
to hunt the English army: it was on December 21 that Lannes
commenced the second siege of Saragossa, and that St. Cyr,
after relieving Barcelona, scattered the army of Catalonia at
the battle of Molins de Rey. But the campaigns of Aragon
and Catalonia were both of secondary importance, when compared with the operations in central Spain. As the whole history
of the war was to show, the progress of events in the valley of
the lower Ebro and in the Catalan hills never exercised much
influence on the affairs of Castile and Portugal. It is not,
therefore, too much to assert that it was Moore's march on
Sahagun, and that march alone, which paralysed the main
scheme of the Emperor for the conquest of Spain.

Between December 21 and January 2 the central reserves

of the French army had been hurried away to the Esla and the plains of northern Leon. It was not till the new year had come that the Emperor began to think of sending some of them back to the neighbourhood of Madrid. The 8th Corps had been incorporated with the 2nd, and sent in pursuit of Moore : the corps of Ney and the division of Lapisse were left to support Soult in his invasion of Galicia. The Imperial Guard marched back to Valladolid. Of all the troops which had been distracted to the north-west, only Dessolles' division of the Central Reserve returned to the capital. Such a reinforcement was far from being enough to enable Joseph Bonaparte, and his military adviser Jourdan, to assume the offensive towards the valleys of the Tagus and Guadiana. The consequences of Moore's diversion were not only far-reaching but prolonged : it was not till the middle of March that the army of the king was able to resume the attempt to march on Seville, and by that time the condition of affairs had been profoundly modified, to the advantage of the Spaniards.

The intervening time was not one of rest for Joseph and his army. Their movements require careful attention. When Napoleon hurried the main body of his troops across the Somosierra in pursuit of the British, he left behind him the corps of Victor, shorn of Lapisse's division, the whole of the corps of Lefebvre[1], and the three independent cavalry divisions of Lasalle, Latour-Maubourg and Milhaud—in all 8,000 horse and 28,000 foot with ninety guns. There was also the Royal Guard of King Joseph, four battalions of foot, and a regiment of horse, beside two skeleton regiments of Spanish deserters, which the 'Intrusive King' was raising as the nucleus of a new army of his own[2].

[1] Save two Dutch and one German regiment of Leval's division, which had been left behind on garrison duty in Biscay and Old Castile.

[2] This was done by the Emperor's orders. The *cadres* of these regiments, called *Royal-Étranger* and *Royal-Napoléon*, were formed partly of Frenchmen, partly of Spanish *Afrancesados*. The rank and file of the first regiment were to be raised from the Swiss and Germans who had served in the old Spanish army : some of them had adhered to the French, others, when taken prisoners in the late campaign, had offered to serve King Joseph. The second regiment was to be composed of native Spaniards. See *Correspondance de Napoléon*, 14,531.

Of these troops the incomplete German division of Leval (2nd of the 4th Corps) and King Joseph's guards formed the garrison of Madrid. This force seeming too small, the division of Ruffin (1st of the 1st Corps) was ordered in to reinforce them. The rest of the army lay in two concentric semicircles outside Madrid : the inner semicircle was formed of infantry : there was a regiment at Guadalajara[1], a whole division under Marshal Victor himself at Aranjuez[2], and two divisions of the 4th Corps under Marshal Lefebvre at Talavera[3]. Outside these troops was a great cavalry screen. In front of Victor the three cavalry brigades of Latour-Maubourg's division lay respectively at Tarancon, Ocaña, and Madridejos, watching the three roads from La Mancha. West of them lay Milhaud's division of dragoons, in front of Talavera, in the direction of Navalmoral and San Vincente, observing the passes of the Sierra de Toledo. Lastly, as a sort of advanced guard in the direction of Estremadura, Lasalle's light cavalry had pushed on to the great bridge of Almaraz, behind which the wrecks of the mutinous armies of Belvedere and San Juan were beginning to collect, under their new commander Galluzzo[4].

The Emperor's parting orders to Jourdan had been to send forward Lasalle and Lefebvre to deal a blow at the Estremaduran army. They had, he wrote, twice the numbers necessary to break up the small force of disorganized troops in front of them. On December 24, Lefebvre was to cross the Tagus, scatter Galluzzo's men to the winds, and then come back to Talavera, after building a *tête de pont* at Almaraz. Lasalle's cavalry would be capable of looking after what was left of this force, for it would not give trouble again for many a week to come. Victor, on the side of La Mancha, must keep watch on any movements of the Spaniards from the direction of Cuenca or the Sierra Morena. He would have no difficulty in holding them off, for ' all the débris of the insurgent armies combined could

---

[1] The 55th, a stray remnant left behind by Dessolles.

[2] Division of Villatte. It had one battalion detached, along with the 26th Chasseurs, at Toledo.

[3] Division of Valence and Sebastiani.

[4] Lasalle's division (often altered in composition) now consisted of the 10th and 26th Chasseurs, 9th Dragoons and Polish Lanceis.

not face even the 8,000 French cavalry left in front of them —
to say nothing of the infantry behind [1].

The first portion of the orders of the Emperor was duly
carried out. On December 24 the Duke of Dantzig advanced
from Talavera upon the bridges of Arzobispo and Almaraz,
behind which lay 6,000 or 7,000 of Galluzzo's dispirited levies.
He made no more than a feint at the first-mentioned passage,
but attacking the more important bridge of Almaraz carried it
at the first rush, and took the four guns which Galluzzo had
mounted on the southern bank to command the defile. The
Spaniards, scattered in all directions, abandoned the banks of
the Tagus, and placed themselves in safety behind the rugged
Sierra de Guadalupe. So far the Emperor's design was carried
out: but Lefebvre then took a most extraordinary step. Instead
of returning, as he had been ordered, to Talavera, and remaining
in that central position till further orders should be sent him,
he went off on an inexplicable adventure of his own. Leaving
only Lasalle's cavalry and two Polish battalions on the Tagus,
he turned north, as if intending to join the Emperor, crossed
the mountains between New and Old Castile, and on January 5
appeared at Avila in the latter province [2]. Not only was the
march in complete contravention of the Emperor's orders, but it
was carried out in disobedience to five separate dispatches sent
from Madrid by Jourdan, in the name of King Joseph. Lefebvre
paid no attention whatever to the 'lieutenant of the Emperor,'
in spite of vehement representations to the effect that he was
exposing Madrid by this eccentric movement. It was indeed
an unhappy inspiration that led him to Avila, for at this
precise moment the Spaniards were commencing a wholly unexpected offensive advance against the Spanish capital, which
Lefebvre, if he had remained at Talavera, might have aided in
repelling. Much incensed at his disobedience Napoleon deprived
him of the command of the 4th Corps, and sent him back to
France. 'This marshal,' he wrote to King Joseph, 'does nothing

---

[1] See for all these details *Nap. Corresp.*, 14,609.

[2] Napier misrepresents this move in the strangest way, saying (i. 364)
merely that 'the Duke of Dantzig recrossed the Tagus and took post
between Talavera and Plasencia.' Avila is fifty miles north of these places,
and on the other side of the Guadarrama.

but make blunders : he cannot seize the meaning of the orders sent him.   It is impossible to leave him in command of a corps ; —which is a pity, for he is a brave enough fellow on the battle-field [1].'   Sebastiani, Lefebvre's senior divisional general, replaced him in command of his corps.

The new Spanish advance upon Madrid requires a word of explanation.   We have seen that the weary and dilapidated Army of the Centre, now commanded by the Duke of Infantado, had reached Cuenca on December 10, after escaping from the various snares which Napoleon had set for it during its march from Calatayud to the valley of the upper Tagus.   When he had escaped from Bessières' pursuit, the duke proceeded to give his army a fortnight's much-needed rest in the mountain villages round Cuenca.   He sent back to Valencia the wrecks of Roca's division, which had originally been raised in that kingdom.   It had dwindled down to 1,455 men, from its original 8,000 [2].   The other troops, the 2nd, 3rd, and 4th divisions of the old army of Andalusia [3], had not suffered quite so much, as they had not been seriously engaged at Tudela, but they were half-starved and very disorderly.   Infantado was forced to shoot an officer and two sergeants for open mutiny before he could restore the elements of discipline [4].

The province of Cuenca is the most thinly peopled and desolate of all the regions of Spain [5], and though some stores and food were procured from Valencia, it was impossible to re-equip the army in a satisfactory way.   Winter clothing, in particular, was absolutely unprocurable, and if the men had not been placed under roofs in Cuenca and the villages around, they

[1] Napoleon to Joseph from Valladolid, Jan. 9, *Nap. Corresp.*, 14,671.

[2] See the figures furnished by the Valencian Junta in Arguelles, ii. 74. It must be remembered that 4,800 of the division had escaped to Saragossa, and took part in its defence.

[3] The 1st division had only four battalions present, the others having been at Madrid, in the army of San Juan.

[4] The officer, a Lieutenant Santiago, had refused to march on Cuenca, and when the order was repeated, unlimbered his battery across the road and threatened to fire on the troops who were marching in that direction. See Arteche, iii. 12.

[5] It had only 311 inhabitants to the square league in 1803, as compared with 926 in Andalusia, and 2,009 in Guipuzcoa.

must have perished of cold.   But a fortnight's rest did much for
them : many stragglers came up from the rear, a few reinforcements were received, and to the surprise of the whole army the
brigade of the Conde de Alacha, which had been cut off from
the rest of the troops on the day of Tudela, turned up intact to
join its division.   This detachment, it will be remembered[1], had
been left in the mountains near Agreda, to observe the advance
of Marshal Ney : after the rout it had nearly fallen into the
hands of the 6th Corps, and had been forced to turn off into
obscure bypaths.   Then, passing in haste between the French
divisions in New Castile, it had finally succeeded in reaching
Cuenca.

Infantado, finding that the French still hung back and
advanced no further into his mountain refuge, proceeded to
reorganize his army ; the three weakened battalions of the old
line regiments were consolidated into two or often into one.
The four divisions of the original Andalusian host were amal-
gamated into two, with an extra 'vanguard' and 'reserve'
composed of the best troops[2]. This rearrangement had not
yet been fully completed when the duke made up his mind
that he would venture on an advance against Madrid.   He could
learn of nothing save cavalry in his front, and he had received
early notice of the departure of Napoleon to the north.
Giving the command of his vanguard and the greater part of his
cavalry to General Venegas, he bade him descend into the plains,
and endeavour to surprise the brigade of dragoons which lay
at Tarancon[3].   This task Venegas attempted to execute on
Christmas Day : he had already turned the town with half
his force, and placed himself across the line of retreat of the
dragoons, before they knew of his approach.   Warned, just in
time of his danger, the French brigadier resolved to cut his
way through : he charged down on the enemy, who fell into
a line of battalion squares with long intervals between them.
Dashing between the squares the two regiments got through
with the loss of fifty or sixty men.   The Spanish cavalry, which
arrived late on the field, made no attempt to pursue.   On the
same day Infantado had sent out another column under

---

[1] See vol. i. p. 437.   [2] For these changes see Appendix I.
[3] Perreimond's brigade of Latour-Maubourg's division.

General Senra, with orders to march on Aranjuez: finding that it was held not only by cavalry but by a heavy force of infantry, the Spanish brigadier wisely halted at a discreet distance, for which he was sharply taken to task by his chief. It is certain that if he had gone on, Victor would have made mincemeat of his little force of 4,000 men.

Although the advance of Venegas and Senra soon stopped short, the news that the Spaniards were descending in force into the plain of New Castile was most discomposing to King Joseph, who was at this moment very weak in troops. Lefebvre had just started on his eccentric march to Avila: Dessolles was not yet back from the north, and there was no disposable reserve at Madrid save the single division of Ruffin, for the king's guards and Leval's Germans were barely enough to hold down the capital, and could not be moved. The situation was made worse by the revolt of several of the small towns of the upper Tagus, including Chinchon and Colmenar, which rose under the belief that Infantado's army would soon be at their gates. There was nothing between the duke and Madrid save the single infantry division of Villatte, which lay with Marshal Victor at Aranjuez, and the six dragoon regiments of Latour-Maubourg, a force of little more than 9,000 sabres and bayonets.

Fortunately for King Joseph, Infantado was a most incapable general, and allowed his opportunity to slip by. By driving in the French cavalry screen, he had given notice of his existence, and spread alarm up to the gates of Madrid. But in order to profit by the situation he should have dashed in at once, before the enemy had time to draw together. If he had marched from Cuenca with his reserves, in the wake of Venegas, he could have brought 20,000 men to bear upon Victor, before the latter could receive the very moderate succours that King Joseph could send him. Instead of doing anything of the kind, he remained quiescent at his head quarters, and did not even send Venegas any further orders, either to advance or to retreat. From December 26 to January 11, the Spanish vanguard lay at Tarancon, as if with the express intention of giving the French time to concentrate. The duke meanwhile, as his dispatches show, was drawing up a grandiose plan of operations, which included not only the eviction of King Joseph from Madrid, but the cutting of Napoleon's communication and the raising of the siege of Saragossa! He was most anxious to induce the Central Junta to move forward all their other forces to aid him. But they could do nothing, so deplorable was the state of their army, but bid the weak division of 6,000 men, which was guarding the Sierra Morena, to begin a demonstration in La Mancha. In pursuance of this order Del Palacio made a forward movement, as dangerous as it was useless, to Villaharta on the upper Guadiana.

Jourdan and the Intrusive King, meanwhile, were for ten days in a state of great anxiety, expecting every moment to hear that the whole Spanish army had descended from the mountains and thrown itself upon the upper Tagus. They ordered Victor to move from Aranjuez to Arganda to parry such a blow, and made preparations for reinforcing him with Ruffin's division, while the rest of the garrison of Madrid, with the French civilians, and the mass of *Afrancesados*, were to shut themselves up in the forts on the Retiro, being too few to hold the entire city. But the expected advance of Infantado never occurred, and Jourdan and Victor were able to put down the insurrection of the little towns in the plain without any interruption. Chinchon was stormed, and the whole male population put to the sword; at Colmenar there were executions on a large scale, and a fine of 50,000 piastres was levied. The rest of the insurgents fled to the hills [1].

On January 8, 1809, the fears of Joseph and Jourdan came to a happy end, for on that day the division of Dessolles marched in from Old Castile, while on the 10th the 4th Corps appeared, having been sent back in haste from Avila by the Emperor. This reinforcement of more than 20,000 men completely cleared the situation. The French line of defence could now be re-established: Valence's Polish division was placed at Toledo: Leval's Germans, completed by the arrival of their belated Dutch brigade, were sent to Talavera. Sebastiani's

---

[1] Jourdan confesses to this massacre in the most open way. ' Le 27e Léger s'étant présenté aux portes de Chinchon, fut reçu à coups de fusil. Cette provocation occasionna la perte des habitants : ils furent *tous* tués, et la ville incendiée.' *Mémoires du Maréchal Jourdan,* 139.

division, with Dessolles and the king's guard, remained to garrison Madrid. Ruffin was sent out to join Victor, who was ordered to march at once on Tarancon and fall upon the Spanish corps which had remained there in such strange torpidity since Christmas day [1]. The Emperor, sending these orders from Valladolid, expressed himself in a somewhat contemptuous strain as to his brother's fears. 'The army of Castaños' (i. e. of Infantado) 'was as great a fiction as that of La Romana: rumour made them 20,000 strong, while really there were not more than 5,000 of them [2]. Victor had ten times as many men as were necessary for clearing off the Spaniards. The panic at Madrid had been absurd and discreditable: all that was wanted was to catch and hang a dozen *mauvais sujets*, and the capital would keep quiet.'

On January 12 Victor marched from Aranjuez with the twenty-one battalions of Villatte's and Ruffin's divisions, the squadrons of light horse which formed his corps-cavalry, and the three brigades of dragoons composing the division of Latour-Maubourg—in all some 12,000 foot and 3,500 horse. He did not find Venegas at Tarancon: on hearing that the French were massing in front of him, that officer had called in the outlying brigade of Senra, and had retired ten miles to Ucles, in the foot-hills of the mountains of Cuenca. He sent news of Victor's approach to Infantado, but the latter gave him no definite orders either to fight or to retreat. He merely forwarded to him three or four more battalions of infantry, and announced that he was coming up from Cuenca with the reserves: he fixed no date for his probable arrival.

Much troubled by the want of definite orders, Venegas doubted whether he ought to hold his ground and await his chief, or fall back into the mountains. After some hesitation he resolved to take the more dangerous course, tempted by the fine position of Ucles, which offered every advantage for a defensive action. He had with him about 9,500 infantry in twenty-two very weak battalions, some of which had no more than 250 or 300 bayonets. Of cavalry he had nine incomplete

---

[1] All these movements are most clearly set forth in Jourdan's *Mémoires*, by far the best authority for the campaign of Ucles.

[2] *Nap. Corresp.*, 14,637 and 14,684.

regiments, giving only 1,800 sabres [1]. There were but five guns with the army, of which one had broken down, and was not fit for service. The town of Ucles lies in the midst of a long ridge stretching north-east and south-west, with a steep slope towards the plain, from which the French were approaching. Venegas drew up his men in a single long line, with the town in the centre. Four battalions were barricaded in Ucles: six took post to the left of it, eight to the right. Only one was held back in reserve, but three with four regiments of cavalry were left out in front, to observe the French advance, in the neighbourhood of the village of Tribaldos. The four guns and the remainder of the cavalry were drawn up before the town. It is almost needless to point out the faults of this order-of-battle—overgreat extension and the want of a reserve. The position was too long for the numbers available. Moreover the men were not in good fighting trim: though several of the old regiments from Baylen were among them, their spirits were low: they had not yet recovered from the dreadful fatigues of the retreat from Tudela, and they had little confidence in their leaders.

Victor marched from Tarancon at daybreak on January 13, with one division on each of the two routes which lead eastward from that place, Villatte's on the southern road which goes directly to Ucles, Ruffin's on the longer and more circuitous path, which, running parallel to the other, ultimately rejoins it at Carrascosa some way behind that town. The majority of Latour-Maubourg's cavalry accompanied the former column.

Already on the previous night Victor's vedettes had discovered the Spanish outpost at Tribaldos: very early on the following morning it was driven in by the advance of Villatte's column, and joined the main body of the army of Venegas. The Marshal then pushed forward to the foot of the hills, to reconnoitre the enemy's position. Having discerned the lie of the ground, and the distribution of the Spanish forces, his mind was soon made up. Orders were promptly sent to Ruffin to leave the road on which he was advancing, and to close in upon the right flank

[1] Beside the twenty battalions given in the Appendix to Arteche, iv, Venegas's narrative shows that at least two more (Baylen and Navas de Tolosa) were present.

and rear of Venegas's army. Meanwhile Villatte and the cavalry drew up in front of Ucles, with a strength of about 7,000 bayonets and 2,500 sabres. The dragoons were placed in the centre; in front of them was ranged a battery, which commenced to shell the town and the Spanish horse drawn up before its gates. This was only a demonstration: the real blow was to be given by an attack on the Spanish left, where the hillside was of easier access than on the steep and rocky northern end of the ridge. Villatte's second brigade, the 94th and 95th regiments, executed a circular march under the eyes of the enemy, and having turned their extreme flank, rapidly climbed the hill and formed up at right angles to the Spanish line. These six battalions fell upon the exposed wing and rolled it up without much difficulty, till they arrived under the very walls of Ucles, driving the enemy before them. Venegas, who was watching the fight from the court of the monastery which dominates the town, had tried to hurry up reinforcements from his right wing: but they arrived too late to be of any use. When the attack on the enemy's left was seen to be making good progress, and the attention of the Spaniards was distracted to that point, Victor directed the first brigade of Villatte's division to assail the steep hill on the Spanish right. They carried it with ease, for half the defenders had been withdrawn to reinforce the left, and the rest were demoralized by the evident disaster on the other flank. The whole of Venegas's army fled eastward without any further endeavour to hold their ground, the considerable force of cavalry in the centre making no attempt, as it would appear, to cover the retreat of the foot. Such rearguard as there was consisted of two or three infantry battalions under General Giron.

Suddenly the Spaniards of the right wing and centre saw rising up in front of them, as they fled, an imposing line of French infantry, barring their further progress. This force consisted of the nine battalions of Ruffin's division. They had lost their way while seeking for the Spanish flank, and (like Ferguson at Roliça) made too wide a circle to enable them to intervene in the actual fighting. But the very length of their turning movement proved advantageous, as they had now got into the direct rear of the retreating army. Driven on by the pursuing dragoons of Latour-Maubourg, the Spaniards found themselves rushing into the very arms of Ruffin's division. The disaster was complete, and more than half of Venegas's army was encircled and captured. Most of the cavalry, indeed, escaped, by dispersing and riding rapidly round the flanks of Ruffin's line. But the slow-moving infantry was trapped: a few battalions from the left wing got off to the south-east, and General Giron with a remnant of his brigade cut his way through a gap between two French regiments. All the rest had to surrender.

Of Venegas's 11,000 men, about 1,000 had been killed or wounded: four generals, seventeen colonels, 306 other officers and 5,560 rank and file were captured [1]. The French secured the four guns which formed the sole artillery of the beaten army, and twenty standards [2]. Their own loss was insignificant —Victor returned his total casualties at 150 men, and probably did not much understate them, as he had met with no serious resistance.

Though they had suffered so little, the French showed great ferocity after the fight. They not only sacked the town of Ucles, but executed in cold blood sixty-nine of its notables, including many monks, who were accused of having fired on the assailants from their convent windows. When the column of Spanish prisoners was sent off to Madrid, orders were given (it is said by Victor himself) that those who would not keep up with the rest should be shot, and we have good French authority to the effect that this was regularly done; thirty or more a day, mostly the wounded and the sick, were shot by the wayside when they dropped behind [3].

What, meanwhile, had happened to the Spanish Commander-in-chief, and the 9,000 men whom he had retained at Cuenca? Infantado had started to join Venegas on January 12: he slept that night at Horcajada, fifteen miles to the east of Ucles.

[1] These numbers are probably exact: Jourdan quotes them from his own official report to Berthier of Jan. 20. See his *Mémoires*, p. 144.

[2] As the wrecks of fifteen or sixteen battalions had surrendered, there seems no reason to doubt the number of standards. But the Spaniards asserted that Victor eked out his trophies, by taking down the old battle-flags of the knights of Santiago from their church in Ucles.

[3] Cf. the *Mémoires* of Rocca (of the 2nd Hussars, Victor's corps-cavalry), p. 68, and Schepeler.

Resuming his march next morning, he had got as far as Carras-cosa, when a disorderly mob of 2,000 routed infantry hurtled into his vanguard. Questioning the fugitives, he learnt the details of the battle of Ucles, and found that the victorious army of the French was only five miles away. Then with a promptitude very different from his torpor of the last three weeks, the duke turned his column to the rear, and made off with all speed. He first returned to his base at Cuenca to pick up his baggage and stores, and then marched by vile cross-roads and in abominable weather to Chinchilla in the kingdom of Murcia, which he reached on January 20. His artillery, forced to go at a snail's pace among the hills and torrents, and escorted by a single cavalry regiment only, was surprised and captured by Digeon's dragoons at Tortola, a few miles to the south of Cuenca (Jan. 18). Fifteen guns were lost on this occasion: several of the French authorities ingeniously add them to the trophies of Ucles, and write as if they had all been taken from Venegas in open battle [1].

Victor after occupying Cuenca, and finding that Infantado was now too far away to be pursued with any chance of success, turned down into the plains of La Mancha, to strike at the small Andalusian force which had advanced under Del Palacio, to lend countenance to Infantado's projects for a march on Madrid. This division, some 6,000 strong, had reached Villa-harta on the upper Guadiana, but when the news of Ucles arrived, its commander hastily drew it back to the foot of the passes. Finding no enemy to attack, Victor, after crossing La Mancha unopposed, took up his post at Madridejos, on the high-road between Madrid and the Despeña-Perros, and waited for further orders from Head Quarters.

It was only after the victory of Ucles that King Joseph was permitted by his brother to make his formal entry into Madrid. Up to this moment he had been told to stop at the Palace of the Pardo, far outside the walls, and only to pay furtive and unostentatious visits to his official abode in the city. When the inhabitants of the capital had been sufficiently impressed by

[1] Notably the ever-inaccurate *Victoires et Conquêtes*, and Thiers. The usually-sensible Belmas makes the Spanish prisoners amount to 13,000 men, two thousand more than Venegas ever put in line.

the arrival of the numerous columns of the 4th Corps and of Dessolles, and had seen the banners and the prisoners taken at Ucles paraded through their streets, their king was once more sent among them. Joseph made his appearance on January 22, passed through a long lane of French bayonets to the church of San Isidro, where a *Te Deum* was chanted for the late victories, and then entered his palace. Here he received numerous deputations of Spaniards who swore him fealty. But the moral effect of these oaths was not very great, for the local notables attended under the pressure of the bayonet. Napoleon had sent orders that every town in Castile of more than 2,000 souls must dispatch delegates to Madrid, or the consequences would be unpleasant[1]. The delegates appeared, but it may be guessed with what feelings they mouthed their oaths and their protestations of joy and loyalty. Yet Joseph, determined to play the part of the benevolent monarch, took the whole farce seriously, and answered with lavish declarations of his love and sympathy for the great Spanish nation. Sentiments of the kind were to be the staple of his fruitless and copious oratory for the next four years. His heart would have sunk within him if only he could have recognized their futility : but 1809 was but just beginning, and he was far from realizing the full meaning of his position : it took a very long time to thoroughly disenchant this hard-working and well-meaning prince.

[1] *Nap. Corresp.*, 14,729, from Valladolid, Jan. 16.

SECTION IX: CHAPTER II

NAPOLEON'S DEPARTURE FROM SPAIN: HIS PLANS FOR
THE TERMINATION OF THE WAR: THE COUNTER-PLANS
OF THE JUNTA

FOUR days after the battle of Ucles Napoleon quitted Spain.
He had rested at Valladolid from January 6 to January 17,
after his return from the pursuit of Sir John Moore. Though
he had failed to entrap the British Army he was not discontented with his achievements. He was fully convinced that he
had broken the back of the Spanish insurrection, and that he
could safely return to France, leaving the completion of the
work to his brother and his marshals. He was anxious to hear
that Saragossa had fallen, and that the English had been driven
out of the Peninsula. When these two events should have come
to pass, his armies might resume, under the guidance of his
subordinates, the original advance against Portugal and Andalusia which had been so effectually frustrated by Moore's daring
move.

Meanwhile he spent full eleven days at Valladolid, busy with
all manner of desk-work, connected not merely with Spain, but
with the affairs of the whole continent. He was evidently
anxious to leave an impression of terror behind him: he hec-
tored and bullied the unfortunate Spanish deputations that
were compelled to come before him in the most insulting fashion.
His harangues generally wound up with the declaration that if
he was ever forced to come back to Spain in arms, he would
remove his brother Joseph, and divide the realm into subject
provinces, which should be governed by martial law. Some
French soldiers (probably marauders) having been assassinated,
he arrested and threatened to hang the whole municipality of
Valladolid, finally releasing them only when three persons
accused (rightly or wrongly) of the murders were delated to him

and executed. He sent advice to King Joseph to deal in the same way with Madrid: nothing would keep the capital quiet, he wrote, but a good string of executions[1]. It was to be many years before he realized that hanging did no good in Spain, and was only repaid by additional assassinations. In return for this good advice to his brother, he extorted from him fifty of the choicest pictures of the royal gallery at Madrid; but in compensation Joseph was invited to annex all that he might choose from the private collections of the exiled Spanish nobility and the monasteries of the capital[2].

Suggestions have sometimes been made that Napoleon hastened his departure from Spain, because he saw that the suppression of the insurrection would take a much longer time than he had originally supposed, and because he wished to transfer to other hands the lengthy and inglorious task of hunting down the last armies of the Junta. This view is certainly erroneous: his three months' stay in Spain had not opened the Emperor's eyes to the difficulties of the business that he had taken in hand. Though many of his couriers and aides-de-camp had already been ambuscaded and shot by the peasantry, though he was already beginning to see that a blockhouse and a garrison would have to be placed at every stage on the high-roads, he believed that these sinister signs were temporary, and that the country-side, after a few sanguinary lessons had been given, would sink down into the quiet of despair.

His final legacy to his brother, on departing, was a long dispatch giving a complete plan of operations for the next campaign. Soult, after forcing the English to embark, was to march on Oporto. Napoleon calculated that he ought to capture it on February 1, and that on February 10 he would be

---

[1] 'Faites donc pendre une douzaine d'individus à Madrid: il n'y manque point de mauvais sujets, et sans cela il n'y aura rien de fait.' *Nap. Corresp.*, 14,684. Compare Lecestre, *Lettres inédites de Napoléon*, i. 275, where orders are given that thirty persons, who had already been acquitted by the civil tribunals, should be rearrested, tried again before a court martial, and promptly shot! Napoleon to Joseph, Jan. 16, 1809.

[2] 'Je préfèrerais que vous prissiez tous les tableaux qui se trouvent dans les maisons confisquées et dans les couvents supprimés, et que vous me fissiez présent d'une cinquantaine de chefs-d'œuvre. Vous sentez qu'il ne faut que de bonnes choses.' *Nap. Corresp.*, 14,717.

in front of Lisbon. The Portuguese levies he practically disregarded as a fighting force, and he was ignorant that there still remained 8,000 or 10,000 British troops on the Tagus, who would serve to stiffen their resistance.

When Soult should have captured Oporto, and be well on the way to Lisbon, Victor was to go forward with his own 1st Corps, the division of Leval from the 4th Corps, and the cavalry of Milhaud, Latour-Maubourg, and Lasalle. He was to strike at Estremadura, occupy Merida and Badajoz, and join hands with Soult along the Tagus. Lisbon being reduced, Victor was to borrow a division from Soult and march on Seville with 40,000 men. With such a force, as the Emperor calculated, he would subdue the whole of Andalusia with ease.

Meanwhile Saragossa must (as Napoleon rightly thought) fall some time in February. When it was disposed of, the 3rd and 5th Corps would provide a garrison for Aragon, and then march on Valencia, which would be attacked and subdued much about the same time that Victor would arrive at Seville. St. Cyr would have made an end of the Catalans long before. Thus the whole Peninsula would be subdued ere the summer was over. There was nowhere a Spanish army that could make head against even 10,000 French troops. The only possible complication would be that Moore's army might conceivably take ship, not for England, but for Lisbon or Cadiz. If the English, 'the only enemy who could create difficulties,' took this course, the Emperor might have to give further orders. But it does not seem that he regarded this as a likely contingency, since he had conceived an even exaggerated idea of the losses and demoralization which the British had suffered in the retreat to Corunna. To Joseph he wrote, 'reserve yourself for the expedition to Andalusia, which may start three weeks hence. With 40,000 men, marching by an unexpected route [i. e. by Badajoz, not by La Carolina], you will surprise the enemy and force him to submit. This is an operation which will make an end of the war : I leave the glory of it to you [1].' To Jerome Napoleon he wrote in the most laconic style, 'the Spanish affair is done with [2],' and then proceeded to discuss the general politics of the

---

[1] Napoleon to Joseph, Jan. 11, 1809, *Nap. Corresp.*, 14,684.
[2] Almost the same words are found in a dispatch to Mollien of Jan. 24,

Continent, as if his whole attention could now be given to the doings of Austria and Russia. On January 18 he rode out of Valladolid, and after six days of incessant travel reached Paris on the 24th. His first care after his arrival was to scare the intriguers of the capital into good behaviour. His second was to endeavour to treat Austria after the same fashion. He had not yet made up his mind whether the ministers of Francis II meant mischief, or whether they had merely been presuming on his long absence in Spain : on the whole he thought that they could be reduced to order by bold language, and by the ostentatious movement of troops on the Rhine and upper Danube. But he was not sure of his conclusion : in his correspondence letters stating that Austria has been brought to reason, alternate with others in which she is accused of incorrigible perversity, and a design to make war in the spring [1]. The Emperor's suspicions are most clearly shown by the fact that in February he ordered the whole of the Imperial Guard, except two battalions and three squadrons, to be brought up from Spain and directed on Paris [2]. In the same month he sent secret orders to the princes of the Confederation of the Rhine, to bid them be ready to mobilize their contingents at short notice.

It is clear that as regards the affairs of Spain the Emperor was in January and February, 1809, as much deluded as he had been seven months before, in June, 1808. The whole plan of campaign which he dictated at Valladolid, and sent as his parting gift to Joseph and Jourdan, was absolutely impracticable, and indicated a fundamental ignorance of the character of the Spanish war. It would have been a perfectly sensible document if the struggle had been raging in Italy or Germany, though even there the calculations of distance and time would have been rather hazardous. Twenty-three days were given to Soult to expel the English, to pacify Galicia, to take Oporto,

'Aujourd'hui les affaires d'Espagne sont à peu près terminées.' This was written *after* the Emperor had returned to Paris.

[1] Cf., for example, *Nap. Corresp.*, 14,741 and 14,749, where Austria is said to have changed her tone and stopped her preparation, with 14,721 and 14,779, which show a most hostile spirit against her.

[2] For the details, see *Nap. Corresp.*, 14,780, written to Bessières from Paris on Feb. 15.

and to march on Lisbon! Even granting that all had gone as the Emperor desired, the estimate was too short by half. It was midwinter; Galicia and northern Portugal form one of the most mountainous regions in Europe: their roads are vile; their food supplies are scanty; their climate at that season of the year detestable. Clearly the task given to Soult could not be executed in the prescribed time [1].

But this is a minor point: it was not so much in his 'logistics' that the Emperor went wrong as in his general conception of the character of the war. He imagined that in dealing with Spain he might act as if he were dealing with Austria or Prussia—indeed that he had an enormous extra advantage in the fact that the armies of Ferdinand VII were infinitely inferior in mere fighting power to those of Francis II or Frederick William III. By all the ordinary rules of modern warfare, a nation whose capital had been occupied, and whose regular armies had been routed and half-destroyed, ought to have submitted without further trouble. The Emperor was a little surprised that the effect of Espinosa and Gamonal, of Tudela and Ucles, had not been greater. He had almost expected to receive overtures from the Junta, asking for terms of submission. But somewhat disappointed though he might be, he had not yet realized that Spain was not as other countries. The occupation of Madrid counted for little or nothing. The insurrectionary armies, when driven into a corner, did not capitulate, but dispersed, and fled in small parties over the hills, to reunite on the first opportunity. Prussian or Austrian troops under similar circumstances would have quietly laid down their arms. But to endeavour to grasp a Spanish corps was like clutching at a ball of quicksilver: the mass dispersed in driblets between the fingers of the manipulator, and the small rolling pellets ultimately united to form a new force. Large captures of Spaniards only took place on the actual battle-field (as at Ucles or Ocaña), or when an army had shut itself up in a fortress and could not get away, as happened at Saragossa and Badajoz. Unless actually penned in between bayonets, the insurgents abandoned cannon and

---

[1] As a matter of fact, as has been stated elsewhere, Soult though working his hardest did not leave Corunna till Feb. 20, 1809, nor take Oporto till March 29.

baggage, broke their ranks and disappeared, to gather again on some more propitious day, either as fresh armies or as guerrilla bands operating upon the victor's lines of communication.

Nor was this all : in Italy, Germany, and Austria Bonaparte had dealt with regions where the population remained quiescent when once the regular army had been beaten. Risings like that of Verona in 1797, or of the Tyrol in 1805, were exceptional. The French army was wont to go forward without being forced to leave large garrisons behind it, to hold down the conquered country-side. A battalion or two placed in the chief towns sufficed to secure the communication of the army with France. Small parties, or even single officers bearing dispatches, could ride safely for many miles through an Italian or Austrian district without being molested. It was not thus in Spain : the Emperor was to find that every village where there was not a French garrison would be a focus of active resistance, and that no amount of shooting or hanging would cow the spirits of the peasantry. It was only after scores of aides-de-camp had been murdered or captured, and after countless small detachments had been destroyed, that he came to realize that every foot of Spanish soil must not only be conquered but also held down. If there was a square of ten miles unoccupied, a guerrilla band arose in it. If a district thirty miles long lacked a brigade to garrison it, a local junta with a ragged apology for an army promptly appeared. Three hundred thousand men look a large force on paper, but when they have to hold down a country five hundred miles broad they are frittered away to nothing. This Great Britain knows well enough from her recent South African experience : but it was not a common matter of knowledge in 1809. If the Emperor had been told, on the day of his entry into Madrid, that even three years later his communication with Bayonne would only be preserved by the maintenance of a fortified post at every tenth milestone, he would have laughed the idea to scorn. Still more ridiculous would it have appeared to him if he had been told that it would take a body of 300 horse to carry a dispatch from Salamanca to Saragossa, or that the normal garrison of Old Castile would have to be kept at 15,000 men, even when there was no regular Spanish army nearer to it than Oviedo or Astorga. In short he, and all

Europe, had much to learn as to the conditions of warfare in the Peninsula. If he had realized them in March, 1808, there would have been no treachery at Bayonne, and the 'running sore,' as he afterwards called the Spanish war, would never have broken forth.

Meanwhile the conquest of Spain was hung up for a month and more after the victory of Ucles. The Emperor had bidden Joseph and Jourdan to wait till the February rains were over, before sending out the great expedition against Andalusia; the siege of Saragossa was prolonged far beyond expectation, and Soult in Galicia (as we shall presently see) found the time-allowance which his master had set him inadequate to the verge of absurdity. The French made no further move of importance till March.

The Central Junta, therefore, were granted three full months from the date of their flight from Aranjuez to Seville, in which to reorganize their armies for the oncoming campaign of 1809— a respite which they gained (as we have already shown) purely and solely through Moore's splendid inspiration of the march to Sahagun.

The members of the Junta trailed into Seville at various dates between December 14 and December 17. Their rapid journey at midwinter through the Sierra de Guadalupe and the still wilder Sierra Morena had been toilsome and exhausting[1]. It proved fatal to their old president, Florida Blanca, who died of bronchitis only eleven days after he had arrived at Seville. In his stead a Castilian Grandee of unimpeachable patriotism but very moderate abilities, the Marquis of Astorga, was elected to the presidential chair. The Junta had no enviable task before it: the news of the disasters on the Ebro and the fall of Madrid had thrown the nation into a paroxysm of unreasoning fury. Ridiculous charges of treason were being raised against all those who had been in charge of the war. Blake and Castaños (of all people!) were being openly accused of having sold themselves to Napoleon. There were a number of political assassinations in the regions to which the French had not yet penetrated: most of the victims were old friends of Godoy. It looked at first as if

---

[1] It will be remembered (see vol. i. p. 529), that they went via Talavera, Merida, and Llerena.

the central government would be unable to restore any sort of order, or to organize any further resistance. Some of the local juntas, whose importance had disappeared with the meeting of the Supreme Junta, showed signs of wishing to resume their ancient independence. Those of Seville and Jaen were especially disobliging. But the evils of disunion were so obvious that even the most narrow-minded particularists settled down after a time into at least a formal obedience to the central government.

The enforced halt made by the French after Napoleon's departure for Madrid was the salvation of Spain. By the month of January things were beginning to assume a more regular aspect, and some attempt was made to face the situation. The most favourable part of that situation was that money at least was not wanting for the moment. The four or five millions of dollars which the British Government had distributed to the provincial Juntas and to the 'Central' had long been spent, and in 1809 no more than £387,000 in specie was advanced to Spain. Spent also was the enormous amount of money accruing from patriotic gifts and local assessments. But there had just arrived at Cadiz a large consignment of specie from America. The Spanish colonies in the New World had all adhered without hesitation to the cause of Ferdinand VII, and their first and most copious contribution had just come to hand. Not only had the Governors of Mexico and Peru and the other provinces strained every nerve to raise money, but a vast patriotic fund had been collected by individuals. There were rich merchants and landholders in America who made voluntary offerings of sums as large as 100,000 or 200,000 dollars apiece. The money which came to hand early in 1809 amounted to more than £2,800,000, and much more was received ere the close of the year. It was with this sum, far more than with British money, that the Spanish armies were paid and fed : but their equipment mainly came from England. The stores of arms, clothing, and munition which had existed in the arsenals of the Peninsula when the war broke out, had all been exhausted in the autumn, and had not even sufficed to equip fully the unfortunate armies which were beaten on the Ebro. The government and the local juntas had set up new manufactories at Seville, Valencia, and elsewhere, which were already turning out a large quantity of weapons, accoutrements, and uniforms: it was now that the armies began to appear in the rough brown cloth of the country and in leather shakos, abandoning the old white uniform and plumed hat which had been the garb of the Spanish line. But the reclothing and rearmament of the troops could never have been completed without the enormous consignments of cloth, powder, muskets, lead, and leather work which came from England. It is true that much was lost by the fortune of war before it could be utilized— notably the considerable amount of muskets, ammunition, and cloth which had been landed in Galicia for La Romana's army. This, as we have seen, was either destroyed by Sir John Moore's army or captured by Soult, because the Galician Junta had kept it waiting too long at the base. But all that went to Andalusia, Valencia, and Catalonia came safely to hand. Palafox's army was re-equipped, just before the second siege of Saragossa began, with British stores sent up by Colonel Doyle from Tarragona. The armies of the south and east also received enormous consignments of necessaries.

It remains to speak of the purely military aspect of the Junta's position. When January began, the wrecks of the Spanish armies were distributed in a wide semicircle reaching from Oviedo to Gerona, while the French lay in their midst. In the Asturias there were still 14,000 or 15,000 men under arms: the relics of Acevedo's division of Blake's army had fallen back, and joined the other levies which the local Junta had assembled. The whole force was watching the two lines on which the French could conceivably move during the winter—the coast route from Santander to Gihon, and the pass of Pajares which leads from Leon to Oviedo.

In Galicia, La Romana's army, now engaged in the miserable retreat from Astorga to Orense, had fallen into the most wretched condition. Of the 22,000 men who had been assembled at Leon in December only 6,000 or 7,000 were now to be found: the Galician battalions had melted home when the army fell back among their native mountains. They cannot be much blamed, for they were suffering acute starvation: in the spring they came back to join the colours readily enough. The regulars, who still hung together, were famished, naked, typhus-ridden, and incapable of any great exertion. Their general's only care was to keep them as far as possible from Soult and Ney, till the winter should have passed by, and food and clothing be procured.

Between La Romana's men at Orense and the army of Estremadura on the Tagus there was no Spanish force in the field. When Lapisse and D'Avenay had occupied Zamora and Salamanca, the only centre of resistance in Leon was the fortress of Ciudad Rodrigo, which was held by a handful of local militia. Portuguese troops were beginning to collect in its rear at Almeida, but with them the Junta had nothing to do.

The Estremaduran army had now passed from the hands of Galluzzo to those of Cuesta. The Junta, in spite of the memories of Cabezon and Rio Seco, had once more given the obstinate and incapable old soldier an important command. Apparently they had been moved by the widespread but idiotic cry imputing treachery to the generals who had been beaten on the Ebro, and gave Cuesta an army because (with all his faults) no one ever dreamed of accusing him of treachery or sympathy with the French. His forces consisted (1) of the wrecks of Belvedere's army from Gamonal, (2) of the débris of San Juan's army from Madrid, (3) of new Estremaduran levies, which had not gone forward to Burgos in October, but had remained behind to complete their organization, (4) of the four dismounted cavalry regiments from Denmark, which had been sent to the south when La Romana landed at Santander, in order to procure equipment and horses. In all, the army of Cuesta had no more than 10,500 foot and 2,000 or 2,500 horse. The spirit of the old troops of San Juan and Belvedere was still very bad, and they were hardly recovered from their December mutinies and murders. After Lefebvre had driven them back from the Tagus, and occupied the bridges of Almaraz and Arzobispo, the Estremadurans had retired to Merida and Truxillo: on January 11 their most advanced position was at the last-named place.

To the east of Estremadura lay the weakest point of the Spanish line: Andalusia and its mountain barrier of the Sierra Morena were almost undefended in January, 1809. It will be remembered that all through the autumn of the preceding year the local juntas, intoxicated with the fumes of Baylen, had let the months slip by without doing much to organize the 'Army of Reserve,' of which they had spoken so much in August and September. It resulted that, when Reding had marched for Catalonia, and the last belated fractions of Castaños' army had been forwarded to Madrid, Andalusia was almost destitute of troops. When the Junta fled to Seville, it looked around for an army with which to defend the passes of the Sierra Morena. Nothing of the kind existed: the only force available consisted of nine or ten battalions, mainly new levies, which were dispersed through the 'Four Kingdoms' completing their armament and organization. They were hastily mobilized and pushed forward to the Sierra Morena, but not more than 6,000 bayonets and 500 sabres could be collected. This was the sole force that lay between the French at Madrid and the Junta at Seville. The charge of the division, whose head quarters were placed at La Carolina, was given to the Marquis del Palacio, who in the general shifting of commanders had just been recalled from Catalonia.

The British Government's knowledge of the danger to which Andalusia was exposed, from the absolute want of troops to defend it, led to an untoward incident, which did much to endanger its friendly relations with the Junta. On hearing of the fall of Madrid, and of Moore's retreat towards Galicia, Canning harked back to one of his old ideas of the previous summer, the notion that British troops might be sent to the south of Spain, if a safe basis for their operations were secured. This, as the Secretary of State for Foreign Affairs believed, would best be provided by the establishment of a garrison in Cadiz. It was all-important that this great centre of commerce should not fall into the hands of the French, and early in January it was known in London that there was no adequate Spanish force ready to defend the passes of Andalusia. If Napoleon had an army large enough to provide, not only for the pursuit of Moore, but for the dispatch of a strong corps for an attack on Seville, it seemed probable that the French might overrun Southern Spain as far as the sea, without meeting with serious opposition. Accordingly, Canning wrote to Frere, on the fourteenth day of the new year, 1809, to offer the assistance of a considerable British force for the defence of Andalusia, if Cadiz were placed in their hands.

'The question of the employment of a British army in the

south of Spain,' he wrote, 'depends essentially upon the disposition of the Spanish Government to receive a corps of that army
into Cadiz. Without the security to be afforded by that fortress,
it is impossible to hazard the army in the interior, after the
example of the little co-operation which Sir John Moore represents himself to have received from the Spaniards in the north.
. . . In consequence of the imminent danger, and of the pressing
necessity for immediate decision arising from Sir John Moore's
retreat, and from the defenceless state in which you represent
Andalusia to be, His Majesty's Government have deemed it
right (without waiting for the result of your communication
with the Central Junta) to send a force direct to Cadiz, to be
admitted into that fortress. Four thousand men under Major-
General Sherbrooke are directed to sail immediately, and he is
informed that he is to expect instructions from you on his
arrival, containing the determination of the Spanish Government respecting his admission into Cadiz. . . . In the event of
a refusal of the Junta to afford this proof of confidence, Major-
General Sherbrooke is directed to proceed to Gibraltar [1].'

The last paragraph of this dispatch shows that Canning's
intentions were perfectly honourable, and that he did not intend
to bring any pressure to bear upon the Junta in the event of their
refusing to admit a British garrison into Cadiz. His views were
founded upon the information available in London when he
wrote, and he was under the impression that a French army
might probably be marching upon Seville at the moment when
his letter would reach Frere's hands. But—as we have seen—
the diversion of the main force of Napoleon's army of invasion
against Moore, had rendered any such expedition impossible,
and no immediate danger was really to be apprehended.

The same idea, however, had entered into Frere's mind, and
long before he received Canning's dispatch he had been sounding
members of the Central Junta as to the way in which they would
look on a proposal to send British troops to Cadiz. The answer
which he received from their secretary, Martin de Garay, was not
reassuring : Don Martin 'energetically repudiated' the project :
there would be no objection, he said, to admit a garrison, if Cadiz
became 'the ultimate point of retreat' of the armies and

[1] Canning to Frere, Jan. 14, 1809 (Record Office).

government of Spain. But the danger that had appeared so pressing some weeks before had passed by, the French had stopped their advance, and the Junta were now hoping to defend Estremadura and the course of the Tagus. The invaders, as they trusted, would be met and checked on the line of Alcantara and Almaraz. They deprecated any sending of British troops to Cadiz, and hoped that Lisbon would be the point to which reinforcements would be dispatched, as its evacuation would have deplorable results. De Garay, in a second letter, spoke of rumours to the effect that Cradock was proposing to evacuate Portugal, and trusted that they were not true. As a matter of fact they were, and that timid commander was already making secret preparations to embark.

Frere gave up for the present any idea of pressing the project further, unless the French should recommence their advance on Andalusia. He had not yet received Canning's dispatch from London, and did not know that the home government had taken to heart the plan for occupying Cadiz and sending a large expedition to Andalusia. But on February 2, before any hint of the kind had reached him, he was informed by a dispatch from Lisbon that troops had been already sent off to Cadiz. This step was the work of Sir George Smith, one of the numerous British military agents in the Peninsula, who had taken upon himself to force events to an issue, without first taking the precaution of communicating either with the home government or the British ambassador at Seville. Smith was a hasty and presumptuous man, full of zeal without discretion. The defencelessness of Andalusia had impressed him, just as it had impressed Canning and Frere. But instead of opening communications with the Junta, as they had both done, he had merely written in very urgent terms to Cradock, and adjured him to detach troops from the scanty garrison of Portugal in order to secure Cadiz. The general, when thus pressed, consented to fall in with the scheme, and set aside a brigade under Mackenzie, which he shipped off from Lisbon at twenty-four hours' notice (February 2). He also ordered the 40th regiment, then in garrison at Elvas, to march on Seville. Both Cradock and Smith were gravely to blame, for they had no authorization

¹ The 29th, 3/27th, and 2/9th regiments.

to attempt to occupy Cadiz, without obtaining the consent of
the Spanish Government [1]. They should have consulted both
Frere and the Junta before moving a man : but it was only
when the troops had actually embarked that they thought fit
to notify their action to the ambassador at Seville.

On receiving their letters Frere was placed in an unenviable
position. Having just seen his own proposals negatived by
the Junta in polite but decisive terms, he now learnt that
a British force had been sent off to carry out precisely the plan
which the Spaniards had refused to take into consideration.
Four days later he was informed that Mackenzie's brigade, which
had chanced upon a favourable wind, was actually lying in Cadiz
harbour, and that Sir George Smith was endeavouring to induce
the local authorities of the place to permit them to land.   The
Junta, as was inevitable, suspected Frere of having been in the
plot, and imagined that he was trying to force their hand by
the display of armed force.   Cadiz was at Smith's mercy, for it
was only garrisoned by its urban guards ; and the populace were
by no means unwilling to see the British land, for the fear of
the French was upon them, and they welcomed the approach of
reinforcements of any kind.

The supreme authority in Cadiz at this moment was the
Marquis of Villel, a special commissioner sent down by the
Central Junta, of which he was a member. He refused to be
cajoled by Smith, and very properly referred his demand for
permission to disembark to the government at Seville. The
latter, not unnaturally incensed, turned for explanations to
Frere. The ambassador's conduct when placed in this dilemma
was by no means wise or straightforward. Instead of frankly
disavowing Smith's action, he adopted the tortuous course [2] of

---

[1] As Canning wrote to Frere, after receiving the news of the abortive
expedition, 'The enclosed copy of the instructions under which Sir G. Smith
was sent out, will show you that the step taken by that officer was not to
have been taken *except at the direct solicitation of the Spanish authorities.*
. . . He has been directed to leave Cadiz at once, and you may assure
the Junta that no separate or secret commission was, has been, or ever
will be entrusted to any officer or other person,' Feb. 26 (Record Office).

[2] Frere, by his own showing, exceeded the bounds of diplomatic evasion.
He writes to Canning (Feb. 9) to say that the dispatch of the Lisbon
troops had been a complete surprise to him, as he had not received any

pretending that the expedition from Lisbon had been sent with his knowledge and consent, but that he would not allow it to land without the leave of the Junta. The Spaniards replied in terms of some indignation, and returned a frank negative to the demand. Their secretary, de Garay, wrote that the unexpected appearance of General Mackenzie's force was 'painful and disagreeable intelligence, Cadiz being no longer in danger from the French, and two Spanish regiments being already on their way to reinforce the garrison. The measure which had been taken would admit of a thousand interpretations, and a consent to hand over the fortress to the British would compromise the Central Junta with the whole nation.' The fact was that Spanish public opinion was strongly opposed to allowing the British to obtain a foothold in Cadiz; there was a deeply-rooted notion abroad that, if once occupied, the place might be kept permanently in our hands, and be turned into a second Gibraltar.

Unfortunately for the credit of Great Britain with her allies, tumults broke out at Cadiz within a few days of the arrival of Mackenzie's army, which supplied an excuse to malevolent Spaniards for attributing the worst motives to their allies. As a matter of fact they were not stirred up by Sir George Smith or any other emissary of the British Government, but were the results of the eccentric behaviour of the Marquis de Villel[1]. This personage was a very strange character, a sort of nineteenth-century Spanish Puritan, with a taste for playing the benevolent despot. He attributed the misfortunes of his country (and not without much reason) to her moral decadence. His idea of the way to commence her regeneration was peculiar, considering the

information on the subject. 'It occurred to me, however, that it was best to take it upon myself, and to affect to consider it a thing of course, and to say that I had sent orders in conformity with the note which I had received from Mr. de Garay. In order to give this some semblance of truth, I did afterwards write a letter to Lisbon to this effect, and sent it off before I dispatched my note to Mr. de Garay. This did not prevent me from being assailed by remonstrances.' Finally he proceeded to tell the Junta 'that he only wished to see Cadiz occupied in the extreme case of an immediate attack by the French' (Record Office).

[1] For Villel's eccentricities in detail see Toreño, i. pp. 375-6, and Arteche, v. p. 107.

circumstances of the time. He issued an edict commanding all married pairs living apart, to reunite, issued laws repressing theatre-going, late hours, and gambling, legislated concerning the length of ladies' skirts, and organized a grand *battue* against women of light reputation, of whom he imprisoned some scores. When he proceeded to engage in a sort of moral inquisition into the private life of all classes, he naturally became very unpopular, and on the first opportunity the populace rose against him. He had ordered into the city a newly-embodied 'Swiss' battalion, raised from the prisoners of Dupont's army and other deserters of all nationalities. The cry was raised by his enemies that he was admitting Frenchmen in disguise into the sacred fortress, with the purpose of betraying it to the enemy. Other rumours were put about to the effect that he was deliberately neglecting the fortifications, and supplying the batteries with powder adulterated with sand[1].

When the foreign battalion drew near to Cadiz on February 22, and began to march up the long spit which connects the city with the Isla de Leon, the storm burst. A mixed multitude of rioters shut the gates against the troops, and then swept the streets, maltreating Villel's subordinates, and slaying Don José Heredia the commander of the coast-guard, a person very unpopular with the smugglers, who formed an appreciable element in the crowd. The High Commissioner himself was besieged in his house, hunted from it, and nearly murdered : he only escaped by the kind offices of the head of a Capuchin convent, who took him within his gates, and made himself responsible to the rioters for keeping the refugee in safe custody. The mob next tried to break open the state prison, for the purpose of slaying General Caraffa and other political captives. Fortunately Felix Jones, the military Governor, succeeded in saving these unhappy persons, by the not over-willing aid of the urban guards, many of whom had joined in the outbreak.

The rioters expressed great friendliness for the British, and many of them kept inviting the troops in the offing to come ashore. It was very lucky that no attention was paid to these solicitations[2], for if they had landed the worst suspicions of

[1] See Col. Leslie (of the 29th), *Memoirs*, p. 94.
[2] Mackenzie wrote that 'it was evident that the people were favourable

the Junta would have appeared justified, and the insurrection would have been attributed to the machinations of Frere or Smith. Fortunately the latter had died, only a few days before the troubles broke out, the victim of a fever which carried him off after no more than twenty-four hours of illness. If he had survived till the twenty-second, he would have been quite capable of taking the fatal step of listening to the appeals of the rioters, and ordering the troops ashore.

As it turned out the whole expedition ended in an absurd fiasco. When the riots had died down, the Junta recalled the eccentric de Villel, but they would not listen to any proposals from Frere for admitting British troops into Cadiz, even when he suggested that only two battalions should remain there, while the rest, including Sherbrooke's division, which was expected to arrive in a few days, should come up and join the 40th regiment at Seville, with the ultimate purpose of marching into Estremadura. The Junta replied that 'the loyalty of the British Ministry and the generosity of its efforts to assist Spain were beyond suspicion : but the National Government must respect national prejudices, and avoid exposing itself to censure. If there were any urgent danger, they would have no hesitation in admitting the troops of their allies into Cadiz. But the French were still far away, and there was no immediate prospect of their approach. The British expedition would be more usefully employed in Catalonia, or in some other theatre of war, than in Cadiz [1].' By March 4, when this final answer was sent to Frere, the state of affairs had so much changed, that the representations made by the Junta were more or less correct. The imminent danger which had existed in January had passed away.

Accordingly, after lying idly for four weeks in their transports, and gazing with much unsatisfied curiosity on the white

to our landing and occupying the town, for it was frequently called for during the tumult.' But 'the utmost care was taken to prevent our officers or soldiers from taking any part whatever on this occasion, and except when I was applied to by the Governor for the interference of some British officers as mediators, we stood perfectly clear.' Dispatch to Castlereagh in the Record Office, dated Lisbon, March 13, 1809.

[1] Martin de Garay to Frere, March 4 (Record Office).

houses, the green shutters, and the flat roofs of Cadiz, across the
beautiful bay, Mackenzie's regiments set sail again for Lisbon
on March 6. As they ran out of the harbour, they met Sherbrooke's belated convoy, whose arrival had been delayed by
fearful tempests in the Bay of Biscay. The whole force, 6,000
bayonets strong, was brought back to Portugal. It might have
been of infinite service to Cradock if it had remained at Lisbon
and had never been sent to Cadiz, and its presence might have
induced him to adopt measures less timid and futile than those
which (as we shall see) he had pursued during January and
February [1].

But this unfortunate incident has detained us too long; we
must return to the state of the Spanish armies at the end of
the month of January. Beyond the levies of the Marquis Del
Palacio at La Carolina, there was a long gap in the Spanish
line of defence. The next force under arms was the army of
Infantado, now engaged in its exhausting winter march from
Cuenca to the Murcian border. After the rout of Ucles it was
still 12,000 strong, though destitute of all supplies and not fit
for immediate service. The Junta ordered it to march from
Chinchilla to join Del Palacio's force at the mouth of the
Despeña Perros, and so to strengthen the defences of Andalusia.

---

[1] Napier enlarges on this incident at great length in pages 14–19 of his
second volume. In his persistent dislike for Canning, Castlereagh and
Mr. Frere, as well as for the Spaniards, he concludes that the business
'indicated an unsettled policy, shallow combination, and bad agents on
the part of the British Cabinet, and an unwise and unworthy disposition
in the Supreme Junta,' while Smith was 'zealous and acute' and Cradock
'full of zeal and moral courage.' It is hard to give an unqualified assent
to any one of these views. Smith was wrong in acting without giving any
notice of his intentions to the Junta: Cradock's zeal was equally un-
tempered by discretion. The British Cabinet, acting on the information
available in the end of December, was right to be anxious about Cadiz,
and equally right to abandon its attempt to occupy the place in March,
when the conditions of the war had changed, and the Junta had shown its
dislike to the proposal. As to the Spaniards, the matter was only broached
to them in February, when the danger of an immediate French advance
had passed away, and they were entirely justified in their answer, which
was framed as politely as could be contrived. We must not blame them
overmuch for their suspicion : England, though now a friend, had long
been an enemy—and the fate of Gibraltar was always before their eyes.

This was done, and the two forces were safely united, so that when a few more new battalions had been brought up from Granada, 20,000 men were placed between Victor and Andalusia. The Junta removed Infantado from command, rightly judging that he had sacrificed Venegas at Ucles by his neglect to send orders and his sloth in coming up to join his subordinate. The charge of the force at La Carolina (still called ' the Army of the Centre ') was made over to General Cartaojal.

Beyond Infantado's depleted corps lay the army of Valencia. Its nucleus was the remains of the old division of Llamas and Roca, which had served with Castaños at Tudela. The local Junta rapidly recruited this skeleton force from 1,500 up to 5,000 men [1]. They added to it several new regiments raised during the winter in Valencia and Murcia, and by February had 10,000 men available for succouring Aragon and Catalonia, though their quality left much to be desired.

A little further north Palafox was still holding out with splendid desperation in Saragossa, where he had shut himself up with the whole army of Aragon. His original 32,000 men were already much thinned by pestilence and the sword, but in January their spirit was yet unbroken, and though it was clear that they were doomed to final destruction, if they were not relieved from the outside, yet they were still doing excellent work in detaining in front of them the whole of the 3rd and 5th French Army Corps.

There yet remains to be described the strongest of all the Spanish armies, that of Catalonia. In addition to the original garrison of the province, and to its gallant *miqueletes* and *somatenes*, there had been gradually drafted into the principality (1) the greater part of the garrison of the Balearic Isles, some 9,000 men ; (2) Reding's Granadan division which started from its home over 10,000 strong ; (3) 2,500 men of Caraffa's old division from Portugal ; (4) the Marquis of Lazan's Aragonese division from the side of Lerida, about 4,000 bayonets. Thus in all some 32,000 men in organized corps had been massed in Catalonia, and the *somatenes* added some 20,000 irregulars. Of course the Spanish strength in January did not reach these figures. Many men had been lost at the siege of Rosas and in

[1] See the table in Arguelles on p. 74 of his Appendix-volume.

the battles of Cardadeu and Molins de Rey : yet there were still
40,000 troops of one sort or another available ; the spirit of the
country was irritated rather than lowered by the late defeats ;
the French only occupied the ground that was within the actual
circle of fire of their garrisons.   If the Catalans had been content to avoid general engagements, and to maintain an incessant
guerrilla warfare, they might have held their own.   Though the
enemy had a very capable commander in General St. Cyr, they
had as yet accomplished nothing more than the capture of the
antiquated fortress of Rosas, the relief of Barcelona, and the
winning of two fruitless battles.   Catalonia remained unsubdued
till the very end of the struggle.

Reckoning up all their armies, the Junta had in the end of
January some 135,000 men in arms,—a force insufficient to face
the French in the open, for the latter (even after the departure
of the Imperial Guard) had still nearly 300,000 [1] sabres and
bayonets south of the Pyrenees, but one quite capable of keeping
up the national resistance if it were only conducted upon the
proper lines.   For, as Napoleon and his marshals had yet to
learn, no Spanish district could be considered conquered unless a
garrison was left in each of its towns, and flying columns kept
in continual motion through the open country.   Of the 288,000
French who now lay in Spain more than half were really wanted
for garrison duty.   A district like Galicia was capable of keeping
40,000 men employed : even the plains of Old Castile and Leon
swallowed up whole divisions.

But, unfortunately for Spain, the mania for fighting pitched
battles was still obsessing the minds of her generals.   Within
a few weeks three wholly unnecessary and disastrous engagements were to be risked, at Valls, Ciudad Real, and Medellin.
Instead of playing a cautious defensive game, and harassing the
French, the Spaniards persisted in futile attempts to face the
enemy in general actions, for which their troops were wholly
unsuited.   The results were so deplorable that but for a second
British intervention—Wellesley's march to Talavera—Andalusia
would have been in as great peril in July, 1809, as it had been
in January.

---

[1] 288,000 on Feb. 15.   See Napier's extracts from the Imperial muster
rolls, i. 514.   These numbers include the sick and detached.

The Central Junta must take its share of the responsibility for this fact no less than the Spanish generals. It still persisted in its old error of refusing to appoint a single commander-in-chief, so that each army fought for its own hand, without any attempt to co-ordinate its actions with those of the others. Indeed several of the generals were at notorious enmity with their colleagues—notably Cuesta and Venegas. It was to no purpose that the Central Government displayed great energy in organizing men and collecting material, if, when the armies had been equipped and sent to the front, they were used piece-meal, without any general strategical scheme, and led ere long to some miserable disaster, such as Ucles, or Medellin, or Ocaña. The Junta, the generals, and the nation were all alike possessed by the delusion that with energy and sufficient numbers they might on some happy morning achieve a second Baylen. But for such a consummation Duponts and Vedels are required, and when no such convenient adversaries were to be found, the attempt to encompass and beat a French army was certain to end in a catastrophe.

The only Spanish fighters who were playing the proper game in 1809 were the Catalonian *somatenes*, and even they gave battle far too often, and did not adhere with a sufficient perti-nacity to the harassing tactics of guerrilla warfare. General Arteche has collected in his fourth volume something like a dozen schemes for the expulsion of the French from Spain, which were laid before the Junta, or ventilated in print, during this year. It is interesting to see that only one of them advocates the true line of resistance—the avoiding of battles, the harassing of the enemy's flanks and communications, and the employment of numerous flying bands instead of great masses [1]. Some of the other plans are the wild imaginings of ignorant fools—one wiseacre wished to run down the French columns with pikemen in a sort of Macedonian phalanx, another to arm one-sixth of the troops with hand-grenades ! But the majority of the Junta's self-constituted advisers thought that numbers were the only necessary thing, and proposed to save Spain by crushing the invaders with levies *en masse* of all persons between sixteen

---

[1] See Arteche, iv. 115–51 : the advocate of the guerrilla game was a certain Faustino Fernandez.

and fifty — one enthusiast makes the age-limit fourteen to seventy !

These were the views of the nation, and the generals and the Junta were but infected with the common delusion of all their compatriots. They would not see that courage and raw multitudes are almost helpless when opposed by equal courage combined with skill, long experience of war, superior tactics, and intelligent leading.

SECTION X

THE AUTUMN AND WINTER CAMPAIGN IN CATALONIA

CHAPTER I

THE SIEGE OF ROSAS

BEFORE we follow further the fortunes of Southern Spain, it is necessary to turn back and to take up the tale of the war on the Eastern coast at the point where it was left in Section V.

The same torpor which was notable in the operations of the main armies of the Spaniards and the French during the months of September and October was to be observed in Catalonia also. On the Ter and the Llobregat the inability of the French to move was much more real, and the slackness of the Spaniards even more inexplicable, than on the Ebro and the Aragon.

In the early days of September the situation of the invaders was most perilous. After the disastrous failure of the second siege of Gerona, it will be remembered that Reille had withdrawn to Figueras, close to the French frontier, while Duhesme had cut his way back to Barcelona, after sacrificing all his artillery and his baggage on the way. Both commanders proceeded to report to the Emperor that there was need for ample reinforcements of veteran troops, or a catastrophe must inevitably ensue. Meanwhile Reille preserved a defensive attitude at the foot of the Pyrenees; while Duhesme could do no more than hold Barcelona, and as much of its suburban plain as he could safely occupy without risking overmuch his outlying detachments. He foresaw a famine in the winter, and devoted all his energies to seizing and sending into the town all foodstuffs that he could find in the neighbourhood. His position was most uncomfortable: the late expedition had reduced his force from 13,000 to 10,000 sabres and bayonets. The men were demoralized, and when sent out to forage saw *somatenes* behind every bush and rock. The populace of Barcelona was awaiting a good opportunity for an *émeute*, and was in constant communication with the insurgents outside.

The blockade was not as yet kept up by any large section of the Captain-General's regular troops, nor had any attempt been made to run lines around the place. It was conducted by an elastic cordon of four or five thousand *miqueletes*, supported by no more than 2,000 infantry of the regular army and possessing five or six field-guns. The charge of the whole line was given to the Conde de Caldagues, who had so much distinguished himself in the previous month by his relief of Gerona. He had been entrusted with a force too small to man a circuit of twelve or fifteen miles, so that Duhesme had no difficulty in pushing sorties through the line of Spanish posts, whenever he chose to send out a sufficiently strong column. But any body that pressed out too far in pursuit of corn or forage, risked being beset and mishandled on its return march by the whole of the *somatenes* of the country-side. Hence there was a limit to the power to roam of even the largest expeditions that Duhesme could spare from his depleted garrison. The fighting along the blockading cordon was incessant, but never conclusive. On September 2 a strong column of six Italian battalions swept aside the Spaniards for a moment in the direction of San Boy, but a smaller expedition against the bridge of Molins de Rey was repulsed. The moment that the Italians returned to Barcelona, with the food that they had scraped together in the villages, Caldagues reoccupied his old positions. There were many skirmishes but no large sorties between September 2 and October 12, when Milosewitz took out 2,000 men for a cattle-hunt in the valley of the Besos. He pierced the blockading line, routing the *miqueletes* of Milans at San Jeronimo de la Murtra, and penetrated as far as Granollers, twenty miles from Barcelona, where he made an invaluable seizure, the food dépôt of the eastern section of the investing force. But he was now dangerously distant from

his base, and as he was returning with his captures, Caldagues
fell upon him at San Culgat with troops brought from other
parts of the blockading line. The Italians were routed with
a loss of 300 men [1], and their convoy was recaptured. After
this Duhesme made no more attempts to send expeditions far
afield: in spite of a growing scarcity of food, he could not
afford to risk the loss of any more men by pushing his sorties
into the inland.

Meanwhile Reille at Figueras was in wellnigh as forlorn
a situation. His communications with Perpignan were open,
so that he had not, like Duhesme, the fear of starvation before
his eyes. But in other respects he was almost as badly off:
the *somatenes* were always worrying his outposts, but this was
only a secondary trial. The main trouble was the want of
clothing, transport, and equipment: the heterogeneous mob of
bataillons de marche, of Swiss and Tuscan conscripts, had been
hurried to the frontier without any proper preparations: this
mattered comparatively little during the summer; but when the
autumn cold began Reille found that troops, who had neither
tents nor greatcoats, and whose original summer uniforms were
now worn out, could not keep the field. His ranks were so
thinned by dysentery and rheumatic affections that he had
to put the men under cover in Figueras and the neighbouring
towns, and even to withdraw to Perpignan some of his battalions,
whose clothing was absolutely dropping to pieces. His cavalry,
for want of forage in the Pyrenees, were sent back into Languedoc,
where occupation was found for them by Lord Cochrane who
was conducting a series of daring raids on the coast villages
between the mouth of the Rhone and that of the Tech [2]. Reille
continued to solicit the war minister at Paris for clothing and
transport, but could get nothing from him: all the resources
of the empire were being strained in September and October
to fit out the main army, which was about to enter Spain
on the side of Biscay, and Napoleon refused to trouble himself
about such a minor force as the corps at Figueras.

The Spaniards, therefore, had in the autumn months a unique
opportunity for striking at the two isolated French forces in

[1] So Vacani. Laffaille gives the incredible figure of 48 !
[2] See Cochrane's *Autobiography*, pp. 269-85.

Catalonia. Two courses were open to them : they might have turned their main army against Barcelona, and attempted to besiege instead of merely to blockade Duhesme : or on the other hand they might have left a mere cordon of *somatenes* around Duhesme, and have sent all their regulars to join the levies of the north and sweep Reille across the Pyrenees. The resources at their disposition were far from contemptible : almost the whole garrison of the Balearic Isles having disembarked in Catalonia, there were now some 12,000 regulars in the Principality, and the local Junta had put so much energy into the equipment of the numerous *tercios* of *miqueletes* which it had raised, that the larger half of them, at least 20,000 men, were more or less ready for the field. Moreover they were aware that large reinforcements were at hand. Reding's Granadan division, 10,000 strong, was marching up from the south, and was due to arrive early in November. The Aragonese division under the Marquis of Lazan, which had been detached from the army of Palafox, was already at Lerida. Valencia had sent up a line regiment[1], and the remains of the division of Caraffa from Portugal were being brought round by sea to the mouth of the Ebro[2]. Altogether 20,000 men of new troops were on the way to Catalonia, and the first of them had already come on the scene.

Unfortunately the Marquis Del Palacio, the new Captain-General of Catalonia, though well-intentioned, was slow and undecided to the verge of absolute torpidity. Beyond allowing his energetic subordinate Caldagues to keep up the blockade of Barcelona he did practically nothing. A couple of thousand of his regulars, based on Gerona and Rosas, lay opposite Reille, but were far too weak to attack him. About 3,000 under Caldagues were engaged in the operations around Barcelona. The rest the Captain-General held back and did not use. All through September he lay idle at Tarragona, to the great disgust of the local Junta, who at last sent such angry complaints

---

[1] Two battalions of the 2nd of Savoia : the old regiment of the name had been completed to four battalions, two were with Castaños and called 1st of Savoia, the other two came to Catalonia.

[2] Four battalions of Provincial Grenadiers of Old and New Castile had already come up.

to Aranjuez that the Central Junta recalled him, and replaced him by Vives the old Captain-General of the Balearic Islands, who took over the command on October 28.

This gave a change of commander but not of policy, for Vives was as slow and incapable as his predecessor. We have already had occasion to mention the trouble that he gave in August, when he refused to send his troops to the mainland till actually compelled to yield by their mutiny. When he took over the charge of operations he found 20,000 foot and 1,000 horse at his disposition, and the French still on the defensive both at Barcelona and at Figueras. He had a splendid opportunity, and it was not yet too late to strike hard. But all that he chose to attempt was to turn the blockade of Barcelona into an investment, by tightening the cordon round the place. To lay siege to the city does not seem to have been within the scope of his intentions, but on November 6 he moved up to the line of the Llobregat with 12,000 infantry and 700 horse, mostly regulars. He had opened negotiations with secret friends within the walls, and had arranged that when the whole forces of Duhesme were sufficiently occupied in resisting the assault from outside, the populace should take arms and endeavour to seize and throw open one of the gates. But matters never got to this point : on November 8 several Spanish columns moved in nearer to Barcelona, and began to skirmish with the outposts of the garrison. But the attack was incoherent, and never pressed home. Vives then waited till the 26th, when he had received more reinforcements, the first brigade of Reding's long-expected Granadan division. On that day another general assault on Duhesme's outlying posts was delivered, and this time with considerable success : several of the suburban villages were carried, over a hundred Frenchmen were captured, and the line of blockade was drawn close under the walls. Duhesme had no longer any hold outside the city. But Barcelona was strong, and its garrison, when concentrated within the place, was just numerous enough to hold its own. Duhesme had thought for a moment of evacuating the city and retiring into the citadel and the fortress of Montjuich : but on mature consideration he resolved to cling as long as possible to the whole circuit of the town. He had heard that an army of relief was at last on the way, and made up his mind to yield no inch without compulsion.

Thus Vives wasted another month without any adequate results : he had, with the whole field army of Catalonia, done nothing more than turn the French out of their first and weakest line of defence.   The fortress was intact, and to all intents and purposes might have been observed as well by 10,000 *somatenes* as by the large force which Vives had brought against it.

Meanwhile the enemy, utterly unopposed on the line of the Pyrenees, was getting together a formidable host for the relief of Barcelona.   When he had recognized that Reille's extemporized army was insufficient alike in quantity and in quality for the task before it, the Emperor had directed on Perpignan (as we have already seen [1]) two strong divisions of the Army of Italy, one composed of ten French battalions under General Souham, the other of thirteen Italian battalions.   The order to dispatch them had only been given on August 10, and the regiments, which had to be mobilized and equipped, and then to march up from Lombardy to the roots of the Pyrenees, did not begin to arrive at Perpignan till September 14 : the artillery, and the troops which came from the more distant points, only appeared on October 28.   Even then there was a further week's delay, for the Emperor had monopolized for the main army, on the side of the Bidassoa, all the available battalions of the military train : the Army of the Eastern Pyrenees had no transport save that which the regiments had brought with them, and it was with the greatest difficulty that a few hundred mules and some open carts were collected from the French border districts.   It was only on November 5 that the army crossed the Pyrenees, by the great pass between Bellegarde and La Junquera.

The officer placed in command was General Gouvion St. Cyr, who afterwards won his marshal's bâton in the Russian war of 1812.   He was a general of first-rate ability, who had served all through the wars of the Revolution with marked distinction : but he disliked Bonaparte and had not the art to hide the fact. This had kept him back from earlier promotion.   St. Cyr was by no means an amiable character : he was detested by his

[1] Vol. i. p. 333.

officers and his troops as a confirmed grumbler, and selfish to an incredible degree [1]. He was one of those men who can always show admirable and convincing reasons for not helping their neighbours. *C'était un mauvais compagnon de lit,* said one of the many colleagues, whom he had left in the lurch, while playing his own game. From his morose bearing and his dislike for company he had got the nickname of '*le hibou.*' He was cautious, cool-headed, and ready of resource, so that his troops had full confidence in him, though he never commanded their liking. Even from his history of the Catalonian war, one can gather the character of the man. It is admirably lucid, and illustrated with original documents, Spanish no less than French, in a fashion only too rare among the military books of the soldiers of the Empire. But it is not only entirely self-centred, but full of malevolent insinuations concerning Napoleon and the author's colleagues. In his first chapter he broaches the extraordinary theory that Napoleon handed over to him the Catalonian army without resources, money, or transport, in order that he might make a fiasco of the campaign and ruin his reputation! He actually seems to have believed that his master disliked to have battles won for him by officers who had not owed to him the beginning of their fortunes [2], and would have been rather pleased than otherwise to see the attempt to relieve Barcelona end in a failure.

These are, of course, the vain imaginings of a jealous and suspicious hypochondriac. It is true that Napoleon disliked St. Cyr, but he did not want to see the campaign of Catalonia end in a disaster. He gave the new general a fine French division of veteran troops, and, as his letter to the Viceroy Eugène Beauharnais shows, the picked regiments of the whole

---

[1] For several curious and interesting stories concerning St. Cyr, the reader may search the third volume of Marbot's *Mémoires.* Marbot is not an authority to be followed with much confidence, but the picture drawn of the marshal is borne out by other and better writers.

[2] 'On ne pourra pas échapper à la pensée que Napoléon, avec sa force immense, a été assez faible pour ne vouloir que des succès obtenus par lui-même, ou du moins sous ses yeux. Autrement on eût dit que la victoire était pour lui une offense : il en voulait surtout à la fortune quand elle favorisait les armes d'officiers qui ne lui devaient pas leur élévation.' *Journal de l'Armée de Catalogne,* p. 26.

Italian army. The Seventh Corps mustered in all more than
40,000 men, and 25,000 of these were concentrated under
St. Cyr's hand at Perpignan and Figueras. It is certain that the
troops were not well equipped, and that the auxiliary services
were ill represented. But this was not from exceptional malice
on Napoleon's part : he was always rather inclined to starve an
army with which he was not present in person, and at this
moment every resource was being strained to fit out the main
force which were to deliver the great blow at Madrid. Catalonia
was but a 'side show': and when St. Cyr tries to prove [1] that it
was the most important theatre of war in the whole peninsula,
he is but exaggerating, after the common fashion of poor
humanity, the greatness of his own task and his own victories.

Before starting from Perpignan St. Cyr refitted, as best he
could, the dilapidated battalions of Reille, which were, he says,
in such a state of nudity that those who had been sent back
within the French border had to be kept out of public view from
motives of mere decency [2]. The whole division had suffered so
much from exposure that instead of taking the field with the
8,000 men which it possessed in August, it could present only
5,500 in November, after setting aside a battalion to garrison
Figueras [3].

But though Reille was weak, and the division of Chabot
(a mere corps of two Neapolitan battalions and one regiment of
National Guards) was an almost negligible quantity, the troops
newly arrived from Italy were both numerous and good in
quality. Souham's ten French battalions had 7,000 bayonets,
Pino's thirteen Italian battalions had 7,300. Their cavalry consisted of one French and two Italian regiments, making 1,700
sabres. The total force disposable consisted of 23,680 men, of
whom 2,096 were cavalry, and about 500 artillery. In this
figure are not included the National Guards and dépôts left
behind to garrison Bellegarde, Montlouis, and other places

[1] St. Cyr, p. 23.

[2] Ibid., p. 19.

[3] For composition see the table of the 7th Corps in Appendix of vol. i.
The figures given by St. Cyr are Pino 8,368, Souham 7,712, Chabot 1,988,
Reille 4,000. The last is an understatement, as shown by the morning
state of Reille's division in Belmas, ii. 456, which shows 4,612 excluding
the garrison of Figueras, more than 1,000 strong.

within the French frontier, but only the troops available for operations within Catalonia.

On his way to Perpignan, St. Cyr had visited the Emperor at Paris, so as to receive his orders in person. Napoleon informed him that he left him *carte blanche* as to all details; the one thing on which he insisted was that Barcelona must be preserved: ' si vous perdiez cette place, je ne la reprendrais pas avec quatre-vingt mille hommes.' This then was to be the main object of the coming campaign : there were about two months available for the task, for Duhesme reported that, though food was growing scarce, he could hold out till the end of December. To lessen the number of idle mouths in Barcelona he had been giving permits to depart to many of the inhabitants, and expelling others, against whom he could find excuses for severity.

The high-road from Figueras to Barcelona was blocked by the fortress of Gerona, whose previous resistance in July and August showed that its capture would be a tedious and difficult matter. St. Cyr calculated that he had not the time to spare for the siege of this place : long ere he could expect to take it, Duhesme would be starved out. He made up his mind that he would have to march past Gerona, and as the high-road is commanded by the guns of the city, he would be forced to take with him no heavy guns or baggage, but only light artillery and pack-mules, which could use the bypaths of the mountains. It was his first duty to relieve Barcelona by defeating the main army of Vives. When this had been done, it would be time enough to think of the siege of Gerona.

But there was another fortress which St. Cyr resolved to clear out of his way before starting to aid Duhesme. On the sea-shore, only ten miles before Figueras, lies the little town of Rosas, which blocks the route that crawls under the cliffs from Perpignan and Port-Vendres to the Ampurdam. The moment that the French army advanced south from Figueras, it would have Rosas on its flank, and even small expeditions based on the place could make certain of cutting the high-road, and intercepting all communications between the base and the field force that had gone forward. But it was more than likely that the Spaniards would land a considerable body of troops in Rosas, for it has an excellent harbour, and every facility for disembarka-

tion. Several English men-of-war were lying there; it served
them as their shelter and port of call while they watched for the
French ships which tried to run into Barcelona with provisions,
from Marseilles, Cette, or Port-Vendres.   Already they had
captured many vessels which endeavoured to pierce the blockade.

St. Cyr therefore was strongly of opinion that he ought to
make an end of the garrison of Rosas before starting on his
expedition to aid Duhesme. The place was strategically important, but its fortifications were in such bad order that he imagined
that it might be reduced in a few days. The town, which counted
no more than 1,500 souls, consisted of a single long street running
along the shore. It was covered by nothing more than a ditch
and an earthwork, resting at one end on a weak redoubt above
the beach, and at the other upon the citadel. The latter formed
the strength of the place: it was a pentagonal work, regularly
constructed, with bastions, and a scarp and counterscarp reveted
with stone. But its resisting power was seriously diminished by
the fact that the great breach which the French had made during
its last siege in 1794 had never been properly repaired. The
government of Godoy had neglected the place, and, when the
insurrection began, the Catalans had found it still in ruins, and
had merely built up the gap with loose stones and barrels filled
with earth.   A good battering train would bring down the
whole of these futile patchings in a few days. A mile to the
right of the citadel was a detached work, the Fort of the Trinity,
placed above a rocky promontory which forms the south-eastern
horn of the harbour. It had been built to protect ships lying
before the place from being annoyed by besiegers. The Trinity
was built in an odd and ingenious fashion: it was commanded
at the distance of only 100 yards by the rocky hill of Puig-Rom:
to prevent ill effects from a plunging fire from this elevation, its
front had been raised to a great height, so as to protect the interior
of the work from molestation. A broad tower 110 feet high
covered the whole side of the castle which faces inland. 'Nothing in short, for a fortress commanded by adjacent heights,
could have been better adapted for holding out against offensive
operations, or worse adapted for replying to them. The French
battery on the cliff was too elevated for artillery to reach, while
the tower, which prevented their shot from reaching the body

of the fort, also prevented any return fire at them, even if the fort
had possessed artillery. In consequence of the elevated position
of the French on the cliff, they could only breach the central portion of the tower. The lowest part of the breach they made
was nearly sixty feet above its base, so that it could only be
reached by long scaling ladders [1].' It is seldom that a besieger
has to complain of the difficulty caused to him by the possession
of ground completely dominating a place that he has to reduce :
but in the course of the siege of Fort Trinity the French were
undoubtedly incommoded by the height of the Puig-Rom. The
garrison below, hidden in good bomb-proofs and covered by the
tower, suffered little harm from their fire. To batter the whole
tower to pieces, by a downward fire, was too long and serious
a business for them ; they merely tried to breach it.

If the ground in front of Fort Trinity was too high for the
French, that of the town of Rosas was too low. It was so
marshy that in wet weather the ditches of their siege works
filled at once with water, and their parapets crumbled into
liquid mud. The only approach on ground of convenient firmness and elevation was opposite a comparatively narrow front
of the south-eastern corner of the place.

The garrison of Rosas, when St. Cyr undertook its siege, was
commanded by Colonel Peter O'Daly, an officer of the Ultonia,
who had distinguished himself at Gerona ; it was composed of
a skeleton battalion (150 men) of the governor's own Irish corps,
of half the light infantry regiment 2nd of Barcelona, of a company of Wimpffen's Swiss regiment, and 120 gunners. These
were regulars : of new levies there were the two *miquelete tercios* of
Lerida and Igualada, with some companies of those of Berga and

---

[1] Lord Cochrane's *Autobiography*, i. 303. He adds ' A pretty correct
idea of our relative positions may be formed if the unnautical reader will
imagine our small force placed in the nave of Westminster Abbey, with
the enemy attacking the great western tower from the summit of a cliff
100 feet higher than the tower, so that the breach in course of formation
corresponds to the great west window of the Abbey. It was no easy
matter to them to scale the external wall of the tower up to the great
window, and more difficult still to get down from the window into the
body of the church. These were the points I had to provide against,
for we could not prevent the French either from breaching or from
storming.'

Figueras. The whole force was exactly 3,000 strong. It would be wrong to omit the mention of the British succours which took part in the defence. There lay in the harbour the *Excellent*, 74, and two bomb-vessels : when the *Excellent* departed on November 21 she was replaced by the *Fame*, another 74-gun ship, and during the last days of the siege Lord Cochrane in his well-known frigate the *Impérieuse* was also present. It is well to remember their exact force, for the French narrators of the leaguer of Rosas are prone to call them 'the British squadron,' a term which seems rather too magnificent to apply to a group of vessels never numbering more than one line-of-battle ship, one frigate, and two bomb-vessels.

St. Cyr moved forward on November 5, with the four divisions of Souham, Pino, Reille, and Chabot, which (as we have seen) amounted in all to about 23,000 men. He had resolved to use Pino and Reille—some 12,000 men—for the actual siege, and Souham and Chabot for the covering work. Accordingly the weak division of the last-named officer was left to watch the ground at the foot of the passes, in the direction of Figueras and La Junquera, while Souham took up the line of the river Fluvia, which lay across the path of any relieving force that might come from the direction of Gerona. St. Cyr remained with the covering army, and gave the conduct of the siege to Reille, perhaps because he had already made one attack on the town in August.

On November 6 Reille marched down to the sea, driving before him the Spanish outlying pickets, and the peasantry of the suburban villages, who took refuge with their cattle in Rosas. On the seventh the investment began, Reille's own division taking its position on the marshy ground opposite the town, while Pino encamped more to the left, upon the heights that face the fort of the Trinity. The head quarters were established at the village of Palau. A battalion of the 2nd Italian light infantry was placed far back, to the north-east, to keep off the *somatenes* of the coast villages about Llanza and Selva de Mar from interfering in the siege.

Next day the civil population of Rosas embarked on fishing-vessels and small merchantmen, and departed to the south, abandoning the whole town to the garrison. They just missed seeing some sharp fighting. The covering party who had been detached to the neighbourhood of Llanza were beset during a dense mist by the *somatenes* of the coast: two companies were cut to pieces or captured; the rest were saved by General Fontane, who led out three battalions from Pino's lines to their assistance. While this engagement was in progress, the garrison sallied out with 2,000 men to beat up the main camp of the Italians; they were repulsed after a sharp fight; the majority got back to the citadel, but one party being surrounded, Captain West of the *Excellent* landed with 250 of his seamen and marines, cut his way to them, and brought them off in safety. West had his horse shot under him (a curious note to have to make concerning a naval officer), and lost ten men wounded.

After the eighth there followed seven days of continuous rain, which turned the camp of Reille's division into a marsh, and effectually prevented the construction of siege works in the low-lying ground opposite to the town. The only active operation that could be undertaken was an attempt to storm the fort of the Trinity, which the French believed to be in far worse condition than was actually the case. It was held by eighty Spaniards, under the Irish Lieutenant-Colonel Fitzgerald, and twenty-five of the *Excellent's* marines. The six voltigeur and grenadier companies of the 2nd Italian light infantry delivered the assault with great dash and resolution. But as the strong frontal tower of the fort was high and unbreached, they could make no impression, their ladders proved useless, and they were repulsed with a loss of sixty men. Their leader, the *chef-de-bataillon* Lange, and several other officers were left dead at the foot of the walls.

Seeing that nothing was to be won by mere escalade, Reille had to wait for his siege artillery, which began to arrive from Perpignan on November 16. He at once started two batteries on the Puig-Rom to breach the Fort of the Trinity, and when the ground had begun to grow dry in front of the town, opened trenches opposite its north-eastern angle. When a good *emplacement* had been found a battery was established which played upon the citadel, and commanded so much of the harbour that Reille hoped that the British ships would be compelled to shift their anchorage further out to sea. The Spaniards and the

[1] James's *Naval History*, v. p. 90.

Excellent replied with such a heavy fire that in a few hours the battery was silenced, after its powder magazine had been exploded by a lucky shell [November 19].

Next day, however, the French repaired the damage and mounted more guns, whose fire proved so damaging that Captain West had to move further from the shore. The assailants had established a marked superiority over the fire of the besieged, and availed themselves of it by pushing out parallels nearer to the town, and building four more breaching batteries. With these additional resources they began to work serious damage in the unstable bastions of the citadel. They also knocked a hole in the Fort of the Trinity : but the breach was so far from the foot of the wall that it was still almost inaccessible, the heaps of rubbish which fell into the ditch did not even reach the lowest part of the gap.

On the twenty-first the *Excellent* was relieved by the *Fame*, and Captain West handed over the task of co-operating with the Spaniards to Captain Bennett. The latter thought so ill of the state of affairs, that after two days he withdrew his marines from the Trinity Fort, an action most discouraging to the Spaniards. But at this juncture there arrived in the bay the *Impérieuse* frigate, with her indefatigable commandant Lord Cochrane, a host in himself for such a desperate enterprise as the defence of the much-battered town. He got leave from his superior officer to continue the defence, and manned the Trinity again with his own seamen and marines. They had hardly established themselves there, when the Italian brigade of Mazzuchelli made a second attempt to storm the fort : but it was repulsed without even having reached the foot of the breach.

Cochrane, seeing that the battery which was playing on the Trinity was on the very edge of a precipitous cliff, resolved to try whether it would not be possible to surprise it at night, by landing troops on the beach at the back of the Puig-Rom ; if they could get possession of the guns for a few minutes he hoped to cast them over the declivity on to the rocks below. O'Daly lent him 700 *miqueletes* from the garrison of the town, and this force was put ashore with thirty of the *Impérieuse's* marines who were to lead the assault. The Italians, however, were not caught sleeping, the attack failed, and the assailants were beaten back to the rocks by the beach, with the loss of ten killed and twenty wounded, beside prisoners[1]. The boats of the frigate only brought off 300 men, but many more escaped along the beach into the hilly country to the east, and were neither captured nor slain [November 23]. The sortie, however, had been disastrous, and the Governor, O'Daly, was so down-hearted at the loss of men and at the way in which the walls of the citadel were crumbling before his eyes, that he began to think of surrender. Nor was he much to blame, for the state of things was so bad that it was evident that unless some new factor was introduced into the siege, the end was not far off. The utter improbability of relief from without was demonstrated on the twenty-fourth. Julian Alvarez, the Governor of Gerona and commander of the Spanish forces in the Ampurdam, was perfectly well aware that it was his duty to do what he could for the succour of Rosas. But his forces were insignificant : Vives had only given him 2,000 regular troops to watch the whole line of the Eastern Pyrenees, and of this small force half was shut up in Rosas. Nevertheless Alvarez sallied out from Gerona with two weak battalions of Ultonia and Borbon, and half of the light infantry regiment of Barcelona. Picking up 3,000 local *miqueletes* he advanced to the line of the Fluvia, where Souham was lying, with the division that St. Cyr had told off to cover the siege. The Spaniards drove in the French outposts at several points, but immediately found themselves opposed by very superior numbers, and brought to a complete stand. Realizing that he was far too weak to do anything, Alvarez retreated to Gerona after a sharp skirmish. If he had pushed on he would infallibly have been destroyed. O'Daly received prompt news of his colleague's discomfiture, and saw that relief was impossible. The fact was that Vives ought to have brought up from Barcelona his whole field army of 20,000 men. With such a host Souham could have been driven back, and Reille compelled to relax the investment, perhaps even to raise the siege. But the

---

[1] Compare the narrative of Lord Cochrane, i. 299–300, with those of Belmas, ii. 441, and St. Cyr. The latter is, of course, wrong in saying that the whole sortie was composed of British seamen and marines. It is curious that Cochrane states his own loss at more than the French claimed to have killed or taken.

Captain-General preferred to waste his men and his time in the futile blockade of Duhesme, who could have been just as well 'contained' by 10,000 *somatenes* as by the main Spanish army of Catalonia. The only attempt which Vives made to strengthen his force in the Ampurdam was to order up to Gerona the Aragonese division of 4,000 men under the Marquis of Lazan, which was lying at Lerida. This force arrived too late for the skirmish on the Fluvia, and when it did appear was far too small to accomplish anything. Alvarez and Lazan united had only 8,000 bayonets, while St. Cyr's whole army (as we have already seen) was 25,000 strong, and quite able to maintain the siege, and at the same time to provide a covering force against a relieving army so weak as that which now lay at Gerona.

The siege operations meanwhile were pushed on. Fresh batteries were established to sweep the harbour, and to render more difficult the communication of the citadel and the Trinity fort with the English ships. A new attack was started against the eastern front of the town, and measures were taken to concentrate a heavier fire on the dilapidated bastion of the citadel, which had been destroyed in the old siege of 1794 and never properly repaired. On the twenty-sixth an assault was directed by Pino's division against the town front. This was defended by no more than a ditch and earthwork : the Italians carried it at the first rush, but found more difficulty in evicting the garrison from the ruined houses along the shore. Five hundred *miqueletes*, who were barricaded among them, made a very obstinate resistance, and were only driven out after sharp fighting. One hundred and sixty were taken prisoners, less than a hundred escaped into the citadel : the rest perished. The besiegers at once established a lodgement in the town, covering themselves with the masonry of the demolished houses. It was in vain that the *Fame* and *Impérieuse* ran close in shore and tried to batter the Italians out of the ruins. They inflicted considerable loss, but failed to prevent the enemy from finding shelter. Next night the lodgement in the town was connected with the rest of the siege works, and used as the base for an attack against a hitherto unmolested front of the citadel.

Just after the storming of the town, the garrison received the only succour which was sent to it during the whole siege ; a weak battalion of regulars from the regiment of Borbon was put ashore near the citadel under cover of the darkness. It would have been more useful on the preceding day, for the defence of the outer works. After the arrival of this small succour the Governor, O'Daly, sent eighty men of the Irish regiment of Ultonia to reinforce Cochrane in the Trinity fort, withdrawing a similar number of *miqueletes* to the citadel.

The guns established by the besiegers in their new batteries among the ruins of the town made such good practice upon the front of the citadel that Reille thought it worth while on the twenty-eighth to summon the Governor to surrender. O'Daly made a becoming answer, to the effect that his defences were still intact and that he was prepared to continue his resistance. To cut him off from his communication with the sea, the only side from which he could expect help, Reille now began to build batteries along the water-front of the town, which commanded the landing-places below the citadel. The English ships proved unable to subdue these new guns, and their power to help O'Daly was seriously diminished. It was only under cover of the darkness that they could send boats to land men or stores for the citadel. On the thirtieth they tried to take off the sick and wounded, who were now growing very numerous in the place : but the shore-batteries having hit the headmost boat, the rest drew off and abandoned the attempt. The prospects of the garrison had grown most gloomy.

Meanwhile the Trinity fort had been perpetually battered for ten days, and the hole in the great frontal tower was growing larger. It can hardly be called a breach, as owing to the impossibility of searching the lower courses of the wall by the plunging fire from the Puig-Rom, the lowest edge of the gap was forty feet from the ground. The part of the tower which had been opened was the upper section of a lofty bomb-proof casemate, which composed its ground story. Lord Cochrane built up, with the débris that fell inwards, and with hammocks filled with earth and sand, new walls inside the bomb proof, cutting off the hole from the interior of the tower : thus enemies entering at the gap would find that they had only penetrated into the upper part of a sort of cellar. The ingenious captain also set a long slide or shoot of greased planks just under the lip of the hole, so that any one stepping in would be precipitated thirty feet into the bottom of the casemate. But the mere sight of this mantrap, as he called it, proved enough for the enemy, who never pushed the attack into it.

On November 30 Pino's division assaulted the fort, the storming party being composed of six grenadier and voltigeur companies of the 1st and 6th Italian regiments. They came on with great courage, and planted their ladders below the great hole, amid a heavy fire of musketry from the garrison. The leaders succeeded in reaching the edge of the ' breach,' but finding the chasm and the ' mantrap' before them, would not enter. They were all shot down : grenades were dropped in profusion into the mass at the foot of the ladders, and after a time the stormers fled back under cover, leaving two officers and forty men behind them. They were rallied and brought up again to the foot of the breach, but recoiled after a second and less desperate attempt to enter. The garrison lost only three men killed and two wounded, of whom four were Spaniards. They captured two prisoners, men who had got so far forward that they dared not go back under the terrible fire which swept the foot of the tower. These unfortunates had to be taken into the fort by a rope, so inaccessible was the supposed breach. After this bloody repulse, the besiegers left Lord Cochrane alone, merely continuing to bombard his tower, and throwing up entrenchments on the beach, from which they kept up an incessant musketry fire on the difficult landing-place by which the fort communicated with the ships.

Their main attention was now turned to the citadel, where O'Daly's position was growing hopeless. 'Their practice,' says Cochrane, ' was beautiful. So accurately was their artillery conducted that every discharge " ruled a straight line " along the lower part of the walls. This being repeated till the upper portion was without support, as a matter of course the whole fell into the ditch, forming a breach of easy ascent. The whole proceedings were clearly visible from the Trinity[1].' On December 3 the Governor played his last card : the worst of the damage was being done by the advanced batteries placed among the ruins of the town, and it was from this point that the

[1] Cochrane, *Autobiography*, i. 307.

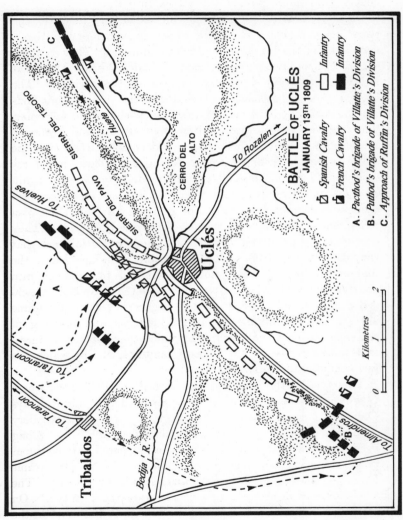

BATTLE OF UCLÉS
JANUARY 13TH 1809

☐ Spanish Cavalry   ☐ Infantry
◼ French Cavalry   ◼ Infantry

A. Pacthod's brigade of Villatte's Division
B. Puthod's brigade of Villatte's Division
C. Approach of Ruffin's Division

Kilometres
0   1   2

To Rozalen

CERRO DEL ALTO

UCLÉS

SIERRA DEL PAVO

SIERRA DEL TESORO

To Huete

To Huelves

To Tarancon

To Tarancon

To Almendros

Tribaldos

Bedija R.

C

A

B

Darbishire & Stanford, L^{td}   *The Oxford Geogl. Inst.*

SIEGE OF ROSAS
NOV. 6 TO DEC. 5 1809

A.A.A.   *French Batteries*
B.B.   *Camps of Pino's Division*
C.C.   *Camps of Reille's Division*
D.D.   *Breached Bastions of the*
     Citadel

PUIG DE LAS AQUILAS

to Palau and Cadaques

to Cadaques

PUIG ROM

Fort Trinity

2nd or Main Attack

Retrenchment

Redoubt

Rosas

Marsh

Citadel

English Ships

ROSAS BAY

to Figueres

Marsh

1st or Right Attack

to Castillon

Metres
0   500   1000

Darbishire & Stanford, L^td

The Oxford Geog^l Inst.

impending assault would evidently be delivered. O'Daly therefore picked 500 of his best men, opened a postern gate, and
launched them at night upon the besiegers' works. The sortie
was delivered with great dash and vigour : the trench guards
were swept away, the breaching batteries were seized, and the
Spaniards began to throw down the parapets, spike the guns,
and set fire to the platforms and fascines. But heavy reserves
came up from the French camp, and their attack could not be
resisted. Before any very serious damage had been done, the
besieged were driven out of the trenches by sheer force of numbers, and forced to retire to the citadel, leaving forty-five dead
behind them. Reille acknowledged the loss of one officer and
twelve men killed, and nineteen men wounded.

On the fourth the siege works were pushed forward to within
200 yards of the walls of the citadel, and the breach already
established in the dilapidated bastion was enlarged to a great
breadth. After dark the French engineers got forward as far
as the counterscarp, and reported that an assault was practicable, and could hardly fail. The same fact was perfectly
evident to O'Daly, who sent out a *parlementaire* to ask for
terms. He offered to surrender in return for leave to take his
garrison off by sea. Reille naturally refused, as the Spaniards
were at his mercy, and enforced an unconditional surrender.

The state of things being visible to Lord Cochrane on the
next morning, he hastily evacuated the Trinity fort, which it
was useless to hold after the citadel had fallen. His garrison,
100 Spaniards and eighty British sailors and marines, had to
descend from the fort by rope ladders, as the enemy commanded
the proper point of embarkation. They were taken off by the
boats of the *Fame* and *Impérieuse* under a heavy musketry fire,
but suffered no appreciable loss. The magazine was left with a
slow match burning, and exploded, ruining the fort, before the
garrison had got on board their ships.

St. Cyr, in his journal of the war in Catalonia, suggests that
Bennett and Cochrane ought to have tried to take off the garrison of the citadel in the same fashion. But this was practically
impossible : the communication between the citadel and the sea
had been lost for some days, the French batteries along the beach
rendering the approach of boats too dangerous to be attempted.

If Captain Bennett had sent in the limited supply of boats that the *Fame*, the *Impérieuse* and the two smaller vessels [1] possessed they would probably have been destroyed. For they would have had to make many return journeys in order to remove 2,500 men, under the fire of heavy guns placed only 200 or 300 yards away from the landing-place. It was quite another thing to remove 180 men from the Trinity, where the enemy could bring practically nothing but musketry to bear, and where the whole of the garrison could be taken off at a single trip. Another futile charge made by the French against the British navy, is that the *Fame* shelled the beach near the citadel while the captive garrison was marching out, and killed several of the unfortunate Spaniards. If the incident happened at all (there is no mention of it in Lord Cochrane or in James) it must have been due to an attempt to damage the French trenches ; Captain Bennett could not have known that the passing column consisted of Spaniards. To insinuate that the mistake was deliberate, as does Belmas, is simply malicious [2].

O'Daly went into captivity with 2,366 men, leaving about 400 more in hospital. The total of the troops who had taken part in the defence, including the reinforcements received by sea, had been about 3,500, so that about 700 must have perished in the siege. The French loss had been at least as great— Pino's division alone lost thirty officers and 400 men killed and wounded [3], besides many sick. It is probable that the total diminution in the ranks of Reille's two divisions was over 1,000, the bad weather having told very heavily on the ill-equipped troops.

So ended an honourable if not a very desperate defence. The place was doomed from the first, when once the torpid and pur-blind Vives had made up his mind to keep his whole force concentrated round Barcelona, and to send no more than the

---

[1] These were the two bomb-vessels *Meteor* and *Lucifer*. The *Magnificent* 74 came up the same day, but after the evacuation of the Trinity.

[2] St. Cyr does not say so (p. 50), but only that the Spaniards imagined that it was done deliberately. Belmas (p. ii. 453) asks if it was not irritation on the part of the British. Arteche does not repulse the silly suggestion, as he reasonably might (iv. 270).

[3] Belmas, ii. 454, and Vacani, ii. 315, agree in these figures.

insignificant division of Alvarez and Lazan to the help of O'Daly. Considering the dilapidated condition of the citadel of Rosas, and the almost untenable state of the town section of the fortifications, the only wonder is that the French did not break in at an earlier date. The first approaches of Reille's engineers were, according to Belmas, unskilfully conducted, and pushed too much into the marsh. When once they received a right direction, the result was inevitable. Even had the artillery failed to do its work Rosas must nevertheless have fallen within a few days, for it was insufficiently provisioned, and, as the communication with the sea had been cut off since November 30, must have yielded ere long to starvation. The French found an ample store of guns (fifty-eight pieces) and much ammunition in the place, but an utterly inadequate supply of food.

[N.B.—Belmas, St. Cyr, and Arteche have all numerous slips in their narration, from not having used the British authorities. Vacani's account is, on the whole, the best on the French side. Much may be learnt from James's *Naval History*, vol. v, but more from Lord Cochrane's picturesque autobiography. From this, e. g., alone can it be ascertained that the column which attacked the Puig-Rom on November 23 was composed of *miqueletes*, not of British soldiers. Cochrane is represented by several writers as arriving on the twenty-fourth or even the twenty-sixth, while as a matter of fact he reached Rosas on the twenty-first. It may interest some to know that Captain Marryat, the novelist, served under Cochrane, and was mentioned in his dispatch. So the description of the siege of Rosas in Marryat's *Frank Mildmay*, wherein his captain is so much glorified, is a genuine personal reminiscence, and not an invention of fiction.]

SECTION X: CHAPTER II

ST. CYR RELIEVES BARCELONA: BATTLES OF CARDADEU AND MOLINS DE REY

WHEN Rosas had fallen St. Cyr was at last able to take in hand the main operation which had been entrusted to him by Napoleon—the relief of Barcelona. While the siege was still in progress he had received two letters bidding him hasten to the relief of Duhesme without delay [1], but he had taken upon himself the responsibility of writing back that he must clear his flank and rear before he dared move, and that he should proceed with the leaguer of Rosas, which could only last a few days longer, unless he received formal orders to abandon the undertaking. He ventured to point out that the moral and political effects of taking such a step would be deplorable [2]. Napoleon's silence gave consent, and St. Cyr's plea was justified by the fall of the place on December 5.

Rosas having been captured, the French general had now at his disposition all his four divisions, those of Souham, Pino, Reille, and Chabot, which even after deducting the casualties suffered in the siege, and the losses experienced by the covering troops from the bad weather, still amounted to 22,000 men. After counting up the very considerable forces which the Spaniards might place in his way, he resolved to take on with him for the relief of Barcelona the troops of Souham, Pino, and Chabot, and to leave behind only those of Reille. With about 5,000 or 5,500 soldiers of not very good quality that officer was to hold Figueras and Rosas, watch Gerona, and protect the high-road to Perpignan. St. Cyr himself with the twenty-six battalions

---

[1] Berthier to St. Cyr, Burgos, Nov. 13. ' Si Roses tarde à être pris, il faut marcher sur Barcelone sans s'inquiéter de cette place, &c.,' and much to same effect from Coubo, Nov. 16 [wrongly printed in St. Cyr, Nov. 10].

[2] St. Cyr to the Emperor, Nov. 17, from Figueras.

and nine squadrons forming the other three divisions, a force of
some 15,000 infantry and 1,500 horse, took his way to the
south.

The first obstacle in his way was Gerona : but if he stopped
to besiege and take it, it was clear that he would never reach
Barcelona in time to save Duhesme from starvation : that
general had reported that his food would only last till the end
of December, and Gerona would certainly hold out more than
three weeks. Indeed, as we shall see, when it was actually
beleaguered in the next year, it made a desperate defence, lasting
for nearly six months [1]. St. Cyr saw from the first that he must
leave the fortress alone, and slip past it. As it commanded the
high-road, this resolution forced him to abandon any intention
of taking forward his artillery and his wheeled transport. They
could not face the rugged bypaths on to which he would be
compelled to throw himself, and he marched without a single
gun, and with his food and provisions borne on pack-horses and
mules, of which he had a very modest provision.

St. Cyr was quite well aware that if General Vives were to
resign the blockade of Barcelona to his *miqueletes* and *somatenes*,
and to come against him with his whole army, the task of
relieving Duhesme would be dangerous if not impossible.
There are but two roads from Gerona to Barcelona, and across
each of them lie half a dozen positions which, if entrenched and
held by superior numbers, he could not hope to force. These
two routes are the coast-road by Mataro and Arens de Mar—
which the French had used for their first march to Gerona in
August—and the inland road up the valley of the Besos by
Hostalrich and Granollers. But the former had been so con-
scientiously destroyed by Lord Cochrane and the local *somatenes* [2]
that St. Cyr regarded it as impassable ; there were places where
it had been blasted away for lengths of a quarter or a half of
a mile. Moreover, at many points the army would have to
defile under the cliffs for long distances, and might be shelled
by any British men-of-war that should happen to lie off the
coast [3]. Accordingly the French general determined to try

---

[1] May 30 to Dec. 10, 1809.

[2] See vol. i. p. 331.

[3] St. Cyr, *Journal de l'Armée de Catalogne*, p. 58.

the inland road, though he would have to march round Gerona and the smaller fortress of Hostalrich, and though it was cut by several admirable positions, where the Catalans might offer battle with reasonable prospects of success.   It was all-important that Vives should be left as long as possible in uncertainty as to his adversary's next move, and that the Catalans should be dealt with in detail rather than in mass.   St. Cyr resolved, therefore, to make a show of attacking Gerona, and to try whether he could not catch Lazan and Alvarez, and rout them, before the Captain-General should come up to their assistance.

On December 9, therefore, St. Cyr had his whole corps, minus the division of Reille, concentrated on the left bank of the river Ter.   On the next day he manœuvred as if about to envelop Gerona.   He had hoped that this move would tempt Lazan and Alvarez to come out and meet him in the open. But fully conscious that their 8,000 men would be exposed to inevitable defeat, the two Spanish officers wisely kept quiet under the walls of their stronghold.   Having worked round their flank, St. Cyr on the eleventh sent back the whole of his artillery and heavy baggage to Figueras, and plunged into the mountains ; at La Bispal he distributed four days' biscuit to his men, warning them that there would be no further issue of rations till they reached Barcelona.   The light carts which had been dragged thus far with the food were burnt.   As to munitions, each soldier had fifty cartridges in his pouch, and the pack-mules carried 150,000 more, a reserve of only ten rounds for each man [1].   The equipment of the army, in short, was such that if it failed to force its way to Barcelona within six days it must starve, while if it was forced to fight three or four heavy engagements it would be left helpless, without a cartridge for a final battle.   The general, if not the men in the ranks, fully realized the peril of the situation.

On the twelfth St. Cyr pushed along the mountains above Palamos and San Feliu, brushing away a body of *miqueletes* from the coast-land under Juan Claros, who tried to hold the defile.

---

[1] St. Cyr says that Napoleon falsified his report, when reprinting it in the *Moniteur,* and put 150 instead of 50 rounds per man, to disguise the risk that had been run (p. 58).

On the thirteenth the French reached Vidreras, where they were again on a decent road, that which goes from Gerona to Malgrat. They now perceived that they were being followed by Lazan and the garrison of Gerona, whose camp-fires were visible on the heights to the north, while troops, evidently detached from the blockade of Barcelona, were visible in front of them. It was clear that St. Cyr had at least succeeded in placing himself between the two main forces which the enemy could oppose to him, and might engage them separately. He might also count on the Spaniards looking for him on the Malgrat-Mataro road, on which he was now established, while it was his intention to abandon it, in order to plunge inland once more, and to fall into the main *chaussée* to Barcelona, south of Hostalrich. That a path existed, along which such a movement could be carried out, was only known to the general by the report of a Perpignan smuggler, who had once kept sheep among these hills. But when exploring parties tried to find it, they lost their way, and reported that no such route existed. If this was the fact, St. Cyr was ruined : but he refused to believe the officers who assured him that the smuggler had erred, and pushing among the rocks finally discovered it himself. During his exploration he was nearly cut off by a party of *somatenes*, and his escort had to fight hard in order to save him.

But the road was found, and on the fifteenth the army followed it, almost in single file, while the dragoons had to dismount and lead their horses. They saw the fortress of Hostalrich in the valley below them, and passed it in sight of the garrison. Some of the latter came out, and skirmished with the rearguard of St. Cyr's long column, but they were too weak to do much harm, while Lazan, whose advent from the north would have caused more serious difficulties, had been completely eluded, and never came in sight.

In the afternoon the whole expeditionary force safely descended into the Barcelona *chaussée* near San Celoni, from which place they drove out four battalions of *miqueletes*, the first troops that the tardy Vives had detached from his main army. The men were much fatigued, and the *somatenes* were beginning to give trouble both in flank and rear, but St. Cyr insisted that they should not encamp by San Celoni, but push southward through the difficult defile of the Trentapassos, so that they might not find it held against them on the following morning. This was done, and the best of the many positions which the Spaniards might have held to oppose the march of the invaders was occupied without the least resistance. St. Cyr encamped at the southern end of the pass, and saw before him, when the night had fallen, a line of watch-fires far down the valley of the Besos which showed that the Spaniards from the leaguer of Barcelona had at last come out to oppose him.

The conduct of Vives during the last six days had been in perfect keeping with the rest of his slow and stupid guidance of the campaign. He had received in due course news of the fall of Rosas, and soon after the additional information that St. Cyr had crossed the Ter and was threatening Gerona. Opinion was divided in the camp of the Catalans as to whether the French were about to lay siege to that fortress, or to pass it by and make a dash for the relief of Duhesme. If they sat down before Gerona there was no need to hurry : if they should pass it by, it would be necessary to move at once, in order to occupy the defiles against them. The opinion of the more intelligent officers was that St. Cyr would be forced to march to aid Duhesme, whose want of provisions was well known by secret intelligence sent out from Barcelona. Unfortunately Vives inclined to the other side : he preferred to believe the alternative which did not impose on him the necessity for instant and decisive action. He did nothing, and pretended to be waiting for further news. It reached him on the night of December 11– 12, in the form of a message from the Junta of Gerona, to the effect that the French had sent back their artillery and were plunging into the mountains in the direction of La Bispal, so that it was clear that they must be marching to relieve Duhesme. It might have been expected that the Captain-General would now at last break up from his lines, and hasten to throw himself across the path of the approaching enemy. But after holding a long and fruitless council of war he contented himself with sending out Reding, with that part of the newly-arrived Grana- dan division which had reached Catalonia. On the twelfth therefore the Swiss General started by the inland road with seven battalions of his own Andalusian levies and a regiment

of cavalry.   Next day he reached Granollers and halted there.
At the same time Francisco Milans, with four tercios of *miqueletes*,
was sent out to guard the coast-road, the other possible line
of approach by which St. Cyr might arrive.   Reding had 5,000
men, Milans 3,000 : but Vives still lay before Barcelona with
two-thirds of his army, at least 16,000 or 17,000 bayonets.   It
was in vain that Caldagues, the preserver of Gerona, implored
him to leave no more than a screen of *miqueletes* in the lines,
and to sally forth to fight with every regular soldier that he
could muster.   The Captain-General refused to listen, supporting
his inactivity by pleading that the advice sent from Gerona did
not speak of the enemy's force as very large : the defiles, he
urged, were so difficult that Reding and Milans, aided by Lazan,
ought to be able to hold them against any small expeditionary
force.

Thus St. Cyr was left to work out his daring plan without
any serious opposition.   The only force with which he came
in contact was Milans' brigade of *miqueletes*, who, finding the
coast-road clear, had crossed the mountains and occupied San
Celoni.   These were the troops whom St. Cyr drove away
on the afternoon of the fifteenth, before entering the defile of
the Trentapassos.

On receiving news of this combat, which had taken place only
twenty-one miles from his lines, Vives at last set out in person.
But persisting in his idiotic notion of blocking Barcelona to the last
moment, he left Caldagues before the place with 12,000 men, and
marched with a single brigade of 4,000 bayonets to join Reding.
Moving all through the night of the fifteenth-sixteenth he joined
the Granadans at daybreak at Cardadeu on the high-road.   Their
united strength was only 9,000 men, of whom 600 were cavalry,
and seven guns[1].   This was the whole force which fought St. Cyr,
for Lazan, moving with culpable slowness, was still far north of
San Celoni, when he should have been pressing on the rear
of the French, while Milans with the *miqueletes*, who had been
beaten on the previous day, was some miles away in the
mountains on the right, and quite out of touch with his commander-in-chief.   Nine thousand Spaniards, in short, were
within ten miles of the field, yet took no part in the battle.

[1] Cf. Cabanes, with Arteche, iv. 276.

St. Cyr in his central position kept them apart, and they failed to combine with Vives and his force at Cardadeu.

The valley of the Besos at this point has broadened out, and is no longer the narrow defile that is seen a few miles further to the north. But there is much broken ground on both sides of the high-road. A little way north of Cardadeu is a low hill covered with pines, lying to the right of the *chaussée*: at the foot of the hill is a ravine which the road has to cross at right angles, and which falls into the stream called the Riera de la Roca. The country-side was composed partly of cultivated ground, partly of thickets of pine and oak, which rendered it difficult for either side to get a general view of its adversaries' movements.

Vives, who had only reached his fighting-ground at dawn, had no time to reconnoitre his position, or to make any elaborate scheme for getting the best use out of the *terrain*. He hastily drew up his army in two lines across the high-road : the front line was behind the ravine, the second higher up on the pine-clad hill. Reding's troops held the right wing on the lowest ground, and extended as far as the river Mogent, a branch of the Besos. Vives' own Catalan regiments formed the centre and left : they were mainly placed on the hill commanding the road, with three guns in front of their centre, and two further to the left on a point from which they could enfilade a turn of the *chaussée*. The *miqueletes* of Vich, on the extreme left, held a spur of the higher mountains which bound the valley of the Besos. The reserve drawn up on the high-road, behind the main position, consisted of two guns, two squadrons of horse (Husares Españoles, lately arrived from Majorca) and two battalions.

St. Cyr could make out very little of his adversaries' force or position ; the woods and hills masked the greater part of the Spanish line. But he knew that he must attack, and that promptly, for every hour that he delayed would give time for Lazan to come up in his rear, and Milans on his left flank. He left behind him at the southern outlet of the Trentapassos the three battalions of Chabot's division, with orders to hold the defile at all costs against Lazan, whenever the latter should appear. With the other twenty-three battalions forming the

divisions of Pino and Souham he marched down the high-road
to deal with Vives. It was necessary to attack at once: 'the
biscuit distributed at La Bispal was just finished: the cartridges
were running low, for many had been spent in the preceding
skirmishes. There was, in fact, only ammunition for one hour
of battle [1].' St. Cyr saw that he must win by one short and
swift stroke, or suffer a complete disaster. Accordingly, he had
resolved to form his two strong divisions—more than 13,000
men—into one great column, which was to charge the Spanish
centre and burst through by its own impetus and momentum.
Pino's thirteen Italian battalions formed the head of the mass:
Souham's ten French battalions its rear. The General's plan is
best expressed in his own words: his orders to Pino, who was
to lead the attack, ran as follows:—

'The corps must fight in the order in which I have arranged
it this morning. There is neither time nor means to make
dispositions to beat the Spaniards more or less thoroughly. The
country-side is so broken and wooded that it would take three
hours to reconnoitre their position, and in two hours Lazan may
be on the spot attacking our rear. Not a minute can be lost:
we must simply rush at and trample down [2] the corps in our
front, whatever its strength may be. Our food is done, our
ammunition almost exhausted. The enemy has artillery, which
is a reason the more for haste: the quicker we attack, the less
time will he have to shell us. There must be no attempt to feel
his position ; not one battalion must be deployed. Though his
position is strong we must go straight at it in column, and burst
through the centre by striking at that one point with our whole
force. The enemy must be given no time to prepare his defence
or bring up his reserves. You must not change the disposition
in column in which we march, even in order to take great
numbers of prisoners. Our sole end is to break through and
to get as close as we can to Barcelona this evening. Our camp-
fires must be visible to the garrison by night, to show that we
are at hand to raise the siege.'

This order of battle was most hazardous: if St. Cyr had found

---

[1] St. Cyr, *Journal de l'Armée de Catalogne*, p. 64.

[2] 'Il faut passer sur le ventre au corps de troupes en face, quel que soit
son nombre.' St. Cyr, p. 66.

in front of him two steady English divisions instead of Reding's raw Granadan levies and the gallant but untrained Catalan *miqueletes*, it is certain that affairs would have gone as at Busaco or Talavera.   Dense columns attacking a fair position held by good troops in line are bound to suffer terrible losses, and ought never to succeed.   But St. Cyr knew the enemies with whom he had to deal, and his method was well adapted to his end.   If he ran some risk of failing at the commencement of the action, it was simply because his subordinates did not follow out his directions.

General Pino, on whom the responsibility of opening the attack devolved, started with every intention of obedience.   But when he arrived at the foot of the Spanish position, and the balls began to fall thickly among his leading battalions, he lost his head.   His column only faced the Spanish right centre, and the heavy flanking fire from the hostile wings daunted him. Instead of pushing straight before him with his whole force, as St. Cyr had ordered, he threw out five battalions of Mazzuchelli's brigade to his left[1], and two battalions under General Fontane to his extreme right[2]; the six battalions of his rear brigade were not yet up to the front, and took no part in the first assault.   Thus he attacked on a front of three-quarters of a mile, instead of at one single point.   His columns, after driving in the Spanish front line, came to a stand halfway up the hill, in a very irregular array, the flanks thrown forward, the centre hanging somewhat back.   Reding, against whom the main attack of Mazzuchelli's brigade had been directed, brought up his second line, and when the Italians were slackening in their advance hurled at them two squadrons of hussars, and led forward his whole division.   The assailants broke, and fell back with loss.

St. Cyr, coming up to the front at this moment, was horrified to mark the results of Pino's disobedience of his orders.   But he had still Souham's division in hand, and flung it, in one solid mass of ten battalions, upon Reding's right ; at the same time he commanded Pino to throw the two regiments of his intact rear brigade upon the Spanish centre[3], while Fontane's two

[1] Three battalions of the 4th of the line, and two of the 2nd Light Infantry.

[2] One battalion of the 2nd Light Infantry and one of the 7th of the line.

[3] Three battalions each of the 1st and 6th of the line.

battalions continued to demonstrate against the enemy's left. The result was what might have been expected : the column of Souham burst through the Granadan division, and completely routed the right wing of the Spanish army : at the same moment Pino's main column forced back Vives and the Catalans along the line of the high-road. All at once fell into confusion, and, when St. Cyr bade his two Italian cavalry regiments charge up the *chaussée*, the enemy broke his ranks and fled to the hills. Five of the seven Spanish guns were captured, with two standards and some 1,500 unwounded prisoners. Reding, who stayed behind to the last, trying to rally a rearguard for the protection of the routed host, was nearly taken prisoner, and had to draw his sword and cut his way out. Vives, whose conduct on this day was anything but creditable, scrambled up a cliff after turning his horse loose, and came almost alone to the sea-shore near Mongat, where he was picked up by the boats of the *Cambrian* frigate, and forwarded to Tarragona. Besides the prisoners the Spaniards lost at least a thousand men, and many of the *miqueletes* dispersed to their homes. St. Cyr acknowledged 600 casualties, nearly all of them, as might have been expected, in Pino's division.

Reding at last succeeded in rallying some troops at Monmalo near San Culgat, and covered the retreat of the main mass of the fugitives to join the troops who had been left in the lines before Barcelona. As to the detached Spanish corps under Milans and the Marquis of Lazan, the former never came down from the hills till the fighting was over, though it was only four or five miles from the scene of action [1]. The latter, which was following in St. Cyr's rear, moved with such extreme slowness that it had not yet reached San Celoni when the battle was fought, and did not even get into contact with Chabot's division, which had been left behind to guard against its approach [2]. On learning of the defeat the Marquis marched back to Gerona, and rejoined Alvarez. Thus Vives got no assistance whatever from his outlying corps : if Lazan is to be trusted, this was largely the fault

---

[1] See the account of Cabanes, who was with Milans this day, in his *History of the War in Catalonia*.

[2] See the narrative of an officer in the division of Lazan, printed by Cabanes as an appendix.

of the Commander-in-chief himself, for no dispatch from him reached his subordinates after December 14, and they had no knowledge of his movements or designs.

Meanwhile Caldagues, who had been left in charge of the blockade, had maintained his post, and repulsed a heavy sortie which Duhesme and the garrison had directed against his posts on the sixteenth. But when the news of the battle of Cardadeu reached him in the evening, he evacuated all the parts of his line which lay to the east of the Llobregat, and concentrated his 12,000 men at Molins de Rey and San Boy, on the further bank of that river. He was forced to abandon at Sarria the large dépôt of provisions from which the left wing of the investing force had been fed.

The road from Cardadeu and San Culgat to Barcelona being thus left open, St. Cyr marched in triumph into Barcelona on the morning of the seventeenth. He complains in his memoirs that he did not discover one single vedette from the garrison pushed out to meet him, and that Duhesme did not come forth to receive him, or give him a single word of thanks. Indeed, when the Governor at last presented himself to meet the commander of the Seventh Corps, he spent his first words not in expressing his appreciation for the service which had been rendered him, but in demonstrating that he had never been in danger, and could have held out for six weeks more. He was somewhat abashed when St. Cyr replied by presenting him with a copy of one of his own former dispatches to Berthier, which painted the condition of the garrison in the blackest colours, and asked for instant succours lest the worst might happen[1].

It was clear that the two generals would not work well together, but as St. Cyr held the supreme command, and was determined to assert himself, Duhesme could do no more than sulk in silence. The conduct of the operations against the Catalans had been taken completely out of his hands.

St. Cyr's daring march to Barcelona had been crowned with complete success. It was by far the most brilliant operation on

---

[1] St. Cyr, as any reader of his *Mémoires* can see, was malicious and sarcastic. But Duhesme has a bad reputation for carelessness and selfishness, and his writings make an even worse impression than those of St. Cyr. Probably the latter's narrative is fairly correct.

the French side during the first year of the war. That it was perilous cannot be denied: if the commander of the Seventh Corps had found the whole army of Vives entrenched at the passage of the Tordera, or across the defile of the Trentapassos, it seems impossible that he could have got forward to Barcelona. Thirty thousand men, of whom half were regular troops, might have been opposed to him, and they could have brought artillery against him, while he had not a single piece. If once checked he must have retreated in haste, for he had only ammunition for a single battle. But the rapid and unexpected character of his movements entirely puzzled the enemy, and he was fortunate in having a Vives to contend against. ' When the enemy has no general,' as Schepeler remarks while commenting on this campaign, ' any stroke of luck is possible.' Against a capable officer St. Cyr would probably have failed, but he had a shrewd suspicion of the character of his opponent from what had happened during the siege of Rosas: he dared much, and his daring was rewarded by a splendid victory.

The campaign, however, was not yet completed. Barcelona had been relieved, but only a fraction of the Spanish army had been met and beaten. Caldagues lay behind the Llobregat with 11,000[1] men who had not yet been engaged. Reding had joined him with the wrecks of the troops which had fought at Cardadeu, some 3,000 or 4,000 men. They lined the eastern bank of the river, only six or seven miles from the suburbs of Barcelona, occupying the entrenchments which had been constructed to shut in Duhesme during the blockade. These were strengthened with several redoubts, some of them armed with heavy artillery, and the positions were good, but too extensive for a force of 14,000 or 15,000 men. Their weak point was that the Llobregat even in December is fordable in many places, and that if the French attacked in mass at one point they were almost certain of being able to force their way through the line. Reding, and his second-in-command Caldagues, were both of opinion that it would be wise to evacuate the lines, if St. Cyr should come out in force against them, and to fall back on the mountains in their rear, which separate the valley

---

[1] Some of his *miqueletes* had absconded during the withdrawal from the eastern half of the river.

of the Llobregat from the coast-plain of Tarragona. Here there
was a strong position at the defile of Ordal, where it was
intended to construct an entrenched camp. But there was
a strong temptation to hold on in the old lines for as long
a time as possible, for by retiring to Ordal the army would
leave open the high-road to Lerida and Saragossa, and give
up much of the plain to the incursions of the French foragers.
Reding sent back to Vives, who had now landed in his rear
and placed himself at Villanueva de Sitjas, to ask whether he
was to retreat at once, or to hold his ground. The Captain-
General sent back the inconclusive reply that 'he might fall
back on Ordal if he could not defend the line of the Llobregat.'
Thus he threw back the responsibility on his subordinate,
and Reding, anxious to vindicate his courage before the eyes
of the Catalans, resolved after some hesitation to retain his
positions, though he had grave doubts of the possibility of
resistance.

He was not allowed much time to ponder over the situation. The reply of Vives only reached him on the night of
December 20–21. On the next morning St. Cyr came out
of Barcelona and attacked the lines. He had brought with
him every available man: Duhesme had been left to hold the
city with Lecchi's Italians alone: his other division (that of
Chabran), together with the three which had formed the army of
succour—those of Souham, Pino, and Chabot—were all directed
against the lines. The plan of St. Cyr was to demonstrate
against the bridge of Molins de Rey, the strongest part of the
Spanish position, with Chabran's 4,000 men, while he himself
crossed the fords lower down the Llobregat with the 14,000
bayonets of the other three divisions, and turned the right flank
of the enemy.

At five o'clock on a miserable gusty December morning the
French came down towards the river: Chabran led off by
making a noisy demonstration opposite the redoubts at the
bridge, on the northern flank of the position. This, as
St. Cyr had intended, drew Reding's attention to that flank:
he reinforced his left with troops drawn from his right wing
on the lower and easier ground down stream. An hour later
the other attacking columns advanced, that of Souham crossing

the ford of San Juan Despi, while Pino and Chabot passed by
that of San Feliu. No proper attempt was made to dispute
their advance. Outnumbered, and strung out along a very
extensive position, the Catalans soon saw their line broken
in several places. The only serious opposition made was by
the centre, which advanced down hill against Souham and tried
to charge him, but gave back long before bayonets had been
crossed.

The most fatal part of Reding's position was that on his
extreme right Chabot's three battalions had got completely round
his flank, and kept edging in on the rear of his southern wing,
which abandoned hill after hill as it saw its retreat threatened.
Pino and Souham had only to press on, and each regiment in
their front gave way in turn when it saw its exposed flank
in danger. At last the whole of the Spanish right and centre
was pushed back in disorder on to the still intact left behind
the bridge of Molins de Rey. Now was the time for Chabran
to turn his demonstration into a real attack : if he had crossed
the river and advanced rapidly, he would have caught the shaken
masses in front, while the rest of the army chased them forward
into his arms. But being timid or unenterprising, he let the
flying enemy pass across his front unmolested, and only forded
the river when they had gone too far to be caught. The
unhappy Vives came up at this moment, just in time to see
his whole army on the run, and headed their flight to the
hills.

Thus the Spaniards got away without any very crushing
losses, though their historian Cabanes confesses that if Chabran
had moved a quarter of an hour earlier he would have captured
half the army of Catalonia. As it was, St. Cyr took about
1,200 prisoners only, though his dragoons pursued the routed
enemy for many miles. It was a great misfortune for the
Catalans that among these captives was the Conde de Caldagues,
the one first-rate officer in their ranks. He was taken by the
pursuers at Vendrell, many miles from the field, when his
exhausted horse fell under him. St. Cyr captured the whole
artillery of the Spaniards, twenty-five cannon[1], of which several

[1] St. Cyr says twenty-five in his report to Napoleon, but increases the
number to fifty in his *Mémoires*, p. 87.

were pieces of heavy calibre, mounted in redoubts. The field-pieces were more useful to him, as he was very short of artillery; he had brought none with him, while Duhesme had been obliged to destroy the greater part of his during the retreat from Gerona in August. He also made prize of a magazine of 3,000,000 cartridges and of many thousands of muskets, which the routed enemy cast away in their haste to escape over the hills. Some of the fugitives fled south, and did not stop till they reached Tortosa and the Ebro: others dispersed in the direction of Igualada and Lerida, but the main body rallied at Tarragona.

The victorious French divisions were pushed far out from the battle-field so as to occupy not only the whole plain of the Llobregat, but also the defiles over the hills leading to Tarragona. Chabran was placed at Martorell, Chabot at San Sadurni, Souham at Vendrell, and Pino at Villanueva de Sitjas and Villafranca. Thus the pass of Ordal was in the victor's hands, and he had it in his power to march against Tarragona without having any further positions to force. But the siege of that place did not form, at present, any part of St. Cyr's designs. His aim was first to collect such magazines at Barcelona as would feed his whole army of 25,000 men till the harvest was ripe, and secondly to reopen his communication with France. The sea route was rendered dangerous by the English ships, which were continually hovering off the coast. The land route was blocked by the fortresses of Hostalrich and Gerona. St. Cyr imagined that it was more important to make an end of these places, and open his route to Perpignan, than to attack Tarragona. The latter place was strong, and the greater part of the Catalan army had taken refuge in it. The siege would need, as he supposed, many months, and could not be properly conducted till a battering-train and a large store of ammunition had been brought down from France.

It is possible that the French general might have come to another conclusion if he had been aware of the state of panic and disorganization among the Catalans at this moment. The *miqueletes* had mostly dispersed to their homes, the regular troops were mutinous, and the populace was crying treason and looking for scape-goats. The incapable Vives was frightened

into resignation, and finally replaced by Reding, whose courage
at least was beyond suspicion, if his abilities were not those
of a great general.   The smaller towns were full of tumults and
assassination :   at Lerida a certain Gomez declared himself
dictator and began to seize and execute all suspected persons.
He did not stop till he was caught and beheaded by a battalion
which Reding sent out against him.   In short, anarchy reigned
in Catalonia for ten days, and it is possible that if St. Cyr had
marched straight to Tarragona he might have taken the place,
though its inhabitants were working hard at their fortifications,
and vowing to emulate Saragossa.   Many historians of the war
have blamed the French general for not making the attempt :
but there was much to urge in his defence.   It is perfectly
possible that the Tarragonese might have made a gallant stand,
in spite of all their troubles, for the garrison was large if
disorderly.   If they held out, St. Cyr had neither a siege
equipage nor sufficient magazines to feed his army when concentrated in a single spot.   The French troops were exhausted,
and suffering dreadfully from the inclement winter weather.
Lazan and Alvarez were in full force in the Ampurdam, and
were giving Reille's weak division much trouble.

Probably therefore St. Cyr was justified in halting for a month,
which he employed in clearing the whole country-side for thirty
miles round Barcelona, and in collecting the stores of food
which his army required before it could make another move.
The halt allowed time for the Catalans to rally, and for Reding
to reorganize his army :   by February he was ready once more to
try his fortune in the field.   Indeed, he was ere long more
formidable than St. Cyr had expected, for he was joined by
the second brigade of his own Granadan division, which came
up from Valencia not long after the battle of Molins de Rey,
and the last reserves from Majorca had also sailed to aid him,
after giving over the fortifications of the Balearic Isles to the
marines of the fleet, and the urban guards of Palma and Port
Mahon.   The *miqueletes*, too, returned to their standards when
the first panic was over, and in a month Catalonia could once
more show an army of 30,000 men.   The first incident which
occurred to encourage the insurgents was that on January 1.
Lazan fell upon and very severely handled a detached battalion

of Reille's division at Castellon in the Ampurdam [1], and when Reille came up against him in person with 2,500 men, inflicted on him a sharp check at the fords of the Muga. Not long after, however, the Marquis withdrew from this region, and marched back toward Aragon, taking with him his own division and leaving only the weak corps of Alvarez to deal with Reille. His retreat was caused by the news of his brother's desperate position in Saragossa. Hoping to make a diversion in favour of Palafox, Lazan marched to Lerida, where he began to gather in all the men that he could collect before moving back to his native province. Thus the pressure on Reille was much reduced.

St. Cyr's men, meanwhile, made many expeditions into the valleys above Barcelona. They cleared the defile of Bruch leading into the upper valley of the Llobregat, which the *somatenes* had held so gallantly against Schwartz and Chabran in June. They took, but did not hold, the almost inaccessible peak of Montserrat, and on the coast-road dominated the country as far as Mataro. But they could not reopen the communications with France: their general did not dare to set about the siege of Gerona while Reding had still the makings of an army in the direction of Tarragona. It was not till that brave but unfortunate officer had received his *third* defeat in February that St. Cyr was able to turn his attention to the north, and the road to Perpignan. For the present, the French general found himself mainly occupied by the imperious necessity for scraping together food not only for his own army, but for the great city of Barcelona, where both the garrison and the people were living from hand to mouth. For the resources of the neighbouring plain were nearly exhausted, and the only external supply came from occasional merchantmen from Cette or Marseilles, whose captains were tempted to run the British blockade by the enormous price which they could secure for their corn if it could be brought safely through. It

---

[1] This was the 4th battalion of the 2nd of the line, which had joined Reille in the late autumn, and did not form part of his original division as detailed in the Appendix to vol. i. St. Cyr says that it only lost sixty prisoners besides some casualties. Lazan wrote that he took ninety prisoners, and killed or wounded over 200 more Frenchmen.

was only somewhat later that the Emperor directed the naval
authorities in Provence to dispatch regular convoys to Barcelona
under a strong escort, whenever the British cruisers were
reported to have been blown out to sea. Meanwhile the
problem of food supplies remained almost as urgent a question
for St. Cyr as the movements of his adversaries in the field.

SECTION X: CHAPTER III

THE CAMPAIGN OF FEBRUARY, 1809: BATTLE OF VALLS

MORE than a month had elapsed since the battle of Molins de Rey before any important movements were made in Catalonia. Early in February St. Cyr drew in his divisions from the advanced positions in the plain of Tarragona, which they had taken up after the victory of Molins de Rey. They had eaten up the country-side, and were being much harassed by the *miqueletes*, who had begun to press in upon their communications with Barcelona, in spite of all the care that was taken to scour the country with small flying columns, and to scatter any nucleus of insurgents that began to grow up in the French rear. Owing to the dispersion of the divisions of the 7th Corps these operations were very laborious; between the new year and the middle of February St. Cyr calculated that his men had used up 2,000,000 cartridges in petty skirmishes, and suffered a very appreciable loss in operations that were practically worthless [1]. Accordingly he drew them closer together, in order to shorten the dangerously extended line of communication with Barcelona.

Reding, during this period of waiting, had been keeping quiet in Tarragona, where he was reorganizing and drilling the harassed troops which had been beaten at Cardadeu and Molins de Rey. He had, as we have already seen, received heavy reinforcements from the South [2] and the Balearic Isles [3]; but it was not in numbers only that his army had improved. St. Cyr's inaction had restored their *morale*. They were too, as regards food and munitions, in a much better condition than their adversaries, as they could freely draw provisions from the plain

---

[1] St. Cyr, *Campagne de Catalogne*, p. 98.

[2] Regiments of Santa Fé, and 1st of Antequera, three battalions with 3,600 men in November, and probably 3,000 in February.

[3] Swiss Regiment of Beschard, about 2,000 strong, and Majorca Militia [sometimes called 'Palma'], 600 strong.

of the Lower Ebro and the northern parts of Valencia, and were besides helped by corn brought in by British and Spanish vessels from the whole eastern Mediterranean. Reding had also got a good supply of arms and ammunition from England. As he found himself unmolested, he was finally able to rearrange his whole force, so as not only to cover Tarragona, but to extend a screen of troops all round the French position. He now divided his army into two wings : he himself, on the right, kept in hand at Tarragona the 1st Division, consisting mainly of the Granadan troops : while General Castro was sent to establish the head quarters of the 2nd Division, which contained most of the old battalions of the army of Catalonia, at Igualada. Their line of communication was by Santa Coloma, Sarreal, and Montblanch. This disposition was probably a mistake : while the French lay concentrated in the middle of the semicircle, the Spanish army was forced to operate on outer lines sixty miles long, and could not mass itself in less than three or four days. By a sudden movement of the enemy, either Reding or Castro might be assailed by superior numbers, and forced to fall back on an eccentric line of retreat before he could be succoured by his colleague.

It would seem that, encouraged by St. Cyr's quiescence, his own growing strength, and the protestations of the Catalans, Reding had once more resolved to resume the offensive. The extension of his left to Igualada was made with no less ambitious a purpose than that of outflanking the northern wing of the French army, and then delivering a simultaneous concentric attack on its scattered divisions as they lay in their canton-ments. Such a plan presupposed that St. Cyr would keep quiet while the preparations were being made, that he would fail to concentrate in time, and that the Spanish columns, operating from two distant bases, would succeed in timing their co-opera-tion with perfect accuracy. At the best they could only have brought some 30,000 men against the 23,000 of St. Cyr's field army—a superiority far from sufficient to give them a rational chance of success. It is probable that at this moment Reding's best chance of doing something great for the cause of Spain would have been to leave a strong garrison in Tarragona, and march early in February with 20,000 men to the relief of Saragossa, which was now drawing near the end of its powers of resistance. Lannes and Junot would have had to raise the siege if an army of such size had come up against them. But, though intending to succour Saragossa in a few weeks, Reding was induced by the constant entreaties of the Catalans to undertake first an expedition against St. Cyr. He sent off no troops to aid the Marquis of Lazan in his fruitless attempt to relax the pressure on his brother's heroic garrison, but devoted all his attention to the 7th Corps.

St. Cyr was not an officer who was likely to be caught unprepared by such a movement as Reding had planned. The extension of the Spanish line to Igualada and the upper Llobregat had not escaped his notice, and he was fully aware of the advantage which his central position gave him over an enemy who had been obliging enough to draw out his fighting strength on an arc of a circle sixty miles from end to end. Without fully realizing Reding's intentions, he could yet see that the Spaniards were giving him a grand opportunity of beating them in detail. He resolved to strike a blow at their northern wing, convinced that if he acted with sufficient swiftness and energy he could crush it long ere it could be succoured from Tarragona.

It thus came to pass that Reding and St. Cyr began to move simultaneously—the one on exterior, the other on interior lines—with the inevitable result. On February 15 Castro, in accordance with the instructions of the Captain-General, began to concentrate his troops at Igualada, with the intention of advancing against the French divisions at San Sadurni and Martorel. At the same time orders were sent to Alvarez, the Governor of Gerona, to detach all the men he could spare for a demonstration against Barcelona, in order to distract the attention of Duhesme and the garrison. Reding himself, with the troops at Tarragona, intended to march against Souham the moment that he should receive the news that his lieutenants were ready to strike.

At the same moment St. Cyr started out on his expedition against Igualada. He took with him Pino's Italian division[1], and ordered Chabot and Chabran to concentrate with him at

---

[1] Troops from Barcelona under Lecchi came out to replace Pino at Villafranca.

Capellades, seven or eight miles to the south-east of Castro's head quarters. By taking this route he avoided the northern bank of the Noya and the defiles of Bruch, and approached the enemy from the side where he could most easily cut him off from reinforcements coming from Tarragona.

The concentration of the three French columns was not perfectly timed, those of Pino and Chabran finding their way far more difficult than did Chabot. It thus chanced that the latter with his skeleton division of three battalions, arrived in front of Capellades many hours before his colleagues. His approach was reported to Castro at Igualada, who sent down 4,000 men against him, attacked him, and beat him back with loss [1] into the arms of Pino, who came on the scene later in the day [Feb. 17]. The Spaniards were then forced to give back, and retired to Pobla de Claramunt on the banks of the Noya, where they were joined by most of Castro's reserves. St. Cyr had now concentrated his three divisions, and hoped that he might bring the enemy to a pitched battle. He drew up in front of them all his force, save one of Pino's brigades, which he sent to turn their right [Feb. 18]. The Spaniards, having a fine position behind a ravine, were at first inclined to fight, and skirmished with the enemy's main body for some hours. They narrowly missed capturing both St. Cyr and Pino, who had ridden forward with their staff to reconnoitre, and fell into an ambush of *miqueletes*, from which they only escaped by the speed of their horses [2].

But late in the day the Spanish General received news that Mazzuchelli, with the detached Italian brigade, was already in his rear and marching hard for Igualada. He immediately evacuated his position in great disorder, and fell back on his head quarters, closely pursued by St. Cyr. The main body of the Spaniards, with their artillery, just succeeded in passing through Igualada before the Italians came up, and fled by the road to Cervera. The rear was cut off, and had to escape in another direction by the path leading to Manresa. Both

---

[1] Chabot lost a Neapolitan colonel (Carascosa) and many other prisoners.

[2] St. Cyr says nothing of his own danger, but the incident is given at length by Vacani, iii. 93, who mentions that one of Pino's aides-de-camp was wounded.

columns were much hustled and lost many prisoners, yet they fairly outmarched their pursuers and got away without any crushing disaster[1]. But their great loss was that in Igualada the French seized all the magazines which had been collected from northern Catalonia for the use of Castro's division. This relieved St. Cyr from all trouble as to provisions for many days : he had now food enough not only to provide for his field army, but to send back to Barcelona.

St. Cyr had now done all the harm that was in his power to the Spanish left wing—he had beaten them, seized their magazines, driven them apart, and broken their line. He imagined that they were disposed of for many days, and now resolved to turn off for a blow at Reding and the other half of the Catalonian army, who might meanwhile (for all that he knew) be attacking Souham with very superior numbers.

Accordingly on Feb. 19 he started off with Pino's division to join Souham and fall upon Reding, leaving Chabot and Chabran, with all the artillery of the three divisions, to occupy Igualada and guard the captured magazines from any possible offensive return on the part of Castro. He marched by cross-roads along the foot-hills of the mountains of the great central Catalonian sierra, intending to descend into the valley of the Gaya by San Magin and the abbey of Santas Cruces, where (as he had learnt) lay the northernmost detachments of Reding's division[2]. Thus he hoped to take the enemy in flank and beat him in detail. He sent orders to Souham to move out of Vendrell and meet him at Villarodoña, halfway up the course of Gaya, unless he should have been already attacked by Reding and forced to take some other line.

At San Magin the French commander came upon some of Reding's troops, about 1,200 men with two guns, under a brigadier named Iranzo. They showed fight, but were beaten

[1] ' Si nous ne fîmes pas dans cette affaire le nombre de prisonniers que nous eussions dû y faire,' says St. Cyr, ' c'est que dans cette journée l'ennemi fit plus usage de ses jambes que de ses armes. Quelques centaines seulement, la plupart blessés, tombèrent entre nos mains ' [*Campagne de Catalogne*, p. 107].

[2] The details of this cross-march in a badly-surveyed country, where the maps are very deficient, are more easily to be made out from Vacani's narrative (pp. 95–8) than from St. Cyr's own account.

and sought refuge further down the valley of the Gaya in the fortified abbey of Santas Cruces. So bare was the country-side, and so bad the maps, that St. Cyr found considerable difficulty in tracking them, and in discovering the best way down the valley. But next day he got upon their trail [1], and beset the abbey, which made a good defence and proved impregnable to a force unprovided with artillery. St. Cyr blockaded it for two days, and then descended into the plain, where he got in touch with Souham's division, which had advanced from Vendrell, and was now pillaging the hamlets round Villarodoña, in the central valley of the Gaya [2] [February 21].

Meanwhile Reding was at last on the move. On receiving the news of the combat of Igualada, he had to choose between the opportunity of making a counter-stroke at Souham, and that of marching to the aid of his lieutenant, Castro. He adopted the latter alternative, and started from Tarragona on February 20 with an escort of about 2,000 men, including nearly all his available cavalry [3]. It was his intention to pick up on the way the outlying northern brigades of his division. This he succeeded in doing, drawing in to himself the troops which were guarding the pass of Santa Cristina, and Iranzo's detachment at Santas Cruces. This force, warned of his approach, broke through the blockade at night, and reached its chief with little or no loss [February 21]. Thus reinforced Reding pushed on by Sarreal to Santa Coloma, where Castro joined him with the rallied troops of his wing, whom he had collected when the French attack slackened. They had between them nearly 20,000 men, an imposing force, with which some of the officers present suggested that it would be possible to

---

[1] St. Cyr (p. 109) has a curious story to the effect that he had failed entirely to find the road, but ultimately discovered it by giving leave to a wounded Spanish officer to return to Tarragona. He was followed at a discreet distance by scouts, who noted the way that he took, and he thus served as a guide of Pino's division as far as the convent of Santas Cruces.

[2] Souham had anticipated St. Cyr's orders, and started to advance from Vendrell before his chief's dispatch from Igualada came to hand.

[3] Two battalions of *miqueletes* (Lerida and 1st of Tarragona), 300 cavalry, a field-battery, and a battalion of Reding's own regiment of Swiss, about 2,100 men in all.

fall upon Igualada, crush Chabot and Chabran, and recover the
lost magazines.   But Reding was nervous about Tarragona,
dreading lest St. Cyr might unite with Souham and fall upon
the city during his absence.   After holding a lengthy council
of war[1] he determined to return to protect his base of operations.
Accordingly, he told off the Swiss General Wimpffen, with some
4,000 or 5,000 of Castro's troops, to observe the French divisions
at Igualada, and started homeward with the rest of his army, about
10,000 infantry, 700 cavalry, and two batteries of field artillery[2].

[1] Col. Doyle was present at this council : his account of it is in the
Record Office.   He declares that he himself was all for fighting, that
Reding wavered, and the majority refused to take risks.

[2] There is a detailed estimate of Reding's army given by St. Cyr
in his Appendix no. 11.   He says that the figures were given him by
'a Spanish general taken prisoner at Valls,' which must mean the Marquis
of Casteldosrius, the only officer of that rank captured.   The names of
nearly all the battalions cited in this list are to be verified, either in Reding's
dispatch or in the narrative of Cabanes—all indeed except the regiment
of Baza, and the three Miquelet Tercios, 1st and 2nd of Tarragona and
Lerida.   But it is probable that Casteldosrius gave St. Cyr a morning
state of the whole army collected at Santa Coloma on the twenty-fourth,
and that these corps (with a total force of 3,000 men) formed part of the
force left with Wimpffen at Santa Coloma.   I am driven to this conclusion
by the statement of Doyle in his letter written from Santa Coloma, on
the day before the battle, that Reding was marching " with 500 horse and
a little over 10,000 foot," for Tarragona.   Doyle is arguing in favour of
fighting, and has no object in understating the numbers.   His figures
are borne out by all the Spanish narratives.   The force must have stood
as follows :—

INFANTRY.					
Granadan Division :			Brought forward		3,530
Reding's Swiss (one batt.)		500	Wimpffen's Swiss (two batts.) . . .		1,140
Iliberia (or 1st of Granada)		1,860	Palma Militia . .		350
Santa Fé (two batts.) .		2,300			5,020
1st of Antequera . .		1,100	CAVALRY.		
		5,760	Husares of Granada .		450
			Husares Españoles . .		250
From the Old Catalan Army :					700
Guards [150 Spanish, 280 Walloons] . . .		430	ARTILLERY.		
Soria		1,000	2 batteries, 8 guns . .		200
2nd of Savoia . . .		800	SAPPERS.		
Provincial Grenadiers of Old and New Castile .		1,300	1 Company . . .		100
Carry forward		3,530	Total		11,800

He had made up his mind to return by the route of Mont-blanch and Valls, one somewhat more remote from the position of St. Cyr on the Gaya than the way by Pla, which he had taken in setting out to join Castro. Reding could only have got home without fighting by taking a circuitous route to the east, via Selva and Reus: the suggestion that he should do so was made, but he replied that having baggage and artillery with him he was forced to keep to a high-road. He chose that by Valls, though he was aware that the place was occupied: but apparently he hoped to crush Souham before Pino could come to his aid. He was resolved, it is said, not to court a combat, but on the other hand not to refuse it if the enemy should offer to fight him on advantageous ground. [February 24.] The truth is, that he was bold even to rashness, could never forget the great day of Baylen, in which he had taken such a splendid part, and was anxious to wash out by a victory the evil memories of Cardadeu and Molins de Rey. He set out on the evening of February 24, and by daybreak next morning was drawing near the bridge of Goy, where the high-road to Tarragona crosses the river Francoli, some two miles north of the town of Valls. His troops, as was to be expected, were much exhausted by the long march in the darkness [1].

St. Cyr, meanwhile, had not been intending to strike a blow at Tarragona. He regarded it as much more necessary to beat the enemy's field army than to close in upon the fortress, which would indubitably have offered a long and obstinate resistance. When he got news of Reding's march to Santa Coloma he resolved to follow him: he was preparing to hasten to the succour of his divisions at Igualada, when he learnt that the Swiss general had turned back, and was hurrying home to Tarragona. He resolved, therefore, to try to intercept him on his return march, and blocked his two available roads by placing Souham's division at Valls and Pino's at Pla. They were only eight or nine miles apart, and whichever road the Spaniards took the unassailed French division could easily come to the aid of the other.

Reding's night march, a move which St. Cyr does not seem to have foreseen, nearly enabled him to carry out his plan. In fact,

[1] These details are from Doyle's letter of Feb. 24, in the Record Office.

as we shall see, he had almost made an end of the French division before the Marshal, who lay himself at Pla with the Italians, arrived to succour it [1].

In the early morning, between six and seven o'clock, the head of the long Spanish column reached the bridge of Goy, and there fell in with Souham's vedettes. The sharp musketry fire which at once broke out warned each party that a combat was at hand. Souham hastily marched out from Valls, and drew up his two brigades in the plain to the north of the town, placing himself across the line of the enemy's advance. Reding at first made up his mind to thrust aside the French division, whose force he somewhat undervalued, and to hurry on his march toward Tarragona. The whole of his advanced guard and part of his centre crossed the river, deployed on the left bank, and attacked the French. Souham held his ground for some hours, but as more and more Spanish battalions kept pressing across the bridge and reinforcing the enemy's line, he began after a time to give way—the numerical odds were heavily against him, and the Catalans were fighting with great steadiness and confidence. Before noon the French division was thrust back against the town of Valls, and Reding had been able to file not only the greater part of his army but all his baggage across the Francoli. The way to Tarragona was clear, and if he had chosen to disengage his men he could have carried off the whole of his army to that city without molestation from Souham, who

---

[1] The French forces engaged at Valls were :—

Souham's Division :
   1st Léger (three batts.).
   42nd of the Line (three batts.).
Provisional regiment :
   [One batt. each of 3rd Léger, and
     67th Line, two batts. 7th Line.]
10 battalions, about 5,500 men.
   24th Dragoons, about 500 men,
   two batteries.

Pino's Division :
   1st Italian Light Regiment (three batts.).
   2nd Italian Light Regiment (three batts.).
   4th Line (three batts.).
   6th ,, ,, ,,
   7th ,, (one batt.).
13 battalions, about 6,500 men.
   7th Italian Dragoons ('Dragoons of Napoleon') and Italian Royal Chasseurs, together about 800 men.

Total about 13,800 men, a force somewhat superior to that of the Spaniards, if the latter had only the corps given in the last table.

was too hard hit to wish to continue the combat. It is even possible that if he had hastily brought up all his reserves he might have completely routed the French detachment before it could have been succoured.

But Reding adopted neither one course nor the other. After driving back Souham, he allowed his men a long rest, probably in order to give the rear and the baggage time to complete the passage of the Francoli. While things were standing still, St. Cyr arrived at full gallop from Pla, where he had been lying with Pino's division, to whom the news of the battle had arrived very late. He brought with him only Pino's divisional cavalry, the 'Dragoons of Napoleon' and Royal Chasseurs, but had ordered the rest of the Italians to follow at full speed when they should have got together. As Pla is no more than eight miles from Valls, it was expected that they would appear within the space of three hours. But, as a matter of fact, Pino did not draw near till the afternoon: one of his brigades, which lay far out, received contradictory orders, and did not come in to Pla till past midday [1], and the Italian general would not move till it had rejoined him. Three hours were wasted by this *contretemps*, and meanwhile the battle might have been lost.

On arriving upon the field with the Italian cavalry, St. Cyr rode along Souham's line, steadied it, and displayed the horsemen in his front. Seeing the French rallying, and new troops arriving to their aid, the Spanish commander jumped to the conclusion that St. Cyr had come up with very heavy reinforcements, and instead of continuing his advance, or pressing on his march toward Tarragona, suddenly changed his whole plan of operations. He would not stand to be attacked in the plain, but he resolved to fight a defensive action on the heights beyond the Francoli, from which he had descended in the morning. Accordingly, first his baggage, then his main body, and lastly his vanguard, which covered the retreat of the rest, slowly filed back over the bridge of Goy, and took position on the rolling hills to the east. Here Reding drew them up in two lines, with the river flowing at their feet as a front defence, and their batteries drawn up so as to sweep the bridge of Goy and the fords. The right wing was covered by a lateral ravine falling into the Francoli; the left, facing the

[1] Vacani, iii. 105-6. This fact is mentioned by no other author.

village of Pixamoxons, was somewhat 'in the air,' but the whole position, if long, was good and eminently defensible.

St. Cyr observed his adversary's movement with joy, for he would have been completely foiled if Reding had refused to fight and passed on toward Tarragona. Knowing the Spanish troops, a pitched battle with superior numbers was precisely what he most desired. Accordingly he took advantage of the long time of waiting, while Pino's division was slowly drawing near the field, to rest and feed Souham's tired troops, and then to draw them up facing the southern half of Reding's position, with a vacant space on their right on which the Italians were to take up their ground, when at last they should arrive.

When St. Cyr had lain for nearly three hours quiescent at the foot of the heights, and no reinforcements had yet come in sight, Reding began to grow anxious. He had, as he now realized, retired with unnecessary haste from in front of a beaten force, and had assumed a defensive posture when he should have pressed the attack. At about three o'clock he made up his mind that he had committed an error, but thinking it too late to resume the fight, resolved to retire on Tarragona by the circuitous route which passes through the village of Costanti. He sent back General Marti to Tarragona to bring out fresh troops from the garrison to join him at that point, and issued orders that the army should retreat at dusk. He might perhaps have got off scatheless if he had moved away at once, though it is equally possible that St. Cyr might have fallen upon his rearguard with Souham's division, and done him some damage. But he waited for the dark before marching, partly because he wished to rest his troops, who were desperately fatigued by the night march and the subsequent combat in the morning, partly because he did not despair of fighting a successful defensive action if St. Cyr should venture to cross the Francoli and attack him. Accordingly he lingered on the hillside in battle array, waiting for the darkness [1].

---

[1] Arteche, v. 207-9, makes Reding deliver a second attack on Souham in the early afternoon. This is, I think, an error, caused by a misreading of Cabanes' somewhat confused account of the fight, from which it might be possible (if no other sources existed) to deduce a second Spanish advance. But Cabanes is really dealing with the later phases of the first combat

This gave St. Cyr his chance; at three o'clock Pino's belated division had begun to come up: first Fontane's brigade, then, an hour and a half later, that of Mazzuchelli, whose absence from Pla had caused all the delay. It was long past four, and the winter afternoon was far spent when St. Cyr had at last got all his troops in hand.

Allowing barely enough time for the Italians to form in order of battle [1], St. Cyr now led forward his whole army to the banks of the Francoli. The two divisions formed four heavy columns of a brigade each: and in this massive formation forded the river and advanced uphill, driving in before them the Spanish skirmishers. The Italian dragoons went forward in the interval between two of the infantry columns; the French cavalry led the attack on the extreme right, near the bridge of Goy.

For a moment it seemed as if the two armies would actually cross bayonets all along the line, for the Spaniards stood firm and opened a regular and well-directed fire upon the advancing columns. But St. Cyr had not miscalculated the moral effect of the steady approach of the four great bodies of infantry which were now climbing the hill and drawing near to Reding's front. Like so many other continental troops, who had striven on earlier battle-fields to bear up in line against the French column-formation, the Spaniards could not find heart to close with the formidable and threatening masses which were rolling in upon them. They delivered one last tremendous discharge at 100 yards' distance, and then, when they saw the enemy looming through the smoke and closing upon them, broke in a dozen different places and went to the rear in helpless disorder, sweeping away the second line, higher up the hill, which

only. It is conclusive that neither Reding himself, in his official dispatch, St. Cyr, Doyle, nor Vacani mention any engagement in the early afternoon.

[1] St. Cyr in his Memoirs (p. 123) makes the curious statement that he silenced his artillery after it had fired only three rounds, lest he should frighten off the Spaniards before he could reach them with his infantry, and so prevent the latter from closing and winning as decisive a victory as possible. One is almost prone to doubt the story, and to suppose that the cessation of fire was due to the fear of killing his own men when they were getting close to the Spanish line. Arteche puts this incident too early in the fight, during Reding's supposed second attack.

ought to have sustained them. The only actual collision was
on the extreme left, near the bridge of Goy, where Reding
himself charged, with his staff, at the head of his cavalry, in
a vain attempt to save the desperate situation. He was met
in full career by the French 24th Dragoons, and thoroughly
beaten. In the *mêlée* he was surrounded, three of his aides-de-
camp were wounded[1] and taken, and he himself only cut his way
out after receiving three sabre wounds on his head and shoulders,
which ultimately proved fatal.

If there had not been many steep slopes and ravines behind
the Spanish position, nearly the whole of Reding's army must
have perished or been captured. But the country-side was so
difficult that the majority of the fugitives got away, though
many were overtaken. The total loss of the Spaniards amounted
to more than 3,000 men, of whom nearly half were prisoners[2].
All the guns of the defeated army, all its baggage, and several
stands of colours fell into the hands of the victors. The French
lost about 1,000 men, mostly in the early part of the engagement, when Souham's division was driven back under the walls
of Valls.

The Spaniards had not fought amiss: St. Cyr, in a dispatch to
Berthier, acknowledges the fact—not in order to exalt the merit
of his own troops, but to demonstrate that the 7th Corps was
too weak for the task set it and required further reinforcements[3].
But Reding did not give his men a fair chance; he hurried
them into the fight at the end of a long night march, drew them
off just when they were victorious, and altered his plan of battle

[1] Among them was an English officer named Reid.

[2] Including Colonels Dumont and Autunez commanding respectively
the Walloon and Spanish guards, the Marquis of Casteldosrius commanding
the cavalry brigade, three of Reding's aides-de-camp, and eighty other
officers. Two colonels were killed, a brigadier-general (Saint Ellier) and
many other superior officers wounded.

[3] 'Votre Altesse me dit qu'il n'y a rien autour de nous qui puisse résister
a 6,000 hommes. Je lui demande pardon. La division Souham a été
quelque temps seule le 25, et nous avons vu qu'il était temps que
l'autre division arrivât. . . . On ne peut nier que les troupes espagnoles
gagnent tous les jours, et nous sommes forcés de leur rendre justice ; à la
bataille de Valls elles se sont très-bien battues.' St. Cyr to Berthier, Valls,
March 6, 1809.

PART OF CATALONIA
TO ILLUSTRATE ST CYR'S CAMPAIGN
NOV. 1808 TO MARCH 1809

Kilometres

0 10 20 30 40 50

The Oxford Geogl. Inst.

Darbishire & Stanford, Ltd.

BATTLE OF
VALLS
FEB. 25 1809

At the moment of
St. Cyr's attack 4 p.m.

French
■ Infantry ◼ Cavalry

Spaniards
▢ Infantry ▢ Cavalry

Souham's Division
A. Dumoulin's Brigade
B. Verge's Brigade
Pino's Division
C. Mazzuchelli's Brigade
D. Fontane's   "
E. 24th Dragoons
F. Italian   "
G. Italian Chasseurs
H. Castro's Division
I. Marti's Division

L.L.L. Site of the engagement in the morning.

Valls
to Valls

La Plana

Pixamoxons

Bridge of Goy

Ford

Ford

Ford

Ford

Ford

SIERRA ALTA

ALTO DEL PUIG

Barranco del Calltart

to Tarragona

to Pla

to Montblanch

Barranco de la Sierra

to Costanti

R. Francoli

Kilometres
0   1   2

The Oxford Geogl. Inst.

Darbishire & Stanford, Ltd

thrice in the course of the day. No army could have done itself justice with such bad leading.

The wrecks of the beaten force straggled into Tarragona, their spirits so depressed that it was a long time before it was possible to trust them again in battle. When they once more took the field it was under another leader, for Reding, after lingering some weeks, died of his wounds, leaving the reputation of a brave, honest, and humane officer, but of a very poor general.

St. Cyr utilized his victory merely by blockading Tarragona. He moved Souham to Reus, and kept Pino at Valls, each throwing out detachments as far as the sea, so as to cut off the city from all its communications with the interior. An epidemic had broken out in the place, in consequence of the masses of ill-attended wounded who cumbered the hospitals. It would seem that the French General hoped that the pestilence might turn the hearts of the garrison towards surrender. If so, he was much deceived: they bore their ills with stolid patience, and being always victualled from the sea suffered no practical inconvenience from the blockade. It seems indeed that St. Cyr would have done far better to use the breathing time which he won at the battle of Valls for the commencement of a movement against Gerona. Till that place should be captured, and the high-road to Perpignan opened, there was no real security for the 7th Corps. Long months, however, were to elapse before this necessary operation was taken in hand.

SECTION XI

THE SECOND SIEGE OF SARAGOSSA

CHAPTER I

THE CAPTURE OF THE OUTWORKS

WHILE Napoleon was urging on his fruitless pursuit of Sir John Moore, while St. Cyr was discomfiting the Catalans on the Besos and the Llobregat, and while Victor was dealing his last blow to the dilapidated army of Infantado, there was one point on which the war was standing still, and where the French arms had made no great progress since the battle of Tudela. Saragossa was holding out, with the same tenacity that she had displayed during the first siege in the July and August of the preceding summer. In front of her walls and barricades two whole corps of the Emperor's army were detained from December, 1808, till February, 1809. As long as the defence endured, she preserved the rest of Aragon and the whole of Valencia from invasion.

The battle of Tudela had been fought on November 23, but it was not till nearly a month later that the actual siege began. The reason for this delay was that the Emperor had called off to Madrid all the troops which had taken part in the campaign against Castaños and Palafox, save Moncey's 3rd Corps alone. This force was not numerous enough to invest the city till it had been strengthened by heavy reinforcements from the North.

After having routed the Armies of Aragon and the Centre, Marshal Lannes had thrown up the command which had been entrusted to him, and had gone back to France. The injuries which he had suffered from his fall over the precipice near Pampeluna [1] were still far from healed, and served as the excuse

---

[1] See vol. i. p. 436.

for his retirement. Moncey, therefore, resumed, on November 25, the charge of the victorious army: on the next day he was joined by Ney, who, after failing to intercept Castaños in the mountains [1], had descended into the valley of the Ebro, with Marchand and Dessolles' divisions of infantry, and Beaumont's light cavalry brigade. On the twenty-eighth the two marshals advanced along the high-road by Mallen and Alagon, and on the second day after appeared in front of Saragossa with all their troops, save Musnier's division of the 3rd Corps and the division of the 6th Corps lately commanded by Lagrange, which had followed the retreating army of Castaños into the hills on the road to Calatayud. They were about to commence the investment of the city, when Ney received orders from the Emperor, dispatched from Aranda, bidding him leave the siege to Moncey, and cross the mountains into New Castile with all the troops of the 6th Corps: he was to find Castaños, and hang on his heels so that he should not be able to march to the help of Madrid.

Accordingly the Duke of Elchingen marched from the camp in front of Saragossa with the divisions of Marchand and Dessolles, and the cavalry brigades of Beaumont and Digeon. At Calatayud he came up with the force which had been dispatched in pursuit of Castaños,—Musnier's division of the 3rd Corps, and that of the 6th Corps which Maurice Mathieu had taken over from Lagrange, who had been severely wounded at Tudela [2]. Leaving Musnier at Calatayud to protect his communications with Aragon, Ney picked up Maurice Mathieu, and passed the mountains into New Castile, where he fell into the Emperor's sphere of operations. We have seen that he took a prominent part in the pursuit of Sir John Moore and the invasion of Galicia.

Moncey, meanwhile, was left in front of Saragossa with his 1st, 3rd, and 4th Divisions—the 2nd being still at Calatayud. This force consisted of no more than twenty-three battalions, about 15,000 men, and was far too weak to undertake the siege. The Marshal was informed that the whole corps of Mortier was

---

[1] See vol. i. pp. 446–7.

[2] Few of the French historians mention these changes, but they are quite certain. On Nov. 23 'the division Maurice Mathieu' means the 1st of the 3rd Corps; on Dec. 1, it means the 2nd of the 6th Corps.

to be sent to his aid, but it was still far away, and with very proper caution he resolved to draw back and wait for the arrival of the reinforcements.   If the Spaniards got to know of his condition, they might sally out from Saragossa and attack him with more than 30,000 men.   Moncey, therefore, drew back to Alagon, and there waited for the arrival of the Duke of Treviso and the 5th Corps.   It was not till December 20 that he was able to present himself once more before the city.

Thus Saragossa gained four weeks of respite between the battle of Tudela and the commencement of the actual siege. This reprieve was invaluable to Palafox and the Aragonese. They would have been in grave danger if Lannes had marched on and assaulted the city only two days after the battle, and before the routed army had been rallied.   Even if Ney and Moncey had been permitted to begin a serious attack on November 30, the day of their arrival before the place, they would have had some chance of success.   But their sudden retreat raised the spirits of the defenders, and the twenty extra days of preparation thus granted to them sufficed to restore them to full confidence, and to re-establish their belief in the luck of Saragossa and the special protection vouchsafed them by its patron saint Our Lady of the Pillar.   Napoleon must take the blame for all the consequences of Ney's withdrawal. He had ordered it without fully realizing the fact that Moncey would be left too weak to commence the siege.   Probably he had over-estimated the effect of the defeat of Tudela on the Army of Aragon.   For the failure of Ney's attempt to surround Castaños he was only in part responsible, though (as we have seen) he had sent him out on his circular march two days too late [1].   But to draw off the 6th Corps to New Castile (where it failed to do any good), before the 5th Corps had arrived to take its place before Saragossa, was clearly a blunder.

Palafox made admirable use of the unexpected reprieve that had been granted him.   He had not, it will be remembered, taken part in person in the battle of Tudela, but had returned to his head quarters on the night before that disaster.   He was occupied in organizing a reserve to take the field in support of his two divisions already at the front, when the sudden

[1] See vol. i. pp. 446-7.

influx of fugitives into Saragossa showed him what had occurred. In the course of the next two days there poured into the place the remains of the divisions of O'Neille and St. March from his own Army of Aragon. With them came Roca's men, who properly belonged to Castaños, but having fought in the right wing had been separated from the main body of the Andalusian army [1]. In addition, fragments of many other regiments of the Army of the Centre straggled into Saragossa. At least 16,000 or 17,000 men of the wrecks of Tudela had come in ere four days were expired. To help them, Palafox could count on all the newly organized battalions of his reserve, which had never marched out to join the field army: they amounted to some 10,000 or 12,000 men, but many of the regiments had only lately been organized and had not received their uniforms or equipment. Nor was this all: several belated battalions from Murcia and Valencia came in at various times during the next ten days [2], so that long ere the actual siege began Palafox could count on 32,000 bayonets and 2,000 sabres of more or less regularly organized corps. He had in addition a number of irregulars—armed citizens and peasants of the country-side— whose numbers it is impossible to fix, for though some had been collected in *partidas* or volunteer companies, others fought in loose bands just as they pleased, and without any proper organization. They may possibly have amounted to 10,000 men at the time of the commencement of the siege, but so many were drafted into the local Aragonese battalions before the end of the fighting, that when the place surrendered in February, there were less than a thousand [3] of these unembodied irregulars under arms.

But it was not so much for the reorganization of his army as for the strengthening of his fortifications that Palafox found

[1] By far the larger part of Roca's division reached Saragossa ; the Spanish returns show that 4,500 men joined Palafox, and only 1,500 escaped to Cuenca with the rest of the 'Army of the Centre.'

[2] Among these were the 1st and 2nd Tiradores de Murcia, the regiment of Florida Blanca, the 3rd and 5th Volunteers of Murcia, and the 3rd Volunteers of Valencia, all of which had arrived too late for Tudela.

[3] To be exact, 756 was the number of *paisanos* as opposed to *tropa* in the return of the garrison on Feb. 20.   See Arteche, Appendix to vol. iv.

the respite during the first three weeks of December profitable. During the first siege it will be remembered that the fortifications of Saragossa had been contemptible from the engineer's point of view : the flimsy mediaeval *enceinte* had crumbled away at the first fire of the besiegers, and the real defence had been carried out behind the barricades.   By the commencement of the second siege everything had changed, and the city was covered by a formidable line of defences, executed, as was remarked by one of the French generals [1], with more zeal and energy than scientific skill, but presenting nevertheless most serious obstacles to the besieger.

After the raising of the first siege by Verdier, the Spaniards had been for some time in a state of such confidence and exultation that they imagined that there was no need for further defensive precautions.   The next campaign was to be fought, as they supposed, on the further side of the Pyrenees.   But the long suspension of the expected advance during the autumn months began to chill their spirits, and, as the year drew on, it was no longer reckoned unpatriotic or cowardly to take into consideration the wisdom of strengthening the inland fortresses in view of a possible return of the French.   In September, Colonel San Genis, the engineer officer who had worked for Palafox during the first siege, received permission to commence a series of regular fortifications for Saragossa.   The work did not progress rapidly, for the Aragonese had not as yet much belief in the possibility that they might be called on once again to defend their capital.   San Genis only received a moderate sum of money, and the right to requisition men of over thirty-five from the city and the surrounding villages. The labour had to be paid, and therefore the labourers were few.   The new works were sketched out rather than executed. Things progressed with a leisurely slowness, till in November the dangers of the situation began to be appreciated, and the approach of the French reinforcements drove the Saragossans to greater energy.   But it was only the thunderclap of Tudela that really alarmed them, and sent soldiers and civilians, men, women, and children, to labour with feverish haste at the com-

[1] See Cavallero's criticism of this statement of Rogniat on p. 17 of his interesting little work.

pletion of the new lines.   Between November 25 and December 20. the amount of work that was carried out was amazing and admirable.   If Ney and Moncey had been allowed to commence the regular siege before the month of November had expired, they would have found the whole system of works in an incomplete condition.   Three weeks later Saragossa had been converted into a formidable fortress.

The only point where San Genis' scheme had not been fully developed was the Monte Torrero.   It will be remembered that this important hill, whose summit lies only 1,800 yards from the walls of Saragossa, overlooks the whole city, and had been chosen during the first siege as the *emplacement* for the main breaching batteries.   To keep the French from this commanding position was most important, and the Spanish engineer had intended to cover the whole circuit of the hill with a large entrenched camp, protected by continuous lines of earthworks and numerous redoubts, with the Canal of Aragon, which runs under its southern foot, as a wet ditch in its front.   But, when the news of Tudela arrived, little or nothing had been done to carry out this scheme: the fortification of the city had absorbed the main attention of the Aragonese, and while that was still incomplete the Monte Torrero had been neglected. In December it was too late to begin the building of three or four miles of new earthworks, and in consequence nothing was constructed on the suburban hill save one large central redoubt, and two small works serving as *têtes-de-pont*, at the points where the Madrid and the La Muela roads cross the Canal of Aragon. St. March's Valencian division, still 6,000 strong, was told off for the defence of the hill, but had no continuous line of works to cover it.   The only strength of the position lay in the canal which runs round its foot: but this was not very broad, and was fordable at more than one point.   In short, the Monte Torrero constituted an outlying defence which might be held for some time, in order to keep the besiegers far off from the body of the place, rather than an integral part of its line of defence.

It was on the works of Saragossa itself that the energy of more than 60,000 enthusiastic labourers, military and civilian, had been expended during the month that followed Tudela.

The total accomplished in this time moves our respect: it will be well to take the various fronts in detail.

On the Western front, from the Ebro to the Huerba, there had been in August nothing more than a weak wall, many parts of which were composed of the rear-sides of convents and buildings. In front of this line there had been constructed by November 10 a very different defence. A solid rampart reveted with bricks taken from ruined houses, and furnished with a broad terrace for artillery, and a ditch forty-five feet deep now covered the entire western side of the city. The convents of the Augustinians and the Trinitarians, which had been outside the walls during the earlier siege, had been taken into this new *enceinte* and served as bastions in it. There being a space 600 yards long between them, where the curtain would have been unprotected by flanking fires, a great semicircular battery had been thrown out, which acted as a third bastion on this side. Strong earthworks had also been built up to cover the Portillo and Carmen gates. As an outlying fort there was the castle of the Aljafferia, which had received extensive repairs, and was connected with the *enceinte* by a ditch and a covered way. It would completely enfilade any attacks made on the north-western part of the new wall.

On the Southern front of the defences the work done had been even more important. Here the new fortifications had been carried down to the brink of the ravine of the Huerba, so as to make that stream the wet ditch of the town. Two great redoubts were pushed beyond it: one called the redoubt of ' Our Lady of the Pillar' lay at the bridge outside the Santa Engracia gate. It was provided with a deep narrow ditch, into which the water of the river had been turned, and armed with eight guns. The corresponding fort, at the south-east angle of the town, was made by fortifying the convent of San José, on the Valencia road, just beyond the Huerba. This was a quadrangle 120 yards long by eighty broad, furnished with a ditch, and with a covered way with palisades, cut in the counterscarp. It held twelve heavy guns, and a garrison of no less than 3,000 men. Between St. José and the Pillar redoubt, the old town wall above the Huerba had been strengthened and thickened, and several new batteries had been built upon it.

It could not well be assailed till the two projecting works in front of it should be reduced, and if they should fall it stood on higher ground and completely commanded their sites. The convent of Santa Engracia, so much disputed during the first siege, had been turned into a sort of fortress, and heavily armed with guns of position.

On the eastern front of the city from San José to the Ebro, the Huerba still serves as a ditch to the place, but is not so steep or so difficult as in its upper course. Here the suburb of the Tanneries (Las Tenerias), where that stream falls into the Ebro, had been turned into a strong projecting redoubt, whose fire commanded both the opposite bank of the Ebro on one side, and the lower reaches of the Huerba on the other. Half way between this redoubt and San José was a great battery (generally called the 'Palafox Battery') at the Porta Quemada, whose fires, crossing those of the other two works, commanded all the low ground outside the eastern front of the city.

It only remains to speak of the fortifications of the trans-pontine suburb of San Lazaro. This was by nature the weakest part of the defences, as the suburb is built in low marshy ground on the river's edge. Here deep cuttings had been made and filled with water, three heavy batteries had been erected, and the convents of San Lazaro and Jesus had been strengthened, crenellated and loopholed, and turned into forts. The whole of these works were joined by palisades and ditches. They formed a great *tête-de-pont*, requiring a garrison of 3,000 men. As an additional defence for the flanks of the suburb three or four gun-boats, manned by sailors brought up from Cartagena, had been launched on the Ebro, and commanded the reach of the river which runs along the northern side of the city.

Yet great as were the works which now sheathed the body of Saragossa, the people had not forgotten the moral lesson of the first siege. When her walls had been beaten down, she had resisted behind her barricades and the solid houses of her narrow streets. They fully realized that this might again have to be done, if the French should succeed in breaking in at some point of the long *enceinte*. Accordingly, every preparation was made for street fighting. Houses were loopholed, and communications were pierced between them, without any regard for private property or convenience. Ground-floor windows were built up, and arrangements made for the speedy and solid closing of all doors. Traverses were erected in the streets, to guard as far as was possible against the dangers of a bombardment, and an elaborate system of barricades, arranged in proper tactical relation to each other, was sketched out. The walls might be broken, but the people boasted that the kernel should be harder than the shell.

Outside the city, where the olive groves and suburban villas and summer houses had given much cover to the French during the first siege, a clean sweep had been made of every stone and stick for 800 yards around the defences. The trees were felled, and dragged into the city, to be cut up into palisades. The bricks and stones were carried off to revet the new ramparts and ditches. The once fertile and picturesque garden-suburbs were left bald and bare, and could be perfectly well searched by the cannon from the walls, so that the enemy had to contrive all his cover by pick and shovel, or gabion and fascine.

The soldiery, whose spirits had been much dashed by the disaster of Tudela, soon picked up their courage when they noted the enthusiasm of the citizens and the strength of the defences. Indeed, it was dangerous for any man to show outward signs of doubt or fear, for the Aragonese had been wrought up to a pitch of hysterical patriotism which made them look upon faintheartedness as treason. Palafox himself did his best to keep down riots and assassinations, but his followers were always stimulating him to apply martial law in its most rigorous form. A high gallows was erected in the middle of the Coso, and short shrift was given to any man convicted of attempted desertion, disobedience to orders, or cowardice. Delations were innumerable, and the Captain-General had the greatest difficulty in preserving from the popular fury even persons whom he believed to be innocent. The most that he could do for them was to shut them up in the prisons of the Aljafferia, and to defer their trial till the siege should be over. The fact was that Palafox was well aware that his power rested on the unlimited confidence reposed on him by the people, and was therefore bent on crossing their desires as little as he could help. He was careful to take counsel not only with his military subordinates, but with all those who had power in the streets. Hence came the prominence which is assigned in all the narratives of the siege to obscure persons, such as the priests Don Basilio (the Captain-General's chaplain) and Santiago Sass, and to the demagogues 'Tio Jorge' and 'Tio Marin.' They represented public opinion, and had to be conciliated. It is going too far to say, with Napier, that a regular 'Reign of Terror' prevailed in Saragossa throughout the second siege, and that Palafox was no more than a puppet, whose strings were pulled by fanatical friars and bloodthirsty gutter-politicians. But it is clear that the Captain-General's dictatorial power was only preserved by a careful observation of every gust of popular feeling, and that the acts of his subordinates were often reckless and cruel. The soldiers disliked the fanatical citizens : the work of Colonel Cavallero, the engineer officer who has left the best Spanish narrative of the siege, is full of this feeling. He sums up the situation by writing that 'The agents of the Commander-in-chief sometimes abused their power. Everything was demanded in the name of King and Country, every act of disobedience was counted as high treason : on the other hand, known devotion to the holy cause gave unlimited authority, and assured impunity for any act to those who had the smallest shadow of delegated power. Even if the citizens had not been unanimous in their feelings, fear would have given them an appearance of unanimity. To the intoxication of confidence and national pride caused by the results of the first siege, to the natural obstinacy of the Aragonese, to the strength of a dictatorial government supported by democratic enthusiasm, there was added an exalted religious fanaticism. Our Lady of the Pillar, patroness of Saragossa, had, it was supposed, displayed her power by the raising of the first siege : it had been the greatest of her miracles. Anything could be got from a people in this frame of mind [1].'

Palafox knew well how to deal with his followers. He kept himself always before their eyes ; his activity was unceasing, his supervision was felt in every department. His unending series

---

[1] Cavallero, pp. 68–9. Belmas translates the paragraph almost word for word in ii. 144–5 of his work, without acknowledgement.

of eloquent, if somewhat bombastic, proclamations was well suited to rouse their enthusiasm.   He displayed, even to ostentation, a confidence which he did not always feel, because he saw that the strength of the defence lay in the fact that the Aragonese were convinced in the certainty of their own triumph. The first doubt as to ultimate success would dull their courage and weaken their arms. We cannot blame him, under the circumstances, if he concealed from them everything that was likely to damp their ardour, and allowed them to believe everything that would keep up their spirits.

Meanwhile he did not neglect the practical side of the defence. The best testimony to his capacity is the careful accumulation which he made of all the stores and material needed for a long siege.   Alone among all the Spanish garrisons of the war, that of Saragossa never suffered from hunger nor from want of resources.   It was the pestilence, not starvation, which was destined to prove the ruin of the defence.   Before the French investment began Palafox had gathered in six months' provisions for 15,000 men ; the garrison was doubled by the arrival of the routed army from Tudela : yet still there was food for three months for the military.   The citizens had been directed to lay in private stocks, and to feed themselves : this they had done, and it was not till the end of the siege that they began to run short of comestibles.   Even when the place fell there were still large quantities of corn, maize, salt fish, oil, brandy, and forage for horses in the magazines [1].   Only fresh meat had failed, and the Spaniard is never a great consumer of that commodity. Military stores had been prepared in vast quantities : there was an ample stock of sandbags, of timber for palisading, of iron work and spare fittings for artillery.   Instead of gabions the garrison used the large wicker baskets employed for the vintage, which were available in profusion.   Of artillery there were some 160 pieces in the place, but too many of them were of small calibre : only about sixty were 16-pounders or heavier.   Of these more than half were French pieces, abandoned by Verdier in August in his siege-works, or fished out of the canal into which he had thrown them.   Of cannon-balls there was also an ample provision : a great part, like the siege-guns, were spoil

[1] Cavallero, pp. 81 and 148.

taken in the deserted camp of the French in August. Shells, on the other hand, were very deficient, and the workmen of the local arsenal could not manufacture them satisfactorily. The powder was made in the place throughout the siege : the accident in July, when the great magazine in the Seminary blew up with such disastrous results, had induced Palafox to order that no great central store should be made, but that the sulphur, salt-petre, and charcoal should be kept apart, and compounded daily in quantities sufficient for all requirements. So many thousand civilians were kept at work on powder- and cartridge-making that this plan never failed, and no great explosions took place during the second siege.

It will be remembered that want of muskets had been one · of the chief hindrances of the Aragonese during the operations in July and August. It was not felt in December and January, for not only had Palafox collected a large store of small arms during the autumn, to equip his reserves, but he received, just before the investment began, a large convoy of British muskets, sent up from Tarragona by Colonel Doyle, who had gone down to the coast by the Captain-General's desire, to hurry on their transport. As the siege went on, the mortality among the garrison was so great that the stock of muskets more than sufficed for those who were in a state to bear arms.

Such were the preparations which were made to receive the French, when they should finally present themselves in front of the walls. All had been done, save in one matter, to enable the city to make the best defence possible under the circum-stances. The single omission was to provide for a field force beyond the walls capable of harassing the besiegers from with-out, and of cutting their communications with their base. From his 40,000 men Palafox ought to have detached a strong division, with orders to base itself upon Upper Aragon, and keep the French in constant fear as to their supplies and their touch with Tudela and Pampeluna. Ten thousand men could easily have been spared, and the mischief that they might have done was incalculable. The city had more defenders than were needed : in the open country, on the other hand, there was no nucleus left for further resistance. Almost every available man had been sent up to Saragossa : with the exception of Lazan's division in Catalonia, and of three other battalions [1], the whole of the 32,000 men raised by the kingdom of Aragon were inside the walls.   Outside there remained nothing but unorganized bands of peasants to keep the field and molest the besiegers.   The only help from without that was given to the city was that supplied by Lazan's small force, when it was withdrawn from Catalonia in January, and 4,000 men could do nothing against two French army corps.   Even as it was, the French had to tell off the best part of two divisions to guard their communications.   What could they have done if there had been a solid body of 10,000 men ranging the mountains, and descending at every favourable opportunity to fall upon some post on the long line Alagon-Mallen-Tudela-Pampeluna by which the besiegers drew their food and munitions from their base?

It would seem that the neglect of Palafox to provide for this necessary detachment arose from three causes.   The first was his want of real strategical insight—which had been amply displayed during the autumn, when he was always urging on his colleagues his ridiculous plan for 'surrounding' the French army, by an impossible march into Navarre and the Pyrenees. The second was his conviction, well-founded enough in itself, that his troops would do much better behind walls than in the open [2].   The third was a strong belief that the siege would be raised not by any operations from without, but by the rigours of the winter.   In average years the months of January and February are tempestuous and rainy in Aragon.   The low ground about Saragossa is often inundated: even if the enemy were not drowned out (like the besiegers of Leyden in 1574), Palafox thought that they would find trench-work impossible in the constant downpour, and would be so much thinned by dysentery and rheumatism that they would have to draw back from their low-lying camps and raise the siege.   Unfortunately for him the winter turned out exceptionally mild, and (what was worse) exceptionally dry.   The French had not to suffer from the awful deluge which in Galicia, during this same month, was rendering

---

[1] The battalions of Alcanitz, Tauste, and *Tiradores de Doyle*; the last were at Jaca, and afterwards served with Blake's army at Maria and Belchite.   They are wrongly put in Saragossa, in Arteche, iv. Appendix.

[2] See the remarks in defence of Palafox in Arteche, iv. 332–4.

the retreat of Sir John Moore so miserable. The rain did no
more than send many of the besiegers to hospital: it never
stopped their advance or flooded their trenches.

When Palafox had nearly completed his defences—the works
on the Monte Torrero alone were still hopelessly behindhand—
the French at last began to move up against him. On December 15 Marshal Mortier arrived at Tudela with the whole of the
5th Corps, veterans from the German garrisons who had not
yet fired a shot in Spain. Their ranks were so full that though
only two divisions, or twenty-eight battalions, formed the corps,
it counted 21,000 bayonets. It had also a brigade of two regiments of hussars and chasseurs as corps-cavalry, with a strength
of 1,500 sabres. The condition of Moncey's 3rd Corps was
much less satisfactory : it was mainly composed of relics of the
original army of Spain—of the conscripts formed into provisional regiments with whom Napoleon had at first intended
to conquer the Peninsula [1]. Its other troops, almost without
exception, had taken part in the first siege of Saragossa under
Verdier, a not very cheerful or inspiriting preparation for the
second leaguer [2]. All the regiments had been thinned by severe
sickness in the autumn ; on October 10 they had already 7,741
men in hospital—far the largest figure shown by any of the
French corps in Spain. The number had largely increased as
the winter had drawn on, and the battalions had grown so weak
that Moncey consolidated his four divisions into three during
his halt at Alagon. The whole of the 4th division was distributed between the 2nd and 3rd, so as to bring the others up to
a decent strength. On December 20 the thirty-eight battalions
only made up 20,000 effective men for the siege, while more
than 10,000 lay sick, some with the army, some in the base
hospitals at Pampeluna. The health of the corps grew pro-
gressively worse in January, till at last in the middle days of the
siege it had 15,000 men with the colours, and no less than 13,000
sick. We find the French generals complaining that one
division of the 5th Corps was almost as strong and effective at

[1] The 114th, 115th, 116th, 117th, 121st, and 2nd Legion of Reserve
were all formed in this way.

[2] These were the 1st, 2nd and 3rd of the Vistula, 44th and 14th of the
line, and one battalion each of the 70th and 5th Léger.

this time as the whole combined force of the 3rd Corps [1].   Nevertheless these weary and fever-ridden troops had to take in charge the main part of the siege operations.

During the twenty days of his halt at Alagon, Moncey had employed his sappers and many of his infantry in the manufacture of gabions, wool-packs, and sandbags for the projected siege.   He was continually receiving convoys of heavy artillery and ammunition from Pampeluna, and when Mortier came up on December 20, had a sufficiency of material collected for the commencement of the leaguer.   The two marshals moved on together on that day, and marched eastward towards Saragossa, with the whole of their forces, save that four battalions were left to guard the camp and dépôts at Alagon, and three more at Tudela to keep open the Pampeluna road [2].   Gazan's division crossed the Ebro opposite Tauste, to invest the transpontine suburb of Saragossa: the rest of the army kept to the right bank. Late in the evening both columns came in sight of the city. They mustered, after deducting the troops left behind, about 38,000 infantry, 3,500 cavalry, and 3,000 sappers and artillerymen.   They had sixty siege-guns, over and above the eighty-four field-pieces belonging to the corps-artillery of Mortier and Moncey.   The provision of artillery was copious—far more than the French had turned against many of the first-class fortresses of Germany.   The Emperor was determined that Saragossa should be well battered, and had told off an extra proportion of engineers against the place, entrusting the general charge of the work to his aide-de-camp, General Lacoste, one of the most distinguished officers of the scientific corps.

When the reinvestment began, Gazan on the left bank established himself at Villanueva facing the suburb of San Lazaro. Mortier with Suchet's division took post at San Lamberto opposite the western front of the city.   Moncey, marching round the place, ranged Grandjean's troops opposite the Monte Torrero, on the southern front of the defences, and Morlot further east near the mouth of the Huerba.   His other division,

---

[1] See the table in Belmas, ii. 381.

[2] These were all detached from Moncey.   The Alagon garrison consisted of four battalions of the 2nd Legion of Reserve, 2,500 strong.   At Tudela were three battalions of the 121st regiment, 1,800 bayonets.

that of Musnier, formed the central reserve, and guarded the artillery and the magazines. The Spaniards made no attempt to delay the completion of the investment, and kept quiet within their walls.

On the next morning the actual siege began. It was destined to last from December 20 to February 20, and may be divided into three well-marked sections. The first comprises the operations against the Spanish outworks, and terminates with the capture of the two great bridge-heads beyond the Huerba, the forts of San José and Our Lady of the Pillar: it lasted down to January 15. The second period includes the time during which the besiegers attacked and finally broke through the main *enceinte* of the city: it lasts from January 16 to January 27. The third section consists of the street-fighting, after the walls had been pierced, and ends with the fall of Saragossa on February 20.

Having reconnoitred the whole circuit of the Spanish defences on the very evening of their arrival before the city (December 20), Moncey and Mortier recognized that their first task must be to evict the Spaniards from the Monte Torrero, the one piece of dominating ground in the whole region of operations, and the spot from which Saragossa could be most effectively attacked. They were rejoiced to see that the broad hill was not protected by any continuous line of entrenchments, but was merely crowned by a large open redoubt, and defended in front by the two small bridge-heads on the Canal of Aragon. There was nothing to prevent an attempt to storm it by main force. This was to be made on the following morning: at the same time Gazan, on the left bank of the Ebro, was ordered to assault the suburb of San Lazaro. Here the marshals had underrated the strength of the Spanish position, which lay in such low ground and was so difficult to make out, that it presented to the observer from a distance an aspect of weakness that was far from the reality.

At eight on the morning of December 21 three French batteries, placed in favourable advanced positions, began to shell the redoubts on the Monte Torrero, with satisfactory results, as they dismounted some of the defender's guns and exploded a small dépôt of reserve ammunition. An hour later the infantry came into action. Moncey had told off for the assault the divisions of Morlot and Grandjean, twenty battalions in all [1]. The former attacked the eastern front of the position, fording the canal and assailing the left-hand *tête-de-pont* on the Valencia road from the flank. The latter, which had passed the canal far outside the Spanish lines, and operated between it and the Huerba, attacked the south-western slopes of the hill. The defence was weak, and when a brigade of Grandjean's men pushed in between the main redoubt on the crest and the Huerba, and took the western part of the Spanish line in the rear, the day was won. St. March's battalions wavered all along the line ; and as his reserves could not be induced to fall upon the French advance, the Valencian general withdrew his whole division into the city, abandoning the entire circuit of the Monte Torrero. The assailants captured seven guns—some of them disabled—in the three redoubts, and a standard of the 5th regiment of Murcia. They had only lost twenty killed and fifty wounded ; the Spanish loss was also insignificant, considering the importance of the position that was at stake, and hardly any prisoners were taken [2]. The besiegers had now the power to bombard all the southern front of Saragossa, and dominated, from the slopes of the hill, the two advanced forts of San José and the Pillar. The leaders of the populace were strongly of opinion that the Valencian division had misbehaved, and they were not far wrong. Palafox had great difficulty in protecting St. March, whose personal conduct had been unimpeachable, from the wrath of the multitude, who wished to make him responsible for the weakness shown by his men [3]. The officer who lost the Monte Torrero in the first siege had been tried and shot [4]: St. March was lucky to escape even without a reprimand.

Meanwhile things had gone very differently at the other point where the French had tried to break down the outer defences of the city. The attack on the transpontine suburb of San Lazaro had been allotted to Gazan's division. This was a very formidable force, 9,000 veterans of the best quality, who were bent on showing that they had not degenerated since they fought at

---

[1] Morlot's division was short of the 121st and the 2nd Legion of Reserve, left behind at Alagon and Tudela, and had only nine battalions present.

[2] Moncey to Berthier, Dec. 23.

[3] Cavallero, pp. 89–90.   [4] See vol. i. p. 153.

Friedland. Owing to some slight mistake in the combination, Gazan only delivered his attack at one o'clock, two hours after the fighting on the Monte Torrero had ceased. His leading brigade, that of Guérin, six battalions strong, advanced against the northern and eastern fronts of the defences of the suburb. The Spaniards were holding as an outwork a large building called the Archbishop's Tower (Torre del Arzobispo)[1] on the Villa-nueva road, 600 yards in front of the main line of entrenchments. This Gazan's men carried at the first rush, killing or capturing 300 men of a Swiss battalion[2] which held it. They then pushed forward towards the inner fortifications, but were taken in flank by a heavy artillery fire from a redoubt which they had overlooked. This caused them to swerve towards the Barcelona road, where they got possession of a house close under the convent of Jesus, and threatened to cut off the garrison of that stronghold from the rest of the defenders of the suburb. At this moment a disgraceful panic seized the defenders of the San Lazaro convent, which lay directly in front of the assailants. They abandoned their post, and began to fly across the bridge into Saragossa. But Palafox came up in person with a reserve, and re-occupied the abandoned post. He then ordered a sortie against the buildings which the French had seized, and succeeded in driving them out and compelling them to retire into the open ground. Gazan doubted for a moment whether he should not send in his second brigade to renew the attack, for the six battalions that had borne the brunt of the first fighting had now fallen into complete disorder. But remembering that if this force failed to break into the suburb he had no reserves left, and that Palafox might bring over the bridge as many reinforcements as he chose, the French general resolved not to push the assault any further. He drew back and retired behind the Gallego stream, where he threw up entrenchments to cover himself, completely abandoning the offensive. For two or three days he did not dare to move, expecting to be attacked at any moment by the garrison. A sudden rise of the Ebro had cut off his communication with Moncey, and he could neither send the

---

[1] Belmas calls it a factory (ii. 151), but Palafox in his dispatch gives the name above.

[2] ' Suizos de Aragon.'

marshal an account of his check, nor get any orders from him [1]. His casualty-list was severe, thirty officers and 650 men killed and wounded : the Spaniards lost somewhat less, even including the 300 Swiss who were cut to pieces at the Archbishop's Tower.

Palafox next morning issued a proclamation, extolling the valour shown in the defence of the suburb, treating the loss of the Monte Torrero as insignificant, and exaggerating the losses of the French.   The Saragossans were rather encouraged than otherwise by the results of the day's fighting, and spoke as if they had merely lost an outwork by the unsteadiness of St. March's Valencians, while the main hostile attack had been repulsed.   But it is clear that the capture of the dominating heights south of the city was an all-important gain to the French.   Without the Monte Torrero they could never have pressed the siege home.   As to the failure at the suburb, it came from attacking with headlong courage an entrenched position that had not been properly reconnoitred.   The assault should never have been delivered without artillery preparation, and was a grave mistake.   But clearly Mortier's corps had yet to learn what the Spaniards were like, and to realize that to turn them out from behind walls and ditches was not the light task that they supposed.

Moncey so thoroughly miscalculated the general effect of the fighting upon the minds of the Spaniards, that next morning he sent in to Palafox a flag of truce, with an officer bearing a formal demand for the surrender of the city.   'Madrid had fallen,' he wrote : 'Saragossa, invested on all sides, had not the force to resist two complete *corps d'armée*.   He trusted that the Captain-General would spare the beautiful and wealthy capital of Aragon the horrors of a siege.   Ample blood had already been shed, enough misfortunes already suffered by Spain.'   Palafox replied in the strain that might have been expected from him—'The man who only wishes to die with honour

---

[1] An officer of sappers named Henri, and one of his privates, tried to reopen communication by swimming the river on an ice-cold night.   They reached the further bank, but died of exhaustion among the reeds, where their corpses were found next morning : thus the message was never delivered.   Belmas, ii. 153.

in defence of his country cares nothing about his position:
but, as a matter of fact, he found that his own was eminently
favourable and encouraging.   In the first siege he had held out
for sixty-one days with a garrison far inferior to that now under
his command.   Was it likely that he would surrender, when he
had as many troops as his besiegers?   Looking at the results
of the fighting on the previous day, when the assailants had
suffered so severely in front of San Lazaro, he thought that he
would be quite as well justified in proposing to the Marshal
that the besieging army should surrender "to spare further
effusion of blood," as the latter had been to make such a proposition to him.   If Madrid had fallen, Madrid must have been
sold: but he begged for leave to doubt the truth of the rumour.
Even at the worst Madrid was but a town, like any other.   Its
fate had no influence on Saragossa [1].'

Having received such an answer Moncey had only to set to
work as fast as possible: his engineer-in-chief, General Lacoste,
after making a thorough survey of the defences, pronounced in
favour of choosing two fronts of attack, both starting on the
Monte Torrero, and directed the one against the fort of San
José and the other against that of the Pillar.   These projecting
works would have to be carried before any attempt could be
made against the inner *enceinte* of the town.   At the same time,
Lacoste ordered a third attack, which he did not propose to press
home, to be made on the castle of the Aljafferia, on the west side
of the town.   It was only intended to distract the attention of
the Spaniards from the points of real danger.   On the further bank
of the Ebro, Gazan's division was directed to move forward again,
and to entrench itself across all the three roads, which issue from
the suburb, and lead respectively to Lerida, Jaca, and Monzon.
He was not to attack, but merely to blockade the northern exits
of Saragossa.   Communications with him were established by
means of a bridge of boats and pontoons laid above the town.
Gazan succeeded in shortening the front which he had to protect
against sorties by letting the water of the Ebro into the low-
lying fields along its banks, where it caused inundations on each
of his flanks.

[1] The two letters may be found in full in the appendices to Belmas,
vol. ii.

On the twenty-third the preliminary works of the siege began, approaches and covered ways being constructed leading down from the Monte Torrero to the spots from which Lacoste intended to commence the first parallels of the two attacks on the Pillar and San José. Preparations of a similar sort were commenced for the false attack on the left, opposite the Aljafferia. Six days were occupied in these works, and in the bringing up of the heavy artillery, destined to arm the siege-batteries, from Tudela. The guns had to come by road, as the Spaniards had destroyed all the barges on the Canal of Aragon, and blown up many of its locks. It was not till some time later that the French succeeded in reopening the navigation, by replacing the sluice-gates and building large punts and floats for the carriage of guns or munitions.

Just before the first parallel was opened Marshal Moncey was recalled to Madrid [December 29], the Emperor being apparently discontented with his delays in the early part of the month. He was replaced in command of the 3rd Corps by Junot, whose old divisions had been made over (as we have seen in the first volume) to Soult's 2nd Corps. This change made Mortier the senior officer of the besieging army, but he and Junot seem to have worked more as partners than as commander and subordinate. Junot, in his report to the Emperor[1] on the state in which he found the troops, enlarges at great length on the deplorable condition of the 3rd Corps. Many of the battalions had never received their winter clothing, hundreds entered the hospitals every day, and there was no corresponding outflow of convalescents. No less than 680 men had died in the base hospital at Pampeluna in November, and the figure for December would be worse. He doubted if there were 13,000 infantry under arms in his three divisions—here he exaggerated somewhat, for even a fortnight later the returns show that his 'present under arms,' after deducting all detachments and sick, were still over 14,000 bayonets: on January 1, therefore, there must have been 15,000. He asked for money, reinforcements, and a supply of officers, the commissioned ranks of his corps showing a terrible proportion of gaps. On the other hand, he conceded that the 5th Corps was in excellent condition, its veterans suffering far

[1] Junot to Berthier, Jan. 1, 1809.

less from disease than his own conscripts. Either of Gazan's and Suchet's divisions was, by itself, as strong as any two of the divisions of the 3rd Corps.

On the night of the twenty-ninth–thirtieth, within twelve hours of Moncey's departure, the first parallel was opened, both in the attack towards St. José and in that opposite the Pillar fort. When the design of the besiegers became evident, Palafox made three sallies on the thirty-first, but apparently more with the object of reconnoitring the siege-works and distracting the workers than with any hope of breaking the French lines, for there were not more than 1,500 men employed in any of the three columns which delivered the sorties. The assault on the trenches before San José was not pressed home, but opposite the false attack at the Aljafferia the fighting was more lively; the French outposts were all driven in with loss, and a squadron of cavalry, which had slipped out from the Sancho gate, close to the Ebro, surprised and sabred thirty men of a picket on the left of the French lines. Palafox made the most of this small success in a magniloquent proclamation published on the succeeding day. He should have sent out 15,000 men instead of 3,000 if he intended to get any profit out of his sorties. An attack delivered with such a force on some one point of the lines must have paralysed the siege operations, and might have proved disastrous to the French.

Meanwhile the besiegers, undisturbed by these sallies, pushed forward their works on the northern slopes of the Monte Torrero. The attack opposite San José got forward much faster than that against the Pillar: its second parallel was commenced on January 1, and its batteries were all ready to open by the ninth. The other attack was handicapped by the fact that the ground sloped down more rapidly towards the Huerba, so that the trenches had to be made much deeper, and pushed forward in perpetual zigzags, in order to avoid being searched by the plunging fire from the Spanish batteries on the other side of the stream, in the *enceinte* of the town. To get a flanking position against the Pillar redoubt, the left attack was continued by another line of trenches beyond the Huerba, after it has made its sharp turn to the south.

Before the engineers had completed their work, and long ere

the breaching batteries were ready, a great strain was thrown
upon the besiegers by fresh orders from Napoleon. On January 2, Marshal Mortier received a dispatch, bidding him march
out to Calatayud with one of his two divisions, and open
up the direct communication with Madrid. Accordingly he
departed with the two strong brigades of Suchet's division,
10,000 bayonets. This withdrawal threw much harder work
on the remainder of the army: Junot was left with not much
more than 24,000 men, including the artillerymen, to maintain
the investment of the whole city. He was forced to spread
out the 3rd Corps on a very thin line, in order to occupy all
the posts from which Suchet's battalions had been withdrawn.
Morlot's division came down from the Monte Torrero to occupy
the ground which Suchet had evacuated: Musnier had to cover
the whole of the hill, and to support both the lines of approach
on which the engineers were busy. Grandjean's division remained on its old front, facing the eastern side of the city, and
Gazan still blockaded the suburb beyond the Ebro. As the
last-named general had still 8,000 men, there were only 15,000
bayonets and the artillery available for the siege, a force far
too small to maintain a front nearly four miles long. If Palafox
had dared to make a general sortie with all his disposable men,
Junot's position would have been more than hazardous. But
the Captain-General contented himself with making numerous
and useless sallies on a petty scale, sending out the most reckless
and determined of his men to waste themselves in bickering
with the guards of the trenches, when he should have saved
them to head a general assault in force upon some weak
point of the siege lines. The diaries and narratives of the
French officers who served at Saragossa are full of anecdotes
of the frantic courage shown by the besieged, generally to no
purpose. One of the strangest has been preserved by the very
prosaic engineer Belmas, who tells how a priest in his robes
came out on January 6 in front of Gazan's lines, and walked
among the bullets to within fifty yards of the trenches, when
he preached with great unction for some minutes, his crucifix
in his hand, to the effect that the French had a bad cause
and were drawing down God's anger upon themselves. To the
credit of his audience it must be said that they let him go off

alive, contenting themselves with firing over his head, in order to see if they could scare him into a run.

At daybreak on January 10, the whole of the French batteries opened upon San José and the Pillar fort. The fire against the latter was distant and comparatively ineffective, but the masonry of San José began to crumble at once : its walls, solid though they were, had never been built to resist siege artillery. The roofs and tiles came crashing down upon the defenders' heads, and most of their guns were silenced or injured. The besiegers suffered little—Belmas says that only one officer and ten men fell, though two guns in the most advanced battery were disabled. The loss of the Spaniards on the other hand was numbered by hundreds, more being slain by the fall of stones and slates than by the actual cannon balls and shells of the assailants. At nightfall Palafox withdrew most of the guns from the convent, but replaced the decimated garrison by three fresh battalions. It was clear that the work would fall next day unless the besiegers were driven off from their batteries. At 1 A.M., therefore, 300 men made a desperate sally to spike the guns. But the French were alert, and had brought up two field-pieces close to the convent, which repressed the sortie with a storm of grape.

Next morning the bombardment of San José recommenced, and by the afternoon a large breach had been established in its southern wall. At four o'clock General Grandjean launched a picked force, composed of the seven voltigeur companies of the 14th and 44th regiments, upon the crumbling defences [1]. The garrison had already begun to quit the untenable post, and only a minority remained behind to fight to the last. The storming column entered without much loss, partly by laying scaling-ladders to the foot of the breach, partly by using a small bridge of planks across the ditch, which the Spaniards had forgotten to remove. They only lost thirty-eight men, and made prisoners of about fifty of the garrison who had refused to retire into the city when the rest fled.

Though San José was thus easily captured, it was difficult to establish a lodgement in it, for the batteries on the *enceinte* of Saragossa searched it from end to end, dominating its ruined

---

[1] Belmas, ii. 175.

quadrangle from a superior height. But during the night the besiegers succeeded in blocking up its gorge, and in connecting the breach with their second parallel by a covered way of sandbags and fascines. The convent was now the base from which they were to attack the town-walls behind it.

But before continuing the advance in this direction it was necessary to carry the fort of Our Lady of the Pillar, the other great outwork of the southern front of Saragossa. The main attention of the besiegers was directed against this point from the twelfth to the fifteenth, and their sapping gradually took them to within a few yards of the counterscarp. The Spanish fire had been easily subdued, and a practicable breach established. On the night of the fifteenth-sixteenth the fort was stormed by the Poles of the 1st regiment of the Vistula. They met with little or no resistance, the greater part of the garrison having withdrawn when the assault was seen to be imminent. A mine under the glacis exploded, but failed to do any harm : another, better laid, destroyed the bridge over the Huerba, behind the fort, when the work was seen to be in the power of the assailants. Lacoste reported to Junot that the Poles lost only one killed and two wounded—an incredibly small casualty list [1].

The fall of the fort of the Pillar gave the French complete possession of all the ground to the south of the Huerba, and left them free to attack the *enceinte* of the city, which had now lost all its outer works save the Aljafferia : in front of that castle the 'false attack' made little progress, for the besiegers did not press in close, and contented themselves with battering the old mediaeval fortress from a distance. On that part of the line of investment nothing of importance was to happen.

[1] Lacoste to Junot, Jan. 16, in Belmas, ii. 378.

SECTION XI: CHAPTER II

SIEGE OF SARAGOSSA: THE FRENCH WITHIN THE WALLS:
THE STREET-FIGHTING: THE SURRENDER

LACOSTE's first care, when the Pillar and San José had both
fallen into his hands, was to connect the two works by his 'third
parallel,' which was drawn from one to the other just above the
edge of the ravine of the Huerba. In order to assail the walls
of the city that stream had to be crossed, a task of some difficulty,
for its bed was searched by the great batteries at Santa Engracia
along the whole front between the two captured forts, while
north of San José the 'Palafox Battery' near the Porta Quemada
completely overlooked the lower and broader part of the river
bed. The Spaniards kept up a fast and furious fire upon the
lost works, with the object of preventing the besiegers from
moving forward from them, or constructing fresh batteries among
their ruins. In this they were not successful: the French, bur-
rowing deep among the débris, successfully covered themselves,
and suffered little.

The second stage of the siege work, the attack on the actual
enceinte of Saragossa, now began. The two points on which it
was directed were the Santa Engracia battery—the southern
salient of the town—and the extreme south-eastern angle of the
place, where lay the Palafox Battery and the smaller work
generally known as the battery of the Oil Mill (Molino de
Aceite). The former was less than 200 yards from the Pillar
fort, the latter not more than 100 from San José, but between
them ran the deep bed of the Huerba.

From the twelfth to the seventeenth the French were busily
engaged in throwing up batteries in the line of their third
parallel, and on the morning of the last-named day no less than
nine were ready. Five opened on Santa Engracia, four on the
Palafox battery: at both points they soon began to do exten-

sive damage, for here the walls had not been entirely reconstructed (as on the western front of the city), but only patched
up and strengthened with earthworks at intervals. The masonry
of the convent of Santa Engracia suffered most, and began to
fall in large patches. Palafox saw that the *enceinte* would be
pierced ere long, and that street-fighting would be the next
stage of the siege. Accordingly he set the whole civil population to work on constructing barricades across the streets and
lanes of the south-eastern part of the city, in the rear of the
threatened points, and turned every block of houses into an
independent fort by building up all the doorways and windows
facing towards the enemy. The spirits of the garrison were
still high, and the Captain-General had done his best to keep
them up by issuing gazettes containing very roseate accounts of
the state of affairs in the outer world. His communication
with the open country was not completely cut, for thrice he had
been able to send boats down the Ebro, which took their chance
of running past the French batteries at night, and always
succeeded. One of these boats had carried the Captain-General's
younger brother, Francisco Palafox, who had orders to appeal to
the Catalans for help, and to raise the peasants of Lower Aragon.
Occasional messengers also got in from without : one arrived on
January 16 from Catalonia, with promises of aid from the
Marquis of Lazan, who proposed to return from Gerona with
his division, in order to fall upon the rear of the besiegers.
Palafox not only let this be known, but published in his Official
Gazette some utterly unfounded rumours, which the courier
had brought. Reding, it was said, had beaten St. Cyr in the
open field : the Duke of Infantado was marching from Cuenca
on Aragon with 20,000 men. Sir John Moore had turned to
bay on the pursuing forces of the Emperor, and had defeated
them at a battle in Galicia in which Marshal Ney had been
killed[1]. To celebrate this glorious news the church bells were
set ringing, the artillery fired a general salute, and military
music paraded the town. These phenomena were perfectly
audible to the besiegers, and caused them many searchings of

---

[1] Was this a distorted rumour of the combat of Cacabellos, and the
death of General Colbert, the commander of Ney's corps-cavalry, on
Jan. 3 ?

heart, for they could not guess what event the Saragossans could be celebrating.

The garrison needed all the encouragement that could be given to them, for after the middle of January the stress of the siege began to be felt very heavily. Food was not wanting—for, excepting fresh meat and vegetables, everything was still procurable in abundance. But cold and overcrowding were beginning to cause epidemic disorders. The greater part of the civil population had taken refuge in their cellars when the bombardment began, and after a few days spent in those dark and damp retreats, from which they only issued at night, or when they were called on for labour at the fortifications, began to develop fevers and dysentery. This was inevitable, for in most of the dwellings from twenty to forty persons of all ages were crowded in mere holes, no more than seven feet high, and almost unprovided with ventilation, where they lived, ate, and slept, packed together, and with no care for sanitary precautions [1]. The malignant fevers bred in these refuges soon spread to the garrison : though under cover, the soldiery were destitute of warm clothing (especially the Murcian battalions), and could not procure enough firewood to cook their meals. By January 20 there were 8,000 sick among the 30,000 regular troops, and every day the wastage to the hospital grew more and more noticeable. Many officers of note had already fallen in the useless sorties, and in especial a grave loss had been suffered on January 13, when Colonel San Genis, the chief engineer of the besieged, and the designer of the whole of the defences of the city, was killed on the ramparts of the Palafox battery, as he was directing the fire against the new entrenchment which the French were throwing up across the gorge of the San José fort [2]. He had no competent successor as a general director, for his underlings had no grasp of siege-strategy, and were only good at details. They built batteries and barricades and ran mines

[1] For the description of these miserable and most insalubrious refuges, see Cavallero, pp. 90–100.

[2] I give the date of San Genis' death from Arteche, iv. Belmas, on the other hand, puts it on Jan. 26, and Cavallero apparently on Jan. 28, for he says that it was three days before that of Lacoste, who was shot on Feb. 1.

in pure opportunism, without any comprehensive scheme of defence before their eyes.

The French meanwhile were very active, though the constant increase of sickness in the 3rd Corps was daily thinning the regiments, till the proportion of men stricken down by fever was hardly less than that among the Spaniards. On the seventeenth and eighteenth Lacoste began to contrive a descent into the bottom of the ravine of the Huerba, by a series of zigzags pushed forward from the third parallel, both in the direction of Santa Engracia and in that of the Palafox battery. The latter was repeatedly silenced by the advanced batteries of the besiegers, but they could not subdue the incessant musketry fire from windows and loopholes which swept the whole bed of the Huerba, and rendered the work at the head of the new sap most difficult and deadly. Sometimes it had to be completely abandoned because of the plunging fire from the city[1]. Yet it was always resumed after a time: the French found that their best and easiest work was done in the early morning, when, for day after day, a dense fog rose from the Ebro, which rendered it impossible for the Spaniards to see what was going on, or to aim with any certainty at the entrenchments. Irritated at the steady if slow progress of the enemy, Palafox launched on the afternoon of January 23 the most desperate sortie that his army had yet essayed against the advanced works of the French. At four o'clock on that day[2] three columns dashed out and attacked the line of trenches: one, as a blind, was sent out opposite the Aljafferia, to distract the attention of Morlot's division from the main sally. The other two were serious attacks, but both made with too small numbers—apparently no more than 200 picked men in each. The left-hand column became hotly engaged with the trenches to the north of San José, and got no further forward than a house a little beyond the Huerba, from which they expelled a French post. But the right-hand force carried out a very bold programme. Crossing

[1] Belmas, ii. 198.

[2] Oddly enough, Belmas places this sortie on Jan. 21, on which day, as Arteche shows, none of the Spanish accounts speak of a sortie, while the latter give at great length details of the fighting on the twenty-third. Probably the Spanish date is the correct one.

the Huerba below Santa Engracia, they broke through the third parallel, and then made a dash at two mortar-batteries in the second parallel which had particularly annoyed the defence on that morning.   The commander of the sortie, Mariano Galindo, a captain of the Volunteers of Aragon, led his men so straight that they rushed in with the bayonet on the first battery and spiked both its pieces.   They were making for the second when they were overwhelmed by the trench guard and by reinforcements hurrying up from Musnier's camp.   Of a hundred men who had gone forward with Galindo from the third parallel twelve were killed and thirty, including their brave leader, taken prisoners.   The French stated their loss at no more than six killed and five wounded, a figure that seems suspiciously low, considering that the first line of trenches had been stormed by the assailants, and a battery in the second line captured and disabled.   Galindo had gone forward more than 500 yards, into the very middle of the French works, before he was checked and surrounded.   It was a very gallant exploit, but once more we are constrained to ask why Palafox told off for it no more than a mere handful of men.   What would have happened had he thrown a solid column of 10,000 men upon the siege-works, instead of a few hundred volunteers ?

On the twenty-second, the day before Galindo's sortie, Junot was superseded in command of the besieging army by Lannes, who had been restored to health by two months' holiday, and was now himself again.   He arrived just in time to take charge of the important task of storming the main *enceinte*, for which Junot's preparations were now far advanced.   But though the siege operations looked not unpromising, he found the situation grave and dangerous.   Belmas and the other French historians describe this as the most critical epoch of the whole Saragossan episode [1].   The fact was that at last there were beginning to be signs of movement in the open country of Aragon.   During the month that had elapsed since the siege began, the peasantry had been given time to draw together.   Francisco Palafox, after escaping from the city, had gone to Mequinenza, and was arming the local levies with muskets procured from Catalonia. He had already a great horde assembled in the direction of

[1] Belmas, ii. 203.

Alcañiz.   On the other bank of the Ebro Colonel Perena had
been organizing a force at Huesca, from northern Aragon and
the foot-hills of the Pyrenees.   Lastly, it was known that Lazan
was on his way from Gerona to aid his brothers, and had
brought to Lerida his division of 4,000 men [1], a comparatively
well-organized body of troops, which had been under arms since
October.   Even far back, on the way to Pampeluna, insurgents
had gathered in the Sierra de Moncayo, and were threatening
the important halfway post of Tudela, by which the besieging
army kept up its communication with France.

Hitherto these gatherings had looked dangerous, but had
done no actual harm.   General Wathier, with the cavalry of
the 3rd Corps, had scoured the southern bank of the Ebro
and kept off the insurgents ; but now they were pressing closer
in, and on January 20 a battalion, which Gazan had sent out to
drive away Perena's levies, had been checked and beaten off at
Perdiguera, only twelve miles from the camp of the besiegers.

Lannes could not fail to see that if he committed himself to
the final assault on Saragossa, and entangled the 3rd Corps in
street-fighting, he might find himself assailed from the rear on
all points of his lines.   There were no troops whatever in front
of Saragossa to form a 'covering-force' to beat off the insurgents, if they should come down upon his camps while he was
storming the city, for the 3rd Corps and Gazan's division had
now only 20,000 infantry for the conduct of the siege.

Accordingly the Marshal resolved to undo the Emperor's
arrangements for keeping up the line of communication with
Madrid, and to draw in Mortier, with Suchet's strong and
intact division, from Calatayud, where he had been lying for
the last three weeks.   This was the only possible force which he
could use to provide himself with a covering army.   The touch
with Madrid, a thing of comparatively minor importance, had to
be sacrificed, except so far as it could be kept up by the division
of Dessolles, which had now come back from the pursuit of
Sir John Moore, and had pushed detachments back to its old
posts at Siguenza and Guadalajara.

Mortier therefore evacuated Calatayud by the orders of

---

[1] Napier (i. 376) calls them ' Catalonians': but they were all Aragonese,
sent to aid Catalonia in October.

Lannes, and came back to the Ebro : passing behind the besieging army he crossed the river and took post at Perdiguera with
10,000 men, facing the levies of Perena in the direction of
Huesca. It was only when he had made certain of having this
powerful reinforcement close at hand, ready to deal with any
interference from without, that Lannes dared to proceed with
the assault. At the same time that Mortier arrived at Perdiguera, he sent out Wathier, with two battalions and two
regiments of cavalry, to deal with the insurgents of the Lower
Ebro, where Francisco Palafox had been busy. Four or five
thousand peasants with one newly-levied regiment of Aragonese
volunteers tried to resist this small column, but were beaten on
the twenty-sixth in front of the town of Alcañiz, which fell
into Wathier's hands, and with it 20,000 sheep and 1,500 sacks
of flour, which had been collected for the revictualling of Saragossa, in case the investment should be broken. They were
a welcome windfall to the besieging army, where food was none
too plentiful, since the plain country where it lay encamped
had now been eaten bare, and convoys of food from Tudela and
Pampeluna were rare and inadequate.

On January 24 the French had succeeded in pushing three
approaches across the Huerba, and were firmly established under
its northern bank. Two days later they made lodgements in
ruins, cellars, and low walls where buildings had been pulled
down, in the narrow space between the town wall and the river
bank, below the Palafox battery. The cannon of the defenders
could only act intermittently : every night the parapets were
repaired, but every morning after a fe hours of artillery duel
the Spanish guns were silenced by the dreadful converging fire
poured in upon them. Meanwhile Palafox was heaping barricade upon barricade in the quarters behind the threatened
points, and fortifying the houses and convents which connected
them.

The final crisis arrived on the twenty-seventh. There were now
three practicable breaches,—two were on the side of the Palafox
battery, one in the convent of Santa Engracia. To storm
the first and second Lannes told off the light companies of the
first brigade of Grandjean's division ; to the third was allotted
the 1st regiment of the Vistula from Musnier's division. Heavy

supports lay behind them, in the third parallel, with orders to rush in if the storming parties should prove successful.

The assault was delivered with great dash and swiftness at noon on the twenty-seventh. On two points it was successful. At the most northern breach the assailants reached the summit of the wall, but could not get down into the city, on account of the storm of musketry from barricades and houses that swept the gap into which they had advanced. They merely made a lodgement in the breach itself, and could penetrate no further. But in the central breach, close beneath the Palafox battery, the voltigeurs not only passed the walls, but seized the 'Oil Mill' which abutted on them, and a triangular block of houses projecting into the town. At the Santa Engracia breach they were even more fortunate: the Poles carried the convent with their first rush: its outer wall had been battered down for a breadth of thirty yards, and entering there the stormers drove out the Spaniards from the interior buildings of the place, and got into the large square which lies behind it, where they seized the Capuchin nunnery. Thus a considerable wedge was driven through the *enceinte,* and the Spaniards had to evacuate the walls for some little distance on each side of Santa Engracia. From the stretch to the west of that convent they were driven out by an unpremeditated assault of Musnier's supports, who ran out from the trenches on the left of the Huerba, and escaladed the dilapidated wall in front of them, when they saw the garrison drawing back on account of the flanking fire from Santa Engracia. They got possession of the whole outer *enceinte* as far as the Trinitarian convent by the Carmen gate.

These successes were bought at the moderate loss of 350 men, of whom two-thirds fell in the fighting on the Santa Engracia front; the Spaniards lost somewhat more, including a few prisoners. In any ordinary siege the day would have settled the fate of the place, for the besiegers had broken through the *enceinte* in two places, and though the space seized inside the Palafox battery was not large, yet on each side of Santa Engracia the assailants had penetrated so far that a quarter of a mile of the walls was in their possession. But Saragossa was not as other places, and the garrison were perfectly prepared with a new front of defence, composed of batteries and crenellated houses in rear of the lost positions. Two wedges, one large and one small, had been driven into the town, but they had to be broadened and driven further in if they were to have any effect.

On the twenty-eighth, therefore, a new stage of the siege began, and the street-fighting, which was to last for twenty-four days more, had its commencement. Lannes had heard, from those who had served under Verdier in the first siege, of the deplorable slaughter and repeated repulses that had followed the attempt to carry by main force the internal defences of the city. To hurl solid columns of stormers at the barricades and the crenellated houses was not his intention. He had made up his mind to advance by sap and mine, as if he were dealing with regular fortifications. His plan was to use each block of houses that he gained as a base for the attack upon the next, and never to send in the infantry with the bayonet till he had breached by artillery, or by mines, the building against which the assault was directed. This form of attack was bound to be slow, but it had the great merit of costing comparatively little in the way of casualties. The fact was that the Marshal had not the numbers which would justify him in wasting lives by assaults which might or might not be successful, but which were certain to prove very bloody. The whole Third Corps, as we have already seen, did not now furnish much more than 13,000 bayonets, while Gazan's men were all occupied in watching the suburb, and Suchet's lay far out, as a covering corps set to watch Perena and Lazan.

There was no one single dominating position in the city whose occupation was likely to constrain the besieged to surrender. The whole town is built on a level, and its fifty-three solidly-built churches and convents formed so many forts, each of which was defensible in itself and could not be reduced save by a direct attack. All that could be done was to endeavour to capture them one by one, in the hope that at last the Saragossans would grow tired of their hopeless resistance, and consent to surrender, when they realized that things had gone so far that they could only protract, but could not finally beat off, the slow advance of the besieging army.

The work of the French, therefore, consisted in spreading out from their two separate lodgements on the eastern and southern sides of the city, with the simple object of gaining ground each day and of driving the Spaniards back towards the centre of the place.   On the right attack the most important objective of the besiegers was the block of monastic buildings to the north of the Palafox battery, the twin convents of San Augustin and Santa Monica, which lay along the northern side of the small wedge that they had driven into the north-eastern corner of the town.   As these buildings lay on ground slightly higher than that which the French had occupied, it was difficult to attack them by means of mines.   But an intense converging fire was brought to bear upon them, both from batteries outside the walls, playing across the Huerba, and by guns brought inside the captured angle of the *enceinte*.   The outer walls of Santa Monica were soon a mass of ruins : nevertheless the first attack on it [January 29] was beaten off, and it was only on the next day, after twenty-four hours more of furious bombardment, that Grandjean's men succeeded in storming, first the convent and then its church, after a furious hand-to-hand fight with the defenders.

After establishing themselves in Santa Monica the French were able to capture some of the adjoining houses, and to turn their attention against its neighbour San Augustin.   They ran two mines under it, and at the same time battered it heavily from the external batteries beyond the Huerba.   On February 1 the explosion took place : it opened a breach in the east end of the convent church, and the storming party, entering by the sacristy, got possession of the choir chapels and the high altar. But the Spaniards rallied in the nave, ran a barricade of chairs and benches across it, and held their own for some time, firing down from the pulpit and the organ loft with effect.   Some climbed up into the roof and picked off the French through the holes which the bombardment had left in the ceiling.   For some hours this strange indoor battle raged within the spacious church.   But at last the French carried the nave, and at night only the belfry remained untaken.   Its little garrison pelted the French with grenades all day, and saved themselves at dusk by a sudden and unexpected dash through the enemy.

In the first flush of success, after San Augustin had been

stormed, the 44th regiment, from Grandjean's division, tried to push on through the streets towards the centre of the town. They captured several barricades and houses, and struggled on till they had nearly reached the Coso. But this sort of fighting was always dangerous in Saragossa: the citizens kept up such a fierce fire from their windows, and swarmed out against the flanks of the column in such numbers, that the 44th had to give back, lost all that it had taken beyond San Augustin, and left 200 dead and wounded behind. Even the formal official reports of the French engineers speak with respect of the courage shown by the besieged on this day. The houses which they had lost in the afternoon they retook in the dusk, by an extraordinary device. Finding the French solidly barricaded in them, and proof against any attack from the street, hundreds of the defenders climbed upon the roofs, tore up the tiles and entered by the garrets, from which they descended and drove out the invaders by a series of charges which cleared story after story[1]. Many monks, and still more women, were seen among the armed crowds which swept the assailants back towards Santa Monica. It was especially noticed that the civilians did far more of the fighting than the soldiers. This was their own special battle.

Irritated at his losses on this day, Lannes issued a general order, expressly forbidding any attempts to storm houses and barricades by main force. After an explosion, the troops were to seize the building that had been shattered, and to cover themselves in it; they were not to go forward and fall upon intact defences further to the front.

While the struggle was raging thus fiercely from January 28 to February 1, in the eastern area of street-fighting, there had been a no less desperate series of combats all around Santa Engracia, on the southern front of attack. Here Musnier's division was endeavouring to drive the Spaniards out of the blocks of houses to the right and left of the captured convent. They worked almost entirely by mines, running tunnels forward from beneath the convent to blow down the walls of the adjoining dwellings. But even when the mines had gutted the doomed buildings, it was not easy to seize them: the few men who

[1] Report of General Laval (commanding in the trenches this day) to Lannes, in Appendix xxvi, of Belmas, vol. ii. Cf. von Brandt, p. 34.

survived the explosion did not fly, but held out among the
ruins, and had to be bayonetted by the assailants who rushed
out from the convent to occupy the new lodgements.   Time
after time the defenders, though perfectly conscious that they
were being undermined, and that by staying on guard they
were courting certain death, refused to evacuate the threatened
houses or to retire into safety.   Hence their losses were awful,
but the French too suffered not a little, while pushing forward
to occupy each building as it was cleared by the explosion.   The
constant rain of musket balls from roofs and church towers
searched out the ruins in which they had to effect their lodgements, and many of the assailants fell before they could cover
themselves among the débris.

On the thirty-first the Spaniards made a sudden rush from
the Misericordia buildings, to recover the Trinitarian convent,
the most western point on the *enceinte* which had fallen into
the hands of the French at the assault of the twenty-seventh.
They charged in upon it with the greatest fury, and blew open
the gate with a four-pounder gun which they dragged up by
hand to the very threshold.   But the French had built up the
whole entrance with sandbags, which held even when the doors
had been shattered ; and, after persisting for some time in
a fruitless attempt to break in, the Saragossans had to retire,
foiled and greatly thinned in numbers.

On the following day (February 1) the French began to move
forward from Santa Engracia towards the Coso, always clearing
their way by explosions, and risking as few men as possible.
Nevertheless they could not always keep under cover, and this
day they suffered a severe loss : their chief engineer, General
Lacoste, was shot through the head, while reconnoitring from
a window the houses against which his next attack was to be
directed [1].   He was succeeded in command by Colonel Rogniat,
one of the French historians of the siege.   That officer, as he
tells us, discovered that his sappers were using too large charges
of powder, which destroyed the roofs and four walls of each

---

[1] There is a full account of his death in Legendre, i. 149 ; that officer
was in the room with him, when he and his aide-de-camp, Lalobe, were
simultaneously shot through the head as they peered out of a side window
where they thought themselves unobserved.

house that they undermined, so that the infantry who followed had no cover when they first took possession. He therefore ordered the substitution of smaller measures of powder, so as to throw down only parts of the wall of the building nearest to the French lines, and to leave the roof and the outer walls uninjured. In this way it was much more easy to establish a lodgement, since the storming-party were covered the moment that they had dashed into the shattered shell. The only plan which the Spaniards could devise against this method of procedure, was to set fire to the ruins, and to prevent the entry of the assailants by burning down all that was left of the house. As the buildings of Saragossa contained little woodwork, and were not very combustible [1], the besieged daubed the walls with tar and resin to make them blaze the better. When an explosion had taken place, the surviving defenders set fire to the débris of floors and roofs before retiring [2]. In this way they sometimes kept the French back for as much as two days, since they could not make their lodgement till the cinders had time to cool. Countermining against the French approaches was often tried, but seldom with success, for there were no trained miners in the city: the one battalion of sappers which Palafox possessed had been formed from the workmen of the Canal of Aragon, who had no experience in subterranean work. On the other hand the French had three whole companies of miners, beside eight more of sappers, who were almost as useful in the demolition of the city. They maintained a distinct ascendent underground, though they not unfrequently lost men in the repeated combats with knife and pistol which ensued when mine and countermine met, and the two sides fought for the possession of each other's galleries.

The first week of February was now drawing to its close, and the advance of the French into the city, though steady, had been extremely slow. Every little block of five or six houses cost a day to break up, and another to entrench. The waste of life, though not excessive, was more than Lannes could really afford, and he waited impatiently, but in vain, for any signs that the

---

[1] The ceilings in all the better sort of houses were made of vaulted arches, not of beams and boards.

[2] See Cavallero, p. 120, and compare Belmas, ii. 253.

obstinacy of the defence was slackening. But though he could
not see it, the garrison were being tried far more hardly than
the besiegers. It was not so much the loss by fire and sword
that was ruining them as the silent ravages of the epidemic
fevers. Since the French had got within the walls, and the
bombardment of the city was being carried on from a shorter
range than before, the civilian population had been forced
to cling more closely than ever to its fetid cellars, and the
infectious fever which had appeared in January was developing
at the most fearful rate. Living under such insanitary conditions, and feeding on flour and salt fish, for the vegetables
had long been exhausted, the Saragossans had no strength to
bear up against the typhus. Whole families died off, and their
bodies lay forgotten, tainting the air and spreading the contagion.
Even where there were survivors, they could not easily dispose
of the dead, for the urban cemeteries were gorged, and burials
took place in trenches hastily opened in streets or gardens.
Outside the churches there were hundreds of corpses, some
coffined, others rolled in shrouds or sheets, waiting in rows for
the last services of the church, which the surviving clergy were
too few to read. The shells from the incessant bombardment
were continually falling in these open spaces, and tearing the
dead to pieces. Ere the siege was over there was a mass of
mutilated and decaying bodies heaped in front of every church
door. Hundreds more lay in the debatable ground for which
the Spaniards and French were contending, and the whole town
reeked with contagion. The weather was generally still and warm
for the time of year, with a thick fog rising every morning from
the low ground by the Ebro. The smoke from the burning
houses lay low over the place, and the air was thick with the
mingled fumes of fire and pestilence. If it nauseated the French,
who had the open country behind them, and were relieved by
regiments at intervals, and allowed a rest in their camps outside
the walls, it was far more terrible to the Spaniards. The death
rate rose, as February drew on, from 300 up to 500 and
even 600 a day. The morning state of the garrison on the
fourth day of the month showed 13,737 sick and wounded, and
only 8,495 men under arms. As the total had been 32,000
when the siege began, nearly 10,000 men must already have

perished by the sword or disease. The civil population, containing so many women, children, and aged persons, was of
course dying at a much quicker rate. Yet the place held out
for sixteen days longer ! Palafox himself was struck down by
the fever, but still issued orders from his bed, and poured out
a string of hysterical proclamations, in which his delirium is
clearly apparent.

The terrible situation of the Saragossans was to a large
extent concealed from the besiegers, who only saw the line of
desperate fighting-men which met them in every house, and
could only guess at the death and desolation that lay behind.
Every French eye-witness bears record to the low spirits of
the troops who were compelled to fight in the long series of
explosions and assaults which filled the early weeks of February.
The engineer Belmas, the most matter-of-fact of all the historians
of the siege, turns aside for a moment from his traverses and
mining-galleries, to describe the murmurs of the weary infantry
of the 3rd Corps. 'Who ever heard before,' they asked, 'of an
army of 20,000 men being set to take a town defended by
50,000 madmen ? We have conquered a quarter of it, and now
we are completely fought out. We must halt and wait for
reinforcements, or we shall all perish, and be buried in these
cursed ruins, before we can rout out the last of these fanatics
from their last stronghold [1].' Lannes did his best to encourage
the rank and file, by showing them that the Spaniards were
suffering far more than they, and by pointing out that the
moment must inevitably come when the defence must break
down from mere exhaustion. He also endeavoured to obtain
reinforcements from the Emperor, but only received assurances
that some conscripts and convalescents for the 3rd Corps should
be sent to him from Pampeluna and Bayonne. No fresh
regiments could be spared from France, when the affairs of
Central Europe were looking so doubtful [2]. The best plan
which the Marshal could devise for breaking down the resolution
of the Spaniards was to lengthen his front of attack, and so
endeavour to distract the attention of the besieged from the
main front of advance towards the Coso.

[1] Belmas, ii. 294.   Cf. Rogniat and Legendre.
[2] Berthier to Lannes, Paris, Feb. 10.

This was only to be done by causing the division of Gazan, which had so long remained passive in front of the suburb, to open an energetic attack on that outlying part of the fortress. The advantage to be secured in this direction was not merely that a certain amount of the defenders would be drawn away from the city. If the suburb were captured it would be possible to erect batteries in it, which would search the whole northern side of Saragossa, the one quarter of the city which was still comparatively unaffected by the bombardment. Here the bulk of the civil population was crowded together, and here too Palafox had collected the greater part of his stores and magazines. If the last safe corner of the city were exposed to a bombardment from a fresh quarter, it would probably do much to lower the hopes of the defenders.

During the last days of January Gazan's division had pressed back the Spanish outposts in front of the suburb, and on the thirtieth of that month Lannes had sent over two companies of siege artillery, to construct batteries opposite the convents of Jesus and San Lazaro. It was not till February 2–3, however, that he ordered a serious and active attack to be pressed in this quarter. From the trench which covered the front of Gazan's investing lines a second parallel was thrown out, and two breaching batteries erected against the Jesus convent : on the fourth an advance by zigzags was pushed still further forward, and more guns brought up. Some little delay was caused by an unexpected swelling of the Ebro, which inundated that part of the trenches which lay nearest to the river : but by the eighth all was ready for the assault. The Jesus convent, as a glance at the map will readily show, was the most projecting point of the defences of the suburb, and was not well protected by any flanking fire from the other works—indeed it was only helped to any appreciable extent by a long fire across the water from the northern side of Saragossa, and by the few gunboats which were moored near the bridge. It was a weak structure—merely a brick convent with a ditch beyond it—and the breaching batteries had found no difficulty in opening many large gaps in its masonry. On the eighth it was stormed by Taupin's brigade of Gazan's division : the garrison made a creditable resistance, which cost the French ninety men, and then

retired to San Lazaro and the main fortifications of the suburb.
The French established themselves in the convent, and connected it with their siege-works, finally turning its ruins into
part of the third parallel, which they began to draw out against
the remaining transpontine works.   They would probably have
proceeded to complete their operations in this direction within
the next two or three days, if it had not been for an interruption from without.   The two brothers, Lazan and Francisco
Palafox, had now united their forces, and had come forward to
the line of the Sierra de Alcubierre, only twenty miles from
Saragossa, the former with his 4,000 men from Catalonia, the
latter with a mass of peasants.   Mortier, from his post at
Perdiguera, reported their approach to Lannes, and the latter
went out in person to meet them, taking with him Guérin's
brigade of Gazan's division, and leaving only that of Taupin to
hold the lines opposite the suburb.   Faced by the 12,000 veteran
bayonets of the 5th Corps, the two Palafoxes felt that they
were helpless, and retreated towards Fraga and Lerida, without
attempting to fight.   On the thirteenth, therefore, Lannes came
back to the siege with the troops that he had drawn away from
it.   While he was absent Palafox had a splendid opportunity for
a sortie on a large scale against Taupin and his isolated brigade,
for only 4,000 men were facing the suburb.   But the time had
already gone by in which the garrison was capable of such an
advance.   They could not now dispose of more than 10,000
men, soldiers and peasants and citizens all included, and none
of these could be drawn away from the city, where the fighting-
line was always growing weaker.   Indeed, its numbers were so
thinned by the epidemic that Palafox was guarding the Aljafferia with no more than 300 men, and manning the unattacked
western front with convalescents from the hospitals, who could
hardly stand, and often died at their posts during the cold and
damp hours of the night.   All his available efficients were
engaged in the street-fighting with the 3rd Corps.

For while the attack on the suburb was being pressed, the
slow advance of the besiegers within the walls was never
slackened.   On some days they won a whole block of houses
by their mining operations : on others they lost many men
and gained no advantage.   The right attack was extending

K 2

itself towards the river, and working from the convent of San Augustin into the quarter of the Tanneries. At the same time it was also moving on toward the Coso, but with extreme slowness, for the Spaniards made a specially desperate defence in the houses about the University and the Church of the Trinity. One three-storied building, which covered the traverse across the Coso to the south of the University, stood *ten* separate assaults and four explosions, and held out from the ninth to the eighteenth, effectually keeping back the advance of the besiegers in this direction[1]. Nor could the French ever succeed in connecting their field of operations on this front with that which centred around Santa Engracia. Down to the very end of the siege the Saragossans clung desperately to the south-eastern corner of the city, and kept control of it right down to the external walls and the bank of the Huerba, where they still possessed a narrow strip of 300 yards of the *enceinte*.

The left attack of the French, that from the Santa Engracia side, made much more progress, though even here it was slow and dearly bought. On February 10, however, in spite of several checks, the besiegers for the first time forced their way as far as the Coso, working through the ruined hospital which had been destroyed in the first siege. On the same day, at the north-western angle of their advance, they made a valuable conquest in the church and convent of San Francisco. A mine was driven under this great building from the ruins of the hospital, and filled with no less than 3,000 pounds of powder. It had not been discovered by the Spaniards, and the convent was full of fighting-men at the moment of the explosion. The whole grenadier company of the 1st regiment of Valencia and 300 irregulars were blown up, and perished to a man[2]. Nor was this all : in the northern part of the building was established the main factory for military equipment of the Army of Aragon : it was crammed with workpeople, largely women, for Palafox had forgotten or refused to withdraw the dépôt to a less convenient and spacious but more safe position. All these unfortunate non-combatants, to the number of at least 400, perished,

[1] Belmas, ii. 314, and before.

[2] In Lejeune, i. 169, the reader will find some horrible anecdotes of this explosion.

and the roof-tops for hundreds of yards around were strewn with their dismembered limbs.

It might have been expected that, as the immediate consequence of this awful catastrophe, the French would have made a long step forward in this direction. But such was not the case: before the smoke had cleared away Spaniards rushed forward from the inner defences, and occupied part of the ruins of San Francisco. A body of peasants, headed by the *émigré* colonel de Fleury, got into the bell-tower of the convent, which had not fallen with the rest, and kept up from its leads a vigorous plunging fire upon the besiegers, when they stole forward to burrow into the mass of débris. But with the loss of some thirty men the French succeeded in mastering two-thirds of the ruins: next day they cleared the rest, and stormed the belfry, where de Fleury and his men were all bayonetted after a desperate fight on the winding stairs. It was first from the commanding height of this steeple that the French officers obtained a full view of the city. The sight was encouraging to them: they could realize how much the inner parts of the place had suffered from the bombardment, and noted with their telescopes the small number of defenders visible behind the further barricades, the heaps of corpses in the streets, and the slow and dejected pace of the few passengers visible. Two great gallows with corpses hanging from them especially attracted the eyes of the onlookers [1]. Other circumstances united on this and the following day (February 11–12) to show that the defence was at last beginning to slacken. A great mob of peasants, mainly women, came out of the Portillo gate towards Morlot's trenches, and prayed hard for permission to go through the lines to their villages. They were not fired on, but given a loaf apiece, and then driven back into the city. It was still more significant that at night, on the eleventh, four or five bodies of deserters stole out to the French; they were all foreigners, belonging to the 'Swiss' battalion [2] which was shut up in Saragossa: several officers were among them. To excuse themselves they said that Palafox and the friars were mad, and that

---

[1] Lejeune, i. 177.

[2] The 'Suizos de Aragon,' of which the unfortunate Fleury had been colonel, had not all perished on Dec. 21.

they judged that all further defence had become impossible. Yet the siege was to endure for nine days longer [1]!

Though the two main attacks continued to press slowly forward, and that on the left had now reached the Coso and covered a front of 100 yards on the southern side of that great street, it was not on this front that the decisive blow was destined to be given. On the eighteenth Lannes determined to deliver the great assault on the suburb, where the batteries in the third parallel and about the Jesus convent had now completely shattered the San Lazaro defences. All Gazan's men being now back in their trenches, since Mortier's expedition had driven off the Marquis of Lazan, Lannes considered that he might safely risk the storm. Fifty-two siege-guns played on San Lazaro throughout the morning of the eighteenth, and no less than eight practicable breaches were opened in it and the works to its right and left. At noon three storming columns leaped out of the trenches and raced for the nearest of these entries. All three burst through : there was a sharp struggle in the street of the suburb, and then the French reached and seized a block of houses at the head of the bridge, which cut the defence in two and rendered a retreat into Saragossa almost impossible. The Spaniards, seeing that all was lost, split into two bodies : one tried to force its way across the bridge ; but only 300 passed ; the rest were slain or captured. The main part, consisting of the defenders of the western front of the suburb, formed in a solid mass and, abandoning their defences, tried to escape westward up the bank of the Ebro, into the open country. They got across the inundation in their front, but when they had gone thus far were surrounded by two regiments of French cavalry, and forced to surrender. They numbered 1,500 men, under General Manso, commanding the 3rd division of Palafox's army, the one which furnished the garrison of the suburb. The officer commanding the whole transpontine defence, Baron de Versage, had been killed by a cannon-ball on the bridge.

This was not the only disaster suffered by the Saragossans on the eighteenth : at three in the afternoon, when the news of the loss of the suburb had had time to spread round the town,

[1] Arteche, iv. 472, and Lejeune, i. 179.

and the attention of the besieged was distracted to this side, Grandjean's division attacked the houses and barricades in the north-eastern part of the city, which had so long held them at bay. A great mine opened a breach in the University, which was stormed, and with it fell the houses on each side, as far as the Coso. At the same time another attack won some ground in the direction of the Trinity convent, and the Ebro. Next day the Spaniards in this remote corner of the town, almost cut off from the main body of the defenders, and now battered from the rear by new works thrown up in the suburb, in and about San Lazaro, drew back and abandoned the quarter of the Tanneries, the quays, and the outer *enceinte* looking over the mouth of the Huerba.

On the nineteenth it was evident that the end had come: a third of the ever-dwindling force of effective men of which Palafox could dispose had been killed or captured at the storm of San Lazaro. The city was now being fired on from the north, the only side which had hitherto been safe. The epidemic was worse than ever—600 a day are said to have died during the final week of the siege. The last mills which the garrison possessed had lately been destroyed, and no more flour was issued, but unground corn, which had to be smashed up between paving-stones, or boiled and eaten as a sort of porridge. The supply of powder was beginning to run low; not from want of material to compound it, but from the laboratories having been mostly destroyed and from the greater part of the arsenal work-men having died. Only about 700 pounds a day [six quintals] could now be turned out, and the daily expenditure in the mines and barricades came to much more.

On this morning the French noted that at many points the defence seemed to be slackening, and that parts of the line were very feebly manned. They made more progress this day than in any earlier twenty-four hours of the siege. Their main work, however, was to run six large mines under the Coso, till they got below the houses on its further side, somewhat to the right of San Francisco. Rogniat placed 3,000 pounds of powder in each, a quantity that was calculated to blow up the whole quarter.

It was not necessary to use them. The spirits of the defenders

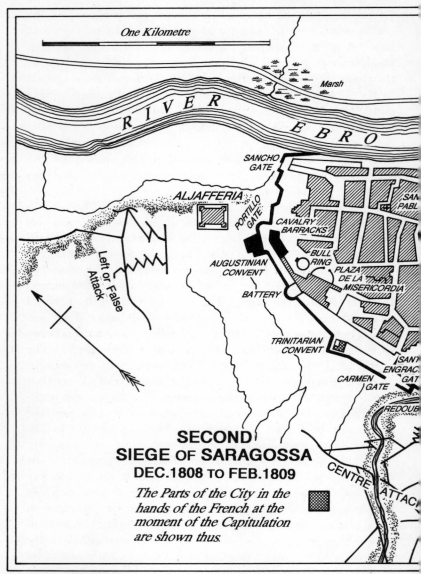

One Kilometre

Marsh

R I V E R   E B R O

SANCHO
GATE

ALJAFFERIA

PORTILLO
GATE

SAN
PABL

CAVALRY
BARRACKS

BULL
RING

Left or False
Attack

AUGUSTINIAN
CONVENT

PLAZA
DE LA
MISERICORDIA

BATTERY

TRINITARIAN
CONVENT

SANT
ENGRAC
GAT

CARMEN
GATE

REDOUB

SECOND
SIEGE OF SARAGOSSA
DEC.1808 TO FEB.1809

*The Parts of the City in the
hands of the French at the
moment of the Capitulation
are shown thus.*

CENTRE ATTAC

Darbishire & Stanford, Ltd.

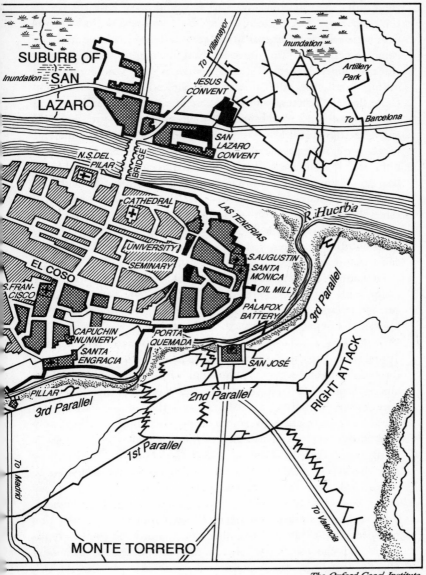

SUBURB OF SAN LAZARO

Inundation

To Villamayor

Inundation

Artillery Park

JESUS CONVENT

To Barcelona

SAN LAZARO CONVENT

N.S.DEL PILAR

BRIDGE

CATHEDRAL

LAS TENERIAS

R. Huerba

UNIVERSITY

SEMINARY

S.AUGUSTIN
SANTA MONICA

EL COSO

OIL MILL

S.FRAN-CISCO

PALAFOX BATTERY

3rd Parallel

CAPUCHIN NUNNERY

PORTA QUEMADA

SANTA ENGRACIA

SAN JOSÉ

RIGHT ATTACK

PILLAR

2nd Parallel

3rd Parallel

1st Parallel

To Madrid

To Valencia

MONTE TORRERO

The Oxford Geogl. Institute.

had at last been broken, and surrender was openly spoken of—
though its mention ten days earlier would have cost the life of
the proposer. Palafox on his sick bed understood that all was
over ; he sent for General St. March and resigned the military
command to him. But in order that he might not seem to be
shirking his responsibility, and trying to put the ignominy of
asking for terms on his successor, he sent his aide-de-camp
Casseillas to Lannes, offering surrender, but demanding that
the troops should march out with the honours of war and join
the nearest Spanish army in the field. Then he turned his face
to the wall, and prepared to die, for the fever lay heavy upon
him, and broken with despair and fatigue he thought that he
had not many hours to live. St. March's appointment not
being well taken—the loss of the Monte Torrero was still
remembered against him—Palafox's last act was to give over
charge of the city to a Junta of thirty-three persons [1], mainly
local notables and clergy, to whom the finishing of the negotiations would fall.

Of course Lannes sent back the Captain-General's aide-de-
camp with the message that he must ask for unconditional
surrender, and that the proposal that the garrison should be
allowed to depart was absurd. The fighting was resumed on
the morning of the twentieth, and the French were making
appreciable progress, when the Junta once more sent to ask
terms from the besiegers. It was not without some bitter debate
among themselves that they took this step, for there was still
a minority, including St. March and the priest Padre Consolation, who wished to continue the resistance. They were
backed by a section of the citizens, who began to collect and to
raise angry cries of Treason. But the whole of the soldiery
and the major part of the civilian defenders were prepared to
yield. At four o'clock in the afternoon they sent out to ask
for a twenty-four hours' truce to settle terms of surrender.
Lannes granted them two hours to send him out a deputation
charged with full powers to capitulate, and ordered the bombardment and the mining to cease. His aide-de-camp, who bore
the message, was nearly murdered by fanatics in the street [2],

[1] Their names can be found on p. 494 of Arteche, vol. iv.

[2] In Lejeune, i. 194–5, will be found a most picturesque account of the

and was rescued with difficulty by some officers of the regular army. But the Junta sent him back with the message that the deputation should be forthcoming, and within the stipulated time eleven of its members came out from the Portillo gate [1], to the Marshal's head quarters on the Calatayud road. There was not much discussion: Lannes contented himself with pointing out to the Spaniards that the place was at his mercy: he had the plan of his siege-works unrolled before them, and pointed out the position of the six great mines under the Coso [2], as well as those of the advanced posts which he had gained during the last two days. The deputies made some feeble attempts to secure that the name of Ferdinand VII should appear in the articles of capitulation, and that the clergy should be guaranteed immunity and undisturbed possession of their benefices. Lannes waved all such proposals aside, and dictated a form of surrender which was on the whole reasonable and even generous. The garrison should march out on the following day, and lay down its arms 100 yards outside the Portillo gate. Those who would swear homage to King Joseph should have their liberty, and might take service with him if they wished. Those who refused the oath should march as prisoners to France. The city should be granted a general pardon : the churches should be respected : private property should not be meddled with. The citizens must surrender all their weapons of whatever sort. Any civil magistrates or employés who wished to keep their places must take the oath of allegiance to King Joseph.

On the following morning the garrison marched out : of peasants and soldiers there were altogether about 8,000 men, 1,500 of whom were convalescents from the Hospitals. 'Never

interview of the French envoy with the fever-ridden and despairing Junta, almost hysterical with rage and shame, but accepting the inevitable.

[1] It is notable that there was not a single churchman among them, though there were eight among the thirty-three members of the Junta. The clergy represented to the last the fighting section.

[2] Lejeune, in his interesting narrative of this interview, says that he saw one of the deputies pore over the map and recognize his own house among the mined buildings ; he crossed himself five or six times, and cried in accents of bitter grief '*Ah la Casa Ciscala.*' The name of Don Joachim Ciscala does occur among the eleven signatures, so the story is probably true. Lejeune, i. 198.

had any of us gazed on a more sad or touching sight,' writes
Lejeune ; 'these sickly looking men, bearing in their bodies the
seeds of the fever, all frightfully emaciated, with long black
matted beards, and scarcely able to hold their weapons, dragged
themselves slowly along to the sound of the drum.   Their clothes
were torn and dirty : everything about them bore witness to terrible misery.   But in spite of their livid faces, blackened with
powder, and scarred with rage and grief, they bore themselves
with dignity and pride.   The bright coloured sashes, the large
round hats surmounted by a few cock's-feathers which shaded
their foreheads, the brown cloaks or *ponchos* flung over their
varied costumes, lent a certain picturesqueness to their tattered
garb.   When the moment came for them to pile their arms and
deliver up their flags, many of them gave violent expression to
their despair.   Their eyes gleamed with rage, and their savage
looks seemed to say that they had counted our ranks, and deeply
regretted having surrendered to such a small army of enemies [1].'

Another and more matter-of-fact eye-witness adds, 'They were
a most motley crowd of men of all ages and conditions, some in
uniform, more without it.   The officers were mostly mounted
on mules or donkeys, and were only distinguished from the men
by their three-cornered hats and their large cloaks.   Many were
smoking their *cigarillos* and talking to each other with an aspect
of complete indifference.   But all were not so resigned.   The
whole garrison, 8,000 to 10,000 strong, defiled in front of us :
the majority looked so utterly unlike soldiers, that our men said
openly to each other that they ought not to have taken so long
or spent so much trouble in getting rid of such a rabble [2].'
The column was promptly put in motion for France, under the
escort of two of Morlot's regiments.   Many died on the way
from the fever whose seeds they carried with them.   Few or
none, as might have been supposed, took advantage of the offer
to save themselves from captivity by taking the oath to King
Joseph.

It is sad to have to confess that the French did not keep to the
terms of the capitulation.   That Lannes could not restrain his
men from plunder, as he had promised, was hardly surprising.

[1] Lejeune, i. 202.
[2] Von Brandt, *Aus meinem Leben*, pp. 43–4.

There were so many empty houses and churches containing valuables, that it was not to be wondered at that the victors should help themselves to all they could find.   But they also plundered occupied houses, and even stole the purses of the captive officers.   What was worse was that many assassinations took place, especially of clergy, for the French looked upon the priests and friars as being mainly responsible for the desperate defence.   Two in especial, Padre Basilio Bogiero, the chaplain of Palafox, and Santiago Sass, a parish priest, were shot in cold blood two days after the surrender [1].   Public opinion in the French ranks was convinced that they, more than any one else, had kept the Captain-General up to the mark.   Palafox himself was treated with great brutality.   As he lay apparently moribund, the French officer who had been made interim governor of Saragossa came to his bedside, and bade him to sign orders for the surrender of Jaca and Monzon.   When he refused, this colonel threatened to have him shot, but left him alone when threats had no effect.   Ere he was convalescent he was sent off to France, where the Emperor ordered that he should be treated, not as a prisoner of war, but as guilty of treason, and shut him up for many years as a close captive in the donjon of Vincennes.

The state in which Saragossa was found by the French hardly bears description.   It was a focus of corruption, one mass of putrefying corpses.   According to a report which Lannes elicited from the municipal officers, nearly 54,000 persons had died in the place since the siege began [2].   Of these about 20,000 were fighting-men, regular or irregular, the rest were non-combatants.   Only 6,000 had fallen by fire and sword : the remainder were victims of the far more deadly pestilence.   A few days after the siege was ended Lannes stated that the total population of the town was now only 15,000 souls, instead of the 55,000 which it had contained when the siege began.   But his estimate does not include some thousands of citizens who had fled into the open country, the moment that they were released from investment, in order to escape from the contagion in the city.   ' Il est impossible que Saragosse se relève,' wrote

[1] For details, see Arteche, iv. 512–3.
[2] Lannes to Berthier, March 19, 1809.

the marshal; 'cette ville fait horreur à voir.' It was weeks indeed before the dead were all buried : months before the contagion of the siege-fever died out from the miserable city. Even after five years of the capable and benevolent government of Suchet it was still half desolate, and no attempt had been made to rebuild the third of its houses and churches which had been reduced to ashes by the mines and the bombardment.

The French losses in front of Saragossa are not easy to calculate. Belmas says that the total of casualties was about 3,000 in the infantry, but he takes no notice of the losses by siege-fever, except to say that many died from it. He does not give the losses of the artillery, except of that small part of it which was not attached either to the 3rd or to the 5th Corps. Considering that the 3rd Corps alone had 13,123 sick on January 15, and that typhus is a notoriously deadly disease, it is probable that the total losses of the French during the siege amounted to 10,000 men. It is hard otherwise to explain the difference between the 37,000 men that the 3rd Corps counted in October, and the 14,000 men which it mustered when Suchet took over its command in April. The sufferings of the 5th Corps were small in comparison, for till February began it took no very serious part in the siege, and its health was notoriously far better than that of Junot's divisions [1]. But we cannot be far wrong in concluding with Schepeler and Arteche that the total French loss must have been 10,000 men, rather than the 4,000 given by Napier, who is apparently relying on Rogniat. That officer gives only the casualties in battle, and not the losses in hospital.

So ended the siege of Saragossa—a magnificent display of civic courage, little helped by strategy or tactics. For Palafox, though a splendid leader of insurgents, was, as his conduct in

---

[1] It seems quite clear that the '1,500 men in hospital' which Belmas mentions on ii. 327 is a misprint for 15,000. For his own figures show that (p. 381) there were 13,000 invalids six weeks earlier, and before the deadly street-fighting had begun. How many died we cannot say, but Suchet in April had only 10,527 men present in nineteen battalions (*Mémoires*, i. 331), with eight more battalions 'on command,' which would give another 4,000. Von Brandt (p. 50) carefully says that the total of 3,000 dead does not include ' the thousands who perished in hospital.'

October and November had shown, a very poor general. He made a gross initial mistake in shutting up 40,000 fighting-men in a place which could have been easily defended by 25,000. If he had sent one or two divisions to form the nucleus of an army of relief in Lower Aragon, with orders to harass, but not to fight pitched battles, it is hard to see how the siege could have been kept up. His second fault was the refusal to make sorties on a large scale during the first half of the siege, while he was still in possession of great masses of superfluous fighting-men. He sent out scores of petty sallies of a few hundred men, but never moved so many as 5,000 on a single day. Such a policy worried but could not seriously harm the French, while it destroyed the willing men of the garrison; if the Captain-General had saved up all the volunteers whom he lost by tens and twenties in small and fruitless attacks on the trenches, he could have built up with them a column-head that would have pierced through the French line at any point that he chose. Anything might have been done during the three weeks while Mortier was at Calatayud, and especially during the days when Gazan with his 8,000 men was cut off by the floods, and isolated on the further bank of the Ebro.

The Captain-General's conduct, in short, was not that of a capable officer. But it is absurd to endeavour to represent him as a coward, or as a puppet whose strings were pulled by fanatical friars. He knew perfectly well what he was doing, and how to manage the disorderly but enthusiastic masses of the population [1]. There can be no doubt that his personal influence was all-important, and the effect of his constant harangues and proclamations immense. It would be quite as true to say that the friars and the mob-orators were his tools, as that he was theirs. He had to humour them, but by humouring them he got out of them the utmost possible service. Against the stories that his proclamations were written for him,

---

[1] The foundation for most of the stories against Palafox seems to be Lannes' letter to Napoleon of 19 mars : 'Ce pauvre misérable prêtait seulement son nom aux moines et aux intrigants.' I cannot find anywhere the source from which Napier draws his statement that Palafox hid himself in a bomb-proof, and lived 'in a disgusting state of sensuality,' shirking all the dangers of the siege (i. 389).

and that he had to be goaded into issuing every order that came from his head quarters, we have the evidence of Vaughan and others who knew him well. It is unanimous in ascribing to him incessant activity and an exuberant fluency in composition. Arteche has preserved some minutes on the siege which he wrote long after the Peninsular War was over : they are interesting and well-stated, but more creditable to him as a patriot than as a military man[1]. There can be no doubt that the garrison might have been much more wisely handled : but it is doubtful whether under any other direction it would have shown so much energy and staying power. There is certainly no other Spanish siege, save that of Gerona, where half so much resolution was shown. If the defence had been conducted by regular officers and troops alone, the place would probably have fallen three weeks earlier. If the monks and local demagogues had been in command, and patriotic anarchy alone had been opposed to the French, Saragossa would possibly have fallen at an even earlier date, from mere want of intelligent direction. Palafox, with all his faults, supplied the connecting link between the two sections of the defenders, and kept the soldiery to work by means of the example of the citizens, while he restrained the citizens by dint of his immense personal influence over them, won in the first siege. In short, he may have been vain, bombastic, and a bad tactician, but he was a good Spaniard. If there had been a few dozen men more of his stamp in Spain, the task of the French in 1808-9 would have been infinitely more difficult. The example of Saragossa was invaluable to the nation and to Europe. The knowledge of it did much to sicken the French soldiery of the whole war, and to make every officer and man who entered Spain march, not with the light heart that he felt in Germany or Italy, but with gloom and disgust and want of confidence. They never failed to do their duty, but they fought without the enthusiasm which helped them so much in all the earlier wars of the Empire.

[1] Arteche, iv. 507-8.

SECTION XII

THE SPRING CAMPAIGN IN LA MANCHA AND ESTREMADURA

CHAPTER I

THE ROUT OF CIUDAD REAL

By the middle of the month of February, as we have already seen, Andalusia was once more covered by two considerable Spanish armies : Cartaojal, with the wrecks of Infantado's host and the new levies of Del Palacio, was holding the great passes at the eastern end of the Sierra Morena. Cuesta had rallied behind the Guadiana the remains of the army of Estremadura. He was at present engaged in reducing it to order by the only method of which he was master, the shooting of any soldier who showed signs of disobedience or mutiny [1]. The army deserved nothing better : its dastardly murder of its unfortunate general in December justified any amount of severity in his successor.

Meanwhile Victor, after his victory at Ucles, and his vain attempt to surprise Del Palacio, had passed away to the west, leaving nothing in the plains of La Mancha save the dragoons of Milhaud and Latour-Maubourg, who were placed as a cavalry screen across the roads to the south, with their divisional head quarters at Ocaña and Madridejos respectively.

The Marshal drew back to the valley of the Tagus, and marched by Toledo on Almaraz ; this was in strict execution of the plan dictated by Napoleon before he left Spain. It will be remembered that he had directed that, when the February rains were over, Victor should move on Badajoz, to assist by his presence

---

[1] There are details in the diary of a citizen of Badajoz in the *Vaughan Papers*.

in that direction the projected attack of Soult on Lisbon. Only when Estremadura and Portugal had been subdued was the attack on Andalusia to be carried out. Soult, as we shall see, was (by no fault of his own) much slower in his movements than Napoleon had expected, and Victor waited in vain at Talavera for any news that the invasion of Portugal was in progress. Hence the Spaniards gained some weeks of respite: the ranks of their armies were filled up, and the spirits of their generals rose.

Cartaojal remained for some time at La Carolina, reorganizing and recruiting the depleted and half-starved battalions which Infantado had handed over to him. He had expected to be attacked by Victor, but when he learnt that the Marshal had gone off to Toledo, and that La Mancha was covered only by a thin line of cavalry, he began to dream of resuming the offensive. Such a policy was most unwise : it shows that Cartaojal, like so many other Spanish generals, was still possessed with the fatal mania for grand operations and pitched battles. He had in his head nothing less than a plan for thrusting back the cavalry screen opposite to him, and for recovering the whole of La Mancha. If Victor's corps had been the only force available to oppose him, there would have been something to say for the plan. An advance on Toledo and Madrid must have brought back the Duke of Belluno from his advance towards Estremadura. But, as a matter of fact, Jourdan and King Joseph had not left the roads to La Mancha unguarded : they had drafted down from Madrid two infantry divisions of the 4th Corps, whose command Sebastiani had now taken over from Lefebvre. The first division lay at Toledo : the third (Valence's Poles) at Aranjuez; thus the former supported Latour-Maubourg, the latter Milhaud.

Ignorant, apparently, of the fact that there was anything but cavalry in his front, Cartaojal resolved to beat up the French outposts. With this object he told off half his infantry and two-thirds of his horse, under the Duke of Albuquerque, a gallant and enterprising, but somewhat reckless, officer, of whom we shall hear much during the next two years of the war. Marching with speed and secrecy, Albuquerque, with 2,000 horse and 9,000 infantry, fell upon Digeon's brigade of dragoons at Mora on February 18. He tried to cut it off with his cavalry, while he attacked it in front with his foot. But Digeon saw the danger in time, and fell back in haste, after losing a few men of the 20th Dragoons and some of his baggage. His demand for assistance promptly brought down Sebastiani, with the 1st division of the 4th Corps, and the two remaining brigades of Latour-Maubourg's cavalry. The moment that he heard that a heavy force had arrived in his front, Albuquerque retired as far as Consuegra, where the French caught up his rear, and inflicted some loss upon it. He then fell still further back, crossed the Guadiana, and took post at Manzanares. Sebastiani did not pursue him beyond Con-suegra, giving as his excuse the exhausted condition of the country-side [1].

Cartaojal meanwhile, with the rest of his army, had come up from the passes to Ciudad Real, following in wake of Albu-querque's advance. When he met with his lieutenant they fell to quarrelling, both as to what had already occurred, and as to what should now be done, for the Duke was anxious to induce his chief to make a general advance on Toledo, while Cartaojal desired him to take a single division of infantry and to try the adventure himself. While they were disputing, orders came from the Supreme Junta that troops were to be detached from the Army of La Mancha to strengthen that of Estremadura. Cartaojal took the opportunity of getting rid of Albuquerque, by putting him at the head of the detachment which was to be sent to Cuesta. The Duke, not loth to depart, went off with a division of 4,500 infantry and a regiment of cavalry [2], and marched down the Guadiana into Estremadura.

Cartaojal remained for the first three weeks of March at Ciudad Real and Manzanares with the main body of his force, about 2,500 horse and 10,000 foot, keeping behind him, at the foot of the passes, a reserve of 4,000 men under La Peña. This was tempting providence, for he was now aware that the whole

---

[1] For these operations compare Jourdan's *Mémoires*, pp. 178-9, and Arteche, v. 228-31.

[2] The cavalry regiment had only 264 sabres : the infantry battalions were Campo Mayor, Tiradores de Cadiz, Granaderos del General, militia of Cordova, Guadix and Osuna. Only the first-named was an old regular corps.

4th Corps, as well as a great mass of cavalry, was in front of him, and that he might be attacked at any moment. His position, too, was a faulty one ; he had descended into the very midst of the broad plain of La Mancha, and had occupied as his head quarters an open town, easy to turn on either flank, and with a perfectly fordable river as its sole defence. As if this peril was not sufficient, Cartaojal suddenly resolved that he would make the dash at Toledo which Albuquerque had proposed to him, though he had refused to send his whole army against that point when the scheme was pressed upon him by his late second-in-command. The nearest hostile troops to him were a regiment of Polish lancers, belonging to Lasalle's division, which lay at Yébenes, twenty miles outside Toledo. Making a swift stroke at this force, while it was far from expecting any advance on his part, Cartaojal drove it in, killing or taking nearly 100 of the Poles (March 24). But Sebastiani came up to their aid with an infantry division and three regiments of Milhaud's dragoons. The Spaniard refused to accept battle, and fell hastily back to Ciudad Real, where he established his whole army behind the river Guadiana, in and about the open town. He was most unsafe in the midst of the vast plain, and was soon to rue his want of caution. Sebastiani had been joined by his Polish division and by part of his corps-cavalry, and having some 12,000 or 13,000 men in hand [1], had resolved to pay back on Cartaojal the beating up of his outpost at Yébenes. On March 26, Milhaud's division of dragoons seized the bridge of Peralvillo, close to Ciudad Real, and crossed to the southern bank of the Guadiana. The Spanish general called up all his cavalry, and some of his foot, and marched to drive the dragoons back. They withdrew across the water, but still held the bridge, behind which they had planted their artillery. Next morning Sebastiani's infantry came up, and he determined to attack Ciudad Real. Cartaojal, who was taken completely off his guard, was suddenly informed that column after column was pressing across the bridge and marching against him. He did

---

[1] He had his own original division of the 4th Corps (twelve batts.), Valence's Poles (six batts.), the 3rd Dutch Hussars (part of his corps-cavalry), the regiment of Polish lancers, and Milhaud's three regiments, the 12th, 16th and 21st Dragoons : apparently in all 12,744 men.

not dream for a moment of fighting, but gave orders for an instant retreat towards the passes. He threw out his cavalry and horse artillery to cover the withdrawal of his infantry, who hurried away in half a dozen small bodies across the interminable plain. Sebastiani charged the Spanish horse with his Polish lancers and Dutch hussars, supported by Milhaud's dragoons. The covering force broke and fled, and the pursuers came up with several of the columns of the retreating infantry. Some of them were dispersed, others were surrounded and taken prisoners. The pursuit was continued next morning, till it was interrupted by a fearful burst of rain, which darkened the horizon, hid the fugitives, and stopped the chase, or Cartaojal's army might have been entirely destroyed. He lost in this rout, which it would be absurd to call a battle, five guns, three standards, and more than 2,000 prisoners, among whom were sixty-one officers. The loss in killed and wounded was probably not very great, for there had been no attempt at a stand, and the troops which were cut off had surrendered without resistance [1]. The loss of the French was insignificant, probably less than 100 men in all. They had stayed their pursuit at Santa Cruz de Mudela, from whence they returned to Ciudad Real, where they lived on the magazines which Cartaojal had collected before his unfortunate march on Yébenes. Sebastiani dared not follow the fugitives into the mountains, as he had received orders to clear La Mancha, but not to invade Andalusia: that was to be the task of Victor.

Cartaojal recrossed the Despeña Perros, and established his head quarters at Sta Elena, in front of La Carolina. His army had been more frightened than hurt, and when the stragglers came in, still numbered 2,000 horse and 12,000 infantry. But he was not allowed to retain its command. Justly indignant at the carelessness with which he had allowed himself to be surprised in front of Ciudad Real, and at his general mismanagement, the Supreme Junta deposed him, and replaced

---

[1] It seems clear that the 2,000 killed and wounded, given by Jourdan (p. 186) and *Victoires et Conquêtes*, is merely a rough estimate. Belmas' figures (i. 69) are still more absurd: he makes the Spaniards lose 9,000 men from an army which did not exceed 16,500 all told, including the rear division of La Peña.

him by Venegas, though the record of the latter's operations at Ucles was hardly encouraging to the soldiery.   By the middle of April the army had been reinforced by new Granadan levies, and could take the field, although its state of discipline was bad and its *morale* much shaken by the late events.

SECTION XII: CHAPTER II

OPERATIONS OF VICTOR AND CUESTA: BATTLE OF MEDELLIN

WHILE Cartaojal and his Andalusian levies were faring so ill in La Mancha, the army of Estremadura and its obstinate old general were going through experiences of an even more disastrous kind. Cuesta, it will be remembered, had rallied about Badajoz and Merida the demoralized troops that had served under San Juan and Galluzzo. He was, contrary to all expectation, allowed to remain unmolested for some weeks. The irrational movement of Lefebvre to Plasencia and Avila[1] had left him for the moment almost without an enemy in his front. Along the middle Tagus he had nothing opposed to him save Lasalle's four regiments of light cavalry, supported by Leval's German division at Talavera. While Victor was engaged in the campaign of Ucles, and in his subsequent circular march through La Mancha to Toledo, the army of Estremadura enjoyed a time of complete rest. Cuesta's fault was not want of energy: after shooting a competent number of mutineers, and disgracing some officers who had shown signs of cowardice, he distributed his troops into three new divisions under Henestrosa, Trias, and the Duke Del Parque, and began to move them back towards the Tagus. As there was nothing in his way except Lasalle's light horse, he was able to take up, at the end of January, the same line which Galluzzo had been forced to evacuate in December. The French cavalry retired behind the river to Oropesa, abandoning the great bridge of Almaraz, the main passage of the Tagus, on January 29. Thereupon Cuesta broke the bridge, a difficult task, for his mines failed, and the work had to be completed with the pick. It was so badly managed that when the key-stone at last gave way, an engineer officer

---

[1] See pp. 4–5 of this volume.

and twenty-six sappers were still upon the arch, and were precipitated into the river, where they were every one drowned. The Captain-General then established his head quarters at Deleytosa, a central point in the mountains, from which he commanded the two passages of the Tagus, that at Almaraz and that by the Puente del Conde, near Meza de Ibor. He arranged his 15,000 men with advanced guards at the water's edge, opposite each of the possible points of attack, and reserves on the high ground to the rear. This forward position gave much encouragement to the peasantry of New Castile, and bands of guerrillas began (for the first time) to be seen on the slopes of the Sierra de Gredos and the Sierra de Toledo. There was a feeling of uneasiness even up to the gates of Madrid.

To restrain the advances of the Spaniards, King Joseph sent out Lasalle's cavalry and Leval's Germans on February 19, with orders to clear the nearer hills. They crossed the Tagus at the bridge of Arzobispo, a little below Talavera, and forced back the division of Trias, which was watching this flank of Cuesta's position. But the country was almost impassable for cavalry, a mere mass of ravines and spurs of the Sierra de Guadalupe, and after advancing as far as the pass of San Vincente, and seeing the Spaniards begin to gather in force on his front and flank, Lasalle retreated, and recrossed the Tagus without having effected anything of importance.

It was not till a month later that the French took the offensive in earnest. Victor was now returned from his excursion into La Mancha, with his two divisions of the 1st Corps, and the six dragoon regiments of Latour-Maubourg, whom he had drawn off to Toledo, handing over the charge of observing Cartaojal to Milhaud and Sebastiani. Uniting these forces to those of Leval and Lasalle, he massed at Talavera an army of some 22,000 or 23,000 men, of whom 5,000 were admirable cavalry [1].

Joseph and Jourdan were now of the opinion that it was time for Victor to move forward on Estremadura, in accordance with the great plan for the conquest of southern Spain, which the Emperor had left behind as his legacy when he

---

[1] This is the estimate of Jourdan (*Mémoires,* p. 181), and exactly agrees with the figures which I give on p. 152.

departed from Valladolid. It was true that this movement was to have been carried out in co-operation with the advance of Marshal Soult upon Portugal; but no news could be got of the Duke of Dalmatia's present position. The last dispatch from him was nearly a month old. Writing from Orense on February 24 he had stated that he hoped to be at Chaves by March 1, and should then march on Oporto and Lisbon. According to Napoleon's calculations he was to be at the last-named city within ten days of the capture of Oporto. It was therefore, in the opinion of Joseph and Jourdan, high time that Victor should start, in order to get in touch with Soult when the Portuguese capital should be occupied.

The Duke of Belluno, however, raised many difficulties, even when he had been shown the Emperor's orders. He complained that he ought to have the help of Lapisse's division, the second of his own Corps, which still lay at Salamanca. He doubted whether he could dare to take on with him, for an expedition into Estremadura, the German division of Leval: he ought, perhaps, to leave it at Talavera and Almaraz, in order to keep up his communications with Madrid. If this were done he would muster only 16,000 men for his great forward movement, and he had the gravest doubt whether Soult could or would give him the assistance of which the Emperor had written, even if he seized Lisbon within the appointed time. Finally, he was short of engineer officers, sappers, horses, and reserve ammunition.

Much of what the Duke of Belluno wrote was true: in particular, the idea of co-operation with Soult was perfectly chimerical: Napoleon had worked out all his logistics to an erroneous result, from want of a real conception of the conditions and difficulties of war in the Peninsula. But some of the pleas which Victor urged merely serve to show his disinclination to accept the task which had been set him; and in especial he under-rated the numbers of his troops beyond the limit of fair statement. He had with him nine battalions of Ruffin's division, twelve of Villatte's, eight of Leval's; of cavalry he had six regiments of Latour-Maubourg's dragoons, three of Lasalle's light cavalry[1], two regiments of his own corps-

---

[1] 26th and 10th Chasseurs and 9th Dragoons; the fourth regiment, the Polish lancers, was with Sebastiani (see pp. 146-7).

cavalry, and the Westphalian regiment of the 4th Corps which was attached to Leval's Germans. The total must have amounted to 15,000 infantry, and about 5,500 cavalry : he had also sixty guns with 1,600 artillerymen [1].

In spite of his reluctance Victor was forced to yield to the pressure of Jourdan and the Emperor's explicit orders. On March 14 he began to make his preparations to cross the Tagus and to attack Cuesta : it was reported to him that the roads starting from the two bridges which were in his power, those of Talavera and Arzobispo, were neither of them practicable for artillery, and that only the route by Almaraz was suitable for the guns and heavy baggage. But the bridge of Almaraz was broken, and beyond it were visible entrenchments thrown up by the Spaniards, and a considerable body of troops—the division of General Henestrosa. The Duke of Belluno determined to clear the way for a crossing at Almaraz, by sending infantry across the Tagus by the passages higher up-stream, with orders to sweep the southern bank till they came opposite to the broken bridge. They were to dislodge the force behind it, and then the artillery, the baggage, and cavalry were to cross on a bridge of rafts, which was being prepared close to Almaraz, in order to be ready the moment that it should be wanted.

On March 15, therefore, Leval's Germans crossed the Tagus by the bridge of Talavera, with some of Lasalle's cavalry, while on the next morning Victor himself passed at Arzobispo with the divisions of Villatte and Ruffin. The combined column pushed westward by a bad road on the hillside overhanging the river, in a difficult country of rocks and woods, seamed with countless ravines, where cavalry could barely act and artillery would have been perfectly useless. Cuesta, on hearing of this movement to turn his flank, threw back his right wing, and bade

---

[1] The February figures for Victor's men *présents sous les armes* are :—

		Brought forward	16,318
1st Division, Ruffin	5,429	Latour-Maubourg's dragoons	2,527
3rd Division, Villatte	6,376	Lasalle's three regiments	1,121
German Division [deducting		Westphalian *Chevaux-Légers*	487
one battalion]	3,127	Artillery of 1st Corps	1,523
Corps-cavalry [two regiments]	1,386	Leval's artillery (two batteries)	184
Carry forward	16,318	Total	22,160

it make a stand behind the ravine of the little river Ibor, which
falls into the Tagus half-way between Arzobispo and Almaraz.
His force in this direction consisted of the division of the
Duke del Parque, about 5,000 strong, with six guns. On
the seventeenth Victor's columns, with the Germans of Leval
at their head, arrived before the defiles of Meza de Ibor, and
found themselves confronted by the Duke, who was firmly
established on the other side of the ravine, in a fine position,
with his guns on a projecting rock which enfiladed the high-road.
Victor directed Leval's eight[1] battalions to cross the ravine, and
storm the heights on the other side. This they did in very
gallant style, but not without heavy losses, for the Estremadurans,
confident in the strength of their rugged fighting-ground, made
a long and vigorous resistance, till the Germans actually came
to close quarters with them and ran in with the bayonet.
Del Parque's line then crumpled up, and dispersed over the
hillsides : finding it impossible to bring off his guns, he cast
them over the precipice into the ravine below. The Germans
lost seventy killed and 428 wounded while climbing the difficult
slopes : Del Parque's men probably suffered far less, as they
absconded when the enemy closed, and had been under cover till
that moment. The supposition of some French authorities that
the defenders of Meza de Ibor lost 1,000 men is most improbable. The country was one exactly suited for a cheap defence,
and for an easy scattering over the hills in the moment of defeat.

The Duke fell back on Deleytosa, higher up the side of the
Sierra de Guadalupe, where Cuesta had established his head
quarters. Here he was joined by another of the Estremaduran
divisions, that of General Trias, nearly 5,000 strong. Henestrosa,
with the rest of the army, was still watching the passage at
Almaraz, where Cuesta had made up his mind that the main
attack of the French would be delivered. He persisted for some
time in believing that Victor's movement across the Talavera
and Arzobispo bridges was merely a feint ; and thus it was that
Del Parque had been left alone to bear the first brunt of the
attack. When he was at last convinced that the bulk of Victor's
infantry was on his flank, and that Almaraz was hopelessly

---

[1] One Hessian battalion was still absent, in garrison at Segovia, so the
total of the division was not much over 3,000.

turned, the old Captain-General hastily sent orders to Henestrosa to abandon his entrenchments opposite the bridge, and to retreat on Truxillo across the mountains. He himself took that path without delay, and got off in safety with his two leading divisions, but Henestrosa had to brush across the front of the advancing French, and was in some danger. Luckily for him Victor was more set on clearing the road from Almaraz than on pursuing the enemy.

When Henestrosa had disappeared, the passage was open, and the cavalry of Latour-Maubourg and Beaumont, guarding the artillery and baggage-train of the 1st Corps, crossed on the rafts which had been prepared long before, and joined the infantry and the Marshal. The passage presented more difficulties than had been expected, for it proved impossible to construct a permanent bridge ; the stream was very fierce, and the anchors by which the floats were moored found no hold in the smooth rocky bottom. The guns passed either by being sent over on rafts or by means of a rope ferry, which was with some difficulty rigged up. It was not till some time later that a solid bridge of boats was built at this most important passage [1]. One cavalry regiment was left behind to protect it [2].

Cuesta, when he had united his three divisions, would have dearly loved to give battle to Victor behind Truxillo, in the excellent position of the Puerto de Santa Cruz, where the *chaussée* from Madrid to Badajoz crosses the Sierra de Guadalupe. His love for general engagements was by no means cured by the event of his experiments at Cabezon and Medina de Rio Seco. But he was withheld from offering battle not by mere prudence, but by the fact that he was expecting to receive two considerable reinforcements. The Marquis de Portago was bringing up a detachment from Badajoz—three battalions [3] which had been intended to form the nucleus of a new Fourth division that was being organized in that fortress. At the same moment Albuquerque was expected from the east, at the head of the 4,500 men whom the Supreme Junta had detached from the

---

[1] Jourdan's *Mémoires*, p. 182.

[2] Apparently the Westphalian *Chevaux Légers*, which had hitherto been attached to Leval's German division.

[3] Four more had to be left behind in the fortress.

army of La Mancha, and had sent down the Guadiana to join that of Estremadura. Cuesta wished to pick up these 7,000 men before he gave battle.

Accordingly he evacuated the pass of Santa Cruz, and fell back southward towards his reinforcements, leaving Henestrosa with the bulk of his cavalry to act as a rearguard. That officer carried out his duty with a dash and a vigour that were rare in Spanish armies at this date. When the fiery Lasalle came pressing up against him with his usual fury, the Spanish general contrived to inflict on him two distinct checks. At Berrocal, half-way down the defile of Santa Cruz, he made a sudden halt and drove in the leading squadron of the French by a charge of his Royal Carbineers, a small remnant of the Guard-Cavalry which had been serving with the Army of Estremadura since its formation [March 20]. The French lost ten killed and fifteen wounded [1].

This was a trifle, but on the next day Henestrosa scored a far more tangible advantage. Noting that Lasalle's leading regiment, the 10th Chasseurs, had got far ahead of the rest of the division, and was pushing on with reckless haste, he laid a trap for it in front of the village of Miajadas. Presenting a small body of cavalry on the high-road, he hid on each side of it a strong regiment of his own horse, with orders to fall upon the flank and rear of the French when they should have passed the ambush. The two corps set aside for this surprise were Infante and Almanza, both regiments of La Romana's army from Denmark, which had not yet drawn their sabres since the war commenced.

Colonel Subervie of the 10th Chasseurs, advancing with heedless confidence to charge the body of Spaniards in front of him, suddenly saw himself enveloped and surrounded by the two regiments placed in ambush. There was a furious *mêlée*, in which the chasseurs lost one officer and sixty-two men killed and about seventy more wounded, before they could cut their way out of the snare. The sight of Lasalle's main body coming up in haste to the rescue made Henestrosa give the order for a prompt retreat, which he accomplished without loss. 'We arrived,' writes a French officer of one of the supporting regiments, 'too late, and saw nothing but a cloud of dust in the distance,

[1] Jourdan, p. 182.

made by the Spaniards as they rode away, and the colonel of
the 10th tearing his hair at the sight of his numerous wounded[1].'
This lesson taught Lasalle more caution : it was creditable to
Henestrosa, though it must be confessed that he had two men
to one in the skirmish, in addition to the advantage of taking
his enemy by surprise. Oddly enough the regiments which
accomplished this successful *coup* on the twenty-first were the
same which behaved worst in the great battle of the next week [2].

At Miajadas, where this skirmish had taken place, the road
descending from the pass of Santa Cruz forks in two directions.
One branch goes towards Merida and Badajoz, the other and
less important to Medellin, La Serena, and the upper Guadiana.
It would have been natural for Cuesta to take the former route,
which brought him nearer to his base at Badajoz, and at the
same time enabled him to cover the main road to Andalusia,
at which Victor was presumably aiming. But the old general
left this line unprotected, and retired by the eastern path to
Medellin. His main object was to secure his junction with
the reinforcements from La Mancha, which Albuquerque was
bringing to him. They were nearing La Serena, and would be
cut off from him if he took the road to Badajoz. At the same
time he argued that, as he had thus placed himself on the flank
of the French, they could not afford to march past him, since
the moment that they left Merida behind them he would
be enabled to cut their communications with Madrid. He
imagined that Victor would prefer to fight him, and would
not dare either to take in hand the siege of Badajoz, or to
advance against Andalusia, without clearing his flank by a general
action. The moment that he should have picked up Albuquerque, Cuesta was prepared to indulge the enemy with a fight,
and if he were not attacked himself he intended to take the
offensive. This was sheer madness ; even when he had drawn
in his last reserves the old general had but 20,000 foot and
3,000 horse [3], a number which only exceeded Victor's total by

---

[1] Rocca, p. 263.   [2] See pp. 162–3.

[3] The Spanish statements that Cuesta had only 2,200 horse seem disproved by a letter from Cuesta's camp, Col. D'Urban to Cradock (April 7),
to the effect that Cuesta had already rallied, after Medellin, fully 3,000
horse, but only 6,000 or 7,000 foot [Record Office].

three or four thousand men because the latter had been dropping detachments between Almaraz and Merida. Considering the relative value of the individual soldiery of the two armies, Cuesta's behaviour was that of a criminal lunatic. We shall see that his tactics were as bad as his strategy.

The Marshal had left the two Dutch battalions of Leval's division at Truxillo, in charge of his sick: he dropped the 1st Dragoons of Latour-Maubourg's division at Miajadas, to guard the cross-roads, and sent out the 4th and 9th from the same division along the upper Guadiana, where they soon learnt of Cuesta's presence on the other side of the river. Lasalle's light horse rode down to Merida, and occupied the old Roman capital of western Spain without having to strike a blow. Learning that the Spaniards had not retreated in this direction, but by the eastern road, the Marshal (as Cuesta had supposed likely) directed the bulk of his infantry on Medellin ; only the division of Ruffin remained behind, at the cross-roads of Miajadas.

Meanwhile Cuesta had evacuated Medellin, and fallen back to La Serena, where Albuquerque joined him on the twenty-seventh. The moment that the army was united, he turned back, and retraced his steps towards his former position. On the twenty-eighth he reached the town of Don Benito, only five miles from Medellin, and learnt to his great pleasure that Victor was before him and quite ready to fight. The Marshal had swept the whole country-side with his numerous cavalry during the last four days, and discovering that there was no Spanish force opposite him in any direction save that of La Serena, had ordered Lasalle and Ruffin to march up and join him from Merida and Miajadas. On the morning of the twenty-ninth he had his entire army united, save the two Dutch battalions left at Truxillo, two more of Leval's battalions left at Merida[1], the 1st Dragoons at Miajadas, and one other cavalry regiment which had been told off to guard the bridge of Almaraz. He cannot have had less than 13,000 infantry and 4,500 horse, even when allowance is made for the sick and the losses at Meza de Ibor and Miajadas. Cuesta outnumbered him by 6,000 infantry,

[1] Frankfort and the 1st of Hesse. See Sausez's *Régiment de Francfort*, p. 30.

but was overmatched in cavalry by more than three to two, since he had but 3,000 sabres, and even more hopelessly in artillery, since Victor had brought over fifty guns to the field, while he had only thirty.

Having been joined in the early morning by Lasalle's and Ruffin's detachments, Victor had drawn out his army in front of Medellin, when his cavalry brought him the news of the approach of the Spaniards. Medellin, an ancient town dominated by a Moorish citadel on a lofty hill, lies in the angle between the river Guadiana and the Hortiga torrent. The latter, easily fordable in March and dry in June, is an insignificant stream but flows at the bottom of a steep ravine. The Guadiana, on the other hand, is a river of the first class : the great bridge which leads into Medellin is no less than 450 yards long. There were several fords up-stream from the bridge, but in March, when the river was high, it is doubtful whether they were practicable. Victor's line, drawn in a quarter of a circle from the Hortiga to the Guadiana, was well protected on either flank by the broad river and the steep ravine. His order of battle was rather odd : its front line was composed of a division of infantry (Villatte's of twelve battalions) in the centre, with two projecting wings, each composed of a cavalry division supported by two battalions of Leval's Germans. On the right, near the Hortiga, was Latour-Maubourg with five of his six regiments of dragoons [1] and ten horse artillery guns. On the left, beside the Guadiana, was Lasalle with three of his own light cavalry regiments, and the 2nd Hussars of Victor's corps-cavalry. The remaining battalion of Leval's division [2] was with Villatte in the centre. Ruffin's division, forming the reserve, lay far to the rear on the further side of the Hortiga. He had with him one cavalry regiment [3] and a reserve of artillery : one

[1] The sixth regiment (1st Dragoons) was still absent at Miajadas.

[2] The division had started with nine battalions, but two (as will be remembered) were left behind at Truxillo, and two more at Merida. Those with Lasalle were the two Baden battalions, those with Latour-Maubourg a Nassau battalion, and one formed of the united light companies of the division. The second Nassau battalion was to the rear, with Villatte. See Séméle's narrative, p. 463.

[3] 5th Chasseurs, of the corps-cavalry of the 1st Corps.

battalion was detached to guard the baggage, which was parked at the bridge-head below the town.

Victor's army, therefore, formed a short and compact arc of a circle, a mile and a half outside of Medellin. Facing him, three or four miles away, was the Spanish army, ranged in a much larger arc, also extending from the Hortiga to the Guadiana, in front of the town of Don Benito. It was deployed along a series of gentle heights, on either side of the main road from Medellin. The position, though rather long for the Spanish numbers, presented many advantages for a defensive battle: but it was Cuesta's intention to go forward, not to receive the attack of the French. He saw with pleasure that the enemy had come half-way to meet him, and was about to fight with a difficult defile (the bridge of Medellin) in his rear. Secure from being outflanked by Victor's numerous cavalry, for the two streams covered his wings, he resolved to march straight before him and to bear down the French line by a direct frontal attack. On his left were the divisions of Del Parque and Henestrosa, eight battalions in a single line, all deployed four deep. They had no supports whatever, save one battalion of grenadiers which marched behind their centre. On their outside flank rode three regiments of cavalry, close to the ravine of the Hortiga[1]. The centre was composed of the four battalions of the division of Trias, all drawn up in the same fashion as the left wing. The right was formed by Portago's incomplete division[2] (only three battalions) and by the contingent from La Mancha which Albuquerque had just brought up—seven strong battalions with 4,500 bayonets. Outside Albuquerque's extreme right, and on the banks of the Guadiana, was placed a cavalry force corresponding to that on the extreme left, and also formed of three regiments[3]. A few remaining squadrons of cavalry were

---

[1] These were the regiments Infante and Almanza (from Denmark) and the new cavalry regiment of Toledo. Letter of Sir Benjamin D'Urban to Cradock, April 8, 1809 (Record Office).

[2] Its remainder was garrisoning Badajoz. Those on the field were Badajoz (two batts.), and 3rd of Seville (one batt.).

[3] Apparently these regiments were Albuquerque's regiment from the Andalusian army, with the Cazadores de Llerena (a new Estremaduran corps) and Del Rey (one of the Baltic regiments).

posted in the intervals between the wings and the centre [1]. The artillery went forward, each battery with the division to which it was attached. This was a most extraordinary order of battle : with the object of securing his flanks and of covering the whole space between the rivers, Cuesta was advancing with a front of nearly four miles and a depth of only four men! There is no parallel in modern history for such a dangerous array. If any single point in the long line gave way, there was no reserve with which to fill the gap and save the day. And it was morally certain that a weak point would be found somewhere, for many of the battalions were raw troops which had never seen fire, and the greater part of the others had graduated in the school of panic under Belvedere and San Juan.

Cuesta, however, was eminently satisfied with himself and with his order of battle : he intended to envelop the shorter French line with converging fire, to thrust it back on to the defile of Medellin, and if possible to seize the bridge behind its left flank, and to endeavour to cut off its retreat. Blind self-confidence could go no further!

When Victor advanced from Medellin he was aware of the proximity of the Spaniards, and could see their cavalry vedettes on all the hills in front of Don Benito, but it was not till his army had marched some distance across the bare and level fields, that Cuesta revealed his order of battle. When the French were well advanced in the plain, the whole Army of Estremadura crowned the heights, and then swept downward from them, in one continuous line forming an exact quarter of a circle. The infantry was well closed up ; each regiment had its mounted officers in front, and the generals were riding up and down the line, perpetually supervising the dressing of their battalions, for they were quite conscious that in the order which Cuesta had chosen any gap or wavering in the line would be ruinous. Each division had its battery in front, and in the long intervals between the guns a very thick line of skirmishers covered the advance of the main body.

Facing this imposing line, as it will be remembered, the

---

[1] These were the two hussar regiments, Voluntarios de España, and Maria Luisa, the latter of which had been re-named ' Hussars of Estremadura.

French had the five dragoon regiments of Latour-Maubourg on the right, and the four light cavalry regiments of Lasalle on the left, each supported by two of Laval's German battalions. The centre under Villatte was somewhat 'refused,' and was much further from the Spaniards than were the two powerful wings of cavalry. As the enemy advanced, Victor bade Latour-Maubourg and Lasalle to seize any good opportunity for a charge, but not to risk, unless circumstances favoured them, a general attack on the Spaniards, until they should have begun to lose their order. The wings of the enemy being covered by the two rivers, there could be no question of flank attacks, and frontal charges by cavalry on unbroken infantry are proverbially dangerous.

When, however, the armies drew near, Latour-Maubourg thought that he saw his chance, and bade one of his brigades (2nd and 4th Dragoons) charge Del Parque's infantry in the Spanish left-centre. The attack completely failed : a fortunate discharge of the Duke's divisional battery blew a gap in the centre of the charging line ; the battalions on each side stood firm and opened a heavy fire, and the dragoons went to the rear in disorder. Their flight exposed the flank of the two German battalions which formed the centre of Latour-Maubourg's line. The Spanish infantry pressed forward, and engaged them with vigour. This determined Victor to order his right wing to fall back and to get into line with Villatte, before making another stand. Accordingly Latour-Maubourg retired, his unbroken regiments moving off in very good order, but suffering considerably from the fire of the Spanish skirmishers, who ran forward with great rapidity and pressed them hard.

The retreat of the right wing made it necessary for Lasalle on the left to conform to the general movement. He also began to draw back towards Medellin. 'For two hours,' writes one of his officers [1], 'we gave back slowly and quietly, facing about at every fifty yards to show a front, and to dispute the ground. Amid the endless whizzing of bullets flying over our heads, and the deafening roar of the shells, which rent the air and tore up the earth around us, we heeded only the voice of our commanders. The further we retired the louder shouted our foes. Their skirmishers were so numerous and daring that

[1] Rocca (of the 2nd Hussars), *Mémoires de la Guerre d'Espagne*, 80.

they sometimes compelled ours to fall back for protection into our ranks. They kept calling to us from a distance that no quarter should be given, and that Medellin should be the Frenchman's grave. General Lasalle was riding backward and forward in front of his division, with a lofty, fearless air. In the space which separated us there might be seen the horses of disabled friends and foes, running on every side, most of them wounded, some of them dragging their dead masters by the stirrup, and struggling to free themselves from the unmanageable load.'

In this fashion the French retired before the advancing army of Cuesta, till they drew near the point where Victor intended to make his stand. The right wing reached the new line of defence first : it halted on the crest of the rising-ground to the north of the point where Villatte's infantry stood. The Marshal placed ten guns in line, ordered the two German battalions to stand firm on each flank of the artillery, and sent up the 94th of the Line from Villatte's division to aid them, as well as a battalion of picked grenadiers. Latour-Maubourg's horsemen, now all in good order again, covered their flanks.

Then came the critical moment of the battle. If the Spaniards could still push their advance, and thrust back the French infantry, Victor's position would be very serious. For a moment it seemed that they might succeed. The battalions of Henestrosa and Del Parque came forward with a steadiness that Spanish troops had not yet often shown during the war. They closed upon the guns, in spite of their rapid fire, and attacked the three battalions on their flanks, which had been thrown into square for fear of cavalry attacks, and were therefore not in very good order for defending themselves against infantry.

The leading Spanish officers had actually ridden into the battery[1], and were cutting down the gunners, when Latour-Maubourg ordered his dragoons to charge. The moment that he saw them on the move, Cuesta, who had been riding on this flank, with the three regiments of cavalry which covered the end of his line, ordered a counter-charge against the flank

---

[1] Cuesta in his dispatch mentions that General Henestrosa, Captain Yturrigarey, and the English Lieutenant-Colonel Benjamin D'Urban were the first three into the battery.

of the advancing French. Then followed a disgraceful scene:
the Spanish squadrons rode forward in an irresolute way for
a few score yards, and then suddenly halted, turned, and
galloped to the rear in a disorderly mass before they had arrived
anywhere near the French dragoons. They collided with Cuesta,
upset him and rode over him [1]: the old man was with difficulty
saved and set upon his horse by his aides-de-camp. The fugitives
never drew rein, and fled far away to the north, almost without
losing a man. Their conduct was all the more disgraceful,
because two of the three regiments were old troops from the
Baltic, which had come back with La Romana and had not
shared in any of the early disasters of the Spanish armies.

The result of this shameful panic was instant disaster to the
whole Spanish right wing. Of Latour-Maubourg's division
one brigade went off in pursuit of the routed cavalry, but the
other three regiments charged in flank the battalions of Henestrosa and Del Parque, just as they stormed the French battery
on which they were intent. A long line without supports, such
as that which these two divisions presented, was helpless when
attacked by cavalry on the flank—it suffered exactly the same
fate which befell Colborne's brigade at Albuera two years later.
While engaged in front with the three battalions already before
it, and with the regiment which Villatte had sent up to aid
them, it could not throw back its flank to face the horsemen:
nor had it any reserve whatever that could be utilized to
hold off Latour-Maubourg. The whole line was rolled up, and
dashed into atoms. Many men were cut down, a few captured,
the remainder fled in utter disorder towards the north. The
French urged the pursuit with cruel vigour, merciless all the
more because they had for a moment doubted of their victory.

While this struggle was raging on the northern part of the
field, Lasalle had been still falling back before the divisions
of Albuquerque, Portago, and Trias, across the plain which
borders the Guadiana. The Spanish line were still moving
forward with great steadiness, but had begun to fall into a sort
of *échelon* formation, with the cavalry near the river most in

---

[1] In a dispatch in the Record Office, Cuesta says that the particular
corps which rode down himself and his staff was the raw 'Toledo'
regiment.

advance, the infantry of Albuquerque a little behind, and the
Estremaduran battalions of the centre still further to the rear.
The fact was that General Eguia, to whom Cuesta had given
the charge of his whole right wing, was trying to edge his
cavalry between Lasalle and the Guadiana, in order to cut him
off from the bridge of Medellin. This end of the line, therefore,
was pushing forward very rapidly, while Trias, on the other
hand, was coming forward rather slowly, from a desire not to
lose touch with Del Parque's division, the nearest troops to him
in the other half of the army.

Lasalle was keeping an anxious eye on the development of the
action further to the north, and the moment that he saw Latour-
Maubourg halt and prepare to charge, followed his example.
His first blow was delivered at the cavalry next the river: he
flung against them the 2nd Hussars, with a chasseur regiment
in support. These two corps, charging with great fury, easily
broke the Andalusian lancers, who were leading the pursuit, and
hurled them back upon the other squadrons of the Spanish
right. The whole body was thrown into disorder and driven off
the field, leaving the flank of Albuquerque's division completely
uncovered. Lasalle then re-formed his men and prepared to
charge the infantry. He had been reinforced meanwhile by one
of Villatte's brigades (63rd and 95th of the Line) and by the
one battalion of Leval's Germans, which had hitherto remained
with the centre. While these seven battalions of fresh troops
delivered a frontal attack on Albuquerque and Trias, Lasalle
hurled his four regiments of cavalry upon their unprotected
right flank. The Spaniards were doomed to destruction, but
for some time kept up a show of resistance; Albuquerque
had got two or three of his battalions out of line into column,
and for a moment these held back Lasalle's chasseurs. But the
fight lasted for a few minutes only: a new French force was
coming up. Latour-Maubourg, returning from the pursuit
of Cuesta with two of his dragoon regiments, appeared upon
the flank and rear of Trias' division and charged in upon it
from behind. This last assault was decisive: the whole Spanish
line broke up and fled eastward over the open ground along
the river. The six regiments of French cavalry were soon in
pursuit, and rode in among the flying horde, using the sabre

with reckless cruelty, and far more intent on slaughter than
on taking prisoners. Lasalle's chasseurs were specially savage,
having to avenge the bloody check which they had received
at Miajadas in the preceding week[1]. 'Our troops,' says a French
witness, 'who had been threatened with no quarter by the
Spaniards if they had been overpowered, and who were enraged
by five hours of preliminary fighting, at first spared no one.
The infantry, following behind at a distance, dispatched the
wounded with their bayonets. Most of all they were pitiless
to such of the Spanish regiments as were without a proper
military uniform[2].' Another eye-witness describes the pursuit
as 'one continuous slaughter till night fell.' Some of the
Spanish battalions dispersed in the most helpless confusion, and
fled in all directions when the line was broken. Others tried
to close up and to defend themselves: this made their flight
slower, and sometimes led to their complete extermination. Rocca
says that he saw the two regiments of Spanish and Walloon
Guards lying dead *en masse* in the order which they had occupied
at the moment of the breaking of the line[3]. The statement is
borne out, at least as to the Walloons, by the fact that the
next morning-state of Cuesta's army which has been preserved
shows that regiment with only 300 men surviving out of two
whole battalions[4]. If any of the infantry of the Spanish right
wing escaped at all, it was partly owing to the fact that the
two cavalry regiments in the centre of the line[5] showed a much
better spirit than their comrades on the wings, and protected
the flight of some battalions. Moreover a frightful thunderstorm swept over the plains late in the afternoon, darkened the
whole horizon, and caused the French squadrons to halt and
cease their pursuit.

[1] Half-a-dozen French authorities speak of the wrath of the chasseurs as
justifiable, because their comrades at Miajadas had been murdered (*égorgés*,
or *lâchement assassinés*). But the Spaniards had killed them in fair
fight.

[2] Rocca, *Mémoires*, p. 82.   [3] Ibid., p. 84.

[4] See the Table in Arteche, vi. 476.

[5] These were the hussar regiments 'Volunteers of Spain' and 'Estremadura' (late Maria Luisa). Cuesta says in his dispatch that they saved
the battalions of Merida, and Provincial of Badajoz, which had been
surrounded and nearly cut off.

The slaughter, nevertheless, had been terrible. Of the 10,000 men whom the Spaniards lost on this fatal day three-fourths fell by the edge of the sword: only 1,850 prisoners were sent back to Talavera, and even if some others had succeeded in escaping during their march to the rear, it is certain that the Spanish casualty-list amounted to at least 7,500 men. Nine standards were taken— less than might have been expected, for the twenty-three Spanish battalions present must have brought forty-six to the field. Twenty pieces of artillery fell into the hands of the French, out of the thirty which Cuesta had possessed. Some few batteries therefore (perhaps the horse artillery of the evasive cavalry brigades) had succeeded in escaping from the rout.

Most French authors unite in stating that the total loss on their side was only 300 men [1]. This figure is as absurd as that given for Soult's losses at Corunna: there were five hours of fighting, and for a long time the battle had gone by no means in favour of Victor's men. It is improbable that they suffered less than 1,000 casualties, and the figure may have been higher, for one brigade of Latour-Maubourg's dragoons was beaten back while charging guns—always a bloody business for cavalry—while the German battalions which retired across the plain in column, played on by artillery and harassed by skirmishers, must also have suffered severely.

Cuesta's cavalry, owing to the disgraceful cowardice shown by the majority of the regiments, had got off comparatively intact. The whole of his dreadful losses had fallen on his infantry, and they had been scattered so far and wide over the Estremaduran plain that it was many days before he could get together a respectable force. He took refuge at Monasterio [2] in the mountains in the direction of Andalusia, and sent urgent appeals for reinforcements to the Central Junta. It might

[1] This is the figure given by Jourdan, and General Sémélé, who ought to have known the facts. It is, of course, reproduced by Thiers, and the other historians. But I agree with Napier (ii. 71) in considering the figure 'scarcely credible.' Rocca says that the French lost 4,000 men, but from the context, I suspect this to be a misprint for 400. Schepeler, always a very well-informed and impartial writer, guesses at 2,000, and he may not be far wrong.

[2] By April 8 he had collected there 3,000 horse and 6,000 or 7,000 foot. Letter of D'Urban to Cradock, April 8.

have been expected that the Junta would disgrace him and remove him from command, as they had Cartaojal, Infantado, and Castaños. But apparently they were rather cheered by the fact that Cuesta had seriously disputed the victory with the French, than angered with the want of generalship which he had shown. They voted that he and his army had deserved well of the State, and distributed honours and promotion to all the officers whom he recommended for good conduct during the action. Rocca remarks that they must have had in their minds the doings of the Romans after Cannae, when the steadfast Senate thanked the consul Varro 'for not having despaired of the republic,' instead of removing him for rashness and incompetence [1]. At any rate, they conferred on Cuesta the post of Captain-General of Estremadura, and hurried up to reinforce him all the troops that they could spare, a strong brigade of new Granadan levies [2], and a division drawn from the army of Cartaojal consisting of nine old battalions of regular troops with a force of 6,000 bayonets [3]. Thus reinforced the host of Cuesta was as strong as on the eve of Medellin, and once more mustered 20,000 foot and 3,000 horse. By the middle of April the whole had been drawn together, and reorganized into five divisions of foot and two of horse. This was the army that was to co-operate with Wellesley in the campaign of Talavera.

'In any other country of Europe,' wrote Marshal Jourdan, 'the gaining of two such successes as Medellin and Ciudad Real would have reduced the country-side to submission, and have enabled the victorious armies to press forward to new conquests. In Spain the reverse was the case: the greater the disaster suffered by the national troops, the more willing were the population to rise and take arms. Already the communications between Victor and Sebastiani were cut: several bearers of dispatches were massacred, and even some detachments cut off. An insurrection almost burst out at Toledo, where a garrison of insufficient strength had been left. It was only averted by

[1] Rocca, *Mémoires*, p. 86.

[2] Regiment of Velez-Malaga (three batts.), and 2nd battalion of Antequera, 3,600 bayonets in all.

[3] Also some stray squadrons of cavalry which had gone to the rear to get horses in Andalusia (Letter of Frere to Castlereagh in Record Office).

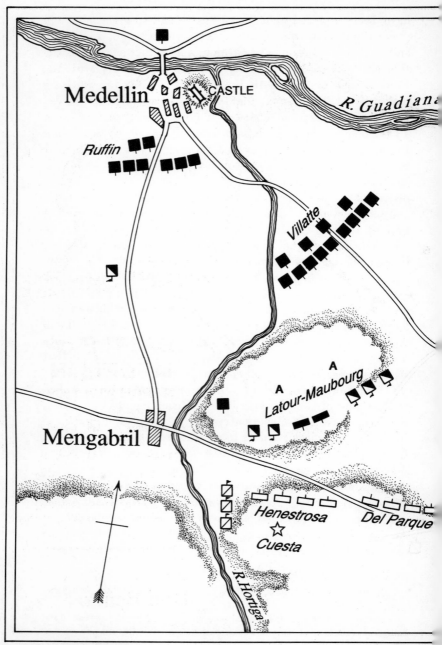

Medellin

CASTLE

R. Guadiana

Ruffin

Villatte

A

A

Latour-Maubourg

Mengabril

Henestrosa

Del Parque

☆
Cuesta

R. Hortiga

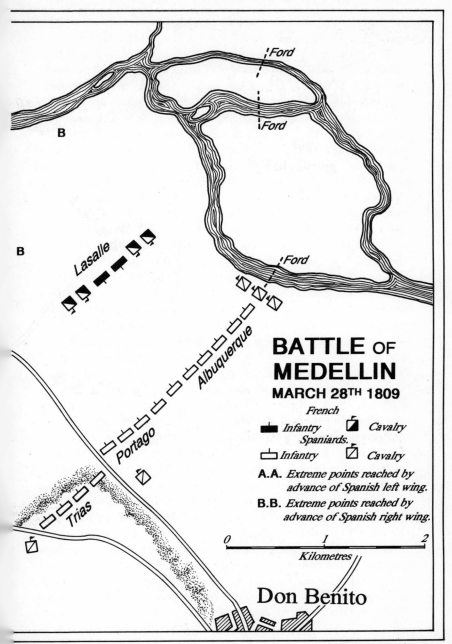

BATTLE OF
MEDELLIN
MARCH 28TH 1809

French

Infantry   Cavalry
Spaniards.
Infantry   Cavalry

A.A. *Extreme points reached by advance of Spanish left wing.*

B.B. *Extreme points reached by advance of Spanish right wing.*

0   1   2

Kilometres

Don Benito

Lasalle

Albuquerque

Portago

Trias

B

B

Ford

Ford

Ford

the providential arrival of an officer with a reinforcement of 500 men. The communications of the 1st Corps with Madrid were in no better state : bands of insurgents gathered in the valley of the Tietar, and threatened to fall upon Almaraz and to break the bridge of boats. The King had to send down in haste 600 bayonets from Madrid to preserve this all-important post[1].' At the same time the road from Almaraz to Salamanca was closed by a trifling Spanish force of two battalions under the brigadier Carlos d'España which had been levied about Caceres and Bejar, and occupied the pass of Baños. It was aided by a battalion of the Loyal Lusitanian legion, which Sir Robert Wilson had sent forward from Almeida. Thus Lapisse at Salamanca could only communicate with Victor at Merida by the circuitous route of Arevalo, Madrid, and Almaraz.

The Duke of Belluno had been ordered by the Emperor to beat the Army of Estremadura, and then to get into touch with Soult, who should have been due at Lisbon long ere this. But no news of the 2nd Corps had come to hand : it was known to have penetrated into northern Portugal, but its exact position could not be learnt. Victor, refusing to move till he had news of his colleague, cantoned his army at Merida and Medellin, and put the old castles of both these places, as well as that of Truxillo, in a state of defence. He would probably have done well to utilize the time of necessary waiting in laying siege to Badajoz. But he contented himself with watching that fortress and observing the reorganized army of Cuesta, which had now grown once more to a respectable force, and might have harassed considerably any part of the 1st Corps which should attempt to molest the capital of Estremadura. Instead of attacking the place, Victor contented himself with sending to it vain summonses to surrender, and with endeavouring to discover whether it might not contain traitors ready to negotiate with King Joseph. He brought down from Madrid, as his agent, a Spanish magistrate named Sotelo, who had become a zealous *Afrancesado*. Through this person he addressed letters both to the governor of Badajoz and to the Central Junta at Seville. After setting forth all the evils which the continuance of the war was bringing upon Spain, Sotelo stated that his king was ready to grant the most

[1] Jourdan, *Mémoires*, pp. 187–8.

liberal and benevolent terms to the Junta, in order to spare further effusion of blood. The letter was duly forwarded to Seville, where it was laid before the government. The ironical answer was promptly returned 'that if Sotelo possessed full powers to negotiate for peace on the basis of the restoration of Ferdinand VII, and the prompt evacuation of Spain by the French armies, peace would be possible. If not, the Junta must continue to carry out the mandate conferred upon it by the nation ; according to which it could conclude no truce or treaty except on the two conditions stated above.' Sotelo tried to continue the negotiation, but his offers were disregarded, and Victor soon realized that he would obtain no further advantages save by his sword. He remained at Merida waiting in vain for the news of Soult's advance on Lisbon, which was, according to Napoleon's orders, to be the signal for the 1st Corps to resume its advance.

N.B.—For the campaign of Medellin I have used the narratives of Rocca and Sémélé (the latter often very inaccurate), the *Mémoires* of Jourdan, the day-book of the Frankfort regiment of Laval's division, and Victor's correspondence with King Joseph, and on the Spanish side the dispatches of Cuesta, also two letters from D'Urban (British attaché on Cuesta's staff) to Cradock, and some enclosures sent by Frere to Castlereagh.

SECTION XIII

SOULT'S INVASION OF PORTUGAL

CHAPTER I

SOULT'S PRELIMINARY OPERATIONS IN GALICIA
(JANUARY 19—MARCH 6, 1809)

AFTER the departure of Bonaparte for Paris there were, as we have already shown, only two points in the Peninsula where the strength of the French armies was such as to allow them to continue the great movement of advance which their master had begun. We have already seen how Victor, after advancing from the Tagus to the Guadiana, found his initiative exhausted, even after his victory at Medellin. He had halted, and refused to take the offensive against Lisbon or Andalusia till he should be heavily reinforced.

It remains to be seen how the other French army available for immediate field operations had fared. Moore's daring march and the ensuing retreat had drawn up into the extreme north-west of the Peninsula the 2nd, 6th, and 8th *corps d'armée*. Of these the last-named had been dissolved at the new year, and the bulk of its battalions had been transferred to Soult's corps, which on January 20 had a nominal effective of more than 40,000 men. Ney's Corps, the 6th, was much smaller, and does not seem to have amounted to more than 16,000 or 18,000 sabres and bayonets. But between Astorga, the rearmost point occupied by Ney, and Corunna, which Soult's vanguard had entered on January 19, there were on paper 60,000 men available for active operations. Nor had they to guard their own communications with Madrid or with France. Lapisse's numerous division had been left at Salamanca ; there was a provisional

brigade at Leon [1]; Bonnet held Santander with another
division; there were detachments in Zamora, Valladolid, and
the other chief towns of the Douro valley. Somewhat later, in
April, the Emperor moved another whole army corps, that of
Mortier, into Old Castile, when it became available after the fall
of Saragossa. Even without this reinforcement he thought that
the rear of the army in Galicia was adequately covered. The
parting instructions of Bonaparte to Soult have already been
cited: when the English should have embarked, the Duke of
Dalmatia was to march on Oporto, and ten days later was to
occupy Lisbon. We have already seen that the scheme of
dates which Napoleon laid down for these operations was impossible, even to the borders of absurdity: Oporto was to be seized
by February 1, and Lisbon by February 10! But putting aside
this error, which was due to his persistent habit of ignoring the
physical conditions of Spanish roads and Spanish weather, the
Emperor had drawn up a plan which seemed feasible enough.
Ney's corps was to move up and occupy all the chief strategical
points in Galicia, taking over both the garrison duty and the
task of stamping out any small lingering insurrections in the
interior. This would leave Soult free to employ the whole of
his four divisions of infantry and his three divisions of cavalry
for the invasion of Portugal. Even allowing for the usual
wastage of men in a winter campaign, the Emperor must have
supposed that, with a nominal effective of 43,000 men, Soult
would be able to provide more than 30,000 efficients for the
expedition against Lisbon [2]. Considering that the Portuguese
army was still in the making, and that no more than 8,000

---

[1] It was composed of the few battalions of the 8th Corps which had not
been drafted into the 2nd.

[2] When the Emperor looked at the half-monthly returns of the army,
which were forwarded to him as regularly as possible, and which pursued
him wheresoever he might go, he must have seen the following statistics—
those of Jan. 15 in the French War Office—for the 2nd Corps, taking the
gross totals :—

Infantry : Merle 12,119 ; Mermet 11,810 ; Delaborde 5,038 ; Heudelet
6,592 : Total 35,559.

Cavalry : Lorges 1,769 ; Lahoussaye 3,087 ; Franceschi 2,512 : Total
7,368. Artillery and Train 1,468.

Total of the whole corps 44,395. By Jan. 30, it had risen to 45,820.

British troops remained in and about Lisbon, the task assigned to the Duke of Dalmatia did not on the face of it appear unreasonable.

But in Spain the old saying that 'nothing is so deceptive as figures—except facts,' was pre-eminently true. No map—those of 1809 were intolerably bad—could give the Emperor any idea of the hopeless condition of Galician or Portuguese mountain-roads in January. No tables of statistics could enable him to foresee the way in which the population would receive the invading army. We may add that even an unrivalled knowledge of the realities of war would hardly have prepared him to expect that the campaign of Galicia would, in one month, have worn down Soult's available effectives to a bare 23,000 men. Such was the modest figure at which the 2nd Corps stood on January 30, for it had no less than 8,000 men detached, and the incredible number of over 10,000—one man in four—in hospital. For this figure it was not the muskets of Moore's host which were responsible : it was the cold and misery of the forced marches from Astorga to Corunna, which seem to have tried the pursuer even more than the pursued. The 8,000 'detached' were strung out in small parties all the way from Leon to Lugo—wherever the Marshal had been obliged to abandon stores or baggage that could not travel fast, he had been forced to leave a guard : he had also dropped small garrisons at Villafranca, Lugo, and Betanzos, to await Ney's arrival ; but the most important drain had been that of his dismounted dragoons [1]. In his cavalry regiments half the horses had foundered or perished : the roads so deadly to Moore's chargers had taken a corresponding toll from the French divisions, and at every halting-place hundreds of horsemen, unable to keep up

[1] The state of the cavalry of the 2nd Corps on Jan. 30 gives the following astounding result :—

	Present under Arms.	Absent.	Sick.
Lorges	809	617	108
Lahoussaye	1,130	1,400	256
Franceschi	1,120	991	208
	3,059	3,008	572

The drain under the second column represents mainly the men who had dropped to the rear, from losing their horses or being unable to take them on.

with the main body, had been left behind. In any other country
than Spain these involuntary laggards would have found their
way to the front again in a comparatively short time. But
Soult was commencing to discover that one of the main features
of war in the Peninsula was that isolated men, or even small
parties, could not move about in safety. The peasantry were
already beginning to rise, even before Moore's army took its
departure; they actually cut the road between Betanzos and
Lugo, and between Lugo and Villafranca, within a few days
after the battle of Corunna. This forced the stragglers to
mass, under pain of being assassinated. Hundreds of them
were actually cut off: the rest gathered in small wayside
garrisons, and could not get on till they had been formed into
parties of considerable strength. The rearmost, who had been
collected at Astorga by General Pierre Soult, the Marshal's
brother, did not join the corps for months—and this body was
no less than 2,000 or 2,500 strong. The other detachments
could not make their way to Corunna even when Marshal Ney
had come up: it was only by degrees, and after delays covering
whole weeks, that they began to rejoin. The only solid reinforcement received by Soult, soon after the departure of the English
army, consisted of his rear division, that of Heudelet, which came
up from Lugo, not many days after the battle of January 16.

Soult was still far from suspecting the full difficulty of the
task that was before him. He had been much encouraged by
the tame way in which the Governor of Corunna had surrendered
on January 19. If Alcedo had made the least semblance of
fight he could have detained the Marshal before his walls for an
indefinite time. The city was only approachable by a narrow
and well-fortified isthmus, and the French could not have
battered this formidable front to any effect with the six-
pounders which formed their only artillery. The surrender of
the place gave Soult some food, the considerable resources
of a rich harbour town, and (most important of all) a large
number of guns of position, suitable for use against the other
fortress which he must take ere he moved on against Portugal.

This place was Ferrol, the second naval arsenal of Spain,
which faces Corunna across the broad inlet of Ares Bay—only
thirteen miles distant by water, though the land road thither

by Betanzos, round the head of the fiord, is forty miles long. To make sure of this place was obviously Soult's first duty : if left unmolested it would prove a dangerous nucleus round which the Galician insurgents could concentrate. For it contained a regular garrison, consisting of the dépôts and half-trained recruits of La Romana's army, and of 4,000 or 5,000 sailors. There were lying in the harbour, mostly half-dismantled and unready for sea [1], no less than eight line-of-battle ships and three frigates. Their crews, much depleted, but still numerous, had been landed to assist the soldiers in garrisoning the forts [2]. In addition several thousand citizens and peasants had taken arms, for muskets abounded in Ferrol, from the stores lately received from England. With these resources it is clear that a governor of courage and resolution might have made a long defence; they were far greater than those with which Palafox had preserved Saragossa; and Ferrol was no open town, but a fortress which had been kept in good repair for fear of the English. But, for the misfortune of Galicia, the commander of Ferrol, Admiral Melgarejo, was a traitor at heart. He was one of the old bureaucrats who had only followed the patriotic cause because it seemed for the moment to be in the ascendant ; if patriotism did not pay, he was perfectly prepared to come to terms and to do homage to Joseph Bonaparte.

On January 23 Soult marched against Ferrol with the infantry division of Mermet, the dragoons of Lorges, and the heavy guns which he had found in Corunna. He left Delaborde in garrison at the latter place, posted Merle at Betanzos, a half-way house between the two fortresses, and directed Franceschi's cavalry division on Santiago and Lahoussaye's on Mellid, in order to see whether there was any Spanish field-force visible in western Galicia. On the twenty-fifth the Marshal presented himself in front of Ferrol, and summoned the place to surrender. Melgarejo was determined not to fight, and several of his chief subordinates supported him. The

---

[1] For the state of this squadron see the report by Admiral De Courcy in the *Parliamentary Papers* for 1809, Spain, March 29, 1809, p. 4.

[2] The marines had been taken away in July, 1808, and formed half a brigade in the division of the Army of Galicia. But the seamen were available.

armed citizens persisted in their idea of defending the place, but when the French broke ground in front of the walls and captured two small outlying redoubts, they allowed themselves to be overpersuaded by their treacherous chief. On January 26 the place surrendered, and on the following day Soult was received within the walls. The capitulation had two shameful clauses: by the first the civil and military authorities undertook to take the oath of allegiance to King Joseph. By the second the splendid men-of-war in the harbour were handed over intact, a most valuable acquisition for the Emperor if Galicia was to remain under his control. Any one but a traitor would have burnt or scuttled them before surrendering. But Melgarejo, after receiving high testimonials from Soult, hastened up to Madrid and took office under the *Rey Intruso*[1]. Along with the squadron 1,500 naval cannon, an immense quantity of timber, cordage, and other stores, and 20,000 muskets newly imported from England, fell into the hands of the French.

On the day after Ferrol was occupied, Soult received the last communication from the Emperor which was to reach him for many a day[2]. It was dated from Valladolid on January 17. We have already had occasion to refer to it more than once, while dealing with the controversies of King Joseph and Marshal Victor. This dispatch repeated the Emperor's former orders, with some slight concession in the matter of dates. Instead of reaching Oporto on February 1 the Marshal was to be granted four extra days, and after taking Oporto on February 5, he was to reach Lisbon on the sixteenth instead of the tenth. Soult was also told that he would not have to depend on his own resources alone: Victor with the 1st Corps would be at Merida by the time that the 2nd Corps was approaching the Portuguese capital: he would be instructed to send a column in the direction of Lisbon, to make a diversion in favour of the attack from the north, and at the same time Lapisse from Salamanca should move on Ciudad Rodrigo and Almeida. Bessières was, so the Emperor said, under strict orders to send Lapisse forward into Portugal the moment that the news should reach him that the

[1] The Supreme Junta very properly condemned him and Alcedo, the governor of Corunna, to the penalties of high treason.

[2] Compare *Instructions de l'Empereur* of Jan. 17, with Berthier to Soult of Jan. 21.

2nd Corps had captured Oporto. This combination sinned against the rules of strategy, as they had to be practised in Spain. The Emperor had yet to realize that in order to make operations simultaneous, when troops starting from bases several hundred miles apart are to co-operate, it is necessary that their generals should be in free communication with each other. But Soult, when he had advanced into Portugal, was as much out of touch with the other French corps as if he had been operating in Poland or Naples. It was literally months before accurate information as to his situation and his achievements reached Salamanca, Merida, or Madrid. The movements of Victor and Lapisse being strictly conditioned by the receipt of news concerning Soult's progress, and that news being never received, or received too late, the combination never did and never could take place. Napoleon had forgotten to reckon with the ubiquitous Spanish insurgent : here, as in so many cases, he was unconsciously assuming that the bearer of dispatches could ride freely through the country, as if he were in Saxony or Lombardy ; and that Soult could make known his movements and his desires as often as he pleased. French critics of the Emperor generally confine themselves to censuring him for sending the 2nd Corps to attempt unaided a task too great for it [1] ; this is not quite fair, for he had intended to support Soult by two strong diversions. The real fault lay in ignoring the fact that in Spain combined operations, which presuppose constant communication between the participants, were practically impossible. The same error was made in 1810, when Drouet was told to co-operate in Massena's invasion of Portugal, and in 1811 when Soult was directed to lend a helping hand to that same invasion. It is impossible to give effective aid to a colleague whose condition and whose whereabouts are unknown.

On January 29 the Duke of Dalmatia set to work to reor-

---

[1] ' Il faut croire,' says St. Chamans, Soult's senior aide-de-camp, ' que Napoléon, au moment où il ordonna une pareille opération, était possédé d'un esprit de vertige. Comment pouvait-il risquer, au milieu d'un royaume insurgé, un si faible corps d'armée, sans communication avec ses autres troupes d'Espagne ? ' [*Mémoires*, p. 117]. ' Tout était en erreur,' says Le Noble, another 2nd Corps writer, ' dans le projet de soumettre le Portugal en 1809 avec une armée si faible et dépourvue de moyens. L'Empereur a montré une confiance aveugle ' (p. 65).

ganize his army for the great expedition that had been assigned to him. It was impossible to march at once, as the Emperor had commanded, because Ney had not yet arrived at the front, and it was necessary to turn over the charge of Corunna and Ferrol to him before departing further south. Moreover, there were many other arrangements to be made : a base hospital had to be organized at Corunna for the thousands of sick and wounded belonging to the 2nd Corps. Its transport had to be reconstructed, for most of the animals had died during the forced marches in pursuit of Moore [1]. A new stock of munitions had to be served out from the stores so fortunately captured at Ferrol. The military chest of the corps had been left behind at Astorga, and showed no signs of appearing : to provide for the more urgent day-by-day needs of the army, the Marshal had to squeeze forced contributions out of the already exhausted towns of Corunna, Ferrol, and Santiago, which had long ago contributed all their surplus resources to the fitting out of Blake's army of Galicia. These same unhappy places had to submit to a heavy requisition of cloth and leather, for the replacing of the garments and boots worn out in the late marches. But even with the aid of 2,500 English greatcoats discovered in store at Corunna, and other finds at Ferrol, the wants of the army could not be properly supplied ; it started on the campaign in a very imperfectly equipped condition [2]. The most dangerous point in its outfit was the want of mules : most of the valleys of inner Galicia and northern Portugal are destitute of carriage roads. To bring up the food and the reserve ammunition pack-animals were absolutely necessary, and Soult could only collect a few hundreds. Even if his men should succeed in living on the country, and so solve the problem of carrying provisions, they could not hope to pick up powder and lead in the same way. When, therefore, the heavy baggage on

---

[1] The authors, English and French, who express a humanitarian horror at the shooting of 3,000 horses and mules before the embarkation of Moore's army, forget what a godsend these would have been to Soult, if the English had left them to fall intact into his hands. The slaughter was dreadful, but perfectly necessary and justifiable.

[2] All these details come from Le Noble, who as *Ordonnateur-en-Chef* of the 2nd Corps, had full experience of the difficulty of equipping it for the Portuguese expedition.

wheels had to be left behind, the 2nd Corps was only able to carry a very insufficient stock of cartridges: twice, as we shall see, it almost exhausted its ammunition and was nearly brought to a standstill on the way to Oporto.

It was not till February had already begun that Soult was able to move forward the whole of his army, for he refused to withdraw Delaborde's division from Corunna and Mermet's from Ferrol, till Ney should have brought up troops of the 6th Corps to relieve them. The Duke of Elchingen, though apprised of the Emperor's orders, lingered long at Lugo, and it was not till he came down in person to the coast that Soult could call up his rear divisions. Meanwhile a small exchange of troops between the two corps was carried out: Ney, being short of cavalry, received a brigade of Lorges' dragoons to add to his own inadequate force of two regiments of light horse. In return he made over to the 2nd Corps three battalions of the 17th Léger, which had accompanied him hitherto. They were added to Delaborde's division, which had been only eight battalions strong.

Even before the troops from Ferrol and Corunna were able to move, Soult had put the rest of his army on the march for Portugal. On January 30 Franceschi's light horsemen started along the coast-road from Santiago to Vigo and Tuy, while further inland Lahoussaye's division of dragoons, quitting Mellid, took the rough mountain path across the Monte Testeyro, by Barca de Ledesma and Cardelle, which leads to Rivadavia and Salvatierra on the lower Minho. Merle's and Heudelet's infantry started several days later, and were many miles behind the advanced cavalry.

Lahoussaye's division met with no opposition in the rugged region which it had to cross, and occupied Salvatierra without difficulty. Franceschi scattered a few peasants at the defile of Redondela outside Vigo, and then found himself at the gates of that harbour-fortress. The governor, no less weak and unpatriotic than those of Ferrol and Corunna, surrendered without firing a shot. His excuse was that he had only recruits, and armed townsfolk, to man his walls and handle his numerous artillery. But his misconduct was even surpassed by that of the Governor of Tuy, who capitulated to Franceschi's 1,200 horsemen three days later in the same style, though he was in command of 500 regular troops, and was implored to hold out by the local junta. Throughout Galicia, in this unhappy month, the officials and military chiefs showed a most deplorable spirit, which contrasted unfavourably with that of the lower classes, both in the towns and the country-side.

The way to the frontier of Portugal had thus been opened, with an ease which seemed to justify Napoleon's idea that the Spaniards would not hold out, when once their field armies had been crushed. Franceschi and Lahoussaye reported to the Duke of Dalmatia that they had swept the whole northern bank of the Minho, and that there was nothing in front of them save the swollen river and a few bands of Portuguese peasantry, who were observing them from Valenza, the dilapidated frontier fortress of the neighbouring kingdom.

Both the French and the Galicians of the coast-line might well have forgotten the fact that there was still a Spanish army in existence within the borders of the province. It is long since we have had occasion to mention the fugitive host of the Marquis of La Romana. After being hunted out of Ponferrada by Soult on January 3, he had followed in the wake of Craufurd's brigades on their eccentric retreat down the valley of the Sil. But while the British troops pushed on to Vigo and embarked, the Spaniards halted at Orense. There the Marquis endeavoured to rally his demoralized and starving host, with the aid of the very limited resources of the district. He had only 6,000 men left with the colours, out of the 22,000 who had been with him at Leon on December 25, 1808. But there were several thousands more straggling after him, or dispersed in the side valleys off the road which he had followed. Most of these men had lost their muskets, many were frost bitten, or suffering from dysentery. The surviving nucleus of the army was composed almost entirely of the old regulars : the Galician militia and new levies had not been able to resist the temptation to desert, when they found themselves among their native mountains. The Marquis hoped that, when the spring came round, they would find their way back to the army : in this expectation, as we shall see, he was not deceived. For nearly a fortnight the wrecks of the army were undisturbed, and La Romana was able to collect enough efficients to constitute two small corps of observation, one of which he posted in the valley of the Sil, to watch for any signs of a movement of the French from the direction of Ponferrada, while the other, in the valley of the Minho, kept a similar look out in the direction of Lugo. The latter force was unmolested, but on January 17 General Mendizabal, who was watching the southern road, reported the approach of a heavy hostile column. This was Marchand's division of Ney's corps: the Marshal had divided his force at Ponferrada; he himself with Maurice Mathieu's division had kept the main road to Lugo, while Marchand had been told off to clear the lateral valleys and seize Orense. La Romana very wisely resolved that his unhappy army was unfit to resist 8,000 French troops. On January 19 he evacuated Orense, and fled across the Sierra Cabrera to Monterey on the Portuguese frontier. Here at last he found rest, for Marchand did not follow him into the mountains, but, after a short stay in Orense, marched to Santiago, where he was directed to relieve Soult's garrison.

The Marquis was completely lost to sight in his frontier fastnesses, and was able to do his best to reorganize his battered host. By February 13 he had 9,000 men under arms, nearly all old soldiers, for the Galician levies were still scattered in their homes. His dispatches during this period are very gloomy reading: he complains bitterly of the apathy of the country-side and the indiscipline of his officers. What could be expected of subalterns, he asks, when a general (Martinengo of the 2nd division) had absconded without asking leave or even report-ing his departure? 'I know not where the patriotism, of which every one boasted, is now to be found, since on the smallest reverse or misfortune, they lose their heads, and think only of saving themselves—sacrificing their country and compromising their commander.' Much harassed for want of food, La Romana kept moving his head quarters; he was sometimes at Verin and Monterey, sometimes at Chaves just inside the Portuguese frontier, more frequently at Oimbra. He had only nine guns left; there was no reserve of ammunition, and the soldiers had but few cartridges remaining in their boxes. The strongest battalion left in the army had only 250 bayonets—many had but seventy or eighty, and others (notably the Galician local

corps) had completely disappeared. He besought the Central
Junta to obtain from the British money, muskets, clothing, and
above all ammunition, or the army would never be fit to take
the field[1]. A similar request in the most pressing terms was
sent to Sir John Cradock at Lisbon.

Soult could not but be aware that La Romana's army, or
some shadow of it, was still in existence : but since it sedulously
avoided any contact with him, and had completely evacuated
the coast-land of Galicia, he appears to have treated it as
a 'negligible quantity' during his first operations. Its dispersion, if it required any further dispersing, would fall to the
lot of Ney and the 6th Corps, not to that of the army sent
against Portugal.

Franceschi and Lahoussaye, as we have already seen, reached
the Minho and the Portuguese border on February 2. It was
only on the eighth that the Duke of Dalmatia set out from
Santiago to follow them, in company with the division of Merle.
Those of Delaborde and Mermet, released by the arrival of Ney,
took the same route on the ninth and tenth respectively. The
rear was brought up by the reserve and heavy artillery, and by
that brigade of Lorges' dragoons which had not been handed
over to the 6th Corps. The coast-road being very good, Soult
was able to concentrate his whole army within the triangle Tuy,
Salvatierra, Vigo by the thirteenth, in spite of the hindrances
caused by a week of perpetual storm and rain.

It was the Marshal's intention to enter Portugal by the great
coast-road, which crosses the Minho at Tuy and proceeds to
Oporto by way of Valenza and Braga. But as Valenza was a
fortress, and its cannon commanded the broad ferry at which the
usual passage was made, it was clearly necessary to choose some

---

[1] Most of these details are from two interesting dispatches of La Romana
in the Foreign Office papers at the Record Office. They are dated from
Chaves on Jan. 28 and Feb. 13. They are unpublished and seem to be
unknown even to General Arteche, who has made such a splendid collection
of the materials in the Spanish archives which bear on this obscure corner
of the war. There was an English officer, Captain Brotherton, with the
army of La Romana : but his reports, which Napier had evidently seen,
are now no longer to be found. No doubt they were bound up in the
January–March 1809 book of Portuguese dispatches, which since Napier's
day has disappeared from the Record Office, leaving no trace behind.

other point for crossing the frontier river. After a careful survey Soult fixed on a village named Campo Saucos, only two miles from the mouth of the Minho, as offering the best starting-point. He established a battery of heavy guns on his own side of the river, and collected a number of fishing-boats[1], sufficient to carry 300 men at a voyage. As he could not discover that the Portuguese had any regular force opposite him, he resolved to attempt the passage with these modest resources.

There would have been no great difficulty in the enterprise during ordinary weather. But the incessant rains had so swelled the Minho that it was now a wild, ungovernable torrent, which it was hard to face and still harder to stem. When the heavy Atlantic surf met the furious current of the stream, during the rising of the tide, the conflict of the waters made the passage absolutely impossible. It had to be attempted at the moment between the flow and the ebb—though there was at that hour another danger—that the boats might be carried past the appointed landing-place and wrecked on the bar at the mouth of the river. But this chance Soult resolved to risk: on February 16, long before daybreak, his twenty or thirty fishing-boats, each with a dozen men on board, launched out from the northern shore, and struck diagonally across the stream, as the current bore them. They were at once saluted by a heavy but ill-directed fire from the Portuguese bank, where hundreds of peasants were at watch even during the hours of darkness. The soldiers rowed and steered badly—Soult had only been able to give them as guides a mere handful of men trained to the water[2]. The furious current swept them away: probably also their nerve was much tried by the fusillade, which, though more noisy

[1] These boats were brought to Campo Saucos overland, for a full mile and more. They came from La Guardia and other fishing-villages on the coast; but finding it impossible to get them over the bar of the Minho in such furious weather, and against the swollen stream, Soult dragged them from the beach north of the mouth to the crossing-point on rollers, much as Mohammed II did with his galleys at the famous siege of Constantinople in 1453. But Soult's vessels were, of course, much smaller.

[2] Soult had got together a few dozen seamen, French prisoners of war, found at Corunna and Ferrol, who had been captured at sea by Spanish cruisers. They were not 'marines' as Napier calls them (ii. 38), but *marins* (see Le Noble, p. 75, and again p. 78).

than dangerous, yet occasionally picked off a rower or a helms-man. The general result was that only three boats with thirty-five or forty men got to the appointed landing-place, where they were made prisoners by the Portuguese. The rest were borne down-stream, and came ashore at various points on the same side from which they had started, barely avoiding shipwreck on the bar.

The attempt to pass the Minho, therefore, ended in a ridicu-lous fiasco : it showed the limitations of the French army, which among its numerous merits did not possess that of good seaman-ship. Soult was deeply chagrined, not because of the insigni-ficant loss of men, but because of the check to his prestige. He resolved that he would not risk another such failure, and at once gave orders for the whole army to march up-stream to Orense, the first point where there was a bridge over the Minho. This entailed a radical change in his general plan of operations, for he was abandoning the good coast-road by Tuy and Valenza for a very poor mountain-way from Orense to Chaves along the valley of the Tamega. There was another important result from the alteration—the new route brought the French army down upon La Romana's camp of refuge : his cantonments in and about Monterey lay right across its path. But neither he nor Soult had yet realized the fact that they were about once more to come into collision. The Marshal did not know where the Marquis was ; the Marquis did not at first understand the meaning of the Marshal's sudden swoop inland. Some of the Spanish officers, indeed, were sanguine enough to imagine that the French, after their failure on the lower Minho, would abandon Galicia altogether [1] !

The whole French army had now made a half-turn to the left, and was marching in a north-easterly direction. Lahoussaye's dragoons, starting from Salvatierra, led the advance, Heudelet's division marched at the head of the infantry ; Delaborde, Mermet, and Merle, each at a convenient interval from the preceding division, stretched out the column to an interminable length. The heavy artillery and wagon train brought up the rear. Nine hundred sick, victims of the detestable weather

[1] Letter of Captain Brotherton [now lost] quoted in Napier, ii. 438, and dated from Oimbra on Feb. 21.

of the first fortnight of February, were left behind at Tuy under the guard of a half-battalion of infantry.

It was on the march from Tuy to Orense that Soult began to realize the full difficulties of his task. He had already met with small insurgent bands, but they had been dispersed with ease, and he had paid little attention to them. Now however, along the steep and tiresome mountain road above the Minho, they appeared in great force, and showed a spirit and an enterprise which were wholly unexpected by the French. The fact was that in the month which had now elapsed since the battle of Corunna, the peasantry and the local notables had found time to take stock of the situation. The first numbing effect of the presence of a large hostile army in their midst had passed away. Ruthless requisitions were sweeping off their cattle, the only wealth of the country. Although Soult had issued pacific proclamations, and had tried to keep his men in hand, he could not restrain the usual plundering propensities of a French army on the march. Enough atrocities had already been committed to make the Galicians forget the misconduct of Moore's men. La Romana, from his refuge at Monterey, had been dispersing appeals to the patriotism of the province, and sending out officers with local knowledge to rouse the country-side. These probably had less effect on the Galicians—the Marquis was a stranger and a defeated general—than the exhortations of their own clergy. In the first rising of the peasantry most of the leaders were ecclesiastics : in the region which Soult was now traversing the peasantry were raised by Mauricio Troncoso, Abbot of Couto, and a friar named Giraldez, who kept the insurgents together until, some weeks later, they handed over the command to military officers sent by La Romana or by the Central Junta. In the valley of the Sil, beyond Orense, it was Quiroga, Abbot of Casoyo, who first called out the country-side[1]. Every narrative of the Galician insurrection, whether French or Spanish, bears witness to the fact that in almost every case the

---

[1] All the details of the Galician insurrection may be found in the very interesting *Los Guerrilleros Gallegos de* 1809, of Pardo de Andrade, reprinted at Corunna in 1892. It is absolutely contemporary and mainly composed of original documents written by men who shared in the rising. But naturally it contains errors and exaggerations.

clergy, regular and secular, were the earliest chiefs of the moun-
taineers. It was characteristic of the whole rising that many of
the bands took the field with the church-banners of their
parishes as substitutes for the national flag.

This much is certain, that as soon as the violent February
rains showed signs of slackening, the whole of rural Galicia flew
to arms. From Corcubion on the surf-beaten headland of
Finisterre, to the remote headwaters of the Sil under the Sierra
de Penamarella, there was not a valley which failed to answer the
appeal which La Romana had made and which the clergy had
circulated. From the weak and sporadic movements of January
there sprang in February a general insurrection, which was all
the more formidable because it had no single focus, was based
on no place of arms, and was directed not by one chief but by
fifty local leaders, each intimately acquainted with the district
in which he was about to operate.

The first result of this widespread movement was to complete
the severance of the communications between the various French
divisions in Galicia. From the earliest appearance of the
invaders, as we have already seen, there had been intermittent
attempts to cut the lines of road by which the 2nd and 6th
Corps kept touch with each other and with Madrid. But hitherto
a convoy, or escort of a couple of hundred men, could generally
brush aside its assailants, and get through from post to post.
In February this power of movement ceased: the insurgents
became not only more numerous and more daring, but infinitely
more skilful in their tactics. Instead of endeavouring to deliver
combats in the open, they broke the bridges, burnt the ferry-
boats, cut away the road in rocky places, and then hung persistently about any corps that was on the move, as soon as it
began to get among the obstacles. They fired on it from
inaccessible side-hills, attacked and detained its rearguard so
as to delay its march, thus causing a gap to grow between it and
the main body, and only closed when the column was beginning
to get strung out into a series of isolated groups. The convoys
which were being sent up from Astorga to the 2nd and 6th
Corps were especially vulnerable to such tactics : the shooting
of a few horses in a defile would hopelessly block the progress
of everything that was coming on from behind. The massing of

men to repair or rehorse disabled wagons only gave the lurking insurgent a larger and an easier target. Hence the bringing up to the front of the heavy transport of the French army became such a slow and costly business, that the attempt to move it was after a time almost abandoned. Another point which the insurgents soon perceived was the helplessness of the French cavalry among rocks and defiles. A horseman cannot get at an enemy who lurks above his head in precipitous crags, refuses to come down to the high-road, and takes careful shots from his eyrie into the squadron below. If, worried beyond endurance, the French officers dismounted some of their men to charge the hillside, the lightly-equipped peasants fled away, and were out of sight before the dragoons in their heavy boots could climb the first fifty yards of the ascent. The copious annals of the Galician guerrilla bands almost invariably begin with tales of the annihilation of insufficiently guarded convoys, or of the defeat and extermination of small bodies of cavalry caught in some defile. A very little experience of such petty successes soon taught them the right way to deal with the French. The invaders could not be beaten *en masse*, but might be cut off in detail, harassed into exhaustion, and so isolated one from the other that it would require the sending out of a considerable expedition to carry a message between two neighbouring garrisons, or to forward a dispatch down the high-road to Madrid.

In a very short time intercommunication between the various sections of the French army in Galicia became so rare and uncertain, that each commander of a garrison or chief of a column found himself in the condition of a man lost in a fog. His friends might be near or far, might be faring ill or prosperously, but it was almost impossible to get news of them. Every garrison was surrounded with a loose screen of insurgents, which could only be pierced by a great effort. Each column on the march moved on surrounded by a swarm of active enemies, who closed around again in spite of all attempts to brush them off. In March and April Ney, on whom the worst stress of the insurrection fell, could only communicate with his outlying troops by taking circular tours at the head of a force of several thousand men. Sometimes he found, instead of the post which he had intended to visit, only a ruined village full of corpses.

Ere the Galician rising was three months old, the bands had
become bold and skilful enough to cut off a strong detachment
or to capture a place held by a garrison several hundreds strong.
In June they actually stopped the Marshal himself, with a whole
division at his back, in his attempt to march from Santiago
to recapture Vigo.

But these times were still far in the future: and when, on
February 17, Soult started on his march along the Minho from
Tuy to Orense, the peasantry were far from being the formidable
opponents that they afterwards became.   Nevertheless, the
progress of the 2nd Corps was toilsome and slow in the extreme.
The troops had been divided between two paths, of which the
so-called high-road, a mile or two from the river, was only
a trifle less impracticable than the rougher path along the
water's edge. Lahoussaye's dragoons had been put upon the
latter track ; Heudelet's infantry division led the advance on
the upper road.   All day long the march was harassed by the
insurgents, who descended from the hills and hung on the left
flank of Heudelet's column, delivering partial attacks whenever
they thought that they saw an opportunity.   The French
advanced with difficulty, much incommoded by the need of
dragging on their cannon, which could hardly be got forward
even with the aid of the infantry. Lahoussaye, on the other
path, was assailed in a similar way, besides being molested by
the Portuguese, who moved parallel to him on the south side
of the Minho, taking long shots at his dragoons wherever the
path was close enough to the water's edge to be within range
of their own bank.   If the peasantry had confined themselves to
these tactics, they might have harassed Soult at small cost
to themselves.   But they had not yet fully learnt the guerrilla's
trade.   At Mourentan on the path by the river, and at
Francelos on the high-road, they had resolved to offer direct
resistance to the enemy, and so put themselves within reach
of the invader's claws. At each place they had barricaded the
village, had run a rough entrenchment across the road, and
stood to receive the frontal shock of the French attack.   They
were, of course, routed with great slaughter when they thus
exposed themselves in close combat : several hundred perished,
among whom were many of their clerical leaders.   Thus Soult

was able to push on and occupy Rivadavia, which he found evacuated by its inhabitants. His soldiery had sacked and burnt all the villages on the way, and (according to the Spanish narratives) shot all adult males whom they could catch, whether found with arms or not [1].

On the eighteenth, having cut his way as far as Rivadavia, the Duke of Dalmatia came to the conclusion that it was hopeless to endeavour to carry on with him his heavy artillery and his baggage. On such roads as he had been traversing, and amid the continual attacks of the insurgents, they would be of more harm than use. In all probability they would ere long fall so far behind that, along with their escort, they would become separated from the army, and perhaps fall into the hands of the Spaniards. Accordingly he sent orders to the rear of the column that Merle's division should conduct back to Tuy all the heavy baggage and thirty-six guns of large calibre. Only twenty pieces, mostly four-pounders, were to follow the expedition. When the wagons had been turned back, there were only pack-horses and mules sufficient to carry 3,000 rounds for the guns, and 500,000 cartridges for the infantry. This was a dangerously small equipment for an army which had a whole kingdom to conquer, and which was forced to waste many shots every day on keeping off the irrepressible insurgents. But Soult was determined that he should not be accused of shrinking from the task imposed on him, or allowing himself to be thwarted by bands of half-armed peasants.

The heavy guns and the train, therefore, were deposited at Tuy, along with the large body of sick and wounded who had already been left there. General Lamartinière, an officer in whom Soult placed much confidence, was left in command. He was warned that he would have to take care of himself, as his communication with the army would be cut the moment that

---

[1] Long details of all this fighting may be found in the narrative of the Alcalde of Rivadavia, on pp. 130–44 of vol. ii. of *Los Guerrilleros Gallegos*. The details are probably exaggerated, but the reader can hardly refuse to believe that there is a solid substratum of truth. The Alcalde notes that the infantry were far better behaved than Lahoussaye's dragoons, of whom he tells tales of quite incredible ferocity, even alleging that they burnt the wounded.

Merle's troops resumed their march to join the rear of the advancing column. Nor did Soult err in this : when the 2nd Corps had gone on its way, Tuy and the neighbouring post of Vigo were immediately beset by a thick swarm of peasants, who kept them completely blockaded.

Having thus freed himself from every possible incumbrance, the Duke of Dalmatia pushed briskly on for Orense and its all-important bridge. The insurgents had not fallen back very far, and on the nineteenth Heudelet's division had two smart engagements with them, and drove them back to Masside, in the hills to the left of the road. The valley was here wider and the route better than on the previous day, and much more satisfactory progress was made. On the twentieth, still pushing on, Soult found that the ferry of Barbantes, ten miles below Orense, was passable. The Galicians had scuttled the ferry-boat in an imperfect fashion : some voltigeurs crossed on a raft, repaired the boat, and set it working again. Soult then pushed across the river some of Mermet's battalions, intending to send them to Orense by the south bank, if it should be found that the bridge was broken. Meanwhile Heudelet continued to advance by the road on the north side : his column arrived at its goal, and found Orense undefended and its bridge intact. The townsfolk made no attempt to resist : they had not left their dwellings like the peasants, and their magistrates came out to surrender the place in due form. They appealed to Soult's clemency, by showing him that they had kept safe and properly cared for 136 sick French soldiers, left behind by Marchand when he had marched through the town in the preceding month.

Where, meanwhile, it will be asked, was the army of La Romana ? The Marquis had now 9,000 men collected at Oimbra and Monterey, and it might have been expected that he would have moved forward to defend the line of the Minho and the bridge of Orense, as soon as he heard of the eastward march of the 2nd Corps. He made no such advance : his dispatches show that the sole precautions which he took were to send some officers with fifty men to aid the peasants of the lower Minho, and afterwards to order another party, only 100 strong, to make sure that the ferry-boats between Tuy and

Orense were all destroyed or removed—a task which (as we have already seen) they did not fully perform. If he had brought up his whole force, instead of sending out these paltry detachments, he would have made the task of Soult infinitely more bloody and dangerous, though probably he could not have prevented the Marshal from carrying out his plan. His quiescence is not to be explained as resulting from a reluctance to fight, though he was fully conscious of the low *morale* of his army, and was at his wits' end to complete its dilapidated equipment. It came from another cause, and one much less creditable to his military capacity. Underrating Soult's force, which he placed at 12,000 instead of 22,000 men, he was labouring under the idea that the 2nd Corps was about to retire from Galicia altogether, in face of the general insurrection and the want of food. The march of the French to Orense appeared in his eyes as the first stage of a retreat up the valley of the Sil to Ponferrada and Astorga, and he imagined that the province would soon be quit of them. Hence he contented himself with stirring up the peasantry, and left to them the task of harassing Soult's columns, being resolved to make the proverbial 'bridge of gold' for a flying enemy. From this vain dream he was soon to be awakened.

From the 21st to the 24th of February the Duke of Dalmatia was busily employed in bringing up the rear divisions of his army to Orense. None of them reached that place without fighting, for the bands which had been driven off by Heudelet and Lahoussaye returned to worry the troops of Delaborde, Merle, and Mermet, when they traversed the route from Salvatierra to Orense. Jardon's brigade of the last-named division had a sharp fight near Rivadavia, and Merle had to clear his way at Crecente by cutting to pieces a body of insurgents which had fortified itself in that village. When the whole army was concentrated between Rivadavia and Orense, the Marshal sent out large detachments to sweep the valleys in the immediate neighbourhood of those places. They found armed peasantry in every direction, but in each case succeeded in thrusting them back into their hills, and returned to Orense driving before them large herds of cattle, and dragging behind them country wagons with a considerable amount of grain. The longest and

most important of these expeditions was one made by Franceschi, who marched, with his own horsemen and one of Heudelet's brigades, along the road which the whole army was destined
to take in its invasion of Portugal. They routed one band of
peasants at Allariz, and another at Ginzo, half way to Monterey
[February 23]. Still there was no sign of La Romana's army,
which remained behind the mountains of the Sierra Cabrera in
complete quiescence, though Franceschi's advanced posts were
only twenty miles away [1].

Soult kept his head quarters at Orense for nine days, during
which he was busied in collecting stores of food, repairing his
artillery, whose carriages had been badly shaken by the villain-
ous roads, and in endeavouring to pacify the country-side by
proclamations and circular letters to the notables and clergy. In
this last scheme he met with little success ; from the bishop of
Orense downwards almost every leading man had taken refuge
in the hills, and refused to return. Silence or defiant replies
answered the Marshal's epistolary efforts. His promises of protection and good government were sincere enough; but the
commentary on them was given by the excesses and atrocities
which his troops were committing in every outlying village. It
was not likely that the Galicians would come down from their
fastnesses to surrender [2].

The general advance of the army towards Portugal had been
fixed for March 4. It was not made under the most cheerful
conditions. Not only were the neighbouring peasantry still
defiant as ever, but bad news had come from the north. An
aide-de-camp of Marshal Ney, who had struggled through to
Orense in despite of the insurgents, brought a letter from his
chief, which reported that the rising had become general
throughout the province, and apparently expressed strong

[1] Le Noble says (p. 96) that at Ginzo the peasants had with them General
Mahy and La Romana's vanguard division. But General Arteche gives
documentary evidence (p. 347) to prove that on that day Mahy and his
troops were at Baltar, twenty miles away behind the mountains. If there
were regulars present they were only detachments or stragglers.

[2] For the bishop of Orense's sarcastic reply see Arteche, v. 351. For
the general effect of the proclamation see St. Chamans : of the atrocities
of the French, *Los Guerrilleros Gallegos* give ample and sometimes incredible
accounts.

doubts as to the wisdom of invading Portugal before Galicia
was subdued. The Duke of Elchingen, as it would seem,
wished his colleague to draw back, and to aid him in suppressing
the bands of the coast and the upper Minho [1]. He might well
doubt whether the 6th Corps would suffice for this task, if the
2nd Corps marched far away towards Oporto, and got completely
out of touch. Soult, however, had the Emperor's orders to
advance into Portugal in his pocket. He knew that if he
disobeyed them no excuse would propitiate his master. Probably he was not sorry to leave to Ney the unenviable task of
dealing with the ubiquitous and irrepressible Galician insurgents. He sent back the message that he should march southward on March 4, and continued his preparations. This resolve
was not to the liking of some of his subordinates : many of the
officers who had served with Junot in Portugal by no means
relished the idea of returning to that country. They did not
conceal their feelings, and made the most gloomy prophecies
about the fate of the expedition. It was apparently Loison
who formed the centre of this clique of malcontents : he found
many sympathizers among his subordinates. Their discontent
was the basis upon which, two months later, the strange and
obscure ' Oporto Conspiracy ' of Captain D'Argenton was to be
based. At the present moment, however, they contented
themselves with denunciations of the madness of the Emperor
in planning the expedition, and of the blind obedience of the
Marshal in undertaking it. They told their comrades that the
numbers, courage, and ferocity of the Galicians were as nothing
compared with those of their southern neighbours, and that
during the oncoming operations those who found a sudden
death upon the battle-field would be lucky, for the Portuguese
not only murdered but tortured the prisoners, the wounded,
and the stragglers. It was fortunate for Soult that the majority
of his officers paid comparatively little attention to these fore-
bodings, which they rightly ascribed to the feelings of resentment and humiliation with which the members of Junot's army
remembered the story of their former disasters [2]. But it did

[1] See Le Noble (p. 98) for this dispatch and its effect on the *morale* of
the army.

[2] For the malcontents and their views see Le Noble, pp. 98–9. St. Chamans,

not make matters easier for the Marshal that even a small section of his lieutenants disbelieved in the feasibility of his undertaking, and expected disaster to ensue. Yet the opening scenes of the invasion of Portugal were to be so brilliant and fortunate, that for a time the murmurs of the prophets of evil were hushed.

On March 4 the Marshal's head quarters were moved forward from Orense to Alariz, on the road to Monterey and the frontier. The main body of the army accompanied him, but Franceschi and Heudelet were already far in front at Ginzo, only separated from La Romana's outposts by the Sierra Cabrera. From that point there are two difficult but practicable roads[1] into Portugal: the one descends the valley of the Lima and leads to Oporto by Viana and the coast. It is easier than the second or inland route, which after crossing the Sierra Cabrera descends to Monterey and Chaves, the frontier town of the Portuguese province of Tras-os-Montes. But every military reason impelled Soult to choose the second alternative. By marching on Viana he would leave La Romana, whose presence he had now discovered, far in his rear. The Marquis would be a bad general indeed if he did not seize the opportunity of slipping back into Galicia, reoccupying Orense, and setting the whole country-side aflame. It was infinitely preferable to fall upon him from the front, rout him, and fling him back among the Portuguese. Accordingly Franceschi, leading the whole army, crossed the mountains on the fifth, and came hurtling into La Romana's cantonments long ere he was expected. Heudelet was just behind him, Mermet and Delaborde a march further back : Merle brought up the rear, guarding a convoy of 800 sick and wounded whom the Marshal had resolved to bring on with him, rather than to leave them at Orense to fall a prey to the insurgents. The dragoons of Lorges and Lahoussaye were kept out on the right and left

on the other hand (p. 119), says that the army started in good spirits and with a great contempt for all insurgents, Spanish or Portuguese. As a trusted staff officer of the Marshal, he no doubt represents the optimistic view at head quarters.

[1] There was also a third road, that by Montalegre and Ruivaens, by which Soult ultimately evacuated Portugal ; but as it was not available for wheeled traffic, it could not be used by an army with artillery.

respectively, watching the one the valley of the Lima, the other the head waters of the Tamega.

Down to the last moment the Marquis had been giving out his intention of retiring into Portugal and co-operating with General Silveira, the commandant of the Tras-os-Montes, in the defence of Chaves and the line of the Tamega. But he was on very strained terms with his ally, who showed no great alacrity to receive the Spaniards across the frontier : his troops had been quarrelling with the Portuguese, and he was very reluctant to expose his half-rallied battalions to the ordeal of a battle, which Silveira openly courted.

On the very day on which Soult started from Orense, La Romana made up his mind that, instead of joining the Portuguese, he would escape eastwards by the single road, over and above that of Chaves, which was open to him. Accordingly his army suddenly started off, abandoning the meagre magazines which it had collected at Oimbra and Verin, and made for Puebla de Senabria, on the borders of the province of Leon, by the road which coasts along the north side of the Portuguese frontier, through Osoño and La Gudina. This sudden move bore the appearance of a mean desertion of the Portuguese in their day of peril : but it was in other respects wise and prudent. It discomfited all Soult's plans, since he failed to catch the army of Galicia, which escaped him and placed itself on his flank and rear instead of on his front. It was small consolation to the Marshal that Franceschi came on the rearguard of the Spaniards at La Trepa near Osoño and routed it. Seven skeleton regiments, only 1,200 bayonets in all, under General Mahy, were caught retiring along a hillside and completely ridden down by the French cavalry. Three standards and 400 prisoners were captured, 300 men more were killed, the rest dispersed. But La Romana's main body, meanwhile, had got away in safety, and Soult had failed to strike the blow which he intended [1]. He was soon to

[1] Compare the narrative of the colonel of the Barcelona Light Infantry, printed by Arteche in v. 359–61 of his *Guerra de la Independencia,* with the highly-coloured account in Le Noble, 104–5. The seven Spanish Corps engaged were Segovia, Zamora, Barcelona, Majorca, Orense, Betanzos, Aragon. None of them had more than 200 bayonets in line : the Galician regiments far less. The three last-named corps lost a flag each. [Betanzos should be substituted for Tuy in the list in Le Noble, p. 105, line 10.]

hear of the Marquis again, in quarters where he little expected and still less desired to find him [1].

Meanwhile the Portuguese were left alone to bear the brunt of the attack of the 2nd Corps.   It is time to relate and explain their position, their resources, and their designs.

[1] Napier (ii. 47) is wrong in saying that La Romana escaped via Braganza ; he did not enter Portugal, but kept on his own side of the frontier, on the Monterey-La Gudina-Puebla de Senabria road.

SECTION XIII: CHAPTER II

PORTUGAL AT THE MOMENT OF SOULT'S INVASION: THE NATION, THE REGENCY, AND SIR JOHN CRADOCK

Soult's vanguard crossed the Portuguese frontier between Monterey and Chaves on March 9, 1809 : it was exactly five months since the last of Junot's troops had evacuated the realm on October 9, 1808. In the period which had elapsed between those two dates much might have been done to develop —or rather to create—a scheme of national defence and a competent army. Unhappily for Portugal the Regency had not risen to the opportunity, and when the second French invasion came upon them the military organization of the realm was still in a state of chaos.

During the autumn months of 1808 the Portuguese Government had been almost as sanguine and as careless as the Spanish Supreme Junta. They had seen Junot beaten and expelled : they still beheld a large British army in their midst ; and they did not comprehend the full extent of the impending danger, when the news came that Bonaparte was nearing the Pyrenees, and that the columns of the ' Grand Army ' were debouching into the Peninsula. It was not till Moore had departed that they began to conceive certain doubts as to the situation : nor was it till Madrid had fallen that they at last realized that the invader was once more at their gates, and that they must prepare to defend themselves.

There were still two months of respite granted to them. Portugal—like Andalusia—was saved for a moment by Moore's march to Sahagun. The great field army which Napoleon had collected for the advance on Lisbon was turned off northwards to pursue the British, and on the New Year's day of 1809 the only French force in proximity to the frontier of the realm was the division of Lapisse, which Bonaparte had dropped at

Salamanca to form the connecting link between Soult and Ney in Galicia, and the troops under Victor and King Joseph in the vicinity of Madrid.

But the danger was only postponed, not averted, by Moore's daring irruption into Old Castile. This the Portuguese Regency understood; and during the first two months of 1809 they displayed a considerable amount of energy, though it was in great part energy misdirected. Their chief blunder was that instead of straining every nerve to complete their regular army, on which the main stress of the invasion was bound to fall, they diverted much of their zeal to the task of raising a vast *levée en masse* of the whole able-bodied population of the realm. This error had its roots in old historical memories. The deliverance of Portugal from the Spanish yoke in the long war of independence in the seventeenth century, had been achieved mainly by the *Ordenanza*, the old constitutional force of the realm, which resembled the English *Fyrd* of the Middle Ages. It had done good service again in the wars of 1703–12, and even in the shorter struggle of 1762. But in the nineteenth century it was no longer possible to reckon upon it as a serious line of defence, especially when the enemy to be held back was not the disorderly Spanish army but the legions of Bonaparte. When there were not even arms enough in Portugal to supply the line-battalions with a musket for every man, it was insane to summon together huge masses of peasantry, and to make over to them some of the precious firearms which should have been reserved for the regulars. The majority, however, of the *Ordenanza* were not even supplied with muskets, they were given pikes—weapons with which their ancestors had done good service in 1650, but which it was useless to serve out in 1809. The Regency had procured some 17,000 [1] from the British Government, and had caused many thousands more to be manufactured. Both on the northern and the eastern frontier great hordes of country-folk, equipped with these useless and antiquated arms, were gathered together. Destitute of discipline and of officers, insufficiently supplied with food, the prey of every rumour, true or false, that ran along the border, they were a source of danger

[1] List of Arms sent to Portugal on p. 9 of *Parliamentary Papers* for 1809.

rather than of strength to the realm. The cry of 'treachery,'
which inevitably arises among armed mobs, was always being
raised in their encampments. Hence came tumults and murders,
for the peasantry had a strong suspicion of the loyalty of the
governing classes—the result of the subservience to the French
invader which had been displayed by many of the authorities,
both civil and military, in 1808. Orders which they did not
understand, or into which a sinister meaning could be read by
a suspicious mind, generally caused a riot, and sometimes the
assassination of the unfortunate commander whom the Regency
had placed over the horde. In Oporto the state of affairs was
particularly bad : the bishop, though a sincere patriot and
a man of energy, had drunk too deeply of the delights of
power during his rule in the summer months. After being
made a member of the Regency by Dalrymple, he should have
remained at Lisbon and worked with his colleagues. But
returning to his own flock, he reassumed the authority which
he had possessed during the early days of the insurrection, and
pursued a policy of his own, which often differed from that of
his Regency at large, and was sometimes in flagrant opposition
to it. His position, in fact, was similar to that of Palafox at
Saragossa, and like the Aragonese general he often practised the
arts of demagogy in order to keep firm his influence over the
populace. He was all for the system of the *levée en masse* ;
and summoned together unmanageable bands which he was able
neither to equip nor to control. He praised their zeal, was
wilfully blind to their frequent excesses, and seldom tried to
turn their energies into profitable channels. Indeed, he was so
ignorant of military matters himself, that he had no useful
orders to give. He ignored the advice of the Portuguese
generals in his district, and got little profit from that of two
foreign officers whom the British Government sent him—the
Hanoverian General Von der Decken and the Prussian Baron
Eben. These gentlemen he seems to have conciliated, and to
have played off against the native military authorities. But if
they gave him good counsel, there are no signs in his actions that
he turned it to account. All the British witnesses who passed
through Oporto in January and February 1809, describe the
place as being in a state of patriotic frenzy, and under mob law

rather than administered by any regular and legal government[1]. The only fruitful military effort made in this part of Portugal was that of the gallant Sir Robert Wilson, who raised there in November and December his celebrated 'Loyal Lusitanian Legion.' This was intended to be the core of a subsidiary Portuguese division in British pay, distinct from the national army. When Wilson arrived in Oporto the bishop welcomed him, and forwarded in every way the formation of the corps. In a few days the Legion had 3,000 recruits of excellent quality, of whom Wilson could arm and clothe only some 1,300, for the equipment which he had brought with him was limited. He soon discovered, however, that the bishop's zeal in his behalf was mainly due to the desire to have a solid force at hand which should be independent of the Portuguese generals. He wished the Legion to be, as it were, his own body-guard. Sir Robert was ill pleased, and being unwilling to mix himself in the domestic feuds of the bishop and the Regency, or to become the tool of a faction, quitted Oporto as soon as his men could march. With one strong battalion, a couple of squadrons of cavalry, and an incomplete battery—under 1,500 men in all— he moved first to Villa Real (Dec. 14), and then to the frontier, where he posted himself near Almeida and took over the task of observing Lapisse's division, which from its base at Salamanca was threatening the Portuguese border. Of his splendid services in this direction we shall have much to tell. The unequipped portion of the Legion, left behind at Oporto, was handed over to Baron Eben, and became involved in the tumultuous and unhappy career of the bishop[2].

Meanwhile Lisbon was almost as disturbed as Oporto, and might have lapsed into the same state of anarchy, if a British garrison had not been on the spot. The mistaken policy of the

---

[1] The Portuguese volume for December 1808 and January–February 1809 in the Record Office being mysteriously lost, Cradock's correspondence and that of the other British officers in Portugal is no longer available. But Napier took copious notes from it, while it was still forthcoming; they will be found on pp. 425–31 of his vol. ii, and bear witness to a complete state of anarchy in Oporto.

[2] The first battalion used to call the second 'Baron Eben's runaways' when they met again, as Mayne assures us in his *History of the Loyal Lusitanian Legion*.

Regency had led to the formation of sixteen so-called 'legions[1]' in the capital and suburbs. These tumultuary levies had few officers and hardly any arms but pikes. They were under no sort of discipline, and devoted themselves to the self-imposed duty of hunting for spies and '*Afrancesados*.' Led by demagogues of the streets, they paraded up and down Lisbon to beat of drum, arresting persons whom they considered suspicious, especially foreign residents of all nationalities. The Regency having issued a decree prohibiting this practice [January 29], the armed levies only assembled in greater numbers next night, and engaged in a general chase after unpopular citizens, policemen, and aliens of all kinds. Many fugitives were only saved from death by taking refuge in the guard-houses and the barracks where the garrison was quartered. Isolated British soldiers were assaulted, some were wounded, and parties of 'legionaries' actually stopped aides-de-camp and orderlies carrying dispatches, and stripped them of the documents they were bearing. The mob was inclined, indeed, to be ill-disposed towards their allies, from the suspicion that they were intending to evacuate Lisbon and to retire from the Peninsula. They had seen the baggage and non-combatants left behind by Moore put on ship-board; early in February they beheld the troops told off for the occupation of Cadiz embark and disappear. When they also noticed that the forts at the Tagus mouth were being dismantled[2] they made up their minds that the British were about to desert them, without making any attempt to defend Portugal. Hence came the malevolent spirit which they displayed. It died down when their suspicions were proved unfounded by the arrival of Beresford and other British officers, at the beginning of March, with resources for the reorganization of the Portuguese army, and still more when a little later heavy reinforcements from England began to pour into the city. But in the last days of January and the first of February matters at

---

[1] They were raised by a decree of Dec. 23, 1808.

[2] This was a proper precaution, as the sea-forts could be of no use for defending Lisbon from a land attack, while, if Lisbon got into French hands again, they would have been invaluable for resisting an attack from the side of the sea. But Cradock was far too precipitate in commencing an operation which betrayed such want of confidence.

Lisbon had been in a most dangerous and critical condition :
the Regency, utterly unable to keep order, had hinted to Sir
John Cradock that he must take his own measures against the
mob, and for several days the British general had kept the
garrison under arms, and planted artillery in the squares and
broader streets—exactly as Junot had done seven months before.
The 'legions' were cowed, and most fortunately no collision
occurred : if a single shot had been fired in anger, there would
have been an end of the Anglo-Portuguese alliance, and it is
more than likely that Cradock—a man of desponding tempera-
ment—would have abandoned the country.

His force at this moment was by no means large : when Moore
marched for Salamanca in October he had left behind in Portugal
six battalions of British and four of German infantry [1], three
squadrons of the 20th Light Dragoons (the regiment that had
been so much cut up at Vimiero), one of the 3rd Light Dragoons
of the King's German Legion, and five batteries, only one of
which was horsed. From Salamanca, when on the eve of starting on the march to Sahagun, Sir John had sent back two
regiments to Portugal, in charge of his great convoys of sick
and heavy baggage [2]. To compensate for this deduction from his
army he had called up a brigade of the troops left in Portugal ;
but only one battalion of it—the 82nd—reached him in time to
join in his Castilian campaign [3]. The net result was that seven
British infantry regiments from Moore's army were left behind,
in addition to the four German corps. Two more had arrived
from England in November [4], and a fresh regiment of dragoons
in December [5].

Thus when Sir John Cradock took over the command at

---

[1] These were the 2/9th, 29th, 1/40th, 1/45th, 82nd, 97th, and 1st, 2nd,
5th, and 7th line battalions of the King's German Legion.

[2] The 1/3rd and 5/60th. The last battalion was mainly composed of
foreigners, and had received more than 200 recruits from the deserters of
Junot's army. Moore would not trust it, and sent it back. It afterwards
did splendid service under Wellesley.

[3] The battalions that did not get up in time were the 1/45th and 97th.

[4] These were the 3/27th and 2/31st, which had sailed with Baird from
Portsmouth, but were sent on from Corunna to Lisbon when the rest
of Baird's expedition landed in Galicia.

[5] The 14th Light Dragoons.

Lisbon on December 14, 1808, he had at his disposal in all thirteen battalions of infantry, seven squadrons of cavalry, and five batteries, a force of about 12,000 men [1]. But not more than 10,000 were effective, for Sir John Moore had left behind precisely those of his regiments which were most sickly, when he marched for Spain. He had moreover discharged more than 2,000 additional sick upon Portugal ere he began field operations: they were encumbering the hospitals of Almeida and Lamego when Cradock appeared. The 10,000 men fit for service were scattered all over Portugal: the two battalions, which had just come back from Spain, and the two others which had been too late to join Moore, were in the north, at Almeida and Lamego [2]. One battalion was in garrison at Elvas [3]. Six lay in Lisbon, as also did the whole of the cavalry and guns [4]: two were on the march from Abrantes to Almeida [5].

Such a dispersion of forces would have appalled the most enterprising of generals, and this was a title to which Cradock had certainly no claims. The two obvious courses between which he had to choose, were either to concentrate his little army on the frontier and make as much display of it in the face of the French as might be possible, or to abandon all idea of protecting exterior Portugal, and collect the scattered regiments in or about Lisbon. Cradock chose the second alternative. He argued that he was too weak to be of any effectual service on the frontier, and moreover found that there would be a vast difficulty in moving forward even the Lisbon garrison, for nearly all the available transport had been requisitioned for the use of Moore's army, and had been carried off into Spain. Neither of these pleas is convincing: with regard to the first, it is merely necessary to point out that Sir Robert Wilson, with 1,500 men of the Lusitanian Legion, not yet three months old, made his

---

[1] Napier (ii. 5) much under-estimates when he calls the whole ' 10,000 including sick.' Cradock's regiments add up to about 12,133 men including those in hospital. In addition there were all Moore's sick, who, though many had died in the interim, presented on Feb. 18 in Portugal convalescents to the number of 2,000 men.

[2] The 1/3rd, 1/45th, 5/60th, and 97th.

[3] The 1/40th.

[4] The four German battalions, the 3/27th and 2/31st.

[5] The 2/9th and 29th.

presence felt on the frontier, checked Lapisse, and kept the whole province of Salamanca in a state of unrest. Ten thousand British bayonets and sabres could have done much more. As to the food and supplies, Cradock was arguing in the old eighteenth-century style, as if a British army was bound to move with all .its baggage and impedimenta, its women and children. If he had chosen to 'march light,' and to take the route through the fertile and well-peopled Estremadura, he could have reached Abrantes or Almeida or any other goal that he chose.

The fact was that the reasons for refusing to adopt a 'forward policy' were moral and not physical. Cradock, in common with Sir John Moore and many other British officers, believed that Portugal could not be defended, and was thinking more of securing himself a safe embarkation than of exercising any influence on the main current of the war.

When Moore's army had passed out of sight, and was known to be retiring in the direction of Galicia, it seemed to Cradock that his own position was hopeless. Even if granted time to concentrate his scattered battalions, he would be forced to fly to the sea and take shipping the moment that any serious French force crossed the frontier. He had not sufficiently accurate information to enable him to see that both Lapisse at Salamanca, and the weak divisions of the 4th Corps which lay in the valley of the Tagus, could not possibly move forward against him. It would have been insane for either of these forces to have attacked Portugal—the one was at this moment less than 10,000, the other about 12,000 strong—they were without communications, and separated by 100 miles of pathless sierras. Moreover the troops in the valley of the Tagus were fully occupied in observing the Spanish army of Estremadura. At the opening of the New Year, therefore, Cradock was in absolutely no danger, and might have gone forward either to Abrantes or to Almeida in perfect security. In the first position he would have menaced the flank of the 4th Corps: in the second he would have exercised a useful pressure on Lapisse. In either case he would have encouraged the Portuguese and lent moral support to the Spaniards.

But Cradock was possessed by that miserable theory which was so frequently expounded by the men of desponding mind

during the early years of the Peninsular War, to the effect that
Portugal was indefensible, and would have to be evacuated
whenever a strong French force approached its frontier [1]. It was
fortunate for England and for Europe that Wellesley had other
views. The history of the next three years was to show that
a British general could find something better to do than to pack
up his baggage and prepare to embark, whenever the enemy came
down in superior strength to the Portuguese border.

No doubt Cradock would have had to take to his transports
if the French had possessed on January 1, 1809, an army of
40,000 men available for the invasion of Portugal, and ready
to advance. They did not happen to own any such force;
and till he was certain that such a force existed, Cradock was
gravely to blame for ordering every British soldier to fall back
on Lisbon, and for openly commencing to destroy the sea-forts
of the capital. It is true that the dispatches which he received
from home gave him many directions as to what he was to do if
the enemy appeared in overpowering strength: he was to blow
up the shore batteries, destroy all military and naval stores, and
embark with the British troops and as many Portuguese as
could be induced to follow. But this was only to take place
'upon the actual approach of the enemy towards Lisbon in such
strength as may render all further resistance ineffectual [2].' To
commence these preparations when the nearest troops of the
enemy were at Salamanca and Almaraz was premature and
precipitate in the highest degree. Till the French began to
move, every endeavour should have been made to encourage
the Portuguese and to maintain a show—even if it were but
a vain show—of an intention to defend the frontier. If Lapisse

---

[1] Sir John Moore himself ventilated this view in a letter to Lord
Castlereagh from Salamanca, Nov. 25, 1808. It is this fact that explains
Napier's very tender treatment of Cradock, who quoted Moore as his
justifying authority. Moreover Cradock had been very obliging in placing
all his papers at Napier's disposal, a fact which prepossessed the historian
in his favour.

[2] Castlereagh to Cradock, Dec. 24, 1808. Napier makes on this the
curious remark that the ministry gave contradictory orders when they
told Cradock to make a show of preparation for resistance, yet to get
ready for embarkation if it should prove necessary.

had heard that Cradock was at Almeida he would have been
nailed down to Salamanca: if Victor had heard that he was at
Alcantara, or even at Abrantes, he would never have dared to
pursue Cuesta into southern Estremadura.

Cradock, however, drew into Lisbon every available man:
Brigadier Cameron, with the troops from Almeida and Oporto,
started back on a weary march from the north, via Coimbra,
bringing not only his own four battalions, but 1,500 convalescents and returned stragglers from Moore's army. Richard
Stewart, with the two battalions that had been at Abrantes,
also came in to the capital, and all the British troops were
concentrated by the beginning of February, save the 40th
regiment, which still lay at Elvas. Having thus got together
about 10,000 men, Cradock, with almost incredible timidity,
began to draw them back to Passo d'Arcos, a place behind
Lisbon near the mouth of the Tagus, from which embarkation
was easy. When Villiers, the British minister at Lisbon,
remonstrated with him on the deplorable political consequences
of assuming this ignoble position on the water's edge, Cradock
replied, "I must object to take up a 'false position,' say Alcantara,
or to occupy the heights in front of Lisbon, which would only
defend a certain position, and leave the remainder [of Portugal?]
to the power of the enemy, one which we must leave upon
his approach, and seek another, bearing the appearance of
flight, and yet not securing our retreat. The whole having
announced the intention of defending Lisbon, but giving up
that idea upon the approach of the enemy, for positions liable
to be turned on every side cannot be persevered in by an inferior
force."

On the day [February 15] upon which Cradock wrote this
extraordinary piece of English prose composition, whose grammar
is as astounding as its argument, the nearest French troops were
at Tuy in Galicia, Salamanca in Leon, and the bridge of Arzobispo on the central Tagus, points respectively 230, 250, and
240 miles distant from Lisbon as the crow flies, and infinitely
more by road. Further comment is hardly necessary.

At this moment Cradock might have had at his disposal
2,000 more British troops, but he had chosen to fall in with
Sir George Smith's hasty and unauthorized scheme for the

occupation of Cadiz [1], and had sent off to that port a whole brigade [2], under General Mackenzie. He also dispatched orders to Colonel Kemmis of the 40th to hand over Elvas to the Portuguese, and march to Seville. The battalion moved into Andalusia, and placed itself at the disposition of Mr. Frere, who found it as useless as the force which Smith had drawn off to Cadiz. It was several months before the 40th rejoined the army of Portugal.

Influenced by the remonstrances of Mr. Villiers, and somewhat comforted by the fact that the French armies had nowhere crossed the Portuguese frontier, Cradock was at last persuaded to give up his position at Passo d'Arcos; he fixed his head quarters at Lumiar, left 2,000 men in garrison at Lisbon, and cantoned the remainder of his army at Saccavem and other places a few miles in front of the city. This was better than leaving them on the sea-shore; but the move was no more than a miserable half measure. It was almost as indicative of an intention to depart without fighting as the retreat to Passo d'Arcos had been. In short, from January to the end of April the British army exercised no influence whatever on the military affairs of the Peninsula. Yet by March it was beginning to grow formidable in numbers: early in that month all the troops which had been drawn off to Cadiz were sent to Lisbon, and by the addition of seven good battalions to his corps [3] Cradock found himself at the head of over 16,000 men. There were but 800 effective cavalry, and of the six batteries only two, incredible as it may seem, were properly horsed, though three months had passed by since the general had begun his first complaints on this point [4]. But 16,000 British troops were a force not to be despised, and if Wellesley or some other competent officer had been in command, we cannot doubt that they would have been

---

[1] See p. 27.

[2] The 3/27th, 2/9th, 29th, and some small details of artillery, &c.

[3] Not only Mackenzie's brigade, but also Tilson's brigade, the 2/87th and 1/88th, and the stronger battalions of H. Campbell, which had gone Cadiz directly from England—the first battalions of the 2nd (Coldstream) and 3rd (Scots Fusilier) Guards.

[4] In a letter of March 20 to Mr. Villiers, Cradock makes the astounding statement that after scouring all Portugal for horses for three months, he was still unable to provide them for four out of his six batteries.

turned to some profitable use.   Under Cradock they remained
cantoned in the suburbs of Lisbon for the whole time during
which Soult was completing his conquest of Oporto and northern
Portugal, and Victor executing his invasion of Estremadura.   It
was not till Soult's advanced guard was on the Vouga [April 6]
that Hill and Beresford[1] succeeded in inducing the general to
carry forward his head quarters to Leiria and his outposts to
Thomar[2].   Fortunately his tenure of command was at last
drawing to an end.   On April 22 Sir Arthur Wellesley arrived
in Lisbon and took over charge of the troops in Portugal.   How
startling were the consequences of this change of generals we
shall soon see: ere May was out the whole Peninsula realized
once more that there was a British Army within its limits—a fact
that might well have passed unnoticed during the last four
months.

[1] Cradock's controversial letters to Lord Londonderry, printed in the
latter's history (ii. 286–7), do no more than bear out Londonderry's
accusations of torpidity against Sir John.

[2] Cradock contended that before the arrival of Hill and Sherbrooke
and the return of Mackenzie from Cadiz, he had only 10,225 men, and,
deducting sick and garrisons for the Lisbon forts, could only have marched
out with 5,221.   [Letter to Londonderry on p. 302, vol. ii. of the latter's
work.] He had sent 3,500 men to Cadiz and Seville, on Sir George Smith's
unhappy inspiration, or his force would have been much larger.   As to
the resolution to march against Soult, which he afterwards claimed to have
made, it is sufficient to say that Wellesley on his arrival wrote to
Castlereagh that 'Sir John Cradock does not appear to have entertained
any decided intention of moving forward : on the contrary he appears
(by his letters to Mr. Villiers) to have intended to go no further till he
should hear of Victor's movements.'   [*Well. Corresp.*, Lisbon, April 24.]

SECTION XIII : CHAPTER III

THE PORTUGUESE ARMY : ITS HISTORY AND ITS REORGANIZATION

WHILE the Regency was wasting much of its energy on the arming of the undisciplined masses of the *Ordenanza*, and while Cradock sat supine at Passo d'Arcos and at Saccavem, one useful piece of work at least was being taken in hand. This was the reorganization of the Portuguese regular army, a task which the Regency determined, though only so late as February, 1809, to hand over to a British general officer.

To explain the chaotic condition of the force at the moment when Soult was just about to enter Portugal, a short account of its previous history is necessary. It had received its existing shape from a foreign hand, that of the well-known 'Conde de La Lippe,' i. e. the German Marshal, Frederick Count of Lippe-Bückeburg, who had been entrusted with its command during the short war with Spain in 1762. He it was who first gave Portugal an army of the modern type, modelled on the ordinary system of the eighteenth century, and showing many traces of adaptations from a Prussian original. The Marshal was a great organizer and a man of mark : his name is perhaps best remembered in connexion with the citadel of Elvas, which he rebuilt, and christened La Lippe after himself : under that designation we shall repeatedly have to mention it while describing the early years of the Peninsular War.

As he left it, the Portuguese army consisted of twenty-four regiments of the line, each forming a single battalion of seven companies and 806 men. There were twelve regiments of cavalry, each originally composed of no more than 240 sabres, and three regiments of artillery of eight batteries each, besides a few garrison companies of that arm. After La Lippe's departure the army had shared in the general decay of strength and organization in the kingdom, which prevailed during the

reign of the mad queen Maria, and her son the feeble Prince-
Regent John. But the lack of mere numerical strength was
not nearly so fatal to its efficiency as the rustiness and rotten-
ness of its internal machinery. Under an octogenarian commander-in-chief, the Duke of Alafoens, every department of
the army had been decaying in the latter years of the eighteenth
century. All the typical faults of an army of the *ancien régime*
after a long period of peace were developed to the highest possible
pitch. Commissions were sold, or given away by intrigue and
corruption, often to persons of unsuitable rank and education [1] :
promotion was slow and perfectly arbitrary : the pay of the
officers was very low, while every incentive to petty jobbing
and embezzlement was afforded by the vicious system under
which the colonel contracted with the government for his
regiment, and the captain with the colonel for his company.
In the Portuguese army, as in all others where this antiquated
practice prevailed, the temptation to fill the muster-rolls with
'dead-heads' and absentees, so that the contractor might save
their food and pocket their pay, had been too strong for the
ordinary officer to resist. Hence came the empty ranks of
the battalions, the ludicrous disproportion of horses to men in

[1] All authorities agree as to the inferior character and status of a great
part of the Portuguese officers. Dumouriez remarks [1766] that ' their
pay does not enable them to live better than the common soldiers, whose
comrades and relatives they often are. The subaltern ranks are filled
from the inferior classes, and their hatred of foreigners prevents their
association with, or receiving any improvement from, them : hence it is
that they remain in such ignorance and wretchedness' (p. 17). Halliday
remarks (p. 106) that ' even captains had not the rank of gentlemen.'
Compare with this Patterson's curious note (vol. i. p. 250), ' The
familiarity that subsists between the native officers and their men renders
ineffective all the authority of the former, at the same time defeating
the object to be attained by discipline. They eat, gamble, and drink
together. I have even seen them waltzing and figuring off in the *contra-
danza*, captains with corporals, majors with drumboys—all Jack-fellows
well met, and excellent boon companions. They will not of themselves
do anything, their good qualities must be elicited by strangers. I know
of nothing that stamps the character of Lord Beresford as a man of energy
and perseverance, more than the way in which he has organized them,
and from a miserable undisciplined rabble produced, in course of time,
a fair body of fighting troops, who performed (encouraged by their English
officers) some spirited service during the war.'

the cavalry, the depleted condition of the regimental stores and equipment.

The short Spanish war of 1801–2 had revealed the complete disorganization of the army. Hasty measures were taken to strengthen it: in the moment of panic every infantry regiment was ordered to raise a second battalion, and though the number of companies per battalion was lowered from seven to five, yet as each of them was now to consist of 150 instead of 116 men, the total strength of each infantry corps was raised to 1,500 officers and men. At the same time the cavalry regiments were supposed to have been increased to 470 sabres [1], and a fourth regiment of artillery was created. Nor was this all: an 'Experimental Legion' for light infantry service, eight companies strong, with a couple of squadrons and a horse-artillery battery attached to it, was soon afterwards raised by the Marquis D'Alorna.

But after the peace of Badajoz had been signed the army was allowed to sink back into its old sloth and inefficiency. When Junot entered Portugal in December, 1807, it is doubtful if there were as many as 20,000 troops really embodied, though the nominal total of the national army reached nearly 50,000 men [2].

Portugal had a few keen soldiers (such as Gomez Freire de Andrade, and the renegade D'Alorna), who had received abroad a good military education, and had even written military books. But the majority of the officers were slack, ignorant, and incompetent; while the men were half-drilled, badly disciplined, and ill-equipped. The only attempt which had been made to introduce any of the modern military discoveries which had been worked out in the wars of the French Revolution,

---

[1] Of these, twelve squadrons were originally cuirassiers (Dumouriez, p. 18), but their armament had been discarded before 1800, and one regiment only was light horse.

[2] Twenty-four regiments of infantry of two battalions each 36,000

twelve regiments of cavalry at 470	5,640
four regiments of artillery at 989	3,956
ten garrison companies of artillery (veterans) . .	1,300
'Experimental Legion,' engineers, &c. . . .	1,500
Total	48,396

Halliday gives an even larger figure, 52,204.

Portuguese Infantry
a Private of the Lisbon Regiment and a man
of the Algarve Ordenanza.
From a drawing of 1809.

Walker & Cockerell Ph. Sc.

consisted in the creation of the already-mentioned 'Experimental Legion' which D'Alorna had been allowed to raise and to train with a new light-infantry drill, adapted by himself from French models. The main body of the army looked with some jealousy and suspicion on this corps, and had made no effort to copy it.

The French invasion of Portugal had dashed to pieces the old regular army. Junot, it will be remembered, had disbanded the greater part of the men, and formed with the remainder a few battalions, which he had begun to send off to France ere the insurrection of June, 1808, broke out. Some of them took an involuntary share in the first siege of Saragossa : others were hurled into the red holocaust of Wagram.

When Portugal rose against the invader, the local juntas endeavoured to call back to arms all the dispersed officers and men, to serve as a nucleus for the insurrectionary hosts. The system of recruiting which La Lippe had introduced made this comparatively easy : he had instituted regimental districts in a very complete form. Each corps was named after a particular town or region [1], drew its conscripts from that locality, and was usually quartered in it. When Junot disbanded the old army, the men naturally returned to their homes. It resulted that when, for example, the Oporto Junta summoned out to service the late members of the 6th and 18th regiments of the line, the two units belonging to the Oporto district, it could be certain of finding the greater part of the rank and file without much difficulty. To reconstitute in a hurry the corps of officers was a much harder matter : a disproportionate number of the more competent holders of commissions had been drafted into the contingent sent to France : comparatively few resided in their proper regimental districts, many in Lisbon, which was still in Junot's hands. Hence the battalions which fought under Leite at Evora, or accompanied Wellesley to Vimiero, bore their old names indeed, but were not merely ill-equipped and low in numbers, but lacked a due supply of officers. Considering the inefficiency of the regiments even before they were destroyed by Junot,

[1] Except two Lisbon regiments, named Viera Tellez and Freire, from former colonels of distinction [Nos. 4 and 16].

they might now be described as no more than 'the shadow of a shade.'

When the French had been driven out of Portugal, and the Junta of Regency took in hand the reconstruction and enlargement of the army, the problem of organization seemed almost insoluble. The government decreed that the regiments of infantry of the line should be raised to their full establishment of 1,500, a figure which they had never really attained in the old days. It was also decided to create six new battalions of riflemen (Cazadores), a class of infantry of which D'Alorna's 'Experimental Legion' had hitherto been the sole representatives in Portugal. As to the cavalry and artillery, it was an obvious fact that the dearth of horses in the kingdom made it impossible to enlarge the number of units. The twelve old regiments of horse[1], the thirty-two old batteries of artillery were to be reconstructed, but no new ones were to be created.

Considering that the old corps of officers in Portugal was notoriously incompetent, it was hard to see how the expanded army was to be drilled and disciplined. About 25,000 recruits were suddenly shot into the old *cadres*; they could be readily procured, for not only were volunteers forthcoming in great numbers, but if they ran short a stringent conscription law was in existence. But how were the regiments to be officered? It was true that a considerable amount of the raw material for officers was obtainable, for patriotic enthusiasm was driving the young men of the upper classes into the army, in a way that had never before been seen—the service had not hitherto been popular, owing to its poor pay and prospects. But one cannot officer raw recruits with equally raw ensigns, and call the result a regular army. Moreover, arms and equipment were lamentably deficient: Junot had confiscated and destroyed almost all the store of arms belonging to the old army: it is said that the insurgents had not 10,000 serviceable muskets among them when Wellesley landed. The British had distributed some 42,000 more between August and December[2]; but what were these among so many? There were to be over 50,000 regulars,

[1] It was intended, however, to give each cavalry regiment an extra squadron.

[2] *Parliamentary Papers*, 1809. Return No. 5, p. 9.

Portuguese Dragoon of the 1st (Alcantara) Regiment

From a drawing of 1809.

Walker & Cockerell Ph. Sc.

when the establishment was completed, and the Regency hoped to call out some 40,000 militia when the first line of defence had been equipped, and after that to arm the vast masses of the *Ordenanza*.

The natural results followed. In obedience to the decree issued by the Regency, a considerable number of men were collected at each regimental dépôt. Of these about one-third, on an average, were old soldiers : but the proportion varied, for some corps had suffered more than others from the drafts of trained men which Junot had sent off to France. A good many of the regiments succeeded, so far as numbers went, in constituting their two battalions without much difficulty. Others were less fortunate, and could only raise one : two were so hopelessly incomplete that Beresford distributed the few hundred men whom they could produce among other corps, and temporarily disbanded them [1]. It was the same with the cavalry, of which two regiments were wholly without horses, and several were so absurdly short of mounts that they could not be used [2]. Even of the corps which were not dissolved, several were so weak that they had not recruited themselves up to half their nominal strength even by September [3]. This was more especially the case in the Alemtejo, where the population displayed an apathy that contrasted strongly with the turbulent enthusiasm prevalent in Lisbon and in the North.

Two invaluable sets of Returns, in the Record Office, show us that, as far as mere numbers went, the Regency had not done so much as it should, in the way of increasing the total of men under arms, during the two months that followed the Convention of Cintra. On September 13, according to a report from Baron Decken, who had gone round the insurrectionary armies of Freire, Leite, and the Monteiro Mor, there were under arms 13,272 line infantry, 3,384 light infantry (Cazadores), 1,812 cavalry, and 19,000 militia : the force of artillery is not

---

[1] The 8th and 22nd, both Alemtejo regiments, were entirely drafted off, and were raised again afresh with recruits in the autumn.

[2] The 2nd and 3rd, both Alemtejo regiments, were never horsed during the whole war, and did foot-service in garrisons of the interior.

[3] In September the 3rd, 5th, 15th, 21st, and 24th had not raised their second battalions. Of these the 5th and 15th were Alemtejo regiments.

given. But of these 37,000 men only 13,600 had serviceable weapons and equipment, and were fit to take the field [1].

On November 26 these figures had risen to 22,361 infantry, 3,422 cavalry, 4,031 artillery, and 20,880 militia. But, owing to the importation of English muskets during the last two months, there were now 31,833 men properly equipped, of whom 2,052 were mounted men. The remaining 19,000 had still nothing more than pikes, or non-military firearms, such as fowling-pieces and blunderbusses : 1,400 cavalry were still without horses [2].

The figures are very moderate, but the worst part of the situation was that a collection of 1,000 or 1,500 men does not constitute a regiment, even if 300 or 400 of them chance to have been old soldiers. There were not, it is clear, muskets enough to arm more than two-thirds of the rank and file : belts, pouches, knapsacks, and other equipment were still more deficient. Yet the really fatal point was that there was a wholly inadequate number of officers, and that of those who were forthcoming the elder men were mostly incompetent, and the younger entirely untrained. In the official correspondence of the early months of 1809 the most prominent fact that emerges is the difficulty that was found in discovering colonels and majors capable of licking into shape the incoherent mass of men at the regimental head quarters, and of teaching the newly-appointed junior officers their duty. It seemed that their long peace-service in small garrison towns had taken all energy and initiative out of the seniors of the army of the *ancien régime*. They gazed with despair on the task before them, and seemed quite incapable of coping with it. When a British general took over the command of the Portuguese army, he complained that ' Long habits of disregard to duty, and consequent laziness, make it not only difficult but almost impossible to induce the senior officers of this service to enter into any regular and continued attention to the duties of their situations, and neither reward nor punishment will induce them to bear up against the fatigue [3].' It was only when a whole generation of colonels had been cleared away

---

[1] Report of Baron Decken, Sept. 13, 1808 (Record Office).
[2] Return of the Portuguese army, Nov. 26 (Record Office).
[3] Beresford to Wellesley, *Wellington Supplementary Dispatches*, vi. p. 774.

that the army grew efficient, and the reorganized regiments began to distinguish themselves in the field.

For the purpose of mobilization every regiment had been sent in the autumn of 1808 to its proper head quarters, in the centre of its recruiting district. There they still lay in the end of February, when Soult was drawing near the frontier. There was absolutely no Portuguese army in the field, only a number of battalions, squadrons, and batteries, in a more or less imperfect state of organization, scattered broadcast over the country. They were, as we have already seen, still insufficiently supplied with arms and equipment. Of transport and train, to enable them to move, there was hardly a trace. The only thing approaching a concentration of force was that in Lisbon and its immediate vicinity there were seven regiments of foot and three of horse, which were there assembled simply because their head quarters and their recruiting ground lay in this quarter[1]. Of the remainder of the infantry two regiments were in Algarve, in the far south ; five in the Alemtejo ; four in Beira ; two in the Tras-os-Montes, four in Oporto and the adjoining province of Entre-Douro-e-Minho. It was with the last six alone that Soult had to deal when he invaded northern Portugal[2] : not one of the others was moved up to aid the northern regiments in holding him back.

Impressed with the state of hopeless disarray in which their army lay, and conscious that for stores and weapons to equip it, and money to pay it, they could look only to Great Britain, the Regency asked in February for the appointment of a British commander-in-chief. This was the best pledge that they could give of their honest intention to place all their military resources at the disposition of their allies. It had another obvious advantage : Bernardino Freire, Leite, Silveira, the Monteiro Mor, and the other Portuguese generals commanding military

[1] These were the 1st, 4th, 7th, 10th, 13th, 16th, 19th of the line, and the 1st, 4th, and 7th cavalry. Of the foot the 1st, 4th, 10th, and 16th were Lisbon regiments, the 7th was named from and belonged to Setubal, the 13th to Peniche, the 19th to Cascaes.

[2] These were the 6th, 9th, 12th, 18th, 21st, and 24th. The 6th and 18th belonged to Oporto, the 9th to Viana, the 12th to Chaves, the 21st to Valenza, the 24th to Braganza.

districts were at feud with each other.   It would be very difficult
to place one above the rest, and to secure for him loyal co-operation from his subordinates.   It was probable that an Englishman,
a stranger to their quarrels and intrigues, would be better obeyed.

The Regency, it would seem, suggested that they would be
glad to see the post of commander-in-chief given to Sir Arthur
Wellesley.   But the victor of Vimiero refused to accept it,
probably because he had already secured from Lord Castlereagh
the promise that he should be sent out again to Portugal to
supersede Cradock.   When he had declined the offer it was, to
the surprise of most men, passed on to General Beresford.   This
officer had the advantage of knowing Portuguese ; he had commanded one of Moore's brigades during the Corunna retreat, and
had seen much service on both sides of the Atlantic.   He
was a comparatively young man, being only in his forty-first
year, and was very junior in his rank, having only become
a major-general in 1807.   Many officers who were his elders
had coveted the post, and some friction was caused by the fact
that with his new Portuguese commission he outranked several
of his seniors in Cradock's army.   Beresford was a good fighting-
man, and a hard worker ; but he was neither a tactician nor
a strategist, and did not shine when placed in independent
command—as witness Albuera.   When Wellington had learnt
his limitations, he never gave him a task of any great difficulty,
and in the later years of the war either kept him under his own
eye or sent him on errands where it was not easy to go wrong.
For really responsible work in 1812–14 he always used Hill, Hope,
or Graham.   But in 1809 Beresford was, but for his undoubted
courage, more or less of an unknown quantity to his colleagues
and his subordinates.   Fortunately he turned out a good
organizer, if a mediocre general.   For what he did in the way
of reforming, and almost recreating, the Portuguese army he
deserves considerable credit.   Every one will remember the
quaint story of how he was received by his army after a short
absence, with the ingenuous cry of ' Long live Marshal Beresford—who takes care of our stomachs [1].'   This in one way was
a high compliment—it was not every general, English, French,

---

[1] The same story is told of General Robert Craufurd and his cazadores,
in Costello's *Memoirs*.

or Spanish, who succeeded in filling his soldiers' bellies during the Peninsular War. The power to do so was not the least among the qualities necessary for a commander-in-chief.

Why the British cabinet chose Beresford, from among many possible candidates, for the very responsible post now put in his charge, it is hard to see. Castlereagh knew him, as being (like himself) one of a powerful Anglo-Irish family connexion, with strong parliamentary influence. This may have told in his favour: it was perhaps also remembered that he was a personal friend of Wellesley, whom Castlereagh was intending to send out to command the British army in Portugal, and moreover his junior. This would facilitate matters when the two generalissimos had to act together; Beresford would probably prove a more tractable colleague and subordinate to the self-confident, autocratic, and frigid Wellesley, than any officer who was a stranger to him or his senior in years and service. It is by no means impossible that Castlereagh nominated him at Sir Arthur's private suggestion. But into the secrets of ministerial patronage it is useless to pry.

Appointed to his new post in February, only a month after he had returned from the Corunna expedition, Beresford at once set sail for Lisbon, and took up the command ere three weeks had expired since his appointment. He arrived at the very moment at which Soult was about to pass the northern frontier, and was at once gazetted as a Portuguese field marshal. After a short survey of those parts of his command which lay in and about Lisbon, he reported to the Regency that the dearth of officers, and especially of competent superior officers, was so great, that he could not hope to reorganize the army unless he were allowed to give commissions in the Portuguese service to many foreigners. As a preliminary measure he asked for volunteers from Sir John Cradock's army, and obtained about enough English officers to give three to each regiment. The main inducement which attracted candidates was Beresford's pledge that every one accepted for the Portuguese service should gain a step—a lieutenant would become a captain, a captain a major. The Marshal at once placed all the battalions with notoriously inefficient commanders in charge of British officers, and drafted into them a larger proportion of his volunteers than was given

to those which were in better state. He also got leave from
the British cabinet to offer Portuguese commissions to officers
serving in corps on the home station. This gave him by the
end of the year some scores of men of the sort required, and it
was by them that the new army was mainly formed and
disciplined [1]. The British drill was introduced, and to teach it
Beresford was allowed to borrow many non-commissioned officers
from Cradock's regiments [2]. As was but natural, there arose
considerable friction between the new comers and the native
Portuguese officers, over whose heads they were often placed.
This was inevitable, but led to less harm than might have been
expected, because the rank and file, quick to recognize soldierly
qualities, took kindly to their new commanders, and served them
loyally and well.

In the beginning Beresford's reorganization only extended
to the regiments in Lisbon and the south. Those stationed
beyond the Douro were already in the field, and actively engaged
with Soult. They had hardly received any assistance, either of
officers or of arms and equipment, before they became involved
in the campaign of March, 1809 [3]. In fairness to them this
must be borne in mind, when their conduct in battle is compared
with that of the reorganized army in the following year. The
Portuguese Regency, in their report on the Oporto campaign
sent to their Prince on May 31, 1809, pleaded with truth 'that
the armies formed in the northern provinces were motley assemblies, whose numbers and good will bore witness to the zeal of
the people, and their determination not to accept the French
yoke, but which could not with any propriety be called regular
troops. They were composed of incomplete and fractional
regiments, and the larger proportion of the rank and file consisted of recruits, many of whom had not been a month under

---

[1] For notes on the difficulties and friction caused by clashing pretensions
of British and Portuguese seniority in rank, see *Wellington Dispatches*,
vol. iv. pp. 368-81, 394-5, and several other letters to Castlereagh and
Beresford.

[2] Largely from the 1/3rd foot. See *Wellington Dispatches*, vol. iv.
p. 463. Other regiments also contributed.

[3] A few British officers had arrived, such as Col. Patrick who commanded
the 12th of the line in Silveira's army.

arms. Some of the corps were short of muskets : those which had them were armed with weapons of bad quality [1], and various calibre. All were deficient in the most essential articles of equipment. It was not fair to expect that such troops could oppose with any prospect of success a well-armed and well-disciplined veteran army like that of France [2].'

The regular troops, and the totally undisciplined *Ordenanza* levies, did not form the whole military force of Portugal. There also existed, mainly on paper, another line of defence for the kingdom. This was the militia : according to the old military system of the realm each regimental district had to supply not only its line battalion, but also two (or sometimes one) battalions of militia. There should have been forty-three such regiments in existence in 1808, and early in 1809 the Regency ordered that they should be raised to forty-eight, and that each should consist of two battalions of 500 men each [3]. This force, however, was purely a paper army : the militia had not been called out since the war of 1802 ; there were a few officers bearing militia commissions, but no rank and file. When the Regency decreed its mobilization, all that could be done was that the local authorities should tell off such eligible young men as had not been embodied in the regular army, for militia recruits. But as there were neither officers to drill them, nor muskets to arm them, the conscription was but a farce. The men were not even called out in many districts, since it was useless to do so till arms could be procured for them. But in the two northern provinces, when Soult crossed the frontier, the militia-men took the field alongside with the *Ordenanza*, from whom they were distinguished by name alone, for they were almost as destitute of uniform, weapons, and officers as the *levée en masse* itself. It would seem that most of the other border regiments

---

[1] Some of the muskets sent by the British were in the hands of the Oporto troops, but none had reached the Tras-os-Montes regiments of Silveira's army.

[2] All this is analysed from the Portuguese historian Da Luz Soriano.

[3] For the local organization and nomenclature of the militia regiments, the reader is referred to the table of the Portuguese army in Appendix II. It will be seen that there were theoretically sixteen regiments in the provinces invaded by Soult, beyond the Douro.

of militia were also mobilized in the spring of 1809, in the neighbourhood of Almeida, Castello Branco, and Elvas. That they were perfectly useless was shown in Mayne's fight with Victor at the bridge of Alcantara (May 14), when their conduct contrasted shamefully with the steady and obstinate fighting of the Lusitanian Legion [1]. In June, Wellesley ordered that all men for whom there were no arms should be sent home on furlough, and that the regiments should endeavour to drill and exercise their men by relays of 200 at a time, each batch being kept two months under arms. This was apparently because there were not arms, officers, or drill-sergeants enough to provide for more than a small proportion of the available number of militia-men [2]. In this way between 8,000 and 10,000 militia were to be out during the times of the year when the country-side could best spare them from the labour of the fields. The rest were to be left at home, unless an actual invasion of Portugal should occur. From the modest scope of this plan, it may easily be guessed what the state of the militia had been four months earlier, when Soult was in the Tras-os-Montes, and Beresford had barely begun his work of reorganization.

The militia-men were supposed to provide their own uniforms, the result of which was that few save the officers ever owned uniforms at all. In 1810 Wellesley had to make formal representation to Masséna that they were part of the armed force of the Portuguese kingdom, and not banditti, as the Marshal threatened to deny the rights of regular combatants to any prisoners not wearing a military dress. The officers, however, had a blue uniform similar to that of the line, save that they had silver instead of gold lace on their collars and wrists. The militia were not entitled to any pay when mobilized within the limits of their own province. When taken over its border officers and men were supposed to draw half the pay of the regulars of corresponding rank, but did not find it easy to obtain the modest stipend to which they were entitled.

Throughout the war the Portuguese militia were only intermittently in the field : the longest continuous piece of service

---

[1] See Mayne, *History of the Loyal Lusitanian Legion,* p. 231, and *Wellington Dispatches,* vol. iv. p. 350.

[2] *Wellington Dispatches,* vol. iv. pp. 389–90 and 478 [June, 1809].

which they performed was that during Masséna's invasion, when they were all mobilized for more than a year on end, from June 1810 to July 1811. At other times, the whole or parts of various regiments were under arms for periods of varying length, either to relieve the regulars from garrison duty, or to watch the less-exposed frontier points in times when the French were active in the neighbouring districts of Spain. They were very seldom exposed to the ordeal of battle, as their presence in the line would have been a source of danger rather than a help. But they were useful for secondary work, such as guarding convoys, maintaining lines of communication, and (most of all) restraining minor raids by small bodies of the enemy. During Masséna's invasion the greater part of them were not drawn within the lines of Torres Vedras, like the Portuguese regulars, but left out in the country-side, to shift for themselves. Here they did invaluable service in cutting the Marshal's line of communication with Spain, and harassing all his detachments. It was they who surprised and captured his wounded and his dépôt at Coimbra, who worried Drouet, and who turned back Gardanne, when he tried to push forward from Almeida in order to join the main French army.

But all this was in the far future when the spring campaign of 1809 began. At that date, as we have already seen, the militia were as undisciplined, as ill-armed, and as useless as the mass of *ordenanza* levies, with which they were confused.

A word must be added as to the theoretical organization of this last force. It dated back to the Middle Ages, and had been regularly used during the days of the enfranchisement of Portugal from the yoke of the Spanish Hapsburgs, in the seventeenth century. The 'ordinance' was a Royal decree summoning to arms all males between sixteen and sixty with the exception of ecclesiastics. In districts owning a feudal lord, that person was ex-officio declared chief-captain (*capitão mor*) of his fief, and charged with the summoning of his vassals to the field. Where manorial customs had disappeared, the senior magistrate of the town, village, or district had to take up the post of *capitão mor*, unless a substitute was named by the crown. It was the duty of this commander to call out all the able-bodied men of his region, to divide them into companies of 250 men, and to name a captain, ensign, sergeant, clerk (*meirinho*), and ten corporals for each of these bodies. Persons able to provide a horse were to serve apart, as cavalry, under separate commanders; but no one ever saw or heard of mounted *ordenanza* troops during the Peninsular War; all the horses of the country did not suffice to provide chargers even for the twelve regiments of the regular army. The whole levy was supposed to be called out twice a year by the *capitão mor*, in order that it might be seen that every man was properly enrolled in a company. But as a matter of fact the *ordenanza* had not been summoned out, save in 1762 and 1802, since the end of the War of the Spanish Succession. Nor had any care been taken to see that every householder possessed a weapon of some sort, as the law directed. When they mustered in 1809, the men with pikes outnumbered those with fowling-pieces or blunderbusses, and the men furnished with no more than scythes on poles, or goads, or such-like rustic weapons, were far more numerous than the pikemen.

The whole mass was perfectly useless; it was cruel to place it in the field and send it against regular troops. Tumultuous, undisciplined, unofficered, it was doomed to massacre whenever it allowed the enemy to approach. It would have been well to refrain from calling it out altogether, and to turn over the few serviceable arms which it possessed to the militia.

NOTE.—By far the best account of the Portuguese army and military system is to be found in Halliday's *Present state of Portugal and the Portuguese Army*, an invaluable book of 1812. Something can be gleaned from Dumouriez's *Essay on the military topography of Portugal* [1766]. A little information comes from Foy, but many of his statements in his vol. ii. are inaccurate. The Wellington and Beresford dispatches in the Record Office are, of course, full of information, but would be very unintelligible but for Halliday's explanatory memoir, as they presuppose knowledge of the details of organization, but do not generally describe them. For the Lusitanian Legion, see Mayne's monograph on that corps, and the dispatches of Sir Robert Wilson. I have inserted in an appendix a table of the reorganized army as it stood in the autumn of 1809.

SECTION XIII: CHAPTER IV

COMBATS ABOUT CHAVES AND BRAGA: CAPTURE OF
OPORTO (MARCH 10-29, 1809)

WHEN La Romana marched off to the east, and abandoned
his Portuguese allies to their own resources, the duty of defending the frontier fell upon General Francisco Silveira, the military
governor of the Tras-os-Montes. He had mobilized his forces
at Chaves the moment that Soult's departure from Orense
became known, and had there gathered the whole levy of his
province. The total amounted to two incomplete line regiments[1]
four battalions of disorderly and ill-equipped militia[2], the
skeletons of two cavalry regiments, with hardly 200 horses
between them[3], and a mass of the local *ordenanza*, armed with
pikes, goads, scythes, and fowling-pieces. The whole mass may
have numbered some 12,000 men, of whom not 6,000 possessed
firearms of any kind[4]. Against them the French marshal was
marching at the head of 22,000 veterans, who had already gained
experience in the art of mountain-warfare from their recent
campaign in Galicia. The result was not difficult to foresee. If
the Portuguese dared to offer battle they would be scattered to
the winds.

Silveira's levies were not the only force in arms on the
frontier. The populous province of the Entre-Douro-e-Minho[5],
roused to tumultuous enthusiasm by the bishop of Oporto, had
sent every available man, armed or unarmed, to the front. A
screen of militia and regulars under General Botilho was watching
the line of the lower Minho: a vast mass of *ordenanza*, backed

---

[1] The 12th and 24th regiments—Chaves and Braganza.
[2] Militia of Chaves, Villa Real, Miranda, and Braganza.
[3] The 6th and 9th cavalry.
[4] Brotherton to Castlereagh, March 13.
[5] Entre-Douro-e-Minho had a population of 500,000 souls, Tras-os-Montes
only 180,000.

by a very small body of line troops lay in and about Braga,
under General Bernardino Freire ; another multitude was still
thronging the streets of Oporto and listening to the windy
harangues of the bishop.   But none of these masses of armed
men were sent to the aid of Silveira.   He was not one of the
bishop's faction, nor was he on good terms with his colleague
Freire.   Neither of them showed any inclination to combine
with him, and their followers, in the true spirit of provincial
particularism, thought of nothing but defending their own
hearths and homes, and left the Tras-os-Montes to take care
of itself.   Yet they had for the moment no enemy in front of
them but the small French garrison of Tuy, and could have
marched without any risk to join their compatriots.

Relying on the aid of La Romana, General Silveira had taken
post at Villarelho on the right bank of the Tamega, leaving the
defence of the left bank to the Spaniards, whom he supposed to
be still stationed about Monterey and Verin.   On the very day
upon which the Army of Galicia absconded, the Portuguese
general sent forward a detachment, consisting of a line regiment
and a mass of peasants, to menace the flank of the French
advance.   This force, having crossed the Spanish frontier, got
into collision with the enemy near Villaza.   Since Franceschi's
horsemen and Heudelet's infantry had turned off to the east in
pursuit of La Romana, the Portuguese fell in with the leading
column of Soult's main body—a brigade of Lahoussaye's
dragoons supported by Delaborde's division.   This force they
ventured to attack, but were promptly beaten off by Foy, the
brigadier of the advanced guard, who routed them and captured
their sole piece of artillery.   The shattered column fell back on
the main body at Villarelho, and then Silveira, hearing of the
departure of the Spaniards, resolved to retire and to look for
a defensive position which he might be able to hold by his own
unaided efforts.   There was none such to be found in front of
Chaves, for the valley of the Tamega widens out between
Monterey and the Portuguese frontier fortress, and offers
no ground suitable for defence.   Accordingly Silveira very
prudently decided to withdraw his tumultuary army to the
heights of San Pedro, a league to the south of the town, where
the space between the river and the mountains narrows down

and offers a short and compact line of resistance. But he waited
to be driven in, and meanwhile left rear-guards in observation at
Feces de Abaxo on the left, and Outeiro on the right bank, of
the Tamega.

Soult halted three days at Monterey in order to allow his
rearguard and his convoy of sick to close up with the main
body. But on March 10 he resumed his advance, using the two
parallel roads on the two banks of the Tamega. Franceschi's
light horse and Heudelet's division pushed down the eastern
side, Caulaincourt's brigade of dragoons[1] and Delaborde's infantry
down the western side of the river. Merle and Mermet were
still near Verin. As the Tamega was unfordable in most places,
the army seemed dangerously divided, but Soult knew well that
he was running little or no risk. Both at Feces and Outeiro
the Portuguese detachments, which covered Silveira's main body,
tried to offer serious resistance. They were of course routed,
with the loss of a gun and many prisoners.

On hearing that his enemy was drawing near, Silveira ordered
his whole army to retreat behind Chaves to the position of San
Pedro[2]. This command nearly cost him his life; the ignorant
masses of militia and *Ordenanza* could only see treason in the
proposed move, which abandoned the town to the French. The
local troops refused to march, and threatened to shoot their
general: he withdrew with such of his men as would still
obey orders, but a mixed multitude consisting of part of
the 12th regiment of the line (the Chaves regiment), and
a mass of *Ordenanza* and militia, remained behind to defend
the dilapidated town. Its walls had never been repaired
since the Spaniards had breached them in 1762; of the
fifty guns which armed them the greater part were destitute of
carriages, and rusting away in extreme old age; the supply of
powder and cannon-balls was wholly insufficient for even a short
siege. But encouraged by the advice of an incompetent
engineer officer[3], who said that a few barricades would make

---

[1] Of Lahoussaye's division.

[2] Brotherton to Cradock, from Povoa de Aguiar, March 13.

[3] He was called Magelhaes Pizarro, but cannot be said to have shown
either the endurance of the Portuguese seaman, or the reckless courage of
the Spanish *conquistador*, whose historic names he bore.

the place impregnable, 3,000 men shut themselves up in it, and
aided by 1,200 armed citizens, defied Soult, and opened a furious
fire upon the vedettes which he pushed up to the foot of the
walls.   The Marshal sent in a fruitless summons to surrender,
and then invested the place on the evening of the tenth ; all
night the garrison kept up a haphazard cannonade, and shouted
defiance to the French.   Next morning Soult resolved to
drive away Silveira from the neighbouring heights, convinced
that the spirits of the defenders of Chaves would fail the
moment that they saw the field army defeated and forced to
abscond.   The divisions of Delaborde and Lahoussaye soon compelled Silveira to give ground : he displayed indeed a laudable
prudence in refusing to let himself be caught and surrounded,
and made off south-eastward towards Villa Real with 6,000 or
7,000 men.   The Marshal then summoned Chaves to surrender
for the second time ; the garrison seem to have tired themselves out with twelve hours of patriotic shouting, and to have
used up great part of their munitions in their silly nocturnal
fireworks.   When they saw Silveira driven away, their spirits
sank, and they allowed their leader, Magelhaes Pizarro, to
capitulate, without remonstrance.   In short, they displayed even
more cowardice on the eleventh than indiscipline upon the tenth
of March.   On the twelfth the French entered the city in
triumph.

Soult was much embarrassed by the multitude of captives
whom he had taken : he could not spare an escort strong
enough to guard 4,000 prisoners to a place of safety.   Accordingly he made a virtue of necessity, permitted the armed citizens
of Chaves to retire to their homes, and dismissed the mass
of 2,500 *Ordenanza* and militia-men, after extracting from them
an oath not to serve against France during the rest of the war.
The 500 regulars of the 12th regiment were not treated in the
same way.   The Marshal offered them the choice between
captivity and enlisting in a Franco-Portuguese legion, which
he proposed to raise.   To their great discredit the majority,
both officers and men, took the latter alternative—though it
was with the sole idea of deserting as soon as possible.   At the
same moment Soult made an identical offer to the Spanish
prisoners captured from Mahy's division at the combats of

Osoño and La Trepa on March 6: they behaved no better than the Portuguese: several hundred of them took the oath to King Joseph, and consented to enter his service [1].

The Duke of Dalmatia had resolved to make Chaves his base for further operations in Portugal. He brought up to it from Monterey all his sick and wounded, including those who had been transported from Orense; the total now amounted to 1,325, of whom many were convalescents already fit for sedentary duty. To guard them a single company of a French regiment, and the inchoate 'Portuguese Legion,' were detailed, while the command was placed in the hands of the *chef de bataillon* Messager. The flour and unground wheat found in the place fed the army for several days, and the small stock of powder captured was utilized to replenish its depleted supply of cartridges.

From Chaves Soult had the choice of two roads for marching on Oporto. The more obvious route on the map is that which descends the Tamega almost to its junction with the Douro, and then strikes across to Oporto by Amarante and Penafiel. But here, as is so often the case in the Peninsula, the map is the worst of guides. The road along the river, frequently pinched in between the water and overhanging mountains, presents a series of defiles and strong positions, is considerably longer than the alternative route, and passes through difficult country wellnigh from start to finish.

The second path from Chaves to Oporto is that which strikes westward, crosses the Serra da Cabrera, and descends into the valley of the Cavado by Ruivaens and Salamonde. From thence it leads to Braga, on the great coast-road from Valenza to Oporto. The first two or three stages of this route are rough and difficult, and pass through ground even more defensible than that on the way to Amarante and Penafiel. But when the rugged defiles of the watershed between the Tamega and the Cavado have been passed, and the invader has reached Braga, the country becomes flat and open, and the coast plain, crossed by two excellent roads, leads him easily to his goal. It has also to be remembered that, by adopting this alternative, Soult

[1] See Naylies, p. 81; St. Chamans, p. 120; Le Noble, p. 120; and Des Odoards, p. 213.

took in the rear the Portuguese fortresses of the lower Minho,
and made it easy to reopen communications with Tuy and the
French forces still remaining in Galicia.

If any other persuasion were needed to induce the Marshal
to take the western, and not the eastern, road to Oporto, it was
the knowledge of the position of the enemy which he had
attained by diligent cavalry reconnaissances. It was ascertained
that Silveira with the remains of his division had fallen back
to Villa Pouca, more than thirty miles away, in the direction of
Villa Real. He could not be caught, and could retreat whithersoever he pleased. Freire, on the other hand, was lying at
Braga with his unwieldy masses, and had made no attempt
to march forward and fortify the passes of the Serra da Cabrera.
By all accounts that the horsemen of Franceschi could gather,
the defiles were blocked only by the *Ordenanza* of the mountain
villages.

This astounding news was absolutely correct. Freire's obvious
course was to defend the rugged watershed, where positions
abounded. But he contented himself with placing mere observation posts—bodies of thirty or 100 men—in the passes, while
keeping his main army concentrated. The truth was that he
was in a state of deep depression of mind, and prepared for
a disaster. Judging from the line which he adopted in the
previous year, while co-operating with Wellesley in the campaign
against Junot, we may set him down as a timid rather than
a cautious general. He had no confidence in himself or in his
troops : the indiscipline and mutinous spirit of the motley levies
which he commanded had reduced him to despair, and he
received no support from the Bishop of Oporto and his faction,
who were omnipotent in the province. Repeated demands for
reinforcements of regular troops had brought him nothing but
the 2nd battalion of the Lusitanian Legion, under Baron Eben.
The Bishop kept back the greater part of the resources of which
he could dispose, for the defence of his own city, in front of
which he was erecting a great entrenched camp. Freire had
also called on the Regency for aid, but they had done no more
than order two line battalions under General Vittoria to join
him, and these troops had not yet crossed the Douro. When
he heard that the French were on the march, and that he

himself would be the next to receive their visit, he so far lost
heart that he contemplated retiring on Oporto without attempting to fight. Instead of defending the defiles of Ruivaens and
Salamonde, he began to send to the rear his heavy stores, his
military chest, and his artillery of position. This timid resolve
was to be his ruin, for the excitable and suspicious multitude
which surrounded him had every intention of defending their
homes, and could only see treason and cowardice in the preparations for retreat. In a few days their fury was to burst forth
into open mutiny, to the destruction of their general and their
own ultimate ruin.

Soult meanwhile had set out from Chaves on March 14, with
Franceschi and Delaborde at the head of his column, as they had
been in all the operations since their departure from Orense.
Mermet and Lahoussaye's dragoons followed on the fifteenth :
Heudelet, with whom were the head quarters' staff and the
baggage, marched on the sixteenth : Merle, covering the rear
of the army, came in from Monterey on that day, and started
from Chaves on the seventeenth. Only Vialannes' brigade of
dragoons [1] was detached : these two regiments were directed
to make a feint upon Villa Real, with the object of frightening
and distracting Silveira, lest he should return to his old post
when he heard that the French army had departed, and fall
upon the rear of the marching columns. They beat up his
outposts at Villa Pouca, announced everywhere the Marshal's
approach with his main body, and retired under cover of the
night, after having deceived the Tras-os-Montes troops for
a couple of days.

The divisions of Delaborde and Franceschi, while clearing the
passes above Chaves, met with a desperate but futile resistance
from the *Ordenanza* of the upper Cavado valley. Practically
unaided by Freire, who had only sent to the defile of Salamonde
300 regular troops—a miserable mockery of assistance—the
gallant peasantry did their best. 'Even the smallest villages,'
wrote an aide-de-camp of Soult, 'tried to defend themselves.
It was not rare to see a peasant barricade himself all alone in his
house, and fire from the windows on our men, till his door was

---

[1] Lorges' other brigade, that of Fournier, had been (as it will be remembered) left behind in Galicia with Marshal Ney.

battered in, and he met his death on our bayonets. The
Portuguese defended themselves with desperation, and never
asked for quarter: if only these brave and devoted fellows had
possessed competent leaders, we should have been forced to give
up the expedition, or else we should never have got out of the
country. But their resistance was individual: each man died
defending his hamlet or his home, and a single battalion of our
advanced guard easily cleared the way for us. I saw during
these days young girls in the fighting-line, firing on us, and
meeting their death without recoiling a step. The priests had
told them that they were martyrs, and that all who died defending
their country went straight to paradise. In these petty combats,
which lasted day after day, we frequently found, among the
enemy's dead, monks in their robes, their crucifixes still clasped
in their hands. Indeed, while advancing we could see from afar
these ecclesiastics passing about among the peasants, and ani-
mating them to the combat[1]. . . . While the columns were on
the march isolated peasants kept up a continual dropping fire
on us from inaccessible crags above the road: at night they
attacked our sentries, or crept down close to our bivouacs to
shoot at the men who sat round the blaze. This sort of war
was not very deadly, but infinitely fatiguing: there was not
a moment of the day or night when we had not to be upon the
qui vive. Moreover, every man who strayed from the ranks,
whether he was sick, drunk, tired, or merely a marauder, was
cut off and massacred. The peasants not only murdered them,
but tortured them in the most horrid fashion before putting
them to death[2].'

Among scenes of this description Franceschi and Delaborde
forced their way down the valley of the Cavado, till they arrived
at the village of Carvalho d'Este, six miles from Braga, where

[1] Every French diarist of Soult's army has tales of the stoic courage
displayed by the Portuguese clergy. A story from Naylies of Lahoussaye's
dragoons may serve as an example. Near Braga he came on a cart escorted
by a single priest with a gun on his shoulder. He was the chaplain of
a convent, who was taking out of harm's way a party of nuns. When he
saw himself overtaken, he quietly waited in the middle of the road, shot
the first dragoon dead, and was killed by the second as he was trying
to reload his musket.

[2] St. Chamans, *Mémoires*, pp. 119–21.

they found a range of hills on both sides of the road, occupied by the whole horde of 25,000 men who had been collected by Freire. The division which followed the French advanced guard had also to sustain several petty combats, for the survivors of the *Ordenanza* whom Delaborde had swept out of the way, closed in again to molest each column, as it passed by the defiles of Venda-Nova, Ruivaens, and Salamonde. Mermet's division, which brought up the rear, had to beat off a serious attack from Silveira's army[1]. For that general, as soon as he discovered that he had been fooled by Lorges' demonstration, sent across the Tamega a detachment of 3,000 men, who fell upon Soult's rear. But a single regiment drove them off without much difficulty: they drew back to their own side of the mountains, and did not quit the valley of the Tamega.

It was on March 17 that Franceschi and Delaborde pushed forward to the foot of the Portuguese position, which swept round in a semicircle on each side of the high-road. Its western half was composed of the plateau of Monte Adaufé, whose left overhangs the river Cavado, while its right slopes upward to join the wooded Monte Vallongo. This latter hill is considerably more lofty than the Monte Adaufé and less easy of access. In front of the position, and bisected by the high-road, is the village of Carvalho d'Este: at the foot of the Monte Vallongo is another village, Lanhozo, whose name the French have chosen to bestow on the combat which followed. To the left-rear of the Monte Adaufé, pressed in between its slopes and the river, is a third village, Ponte do Prado, with a bridge across the Cavado, which is the only one by which the position can be turned. The town of Braga lies three miles further to the rear. The invaders halted on seeing the whole range of hills, some six miles long, crowned with masses of men in position. Franceschi would not take it upon himself to attack such a multitude, even though they were but peasantry and militia, of the same quality as the horde that had been defeated near Chaves a few days before. He sent back word to the Marshal, and drew up in front of the position to await the arrival of the main body.

---

[1] For combats waged by Lahoussaye's dragoons, who were in the middle of the long column, see the journal of Naylies (pp. 83–4). For attacks on Mermet, in the rear column, see Fantin des Odoards (p. 214).

But noting that a long rocky spur of the Monte Adaufé projected from the main block of high ground which the enemy was
holding, he caused it to be attacked by Foy's brigade of infantry,
and drove back without much difficulty the advanced guard of
the Portuguese. The possession of this hill gave the French
a foothold on the heights, and an advantageous *emplacement*
for artillery such as could not be found in the plain below.

It was three days before the rest of Soult's army joined the
leading division—not until the twentieth was his entire force,
with the exception of Merle's infantry, concentrated at the foot
of the enemy's position, and ready to attack. This long period of
waiting, when every mind was screwed up to the highest pitch
of excitement, had completely broken down the nerve of the
Portuguese, who spent the hours of respite in hysterical tumult
and rioting. Freire, as we have already seen, had been planning
a retreat on Oporto, but he found the spirit of his army so
exalted that he thought it better to conceal his project. He
pretended to have abandoned the idea of retiring, and gave
orders for the construction of entrenchments and batteries on
the Monte Adaufé, to enfilade the main approach by the high-
road. But he could not disguise his down-heartedness, nor
persuade his followers to trust him. Presently the wrecks of the
Ordenanza levies, who had fought at Salamonde, fell back upon
Braga, loudly accusing him of cowardice, for not supporting
them in their advanced position. The whole camp was full
of shouting, objectless firing in the air, confused cries of treason,
and mutinous assemblies. On the day when the French appeared
in front of the position Freire grew so alarmed at the threats
against his life, which resounded on every side, that he secretly
quitted Braga to fly to Oporto. But he was recognized and
seized by the *Ordenanza* of Tobossa, a few miles to the rear.
They brought him back to the camp as a prisoner, and handed
him over to Baron Eben, the colonel of the 2nd battalion of
the Lusitanian Legion, who had been acting as Freire's second-
in-command. This officer, an ambitious and presumptuous man,
and a great ally of the Bishop of Oporto, played the demagogue,
harangued the assembled multitude, and readily took over the
charge of the army. He consigned his unfortunate predecessor
to the gaol of Braga, and led on the mutineers to reinforce the

array on Monte Adaufé. When Eben had departed, a party of
Ordenanza returned to the city, dragged out the wretched Freire,
and killed him in the street with their pikes. The same afternoon they murdered Major Villasboas, the chief of Freire's
engineers, and one or more of his aides-de-camp. They also
seized and threw into prison the *corregidor* of Braga, and several
other persons accused of sympathy with the French. Eben
appears to have winked at these atrocities—much as his friend
the Bishop of Oporto ignored the murders which were taking
place in that city. By assuming command in the irregular
fashion that we have seen, he had made himself the slave of
the hysterical horde that surrounded him, and had to let
them do what they pleased, lest he should fall under suspicion
himself [1].

It would seem, however, that Eben did the little that was
possible with such material in preparing to oppose Soult. He
threw up more entrenchments on the Monte Adaufé, mounted
the few guns that he possessed in commanding situations, and
did his best to add to the lamentably depleted store of munitions on hand. Even the church roofs were stripped for lead,
when it was found that there was absolutely no reserve of cartridges, and that the *Ordenanza* had wasted half of their stock
in demonstrations and profitless firing at the French vedettes.
On the morning of the nineteenth he extended his right wing
to some hills below the Monte Vallongo, beyond the village of
Lanhozo, a movement which threatened to outflank and surround that part of the French army which was in front of him,
and to cut it off from the divisions still in the rear. This could
not be tolerated, and Mermet's infantry were dispatched to

---

[1] I agree with General Arteche in thinking that Eben's dispatch to
Cradock, from which this narrative is mainly drawn, does him no credit.
Indeed, it is easy to adopt the sinister view that Eben was aiming at
getting the command, did nothing to discourage the mob, and was
indirectly responsible for Freire's murder. As Arteche remarks ' with
a little more resolution and a little less personal ambition, the Baron
could probably have prevented the catastrophe' (vol. v. p. 393). But
Freire's conduct had been so cowardly and incapable that the peasants
were reasonably incensed with him. Why had he not defended the rugged
defiles of Venda Nova and Salamonde, and what could excuse his absconding
and abandoning his army ?

dislodge the 2,000 men who had taken up this advanced position. They were easily beaten out of the village and off the hill, and retired to their former station on the Monte Vallongo. The French here captured two guns and some prisoners. Soult gave these men copies of a proclamation which he had printed at Chaves, offering pardon to all Portuguese who should lay down their arms, and sent them back into Eben's lines under a flag of truce. When the *Ordenanza* discovered what the papers were, they promptly put to death the twenty unfortunate men as traitors, without listening to their attempts to explain the situation.

On the morning of March 20, Soult had been joined by Lorges' dragoons and his other belated detachments, and prepared to attack the enemy's position. To defend it Eben had now, beside 700 of his own Legion [1], one incomplete line regiment (Viana, no. 9), the militia of Braga and the neighbouring places, and some 23,000 *Ordenanza* levies, of whom 5,000 had firearms, 11,000 pikes, and the remaining 7,000 nothing better than scythes, goads, and instruments of husbandry. There were about fifteen or twenty pieces of artillery distributed along the front of the six-mile position, the majority of them in the entrenchments on the Monte Adaufé, placed so as to command the high-road.

Knowing the sort of rabble that was in front of him, Soult made no attempt to turn or outflank the Portuguese, but resolved to deliver a frontal attack all along the line, in the full belief that the enemy would give way the moment that the charge was pushed home. He had now about 3,000 cavalry and 13,000 infantry with him—Merle being still absent. He told off Delaborde's division with Lahoussaye's dragoons to assail the enemy's centre, on both sides of the high-road, where it crosses the Monte Adaufé. Mermet's infantry and Franceschi's light horse attacked, on the left, the wooded slopes of the Monte Vallongo. Heudelet's division, on the right, sent one brigade to storm the heights above the river, and left the other brigade as a general reserve for the army. Lorges' dragoons were also held back in support.

---

[1] Eben's dispatch is in the Record Office, in the miscellaneous volume at the end of the Portugal 1809 series.

As might have been expected, Soult's dispositions were completely successful. When the columns of Delaborde and Heudelet reached the foot of the enemy's position, the motley horde which occupied it broke out into wild cheers and curses, and opened a heavy but ineffective fire. They stood as long as the French were climbing up the slopes, but when the infantry debouched on to the plateau of Monte Adaufé they began to waver and disperse[1]. Then Soult let loose the cavalry of Lahoussaye, which had trotted up the high-road close in the rear of Delaborde's battalions, the 17th Dragoons leading. There was no time for the reeling mass of peasants to escape. 'We dashed into them,' wrote one officer who took part in the charge[2]; ' we made a great butchery of them; we drove on among them pell-mell right into the streets of Braga, and we pushed them two leagues further, so that we covered in all four leagues at full gallop without giving them a moment to rally. Their guns, their baggage, their military chest, many standards fell into our power[3].'

Such was the fate of the Portuguese centre, on each side of the high-road. Further to the right, above the Cavado, Heudelet was equally successful in forcing his way up the northern slopes of the Monte Adaufé; the enemy broke when he reached the plateau, but as he had no heavy force of cavalry with him, their flight was not so disastrous or their loss so heavy as in the centre. Indeed, when they had been swept down into the valley behind the ridge, some of the Portuguese turned to bay at the Ponte do Prado, and inflicted a sharp check on the Hanoverian legion, the leading battalion in Heudelet's advance. It was not till the 26th of the line came up to aid the Germans that the rallied peasantry again broke and fled. They only lost 300 men in this part of the field.

---

[1] Eben, in his report, says that at the moment of the French assault one of his guns in the battery commanding the high-road burst, and killed many of those standing about, and that the rout commenced with the stampede caused by this explosion.

[2] Naylies [of the 19th Dragoons], p. 87.

[3] Even while flying through the streets of Braga, some of the routed horde found time to pay a visit to the town gaol, and to murder the *corregidor* and the other prisoners who had been placed there on the eighteenth.

Far to the left, in the woods on the slope of the Monte
Vallongo, Mermet and Franceschi had found it much harder to
win their way to the edge of the plateau than had the troops in
the centre. But it was only the physical obstacles that detained
them : the resistance of the enemy was even feebler than in the
centre. By the time that the infantry of Mermet emerged on
the crest of the hill, the battle had already been won elsewhere.
The Portuguese right wing crumpled up the moment that it
was attacked, and fled devious over the hillsides, followed by
Franceschi's cavalry, who made a dreadful slaughter among the
fugitives. Five miles behind their original position a body of
militia with four guns rallied under the cliffs on which stands
the village of Falperra. The cavalry held them in check till
Mermet's leading regiment, the 31st Léger, came up, and then,
attacked by both arms at once, the whole body was ridden
down and almost exterminated. ' The commencement was
a fight, the end a butchery,' wrote an officer of the 31st; 'if our
enemies had been better armed and less ignorant of the art of
war, they might have made us pay dearly for our victory. But
for lack of muskets they were half of them armed with pikes
only : they could not manœuvre in the least. How was such
a mob to resist us ? they could only have held their ground if
they had been behind stone walls [1].'

The rout and pursuit died away in the southern valleys
beyond Braga, and Soult could take stock of his victory. He
had captured seventeen guns, five flags, and the whole of the
stores of Eben's army : he had killed, according to his own
estimate, some 4,000 men [2], and taken only 400 prisoners. This
shocking disproportion between the dead and the captives was
caused by the fact that the French in most parts of the field
had given no quarter. Some of their historians explain that
their cruelty resulted from the discovery that the Portuguese
had been murdering and mutilating the stragglers who fell
into their hands [3]. But it was really due to the exasperation of

[1] Fantin des Odoards, p. 216.

[2] Eben, in his report to Cradock at the Record Office, says 1,000 only,
of whom more than 200 belonged to the Lusitanian Legion.

[3] Le Noble, p. 142. St. Chamans, p. 121. Naylies and Fantin des
Odoards, though both mentioning the slaughter in which they took part,

spirit that always accompanies guerrilla warfare. Constantly worried by petty ambushes, 'sniped' in their bivouacs, never allowed a moment of rest, the soldiers were in a state of nervous irritation which found vent in needless and unjustifiable cruelty. In the fight they had lost only forty killed and 160 wounded, figures which afford no excuse for the wholesale slaughter in the pursuit to which they gave themselves up.

In the first flush of victory the French supposed that they had made an end of the *Ordenanza*, and that northern Portugal was at their feet. 'Cette journée a été fatale à l'insurrection portugaise,' wrote one of the victors in his diary[1]. But no greater mistake could have been made: though many of the routed horde dispersed to their homes, the majority rallied again behind the Avé, only ten or twelve miles from the battle-field. Nor did the battle of Braga even open the way to Galicia: General Botilho, with the levies of the Valenza and Viana district, closed in behind Soult and blocked the way to Tuy, the nearest French garrison. The Marshal had only conquered the ground on which he stood, and already his communication with Chaves, his last base, had been intercepted by detachments sent into the passes by Silveira.

Soult halted three days at Braga, a time which he utilized for the repair of his artillery, and the replenishing of the cartridge boxes of his infantry from the not too copious supply of munitions captured from the Portuguese. His cavalry scoured the country down the Cavado as far as Barcellos, and southward to the line of the Avé, only to find insurgents everywhere, the bridges broken, and the fords dredged up and staked.

The Marshal, however, undaunted by the gloomy outlook, resolved to march straight for his destined goal, without paying any attention to his communications. He now made Braga a temporary base, left there Heudelet's division in charge of 600 sick and wounded, and moved on Oporto at the head of his three remaining infantry divisions and all his cavalry.

Two good *chaussées*, and one additional mountain road of inferior character, lead from Braga to Oporto, crossing the Avé,

do not give this justification for it. The latter says that the French gave no quarter save to men in uniform.

[1] Fantin des Odoards, p. 216.

the one four, the next six, the third twenty-four miles from the
sea. The first and most westerly passes it at Ponte de Avé, the
second at Barca de Trofa, where there is both a bridge and
a wide ford, the third and least obvious at Guimaraens not far
from its source in the Serra de Santa Catalina. Soult resolved
to use all three for his advance, wisely taking the difficult road
by Guimaraens into his scheme, since he guessed that it would
probably be unwatched by the Portuguese, precisely because it
was far less eligible than the other two. He was perfectly right :
the Bishop of Oporto, the moment that he heard of the fall of
Braga, pushed up some artillery and militia to aid the *Ordenanza*
in defending both the Ponte de Avé and the Barca de Trofa
bridges. Each was cut : batteries were hastily thrown up commanding their approaches, and entrenchments were constructed
in their rear. At Barca de Trofa the ford was dredged up and
completely blocked with *chevaux de frise*. But the remote and
secondary passage at Guimaraens was comparatively neglected,
and left in charge of such of the local *Ordenanza* as had returned
home after the rout of Braga.

Soult directed Lorges' dragoons against the western road : he
himself with Delaborde's and Merle's infantry and Lahoussaye's
cavalry took the central *chaussée* by Barca de Trofa. On the
difficult flanking path by Guimaraens he sent Franceschi's light
horse and Mermet's infantry. On both the main roads the
Portuguese positions were so strong that the advancing columns
were held back : Soult would not waste men—he was beginning
to find that he had none to spare—in attempting to force the
entrenched positions opposite him. After feeling them with
caution, he pushed a column up-stream to a small bridge at
San Justo, which had been barricaded but not broken. Here
he established by night a heavy battery commanding the
opposite bank. On the morning of the twenty-sixth he opened
fire on the Portuguese positions across the water, and, when the
enemy had been well battered, hurled the brigade of General
Foy at the fortified bridge. It was carried, and Delaborde's
division was beginning to pass, when it met another French
force debouching on the same point. This was composed of
Mermet and Franceschi's men : they had beaten the local
Ordenanza at Guimaraens, crossed the Avé high up, and were

now pushing along the southern bank to take the Barca de Trofa position in the flank. Thus Soult found that, even if his frontal assault at San Justo had failed, his left-hand column would have cleared the way for him a few hours later, being already across the river and in the enemy's rear. Indeed his lateral detachment had done all that he had expected from it, and at no great cost. For though the *Ordenanza* had opposed it bravely enough, they had never been able to hold it back. The only notable loss that had been sustained was that of General Jardon, one of Mermet's brigadiers, who had met his death by his own recklessness. Finding his men checked for a moment, he had seized a musket and charged on foot at the head of his skirmishing line. This was not the place for a brigadier-general, and Jardon died unnecessarily, doing the work of a sub-lieutenant.

Finding the French across the river at San Justo, the Portuguese, who were defending the lower bridges, had to give way, or they would have been surrounded and cut off. They yielded unwillingly, and at Ponte de Avé actually beat off the first attempt to evict them. But in the end they had to fly, abandoning the artillery in the redoubts that covered the two bridges [1].

On the twenty-seventh, therefore, Soult was able to press close in to Oporto, for the line of the Avé is but fifteen miles north of the city. On approaching the heights which overhang the Douro the French found them covered with entrenchments and batteries ranged on a long front of six or seven miles, from San João de Foz on the sea-shore to the chapel of Bom Fin overlooking the river above the town. Ever since the departure of the French from Orense and their crossing of the frontier had become known, the whole of the populace had been at work on the fortifications, under the direction of Portuguese and British engineer officers. In three weeks an enormous amount of work had been done. The rounded summits of the line of hills, which

---

[1] Le Noble (pp. 157–8), and Napier following him, say that the Portuguese murdered their commander, Brigadier-General Vallongo, when the bridges were forced, tore him in pieces, and buried his scattered members in a dunghill. It is a relief to know from Da Luz Soriano, the Portuguese historian, that nothing of the kind occurred, and that there was no officer of the name of Vallongo in the Portuguese army.

rise immediately north of the city, and only half a mile in advance
of its outermost houses, had been crowned with twelve redoubts
armed with artillery of position.   The depressions between the
redoubts had been closed by palisades and abattis.   Further
west, below the city, where the line of hills is less marked, the
front was continued by a deep ditch, fortified buildings, and four
strong redoubts placed in the more exposed positions.   It ended
at the walls of San João da Foz, the old citadel which commands
the mouth of the Douro, and had in this direction an outwork
in another ancient fort, the castle of Quejo, on the sea-shore
a mile north of the estuary.   There were no less than 197 guns
of various calibres distributed along the front of the lines.   Nor
was this all : the main streets of the place had been barricaded
to serve as a second line of defence, and even south of the river
a battery had been constructed on the height crowned by the
Serra Convent, which overlooks the bridge and the whole city.

To hold this enormous fortified camp the Bishop of Oporto
had collected an army formidable in numbers if not in quality.
There was a strong nucleus of troops of the regular army : it
included the two local Oporto regiments (6th and 18th of the
line), two more battalions brought in by Brigadier-General
Vittoria, who had been too late to join in the defence of Braga,
a battalion of the regiment of Valenza (no. 21), a fraction of
that of Viana (no. 9), with the wrecks of the 2nd battalion of
the Lusitanian Legion, which had escaped from Eben's rout of
the twentieth, and the skeleton of an incomplete cavalry
regiment (no. 12, Miranda).   In all there cannot have been
less than 5,000 regular troops in the town, though many of the
men were recruits with only a few weeks of service.   To these
may be added three or four militia regiments in the same condition as were the rest of the corps of that force, i. e. half-armed
and less than half-disciplined [1].   But the large majority of the
garrison was composed of the same sort of levies that had
already fought with such small success at Chaves and Braga—
there were 9,000 armed citizens of Oporto and a somewhat
greater number of the *Ordenanza* of the open country, who had
retired into the city before Soult's advancing columns.   The

[1] Apparently the regiments of Oporto, Baltar, Feira, and Villa de
Conde.

whole mass—regulars and irregulars—may have made up a force
of 30,000 men—nothing like the 40,000 or 60,000 of the French
reports [1]. Under the Bishop the military commanders were
three native brigadier-generals, Lima-Barreto, Parreiras, and
Vittoria. Eben had been offered the charge of a section of the
defences, but—depressed with the results of his experiment in
generalship at Braga—he refused any other responsibility than
that of leading his battalion of the Lusitanian Legion. The
Bishop had allotted to Parreiras the redoubts and entrenchments on the north of the town, to Vittoria those on the north-
east and east, to Lima-Barreto those below the town as far as
St. João da Foz. The regulars had been divided up, so as to
give two or three battalions to each general; they were to form
the reserve, while the defences were manned by the militia and
Ordenanza. There was a lamentable want of trained gunners—
less than 1,000 artillerymen were available for the 200 pieces in
the lines and on the heights beyond the river. To make up the
deficiency many hundreds of raw militia-men had been turned
over to the commanders of the batteries. The natural result
was seen in the inferior gunnery displayed all along the line
upon the fatal twenty-ninth of March.

To complete the picture of the defenders of Oporto it must
be added that the anarchy tempered by assassination, which had
been prevailing in the city ever since the Bishop assumed
charge of the government, had grown to a head during the last
few days. On the receipt of the news of the disaster at Braga
it had culminated in a riot, during which the populace constituted a sort of Revolutionary Tribunal at the Porto do Olival.

[1] I draw these deductions from Beresford's and Eben's reports in the
Record Office. Beresford (writing to Castlereagh on March 29, the day of
the storm) complains that he can get no proper ' morning states' out of
the officers at Oporto, but says that the Bishop has there nos. 6 and
18 of the line, Vittoria's two battalions and the wrecks of the 2nd
Lusitanian Legion. He speaks of two or three militia regiments, 9,000
armed citizens, and an indefinite number of *Ordenanza.* Eben gives some
details concerning his own doings. Da Luz Soriano mentions Champlemond
and his battalion of the 21st of the line. As to the *Ordenanza,* 9,000
seems a high estimate for the local Oporto horde, for that town with
70,000 souls had already supplied two regiments of the line, two battalions of the Lusitanian Legion, and a militia regiment, 6,500 men in all.

They haled out of the prisons all persons who had been consigned to them on a charge of sympathizing with the French, hung fourteen of these unfortunates, including the brigadier-general Luiz da Oliveira, massacred many more in the streets, and dragged the bodies round the town on hurdles. ' The Bishop, though he had 5,000 regular troops at hand, made no attempt to intervene—' he could not stand in the way of the righteous vengeance of the people upon traitors.' On the night of the twenty-eighth he retired to a place of safety, the Serra Convent across the river, after bestowing his solemn benediction upon the garrison, and handing over the further conduct of the defence to the three generals whose names we have already cited.

The town of Oporto was hidden from Soult's eyes by the range of heights, crowned by fortifications, which lay before him. For the place was built entirely upon the downslope of the hill towards the Douro, and was invisible till those approaching it were within half a mile of its outer buildings. It is a town of steep streets running down to the water, and meeting at the foot of the great pontoon-bridge, more than 200 yards long, which links it to the transpontine suburb of Villa Nova, and the adjacent height of the Serra do Pilar. The river front forms a broad quay, along which were lying at the time nearly thirty merchant ships, mostly English vessels laden with port wine, which were wind-bound by a persistent North-Wester, and could not cross the bar and get out to sea.

Although his previous attempts to negotiate with the Portuguese had not been very fortunate, the Marshal thought it worth while to send proposals for an accommodation to the Bishop. He warned him not to expose his city to the horrors of a sack, pointed out that the raw levies of the garrison must inevitably be beaten, and assured him that ' the French came not as enemies, but as the deliverers of Portugal from the yoke of the English. It was for the benefit of these aliens alone that the Bishop would expose Oporto to the incalculable calamities attending a storm [1].' The bearer of the Marshal's letter was a Portuguese major taken prisoner at Braga, who would have been massacred at the outposts if he had not taken the precaution

[1] Le Noble, p. 161.

of explaining to his countrymen that Soult had sent him in to propose the surrender of the French army, which was appalled at the formidable series of defences to which it found itself opposed! The reply sent by the Bishop and his council of war was, of course, defiant, and bickering along the front of the lines immediately began. While the white flag was still flying General Foy, the most distinguished of Soult's brigadiers, trespassed by some misconception within the Portuguese picquets and was made prisoner. While being conducted into the town he was nearly murdered, being mistaken for Loison, for whom the inhabitants of Oporto nourished a deep hatred [1].

On finding that the Portuguese were determined to fight, Soult began his preparations for a general assault upon the following day. He drove in the enemy's outposts outside the town, and captured one or two small redoubts in front of the main line. Having reconnoitred the whole position, he told off Delaborde and Franceschi to attack the north-eastern front, Mermet and one brigade of Lahoussaye's dragoons to storm the central parts of the lines, due north of the city, where the fortifications were most formidable, Merle and the other brigade of Lahoussaye to press in upon the western entrenchments below the city. There was no general reserve save Lorges' two regiments of cavalry, and these had the additional task imposed upon them of fending off any attack on the rear of the army which might be made by scattered bodies of *Ordenanza*, who

---

[1] Some of the French writers say that Foy was taken prisoner while carrying a flag of truce and a second letter for the Bishop's eye. But what really seems to have happened was that he conceived a notion that one of the Portuguese outposts wished to surrender, rode in amongst them, and began to urge them to lay down their arms. But they seized him and sent him to the rear ; his companion, the *chef de bataillon* Roger, drew his sword and tried to cut his way back to his men, whereupon he was bayonetted. One cannot blame the Portuguese, for officers, in time of truce, have no right to come within the enemy's lines, still less to urge his troops to desertion. Foy proved that he was not Loison by holding up his two hands. Loison being one-handed (as his nickname *Maneta* shows), the populace at once saw that they had made a mistake. I follow the narrative in Girod de l'Ain's new life of Foy (p. 78), corroborated by Le Noble (p. 162). Napier (ii. p. 57), of course, gives a version unfavourable to the Portuguese.

were creeping out into the woods along the sea-coast, and
threatening to turn the Marshal's right flank.

Soult had but 16,000 men available,—of whom 3,000 were
cavalry, and therefore could not be employed till the infantry
should have broken through the line of fortifications which
completely covered the Portuguese front.   Nevertheless he had
no doubts of the result, though he had to storm works defended
by 30,000 men and lined with 197 cannon.   He now knew the
exact fighting value of the Portuguese levies, and looked upon
Oporto as his own.

The Marshal's plan was not to repeat the simple and simultaneous frontal attack all along the line by which he had
carried the day at Braga.   There was a good deal of strategy in
his design: the two flank divisions were ordered to attack,
while the centre was for a time held back.   Merle, in especial,
was directed to do all that he could against the weakest point
of the Portuguese line, in the comparatively level ground to the
west of the city.   Soult hoped that a heavy attack in this
direction would lead the enemy to reinforce his left from the
reserves of his centre, and gradually to disgarnish the formidable
positions north of the city, when no attack was made on
them.   If they committed this fault, he intended to hurl
Mermet's division, which he carefully placed under cover till the
critical moment, at the central redoubts.   A successful assault
at this point would finish the game, as it would cut the Portuguese
line in two, and allow the troops to enter the upper quarters of
the city in their first rush.

The French were under arms long ere dawn, waiting for the
signal to attack.   The Portuguese also were awake and stirring
in the darkness, when at three o'clock a thunderstorm, accompanied by a terrific hurricane from the north-west, swept over the
city.   In the midst of the elemental din some of the Portuguese
sentinels thought that they had seen the French columns
advancing to the assault : they fired, the artillery followed their
example, and for half an hour the noise of the thunderstorm
was rivalled by that of 200 guns of position firing at nothing.
Just as the gunners had discovered their mistake, the tempest
passed away, and soon after the day broke.   So drenched and
weary were the French, who had been lying down under the

torrential rain, that Soult put off the assault for an hour, in order to allow them to dry themselves and take some refreshment; the pause also allowed the sodden ground to harden.

At seven all was again ready, and Merle's and Delaborde's regiments hurled themselves at the entrenchments above and below the city. Both made good progress, especially the former, who lodged themselves in the houses and gardens immediately under the main line of the Portuguese left wing, and captured several of its outlying defences. Seeing the position almost forced, Parreiras, the commander of the central part of the lines, acted just as Soult had hoped, and sent most of his reserve to reinforce the left. The Marshal then bade Merle halt for a moment, but ordered Delaborde, on his eastern flank, to push on as hard as he could. The general obeyed, and charged right into the Portuguese entrenchments, capturing several redoubts and actually breaking the line and getting a lodgement in the north-east corner of the city. Parreiras, to aid his colleague in this quarter, drew off many of his remaining troops, and sent them away to the right, thereby leaving his own section of the line only half manned. Thereupon Soult launched against the central redoubts his main assaulting column, Mermet's division and the two regiments of dragoons. The central battalion went straight for the main position above the high-road, where the great Portuguese flag was flying on the strongest redoubt. The others attacked on each side. This assault was decisive: the Portuguese gunners had only time to deliver two ineffective salvos when the French were upon them. They charged into the redoubts through the embrasures, pulled down the connecting abattis, and swept away the depleted garrison in their first rush. The line of the defenders was hopelessly broken, and Mermet's division hunted them down the streets leading to the river at full speed.

The centre being thus driven in, the Portuguese wings saw that all was lost, and gave way in disorder, looking only for a line of retreat. Vittoria, with the right wing, abandoned his section of the city and retreated east along the Vallongo road, towards the interior: he got away without much loss, and even turned to bay and skirmished with the pursuing battalions of Delaborde when once he was clear of the suburbs. Far other

was the lot of the Portuguese left wing, which had the sea behind
it instead of the open country. General Lima-Barreto, its commander, was killed by his own men: he had given orders to spike
the guns and double to the rear the moment that he saw the
central redoubts carried. Unfortunately for himself, he was
among a mass of men who wished to hold on to their entrenchments in spite of the disaster on their right. When he reiterated
his order to retreat, he was shot down for a traitor. But Merle's
division soon evicted his slayers, and sent them flying towards
St. João da Foz and the sea. There was a dreadful slaughter of
the Portuguese in this direction : some escaped across the river
in boats, a large body slipped round Merle's flank and got away
to the north along the coast (though Lorges' dragoons pursued
them among the woods above the water and sabred many):
others threw themselves into the citadel of St. João and capitulated on terms. But several thousands, pressed into the angle
between the Douro and the ocean, were slaughtered almost
without resistance, or rolled *en masse* into the water.

The fate of the Portuguese centre was no less horrible. Their
commander, Parreiras, fled early, and got over the bridge to
report to the Bishop the ruin of his army. The main horde
followed him, though many lingered behind, endeavouring to
defend the barricades in the streets. When several thousands
had passed the river, some unknown officer directed the drawbridge between the central pontoons to be raised, in order to
prevent the French from following. This was done while the
larger part of the armed multitude was still on the further bank,
hurrying down towards the sole way of escape. Nor was it
only the fighting-men whose retreat was cut off: when the news
ran round the city that the lines were forced, the civil population
had rushed down to the quays to escape before the sack began.
It was fortunate that half the people had left Oporto during the
last two days and taken refuge in Beira. But tens of thousands
had lingered behind, full of confidence in their entrenchments
and their army of defenders. A terrified mass of men, women,
and children now came pouring down to the bridge, and mingled
with the remnants of the routed garrison. The pontoons were
still swinging safely on their cables, and no one, save those in
the front of the rush, discovered that there was a fatal gap

in the middle of the passage, where the drawbridge had been raised. There was no turning back for those already embarked on the bridge, for the crowds behind continued to push them on, and it was impossible to make them understand what had happened. The French had now begun to appear on the quays, and to attack the rear of the unhappy multitude: their musketry drowned the cries of those who tried to turn back. At the same time the battery on the Serra hill, beyond the river, opened upon the French, and the noise of its twenty heavy guns made it still more impossible to convey the news to the back of the crowd. For more than half an hour, it is said, the rush of fugitives kept thrusting its own front ranks into the death-trap, forty feet broad, in the midst of the bridge. If anything more was needed to add to the horror of the scene, it was supplied by the sudden rush of a squadron of Portuguese cavalry, which—cut off from retreat to the east—galloped down from a side street and ploughed its way into the thickest of the crowd at the bridge-head, trampling down hundreds of victims, till it was brought to a standstill by the mere density of the mass into which it had penetrated. So many persons, at last, were thrust into the water that not only was the whole surface of the Douro covered with drowning wretches, but the gap in the bridge was filled up by a solid mass of the living and the dead. Over this horrid gangway, as it is said, some few of the fugitives scrambled to the opposite bank [1].

At first the French, who had fought their way down to the quay, had begun to fire upon the rear of the multitude which was struggling to escape. But they soon found that no resistance was being offered, and saw that the greater part of the flying crowd was composed of women, children, and non-combatants. The sight was so sickening that their musketry died

[1] Le Noble, and Napier following him, state that the breach in the bridge was caused merely by some of the central pontoons sinking under the weight of the passing multitude. Hennegan, who was present in Oporto that day, says the same. But it seems safer to follow Da Luz Soriano and other Portuguese witnesses, who state that no such accident occurred, but that the early fugitives pulled up the drawbridge in order to stay the pursuit, reckless as to the fate of those who were behind them. Historians telling a story to the discredit of their own party may generally be trusted.

down, and when they saw the unfortunate Portuguese thrust by
thousands into the water, numbers of them turned to the
charitable work of helping the strugglers ashore, and saved
many lives.   The others cleared the bridge-head by forcing
the fugitives back with the butt ends of their muskets, and
edging them along the quays and into the side streets, till the
way was open.   In the late afternoon some of Mermet's troops
mended the gap in the bridge with planks and rafters, and
crossed it, despite of the irregular fire of the Portuguese battery
on the heights above.   They then pushed into the transpontine suburb, expelled its defenders, and finally climbed the Serra
hill and captured the guns which had striven to prevent their
passage.

Meanwhile the parts of Oporto remote from the pontoon-
bridge had been the scene of a certain amount of desultory
fighting.   Many small bodies of the garrison had barricaded
themselves in houses, and made a desperate but ineffectual
attempt to defend them.   In the Bishop's palace at the south
end of the town 400 militia held out for some hours, and were
all bayonetted when the gates were at last burst open.   Street-
fighting always ends in rapine, rape and arson, and as the
resistance died down the victors turned their hands to the usual
atrocities that follow a storm.   It was only a small proportion
of them who had been sobered and sickened by witnessing the
catastrophe on the bridge.   The rest dealt with the houses and
with the inhabitants after the fashion usual in the sieges of that
day, and Oporto was thoroughly sacked.   It is to the credit of
Soult that he used every exertion to beat the soldiers off from
their prey, and restored order long ere the following morning.
It is to be wished that Wellington had been so lucky at Badajoz
and San Sebastian.

The French army had lost, so the Marshal reported, no more
than eighty killed and 350 wounded, an extraordinary testimony
to the badness of the Portuguese gunnery.   How many of the
garrison and the populace perished it will never be possible to
ascertain—the figures given by various contemporary authorities
run up from 4,000 to 20,000.   The smaller number is probably
nearer the truth, but no satisfactory estimate can be made.   It
is certain that some of the regiments which took part in the

COMBAT OF BRAGA
(OR LANHOZO)
MARCH 20TH 1809

French Infantry ▬ Cavalry ▭
Portuguese

San Joao de Rey

Val de Geras

R. Cavado

Ponte de Prado

R. Cavado

Braga

Palmera

Falperra

MONTE ADAUFE PLATEAU

Graindorges
Brigade

Lahoussaye's
Dragoons

Delaborde's Division

Carvalho D'Este

Convent

Loĝge's
Dragoons

Maranzin's
Brigade

Lanhozo

Mermet's and Franceschi's Divisions

MONTE VALLONGO PLATEAU

Kilometres

0 1 2 3 4

Darbishire & Stanford, Lᵗᵈ

The Oxford Geogᶦ Inst.

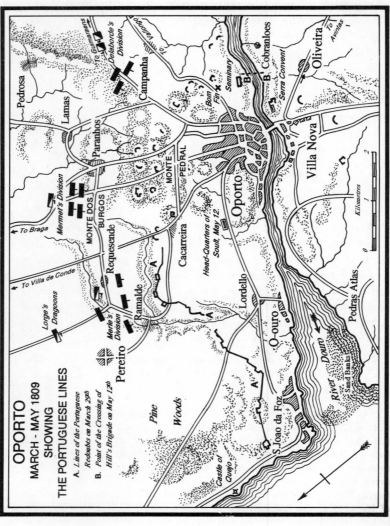

OPORTO
MARCH - MAY 1809
SHOWING
THE PORTUGUESE LINES

A. Lines of the Portuguese
   Redoubts on March 29th
B. Point of the Crossing of
   Hill's Brigade on May 12th

Pedrosa

To Guimaraens

Delaborde's
Division

Lamas

Campanha

Paranhos

Mermet's Division

To Braga

MONTE DOS BURGOS

Requesende

To Villa de Conde

MONTE

PEDRAL

Bom
Fim

Seminary

Cobranloes

To
Avintas

Serra Convent

Oliveira

Lorge's
Dragoons

Ramalde

Merle's
Division

Pereiro

Cacarreira

Head-Quarters of
Soult, May 12.

Oporto

Villa Nova

Lordello

O-ouro

River Douro

Pedras Atlas

Sand Banks

Pine
Woods

Castle of
Quejo

S. Joao da Foz

Kilometres

0   1   2

The Oxford Geogl Inst.

Darbishire & Stanford, Lrd

defence were almost annihilated [1], and that thousands of the inhabitants were drowned in the river. Yet the town was not depopulated, and of its defenders the greater proportion turned up sooner or later in the ranks of Silveira, Botilho, and Trant. The slain and the drowned together may perhaps be roughly estimated at 7,000 or 8,000, about equally divided between combatants and non-combatants.

Soult meanwhile could report to his master that the first half of his orders had been duly carried out. He had captured 200 cannon, a great store of English ammunition and military equipment, and more than thirty merchant vessels, laden with wine. He had delivered Foy and some dozens of other French captives—for it would be doing the Portuguese injustice to let it be supposed that they had killed or tortured all their prisoners. In short, the victory and the trophies were splendid: yet the Marshal was in reality almost as far from having completed the conquest of northern Portugal as on the day when he first crossed its frontier. He had only secured for himself a new base of operation, to supersede Chaves and Braga. For the next month he could do no more than endeavour ineffectually to complete the subjugation of one single province. The main task which his master had set before him, the capture of Lisbon, he was never able to contemplate, much less to take in hand. Like so many other French generals in the Peninsula, he was soon to find that victory is not the same thing as conquest.

[1] E. g. the 21st of the line had even in September, nearly six months after the storm, only 193 men under arms.

N.B.—The sources for this part of the Portuguese campaign are very full. On the French side we have, besides the Marshal's dispatches, the following eye-witnesses: Le Noble, Soult's official chronicler; St. Chamans (one of the Marshal's aides-de-camp); General Bigarré, King Joseph's representative at the head quarters of the 2nd Corps; Naylies of Lahoussaye's dragoons; and Fantin des Odoards of the 31st Léger. On the Portuguese side we have the lengthy dispatches of Eben, the narrative of Hennegan (who had brought the British ammunition to Oporto), some letters from Brotherton, who was first with La Romana and then with Silveira, and a quantity of official correspondence in the Record Office, between Beresford and the Portuguese.

SECTION XIII: CHAPTER V

SOULT'S HALT AT OPORTO: OPERATIONS OF WILSON ON
THE PORTUGUESE FRONTIER: SILVEIRA'S DEFENCE
OF AMARANTE

OPORTO had been conquered: the unhappy levies of the
Bishop had been scattered to the winds: by the captures which
it had made the French army was now, for the first time since
its departure from Orense, in possession of a considerable store
of provisions and an adequate supply of ammunition. Soult
was no longer driven forward by the imperative necessity for
finding new resources to feed his troops, nor forced to hurry on
the fighting by the fear that if he delayed his cartridges would
run short. He had at last leisure to halt and take stock of his
position. The most striking point in the situation was that he
was absolutely ignorant of the general course of the war in the
other regions of the Peninsula. When he had been directed to
march on Oporto, he had been assured that he might count on
the co-operation of Lapisse, who was to advance from Salamanca
with his 9,000 men, and of Victor, who was to stretch out to
him a helping hand from the valley of the Tagus. It was all-
important to know how far the promised aid was being given:
yet the Marshal could learn nothing. More than two months
had now elapsed since he had received any dispatches from the
Emperor. It was a month since he had obtained his last news
of the doings of his nearest colleague, Ney, which had been
brought to him, as it will be remembered, just as he was about
to leave Orense. At that moment the Duke of Elchingen had
been able to tell him nothing save that the communications
between Galicia and Leon had been broken, and that the insurrection was daily growing more formidable. After this his only
glimpse of the outer world had been afforded by Portuguese
letters, seized in the post-offices of Braga and Oporto, from which

he had learnt that his garrisons left behind at Vigo and Tuy
were being beleaguered by a vast horde of Galician irregular
levies. 'The march of the 2nd Corps,' wrote one of Soult's
officers, ' may be compared to the progress of a ship on the
high seas : she cleaves the waves, but they close behind her, and
in a few moments all trace of her passage has disappeared [1].'
To make the simile complete, Fantin des Odoards should have
compared Soult to the captain of a vessel in a dense fog,
forging ahead through shoals and sandbanks without any possibility of obtaining a general view of the coast till the mists may
lift.   To all intents and purposes, we may add, the fog never
dispersed till May had arrived, and Wellesley hurtled down in
a dreadful collision on the groping commander, ere he had fully
ascertained his own whereabouts.

When the whole country-side is up in arms, as it was in
Galicia and northern Portugal in the spring of 1809, it is
useless to dispatch small bodies of men in search of news. They
are annihilated in a few hours : but to make large detachments
and send them out on long expeditions, so weakens the main
army that it loses its power of further advance. This was the
fate of the 2nd Corps after the fall of Oporto. Soult, compelled
to seek for information at all costs, had to send one of his four
infantry divisions back towards Galicia, to succour Tuy and
Vigo and obtain news of Ney, while another marched eastward
to the Tras-os-Montes, to look for signs of the advance of
Lapisse from Salamanca. When these detachments had been
made, the remainder of the army was too weak to resume the
march on Lisbon which the Emperor had commanded, and was
forced to remain cantoned in the neighbourhood of Oporto.

The details of Soult's disposition of his troops after the fall
of Oporto were as follows : Franceschi's cavalry, supported by
Mermet's division of infantry, were pushed forward across the
Douro on the road to Coimbra, to watch the movements
of the wrecks of the Bishop's army, which had retired to the
line of the Vouga. Merle's division and half Delaborde's
remained in garrison at Oporto, while Lorges' and one brigade
of Lahoussaye's dragoons were kept not far from them, in the
open country north of the city, about Villa de Conde and

[1] Fantin des Odoards, *Journal*, April 28, p. 226.

Vallongo. The other brigade of Lahoussaye's division, supported by Foy's infantry, was sent out on an expedition towards the Tras-os-Montes, with orders to brush away Silveira and seek for news of the expected approach of Lapisse. Loison was placed in command of this detachment. Finally, Heudelet's division, which had been guarding the sick and the stores of the army at Braga, was ordered to send on all the *impedimenta* to Oporto, and then to prepare to march northward in order to relieve Tuy and Vigo, and to get into touch with Ney and the 6th Corps.

It was clear that the further movements of the Duke of Dalmatia would depend on the intelligence which Loison and Heudelet might obtain. If Ney should have crushed the Galician insurgents, if Lapisse should be met with somewhere on the borders of Spain, matters would look well for the resumption of the advance on Lisbon. It was also to be hoped that Lapisse would be able to give some information as to the doings of Victor and the 1st Corps. For it was necessary to find out how the Duke of Belluno had been faring in Estremadura, and to know whether he was prepared to co-operate in that general movement against the Portuguese capital which the Emperor had prescribed in his parting instructions from Valladolid.

As a matter of fact, Victor, having beaten Cuesta at Medellin on the day before Soult captured Oporto (March 28), had reached the end of his initiative, and was now lying at Merida, incapable, according to his own conception, of any further offensive movement till he should have received heavy reinforcements. Ney in Galicia was fighting hard against the insurgents, and beginning to discover that though he might rout them a dozen times he could not make an end of them. He had not a man to spare for Soult's assistance.

There remained Lapisse, who in his central position at Salamanca should have been, according to Napoleon's design, the link between Ney, Victor, and Soult. He had been directed, as it will be remembered [1], to move on Ciudad Rodrigo and Almeida, to capture both these fortresses, and then to advance into Portugal and to strike at Abrantes : when he arrived there it was hoped that he would find Soult on his right and Victor

[1] See p. 175.

on his left, and would join them in the general assault on Lisbon. There can be no doubt that Napoleon was giving too heavy a task to Lapisse : he had but a single division of infantry —though it was a strong one of twelve battalions—and one provisional brigade of cavalry [1], in all about 9,000 men. This was ample for the holding down of the southern parts of the kingdom of Leon, or even for the attack on Almeida and Rodrigo : but it was a small force with which to advance into the mountains of central Portugal or to seize Abrantes. If he had carried out his instructions, Lapisse would have had to march for nearly 200 miles through difficult mountain country, beset every day by the *Ordenanza*, as Soult had been in his shorter route from Orense to Oporto. And if he had ever cut his way to Abrantes, he ought to have found himself faced by Cradock's 9,000 British troops and by the reorganized Portuguese regular army, which lay in and about Lisbon, with a strength which even in February was not less than 12,000 men.

Napoleon had given Lapisse too much to do : but on the other hand that general performed far too little. Though he could never have reached Abrantes, he ought to have reached Almeida, where his presence would have been of material assistance to Soult, more especially if he had from thence pushed exploring columns towards Lamego and Vizeu, before plunging into the mountains on the road to the south. As a matter of fact, Lapisse in February and March never advanced so much as fifty miles from Salamanca, and allowed himself to be ' contained' and baffled, for two whole months, by an insignificant opposing force, commanded by a general possessing that enterprise and initiative which he himself entirely lacked.

The officer who wrecked this part of Napoleon's plan for the invasion of Portugal was Sir Robert Wilson, one of the most active and capable men in the English army, and one who might have made a great name for himself, had fortune been propitious. But though he served with distinction throughout the Napoleonic war, and won golden opinions in Belgium and Egypt, in Prussia and Poland, no less than in Spain, he never obtained that command on a large scale which would have

---

[1] On Feb. 1 the force was, *présents sous les armes*, 7,692 infantry, about 1,000 cavalry, and 200 gunners.

enabled him to show his full powers. It may seem singular
that a man who won love and admiration wherever he went,
who was decorated by two emperors for brilliant feats of arms
done under their eyes, who was equally popular in the Russian,
the Austrian, or the Portuguese camp, who had displayed on
a hundred fields his chivalrous daring, his ready ingenuity, and
his keen military insight, should fail to achieve greatness. But
Wilson, unhappily for himself, had the defects of his qualities.
When acting as a subordinate his independent and self-reliant
character was always getting him into trouble with his hier-
archical superiors. He was not the man to obey orders which
he believed to be dangerous or mistaken : he so frequently
'thought for himself' and carried out plans quite different from
those which had been imposed upon him, that no commander-
in-chief could tolerate him for long. His moves were always
clever and generally fortunate, but mere success did not atone
for his disobedience in the eyes of his various chiefs, and he
never remained for long in the same post. All generals, good
and bad, agree in disliking lieutenants who disregard their
orders and carry out other schemes—even if they be ingenious
and successful ones [1]. It must be added that Wilson dabbled
in politics on the Whig side, and was not a favourite with
Lord Castlereagh, a drawback when preferments were being
distributed.

But when trusted with any independent command, and
allowed a free hand, Wilson always did well. Not only had he
all the talents of an excellent partisan chief, but he was one of
those genial leaders who have the power to inspire confidence
and enthusiasm in their followers, and are able to get out of
them double the work that an ordinary commander can extort.
He was in short one of those men who if left to themselves
achieve great things, but who when placed in a subordinate
position quarrel with their superiors and get sent home in
disgrace. From the moment when Beresford assumed command
of the Portuguese army his relations with Wilson were one
long story of friction and controversy, and Wellesley (though

[1] Wellington, e. g., writes to him on August 5, 1809, ' It is difficult for
me to instruct you, when every letter that I receive from you informs me
that you have gone further off, and are executing some plan of your own.'

acknowledging his brilliant services) made no attempt to keep him in the Peninsula. He wanted officers who would obey orders, even when they did not understand or approve them, and would not tolerate lieutenants who wished to argue with him [1].

It was Wilson who first showed that the new levies of Portugal could do good service in the field. While Silveira and Eben were meeting with nothing but disaster in the Tras-os-Montes and the Entre-Douro-e-Minho, he was conducting a thoroughly successful campaign on the borders of Leon. From January to April, 1809, he, and he alone, protected the eastern frontier of Portugal, and with a mere handful of men kept the enemy at a distance, and finally induced him to draw off and leave Salamanca, just at the moment when Soult's operations on the Douro were becoming most dangerous.

The force at his disposal in January, 1809, consisted of nothing more than his own celebrated 'Loyal Lusitanian Legion.' We have already had occasion to mention this corps while speaking of the reorganization of the Portuguese army (see page 199). On December 14, as we have seen, he had led out his little brigade of Green-coats towards the frontier [2].

Wilson's reasons for moving forward were partly political, partly military : on the one hand he wished to get away from the neighbourhood of the Bishop of Oporto, whose intrigues disgusted him ; on the other he saw that it was necessary to

---

[1] It is most unfortunate that while Wilson wrote and published admirable narratives of his doings in Prussia and Poland in 1806-7, and of his Russian and German campaign of 1812-3, he has left nothing on record concerning Portugal in 1808-9. Moreover the life, by his son-in-law, breaks off in 1807, and was never finished. My narrative is constructed from his dispatches in the Record Office, the correspondence of Wellesley and Beresford, and Mayne and Lillie's *Loyal Lusitanian Legion*.

[2] It will be remembered that it was only the first division of the Legion that marched. The second, which could not go forward for want of uniforms and arms, was left behind in charge of Baron Eben. That officer had strict orders to move out to Almeida the moment that he should receive the muskets, &c. that were on their way from England. Eben, however, disregarded his instructions, became one of the Bishop's clique, and involved his men in the campaign against Soult, thereby marring Wilson's plans and depriving him of half his proper force.

bring up a force to cover the frontier of Portugal, when Moore marched forward into Spain. As long as Moore had remained at Salamanca, there was a strong barrier in front of Portugal : but when he departed it was clear that the kingdom must defend itself. Wilson therefore advanced to Pinhel, near Almeida, and there established his little force in cantonments.

He was at this place when the startling developments of the campaign in the last ten days of December, 1808, took place. Moore retired on Galicia, Napoleon's army swept on into Leon, and Wilson found himself left alone with the whole defence of the north-eastern frontier of Portugal thrown on his hands. He soon heard of the storming of Zamora and Toro, and learnt that Lapisse's division had arrived at Salamanca. Three marches might bring that general to the border.

A few days later Wilson received from Sir John Cradock the news that he had ordered the British garrison to evacuate Almeida[1], and to retire on Lisbon, as the whole remaining force in Portugal would probably have to embark in a few days. The new commander-in-chief added that he should advise Wilson to bring off his British officers and depart with the rest, as the Portuguese would be unable to make any head against Bonaparte, and it would be a useless sacrifice to linger in their company and be overwhelmed. This pusillanimous counsel shocked and disgusted Wilson : he called together his subordinates, and found that they agreed with him in considering Cradock's advice disgraceful. They resolved that they could not desert their Portuguese comrades, and were in honour bound to see the campaign to an end, however black the present outlook might appear [2].

When therefore the British garrison of Almeida was withdrawn, Wilson entered that fortress with the Legion and took charge of it. He obtained from the Regency leave to appoint his lieutenant-colonel, William Mayne, as the governor, and also received permission to assume command of the local levies

---

[1] It consisted of the 45th and 97th regiments.

[2] Napier, who is very friendly to Cradock, makes no mention of this extraordinary dispatch. But it is fully substantiated by Mayne and Lillie, who were both present at Wilson's council of war, and heard the matter discussed. See their *History of the Lusitanian Legion*, p. 43.

in the neighbourhood. These consisted of the skeletons of two line regiments (nos. 11 and 23) whose reorganization had but just begun. There were also two militia regiments (Guarda and Trancoso) to be raised in the district, but at this moment they existed only in name, and possessed neither officers nor arms. For immediate action Wilson could count upon nothing but the 1,300 men of the Lusitanian Legion.

Nevertheless he resolved to advance at once, and to endeavour to impose on Lapisse by a show of activity. Leaving the Portuguese regulars and 700 men of the Legion to garrison Almeida, he crossed the frontier with his handful of cavalry (not 200 sabres), two guns, and 300 men of his light companies. Passing the Spanish fortress of Ciudad Rodrigo he advanced some distance on the Salamanca road, and took up his position behind the Yeltes river, with his right resting on the inaccessible Sierra de Francia, and his left at San Felices, half way to the Douro. His whole force constituted no more than a thin line of pickets, but he acted with such confidence and decision, beating up the French outposts with his dragoons, raiding well forward in the direction of Ledesma and Tamames, and stirring up the peasants of the mountain country to insurrection, that Lapisse gave him credit for having a considerable force at his back. The French general had expected to meet with no opposition on his way to Almeida, believing that Cradock was about to embark, and that the Portuguese would not fight. He was accordingly much surprised to find a long line in his front, occupied by troops dressed like British riflemen, and commanded by British officers—whose strength he was unable to ascertain. He halted, in order to take stock of his opponent, when a bold push would have shown him that only a skeleton army was before him. In an intercepted dispatch of February [1] he reported that the peasantry informed him that Wilson had 12,000 men, and that as many more were in garrison at Ciudad Rodrigo and Almeida.

As the weeks wore on, and the winter drew to an end, Wilson obtained some slight reinforcements. When he first advanced the Spaniards could give him no help, for the garrison of Ciudad Rodrigo itself consisted of nothing but its six companies of

[1] See the *Lusitanian Legion*, p. 47.

urban militia, and a new battalion of 500 men, which had been on the point of setting out to join La Romana when its way to Leon was intercepted by the French.   There were 1,400 men to man a fortress which required a garrison of 4,000[1]!   But before January was out, Pignatelli, the captain-general of Castile, had sent into the place a regiment which he had raised in the mountains of Avila, and Carlos d'España[2] had begun to form some new battalions from the peasantry of the Ciudad Rodrigo district, stiffened by stragglers from La Romana's army[3].   In February the Central Junta gave Wilson a provisional command over the Spanish forces in Leon, and he used his authority to draw upon the garrison of Rodrigo for detachments to strengthen his outposts.   He also requisitioned men from Almeida, when the Portuguese regiments there placed had begun to fill up their ranks to a respectable strength.   A few cavalry of the re-formed 11th of the line were especially useful to him for scouting work.

With this small assistance, Wilson, whose total force never exceeded 400 horse and 3,000 infantry, kept Lapisse employed throughout February and March.   He beat up the French quarters on several occasions, and twice captured large convoys of provisions which were being directed on Salamanca ; to fall upon one of these, a great requisition of foodstuffs from Ledesma, he dashed far within Lapisse's lines, but brought out all the wagons in safety and delivered them to the governor of Ciudad Rodrigo.   At last, emboldened by his adversary's timidity, he extended his right beyond the Sierra de Francia, and established part of the Legion under Colonel Mayne in the Puerto de Baños, the main pass between Salamanca and Estremadura. Thus Lapisse was completely cut off from all communication

[1] This fact comes from a letter of Ramon Blanco, governor of Ciudad Rodrigo, dated Jan. 13, which Frere sent home to Castlereagh, and which is therefore now in the Record Office.   Blanco complains that he is absolutely without trained artillerymen of any sort.

[2] Carlos d'España, whose name we shall so frequently meet during the succeeding years, was no Spaniard, but a French *émigré* officer of the name of D'Espagne.   Englishmen, on account of his name, sometimes took him for a prince of the Spanish royal family.

[3] Sir Robert Wilson to Frere, dated Jan. 29, in the Record Office. The regiment sent by Pignatelli was called ' Volunteers of Avila.'

with Victor and the French army on the Tagus, save by the circuitous route through Madrid.

Jourdan, writing in the name of King Joseph, had duly transmitted to Lapisse the Emperor's orders to march on Abrantes, the moment that it should be known that Soult had arrived at Oporto. He had even reiterated these directions in February, though both he and the King doubted their wisdom. Victor had written to Madrid to suggest that Alcantara would be a much better and safer objective for the division to aim at than Abrantes[1]. He wished to draw Lapisse's troops (which properly belonged to the 1st Corps) into his own sphere of operations, and repeatedly declared that without them he had no hope of bringing his Estremaduran campaign to a happy end, much less of executing any effective diversion against Portugal. Jourdan agreed with him, opining that Lapisse would miscarry, if he invaded central Portugal on an independent line of operations. But no one was so convinced of this as Lapisse himself, who, with his exaggerated ideas of the strength of Wilson, was most reluctant to move forward. As late as the end of March the Emperor's orders were still ostensibly in vigour[2], and the general only excused himself for not marching, by pretending that he could not venture to advance till he had certain news of Soult's movements. This the Galician insurgents were obliging enough to keep from him.

At last, however, Jourdan yielded to Victor's wishes, and authorized Lapisse to drop down on to Alcantara, keeping outside the limits of Portugal, instead of making the attack on Rodrigo and the subsequent dash at Abrantes which the Emperor had prescribed[3]. Overjoyed at escaping from the responsibility which he dreaded, Lapisse first prepared to march

---

[1] Victor to King Joseph, from Toledo, Feb. 3, 1809.

[2] This is shown by a letter of March 23 from Solignac, one of Lapisse's brigadiers, which was intercepted by guerrillas. The general writes to his friend Raguerie that the march on Abrantes is certain, and that letters for him had better be readdressed to Lisbon [Record Office].

[3] Jourdan's *Mémoires*, p. 189, show that he and Joseph authorized the move, at Victor's instance, and prove that it was not made on Lapisse's own responsibility, as Napier supposes [ii. 72], but in obedience to superior orders.

southward by the Puerto de Baños. But when he found it held by Mayne and the troops of Wilson's right wing, he made no attempt to force the passage, but resolved to carry out his design by stratagem. Massing his division, he marched on Ciudad Rodrigo upon April 6. He pierced with ease the feeble screen of Wilson's outposts and appeared in front of the Spanish fortress, which he duly summoned to surrender. But though the place might easily have been carried by a *coup de main* in January, it was now safe against anything but a formal siege, and Lapisse had neither a battering-train nor any real intention of attacking. When the governor returned a defiant answer, the French division made a show of sitting down in front of the walls. This was done in order to draw Wilson to the aid of the place, and the move was successful. Calling in all his outlying detachments from the nearer passes and collecting some of Carlos d'España's levies, Sir Robert took post close to the walls of Ciudad Rodrigo, with a battalion of the Legion under Colonel Grant, some other Portuguese troops and four guns [1].

Having thus lured Wilson away from the passes, the French general suddenly broke up by night, and made a forced march for the Puerto de Perales, the nearest mountain - road to Alcantara. He thus obtained a full day's start, and got off unmolested. Sir Robert and Carlos d'España followed on his track as soon as they discovered his departure, and Mayne also pursued, from the Puerto de Baños, but none of them could do more than harass his rearguard, with which they skirmished for three days in the passes. It would not have been wise of them to attempt more, even if they could have got into touch with the main body, for the French division was double their strength. Meanwhile the peasantry of the Sierra de Gata endeavoured to stop Lapisse's progress, by blocking the defiles; but he swept them away with ease, and they never succeeded in delaying him for more than a few hours. Their incessant 'sniping' and night attacks exasperated the French, who dealt most ruthlessly with the country-side as they passed. When

[1] This narrative is from Mayne and Lillie, supplemented by Jourdan and other French sources. Wilson thought that he had foiled a real attack on Rodrigo, but was mistaken: Lapisse was only feinting.

they arrived at Alcantara, and found the little town barricaded, they not only refused all quarter to the fighting-men when they stormed the place, but committed dreadful atrocities on the non-combatants. Not only murder and rape but mutilation and torture are reported by credible witnesses[1]. After the houses had been sacked, the very tombs in the churches were broken open in search of plunder. Leaving Alcantara full of corpses and ruins [April 12], the division marched on by Caceres and joined Victor in his camp near Merida[2] [April 19].

Since Lapisse, then, had moved off far to the south, and thrown in his lot with his old comrades of the 1st Corps, it was in vain that Soult sought for news of him on the Douro after the fall of Oporto. When Loison set out to cross the Tamega and to enter the Tras-os-Montes, in order that he might obtain information of the movements of the division at Salamanca, that division was making ready for its march to Alcantara; a fortnight later it had disappeared from the northern theatre of operations altogether, and Soult's last chance of obtaining external help for his invasion of Portugal was gone. This section, in short, of Napoleon's great plan for the march on Lisbon had been foiled, and foiled almost entirely by Sir Robert Wilson's happy audacity and resourceful generalship. But for

[1] It is impossible to make out why Alcantara was treated so much worse than other places taken by storm, but the facts are well vouched for. The report of the local authorities to Cuesta says that not only all peasants taken with arms in their hands, but more than forty non-combatants were butchered, and that not a woman who had remained in the place escaped rape. Lillie, the historian of the Lusitanian Legion, who was with the force that pursued Lapisse from Rodrigo, says that he saw the traces of 'acts of barbarity that would disgrace the most savage and uncivilized of mankind'—corpses deliberately mutilated and laid out to roast on piles of burning furniture, with the bodies of domestic animals, such as pigs and dogs, placed on the top of the pile as if in jest [*Lusitanian Legion*, pp. 66–7]. The German historian Schepeler gives very similar details, adding the note about the dragging up of bones and coffins from the churches.

[2] All Napier's criticism (ii. 85–6) on Lapisse's movement to Alcantara is vitiated by his ignorance of the fact that Jourdan and the King, at Victor's instance, had sent him orders to go there. But nothing can excuse his previous inaction in February and March. He ought to have attacked Rodrigo before the end of January, when it was still almost without a garrison, and in a state of great disrepair.

him, the timidity of Cradock, the impotence of the Spaniards, and the disorganization of the Portuguese army might. have brought about the fall of Ciudad Rodrigo and Almeida, at the same moment that Soult was entering Portugal on its northern frontier.   His services have never received their proper meed of praise, either from the government which he served so well, or from the historians who have told the annals of the Peninsular War.

We must now return to the details of the Duke of Dalmatia's operations.   His movements were clearly dependent on the results of the two expeditions under Heudelet and Loison, which he had sent out to the north and the east after his victory of March 29.

Heudelet, after discharging on to Oporto the sick and wounded and the stores which he had been guarding at Braga, started out northward on April 6, with the 4,000 infantry of his own division and Lorges' dragoons, whom the Marshal had ordered up to his aid from Villa de Conde.   Heudelet was ordered to disperse the insurgents in the valleys of the Lima and Minho, and to relieve Tuy and Vigo, where the French garrisons were known to be in a state of siege.   To reach them it was necessary to pierce through the screen of militia and *Ordenanza* under General Botilho, which had cut off all communication between Galicia and the army of Portugal since the month of February.

On April 7 the French general neared the line of the Lima, only to find the bridges barricaded and Botilho's horde entrenched behind them.   After some preliminary skirmishing, fords were discovered, which Heudelet's infantry passed upon the following morning, sending the unfortunate Portuguese flying in every direction and capturing the three guns which formed their sole artillery.   On the tenth the frontier fortress of Valenza was reached: it was found to be in a dilapidated condition, and garrisoned by only 200 men, who surrendered at the first summons.   Tuy, where General Lamartinière had been shut up for the last seven weeks, faces Valenza across the broad estuary of the Minho, so that Heudelet was now in full communication with it.

Lamartinière, as it will be remembered [1], had been left behind,

[1] See p. 188.

with Soult's heavy artillery, wheeled transport, and sick, when
the 2nd Corps marched for Orense on February 16. He had
gathered in several belated detachments which had started from
Santiago in the hope of joining the rear of the marching
column, so that he had the respectable force of 3,300 men,
though 1,200 of them were invalids or convalescents. The
walls of Tuy were in a bad state of repair, but the governor
had found no great difficulty in maintaining himself against the
Galician insurgents on his own side of the Minho, and the
Portuguese levies from the other bank which Botilho sent to
the aid of the Spaniards. But he had been completely shut in
since Soult's departure, and could give no information concerning Ney's operations in northern Galicia, or the general progress
of the war in the other parts of Spain. The only news which
he could supply was that Vigo, the next French garrison, had
fallen into the hands of the enemy. On his way to Portugal
Soult had dropped a force of 700 men at that fortress, lest its
excellent harbour should be utilized by the British for throwing
in supplies to the Galician insurgents. The paymaster-general
of the 2nd Corps, with his treasure and its escort, had lagged
behind during the Marshal's advance, and, being beset by the
peasantry, had entered Vigo instead of pushing on to Tuy.

When Soult had passed out of sight on the way to Orense,
the Galicians of the coast-land, headed by Pablo Morillo, a
lieutenant of the regular army whom La Romana had sent
down from the interior, and by Manuel Garcia Del Barrio [1],
a colonel dispatched by the Central Junta from Seville, had
taken arms in great numbers, and blockaded Vigo. The French
commander, Colonel Chalot, found himself unable to defend the
whole extent of the fortifications for sheer want of men, and
could not prevent the insurgents from establishing themselves
close under the walls and keeping up a continual fire upon the
garrison. He believed that a serious assault would infallibly
succeed, and only refused to surrender because he was ashamed
to yield to peasants. On March 23 two English frigates, the
Lively and *Venus*, appeared off the harbour mouth, and began
to supply the insurgents with ammunition, and to land heavy

---

[1] Napier's 'Colonel Barrois.'

naval guns for their use. On the twenty-seventh one of the gates was battered in, and the Galicians were preparing to storm the place, when Chalot surrendered at discretion, only stipulating that he and his men should be handed over to the British, and not to the Spaniards. This request was granted, and Captain Mackinley received twenty-three officers and nearly 800 men as prisoners, besides a number of sick and several hundred non-combatants belonging to the train, and camp-followers. The plunder taken consisted of sixty wagons, 339 horses, and more than £6,000 in hard cash, composing the military chest of the 2nd Corps [March 28].

The Galicians had somewhat relaxed the blockade of Tuy in order to press that of Vigo, and on the very day when Chalot surrendered, General Lamartinière had sent out a flying column to endeavour to communicate with his colleague. It returned pursued by the Spaniards, to report to the governor that Vigo had fallen[1]. On its way back to Tuy it suffered a loss of seventy prisoners and nearly 200 killed and wounded.

Heudelet and Lamartinière had now some 7,000 men collected at Tuy, a force with which they could easily have routed the whole of the insurgents of the Minho, and forced them to retire into the mountains. But Soult's orders to his lieutenants were to avoid operations in Galicia, and to concentrate towards Portugal. Tuy was evacuated, and its garrison transferred across the frontier-river to the Portuguese fortress of Valenza. Before the transference was completed, the French generals received an unexpected visit from some troops of the 6th Corps. Ney, disquieted as to the condition of Tuy and Vigo, had sent a brigade under Maucune to seek for news of their garrisons. This force, cutting its way through the insurgents, came into

---

[1] Most of these details as to the fall of Vigo come from a contemporary account in Andrade's collection, printed in *Los Guerrilleros Gallegos*, pp. 129–37. Le Noble asserts that only 794 men were captured, but Captain Mackinley says that he received nearly 1,300 prisoners, including 300 sick and many non-combatants. He had the best opportunities of knowing, and must be followed. Le Noble and the Spaniards do not give the French commander's name, but I find that of Chalot as the senior officer among the prisoners in the list in the Record Office. Next to him is the paymaster-general Conscience. Toreno and Schepeler agree with Captain Mackinley in giving the number of the prisoners at over 1,200.

Tuy on April 12. Thus Heudelet was at last able to get news of the operations of Ney. The information received was not encouraging : the Duke of Elchingen was beset by the Galicians on every side : La Romana had cut off one of his outlying garrisons, that of Villafranca, and his communications with Leon were so completely cut off that he had no reports to give as to the progress of affairs in the rest of Spain. Finding that Vigo was lost, and the garrison of Tuy relieved, Maucune retraced his steps and returned to Santiago, harassed for the whole of his march by the insurgents of the coast-land.

Meanwhile Heudelet's communication with Oporto had been interrupted, for the Portuguese, routed on the Lima a week before, had come back to their old haunts, seized Braga, and blocked the high-road and the bridges. Soult only got into touch with his expeditionary force by sending out Lahoussaye with 3,000 men to reopen the road to the North. When this was done, he bade Heudelet evacuate Valenza (whose fortifications turned out to be in too bad order to be repaired in any reasonable space of time), and to disperse his division in garrisons for Braga, Viana, and Barcelos. The whole of the convoy and the sick from Tuy were sent up to Oporto.

The net result of Heudelet's operations was that the Marshal, at the cost of immobilizing one of his four infantry divisions, obtained a somewhat precarious hold upon the flat country of Entre-Douro-e-Minho. The towns were in his hands, but the *Ordenanza* had only retired to the hills, and perpetually descended to worry Heudelet's detachments, and to murder couriers and foraging parties. Meanwhile 4,000 men were wasted for all purposes of offensive action. Vigo, Tuy, and Valenza had all been abandoned, and touch with the army of Galicia had been completely lost.

Even this modest amount of success had been denied to Soult's second expedition, that which he had sent under Loison towards the Tras-os-Montes. The enemy with whom the French had to deal in this region was Silveira, the same officer who had been defeated between Monterey and Chaves in the early days of March, when the 2nd Corps crossed the Portuguese frontier. He had fled with the wrecks of his force towards Villa Real, at the moment when Soult marched on Braga, and the Marshal had fondly hoped that he was now a negligible quantity in the campaign.   This was far from being the case : the moment that Silveira heard that the French had crossed the mountains and marched on Braga, he had rallied his two regular regiments and his masses of *Ordenanza*, and pounced down on the detachment under Commandant Messager, which Soult had left in garrison at Chaves.   This, it will be remembered, consisted of no more than a company of infantry, a quantity of convalescents and stragglers, and the untrustworthy Spanish-Portuguese ' legion,' which had been formed out of the prisoners captured on March 6 and 12 [1].   On the very day upon which Soult was routing Eben in front of Braga, Silveira appeared before the walls of Chaves with 6,000 men.   Messager retired into the citadel, abandoning on the outer walls of the town a few guns, which the Portuguese were thus enabled to turn against the inner defences.   After a siege of five days and much ineffective cannonading, the governor surrendered, mainly because the native 'legion' was preparing to open the gates to Silveira.   Twelve hundred men were captured, of whom only one-third were Frenchmen capable of bearing arms, the rest being sick or 'legionaries.'

Having made this successful stroke, Silveira marched down the Tamega to Amarante, making a movement parallel to Soult's advance on Oporto.   His recapture of Chaves brought several thousands more of *Ordenanza* to his standard, and at Amarante he was joined on the thirtieth by many of the fugitives who had escaped from the sack of Oporto on the previous day.   He spread his army, now amounting to 9,000 or 10,000 men, along the left bank of the Tamega, whose bridges and fords he protected with entrenchments.   Advanced

---

[1] Le Noble, though he mentions the formation of the legion (p. 120), omits to state that it was left at Chaves.   But St. Chamans establishes this fact (p. 120) ; he calls the corps ' les Espagnols et Portugais qui se disaient de notre parti.'   Des Odoards (p. 212) also speaks of the ' legion,' as does Naylies (p. 81).   Its existence explains both the feebleness of Messager's defence, and the large number of prisoners whom Silveira captured.   The fighting force of the garrison was only the one company, plus some hundreds of convalescents, who in the fortnight since Soult's departure had been able to resume their arms.

guards were pushed out on the further side of the river on the three roads which lead to Oporto.

When, therefore, the troops under Loison, which Soult had sent out towards the Tras-os-Montes, drew near the Tamega, they found the Portuguese in force. The cavalry could get no further forward than Penafiel; when Foy's infantry came up (April 7) Loison tried to force the enemy back, both on the Amarante and on the Canavezes road. He failed at each point, and sent back to the Marshal to ask for reinforcements. Seeing him halt, Silveira, whose fault was not a want of initiative, actually crossed the river with his whole army, and fell upon the two French brigades. He was checked, but not badly beaten, and Loison remained on the defensive (April 12).

At this moment Soult heard of the fall of Chaves, full seventeen days after it had happened. Realizing that Silveira was now growing formidable, he sent to Loison's aid General Delaborde with the second of his infantry brigades, and Lorges' dragoons. These reinforcements brought the troops facing Silveira up to a total of some 6,500 men—nearly a third of Soult's whole disposable force. As Heudelet was still absent on the Minho with 4,000 men more, the Marshal had less than 10,000 left in and about Oporto. It was clear that the grand march on Lisbon was not likely to begin for many a long day.

On April 18 Loison advanced against Silveira, who boldly but unwisely offered him battle on the heights of Villamea in front of Amarante. Considering that he had but 2,000 regulars and 7,000 or 8,000 half-armed militia and *Ordenanza*, his conduct can only be described as rash in the extreme. He was, of course, beaten with great loss, and hustled back into the town of Amarante. He would have lost both it and its bridge, but for the gallantry of Colonel Patrick, an English officer commanding a battalion of the 12th of the line, who rallied his regiment in the streets, seized a group of houses and a convent at the bridge-head and beat off the pursuers[1]. Patrick was mortally wounded, but the passage of the river was prevented. This saved the situation: Silveira got his men together, planted

---

[1] Silveira to Beresford (Record Office). Cf. Foy's dispatch to Loison (April 19), in which he owns that he failed to hold the convent, and retired with a loss of ninety-one men of the 17th regiment.

his artillery so as to command the bridge, and took post in entrenchments already constructed on the commanding heights on the left bank. Next day Loison stormed the buildings at the bridge-head, but found that he could get no further forward. The town was his, but he could not debouch from it, as the bridge was palisaded, built up with a barricade of masonry and raked by the Portuguese artillery. Soult now sent up to aid Loison still further reinforcements, Sarrut's brigade of infantry from Merle's division and the second brigade of Lahoussaye's dragoons. Thus no less than 9,000 French troops, nearly half the army of Portugal, were concentrated at Amarante.

The fact that twelve whole days elapsed between the arrival of these last succours and the forcing of the passage of the Tamega had no small influence on the fate of Soult's campaign. Hitherto the initiative had lain with him, and he had faced adversaries who could only take the defensive. This period was nearly at an end, for on April 22 Wellesley had landed at Lisbon, the English reinforcements had begun to arrive, and an army, differing in every quality from the hordes which the Marshal had encountered north of the Douro, was about to assume the offensive against him. By the time that Loison at last forced the bridge of Amarante, the British were already on the march for Coimbra and Oporto.

Silveira and his motley host, therefore, were doing admirable service to the cause of their country when they occupied 9,000 out of Soult's 21,000 men from April 20 to May 2 on the banks of the Tamega. The ground was in their favour, but far stronger positions had been forced ere now, and it was fortunate that this one was maintained for so many days. The town of Amarante, it must be remembered, lies on comparatively low ground : its bridge is completely commanded by the heights on which Silveira had planted his camp and his batteries. The river flows in a deep-sunk ravine, and was at this moment swollen into an impassable torrent by the melting of the mountain snows. Loison more than once sent swimmers by night, in search of places where the strength of the current might be sufficiently moderate to allow of an attempt to pass on rafts or boats. Not one of these explorers could get near the further bank : they were swept off by the rushing water and cast ashore far down stream, on the same side from which they had started. There had been bridges above Amarante at Mondin and Aroza, and below it at Canavezes, but reconnaissances showed that they had all three been blown up, and that Portuguese detachments were watching their ruins, to prevent any attempt to reconstruct them. Loison found, therefore, that he could not turn Silveira's position by a flanking movement : there was nothing to do save to wait till the river should fall, or to attempt to force the bridge of Amarante at all costs. Continual rains made it hopeless to expect the subsidence of the Tamega for many days, wherefore Loison devoted all his energies to the task of capturing the bridge. Even here there was one difficulty to be faced which might prove fatal : the French engineers had discovered that the structure was mined. It was necessary, therefore, not only to drive back the Portuguese, but to prevent them from blowing up the bridge at the moment of their retreat.

Loison had entrusted the details of the attack on the bridge to Delaborde, whose infantry held the advanced posts. That officer first tried to approach the head of the bridge by means of a flying sap ; but when it had advanced a certain distance the fire of the Portuguese from across the river became so deadly, that after many men had been killed in the endeavour to work up to the palisades on the bridge, the attempt had to be abandoned. The next device recommended by the engineers was that an attempt should be made to lay a trestle bridge at a spot some way below the town, where a mill-dam contracted the width of the angry river. This was found to be impossible, the stream proving to be far deeper than had been supposed, while the Portuguese from the left bank picked off many of the workmen [April 25].

Soult was now growing vexed at the delay, and sent two guns of position from Oporto to Loison, to enable him to subdue the fire of the enemy's batteries. He also offered to call up Heudelet's division from Braga, even at the cost of abandoning his hold on the northern part of the province of Entre-Douro-e-Minho. But a mere increase of his already considerable force would have been of no service to Loison ; it was a device for passing the Tamega that he needed.

Such a scheme was at last laid before him by Captain
Bouchard, one of his engineers [1].   The French officers had
discovered, by a careful use of their glasses, that the Portuguese
mine, which was to destroy the bridge, was situated in its left-
hand arch, and that the mechanism by which it was to be
worked was not a 'sausage' or a train of powder [2], but a loaded
musket, whose muzzle was placed in the mine, while to its
trigger was attached a cord which ran to the nearest trenches
beyond the river.   The musket was concealed in a box, but its
cord was visible to those provided with a good telescope.
Bouchard argued that if the cord could be cut or broken, the
enemy would not be able to touch off the mine, and he had
thought out a plan for securing his end.   He maintained that
an explosion at the French side of the bridge would probably
sever the cord without firing the mine, and that a sudden
assault, made immediately after the explosion, and before the
Portuguese could recover themselves, might carry the barricades.   In spite of the strongly-expressed doubts of Foy and
several other generals, Bouchard was finally permitted to carry
out his scheme.

He executed it on the night of May 2, when a dense fog
chanced to favour his daring and hazardous proceedings.   Having
first told off some *tirailleurs* to keep up a smart fire on the
enemy's trenches and distract his attention, he sent four sappers,
each provided with a small powder-barrel, on to the bridge.
The men, dressed in their grey *capotes*, crawled on hands and
knees, each rolling his barrel (which was wrapped in cloth to
deaden the sound) before him.   They kept in the shadow, and
getting close under the parapet of the bridge crept on till they
reached the outermost Portuguese palisade.   One after another,
at long intervals, each got forward unobserved, left his barrel
behind, and crawled back.   The fourth sapper, starting to his
feet on his return journey, was observed by the Portuguese and
shot down, but Silveira's men did not realize what he had been
doing, and merely took him for some daring explorer who was

[1] Napier, ii. pp. 80–1, consistently mis-calls him Brochard.

[2] Either of these might easily have been fired by a casual shot, during
the long cannonading which had been in progress. The Portuguese, therefore, avoided them.

endeavouring to spy out the state of the defences. After
waiting for an hour, Bouchard sent out a fifth sapper, who
dragged behind him a 'sausage' of powder thirty yards long,
which he successfully connected with the four barrels. All was
now ready, and a battalion of picked grenadiers from Delaborde's
division, filed silently down into the street near the bridge-head:
a whole brigade came behind them.

At two o'clock Bouchard fired his sausage, and the explosion
followed. There were two chances of failure—one that the
apparatus for firing the mine might not be disturbed by the
concussion, the other that the shock might prove too strong,
reach the mine, and destroy the bridge. Neither of these fatali-
ties took place : the explosion duly broke the cord, shattered
the nearest palisades, but did not affect the mine. Before the
smoke had cleared away Delaborde's grenadiers had dashed
out on to the bridge, scrambled over the barricades, and
driven off the guard on the further side. Regiment after
regiment followed them, and charged up the mountain-side
towards Silveira's batteries and entrenchments. None of the
Portuguese were under arms, save the few companies guarding
the debouches from the bridge. These were swept away, and
the French columns came storming into the bivouacs of the
enemy before he was well awake. Hardly half a dozen cannon
shots were fired on them from the batteries, and the greater
part of the army of the Tras-os-Montes fled without firing
a shot. Silveira escaped almost naked by the back window of
the house above the bridge in which he had been sleeping.

All the ten guns in the Portuguese batteries, five standards,
and several hundred prisoners fell into the hands of the
victorious French, who lost (it is said) no more than two killed
and seven wounded. Their good fortune had been extraordinary : without the opportune fog which hid their advance,
their preliminary operations would probably have been discovered. If their explosion had done a little more or a little
less than was hoped, the bridge might have been totally
destroyed, or its barricades left practically uninjured—either of
which chances would have foiled Bouchard's plan. But the
luck of the army of Portugal was still in the ascendant, and all
went exactly as had been intended.

Thus the Tamega was passed, and Silveira decisively beaten : his levies had fled in all directions, and Soult opined that it would take a long time to rally them.   The day after the fight Loison was joined at Amarante by Heudelet's division from Braga, which, in obedience to the Marshal's orders, had marched to join the expeditionary force, leaving only a single battalion behind to hold Viana.   This was an unfortunate move, as on Heudelet's departure the *Ordenanza* came down from the Serra de Santa Catalina, and overran the district which had been evacuated, in spite of Lorges' dragoons, who had been directed to keep the roads clear after the infantry had been withdrawn.

Meanwhile there were far more troops at Amarante than were needed for the pursuit of Silveira, so Soult called back to Oporto the division of Delaborde, leaving to Loison the infantry of Heudelet and Sarrut, with Lahoussaye's two brigades of dragoons, a force of about 7,000 men.   He ordered his lieutenant to scour the country as far as Villa Real, and to send reconnaissances on the roads toward Chaves and Braganza, with the object of frightening the insurgents to retreat as far as possible.   But Loison was not to advance for more than two days' march into the Tras-os-Montes, for rumours were beginning to arrive concerning the appearance of British troops in the direction of Coimbra, and the Marshal wished to keep his various divisions close enough to each other to enable them to concentrate with ease.   If there were any truth in the news from the south, it would be dangerous to allow a force which formed a third of the whole army of Portugal to go astray in the heart of the mountains beyond the Tamega.   Loison accordingly marched off on May 8 towards Villa Real, which he occupied without meeting with resistance.   He learnt that Silveira and his regulars had crossed the Douro, and gone off in the direction of Lamego ; but Botilho had fled up the Tamega towards Chaves, and the *Ordenanza* were lurking in the hills.   He then returned to Amarante, where we may leave him, at the end of his tether, while we describe the state of affairs in Oporto.

SECTION XIII: CHAPTER VI

INTRIGUES AT OPORTO : THE CONSPIRACY OF ARGENTON

It will have occurred to every student of the operations of the army of Portugal during the month of April, that it was strange that Marshal Soult should have remained quiescent at Oporto, while the fate of his entire campaign was at stake during the fighting on the Tamega. His head quarters were only thirty miles from Amarante—but one day's ride for himself and his staff—yet he never paid a single flying visit to the scene of operations, even after he had come to the conclusion that Loison was mismanaging the whole business. He sent his lieutenant many letters of reproach, forwarded to him guns of position, and ample reinforcements, but never came himself to the spot to urge on the advance, even when ten and twelve days had elapsed since the first unsuccessful attempts to force the passage of the Tamega.

The explanation of this persistent refusal of the Marshal to quit Oporto is to be found in the political not the military state of affairs. At Chaves he had proclaimed himself Viceroy of Portugal: his viceroyalty at that moment embraced only just so much soil as was covered by the encampments of his battalions. But after the capture of Oporto and the occupation of the neighbouring towns of the Entre-Douro-e-Minho, his position assumed an air of reality, and he himself allowed the duties of the viceroy to trespass on those of the commander of the Second Corps d'Armée. Nay more, there is good reason to believe that he was not merely dreaming of setting up a stable government in northern Portugal, but of something else. The evidence as to his intentions is hard to weigh, for most of it comes from the letters and diaries of men who disliked him, but there are certain facts which cannot be disguised, and the inference from them is irresistible.

With the example of Murat's exaltation before them, the more ambitious and capable of Napoleon's marshals could not refrain from dreaming of crowns and sceptres. Nothing seemed impossible in those astounding days, when the Emperor was creating sovereigns and realms by a stroke of the pen, whenever the notion seized him. The line between an appanaged duke and a vassal prince was a very thin one—as the case of Berthier shows. Junot had dreamed of royalty at Lisbon in 1808, and there seems little doubt that the same mirage of a crown floated before Soult's eyes at Oporto in 1809. The city itself suggested the idea: in the Treaty of Fontainebleau Napoleon had put on paper the project for creating a 'king of Northern Lusitania,' with Oporto as his capital and the Entre-Douro-e-Minho as his realm. Soult was cautious and wary, but he was also greedy and ambitious. If, on the one hand, he had a wholesome fear of his master, he had on the other good reasons for believing that it might be possible to force his hand by presenting him with a *fait accompli.*

There was in the city the nucleus of a party which was not wholly indisposed to submit to the French domination. It was mainly composed of those enemies of the Bishop of Oporto who had been suffering from his anarchical rule of the last two months. They were the friends and relatives of those who had perished by the dagger or the rope, during the mob-law which had prevailed ever since Dom Antonio returned from Lisbon. To these may be added some men of purely material interests, who saw that the insurrection was ruining them, and a remnant of the old corrupt bureaucracy which had submitted once before to Junot—whose only thought was to keep or gain profitable posts under the government of the day, whatever that government might be. The whole body of dissidents from the cause of patriotism and independence was so small and weak, that it is impossible to believe that they would have taken any overt action if they had not received encouragement from Soult.

This much is certain—that when the disorders which accompanied the capture of Oporto were ended, Soult showed himself most anxious to conciliate the Portuguese, not only by introducing a regular and orderly government, but by going out of his way to soothe and flatter any notable who lingered in the city. In his anxiety to win over the clergy he caused new silver vessels and candelabra to be made to replace those which had been stolen from the churches in the sack[1]. He filled up all civil appointments, whose holders had fled, from the small number of persons who were ready to adhere to the French. He again, as already at Chaves, endeavoured to enlist a native military force, by putting tempting offers before those officers of the regular army who had been made prisoners. All this might have had no other cause than the wish to build up a party of *Afrancesados*, such as already existed in Spain, and Soult openly declared that such was his object[2]. This was the only purpose that he avowed in his dispatches to the Emperor, and in his communications with his colleagues.

But if the Marshal had no ulterior object in view, it is singular that all his native partisans concurred in setting on foot a movement for getting him saluted as king of northern Portugal. The new municipal authorities, whom he had established in the half-deserted towns occupied by his troops, sent in petitions begging him to assume the position of sovereign. Documents of this kind came in from Braga, Barcellos, Guimaraens, Feira, Oliveira and Villa de Conde. In Oporto proclamations were posted on the walls declaring that ' the Prince Regent by his departure to Brazil had formally resigned his crown, and that the only salvation for Portugal would be that the Duke of Dalmatia, the most distinguished of the pupils of the great Napoleon, should ascend the vacant throne[3].' A priest named Veloso and other persons went about in the street delivering harangues in favour of the creation of the 'kingdom of Northern Lusitania.' A register was opened in the municipal buildings

[1] See Le Noble (Soult's partisan and official vindicator), p. 207, and Fantin des Odoards, p. 227.

[2] See his conversation with his aide-de-camp, St. Chamans, in the latter's *Mémoires*, p. 139. The Marshal said that he was in a hazardous military position and that ' je ne puis m'en tirer qu'en divisant les Portugais entre eux, et j'emploie pour cela le meilleur moyen politique qui soit en mon pouvoir.' Compare Fantin des Odoards, p. 227.

[3] Fantin des Odoards, writing at Oporto under the date May 5, says that he had just read this proclamation on the walls, and was astounded at it, for the great bulk of the population was so hostile that the project seemed absolutely insane.

to be signed by all persons who wished to join in the petition
to the Marshal to assume the regal title, and a certain number
of signatures were collected. A newspaper, called the *Diario do
Porto*, was started, to support the movement, and ran for about
a month. It is said that Soult's partisans even succeeded in
gathering small crowds together, before the mansion where his
head quarters were established, to shout *Viva o Rei Nicolao!*
and that the acclamations were acknowledged by showers of
copper coins thrown from the windows[1]. The latter part
of this story is no doubt an invention of Soult's enemies, but
it was believed at the time by the majority of the French
officers, and '*Le Roi Nicolas*' was for the future his nickname
in the army of Portugal[2]. On April 19 the Marshal ordered
his chief of the staff, General Ricard, to issue a circular letter to
the generals of divisions and brigades[3], inviting their co-operation in the movement, and assuring them that no disloyalty to
the Emperor would be involved even if the Marshal assumed
regal powers[4]. This document is the most convincing piece
of evidence that exists as to Soult's intentions. In it there
is no attempt made to conceal the movement that had been set
on foot: the writer's only preoccupation is to show that it was
not directed against Napoleon. When, five months later,
Ricard's circular came under the Emperor's eye, it roused
his wrath to such a pitch that he wrote in the most stinging
and sarcastic terms to Soult. 'He is astounded,' he says, 'to find
the chief of the staff suggesting to the generals that the Marshal
should be requested to take up the reins of government, and
assume the attributes of supreme authority. If he had assumed

---

[1] St. Chamans, aide-de-camp to Soult, speaks of the crowds assembled
by Veloso and others (p. 134) : Bigarré says that General Ricard threw
money to the crowd for seven days running from the Marshal's balcony,
and then stopped because the harvest of *vivas* was not large enough (p. 245).

[2] See Fantin des Odoards, p. 229, and Jourdan, p. 218.

[3] This strange document will be found printed in the Appendix.

[4] See Chamans, pp. 134 and 140. He ends with observing that Soult
'aurait voulu se faire demander pour roi de Portugal par les habitants,
qu'alors, le premier pas fait, il aurait sollicité les suffrages de l'armée, ils
auraient été consignés sur des registres pour chaque corps, et il aurait mis
toutes ces pièces sous les yeux de l'Empereur, en lui demandant son
approbation.'

sovereign power on his own responsibility, it would have been a crime, clear *lèse-majesté*, an attack on the imperial authority. How could a man of sense, like Soult, suppose that his master would permit him to exercise any power that had not been delegated to him? No wonder that the army grew discontented, and that rumours got about that the Marshal was working for himself, not for the Emperor or France. After receiving this circular, it is doubtful whether any French officer would not have been fully justified in refusing to obey any further orders issued from Oporto [1].'

This was written from Vienna, before the Emperor had received any full and exact account of the details of Soult's intrigues. Had he but known them all, it is doubtful if he would have granted his lieutenant the complete pardon and restoration to favour with which his dispatch concludes [2].

There can be no doubt that the Duke of Dalmatia might have put a stop to all the activity of his Portuguese friends by merely raising his hand. It would have sufficed for him to assure the deputations which visited him that his duty as the lieutenant of the Emperor forbade him to listen to their proposals. He

---

[1] Napoleon to Soult from Schönbrunn, Sept. 26, *Nap. Corresp.*, 15,871.

[2] Napier's conclusions as to Soult's conduct are wholly warped by his strong predilection for the Marshal—which dated back to the time when the latter dealt kindly with his wounded brother on the day after Corunna. He understates Soult's encouragement of the movement, and will have us believe that it was purely the work of the Portuguese. He omits all mention of Ricard's circular, and finally suppresses all mention of Napoleon's angry upbraidings except the following (ii. p. 75): 'The Emperor wrote to Soult that the rumour had reached him, adding, with a delicate allusion to the Marshal's previous services, "I remember nothing but Austerlitz."' Now it was not a *rumour* which had reached Schönbrunn, but a copy of Ricard's circular, which the Emperor quotes *verbatim*. Therefore Napoleon was writing with tangible evidence, not with camp reports, to guide him. How far Napier's sentence above gives a fair impression of the tone of the dispatch which I have reproduced, I leave the reader to judge. It was a surprise to myself when I put the two together. Once and for all, it must be remembered that Napier can never be trusted when Soult is in question—the Marshal's intrigues, his greed, his shameful plundering of Andalusian churches, are all concealed.

could have caused the proclamations to be torn down, and have silenced the street orators. 'They could not have made him king against his own will,' as one of his officers remarked[1]. But no action of the kind was taken; and the movement was openly encouraged. The Marshal's explanation, that he was only taking the best means in his power to build up a French party in Oporto, will not stand examination. Why should the scheme involve his own promotion to the throne, if his views were disinterested, and his actions merely intended to serve his master's ends? Is it conceivable that the Portuguese should, of their own accord, and without any suggestion from without, have hit upon the idea of crowning a conqueror whose very name was strange to them three weeks before, and whose hands were red with the blood of thousands of their fellow country-men? Clever and cautious though the Marshal was, it is impossible to avoid the conclusion that he had for once allowed his ambition to take the bit between its teeth, and to whirl him off into an enterprise that was worthy of the most hair-brained of adventurers.

Meanwhile the consequences of his intrigue were strange and various. The army received the news of what was going on at Oporto with puzzled surprise. Of those who were not present at the centre of affairs, some refused to believe the stories that reached them, and merely observed that the Marshal was not such a fool as to take in hand a plan that was both treasonable to his master and preposterous in itself[2]. Others, particularly his personal enemies, not only credited the informa-tion but began to concert measures for resisting him if he should try to carry out his scheme. This party was very strong among the officers of Junot's old army of Portugal, who had been transferred in large numbers to the 2nd Corps. They disliked the expedition, had been prophesying disaster from the first, and had criticized every move of the Marshal. Now they found in the news of his intrigue another excuse

---

[1] Fantin des Odoards, p. 220.

[2] So writes Naylies, of Lahoussaye's dragoons, who, being absent at Amarante and elsewhere, never saw the doings in Oporto: 'Il s'est répandu dans l'armée qu'il aspirait à la souveraineté du pays : on en conçut d'abord quelques inquiétudes, qui furent bientôt dissipées' (p. 119).

for running counter to his orders.   There is good reason for
believing that Loison and Delaborde had actually conferred
on the necessity for seizing and imprisoning the Marshal if he
should take the final step and allow himself to be proclaimed
king.   Both these generals were faithful adherents of Napoleon,
and had no thought save that of serving their master.   But
there were other officers who watched the progress of affairs
with very different eyes.

There had existed in the French army from the day when
the empire was first proclaimed, a party of malcontents who
still regarded Bonaparte as a usurper, and were only biding
their time till it might be safe to deal a blow at him.   Hitherto
his career had been so uniformly successful that no opportunity
had arisen.   But secret societies, of which the *Philadelphes* was
the best known, were at work all through the years of the
Emperor's reign : their one object was to be ready for a *coup
d'état* when the favourable moment should arrive.   The history
of these associations is so obscure that it is impossible to estimate
their strength at any given time—no trustworthy historian ever
arose from their ranks to tell the story of their schemes, when
lips were unsealed by the fall of Napoleon [1].   It is only by
the sudden appearance of phenomena like Malet's conspiracy
of 1812, and the plot which we are now about to describe, that
the reality of the existence of these secret societies is proved.

In the army of Portugal there was a group of officers who
belonged to the band of the discontented, and were perfectly
prepared to execute a *pronunciamento* against the empire if
the times and circumstances proved propitious.   We know
the names of four [2]: Donadieu, colonel of the 47th of the line ;
Lafitte, colonel of the 18th Dragoons ; his brother, a captain in
the same regiment, who was serving on Soult's staff; and Argenton, another captain, who was adjutant of Lafitte's regiment ; two
other plotters are hidden under the assumed names of ' Dupont '
and ' Garis,' by which they were introduced to Wellesley.

---

[1] Charles Nodier's *Histoire des conspirations militaires sous l'Empire* is
unfortunately quite untrustworthy.   He was never among the *Philadelphes*,
and writes as a credulous and ill-informed outsider.   Nevertheless there is
a basis of fact underlying his work.

[2] The names of Argenton, Lafitte, and Donadieu are public property.

There were *certainly* other officers implicated, for it is inconceivable that six men could have planned an insurrection unless they were sure of a certain measure of support. At this moment they were carrying on an active propaganda of discontent, especially among the officers of Delaborde's division and of Lahoussaye's dragoons. There were many men who saw the full iniquity of the Spanish War, and were disgusted at finding themselves involved in it [1]. Others loathed the hanging and burning, the shooting of priests and women, the riding down of half-armed peasants, which had been their lot for the last two months. Still more were simply discontented at being lost in a remote corner of Europe, where glory and profit were both absent, and where ignominious death at the hands of the lurking 'sniper' or the midnight assassin came all too frequently —sometimes death accompanied by torture. It was three months since the army had received a mail from France ; they might as well have been in Egypt or America, and they felt themselves forgotten by their master. In many a mind the question arose whether the game was worth playing : must they for ever persist in this wretched interminable campaign, in order that the Duke of Dalmatia might become a king, or even in order that the Emperor might be able to apply the Continental System in its full rigour to this land of brutish peasants and fanatical monks ? A speedy return to France seemed the one thing desirable.

It is easy to understand that the conspirators found many sympathizers, so long as they confined themselves to setting forth the miseries of the campaign, and to criticizing the Marshal and the Emperor. But they erred when they took a general readiness to grumble for a sign that the army was ripe for revolt. However discontented the officers might be, there were very few of them who were prepared to engage in the game of high treason. The vast majority were still unable to dissociate the idea of the Emperor from the idea of France.

Napier gives them, as does Bigarré. The names of ' Dupont ' and ' Garis ' are in suppressed paragraphs of the *Wellington Dispatches* which Gurwood chose to omit, and are also found in the minutes of Argenton's trial at Paris.

[1] The reader may trace this feeling in Foy's diaries, and Naylies (p. 67).

It was only a few who could rise (or sink) to the conception of turning their arms against Bonaparte in order to free France from autocracy. This bore too close a resemblance to treachery to be palatable to men of honour. None save exalted Jacobins, or men of overweening ambition and few scruples, could contemplate the idea with patience. When we find that the plans of the conspirators included not merely a *pronunciamento*, but the conclusion of a secret pact with the enemies in arms against them, we are driven to conclude that they belonged to the last-named of these classes—that their heads were turned with the grandiose notion of getting an army into their power and changing the fate of Europe.

The conspirators, observing the course of affairs at Oporto, were fully convinced that Soult would within a few days declare himself ' King of Northern Lusitania.' This act would produce an outburst of wrath in the army, and they hoped to turn the inevitable mutiny to their own profit. They intended to seize the Marshal, and then to make an appeal to the soldiery, not in the name of Napoleon but in that of France. They were also prepared to lay hands on any general who might attempt to assume command of the troops in the Emperor's interest [1]. Donadieu and Lafitte had secured some of the officers of their own regiments, and believed that the men would follow them. The other corps, as they hoped, would be drawn away after them, and the cry of liberty and the promise of an instant return to France would lure the whole army into rebellion. So far the plot, though rash and hazardous, might conceivably have been carried out. But their next step was to be the issue of an appeal to Ney's divisions and the other French troops in northern Spain to join them, and march upon the Pyrenees. Even though there were members of the secret societies scattered all through the army, it seems absolutely impossible to believe

---

[1] Napier and Le Noble both hint that Loison was in the plot, and perhaps Delaborde, though they do not actually name these officers. But I think that their innocence is proved by Argenton's declaration to Wellesley (Wellesley to Castlereagh, May 7, Record Office), that Loison was attached to Bonaparte, and would certainly seize Soult if he proclaimed himself king for 'ambitious abuse of his authority and disobedience to his master.'

that they could have carried away with them into open revolt the whole of their companions. The movement of protest against Napoleon would have begun and ended with the 2nd Corps, if even it got so far as the initial *pronunciamento*[1]. To be effective it would have required a strong backing in France, and the list of the leaders in that country, on whom the conspirators said that they relied for aid, does not give us a high opinion of the strength and organization of the plot. The persons named were the old Jacobin general Lecourbe, Macdonald who—though they did not know it—had just been taken back into favour by the Emperor, and Dupont, who was in prison and incapable for the moment of helping himself or any one else[2]. They also spoke of sending for Moreau from America, and placing him at the head of the whole movement. But it is clear that they were not in actual communication with the generals in France, much less with the exiled victor of Hohenlinden. The whole plan was ill-considered; it was the result of the intense irritation against Soult and Bonaparte felt by the officers of the army of Portugal, acting upon the disordered ambition of a knot of intriguers. Anger and vain self-confidence blinded them to the inadequacy of their resources.

It was a main condition of the projected outbreak that Soult's position should be made impossible: the most favourable course of events, so the conspirators held, would be that he should persist in his monarchical ambitions and proclaim himself king. When he did so, the party loyal to Bonaparte among his officers would make an attempt—successful or unsuccessful—to seize his person. Chaos and civil strife within the army would result, and it was then that the conspirators intended to show their hand. It would seem that their Machiavellian foresight

---

[1] This, at the time, was Wellesley's eminently sensible conclusion. He wrote to Castlereagh on April 27, ' I doubt whether it will be quite so easy as their emissary thinks to carry their intentions into execution : I also doubt whether it follows that the successful revolt of this one corps would be followed by that of others, and I am convinced that the method proposed by M. D'Argenton would not answer that purpose.' *Wellington Dispatches*, iv. 276.

[2] These are the names omitted in the printed version of the *Wellington Dispatches* : that of Moreau does not occur there, but is to be found in the confession which Argenton made to Soult : see Le Noble, p. 236.

went so far that they proposed to wait till the Marshal should be imprisoned, or should find himself involved in hostilities with the Bonapartists, and then offer him the aid of their regiments, on condition that he should put himself at the head of the anti-imperialist movement. All this was too ingenious for practical work. But the next development of the plot was even more astonishing in its futile cunning.

The conspirators wished to draw the English commander at Lisbon into their scheme—it was Cradock whom they had in view, for Wellesley was in England when the plot began, and when it developed he had landed indeed, but his arrival was not known. The part which they had allotted to Cradock was twofold—he was to be asked to send secret advice to the Portuguese notables of the north, ordering them to feign an enthusiastic approval of Soult's designs on the crown, and to join with all possible clamour in the demonstrations at Oporto. When this unexpected outburst of devotion to his person should be forthcoming, they supposed that the Marshal would not hesitate any longer to assume the crown. Then would follow civil strife and the desired opportunity for intervention by the conspirators. The second request which they intended to make was that Cradock should bring up the British army to the front, and place it so as to make it dangerous or impossible for Soult to force his way out of Portugal in the direction of the middle Douro and Salamanca. They suggested Villa Real in the Tras-os-Montes as a suitable position for him. Their idea in making this proposal was that the army would be filled with despair at seeing its best line of retreat cut off (that by Galicia was growing to be considered impossible), and would therefore be more incensed against Soult, and at the same time more inclined to secure safety by coming to a pact and agreement with the enemy [1].

[1] It must be remembered that the whole plot was far advanced, and that Argenton had placed himself in treasonable communication with the British, before Wellesley landed. Sir Arthur came ashore on the night of April 22. On the morning of the twenty-fifth, he received a visit from Beresford, who came down from Coimbra to tell him that a French officer, bearing the message of the conspirators, had come within the Portuguese lines on the Vouga on the twenty-first. Argenton arrived at Lisbon the same night, and had his first interview with the new

The officer who volunteered for the dangerous task of going within the English lines was Captain Argenton, the adjutant of Lafitte's regiment of dragoons. He was a vain, ready, plausible man, full of resources but destitute of firmness: his character is sufficiently shown by the fact that he ultimately wrecked the plot by his indiscretion in tampering with loyal Bonapartists, who delated him, and that when seized he betrayed the whole scheme to Soult in the hope of saving his life. Clearly he was deficient both in the caution and in the stoic courage required for a conspirator—successful or unsuccessful.

We must note that he started from the camp of Lahoussaye's dragoons, near Amarante, on April 19, that he reached the French outposts on the Vouga and got into communication with Major Douglas, one of Beresford's officers in the Portuguese service, on the twenty-first, finally, that at the invitation of Douglas and Beresford he came into Lisbon and reached that city on the twenty-fifth, just in time to meet the newly-landed Wellesley. The plot meanwhile stood still in his absence, for the Duke of Dalmatia did not take the overt step which would have given the plotters their opportunity—he refrained from accepting the crown which his Portuguese partisans were so continually pressing him to assume. Nothing decisive had occurred, when the situation was suddenly changed by the appearance of the British army upon the offensive on May 7 [1].

commander-in-chief, whom he found in charge of the British army, and not (as he had expected) Sir John Cradock. The three requests made were (1) that Wellesley would ' press upon Soult's Corps '—the seizure of Villa Real being suggested, (2) that he would give passports to Argenton and two others to go to France, (3) that he would stir up the Portuguese to flatter and deceive Soult into taking overt steps of treason. Cf. *Wellington Dispatches*, iv. 274 [Lisbon, April 27] and 308 [Coimbra, May 7].

[1] It is to these days, and probably to some date about May 4–7, that belongs General Bigarré's curious story about the conspirators (see his *Mémoires*, p. 235, and Le Noble, p. 238; the latter printed the story in 1821 without names, the former's version was only given to the light a few years ago; they agree in every point). The story is too good to be omitted. Bigarré says that, walking the quay of Oporto on a moonlight night, he came on Lafitte and Donadieu, muffled in their cloaks and vehemently discussing something in a dark corner. He stole up to them

unnoticed, slapped his friend Donadieu on the back, and suddenly shouted in their ears '*Ah! je vous y prends, Messieurs les conspirateurs.* Lafitte whipped out a pistol, and had nearly shot the practical joker, before Donadieu could reassure him that this was only a boisterous piece of fun and that Bigarré knew nothing. It was not till much later that the latter found out what had been brewing.

N.B.—For some documents bearing on Argenton's conspiracy see Appendix at the end of this volume.

SECTION XIV

WELLESLEY'S CAMPAIGN IN NORTHERN PORTUGAL

CHAPTER I

SIR ARTHUR WELLESLEY

On Nov. 25, 1808, Sir John Moore, in answer to a question from Lord Castlereagh, wrote the following conclusions as to the practicability of defending Portugal[1]:

'I can say generally that the frontier of Portugal is not defensible against a superior force. It is an open frontier, all equally rugged, but all equally to be penetrated. If the French succeed in Spain it will be vain to attempt to resist them in Portugal. The Portuguese are without a military force . . . no dependence can be placed on any aid that they can give. The British must in that event, I conceive, immediately take steps to evacuate the country. Lisbon is the only port, and therefore the only place from whence the army, with its stores, can embark. . . . We might check the progress of the enemy while the stores are embarking, and arrangements are being made for taking off the army. Beyond this the defence of Lisbon or of Portugal should not be thought of.'

Four months later, on March 7, 1809, Sir Arthur Wellesley answered the same question, put to him by the same minister, in very different terms.

---

[1] In common fairness to Moore, it is necessary to quote Wellesley's own words on their fundamental difference of opinion as to the possibility of defending Portugal. 'I have as much respect as any man can have for the opinion and judgement of Sir J. Moore, and I should mistrust my own (if opposed to his) in a case where he had an opportunity of knowing and considering. But he positively knew nothing of Portugal, and *could*

'I have always been of opinion that Portugal might be defended, whatever might be the result of the contest in Spain, and that in the meantime measures adopted for the defence of Portugal would be highly useful to the Spaniards in their contest with the French. My notion was that the Portuguese military establishment ought to be revived, and that in addition to those troops His Majesty ought to employ about 20,000 British troops, including about 4,000 cavalry. My opinion was that, even if Spain should have been conquered, the French would not be able to overrun Portugal with a smaller force than 100,000 men. As long as the contest may continue in Spain, this force [the 20,000 British troops], if it could be placed in a state of activity, would be highly useful to the Spaniards, and might eventually decide the contest.'

Between these two divergent views as to the practicability of defending Portugal, Lord Castlereagh had to make his decision. On it—though he could not be aware of the fact—depended the future of Britain and of Bonaparte. He carefully considered the situation; after the disasters of the Corunna retreat it required some moral courage for a minister to advise the sending of another British army to the Peninsula. Moore's gloomy prognostications were echoed by many military experts, and there were leading men—soldiers and politicians—who declared that the only thing that now remained to be done was to withdraw Cradock's 10,000 sabres and bayonets from Lisbon, before the French came near enough to that city to make their embarkation difficult.

Castlereagh resolved to stake his faith on the correctness of Wellesley's conclusions: all through these years of contest he had made him his most trusted adviser on things military, and now he did not swerve from his confidence. He announced to him, privately in the end of March, and officially on April 2[1], that the experiment of a second expedition to Portugal should

know nothing of its existing state.' Yet he says that 'The greatest disadvantage under which I labour is that Sir John Moore gave an opinion that the country could not be defended by the army under his command.' Wellington to Lord Liverpool, from Vizeu, April 2, 1810.

[1] The official notice is dated April 2 (*Wellington Supplementary Dispatches*, vi. p. 210), but several letters dated late in March show that the matter had been already settled.

be tried, and that he himself should have the conduct of it.
Reinforcements should at once be sent out to bring the British
army at Lisbon up to a total of 30,000 men—the number to
which Wellesley, on consideration, raised the original 20,000
of which he had spoken.   Beresford had already sailed, with
orders to do all that he could for the reorganization of the
disorderly native forces of Portugal.   The few regiments
in England that were ready for instant embarkation were
sent off ere March ended, and began to arrive at Lisbon early
in April [1].   Others were rapidly prepared for foreign service;
but it was a misfortune that the Corunna battalions were still
too sickly and depleted to be able to sail, so that troops who
had seen nothing of the first campaign had to be sent out.   The
majority of them were 'second battalions' from the home
establishment [2], many of them very weak in numbers and full
of young soldiers, as they had been drained in the previous
year to fill their first battalions up to full strength.   Finally,
just behind the first convoys of reinforcements, Wellesley himself
set sail from Portsmouth, after resigning his position as Under
Secretary for Ireland, which, by a curious anomaly, he had
continued to hold all through the campaign of Vimiero, and
the proceedings of inquiry concerning the Convention of Cintra.
He sailed upon April 14, in the *Surveillante* frigate, had the
narrowest of escapes from shipwreck on the Isle of Wight during
the first night of his voyage, but soon obtained favourable winds
and reached Lisbon on the twenty-second, after a rapid passage
of less than eight days.   Just before he started there had been
received from Portugal not only the correct intelligence that
Soult had stormed Oporto upon March 29, but a false rumour
that Victor had been joined by the corps of Sebastiani [3] and

[1] The troops from the abortive expedition to Cadiz, under Mackenzie,
Sherbrooke and Tilson, turned up about the middle of March at Lisbon.
But Hill, with the first body of the second batch of reinforcements, only
appeared upon April 5.

[2] Of the first ten battalions to appear, seven were 2nd battalions—those
of the 7th, 30th, 48th, 53rd, 66th, 83rd, 87th regiments.   Some were very
weak, with less than 750 bayonets, e. g. the 7th (628 men), 30th (698 men),
66th (740 men).

[3] This came from Beresford at Lisbon (see *Wellington Supplementary
Dispatches*, vi. p. 219).

had after his victory at Medellin laid siege to Badajoz [1]. If this had been true, the Duke of Belluno would have been strong enough to move against Portugal with 25,000 men, after detaching a competent force to watch the wrecks of Cuesta's army. Fortunately the whole story was an invention : but it kept Wellesley in a state of feverish anxiety till he reached Lisbon. His fears are shown by the fact that he drew up a memorandum for Lord Castlereagh, setting forth the supposed situation, and asking what he was to do on arriving, if he should find that Cradock had already embarked his troops and quitted Portugal [2]. The Secretary of State, equally harrassed by the false intelligence, replied that he was to make an effort to induce the Spaniards to let him land the army at Cadiz, and, if they should refuse, might reinforce the garrison of Gibraltar to 8,000 men, and bring the rest of the expeditionary force back to England [3].

It was therefore an immense relief to Wellesley to find, when he landed, that the news from Estremadura was false, that Victor had not been reinforced, and that the 1st Corps was lying quiescent at Merida. Soult was still at Oporto, Cradock had not been molested, and the French invasion was at a standstill.

It is comparatively seldom that the historian is able to compare in detail a general's original conception of a plan of campaign with the actual scheme which he carried out. Still less common is it to find that the commander has placed on record his ideas as to the general policy to be pursued during a war, before he has assumed charge of his army or issued his first orders. It is therefore most fortunate that we have three documents from Wellesley's hand, written early in 1809, which enable us to understand the principles on which

[1] Wellesley to the Duke of Richmond, April 14 (*Supplementary Dispatches*, vi. 227).

[2] *Wellington Supplementary Dispatches*, vi. 221–2. It is very creditable to Sir Arthur that, adverting to another possibility, viz. that Cradock may have plucked up courage to go out against the French, and have successfully beaten them off, he declares that ' he could not reconcile it with his feelings' to supersede a successful general. He remembered his own state of mind when supplanted by Burrard on the day of Vimiero.

[3] Castlereagh to Wellesley, *Supplementary Dispatches*, vi. 222 and 228.

he believed that the Peninsular War should be fought out. These are his *Memorandum on the Defence of Portugal,* which we have already had occasion to quote, and the two dispatches to Lord Castlereagh and to Mr. Frere which he wrote immediately after his arrival in Lisbon. The first gives us his general view of the war. He believed that an English army of 20,000 or 30,000 men, backed by the levies of Portugal, would be able to maintain itself on the flank of the French army in Spain. Its presence there would paralyse all the offensive actions of the enemy, and enable the Spaniards to make head against the invaders as long as Portugal remained unsubdued. The news that a British army had once more taken the field would, he considered, induce the French to turn their main efforts against Portugal [1], but he believed that considering the geography of the country, the character of its people, and the quality of the British troops, they would fail in their attempt to overrun it. They could not succeed, as he supposed, unless they could set aside 100,000 men for the task, and he did not see how they would ever be able to spare such a large detachment out of the total force which they then possessed in the Peninsula—a force whose numerical strength (in common with all British statesmen and soldiers of the day) he somewhat underrated. Being in the secrets of the Ministry, he was already aware in March that a new war in Germany was about to break out within the next few months. When Austria took the field, Napoleon would not be able to spare a single battalion of reinforcements for Spain. If the Spaniards pursued a reasonable military policy, and occupied the attention of the main armies of the French, the enemy would never be able to detach a force of 100,000 for the invasion of Portugal. He would underrate the numbers required, make his attempt with insufficient resources, and be beaten. When Wellesley landed at Lisbon, and found that Soult had halted at Oporto, that Victor lay quiescent at Merida, and that Lapisse with the troops from Salamanca

[1] Memorandum of March 7, ' As soon as the newspapers shall have announced the departure of officers for Portugal, the French armies in Spain will receive orders to make their movements towards Portugal, so as to anticipate our measures for its defence,' &c.

had gone southward to join the 1st Corps, and so severed
the only link which bound together the army in Northern
Portugal and the army in Estremadura, he was reassured as
to the whole situation. Soult and Victor, isolated as they now
were, would each be too weak to beat the Anglo-Portuguese
army. They were too far apart to make co-operation between
them possible, considering the geography of Central Portugal,
and the fact that the whole country behind each was in a state
of insurrection [1].

But 'the best defensive is a vigorous local offensive,' and
Wellesley saw the advantage of the central position of the
British army upon the Tagus. A few marches would place
it at a point from which it could fall either upon Victor to the
right or Soult to the left, before either marshal could be in
a position to lend help to his colleague, probably long before
he would even be aware that his colleague was in danger.
Wellesley could strike at the one or the other, with almost
perfect certainty of catching him unreinforced. Ney, it was
true, lay behind Soult, but he was known to be entangled in
the trammels of the vigorous Galician insurrection. Victor had
Sebastiani in his rear, but the 4th Corps was having occupation
found for it by the Spanish army of La Mancha. It was improbable that either Soult or Victor, if suddenly attacked, could
call up any appreciable reinforcements. Victor, moreover, had
Cuesta to observe, and could not move off leaving 20,000
Spaniards behind him. Soult was known to be distracted by
Silveira's operations on the Tamega. Wellesley, therefore, saw
that it was well within his power to strike at either of the
marshals. He would, of course, be obliged to place a 'containing force' in front of the one whom he resolved to leave
alone for the present. But this detachment need not be very
large, and might be composed for the most part of Portuguese

---

[1] It is noteworthy that Wellesley, when he was placed in communication
with Argenton three days later, considered that one of the few useful
facts which he had got from the plotter was that Soult and his army had no
knowledge of where Victor might be, or of what he was doing. This was
a far more precious piece of information than any details as to the conspiracy, which Wellesley regarded from the first as doomed to failure: see
Wellington Dispatches, iv. 274.

troops : its duty would be to distract, but not to fight the enemy.

On the whole Wellesley thought it would be best to make the first onslaught on Soult. 'I should prefer an attack on Victor,' he wrote, two days after landing, 'in concert with Cuesta, if Soult were not in possession of a fertile province of this kingdom, and of the favourite town of Oporto, of which it is most desirable to deprive him. Any operation upon Victor, connected with Cuesta's movements, would require time to concert, which may as well be employed in dislodging Soult from the north of Portugal, before bringing the British army to the eastern frontier [1]. . . . I intend to move upon Soult, as soon as I can make some arrangement, on which I can depend, for the defence of the Tagus, to impede or delay Victor's progress, in case he should come on while I am absent.' 'I think it probable,' he wrote on the same day but in another letter, 'that Soult will not remain in Portugal when I pass the Mondego : if he does, I shall attack him. If he should retire, I am convinced that it would be most advantageous for the common cause that we should remain on the defensive in the North of Portugal, and act vigorously in co-operation with Cuesta against Victor [2].'

Further forward it was impossible to look : a blow at Soult, followed by another at Victor, was all that could at present be contemplated. Wellesley was directed, by the formal instructions which he had received from Castlereagh, to do all that was possible to clear Portugal and the frontier provinces of Spain from the enemy, but not to strike deep into the Peninsula till he should have received permission from home to do so. Nevertheless he had devoted some thought to the remoter possibilities of the situation. If Portugal were preserved, and Soult and Victor beaten off, more ambitious combinations might become possible. He expressed his conviction that the French occupa-

---

[1] Wellesley to Castlereagh, from Lisbon, April 24. I have ventured to substitute ' before bringing ' in the last sentence for the unmeaning ' and to bring ' which is clearly a *lapsus calami*.

[2] Wellesley (to Mr. Frere, at Seville) from Lisbon, April 24. In many sentences this dispatch is only a repetition of that to Castlereagh. But in others Sir Arthur makes his meaning more clear, by a more detailed explanation.

tion of Spain would only be endangered when a very large force, acting in unison under the guidance of a single mind, should be brought together. The co-operation of the English army and that of Cuesta 'might be the groundwork of further measures of the same and a more extended description [1].' He was under no delusions as to the easiness of the task before him : he did not hurry on in thought, to dream of the expulsion of the French from the Peninsula as a goal already in sight. But he believed that he and his army 'might be highly useful to the Spaniards and might eventually decide the contest [2].'

It is the survey of documents such as these that enables us to appreciate Wellesley at his best. He had gauged perfectly well the situation and difficulties of the French. He saw exactly how much was in his own power. The whole history of the Peninsular War for the next two years is foreseen in his prophetic statement, that with 30,000 British troops and the Portuguese levies he would guarantee to hold his own against any force of less than 100,000 French, and that he did not think that the enemy would find it easy to collect an army of that size to send against him. This is precisely what he accomplished : for the first fifteen months after his arrival he held with ease that frontier which Moore had described as 'indefensible against a superior force.' When at last Napoleon, free from all other continental troubles, launched against him an army under Masséna, which almost reached the figure that he had described as irresistible in 1809, he showed in 1810–11 that he had built up resources for himself which enabled him to beat off even that number of enemies. Though four-fifths of Spain had been subdued, he held his own, because he had grasped the fundamental truth that (to use his own words) 'the more ground the French hold down, the weaker will they be at any given point.' In short, he had fathomed the great secret, that Napoleon's

---

[1] Wellesley to Frere, Lisbon, April 24, 1809.

[2] *Memorandum on the Defence of Portugal,* of March 7.

[3] If to Masséna's field army of 60,000 men we add the troops on his communications (viz. the 9th Corps and the garrisons of Rodrigo and Almeida) and also the force which Soult and Mortier brought up against Badajoz and Elvas—a force against which Wellesley had to provide, by making large detachments—the full number of 100,000 is reached.

military power—vast as it was—had its limits: that the
Emperor could not send to Spain a force sufficient to hold down
every province of a thoroughly disaffected country, and also
to provide (over and above the garrisons) a field army large
enough to beat the Anglo-Portuguese and capture Lisbon. If the
French dispersed their divisions, and kept down the vast tracts
of conquered territory, they had no force left with which to take
the offensive against Portugal: if they massed their armies, they
had to give up broad regions, which immediately relapsed into
insurrection and required to be subdued again. This was as
true in the beginning of the war as in the end. In 1809 the
army that forced Wellesley to retreat after Talavera was only
produced by evacuating the whole province of Galicia, which
passed back into the hands of the insurgents. In 1812, in
a similar way, the overpowering force which beat him back
from Burgos, had been gathered only by surrendering to the
Spanish Government the whole of the four kingdoms of Andalusia. On the other hand, during the long periods when the
enemy had dispersed himself, and was garrisoning the whole
south and centre of Spain, e.g. for the first six months of 1810,
and for the last six months of 1811, Wellesley held his own on
the Portuguese frontier in complete confidence, assured that
no sufficient force could be brought up against him, till the
enemy either procured new troops from France or gave up some
great section of the regions which he was holding down.
A detailed insight into the future is impossible to any general,
however great, but already in April 1809 Wellesley had grasped
the main outlines of the war that was to be.

Before passing on to the details of the campaign on the
Douro, with which Wellesley's long series of victories began,
it is well to take a glance at the man himself, as he sat at his
desk in Lisbon dictating the orders that were to change the face
of the war.

Arthur Wellesley was now within a few days of completing
his fortieth year. He was a slight but wiry man of middle
stature, with a long face, an aquiline nose, and a keen but cold
grey eye. Owning an iron constitution on which no climate
or season seemed to make the least impression, he was physically
fit for all the work that lay before him—work more fatiguing

than that which falls to most generals. For in the Peninsula he was required, as it soon appeared, to be almost as much of a statesman as of a general; while at the same time, owing to the inexperience of the British officers of that day in warfare on a large scale, he was obliged for some time to discharge for himself many of the duties which properly fall to the lot of the chief of the staff, the commissary-general, the paymaster-general, and the quartermaster-general in a well organized army. No amount of toil, bodily or mental, appeared too much for that active and alert mind, or for the body which seven years of service in India seemed to have tanned and hardened rather than to have relaxed. During the whole of his Peninsular campaigns, from 1808 to 1814, he was never prostrated by any serious ailment. Autumn rains, summer heat, the cold of winter, had no power over him. He could put up with a very small allowance of sleep, and when necessary could snatch useful moments of repose, at any moment of the twenty-four hours when no pressing duty chanced to be on hand. His manner of life was simple and austere in the extreme; no commander-in-chief ever travelled with less baggage, or could be content with more Spartan fare. Long after his wars were over the habit of bleak frugality clung to him, and in his old age men wondered at the bare and comfortless surroundings that he chose for himself, and at the scanty meals that sustained his spare but active frame. Officers who had long served in India were generally supposed to contract habits of luxury and display, but Wellesley was the exception that proved the rule. He hated show of any kind; after the first few days of the campaign of 1809 he discarded the escort which was wont to accompany the commander-in-chief. It was on very rare occasions that he was seen in his full uniform: the army knew him best in the plain blue frock coat, the small featherless cocked hat, and the short cape, which have been handed down to us in a hundred drawings. Not unfrequently he would ride about among his cantonments dressed like a civilian in a round hat and grey trousers[1]. He was as careless about the dress of his subordinates as about his

---

[1] See, for example, the anecdote in Sir G. L'Estrange's *Reminiscences*, p. 194. Picton was equally given to the use (or abuse) of *mufti*, and fought Quatre Bras in a tall hat!

own, and there probably never existed an army in which so little fuss was made about unessential trappings as that which served in the Peninsula from 1809 to 1814[1]. Nothing could be less showy than its head-quarters' staff—a small group of blue-coated officers, with an orderly dragoon or two, riding in the wake of the dark cape and low glazed cocked hat of the most unpretentious of chiefs. It contrasted in the strangest way with the plumes and gold lace of the French marshals and their elaborately ornate staffs[2].

Considered as a man Wellesley had his defects and his limitations; we shall have ere long to draw attention to some of them. But from the intellectual point of view he commands our undivided admiration as a practical soldier[3]. A careful study of his dispatches leaves us in a state of wonder at the imbecility of the school of writers—mostly continental—who have continued to assert for the last eighty years that he was no more than a man of ordinary abilities, who had an unfair share of good luck, and was presented with a series of victories by the mistakes and jealousies of the generals opposed to him. Such assertions are the results of blind ignorance and prejudice. When found in English writers they merely reflect the bitter hatred that was felt toward Wellesley by his political opponents during the second and third decades of the nineteenth century. In French military authors they only represent the resentful

[1] 'Provided we brought our men into the field well appointed, and with sixty good rounds in their pouches, he never looked to see whether our trousers were black or blue or grey. Scarcely any two officers dressed alike. Some wore grey braided coats, others brown, some liked blue : many from choice or necessity stuck to the "old red rag." We were never tormented with that greatest of *bores* on active service, uniformity of dress.' Grattan's *With the 88th*, p. 50.

[2] To find a humorous contrast to Wellington's staff, the reader might consult Lejeune's account of that of Berthier, who had allowed him to design a special and gorgeous uniform, all fur feathers and braid, for his aides-de-camp. Lejeune dwells with the enthusiasm of a tailor on his efforts and their glorious effect on parade [Lejeune, i. p. 95].

[3] Lord Roberts, in his *Rise of Wellington*, only slightly overstates his case when he observes that the more we study Wellesley's life in detail, the more we respect him as a general and the less we like him as a man. If we come upon much that is hard and unsympathetic, there are too many redeeming traits to justify the statement in its entirety.

carpings of the vanquished army, which preferred to think that
it was beaten by anything rather than by the ability of the conqueror. In 1820 every retired colonel across the Channel was
ready to demonstrate that Toulouse was an English defeat, that
Talavera was a drawn battle, and that Wellesley was over-rash
or over-cautious, a fool or a coward, according as their thesis
of the moment might demand[1]. They were but echoing their
Emperor's rancorous remark to Soult, on the hillside of La Belle
Alliance, when after telling the Marshal that he only thought
his old adversary a good general because he had been beaten
by him, he added, ' Et moi, je vous dis que Wellington est un
mauvais général, et que les Anglais sont de mauvaises troupes[2].'

Bonaparte consistently refused to do justice to the abilities of
the Duke. He regarded him as a bitter personal enemy, and
his whole attitude towards Wellesley was expressed in the
scandalous legacy to Cantillon[3] which disgraces his last will and
testament. In strict conformity with their master's pose, his
followers, literary and military, have refused to see anything
great in the victor of June 18, 1815. Even to the present day
too many historians from the other side of the straits continue
to follow in the steps of Thiers, and to express wonder at the
inexplicable triumphs of the mediocre general who routed in
succession all the best marshals of France.

To clear away any lingering doubts as to Wellesley's extraordinary ability, the student of history has only to read a few
of his more notable dispatches. The man who could write the
two Memoranda to Castlereagh dated September 5, 1808, and
March 7, 1809[4], foresaw the whole future of the Peninsular
War. To know, at that early stage of the struggle, that the
Spaniards would be beaten when- and wherever they offered
battle, that the French, in spite of their victories, would never

---

[1] The reader curious in such things may find as much as he desires
of this sort of stuff in Thiébault, Marbot, Le Noble and Lemonnier
Delafosse.

[2] These phrases are preserved in the notes of Soult's aide-de-camp Baudus.

[3] Cantillon was the assassin who fired on Wellington in Paris on
Sept. 10, 1818.

[4] Wellington to Castlereagh, Zambujal, Sept. 5, 1808, and London,
March 7, 1809.

be able to conquer and hold down the entire country, that 30,000 British troops would be able to defend Portugal against any force that could be collected against them, required the mind of a soldier of the first class.   When the earliest of those memoranda was written, most Englishmen believed that the Spaniards were about to deliver their country by their own arms: Wellesley saw that the notion was vain and absurd. When, on the other hand, he wrote the second, the idea was abroad that all was lost, that after Corunna no second British army would be sent to the Peninsula, and that Portugal was indefensible.   Far from sharing these gloomy views he asks for 30,000 men, and states that though Spain may be overrun, though the Portuguese army may be in a state of hopeless disarray, he yet hopes with this handful of men to maintain the struggle, and eventually to decide the contest.   How many generals has the world seen who could have framed such a prophecy, and have verified it ?

To talk of the good fortune of Wellesley, of his 'lucky star,' is absurd.   He had, like other generals, his occasional uncovenanted mercies and happy chances : but few commanders had more strokes of undeserved disappointment, or saw more of their plans frustrated by a stupid subordinate, an unexpected turn of the weather, an incalculable accident, or a piece of false news. He had his fair proportion of the chances of war, good and bad, and no more.   If fortune was with him at Oporto in 1809, or at El Bodon in 1811, how many were the occasions on which she played him scurvy tricks ?   A few examples may suffice.   In May 1809 he might have captured the whole of Soult's army, if Silveira had but obeyed orders and occupied the impregnable defile of Salamonde.   On the night of Salamanca he might have dealt in a similar fashion with Marmont's routed host, if Carlos d'España had not withdrawn the garrison of Alba de Tormes, in flat disobedience to his instructions, and so left the fords open to the flying French.   It is needless to multiply instances of such incalculable misfortune ; any serious student of the Peninsular War can cite them by the dozen.   Masséna's invasion of Portugal in 1810 would have been checked by the autumn rains, and never have penetrated far within the frontier, but for the unlucky bomb which blew up the grand magazine at

Almeida, and reduced in a day a fortress which ought to have held out for a month. In the autumn of 1812 the retreat beyond the Douro need never have been made, if Ballesteros had obeyed orders, and moved up from Granada to threaten Soult's flank, instead of remaining torpid in his cantonments 200 miles from the theatre of war.

Wellington was not the child of fortune; he was a great strategist and tactician, placed in a situation in which the military dangers furnished but half his difficulties. He had to cherish his single precious British army corps, and to keep it from any unnecessary loss, because if destroyed it could not be replaced. With those 30,000 men he had promised to keep up the war; the home government was reluctant to risk the whole of its available field army in one quarter, and for years refused to raise his numbers far above that total. It was not till the middle of 1810 that his original five divisions of infantry were increased to six, nor till 1811 that his seventh and eighth divisions were completed [1]. Right down to 1812 it was certain that if he had lost any considerable fraction of his modest army, the ministry might have recalled him and abandoned Portugal. He had to fight with a full consciousness that a single disaster would have been irreparable, because it would have been followed not by the sending off of reinforcements to replace the divisions that might be lost, but by an order to evacuate the Peninsula. His French opponents fought under no such disabilities; when beaten they had other armies at hand on which to fall back, and behind all the inexhaustible reserve of Napoleon's conscription. Considering the campaigns of 1809–10–11 it is not Wellington's oft-censured prudence that we find astonishing, but his boldness. Instead of wondering that he did not attempt to relieve Rodrigo or Almeida in July–August 1810, or to fall upon Masséna at Santarem in January 1811, we are filled with surprise at the daring which inspired the storming of Oporto, and the offering of battle at Busaco and Fuentes d'Oñoro. When a defeat spelt ruin and recall, it required no small courage to take any risks : but Wellesley had the sanest of minds ; he could draw the line with absolute accuracy between enterprise and rashness, between

[1] The Fifth Division was not completed till Oct. 8, 1810, the Sixth and Seventh on March 8, 1811.

the possible and the impossible.   He had learned to gauge with
wonderful insight the difficulties and disabilities of his enemies,
and to see exactly how far they might be reckoned upon in dis-
counting the military situation.   After some time he arrived
at an accurate estimate of the individual marshals opposed to
him, and was ready to take the personal equation into consideration, according as he had to deal with Soult or Masséna,
Marmont or Jourdan.   In short, he was a safe general, not
a cautious one.   When once the hopeless disparity between his
own resources and those of the enemy had ceased to exist, in the
year 1812, he soon showed the worth of the silly taunts which
imputed timidity to him, by the smashing blows which reduced
Ciudad Rodrigo and Badajoz, and the lightning-stroke which
dashed to pieces Marmont's army at Salamanca.   In the next
year, when for the first time he could count on an actual
superiority of force [1], his irresistible march to Vittoria displayed
his mastery of the art of using an advantage to the uttermost.
Napoleon himself never punished a strategic fault on the part of
the enemy with such majestic ease and confidence.

Of Wellington as a tactician we have already had occasion to
speak in the first volume of this work [2].   It is only necessary to
repeat here that the groundwork of his tactics was his knowledge
of the fact that the line could beat the column, whether on the
offensive or the defensive.   The *data* for forming the conclusions
had been in possession of any one who chose to utilize them,
but it was Wellesley who put his knowledge to full account.
Even before he left India, it is said, he had grasped the great
secret, and had remarked to his confidants that 'the French
were sweeping everything before them in Europe by the use of
the formation in column, but that he was fully convinced that
the column could and would be beaten by the line [3].'   Yet even

---

[1] Though even then the superiority, such as it was, consisted entirely
of Spanish troops of doubtful quality.

[2] See pp. 114–22 of vol. i.

[3] The same idea is well marked in a conversation reported by Croker,
which took place in London, on the eve of Wellesley's departure to assume
command of the troops at Cork with whom he was about to sail for the
Peninsula.   After a long reverie, he was asked the subject of his thoughts.
'To say the truth,' he replied, 'I am thinking of the French I am going to
fight.   I have not seen them since the campaign in Flanders [1794–5]

though the epoch-making, yet half-forgotten, fight of Maida had occurred since then, the first Peninsular battles came as a revelation to the world. After Vimiero and Talavera it became known that the line was certainly superior for the defensive, but it was only the triumphant line-advance of Salamanca that finally divulged the fact that the British method was equally sure and certain for the attack. If Wellesley's reputation rested on the single fact that he had made this discovery known to the world, he would have won by this alone a grand place in military history. But his reputation depends even more on his strategical than on his tactical triumphs. He was a battle-general of the first rank, but his talents on the day of decisive action would not have sufficed to clear the French out of Spain. His true greatness is best shown by his all-embracing grasp of the political, geographical, and moral factors of the situation in the Peninsula, and by the way in which he utilized them all when drawing up the plans for his triumphant campaigns.

As to tactics indeed, there are points on which it would be easy to point out defects in Wellesley's method—in especial it would be possible to develop the two old, but none the less true, criticisms that he was ' pre-eminently an infantry general,' and that 'when he had won a battle he did not always utilize his success to the full legitimate end.' The two charges hang closely together, for the one defect was but the consequence of the other ; a tendency to refrain from making the greatest possible use of his cavalry for breaking up an enemy who had already begun to give ground, and for pursuing him *à outrance* when he was well on the run, was the natural concomitant of a predilection for the use of infantry in the winning of battles. If Napoleon

when they were capital soldiers, and a dozen years of victory under Buonaparte must have made them better still. They have besides a new system of strategy, which has outmanœuvred and overwhelmed all the armies of Europe. 'Tis enough to make one thoughtful ; but no matter, the die is cast : they may overwhelm me, but I don't think they will outmanœuvre me. First, because I am not afraid of them, as everybody else seems to be ; and secondly, because, if all I hear of their system be true, I think it a false one against steady troops. I suspect all the continental armies are half beaten before the battle begins. I, at least, will not be frightened beforehand.' Croker's *Diary and Correspondence*, vol. i. p. 13, under the date June 14, 1808.

had commanded the British army at Salamanca, Marmont's
troops would have been annihilated by a rapid cavalry pursuit,
instead of merely scattered.   If Wellington had commanded the
French army in the Jena-Auerstadt campaign, it is reasonably
certain that Hohenlöhe's broken divisions would have escaped
into the interior, instead of being garnered in piecemeal by the
inexorable and untiring chase kept up by the French horse.
The very distrust which Wellington expressed for the capacities
of the British cavalry [1], who after all were admirable troops when
well handled, is but an illustration of the fact that he was no true
lover of the mounted arm.   But of this we have already spoken,
and it is unnecessary to dwell at greater length on his minor
deficiencies than on his numerous excellencies on the day of
battle.

A far more serious charge against Wellesley than any which
can be grounded on his tactical faults, is that, though he
won the confidence of his army, he could never win their affection.
'The sight of his long nose among us on a battle morning,'
wrote one of his veterans, 'was worth ten thousand men, any
day of the week [2].'   But it was not personal attachment to
him which nerved his soldiers to make their best effort : he
was feared, respected, and followed, but never loved.   He was
obeyed with alacrity, but not with enthusiasm.   His officers and
his men believed, and believed rightly, that he looked upon them
as admirable tools for the task that had been set him, and did
his best to keep those tools unbroken and in good repair, but that
he felt no deep personal interest in their welfare.   It is seldom
that the veterans who have served under a great commander
have failed to idolize as well as to respect him.   But Wellesley's
men, while acknowledging all his greatness, complained that he
systematically neglected both their feelings and their interests [3].

[1] See vol. i. p. 119.

[2] See Kincaid, chap. v, May 3, 1811.

[3] The feelings, expressed more or less clearly in a hundred memoirs,
may be summed up in a paragraph by Wm. Grattan of the 88th.   'In his
parting General Order to the Peninsular army he told us that he would
never cease to feel the warmest interest for our welfare and honour.   How
this promise was kept every one knows.   That the Duke of Wellington is
one of the most remarkable (perhaps the greatest) man of the present age,
few will deny.   But that he neglected the interests and feelings of his

It was but too true : he showed for his army, the officers no less
than the rank and file, a certain coldness that was partly bred
of intellectual contempt, partly of aristocratic hauteur.   There
are words of his on record concerning his men which can never
be forgiven, and words, too, not spoken in the heat of action or
the moment of disappointment, but in the leisure of his later
years.   Take, for example, the passage in Lord Stanhope's *Conversations with the Duke of Wellington*, where he is speaking of
the rank and file : ' they are the scum of the earth ; English
soldiers are fellows who have enlisted for drink.   That is the
plain fact—they have *all* enlisted for drink [1].'   He described
the men who won Talavera as ' a rabble who could not bear
success,' and the Waterloo troops as ' an infamous army '—
the terms are unpardonable.   His notions of discipline were
worthy of one of the drill sergeants of Frederic the Great.
' I have no idea of any great effect being produced on British
soldiers,' he once said before a Royal Commission, ' by anything
but the fear of immediate corporal punishment.'   Flogging was
the one remedy for all evils, and he declared that it was
absolutely impossible to manage the army without it.   For
any idea of appealing to the men's better feeling, or moving
them by sentiment, he had the greatest contempt.

The most distressing feature in Wellington's condemnation of
the character of his soldiery is that he was sinning against the
light : officers, of less note but of greater heart, were appealing
to the self-respect, patriotism, and good feeling of their men,
with the best results, at the very moment that Wellesley was
denouncing them as soulless clods and irreclaimable drunkards.
It was not by the lash that regiments like Donnelau's 48th or
Colborne's 52nd, or many other corps of the Peninsular army
were kept together.   The reminiscences of the Napiers, and many
other regimental officers of the better class, are full of anecdotes
illustrating the virtues of the rank and file.   There are dozens
of diaries and autobiographies of sergeants and privates of
Wellesley's old divisions, which prove that there were plenty of

Peninsular army, as a body, is beyond all question.   And were he in his
grave to-morrow, hundreds of voices that now are silent would echo what
I write ' (p. 332).

[1] *Conversations with the Duke of Wellington*, p. 14.   [Nov. 4, 1831.]

well-conditioned, intelligent, sober and religious men in the ranks
—it is only necessary to cite as examples the books of Surtees,
Anton, Morris, and Donaldson [1].   If there were also thousands
of drunkards and reckless brutes in the service, the blame for
their misdoings must fall to a great extent on the system under
which they were trained.   The ruthless mediaeval cruelty of the
code of punishment alone will account for half the ruffianism of
the army.

The same indiscriminate censure which Wellesley poured on
his men he often vented on his officers, denouncing them *en
masse* in the most reckless fashion.   There were careless colonels
and stupid subalterns enough under him, but what can excuse
such sweeping statements as that ' When I give an order to an
officer of the line it is, I venture to say, a hundred to one
against its being done at all,' or for his Circular of November,
1812, declaring that all the evils of the Burgos retreat were due
' to the habitual inattention of the officers of regiments to their
duty.'   It was a bitter blow to the officers of the many battalions which had kept their order and discipline, to find themselves
confused with the offending corps in the same general blast of
censure.   But by 1812 they were well accustomed to such
slashing criticism on the part of their commander.

Such a chief could not win the sympathy of his army, though
he might command their intellectual respect.   Equally unfortunate were his autocratic temper and his unwillingness to
concede any latitude of instructions to his subordinates, features
in his character which effectually prevented him from forming
a school of good officers capable of carrying out large independent operations.   He trained admirable generals of division, but
not commanders of armies, for he always insisted on keeping the
details of operations, even in distant parts of the theatre of war,
entirely under his own hand.   His preference for Hill as a com-

---

[1] It is often forgotten that there was a strong religious element in the
rank and file of the Peninsular army.   In a letter from Cartaxo [Feb. 6,
1811], Wellington mentions, with no great pleasure, the fact that there
were three separate Methodist meetings in the Guards' brigade alone, and
that in many other regiments there were officers who were accustomed
to preach and pray with their men.   For the spiritual experiences of a
sergeant in the agonies of conversion, the reader may consult the diary
of Surtees of the 95th during the year 1812.

mander of detached corps came entirely from the fact that he could trust that worthy and gallant officer to make no movements on his own initiative, and to play a safe waiting game which gave his chief no anxiety. In his younger days, while serving under other generals, Wellesley had been by no means an exponent of blind obedience or unquestioning deference to the orders of his superiors. But when placed in command himself he was autocratic to a fault. He was prone to regard any criticism of his directions as insubordination. He preferred a lieutenant on whom he could rely for a literal obedience to orders, to another of more active brain who possessed initiative and would 'think for himself.' There was hardly an officer in the Peninsular army to whom he would grant a free hand even in the carrying out of comparatively small tasks[1]. His most trusted subordinates were liable to find themselves overwhelmed with rebukes delivered in the most tempestuous fashion if they took upon themselves to issue a command on their own responsibility, even when the great chief was many leagues away. Sometimes when their inspirations had been obviously useful and successful, he would wind up his harangue, not with an expression of approval, but with a recommendation to the effect that 'matters had turned out all right, but they must never again act without orders[2].' This was not

[1] Robert Craufurd and Hill were perhaps the only exceptions.

[2] Take, for example, his behaviour to Sir James McGrigor, perhaps the most successful of his chiefs of departments. M Grigor, being at Salamanca, while Wellesley was at Madrid [Aug. 1812], ordered on his own authority the bringing up of stores for the mass of wounded left behind there after the battle. He then came to bring his report to Madrid. 'Lord Wellington was sitting to a Spanish painter [Goya] for his portrait when I arrived, and asked me to sit down and give him a detail as to the state of the wounded at Salamanca. When I came to inform him that for their relief I had ordered up purveying and commissariat officers, he started up, and in a violent manner reprobated what I had done. His Lordship was in a passion, and the Spanish artist, ignorant of the English language, looked aghast, and at a loss to know what I had done to enrage him so much. "I shall be glad to know," he asked, "who is to command the army, I or you? I establish one route, one line of communications for the army; you establish another, and order up supplies by it. As long as you live, sir, never do that again; never do *anything* without my orders." I pleaded that there was no time to consult him, and that I had to save lives. He peremptorily desired me "never again to act without his

the way to develop their strategical abilities, or to secure that intelligent co-operation which is more valuable than blind obedience.   It may be pleaded in Wellesley's defence that at the commencement of the war he had many stupid and discontented officers under him, and that their carpings at his orders were often as absurd as they were malevolent.   But it was not only for them that he reserved his thunders.   They fell not unfrequently on able and willing men, who had done no more than think for themselves, when an urgent problem had been presented to them. He was, it must be confessed, a thankless master to serve: he was almost as pitiless as Frederic the Great in resenting a mistake or an apparent disobedience to orders.   The case of Norman Ramsay may serve as an example.   Ramsay was perhaps the most brilliant artillery officer in the Peninsular army: the famous charge of his guns through a French cavalry regiment at Fuentes d'Oñoro is one of the best-known exploits of the whole war. But at Vittoria he made an error in comprehending orders, and moved forward from a village where the commander-in-chief had intended to keep him stationed.   He was placed under arrest for three weeks, cut out of his mention in dispatches, and deprived of the brevet-majority which had been promised him. His career was broken, and two years later he fell, still a captain, at Waterloo.

It would almost seem that Wellesley had worked out for himself some sort of general rule, to the effect that incompetent being more common than competent subordinates, it would be safer in the long run to prohibit all use of personal initiative, as the occasions on which it would be wisely and usefully employed would be less numerous than those on which it would result in blunders and perils.   He had a fine intellectual contempt for many of the officers whom he had to employ, and never shrank from showing it.   When once he had made up his mind, he could not listen with patience to advice or criticism.   It was

orders." . . . A month later I was able to say to him, " My Lord, recollect how you blamed me at Madrid for the steps which I took on coming up to the army, when I could not consult your Lordship, and acted for myself.   Now, if I had not, what would the consequences have been ? " He answered, " It is all right as has turned out ; but I recommend you still *to have my orders for what you do.*"   This was a singular feature in the character of Lord Wellington.'   McGrigor's *Autobiography,* pp. 302–3 and 311.

this that made him such a political failure in his latter days : he carried into the cabinet the methods of the camp, and could not understand why they were resented. His colleagues ' started up with crotchets,' he complained: ' I have not been used to that in the early part of my life. I was accustomed to carry on things in quite a different manner. I assembled my officers and laid down my plan, and it was carried into effect without any more words [1].' For councils of war, or other devices by which a weak commander-in-chief endeavours to discharge some of the burden of responsibility upon the shoulders of his lieutenants, Wellesley had the greatest dislike. He never allowed discussion as long as he held supreme authority in the field : he would have liked to enforce the same rule in the cabinet when he became prime minister of England. Sometimes he had glimpses of the fact that it is unwise to show open scorn for the opinion of others, especially when they are men of influence or capacity [2]. But it was not often that the idea occurred to him. His reception of an officer who came with a petition or a piece of advice was often such that the visitor went away boiling with rage, or prostrated with nervous exhaustion. Charles Stewart is said to have wept after one stormy interview with his chief, and Picton, whose attempts at familiarity were particularly offensive to the Duke, would go away muttering words that could not be consigned to print [3]. A passage from the memoir of the chief of one of his departments may suffice to paint the sort of scene which used to occur :—

' One morning I was in his Lordship's small apartment, when two officers were there, to request leave to go to England. A general officer, of a noble family, commanding a brigade, advanced, saying, " My Lord, I have of late been suffering much from rheumatism—." Without allowing him time to proceed further, Lord Wellington rapidly said — " and you must go to

[1] Salisbury MSS., 1835. Quoted in Sir Herbert Maxwell's *Wellington*, ii. 194.

[2] Take, as a rare instance of recognition of this fact, his remark in 1828 that ' When the Duke of Newcastle addressed to me a letter on the subject of forming an Administration, I treated him with contempt. No man *likes* to be treated with contempt. I was wrong.' Ibid. ii. 213.

[3] For a record of such an interview by an eye-witness see Gronow's *Reminiscences*, p. 66.

x 2

England to get cured of it. By all means. Go there immediately." The general, surprised at his Lordship's tone and manner, looked abashed, while he made a profound bow. To prevent his saying anything more, his Lordship turned to address me, inquiring about the casualties of the preceding night [1],' &c.

Hardly less humiliating to many of Wellesley's subordinates than personal interviews of this kind, were the letters which they received from him, when he chanced to be at a distance. He had not the art, probably he had not the wish, to conceal the fact that he despised as well as disliked many of those whom the fortune of war, or the exigencies of home patronage, placed under his command. The same icy intellectual contempt which he showed for the needy peers, the grovelling place-hunters, and the hungry lawyers of Dublin, when he was under-secretary for Ireland, pierces through many of his letters to the officers of the army of Portugal. Very frequently his mean opinion of their abilities was justifiable—but there was no need to let it appear. In this part of the management of men Wellesley was deficient: he failed to see that it is better in the end to rule subordinates by appealing to their zeal and loyalty than to their fears, and that a little commendation for work well performed goes further in its effect on an army than much censure for what has been done amiss. When he has to praise his officers in a dispatch, the terms used are always formal and official in the extreme—it is the rarest thing to find a phrase which seems to come from the heart. The careful reader will know what importance to attach to these expressions of approval, when he notes that the names of subordinates whom Wellesley despised and distrusted are inserted, all in due order of seniority, between those of the men who had really done the work [2]. All commanders-in-chief have to give vent to a certain amount of these empty and meaningless commendations, but few have shown more neglect in discriminating between the really deserving men and the rest than did the victor of Salamanca and Waterloo. Occasionally this carelessness as to the merits and the feelings of others took the form of gross injustice, more frequently it led to nothing worse

---

[1] Sir James McGrigor's *Memoirs*, pp. 304–5.

[2] He honourably mentioned Murray in his Oporto dispatch, and Tripp in his Waterloo dispatch! Both had behaved abominably.

than a complete mystification of the readers of the dispatch as to the relative merits of the persons mentioned therein [1].

The explanation of this feature in Wellesley's correspondence is a fundamental want of broad sympathy in his character. He had a few intimates to whom he spoke freely, and it is clear that he often showed consideration and even kindness to his aides-de-camp and other personal retainers; there were one or two of his relatives to whom he showed an unswerving affection, and whose interests were always near his heart [2]. Among these neither his wife nor his elder brother Richard, the great Governor-General of India, were to be numbered. He quarrelled so bitterly with the latter that for many years they never met. No doubt there were faults on both sides, yet Wellington might have borne much from the brother who started him on his career. But for him the position of Resident in Mysore would not have been given to so junior an officer, nor would the command of the army that won Assaye and Argaum have been placed in his hands. It is small wonder that the grievances and petty ambitions of the average line officer never touched the heart of the man who could be estranged from his own brother by a secondary political question.

It has often been noted that when the wars were over he showed little predilection for the company of his old Peninsular officers. Some of his most trusted subordinates hardly looked upon his face after 1815: he clearly preferred the company of politicians and men of fashion to that of the majority of his old generals. They only met him at the formal festivity of the annual Waterloo Banquet.

[1] Take, for example, the case of Baring of the K. G. L. at Waterloo. In a dispatch, not written immediately after the battle (when accurate information might have been difficult to procure), but *two months* later, Wellesley says that La Haye Sainte was taken at two o'clock, 'through the negligence of the officer who commanded the post.' Yet if anything is certain, it is that Baring held out till six o'clock, that his nine companies of the K. G. L. kept back two whole French divisions, and that when he was driven out, the sole cause was that his ammunition was exhausted, and that no more could be sent him because the enemy had completely surrounded the post. If Wellington had taken any trouble about the ascertaining of the facts, he could not have failed to learn the truth.

[2] See especially his charming letters to his niece, Lady Burghersh, lately published.

The remembrance of the countless panegyrics upon Wellington, not only as a general but as a man, which have appeared during the last sixty years, has made it necessary, if painful, to speak of his limitations. For two whole generations it seemed almost treasonable to breathe a word against his personal character— so great was the debt that Britain owed him for Salamanca and Waterloo. His frigid formalism was regarded with respect and even admiration: his lack of geniality and his utter inability to understand the sentimental side of life were even praised as signs of Spartan virtue. Certain episodes which did not fit in too happily with the 'Spartan hero' theory were deliberately ignored[1]. The popular conception of Arthur Wellesley has been largely built up on laudatory sketches written by those who knew him in his old age alone. He lives in our memories as a kind of Nestor, replete with useful and interesting information, as Lord Stanhope drew him in his *Conversations with the Duke of Wellington*. This was not the man known to his contemporaries in the years of the Peninsular War.

Yet there was much to admire in Wellesley's personal character. England has never had a more faithful servant. Though intensely ambitious, he never allowed ambition to draw him aside from the most tedious and thankless daily tasks. When once convinced that it was his duty to undertake a piece of work, he carried it through with unswerving industry and perseverance, if not always with much tact or consideration for the feelings of others[2]. He was unsparing of himself, careless of praise or blame, honest in every word and deed. He was equally ready to offend his king or to sacrifice his popularity with the multitude, when he

---

[1] His relations with the other sex were numerous and unedifying. From his loveless and unwise marriage, made on a point of duty where affection had long vanished, down to his tedious 'correspondence with Miss J.,' there is nothing profitable to be discovered. See Greville's *Diaries* [2nd Series], iii. 476.

[2] When we read Wellington's interminable controversies with the Portuguese Regency and the Spanish Junta, we soon come to understand not merely the way in which they provoked him by their tortuous shuffling and their helpless procrastination, but still more the way in which he irritated them by his unveiled scorn, and his outspoken exposure of all their meannesses. A little more diplomatic language would have secured less friction, and probably better service.

thought that he had to face a question in which right and wrong were involved. He was essentially, what he once called himself, using a familiar Hindustani phrase, 'a man of his salt.' In spite of all his faults he stands out a majestic figure in the history of his time. It is the misfortune of the historian that when he sees so much to admire and to respect, he finds so little that commands either sympathy or affection.

SECTION XIV: CHAPTER II

WELLESLEY RETAKES OPORTO

On arriving at Lisbon, Wellesley, as we have already seen, was overjoyed to find that the situation in Portugal remained just as it had been when he set sail from Portsmouth: Victor was still quiescent in his cantonments round Merida: Soult had not moved forward on the road toward Coimbra, and was in the midst of his unfruitful bickerings with the army of Silveira. Lapisse had disappeared from his threatening position in front of Ciudad Rodrigo, and had passed away to Estremadura. All the rumours as to an immediate French advance on Badajoz and Abrantes, which had arrived just as the new commander-in-chief was quitting England, had turned out to be baseless inventions. There were reassuring dispatches awaiting him from the English attachés with the armies of Cuesta and La Romana [1], which showed that Galicia was in full insurrection, and that a respectable force was once more threatening Victor's flank. Accordingly it was possible to take into consideration plans for assuming the offensive against the isolated French armies, and the defensive campaign for the protection of Lisbon, which Wellesley had feared to find forced upon him, was not necessary.

Within thirty-six hours of his arrival the British commander-in-chief had made up his mind as to the strategy that was incumbent on him. He resolved, as we have already seen, to leave a containing force to watch Victor, while he hastened with the main body of his army to strike a blow at Soult, whose corps was clearly in a state of dispersion, which invited attack. The Duke of Dalmatia was operating at once upon the Minho, the Tamega, and the Vouga, and it seemed likely that a prompt stroke might surprise him, in the midst of the movement for

[1] Monro to Beresford, April 15, and McKinley's inclosure from Vigo of April 16, 1809.

concentration which he would be compelled to make, when he should learn that the British were in the field.

The forces available for Wellesley's use consisted of some 25,000 British[1] and 16,000 Portuguese troops. Cradock, urged on by Hill and Beresford, had advanced with the main body of his army to Leiria and lay there upon the twenty-fourth, the day upon which he received Wellesley's notification that he had been superseded and was to sail to take up the governorship of Gibraltar. But four or five newly arrived corps still lay at Lisbon, and more were expected. The army was very weak in cavalry, there were but four regiments and fractions of two others available[2]. Of the infantry there were only present five of the battalions[3] which had served at Vimiero and knew the French and their manner of fighting. The rest were all inexperienced and new to the field, and the majority indeed were weak second battalions, which had not originally been intended for foreign service, and had been made up to their present numbers by large and recent drafts from the militia[4]. Even at Talavera, six months after the campaign had begun, it is on record that many of the men were still showing the names and numbers of their old militia regiments on their knapsacks. The battalions which had joined in Moore's march into Spain only began to reappear in June, when Robert Craufurd brought back to Lisbon the 1/43rd, 1/52nd and 1/95th, which were to form the nucleus of the famous Light Division. The remainder of the Corunna troops, when they had been rested and recruited, were drawn aside to take part in the miserable expedition to Walcheren. When Wellesley first took the field therefore, these veterans of the campaign of 1808 were only represented

[1] Excluding troops that arrived at Lisbon just after Wellesley's arrival.

[2] The 3rd Dragoon Guards, 4th Dragoons, 14th and 16th Light Dragoons, with one squadron of the 3rd Light Dragoons of the K. G. L., and two of the 20th Light Dragoons.

[3] The 2/9th, 1/45th, 29th, 5/60th and 97th.

[4] Of Wellesley's twenty-one British battalions, ten were 2nd battalions, [of the 7th, 9th, 24th, 30th, 31st, 48th, 53rd, 66th, 83rd, 87th], two were single-battalion regiments [the 29th and 97th], three first battalions [of the 3rd, 45th and 88th], two Guards' battalions [1st Coldstreams and 1st Scots Fusiliers], two 'battalions of detachments,' one a 3rd battalion (27th), one a 5th battalion [60th].

by the two 'battalicns of detachments' which General Cameron
had organized from the stragglers and convalescents of Moore's
army.

The Portuguese troops which Wellesley found available for
the campaign against Soult consisted entirely of the line regiments from Lisbon and the central parts of the realm, which
Beresford had been reorganizing during the last two months.
The troops of the north had been destroyed at Oporto, or were
in arms under Silveira on the Tamega. Those of the south
were garrisoning Elvas, or still endeavouring to recruit their
enfeebled *cadres* at their regimental head quarters. But Beresford
had massed at Thomar and Abrantes ten [1] line regiments, some
with one, some with their statutory two battalions, three newly
raised battalions of Cazadores, and three incomplete cavalry
regiments, a force amounting in all to nearly 15,000 sabres and
bayonets. Though Wellesley considered that they 'cut a bad
figure,' and that the rank and file were poor and the native
officers 'worse than anything he had ever seen,' he was yet resolved
to give them a chance in the field. Beresford assured him that
they had improved so much during the last few weeks, and were
showing such zeal and good spirit, that it was only fair that
they should be given a trial [2].

Accordingly Wellesley resolved to brigade certain picked
battalions among his English troops, and to take them straight
to the front, while he told off others to form part of the
'containing force' which was to be sent off to watch Victor

---

[1] These regiments were the 1st, 3rd, 4th, 7th, 10th, 13th, 15th, 16th,
19th, raised respectively at Lisbon (1st, 4th, 10th, 16th), Estremoz (3rd),
Setubal (7th), Peniche (13th), Villa Viciosa (15th), Cascaes (19th), Campomayor (20th), the 1st, 4th and 5th Cazadores, and 1st, 4th and 7th
Cavalry.

[2] It is fair to the Portuguese to note that other witnesses of May 1809
speak much more favourably of them. Londonderry (i. p. 305) writes
that ' they had applied of late so much ardour to their military education
that some were already fit to take the field, and it only required a little
experience to put them on a level with the best troops in Europe. There
was one brigade under General Campbell (the 4th and 10th regiments),
which struck me as being in the finest possible order : it went through
a variety of evolutions with a precision and correctness which would have
done no discredit to our own army.'

and the French army of Estremadura. The remainder, under Beresford himself, were to act as an independent division during the march on Oporto.

Five days of unceasing work had to be spent in Lisbon before Wellesley could go forward, but while he was making his arrangements with the Portuguese regency, drawing out a new organization for Beresford's commissariat, and striving to get into communication with Cuesta, the British troops were already being pushed forward from Leiria towards Coimbra, and the Portuguese were converging from Thomar on the same point, so that no time was being lost. It was during this short and busy stay at Lisbon that Wellesley was confronted with the conspirator Argenton, who had come up to the capital in company with Major Douglas. He did not make a good impression on the commander-in-chief, who wrote home that he had no doubt as to the reality of the plot against Soult, and the discontent of the French army, but thought it unlikely that any good would come from the plot[1]. He refused to promise compliance with Argenton's two requests, that he would direct the Portuguese to fall in with Soult's plans for assuming royal power, and that he would bring the British army forward to a position in which it would threaten the retreat of the 2nd Corps on Leon. The former savoured too much of Machiavellian treachery: as to the latter, he thought so little of the profit likely to result from the plot, that he would not alter his plans to oblige the conspirators. The only information of certain value that he had obtained from the emissary was that Soult had no idea of Victor's position or projects. All that he granted to Argenton was passports to take him and his two friends, 'Captains Dupont and Garis,' to England, from whence they intended to cross into France, in order to set their friends in the interior on the move. Great care was taken that Argenton on his return journey to Oporto should see as little as possible of the British army, lest he should be able to tell too much about its numbers

---

[1] *Wellington Dispatches*, iv. 273-5, 276. To Castlereagh. Wellesley says that the plot will probably fail, and that even if the 2nd Corps mutinied, they would not carry away the other French armies, as Argenton hoped. He had therefore refused to commit himself to anything.

and dispositions. He was conducted back by Douglas to the
Vouga, by a circuitous route, and safely repassed Franceschi's
outposts.

On the twenty-ninth Wellesley at last got clear of Lisbon,
where the formal festivities and reception arranged in his
honour had tried him even more than the incessant desk-work
which had to be got through before the organization of his base
for supplies was completed.   On April 30 he pushed forward to
Leiyria, on May 1 to Pombal, on the second he reached Coimbra
and found himself in the midst of his army, which had only
concentrated itself at that city during the last five days.

All was quiet in the front: Trant, who was holding the line
of the Vouga with 3,000 disorderly militia and some small
fragments rallied from the line regiments which had been dispersed at Oporto, reported that Franceschi and the French light
cavalry had remained quiescent for many days.   The same news
came in from Wilson, who, after pursuing Lapisse to Alcantara,
had come back with part of his troops to the neighbourhood of
Almeida, and had a detachment at Vizeu watching the flank of
the French advance.   Silveira reported from Amarante that he
was still holding the line of the Tamega, and had at least
10,000 enemies in front of him.   All therefore seemed propitious
for the great stroke.

Wellesley's plan, as finally worked out in detail, was to push
forward his main body upon Oporto with all possible speed,
while sending a flanking column under Beresford to cross the
Douro near Lamego, join Silveira, and intercept Soult's line of
retreat upon the plains of Leon by way of the Tras-os-Montes.
If he could move fast enough, he hoped to catch the Marshal
with his army still unconcentrated.   His design, as he wrote to
Castlereagh, was 'to beat or cripple Soult,' to thrust him back
into Galicia; he doubted whether it would be possible to
accomplish more with the force that was at his disposal, but if
any chance should occur for destroying or surrounding the
enemy he would do his best.   Rumours that the Marshal was
preparing to evacuate Oporto were in the air: if they were true,
and the French were already making ready to retreat, it was
unlikely that they would stand long enough to run into danger.

[1] *Wellington Dispatches,* ii. 306.

The detailed arrangements for the distribution of the troops were as follows :—

It was first necessary to provide a 'containing force' to hold back Victor, in case he should make an unexpected move down the Tagus or the Guadiana. For this purpose Wellesley told off one of his brigades, that of Mackenzie, together with two regiments of heavy cavalry and one of infantry which had lately arrived at Lisbon, and were now on their march to Santarem. With these four battalions, one field battery, and eight squadrons, Mackenzie was to take post at Abrantes, and behind the line of the Zezere[1]. There he was to be joined by the larger half of Beresford's reorganized Portuguese army—seven battalions of line troops, three of Cazadores, five squadrons of cavalry, and three batteries[2]. He would also have three regiments of militia at his disposal, to garrison the fortress of Abrantes. His whole force, excluding the militia, would amount to 1,400 British and 700 Portuguese cavalry, nearly 3,000 British infantry, 6,000 Portuguese infantry, and four batteries.   These 12,000 men ought to be able to hold back any force that Victor could detach for a raid along the Tagus : for, having Cuesta's army in his front, it was absolutely impossible that he could march with his whole corps into Portugal. If the Marshal moved forward south of the Tagus, that river should be held against him, and since it was in full flood it would be easy to keep him back, as all the boats and ferries could be destroyed, and it would be useless for him to present himself opposite Vella Velha, Abrantes,

---

[1] The regiments were, giving their force present with the colours from the return of May 5 :—

3/27th Foot . . .	726	3rd Dragoon Guards . .	698
2/31st ,, . . .	765	4th Dragoons . . .	716
1/45th ,, . . .	671	One battery Field Artillery	
2/24th ,, [From Lisbon]	750	[Captain Baynes's], six-pounders . . .	120
	2,912		1,534
		Total	4,446

[2] The Portuguese regiments were :—1st Foot [La Lippe] one batt., 3rd and 15th Foot [1st and 2nd of Olivenza] each one batt., 4th Foot [Freire] and 13th Foot [Peniche] two batts. each. 1st, 4th and 5th Cazadores, one batt. each. Five squadrons of the 4th and 7th cavalry. Total, 6,000 foot, 700 horse, and three field-batteries, about 7,100 men.

or Santarem. If he advanced north of the Tagus, the line of
the Zezere was to be maintained against him as long as possible,
then those of the Nabao and Rio Mayor. But the main army
would be back from the north, to reinforce the 'containing
force,' long ere the Marshal could push so far. As an outlying
post on this front Wellesley ordered Colonel Mayne, with the
part of Wilson's Lusitanian Legion that had not returned to
the north and a militia regiment, to occupy Alcantara. He was
to break its bridge if forced out of the position.

Victor being thus provided for, Wellesley could turn the rest
of his army against Soult at Oporto. For the main operation
he could dispose of 17,000 British and 7,000 Portuguese troops
present with the colours, after deducting the sick, the men on
detached duty, and one single battalion left in garrison at
Lisbon. He divided them, as we have already stated, into
a larger force destined to execute the frontal attack upon Soult,
and a smaller one which was to cut off his retreat into central
Spain.

The flanking column, 5,800 men in all, was entrusted to Beresford: it was composed of one British brigade (that of Tilson)
consisting of 1,500 bayonets[1], a single British squadron (the 4th
of the 14th Light Dragoons) with five battalions[2], three
squadrons[3], and two field-batteries of Portuguese. These troops
were originally directed to join Silveira at Amarante, and
co-operate with him in defending the line of the Tamega. But
on May 3 there arrived at Coimbra the unwelcome news that
Loison had forced the bridge of Amarante, and that Silveira in
consequence had retired south of the Douro and was lying at
Lamego with the wrecks of his army, some 4,000 men at most.
This untoward event did not cause Wellesley to change the
direction of Beresford's column, but rendered him more cautious
as to pushing it beyond the Douro. He ordered his lieutenant
to pick up Sir Robert Wilson's small force at Vizeu[4], to join

[1] Viz. 2/87th, 669 bayonets, 1/88th, 608 bayonets, five companies of the
5/60th, 306 bayonets.

[2] Two battalions each of the regiments nos. 7 (Setubal), 19 (Cascaes),
and one of no. 1 (La Lippe), as far as I can ascertain, composed this
force.   [3] Regiment, no. 1.

[4] Wilson had been removed by Beresford from his own Lusitanian
Legion, and told to take up the command of the Brigade at Almeida :

Silveira at Lamego, and then to guide his further operations by the attitude of the French. If they tried to pass the Douro he was to oppose them strenuously; if they still clung to the northern bank and had not advanced far beyond Amarante, he might cross, and occupy Villa Real, if he thought the move safe and the position behind that town defensible. But he was to risk nothing; if the whole of Soult's corps should retreat eastward he was not to attempt to stop them, ' for,' wrote Wellesley, ' I should not like to see a single British brigade, supported by 6,000 or 8,000 Portuguese, exposed to be attacked by the French army in any but a very good post [1].' If Loison alone were left on the Tamega, Beresford might take post at Villa Real and fight: if, however, Soult should appear at the head of his entire force, it would be madness to await him : the column must fall back and allow him to pass. ' Remember,' added Wellesley in another letter [2], ' that you are a commander-in-chief *and must not be beaten* : therefore do not undertake anything with your troops if you have not some strong hope of success.' Beresford's column was sent off a day before the rest of the army, in order to allow the flanking movement time to develop before the frontal attack was pushed home. He left Coimbra on May 6, was at Vizeu on the eighth, and joined Silveira at Lamego on the tenth; all his movements passed completely unobserved by the enemy, owing to the wide sweep to the right which he had been ordered to make.

The infantry of Wellesley's main force, with which the frontal attack on Oporto was to be made, consisted of six brigades of British, one of the King's German Legion, and four picked battalions of Portuguese who were attached respectively to the brigades of A. Campbell, Sontag, Stewart, and Cameron. Of cavalry, in which he was comparatively weak, he had the whole of the 16th, three squadrons of the 14th, and two of the 20th Light Dragoons, with one squadron more from the 3rd Light Dragoons of the King's German Legion. The artillery, twenty-four guns in all, was composed of two British and two German field-batteries.

---

it was, apparently, with two battalions drawn from the garrison of that fortress that he now joined Beresford.

[1] Wellesley to Beresford, Coimbra, May 7. *Wellington Dispatches,* iv. 309.   [2] Ibid. iv. 320.

No horse artillery had yet been received from England, though Wellesley had been urging his need for it on the home authorities, at the same time that he made a similar demand for good light infantry, such as that which had formed the light brigade of Moore's army [1], and for remounts to keep his cavalry up to full fighting strength. The army was not yet distributed into regular divisions, but the beginnings of the later divisional arrangement were indicated by the telling off the brigades of Richard Stewart and Murray to serve together under Edward Paget (who had commanded Moore's reserve division with such splendid credit to himself during the Corunna retreat), while those of H. Campbell, A. Campbell, and Sontag were to take their orders from Sherbrooke, and those of Hill and Cameron to move under the charge of the former brigadier. The cavalry was under General Cotton, with Payne as brigadier; the senior officer of artillery was General E. Howorth [2].

[1] *Wellington Dispatches*, iv. pp. 270, 281, 305.

[2] The whole force consisted of the following, present with the colours:—

CAVALRY :	Officers.	Men.		Officers.	Men.
14th Light Dragoons	20	471	R. Stewart's brigade :		
16th ,, ,,	37	673	29th Foot	26	596
20th ,, ,,	6	237	1st Batt. Detachments	27	803
3rd ,, ,, K.G.L.	3	57	1/16th Portuguese	—	—
INFANTRY :			Murray's brigade :		
H. Campbell's brigade :			1st Line Batt. K.G.L.	34	767
Coldstream Guards	33	1,194	2nd ,, ,,	32	804
3rd Foot Guards	34	1,228	5th ,, ,,	28	720
One company 5/60th	2	61	7th ,, ,,	22	688
A. Campbell's brigade :			Hill's brigade :		
2/7th Foot	26	559	1/3rd Foot	28	719
2/53rd Foot	35	787	2/48th Foot	32	721
One company 5/60th	4	64	2/66th Foot	34	667
1/10th Portuguese	—	—	One company 5/60 Foot	2	61
Sontag's brigade :			Cameron's brigade :		
97th Foot	22	572	2/9th Foot	27	545
2nd Batt. Detachments	35	787	2/83rd Foot	29	833
One company 5/60th	2	61	One company 5/60 Foot	2	60
2/16th Portuguese	—	—	2/10th Portuguese	—	—

With Lawson's battery of 3-pounders, and Lane's, Heyse's, and Rettberg's of 6-pounders. Allowing 600 each for the Portuguese battalions, the total comes to 16,213 infantry, 1,504 cavalry, and 550 gunners, also sixty-four men of the wagon train, and thirty-nine engineers. Total, 18,370.

It will be noted that of the total force with which Wellesley was about to assail the 2nd Corps, about 16,400 were British troops and 11,400 Portuguese. Considering that Soult had at least 23,000 sabres and bayonets, of whom not more than 2,200 were in his hospitals, and that over three-eighths of the allies were untried and newly-organized levies, it cannot be denied that the march on Oporto showed considerable self-confidence, and a very nice and accurate calculation of the chances of war on the part of the British Commander-in-chief.

On the very day on which the vanguard marched out from Coimbra upon the northern road, Wellesley received a second visit from the conspirator Argenton, who had returned from consulting his friends at Oporto and Amarante. He brought little news of importance : Soult had not yet proclaimed himself king, and therefore the plotters had taken no open steps against him. The French army had not begun to move, but it appeared that the Marshal was pondering over the relative advantages of the lines of retreat available to him, for Argenton brought a memorandum given him by (or purloined from) some staff-officer, which contained a long exposition of the various roads from Oporto, and stated a preference for that by Villa Real and the Tras-os-Montes[1]. He had a number of futile propositions to lay before Wellesley, and especially urged him to make sure of Villa Real and to cut off the Marshal's retreat on Spain. The traitor was sent back, with no promises of compliance ; and every endeavour was made to keep from him the fact that the allied army was already upon the move. Unfortunately he had passed many troops upon the road from Coimbra to the Vouga, and had guessed at what he had not seen. On the following day he passed through the French lines on his return journey, and by the way endeavoured to spread the propaganda of treason. One of the infantry brigades which lay in support of Franceschi's cavalry was commanded by a general Lefebvre, with whom Argenton had long served as aide-de-camp. Knowing that his old chief was weak and discontented[2], the emissary of

---

[1] Wellington to Beresford, from Coimbra, May 7, 1809.

[2] He told Wellesley that the general was ' a man of weak intellect,' and that he thought that he had won him over to the plot from the way in which he received the news of it. Wellesley to Castlereagh, May 15, from Oporto.

the malcontents paid a midnight visit to him, revealed to him
the outlines of the conspiracy, and endeavoured to enroll him as
a fellow plotter.   He had misjudged his man : Lefebvre listened
to everything without showing any signs of surprise or anger,
but hastened to bear the tale to Soult, and arranged for
Argenton's arrest on his return to Oporto upon the following
morning.   Confronted with the Marshal, the traitor held his
head high, and boasted that he was the agent of a powerful
body of conspirators.   He invited Soult to declare against the
Emperor, and deliver France from servitude.   He also warned
him that Wellesley had arrived at Coimbra, and told him that
30,000 British troops of whom 3,000 at least were cavalry, would
fall upon Franceschi that day.   Thus, owing to his conference
with Argenton, Wellesley lost the chance of surprising Soult,
who was warned of the oncoming storm exactly at the moment
when it was most important that he should still be kept in the
dark as to the force that was marching against him [May 8].

Soult sent back Argenton to his prison, after threatening him
with death : but uncertain as to the number of the conspirators,
he was thrown for a moment into a state of doubt and alarm.
He probably suspected Loison and Lahoussaye of being in the
plot against him, as well as the real traitors—possibly Mermet
also [1].   Feeling the ground, as it were, trembling beneath his
feet, he began to make instant preparations for retreat : orders
were sent to Franceschi to fall back on Oporto, and not to risk
anything by an attempt to hold off Wellesley longer than was
prudent.   Loison was informed that he must clear the road
beyond Amarante, as the army was about to retire by the Tras-
os-Montes, and he would now form its advanced guard.   Lorges
at Braga was directed to gather in the small fractions of Heudelet's division which had been left at Viana and other places in

---

[1] This may be perhaps inferred from Soult's letter to King Joseph,
written after the retreat, in which he says that he had intended to pack off
Lahoussaye and Mermet from the front : ' À cette époque j'ai voulu faire
partir ces généraux, qui n'ont pas toujours fait ce qui était de leur pouvoir
pour le succès des opérations ; mais j'ai preféré attendre d'être arrivé
à Zamora, afin de ne pas accréditer les bruits d'intrigues et de conspirations qui eurent lieu à Oporto, auxquels ils n'ont pas certainement
pris aucune part.' [Intercepted letter in Record Office.]

the north, and to march in their company upon Amarante by the way of Guimaraens. The Marshal saw, with some dismay, that these isolated detachments would not be able to join the main body till the fourteenth or fifteenth of May; it was necessary to hold Oporto as long as possible in order to give them time to come up.

Next day Soult contrived to extort some more information from the unstable Argenton. Receiving a promise of life for himself and pardon for his fellow conspirators (which the Marshal apparently granted because he thought that accurate information concerning the plot would be worth more to him than the right to shoot the plotters), the captain gave up the names of all the leaders. Much relieved to find that none of his generals were implicated, Soult did no more than arrest the two colonels, Lafitte and Donadieu, leaving the smaller fry untouched [1]. He kept his promise to Argenton by hushing up the whole matter. The colonels suffered no harm beyond their arrest: Argenton escaped from custody (probably by collusion with the officer placed in charge of his person) [2], and got back to the English lines the day after the capture of Oporto [3]. Some months later he secretly revisited France, was recognized, captured, and shot on the Plain of Grenelle [4].

At the very moment when Soult was cross-examining Argenton, issuing hurried orders for the concentration of his troops, and preparing for a retreat upon Amarante, Wellesley's advanced guard was drawing near the Vouga and making ready to pounce

[1] Soult so far managed to forget the whole business that he, two years later, sent the younger Lafitte to present to the Emperor the English flags captured at Albuera! [See St. Chamans, p. 133.]

[2] Most of this comes from Argenton's confession to Wellesley on May 13. See *Wellington Dispatches*, iv. p. 339. He said that he slipped away from the gendarmes at the advice of Lafitte, who told him that his friends would come to no harm if the chief witness against them vanished.

[3] The extraordinary clemency shown to the conspirators by Soult, the providential escape of Argenton, the favours which the Marshal afterwards lavished on Lafitte, and the trouble which he took to hush up the whole matter, led many of his enemies to suspect that he himself had been in the plot, and had intended to combine his scheme for Portuguese kingship with a rising against Bonaparte at the head of his *corps d'armée* : Argenton's confession made this impossible.

[4] For further details on Argenton's fate, see the Appendix.

upon Franceschi.   Two roads lead northward from Coimbra, the
main *chaussée* to Oporto which runs inland via Ponte de Vouga
and Feira, and a minor route near the coast, which passes by
Aveiro and Ovar.   Five of Wellesley's brigades and the whole of
his cavalry marched by the former route.   Moving forward under
the screen of Trant's militia, which still held the line of the
Vouga, they were to fall on the enemy's front at dawn on
May 10.   The five squadrons of the 14th and 16th Light
Dragoons under Cotton led the advance : then followed the
infantry of Edward Paget—the two brigades of Murray and
Richard Stewart.   Sherbrooke's column marched in support, ten
miles to the rear.   It was intended that the whole mass should
rush in upon Franceschi's pickets, and roll them in upon his main
body before the advance from Coimbra was suspected.   Unhappily
Soult had already warned his cavalry commander of the coming
storm upon the ninth, and he was not caught unprepared.

Meanwhile the remaining two infantry brigades of Wellesley's
army, those of Hill and Cameron, were to execute a turning
movement against Franceschi's flank.   Orders had been sent
to the magistrates of the town of Aveiro, bidding them collect
all the fishing-boats which were to be found in the great lagoon
at the mouth of the Vouga—a broad sheet of shallow water
and sandbanks which extends for fifteen miles parallel to the
sea, only separated from it by a narrow spit of dry ground.
At the northern end of this system of inland waterways is the
town of Ovar, which lay far behind Franceschi's rear.   Hill was
directed to ship his men upon the boats, and to throw them
ashore at Ovar, where they were to fall upon the flank of the
French, when they should be driven past them by the frontal
advance of the main body.

If all had gone well, the French detachment might have been
annihilated.   Franceschi had with him no more than the four
weak cavalry regiments of his own division[1], not more than
1,200 sabres, with one light battery, and a single regiment of
infantry.   But not far behind him was the rest of Mermet's
division, eleven battalions of infantry with a strength of some
3,500 men.   One regiment, the 31st Léger, lay at Feira, near

---

[1] 1st Hussars, 8th Dragoons, 22nd Chasseurs and Hanoverian Chevaux-
légers.

Ovar, while Ferrey's brigade was five miles further back, at Grijon.

On the night of the ninth the British advanced guard reached the Vouga : after only a few hours' repose the cavalry mounted again at 1 a.m., and pushed forward in order to fall upon the enemy at daybreak. The night march turned out a failure, as such enterprises often do in an unexplored country-side seamed with rocks and ravines. The rear of the cavalry column got astray and fell far behind the leading squadrons : much time was lost in marching and countermarching, and at dawn the brigade found itself still some way from Albergaria Nova, the village where Franceschi's head quarters were established[1]. It was already five o'clock when they fell in with and drove back the French outlying pickets : shortly after they came upon the whole of Franceschi's division, drawn out in battle array on a rough moor behind the village, with a few companies of infantry placed in a wood on their flank and their battery in front of their line. General Cotton saw that there was no chance of a surprise, and very wisely declined to attack a slightly superior force of all arms with the 1,000 sabres of his two regiments. He resolved to wait for the arrival of Richard Stewart's infantry brigade, the leading part of the main column. When Franceschi advanced against him he refused to fight and drew back a little [2]. Thus some hours of the morning were wasted, till at last there arrived on the field Lane's battery and a battalion of the 16th Portuguese, followed by the 29th and the 1st Battalion of Detachments. Like the cavalry, the infantry had been much delayed during

[1] For details of this fatiguing night march and its gropings in the dark see Tomkinson's (16th Dragoons) *Diary*, pp. 4–5, and Hawker's (14th Light Dragoons) *Journal*, p. 47.

[2] The Light Dragoons, says Hawker (*Journal*, p. 48), 'finding ourselves opposed by a heavy column of cavalry, retired a little.' Their total loss was one officer and two men wounded, and one man missing. On this slender foundation Le Noble founds the following romance (p. 240). 'Le général Franceschi charge à la tête de sa division ceux qui l'attaquent en front, renverse la première ligne, et tandis qu'elle se rétablit, se retire, et fond avec 6 pièces et deux régiments sur la colonne qui le tournait par sa droite. L'ennemi est culbuté, la colonne recule, et le général se retire sur Oliveira avec quelques prisonniers.' All this fuss produced *four* casualties in the two English regiments. See official report of casualties for May 10, 1809.

the hours of darkness, mainly by the impossibility of getting the guns up the rocky defile beyond the Vouga, where several caissons had broken down in the roadway. It was only after daylight had come that they were extricated and got forward on to the upland where lies the village of Albergaria.

Wellesley himself came up along with Stewart's brigade, and had the mortification of seeing all his scheme miscarry, owing to the tardiness of the arrival of his infantry. For at the very moment when Franceschi caught sight of the distant bayonets winding up the road, he hastily went to the rear, leaving the 1st Hussars alone in position as a rearguard. This regiment was charged by the 16th Light Dragoons, and driven in with some small loss. Under cover of this skirmish the French division got away in safety through the town of Oliveira de Azemis, which lay behind them, and after making two more ineffectual demonstrations of a desire to stand, fell back on the heights of Grijon, where Mermet's infantry division was awaiting them.

The whole day's fighting had been futile but spectacular. 'I must note,' says an eye-witness, 'the beautiful effect of our engagement. It commenced about sunrise on one of the finest spring mornings possible, on an immense tract of heath, with a pine wood in rear of the enemy. So little was the slaughter, and so regular the manœuvring, that it all appeared more like a sham-fight on Wimbledon Common than an action in a foreign country[1].' The picturesque side of the day's work must have been small consolation to Wellesley, who thus saw the first stroke of his campaign foiled by the chances of a night march in a rugged country—a lesson which he took to heart, for he rarely, if ever again, attempted a surprise at dawn in an unexplored region.

An equal disappointment had taken place on the flank near the sea. Hill's brigade had marched down to Aveiro, where the local authorities had worked with excellent zeal and collected a considerable number of boats, enough to carry 1,500 men at a

[1] Hawker, pp. 49–50. Tomkinson has words to much the same effect, 'it was more like a field-day than an affair with the enemy : all the shots went over our heads, and no accident appeared to happen to any one' (p. 6).

trip. During the night of the ninth–tenth the flotilla was engaged in sailing up the long lagoon which leads to Ovar. It was quite early in the morning when the brigade came to land, and if Franceschi had been driven in at an early hour he would have found Hill in a most threatening position on his flank. But the French cavalry was still ten or twelve miles away, engaged in its bloodless demonstration against Cotton's brigade. Finding from the peasants that there were French infantry encamped quite close to him, at Feira, and that the English main column was still at a distance, Hill kept his men within the walls of Ovar, instead of engaging in an attempt to intercept Franceschi's retreat. He was probably quite right, as it would have been dangerous to thrust three battalions, without cavalry or guns, between Mermet's troops at Feira and the retiring columns of the French horsemen. Hill therefore sent back his boats to bring up Cameron's brigade from Aveiro, and remained quiet all the morning. At noon his pickets were driven in by French infantry: Mermet had at last heard of his arrival, and had sent out the three battalions of the 31st Léger from Feira to contain him and protect Franceschi's flank. The *voltigeur* companies of this force pressed in upon Hill, but would not adventure themselves too far. The afternoon was spent in futile skirmishing, but at last the retreating French cavalry went by at a great pace, and the English Light Dragoons, following them in hot pursuit, came up with the 31st Léger. Hill, seeing himself once more in touch with his friends, now pushed out of Ovar in force, and pressed on the French *voltigeur* companies, which hastily retired, fell back on their regiment, and ultimately retired with it and rejoined Mermet's main body on the heights above Grijon. The skirmishing had been almost bloodless— Hill lost not a single man, and the French infantry only half-a-dozen wounded [1].

On the morning of May 11, therefore, Hill's troops on the left and Cotton's and Paget's on the right lay opposite the posi-

---

[1] The best account of this little skirmish is in the *Journal* of Fantin des Odoards of the 31st Léger (p. 230). Napier does not mention that the reason why Hill did not move in the afternoon was simply that he was already ' contained,' and engaged with a force of French infantry of nearly his own strength.

tion which Mermet and Franceschi had taken up. Sherbrooke
was still more than ten miles to the rear, having barely crossed
the Vouga, while Cameron had not yet sailed up from Aveiro.
Wellesley had therefore some 1,500 cavalry and 7,000 infantry
under his hand, with which to assail the 1,200 horse and 4,200
foot of the two French divisions. The enemy were strongly
posted: Grijon lies in a valley, with woods and orchards around
it and a steep hillside at its back. The French *tirailleurs* held
the village and the thickly-wooded slopes on each side of it:
behind them the fifteen battalions of Mermet were partly visible
among the trees on the sky-line of the heights.

Wellesley was anxious to see whether the enemy intended to
hold his ground, or would retire before a demonstration: he
therefore threw the light companies of Richard Stewart's brigade
into the woods on each side of Grijon. A furious fire at once
broke out, and the advancing line of skirmishers could make no
headway. Realizing that the French intended to fight a serious
rearguard action, Wellesley refused to indulge them with a
frontal attack and determined to turn both their flanks. While
Cotton's cavalry and the two English battalions of Stewart's
brigade drew up opposite their centre, Murray's Germans
marched off to the left, to get beyond Mermet's flank, while
Colonel Doyle, with the battalion of the 16th Portuguese which
belonged to Stewart's brigade, entered the woods on the extreme
right. Hill's brigade, a mile or two to the left of Murray,
pushed forward on the Ovar-Oporto road, at a rate which would
soon have brought them far beyond the enemy's rear.

The meaning of these movements was not long hidden from
the French: the 1st and 2nd battalions of the King's German
Legion, led by Brigadier Langwerth, were soon pressing upon
their right flank, while the Portuguese battalion plunged into
the woods on the other wing with great resolution. Wellesley
himself was watching this part of the advance with much interest:
it was the first time that he had sent his native allies into the
firing line, and he was anxious to see how they would behave.
They surpassed his expectations: the 16th was a good regiment,
with a number of students of the University of Coimbra in its
ranks. They plunged into the thickets without a moment's
hesitation, and in a few minutes the retiring sound of the

musketry showed that they were making headway in the most promising style. This sight was an enormous relief to the Commander-in-chief: if the Portuguese could be trusted in line of battle, his task became immeasurably more easy. 'You are in error in supposing that these troops will not fight,' he wrote to a downhearted correspondent: 'one battalion has behaved remarkably well under my own eyes[1].'

Mermet and Franceschi did not hesitate for long, when they saw their flank guard beaten in upon either side, and heard that Hill was marching upon their rear. They gave orders for their whole line to retire without delay: the plateau behind them was so cut up with stone walls enclosing fields, that the cavalry could be of no use in covering the retreat, so Franceschi went to the rear first at a round trot. Mermet followed, leaving the three battalions of the 31st Léger to act as a rearguard[2].

The whole British line now pressed in as fast as was possible in the woods and lanes: the infantry could never overtake the enemy, but two squadrons of the 16th and 20th Light Dragoons, galloping along the high road, came up with Mermet's rear a mile beyond the brow of the hill. Charles Stewart, who was leading them on, was one of those cavalry officers who thoroughly believe in their arm, and think that it can go anywhere and do anything. He at once ordered Major Blake of the 20th to charge the enemy, though the French were retiring along a narrow *chaussée* bordered with stone walls. Fortunately for the dragoons their opponents were already shaken in *morale* : the three battalions were not well together, isolated companies were still coming in from the flanks, and the colonel of the 31st had completely lost his head. On being charged, the rearguard fired a volley, which brought down the front files of the pursuing cavalry, but then wavered, broke, and began scrambling over the walls to escape out of the high road into the fields. There followed a confused *mêlée*, for the English dragoons also leaped the walls, and tried to follow the broken enemy among thickets and ploughland. Of those of the French

---

[1] Wellesley to Mackenzie [the latter had written that he dared not trust his Portuguese battalions], *Wellington Dispatches*, iv. p. 350.

[2] See Fantin des Odoards. Le Noble (incorrect as always) says that the 47th brought up the rear.

who fled down the high road many were sabred, and a considerable number captured : indeed the eagle of the regiment was in
considerable danger for some time.   But the British had no
supports at hand ; they scattered in reckless pursuit of the men
who had taken to the fields, and many were shot down when
they had got entangled among trees and walls.   However, the
charge, if somewhat reckless, was on the whole successful : the
dragoons lost no more than ten killed, one officer and thirty
troopers wounded, with eight or ten missing, while the French
regiment into which they had burst left behind it over 100
prisoners and nearly as many killed and wounded[1].

For the rest of the day Mermet and Franceschi continued to
fall back before the advancing British, without making more
than a momentary stand.   At dusk they reached Villa Nova,
the transpontine suburb of Oporto, which they evacuated during

---

[1] There are two excellent accounts of this charge in the diaries of
Tomkinson of the 16th Light Dragoons and Fantin des Odoards of the
31st Léger. The former (pp. 9–11) holds that the charge was indefensible,
and blames Charles Stewart for ordering it, and Major Blake for carrying
it out.   A different impression is received from the French diarist, who
speaks of it as a complete rout of his regiment and very disastrous.
' Assaillis en détail nous avons été facilement mis en désordre, attendu
notre morcellement et la confusion que des charges audacieuses de cavalerie
mettaient dans nos rangs.   Les trois bataillons ont lâché pied et se sont
enfuis à vau de route.   Si le pays n'avait pas offert des murs, des fossés
et des haies, ils auraient été entièrement sabrés. . . . Peu à peu les
débris du régiment se sont ralliés à la division, qui était en position à une
lieue de Porto. Notre perte a été considérable, mais notre aigle, qui a couru
de grands dangers dans cette bagarre, a fort heureusement été sauvée. . . .
Les dragons étaient acharnés à nous poursuivre, et mal a pris ceux qui
au lieu de gagner les collines ont suivi le vallon et la grande route ' (p. 231).
It seems probable (a thing extremely rare in military history) that
Tomkinson and Des Odoards, the two best narrators of the fight, actually
met each other.   The former mentions that he chased an isolated French
infantry man, fired his pistol at his head, but missed, and that he was
at once shot in the shoulder by another Frenchman and disabled.   Then
turning back, he was again fired at by several men and brought down.
Des Odoards says that he was chased by a single English dragoon, who
got up to him, fired at him point blank and missed, whereupon a corporal
of his company, who had turned back to help him, shot the dragoon, who
dropped his smoking pistol at Des Odoards' feet, and rolled off his
horse. The narratives seem to tally perfectly.

the night. The moment that they had crossed the bridge of boats Soult caused it to be blown up, and vainly believed himself secure, now that the broad and rapid Douro was rolling between him and his enemy. The total loss of the French in the day's fighting had been about 250 men, of whom 100 were prisoners. That of the British was two officers and nineteen men killed, six officers and sixty-three men wounded, and sixteen men missing. Nearly half the casualties were in the ranks of the two squadrons of dragoons, the rest were divided between the light companies of the 1st Battalion of Detachments, the 1st and 2nd battalions of the German Legion, and the 16th Portuguese[1].

On the night of the eleventh–twelfth, when Mermet and Franceschi had joined him, Soult had collected in Oporto the main body of his army: he had in hand of cavalry Franceschi's four regiments, and of infantry fifteen battalions of Mermet's division, seven battalions of Merle's (forming Reynaud's brigade), and seven of Delaborde's, a force in all of about 10,000 bayonets and 1,200 sabres. Only a few miles away, at Baltar, on the road to Amarante, were Caulaincourt's dragoons and the remaining regiment of Delaborde's division, an additional force of somewhat over 2,000 men. With 13,000 men at his disposal and a splendid position behind the Douro, he imagined that he might retreat at leisure, maintaining the line of the impassable river for some days more. He intended to hold Oporto long enough to enable Loison to clear the road to Villa Real, and to allow Lorges and the belated troops from the north time to march in to Amarante. He was somewhat vexed to have received no news from Loison for four days, but, when last heard of [on May 7], that general was moving forward into the Tras-os-Montes, with orders to push on and open a way for

---

[1] The officers killed were Captain Detmering of the 1st K. G. L., and a Portuguese ensign of the 1/16th. Those wounded were Captain Ovens and Lieutenant Woodgate of the 1st Battalion of Detachments, Lieutenants Lodders and Lahngren of the K. G. L., Cornet Tomkinson of the 16th Light Dragoons, and a Portuguese lieutenant of the 1/16th. It would seem that some of the fourteen 'missing' were infantry killed in the woods, whose bodies were never found, but several belonged to the maltreated dragoon squadrons, and were taken from having pursued too fast and far.

the army as far as the Spanish border. Silveira having retired
to the south bank of the Douro, the Marshal had no doubt that
Loison would easily brush away the *Ordenanza*, and open for the
whole *corps d'armée* the passage to Zamora and the plains of
Leon.

Meanwhile the only danger which the Marshal feared was
that Wellesley might send forward the fleet of fishing-boats
which had carried Hill to Ovar, bring them to the estuary of
the Douro, and use them to pass troops across its lowest reach,
just within the bar at its mouth. Accordingly he told Franceschi to patrol carefully the five miles of the river that lie
between Oporto and the sea. The infantry was comfortably
housed in the city, with pickets watching the quays: every
boat on the river, as it was supposed, had either been destroyed
or brought over to the north bank. Wellesley would, as Soult
calculated, be compelled to spend several days in making his
preparations for passing the Douro, since he had no means of
pushing his army across the broad stream, save the fishing-
smacks which he might bring round from the lagoon of Ovar.

The Marshal therefore was quite at his ease, even though he
knew that Wellesley's vanguard was at Villa Nova in force. He
imagined that he could count on ample time for the evacuation
of Oporto, and began to make arrangements for a leisurely
retreat. His first care was to send off eastward all his convalescents, his reserve ammunition, and his wheeled vehicles, of
which he had collected a fair supply during his seven weeks' halt
at Oporto. These were to march, under the convoy of Mermet's
division, during the course of the morning. The other troops
from Merle's and Delaborde's divisions, together with Franceschi's
horse, were to watch the lower Douro and check any attempt of
the British to cross. The Marshal was himself lodged at a
villa on the high ground west of the city, from which he commanded a fine view of the whole valley from Oporto to the sea:
the view up-stream was blocked by the hill crowned by the Serra
Convent, where the river makes a slight bend in order to get
round the projecting heights on the southern bank. So
thoroughly were both Soult and his staff impressed with the
idea that Wellesley would endeavour to operate below, and not
above, the city, that while the lower reaches of the Douro were

watched with the greatest care, a very inefficient look-out was
kept on the banks above Oporto: there would seem to have
been but a single battalion placed in that direction, and this
small force was lying far back from the river, with no proper
system of pickets thrown forward to the water's edge.   Yet the
opposite bank was full of cover, of thickets, gardens and olive
groves, screening several lanes and by-paths that had led down
to ferries.   Such of the boats as had not been scuttled had been
brought over to the north bank, but they were not all protected
by proper guards.   All this was inexcusably careless—the main
blame must fall on the Marshal for his *parti pris* in refusing to
look up-stream : though some must also be reserved for General
Quesnel, the governor of Oporto, and for Foy, the brigadier
whose battalions were in charge of the eastern suburb of the
city.   But the fact was that none of the French officers dreamed
of the possibility that Wellesley might make an attempt, on the
very morning of his arrival, to cross the tremendous obstacle
interposed in his way by the rolling stream of the Douro.   That
he would deliver a frontal attack on them in full daylight was
beyond the limits of the probable.   They had no conception of
the enterprise of the man with whom they had to deal.

There was this amount of truth in their view, that the
British General would not have made his daring stroke at
Oporto, unless he had ascertained that the carelessness of his
adversaries had placed an unexpected chance in his hands.   By
ten o'clock in the morning Wellesley had concentrated behind
Villa Nova the whole of his force—the three columns of Paget,
Hill, and Sherbrooke were now up in line.   They were kept out
of sight of the enemy, some in the lateral lanes of the suburb,
but the majority hidden behind the back slope of the hills,
where orchards and vineyards gave them complete cover from
observers on the northern bank.

While the troops were coming up, Sir Arthur mounted the
Serra height, and reconnoitred the whole country-side from the
garden of the convent.   He had with him Portuguese notables
who were well acquainted with Oporto and its suburbs, including several persons who had come over the river on the preceding
day, and could give him some notion of the general disposition and
emplacement of the French army.   Sweeping the valley with his

glasses he could see Franceschi's vedettes moving about on the heights down-stream, and heavy columns of infantry forming up outside the north-eastern gates of the city.   At eleven o'clock this body moved off, escorting a long train of wagons—it was Mermet's division starting for Amarante in charge of Soult's convoy of sick and reserve artillery.   On the quays, below the broken bridge, many French pickets were visible, ensconced at the openings of the streets which lead down to the water.   But turning his glass to the right, Wellesley could note that up-stream matters looked very quiet, the rocky banks above the deep-sunk river were deserted, and nothing was visible among the gardens and scattered houses of the south-eastern suburb. It was possible that French troops might be ensconced there, but no sign of them was to be seen.

Many intelligence-officers had already been sent off, to scour the southern bank of the river, and to ascertain whether by any chance the enemy had overlooked some of the boats belonging to the riverside villages.   In a short time two valuable pieces of news were brought up to the Commander-in-chief.   The large ferry-boat at Barca d'Avintas, four miles above the city, had been scuttled, but not injured beyond the possibility of hasty repairs.   It was already being baled out and mended by the villagers.   Nearer at hand a still more important discovery was made.   Colonel Waters, one of the best scouts in the army, had met, not far south of the suburban village of Cobranloes, an Oporto refugee, a barber by trade, who had crossed over from the north bank in a small skiff, which he had hidden in a thicket.   The man reported that the opposite bank was for the moment unguarded by the French, and pointed to four large wine-barges lying stranded below the brink of the northern shore, with no signs of an enemy in charge.   Yet the position was one which should have been well watched : here a massive building, the bishop's Seminary, surrounded by a high garden wall, lies with its back to the water.   It was an isolated struc-ture, standing well outside the eastern suburb, in fairly open ground, which could be easily swept by artillery fire from the dominating position of the Serra heights.   Waters had with him as guide the prior of Amarante, and by his aid collected three or four peasants from the neighbouring cottages.   After some persuasion from the ecclesiastic, these men and the barber consented to join the British officer in a raid on the stranded barges on the further bank. It was a hazardous undertaking, for one French picket had lately been seen to pass by, and another might appear at any moment. But the necessary half-hour was obtained; Waters and his fellows entered the barber's skiff, crossed the river unseen, got the four barges afloat, and returned with them to the southern bank. They turned out to be big clumsy vessels, capable of holding some thirty men apiece. The explorer had noted that the Seminary buildings above were perfectly empty.

On receiving this intelligence, Wellesley resolved to take the chance which the fates offered him. If the French had shown themselves alert and vigilant, he could not have dared to throw troops across the river into their midst. But they seemed asleep at high noon, and their manifest negligence encouraged him. His mind was soon made up: he ordered Murray with two battalions of his brigade [1], two guns, and two squadrons of the 14th Light Dragoons, to march hard for Barca d'Avintas, cross on the ferry, and seize a position on the opposite bank capable of being defended against superior numbers. But this (as the small force employed sufficiently demonstrates) was only intended as a diversion. The main blow was to be delivered nearer at hand. Wellesley had resolved to endeavour to seize the abandoned Seminary, and to throw his main body across the river at this point if possible. The local conditions made the scheme less rash in fact than it appears on the map. The east end of the Serra hill completely commands all the ground about the Seminary: three batteries [2] were quietly pushed into the convent garden and trained upon the roads leading to that isolated building—one along the shore, the other further inland. If the place could once be seized, it would be possible to protect its garrison by fire across the water. There were only two artillery positions on the French bank, from which the Seminary could be battered: one, close to the water's edge, was completely under the guns of the Serra convent. The other, on the

---

[1] 1st and 2nd Line battalions of the K. G. L., also a detached company of rifles of the K. G. L.

[2] Lane's and Lawson's British guns, and one K. G. L. battery.

heights by the chapel of Bom Fin, was rather distant, and could not be used against boats crossing the river, as they would be invisible to gunners working on this emplacement.   Cannon placed there might do some damage to the Seminary buildings, but could not prevent the garrison from being reinforced.   Realizing all this at a glance, Wellesley hurried down Hill's brigade to the water's edge, and the moment that the leading company of the Buffs had got on board the barges, bade them push off.   In a quarter of an hour the first vessel was over, and a subaltern and twenty-five men rushed up into the empty enclosure of the Seminary, and closed the big iron gate opening into the Vallongo road, which formed its only land-exit.   The men from the other barges were just behind: they set themselves to lining the garden wall and to piling up wood and earth against it, in order to give themselves a standing-place from which they could fire over the coping.   The barges went back with all speed, and were again loaded and sent off.   Meanwhile Wellesley and his staff were looking down in breathless anxiety on the quiet bend of the river, the silent suburb, and the toiling vessels.   At any moment the alarm might be given, and masses of the enemy might debouch from the city and dash in upon the Seminary before enough men were across to hold it.   For the best part of an hour the Commander-in-chief must have been fully aware that his daring move might end only in the annihilation of two or three companies of a good old regiment, and a check that would appear as the righteous retribution for recklessness.

But no stir was seen in Oporto: the barges crossed for a second time unmolested: on their third trip they carried over General Edward Paget, whom Wellesley had placed in command of the whole movement.   More than half the Buffs had passed, and the Seminary was beginning to be adequately manned, when at last some shots were heard outside the gates, and a few minutes later a line of French *tirailleurs*, supported by three battalions in column, came rushing down upon the enclosures. A full hour had passed between the moment when the first boat-load of British soldiers had been thrown across the river, and the time when the French discovered them!

The fact was that the enemy's commander was in bed, and his staff breakfasting!   The Duke of Dalmatia had sat up all night

WELLESLEY'S PASSAGE OF THE DOURO.

N.B. The trees on the cliff to the right are close outside the enclosure of the Serra Convent : the roof of the Seminary is just visible over the crest of the hill on the other bank. In the background are the low slopes above Avintas.

dictating dispatches, and making his arrangements for a leisurely
flitting, for he intended to stay two days longer in Oporto, so
as to cover the march of his other divisions towards Amarante
and Villa Real.   His desk-work finished, he went to bed at
about nine o'clock [1], in full confidence that he was well protected
by the river, and that Wellesley was probably engaged in the
laborious task of bringing up boats to the mouth of the Douro,
which would occupy him for at least twenty-four hours.   The
staff were taking their coffee, after a late *déjeuner*, when the
hoof-beats of a furious rider startled them, and a moment later
Brossard, the aide-de-camp of General Foy, burst into the Villa
shouting that the English had got into the town.   Led to the
Marshal's bedside, he hurriedly explained that Foy had just
discovered the enemy passing by boats into the Seminary, and
was massing his brigade for an attack upon them.   The Marshal
started up, sent his staff flying in all directions to warn the outlying troops, ordered all the remaining *impedimenta* to be sent
off on the Vallongo road, and dispatched Brossard back to Foy
to tell him to 'push the English into the river.'   He was hardly
dressed and on horseback, when the noise of a distant fusillade,
followed by heavy artillery fire, gave the news that the attack
on the Seminary had already begun.

It had been only at half-past ten that Foy, riding along the
heights by the Chapel of Bom Fin, had been informed that
there were boats on the river, filled with red-coated soldiery.
It took him wellnigh three-quarters of an hour to bring up his
nearest regiment, the 17th Léger, and only at 11.30 did the
attack on the Seminary begin.   The three battalions beset the

---

[1] Soult's doings on this day are best told by his aide-de-camp St. Chamans,
who was with him all the morning. No attention need be paid to the
narrative of his panegyrist Le Noble, who tells a foolish story to the effect
that a commandant Salel came at six o'clock (more than four hours
before the Buffs began to pass), and assured some of Soult's staff that
the English were already crossing the river. ' On hearing this,' says
Le Noble, ' the Marshal sent for Quesnel, the governor of Oporto, and
asked if there was any truth in the rumour. The latter denied it and
Soult was reassured. If only Salel had been believed, all the English
who had then passed might have been killed or captured,' and a disaster
avoided. As a matter of fact Quesnel was right, and not a British soldier
had yet crossed [*Campagne de Galice*, p. 247].

northern and western sides of the Seminary, and made a vigorous
attempt to break in, while some guns were hurried down to the
river bank, just below the building, to fire upon the barges
that were bringing up reinforcements.

Wellesley, from his eyrie on the Serra heights, had been
watching for the long-expected outburst of the French. The
moment that they came pressing forward, he gave orders for
the eighteen guns in the convent garden to open upon them.
The first shot fired, a round of shrapnel from the 5½-inch
howitzer of Lane's battery, burst just over the leading French
gun on the further bank, as it was in the act of unlimbering,
dismounted the piece, and by an extraordinary chance, killed or
wounded every man and horse attached to it [1]. A moment later
came the blast of the other seventeen guns, which swept the level
ground to the west of the Seminary with awful effect. The
French attack reeled back, and the survivors fled from the open
ground into the houses of the suburb, leaving the disabled
cannon behind them. Again and again they tried to creep
forward, to flank the English stronghold, and to fire at the
barges as they went and came, but on every occasion they were
swept away by the hail of shrapnel. They could, therefore, only
attack the Seminary on its northern front, where the buildings
lay between them and the Serra height, and so screened them
from the artillery. But in half an hour the 17th Léger was
beaten off and terribly mauled ; they had to cross an open space,
the Prado do Bispo, in order to get near their adversaries, and
the fire from the garden wall, the windows, and the flat roof of
the edifice, swept them away before they could close.

Meanwhile the English suffered little : the only serious loss
sustained was that of General Edward Paget, whose arm was
shattered by a bullet. He was replaced in command by Hill,
who (like him) had crossed in one of the earlier barges. The
number of troops in the building was always growing larger, the
Buffs were all across, and the 66th and 48th were beginning to follow.

After a short slackening in the engagement, General Delaborde
came up, with the three battalions of the 70th of the line, to

[1] This interesting fact I owe to the diary of Captain Lane, still in
manuscript, of which a copy has been sent me by Col. Whinyates, R.A.,
a specialist on the history of the British artillery in the Peninsula.

support his brigadier.   This new force executed a far more sustained and desperate attack on the Seminary than had their
predecessors.   Hill in his letters home called it 'the *serious*
attack.'   But it had no better fortune than the last: a thousand
English infantry, comfortably ensconced behind stone walls, and
protected on their flanks by the storm of shot and shell from the
opposite bank of the river, could not easily be moved.   So well,
indeed, were they covered, that in three hours' fighting they
only lost seventy-seven men [1], while the open ground outside
was thickly strewn with the dead and wounded Frenchmen.

Soult was now growing desperate : he ordered up from the
city Reynaud's brigade, which had hitherto guarded the quays
in the neighbourhood of the broken bridge.   His intention was
to make one more attack on the Seminary, and if that failed to
draw off in the direction of Vallongo and Amarante.   This move
made an end of his chances ; he had forgotten to reckon with
the Portuguese.   The moment that the quays were left unguarded, hundreds of citizens poured out of their houses and ran
down to the water's edge, where they launched all the boats that
had been drawn ashore, and took them over to the English bank.
Richard Stewart's brigade and the Guards who had been waiting
under cover of the houses of Villa Nova, immediately began to
embark, and in a few moments the passage had begun.   The 29th
was first formed up on the northern bank, and dashed up the main
street into the city, meeting little or no opposition ; the 1st
Battalion of Detachments and the Guards' brigade soon followed.
In half an hour they had come upon the flank of the French force
which was attacking the Seminary, and had taken in the rear
and captured one of Soult's reserve batteries, whose horses were
shot down before they could escape along a narrow lane.   As
the British went pouring through Oporto the whole population,
half mad with joy, stood cheering at the windows and on the
roofs, waving their handkerchiefs and shouting *Viva*.   The
rabble poured down into the streets, and began to attack the
French wounded, so that Sherbrooke had to detach a company to
protect them from assassination [2].

[1] Viz. 1/3rd, fifty men, 2/48th, seventeen men, 2/66th, ten men, killed
and wounded.   The French 17th alone lost 177 [Foy's Dispatch].

[2] All this is well described by Leslie of the 29th (p. 113), Stotherd

When Soult found himself thus attacked in the flank, he saw that there was no more to be done, and bade the whole army retreat at full speed along the road to Vallongo and Baltar. They went off in a confused mass, the regiments all mingled together, and the artillery jammed in the midst of the column. Hill came out of the Seminary and joined in the pursuit, which was urged for three miles. 'They made no fight,' writes an eye-witness, 'every man seemed running for his life, throwing away their knapsacks and arms, so that we had only the trouble of making many prisoners every instant, all begging for quarter and surrendering with great good humour [1].'

The French army might have been still further mauled, and indeed almost destroyed, if Wellesley's detached force under Murray had been well handled by its commander. The two battalions of the German Legion, with their attendant squadrons of the 14th Light Dragoons, had crossed the Douro at the ferry of Barca d' Avintas wholly unopposed. It was a slow business, but the detachment was over long ere Soult had abandoned his attack on the Seminary. Advancing cautiously along the river bank, Murray suddenly saw the whole French army come pouring past him in total disorder on the line of the Vallongo road. He might have made an attempt to throw himself across their path, or at least have fallen upon their flank and endeavoured to cut the column in two; but thinking them far too strong for his small force, and forgetting their demoralization, he halted and allowed them to go by. When all had passed, General Charles Stewart, who had been sent in search of Murray by the Commander-in-chief, came galloping up to the force, and took from it a squadron of the 14th [2], with which he made a dash at the enemy's last troops. The French had now formed a sort of rear-guard, but the dragoons rode into it without hesitation. The French generals were bringing up the rear, and trying to keep their men steady. Delaborde was unhorsed and for a moment

of the Scots Fusilier Guards (p. 41), and Cooper of the 2/7th, who crossed later.

[1] Leslie, ibid.

[2] So Hawker of that regiment, who took part in the charge, and describes it well. In Wellesley's dispatch, *two* squadrons are wrongly named.

was a prisoner, but escaped owing to his captor being killed. Foy received a sabre cut on the shoulder. The infantry broke, and nearly 300 of them were cut off and captured. But the dragoons also suffered heavily; of about 110 men who took part in the charge no less than thirty-five men were killed and wounded. Murray, who watched the whole skirmish from his position on a neighbouring hillside, gave no assistance to his cavalry, though the intervention of his two battalions would have led to the capture of the whole of Soult's rearguard. It was to infantry of Sherbrooke's division that the dragoons turned over their prisoners before rejoining their other squadron [1].

So ended the battle of Oporto, daring in its conception, splendidly successful in its execution, yet not so decisive as it might have been, had Murray but done his duty during the pursuit. The British loss was astoundingly small—only twenty-three killed, ninety-eight wounded, and two missing : among the dead there was not a single officer : the wounded included a general (Paget) and three majors. The casualties of the French were, as was natural, much greater : the attacks on the Seminary had cost them dear. They lost about 300 killed and wounded and nearly as many prisoners in the field, while more

[1] The best account of this charge is the diary of Hawker ; it runs as follows : ' After going at full speed, enveloped in a cloud of dust for nearly two miles, we cleared our infantry, and that of the French appeared. A strong body was drawn up in close column, with bayonets ready to receive us on their front. On each side of the road was a stone wall, bordered outwardly with trees. On our left, in particular, numbers of the French were posted with their pieces resting on the wall, which flanked the road, ready to give us a running fire as we passed. This could not but be effectual, as our men (in threes) were close to the muzzles of their muskets, and barely out of the reach of a *coup de sabre*. In a few seconds the ground was covered with our men and horses. Notwithstanding this we penetrated the battalion in the road, the men of which, relying on their bayonets, did not give way till we were close upon them, when they fled in confusion. For some time the contest was kept up hand to hand. After many efforts we succeeded in cutting off 300, of whom most were secured as prisoners. But our loss was very considerable. Of fifty-two men in the leading troop ten were killed, and eleven severely wounded (besides others slightly), and six taken prisoners.' (Of the last all save one succeeded in slipping off and got back.) Out of four officers engaged three were wounded : Hervey, the major in command, lost an arm. Foy called the attack ' une charge incroyable.'

than 1,500 sick and wounded were captured in the hospitals of
Oporto [1]. The trophies consisted of the six field-pieces taken
during the fighting, a great number of baggage wagons, and
fifty-two Portuguese guns, dismounted but fit for further service,
which were found in the arsenal. Soult had destroyed, before
retreating, the rest of the cannon which he had captured in the
Portuguese lines on March 29.

[1] Fantin des Odoards (p. 233) says that the French left 1,800 men
in the hospitals. This is probably a little too high an estimate : there
were only 2,150 French sick in Braga, Viana, and Oporto on May 10 —
five-sixths of them at Oporto. But many convalescents had marched with
Mermet early on the eleventh. Wellington in his first dispatch merely
says that he had taken 700 sick in the hospitals. But three days later, in
a letter to Admiral Berkeley, he writes that he has 2,000 sick, wounded
and captured French in his hands, and must send them to England at
once (*Wellington Dispatches*, iv. 337). He therefore asks for shipping for
them at the rate of two tons per man. Allowing for 300 unwounded
prisoners at Oporto, and 100 at Grijon, there remain 1,500, or somewhat
more, for the men in hospital.

SECTION XIV: CHAPTER III

SOULT'S RETREAT FROM OPORTO

THE headlong charge of Hervey's squadron of the 14th Light Dragoons was the last molestation which fell to the lot of Soult's retreating column on the afternoon of May 12. Marching till dark, the disordered infantry encamped at Baltar, ten miles from Oporto, where they fell in with the detached regiment of Delaborde's division and with Caulaincourt's dragoons, who had been guarding this half-way stage between Amarante and Oporto, ever since Loison had marched on into the Tras-os-Montes ten days before. Of the rest of the French army, Franceschi (always in the post of danger) covered the rear at Vallongo, just west of Baltar. Mermet, with the division that had marched from Oporto before Wellesley's attack was developed, had encamped on the Souza river, four miles ahead of the main column. The Marshal had thus nearly 13,000 men concentrated, and proposed next day to push on for Amarante, in the wake of Loison, who (as he supposed) must now be well ahead in the Tras-os-Montes, clearing for him the way into Spain. It was disquieting, however, to find that no news from that general had yet come to hand—indeed he had not been heard of since May 7, when he was just starting out on his expedition. Wherever Loison might be, the Marshal was bound to follow him in haste, since it was certain that Wellesley would be close at his heels, and that no time was to be lost in lingering.

At half-past one in the morning Soult was roused from sleep, and informed that the long-expected messenger from Loison had at last arrived. The news which he brought was nothing less than appalling: the French detached corps had been not only checked but beaten, the bridge of Amarante had been lost,

---

[1] See Le Noble, *Campagne de Galice*, pp. 250-2.

and Loison was hastily retreating to the north-west at the moment that his chief was moving eastward to join him.

Beresford's turning movement, in fact, had been completely successful—far more so than Wellesley had thought likely; he had not only succeeded in placing himself across the French line of retreat into Spain, but had beaten Loison and thrown him back into Soult's arms.

What had happened was shortly this. On May 8 Beresford had picked up Wilson's detachment at Vizeu: on the tenth he had met Silveira at Lamego. He had thus concentrated some 10,500 or 11,000 men, all Portuguese save Tilson's brigade and the single squadron of the 14th Light Dragoons. Learning at Lamego that, as late as the ninth, Loison was still in the neighbourhood of Amarante, and had not yet penetrated far into the Tras-os-Montes, Beresford resolved to take the risk of passing the Douro and to throw his army directly across the path of the advancing French. On the tenth, the same day on which the force from Coimbra reached Lamego, he sent Silveira over the river by the bridge of Peso da Regoa, which had never passed out of the hands of the Portuguese and had a strong *tête de pont* on its northern side. Silveira had barely crossed when Loison, who had spent the previous day at Mezamfrio, ten miles away on the Amarante road, came up against him with Heudelet's and Sarrut's infantry and Marisy's dragoons—about 6,500 sabres and bayonets. Emboldened by having entrenchments to help him, and by knowing that Beresford was close behind, Silveira stood firm at the *tête du pont* and accepted battle.

Loison was somewhat discouraged by his adversary's confidence, and did not fail to note the masses of troops on the southern bank of the Douro, which were moving up to the bridge to support Silveira. However, late in the afternoon he attacked the Portuguese, but was steadily met and beaten off with some loss[1]. Thereupon he drew back and retired to Mezamfrio. On the following day (May 11) he continued his

---

[1] Loison reported to Soult that he lost only a *chef de bataillon* and eighty men, but that the horses of himself and Generals Heudelet and Maransin were killed under them. The figures given are probably an understatement.

retreat to Amarante, closely pursued by Silveira, who kept driving in his rearguard wherever it attempted to make a stand.

Beresford meanwhile brought his own troops across the Douro on May 11, in the wake of Silveira's division. On the twelfth he pushed forward to Amarante, intending to fight Loison if the latter should try to hold his ground beyond the bridge. But on his approach he found that the French rearguard (Sarrut's brigade) had already been driven across the water by the Portuguese [1]. The bridge, however, still remained in Loison's hands, and as it was no less defensible from the eastern than from the western bank, the army could get no further forward.

Matters were now at a deadlock, for if Beresford could not cross the Tamega, it was clear that Loison, even if heavily reinforced from Oporto, would not be able to force the imposing position on the heights commanding the bridge, which was now held by 11,000 men, including a British brigade. But he might, and should, have continued to hold the town and the bridge-head, till further orders reached him from Soult. Instead of doing so, he made up his mind to retreat at once, and marched off early on the evening of May 12 along the road to Guimaraens and Braga. Thus at the moment when Soult was retiring on Amarante, Loison abandoned the position which covered his chief's chosen line of retreat. Moreover, he was so tardy in sending news of his intentions to head quarters, that the aide-de-camp who bore his dispatch only reached Baltar after midnight on the twelfth–thirteenth: this was the first report that Soult had received from him since May 8. It was a military crime of the highest magnitude that he had neither informed his chief of the check at Peso da Regoa on the tenth, nor of his retreat to Amarante on the eleventh. Knowledge of these facts would have been invaluable to the Marshal, since it would have shown him that the route through the Tras-os-Montes was

---

[1] The British brigade of Tilson was to have led the attack. They were burning for a fight. 'I never witnessed so much enthusiasm,' writes an eye-witness, 'as was shown by the men. The advance was a perfect trot, but on our arrival we found the enemy had fled.' (From an unpublished letter of Lord Gough, then colonel of the 87th regiment, which has been placed at my disposal by the kindness of Mr. R. Rait of New College, who is preparing a life of that officer.)

blocked, and that he must not count upon an undisturbed retreat into Spain. If he had known of this, he would not have evacuated Oporto by the Baltar road, but would have been forced to march northward on Braga or Guimaraens, instead of due east. So strange, in fact, was Loison's slackness, that Soult's advocates have not hesitated to accuse him of deliberate treachery, and have hinted that he was engaged in Argenton's plot—a hypothesis which would have explained his conduct clearly enough. But, as a matter of fact, Argenton's revelations to Wellesley show that this was not the case, and that the conspirators looked upon Loison and Delaborde as the two officers who were most likely to give them trouble. It must therefore have been sheer military incapacity, and disgust at the whole Portuguese expedition, which lay at the bottom of Loison's misbehaviour. Disbelieving in Soult's plan of campaign, he was probably bent on compelling his chief to retire to Braga, and was (of course) quite ignorant of the fact that Wellesley's capture of Oporto had changed the whole face of affairs, and that the retreat in that direction was no longer open.

Despondent, tired out by the work of the preceding day, and suffering physically from a heavy fall from his horse during the retreat, Soult was roused from his slumbers to read Loison's disastrous dispatch. When he had made out its full meaning he was appalled. All his plans were shattered, and he was clearly in imminent danger, for Wellesley from Oporto and Beresford from Amarante might converge upon him in the morning, with nearly 30,000 men, if it should chance that they had made out his position. No help could come from Loison, who, having now reached Guimaraens, was separated from the main body by the roadless expanse of the rugged Serra de Santa Catalina. Eastward lay one hostile force, westward another, to the south was the impassable Douro, to the north the inhospitable mountains. It was useless to think of making a desperate dash at Beresford's army : in open ground an attack on the Portuguese might have been practicable, but the bridge of Amarante was a post impossible to force in a hurry, and while the attack on it was in progress, it was certain that Wellesley would come up from the rear. The situation and the results of Baylen would inevitably be reproduced.

Realizing this, the Duke of Dalmatia came to the conclusion that the only course open to him was to abandon everything that could not be carried on his men's backs, and to make a desperate attempt to cross the Serra de Santa Catalina before the news of his straits had reached the enemy. He imagined that there must be some sort of a footpath from Baltar or Penafiel to Guimaraens: in a thickly peopled country like Northern Portugal, the hill-folk have short cuts of their own— the only difficulty for the stranger is to discover them. Hasty inquiries in the bivouac of the army produced a Navarese camp-follower, who said that he knew the localities and could point out a bad mule-track, which climbed the hillside above the Souza torrent, and came down into the valley of the Avé, not far south of Guimaraens[1]. It was the kind of path in which the army would meet every sort of difficulty, and where the head of the column might be stopped by a couple of hundred *Ordenanza*, if it should chance that the Portuguese peasantry were on the alert. But it seemed the only practicable way out of the situation, and the Marshal resolved to try it.

At daybreak the army was warned of its danger ; and wasting no time on councils of war or elaborate orders, Soult sent round word that the troops were to abandon everything that could not be carried on the backs of men or horses, and to take to the hills. An immense mass of baggage and plunder had to be left on the banks of the Souza, including the whole of the heavy convoy which Mermet had escorted out of Oporto on the previous day. The Marshal even decided that the infantry should turn out of their knapsacks everything except food and cartridges, an order which those who had in their possession gold plate and other valuable plunder of small bulk took care to disobey. The cannon were destroyed by being placed mouth to mouth and discharged simultaneously in pairs. As much of the reserve ammunition for infantry as could be packed in convenient bundles was laden on the backs of the artillery horses. The rest, with all the powder wagons, was collected in

---

[1] 'Un de ces Navarrins, qui vont tous les ans en Portugal parcourir les villages pour y couper les cochons qu'on veut engraisser,' says Le Noble [p. 254]. 'Une espèce de contrebandier que le général Dulauloi avait trouvé,' says St. Chamans, Soult's aide-de-camp (p. 147).

a mass, ready to be fired when the army should have absconded. One curious circumstance, which displays better than anything else the hurry of the retreat, is worth mentioning. The military chest of the 2nd Corps was well filled—it is said to have contained nearly £50,000 in Portuguese silver. The Marshal ordered the paymaster-in-chief to serve out all that he could to the regimental paymasters. Only two of these officials could be found, and they were unable to carry off more than a fraction of the money. Soult then ordered the treasure-chests to be broken open, and sent word that the men, as they passed, might help themselves. But hardly a soldier took advantage of the offer: they looked at the bulky bags of *cruzados novos*, shook their heads, and hurried on. Those who were tempted at first were seen, later in the day, tossing the weighty pieces into the ravine of the Souza. Perceiving that there was no way of getting rid of the mass of silver, Soult at last ordered the *fourgons* containing it to be dragged alongside of the powder wagons. When the train was exploded, after the rearguard had passed, the money was scattered to the winds. For years after the peasants of Penafiel were picking up stray coins on the hillside [1].

As the French army was beginning its weary climb over the Serra de Santa Catalina a heavy drenching rain commenced to fall. It lasted for three days, and added much to the miseries

---

[1] Several of the French diarists relate this curious incident. ' L'argent blanc ne tentait personne,' says Fantin des Odoards, p. 234, ' à cause de sa pesanteur et de son inutilité momentaire. On permit le pillage des fourgons du payeur, et chose inouïe, il n'y fut presque pas touché. Les soldats regardaient en passant les sacs, secouaient la tête et s'éloignaient sans y mettre la main. Pour moi, je m'emparai d'un sac de 2,400 francs ; cette lourde somme m'embarassait : elle aurait blessé mon cheval, et après l'avoir portée pendant une lieue je l'abandonnai' [p. 234]. ' Les grenadiers du 70e servaient d'escorte au trésor,' says Le Noble, ' l'in- tendant-général les invita de prendre des fonds. Ayant rencontré leur officier, le lieutenant Langlois, à Toro, il lui demanda ce qu'avaient pu emporter ses soldats. " *Rien*," répliqua-t-il, " ils portaient la caisse à tour de rôle pour quelque distance, et la jetèrent ensuite." ' Naylies also mentions the dispersion of the treasure. The reader will compare this incident with the rolling of Moore's treasure down the cliffs of Herrerias during the Corunna retreat. Soult certainly scattered his cash more widely.

of the retreat; but it was not without its advantages to the
fugitive host, for it kept the Portuguese peasantry indoors,
and it would seem that no one in the mountain villages got
wind of the movement for many hours. It was not till the
French had crossed the ridge and descended, late in the dusk, on to
the village of Pombeiro in the valley of the Avé that they began
to be molested by the *Ordenanza*. After a few shots had been
fired the peasants were driven off. Next morning [May 14]
Soult got into communication with Loison, who was still lying
at Guimaraens with all his troops. On the same day Lorges'
dragoons and the garrison of Viana came in from the north, and
the whole army, still over 20,000 strong, was reconcentrated.
The first danger, that of destruction piecemeal, had been
avoided. But Soult's desperate move had only warded off the
peril for the moment: he had still to fear that Wellesley and
Beresford might close in upon him before he could get clear
of the mountains.

It remains to be seen how the two British generals had
employed the day during which the French were scaling the
heights of the Serra de Santa Catalina. Wellesley had crossed
in person to Oporto long ere the fighting was over, and had
established his head quarters in Soult's villa on the heights,
where he and his staff thought themselves fortunate in finding
ready for their consumption the excellent dinner which had
been prepared for the Marshal. As long as daylight lasted
the British infantry continued to be ferried over to the city,
but they were not all across when night fell. The artillery, the
train, and all the regimental baggage were still on the wrong
side of the river, and as the great bridge was destroyed beyond
hope of repair, all the *impedimenta* had to be brought over in
boats and barges. It was mainly this fact that delayed
Wellesley from making an early move on the thirteenth. He
could not advance without his guns and his reserve ammunition,
and did not receive them till the day was far spent and the
natural hour for marching was past. There were other circumstances which hindered him from pressing on as he would have
liked to do. The infantry were tired out: they had marched
more than eighty miles during the last four days, and had
fought hard at Grijon and Oporto. Human nature could do no

more without a halt, and Wellesley was forced to grant it.
Moreover, there was the question of food to be taken into
consideration. The troops had outrun their supplies, and the
provision wagons were still trailing up from Coimbra. In Oporto
no stores of any importance were discovered, for Soult had
stopped collecting more than he could carry, the moment that
he made up his mind to retreat, and had been living from hand
to mouth during the last few days of his sojourn in the city.
The only thing that abounded was port wine, and from that the
soldiers had to be kept away, or results disastrous to discipline
would have followed [1].

With great reluctance, therefore, Wellesley resolved to halt
for a day, only sending forward Murray and the German Legion,
with a couple of squadrons, along the Baltar road. This brigade
did not come up with Soult's rearguard, though they found
ample traces of his passage in the shape of murdered stragglers
and abandoned plunder. No doubt the Commander-in-chief
would have directed them to push on further, and have supported them with every battalion that could still march ten miles,
if only he had been aware of the fact that Beresford had got
possession of the bridge of Amarante, and that the enemy was
therefore in a trap. But he was only in communication with
his lieutenant by the circuitous route of Lamego and Mezamfrio,
and the last news that he had received of the turning column
led him to believe that it was still in the neighbourhood of
Villa Real, and that Loison continued to hold the passage
of the Tamega. Writing to Beresford on the night of the
capture of Oporto, he desired him to make every effort to hold
on to Villa Real, and to keep Soult in check till he himself
could overtake him [2].

It was not till the afternoon of the thirteenth that Wellesley
obtained information that put him on the right track. The
intelligence officer with Murray's column [3] sent him back word

[1] When the troops got at the wine they drank only too well: Hartmann
in his *Journal* records that twenty of his German Legion gunners drank
forty-one bottles of port at a sitting (p. 71).

[2] *Wellington Dispatches*, iv. 327. To Marshal Beresford, from Oporto,
night of the twelfth.

[3] A Captain Mellish, *Wellington Dispatches*, iv. 330 [to Murray] and 332
[to Beresford].

that heavy explosions had been heard at Penafiel, and that the smoke of large fires was visible along the hillside above it. This gave a strong hint of what was probably taking place in that direction, but it was not till five in the afternoon that full information came to hand. This was brought by the Portuguese secretary of General Quesnel, who had deserted his employer and ridden back to Oporto, to give the valuable news which would save him from being tried for treason for serving the enemy. He gave an accurate and detailed account of all that had happened to Soult's column, and had seen it start off on the break-neck path to Guimaraens. Only about Loison was he uncertain—that officer, he said, was probably still at Amarante, holding back Silveira and Beresford [1].

On receipt of this important intelligence Wellesley sent orders to Murray to press on his small force of cavalry, and some mounted rifles (if he could secure horses or mules) as far as Penafiel, to verify the secretary's information [2]. A later dispatch bade him press on to Amarante, if Loison was still there, in order to take that officer in the rear; but if he were gone, the Legionary brigade was to follow Soult over the hills towards Guimaraens and Braga, and endeavour to catch up his rearguard [3]. The orders arrived too late: Murray, on the morning of the fourteenth, learnt that Loison had long ago departed, and that Soult was far on his way. He followed the Marshal across the Serra de Santa Catalina, but never got near him, though he picked up many French stragglers, and saw the bodies of many more, who had been assassinated by the peasantry [4].

Meanwhile Beresford had acted with great decision, and with an intelligence which he did not always display. When, on the morning of the thirteenth, he found that the French had disappeared, and that Amarante (after having been thoroughly sacked) [5] had been abandoned to him, he did not waste time in

---

[1] Deposition of the Secretary to the late Governor of Oporto. *Wellington Supplementary Dispatches*, vi. 262 [May 13, afternoon].

[2] *Wellington Dispatches*, iv. 330, afternoon of May 13.

[3] Ibid. iv. 332, morning of May 14.

[4] It is astonishing to find that Murray succeeded in taking two light three-pounder guns over this difficult path. The fact reflects great credit on his gunners.

[5] The state of Amarante was dreadful. ' I was never witness to such

a fruitless pursuit of Loison in the direction of Guimaraens, but resolved to endeavour to cut off the retreat of the whole French army towards the north. If they had absconded by way of Braga, the chase would fall to Wellesley's share, but if they had taken the other road by Chaves, all would depend on his own movements. Accordingly he resolved to march at once on the last named town, without waiting for orders from the Commander-in-chief. Having hastily collected three days' provisions, he moved off himself by the high-road up the valley of the Tamega, detaching Silveira and his division to strike across country, and occupy the defiles of Ruivaens and Salamonde on the Braga-Chaves road, where it would be possible to detain, if not to stop, the retreating columns of Soult if they should take this way [May 14]. While on his march Beresford received Wellesley's letters, which prescribed to him exactly the line of conduct that he had already determined to pursue[1]. After three difficult marches in drenching rain, which turned every rivulet into an almost impassable torrent, and spoilt the inadequate provision of bread which had been served out to the men, the division reached Chaves about 12 p.m. on the night of the sixteenth–seventeenth. The men were absolutely exhausted; though the distance covered had not exceeded some fourteen or fifteen miles per day, yet the rain, the starvation, and the bad road had much thinned the ranks, and those who had kept up with the colours were dropping with fatigue. The slowness of the column's advance was certainly not Beresford's fault; he had allowed only a six hours' halt each day on the fourteenth, fifteenth, and sixteenth, and had been pushing on as hard as was, humanly speaking, possible. Nevertheless he was too late: on the seventeenth, the all-important day of the campaign, he held Chaves, but his

---

a scene of misery and horror as here presented itself,' says Lord Gough in an unpublished letter to his father. 'Every house and public building of every description, with the exception of a monastery which covered the passage of the bridge, a chapel, and about five detached houses, was burnt to the ground, with many of the late inhabitants lying dead in the streets.'

[1] The best testimony to Beresford's good conduct is that Wellesley (*Wellington Dispatches*, iv. 343) says that he had exactly anticipated the instructions sent him, and carried them out on his own initiative. Napier's criticism (ii. 116–7) is unfair and misleading.

troops were too tired to start early or to march far. The bad
weather which made the French retreat so miserable, had at
least saved the flying army from its pursuers [1].

Soult meanwhile had gathered in Loison and Lorges, and his
whole army was concentrated at Guimaraens on the morning
of the fourteenth. From the point where he now lay, in the
upper valley of the Avé, there are only two carriage roads, that
to Amarante by which Loison had arrived, and that to Braga.
There was a bare chance that if Wellesley had received his
information late, and moved slowly, it might be possible to
escape from him by the road to Braga. If, however, he had
marched promptly from Oporto, he would be able to intercept
the retreating army at that place. Soult refused to take this
risk, and resolved instead to plunge once more into the mountains, and to cross the watershed between the Avé and the
Cavado by a rugged hill-path, no better than that which had
served him between Penafiel and Guimaraens. It was accordingly necessary to sacrifice all the guns, munitions, and baggage
belonging to Loison and Lorges, just as those of Mermet and
Delaborde had been destroyed on the banks of the Souza. The
guns were burst, the ammunition exploded, the baggage piled

---

[1] The best account of Beresford's forced march is to be found in the
unpublished letter of Lord Gough (then major of the 87th) which, as I have
already mentioned, has been shown me by Mr. R. Rait of New College.
He says : ' The business of crossing the river took the Brigade (Tilson's)
four hours : the evening set in with a most dreadful fall of rain, which
continued all night, and the next three days and nights. Our road lay
over almost impassable mountains, made more so by the rain that swelled
the mountain rivulets into rivers. In the dark many men lost the column,
several fell into pits excavated by the falling water : many lay down in
the road from fatigue and hunger, and the greater part lost their shoes.
. . . Next day we pursued our melancholy march at five o'clock, the men
nearly fainting with hunger : about twelve we fell in with some cars of
bread belonging to a Portuguese division, which Gen. Tilson pressed for
the men ; this (with some wine) enabled us to proceed, and that night
at twelve we reached Chaves, after a forced march of three days, with
only twelve hours' halt. The men were without a shoe to their feet, and
hundreds fallen out from fatigue and hunger. . . . The 88th had, of
700 with which they joined us, only 150 in the ranks. . . . Part of the
officers and nearly all the men had their feet cut to the bone for want of
shoes.'

in heaps and burned. After this second holocaust the army struck up a track by the Salto torrent, which ultimately brought them over the crest, and down upon the village of Lanhozo, eight miles from Braga, and just at the foot of the position which Eben had occupied during his unhappy battle on March 20. The weather had been abominable, and the rearguard had been forced to bivouac in misery on the hills, the darkness having come down upon them before the descent into the valley of the Cavado was completed.

Next morning Soult sent out Lahoussaye's dragoons down the valley of the Cavado towards Braga, to see if that city was already in Wellesley's hands or whether it was still possible to escape across his front and gain the high road to Galicia. As the Marshal had feared would be the case, they met British light cavalry pushing briskly up the road towards them ; it was clear that the pursuers were already in Braga, and Soult at once ordered his columns to turn their faces to the north-east, and follow the road up the Cavado towards Salamonde and Ruivaens. The British were ere long visible in close pursuit.

Sir Arthur had quitted Oporto on the fourteenth with his whole force except the brigade of Murray, which had already gone forth on the eastern line of pursuit, and the 20th Light Dragoons, which he had been ordered to send back to Lisbon. On that day his army covered twenty-two miles of road in vile weather, and slept at Villa Nova de Famelicção. On the fifteenth the British started early, and their vanguard had already marched twelve miles and reached Braga when the French dragoons were descried. The latter, seeing themselves fore-stalled, retired on their main body, and when Wellesley's men mounted the crest of the Monte Adaufé (Eben's old position in the battle of March 20), they caught a glimpse of the whole French army retiring up the valley. Soult, immediately on hearing that the pursuers were in Braga, had commenced a new retreat. He had rearranged his order of march. Loison now led the column, with Heudelet's division and Lorges' dragoons: then came the droves of artillery horses and pack-mules, with the reserve ammunition and the little baggage that had been saved, followed by Delaborde and Mermet. Merle's infantry and Franceschi's horse were in the rear, under the Marshal's

own command. In this order the French remounted the stream
of the Cavado as far as Salamonde, where the broad valley
narrows down to a defile. They were followed by the British
light dragoons, but the infantry of the pursuing column had
not got far beyond Braga, where Wellesley's head quarters were
established that night. Murray's German brigade, which had
crossed the mountains from Guimaraens in Soult's wake, joined
the main body on this evening.

On reaching Salamonde Soult was informed by the cavalry in
his front that they had been brought to stand at the bridge of
Ponte Nova, a few miles up the defile, by a body of *Ordenanza*,
who had taken up the wooden flooring of the bridge, torn down
its balustrades, and barricaded themselves upon the further side.
Unless they could be dislodged ruin stared the Marshal in the
face : for the British were close in his rear, and there was no
lateral line of escape from the precipitous defile. Surrender
next morning must follow. In this crisis Soult saw no chance
of safety before him save a dash at the half-demolished bridge.
When darkness had fallen he sent for Major Dulong, an officer
of the 31st Léger, who enjoyed the reputation of being the most
daring man in the whole army, and told him that he must
surprise the Portuguese by a sudden rush at midnight, and win
the passage at all costs. He was allowed to pick 100 volunteers
from his own regiment for the enterprise.

The safety of a whole army has seldom depended upon a
more desperate venture than that which Dulong took in hand.
Nothing remained of the bridge save the two large cross-beams,
no more than three or four feet broad ; they were slippery with
continuous rain, and had to be passed in complete darkness
under the driving sleet of a bitter north wind. Fortunately for
the assailants the same cold and wet which made their enterprise
so dangerous had driven the *Ordenanza* under cover : they had
retired to some huts a little way beyond the bridge. If they
left any one on guard, the sentinel had followed his friends, for
when Dulong and his party crept up to the passage they found
it absolutely deserted. They crossed in single file, and reached
the further side unobserved, losing one man who slipped and fell
into the fierce river below. A moment later they came on
the Portuguese, who were surprised in their sleep : many were

bayonetted, the rest fled in dismay—they were but a few score of peasants, and were helpless when once the passage had been won.

For six hours Soult's sappers were working hard to replace the flooring of the ruined bridge with tree trunks, and boards torn from the houses of the neighbouring village. At eight it was practicable, and the troops began to cross. It was a long business : for 20,000 men with 4,000 cavalry horses and a great drove of pack-animals had to be passed over the narrow, rickety, and uneven structure, whose balustrades had not been replaced. All the day was spent in hurrying the troops across, but they got forward so slowly that Soult saw himself forced to place a strong rearguard in position, to hold back the pursuers till the main body was safe. He left behind a brigade of Merle's division, and two of Franceschi's cavalry regiments, ranged behind a lateral ravine which crosses the road some distance below the bridge. They were placed with their right on the rough river bank and their left on the cliffs which overhang the road; orders were given to the effect that they must hold on at all costs till the army had completed the passage of the Ponte Nova. At half-past one the British light dragoons arrived in front of the position, saw that they could not force it, and started a bickering fire with the French pickets, while they waited for the main body to come up.

Owing to the long distance which Wellesley's infantry had to cover, the day wore on without any serious collision on this point. But meanwhile Soult found that another and more serious danger lay ahead of him. After crossing the Cavado at the Ponte Nova there were two paths available for the army— the main road leads eastward to Chaves by way of Ruivaens, a branch, however, turns off north to Montalegre and the sources of the Misarella, the main affluent of the Cavado. The former was the easier, but there was a grave doubt whether Chaves might not already be in the hands of Beresford and his turning column—as a matter of fact it only arrived there a few hours after Soult stood uncertain at the parting of the ways. Bearing this in mind, the Marshal resolved to take the more rugged and difficult path; but when Loison and the vanguard were engaged in it they found that the bridge over the Misarella, the

Saltador as it was called from the bold leap which its single arch makes across the torrent, was held against them. Again it was only with *Ordenanza* that the army had to deal: Beresford had just reached Chaves, but his troops were some miles further back; Silveira, who ought to have been at Ruivaens that morning, had not appeared at all. But Major Warre, an officer of Beresford's staff, had ridden ahead to rouse the peasantry, and had collected several hundred half-armed levies at the *Saltador* bridge, which he encouraged them to hold, promising that the regulars would be up to support them before nightfall. Unfortunately he could not persuade them to destroy the bridge, on which all the cross-communications of the Misarella valley depend. But they had thrown down its parapets, built an *abattis* across its head, and thrown up earthworks on each side of it so as to command the opposite bank. This, unhappily, was not enough to hold back 20,000 desperate men, who saw their only way of salvation on the opposite bank.

When Loison found his advance barred, he made an appeal to that same Major Dulong who had forced the Ponte Nova on the preceding night. Again that daring soldier volunteered to conduct the forlorn hope: he was given a company of *voltigeurs* to lead the column, and two battalions of Heudelet's division to back them. Forming the whole in one continuous mass—there was only room for four men abreast—he dashed down towards the bridge amid a spluttering and ineffective fire from the Portuguese entrenchments on the opposite bank. The column reached the arch, passed it, was checked but a moment while tearing down the *abattis*, and then plunged in among the scared *Ordenanza*, who fled in every direction, leaving the passage free. Dulong was wounded, but no more than eighteen of his companions were hit, and at this small sacrifice the army was saved. Late in the afternoon the whole mass began to stream up the Montalegre road; they had no longer anything more to fear than stray shots from the scattered *Ordenanza*, who hung about on the hillsides, firing into the column from inaccessible rocks, but doing little damage.

If Dulong had failed at the Saltador Soult would have been lost, for just as the passage was forced the rumbling of cannon began to be heard from the rear. Merle was attacked by the

British, and was being driven in. At five o'clock the Guards' brigade, forming the head of Wellesley's infantry, had come up with the French rearguard. It was formidably posted, but Sir Arthur thought that it might be dislodged. Accordingly he placed the two three-pounders, which accompanied the column, on the high road, and began to batter the French centre, while he sent off the three light companies of the brigade [1] to turn the French left flank on the cliffs to the south. When the crackling of their musketry was heard among the rocks, he silenced his guns and flung the Guards upon the enemy's main body: They broke, turned, and fled in confusion, though the regiment on the road, the 4th Léger, was considered one of the best in the French army [2].

The chase continued as far as the Ponte Nova, which the broken troops crossed in a struggling mass, thrusting each other over the edge (where the balustrades were wanting) till the torrent below was choked with dead men and horses. The British guns were brought up and played upon the weltering crowd with dreadful effect. But the night was already coming on, and the darkness hid from the pursuers the full effect of their own fire. They halted and encamped, having slain many and taken about fifty prisoners, of whom one was an officer. It was only at daybreak that they realized the terrors through which the French had passed. 'The rocky bed of the Cavado,' says an eye-witness, 'presented an extraordinary spectacle. Men and horses, sumpter animals and baggage, had

---

[1] The brigade had a company of the 5/60th attached, so had three instead of two light companies.

[2] 'Il y avait à l'arrière-garde un excellent régiment d'infanterie légère, qui (vu la nature du terrain) pouvait facilement braver une armée entière : et bien, à l'apparition de l'ennemi, il s'est débandé sans qu'on ait pu lui faire entendre raison. La confusion qui a été le résultat de cette terreur panique a été épouvantable. Fantassins et cavaliers se précipitaient les uns sur les autres, jetaient leurs armes, et luttaient à qui courrait le plus vite. Le pont étroit et sans parapet ne pouvait suffire à l'impatience des fuyards, ils se pressaient tellement que nombre d'hommes furent précipités et noyés dans le torrent ou écrasés sous les pieds des chevaux. Si les Anglais avaient été en mesure de profiter de cette épouvante, je ne sais pas en vérité ce que nous serions devenus, tant la peur est contagieuse, même chez les plus braves soldats.' Fantin des Odoards, p. 236.

been precipitated into the river, and literally choked its course. Here, with these fatal accompaniments of death and dismay, was disgorged the last of the plunder of Oporto. All kinds of valuable goods were left on the road, while above 300 horses, sunk in the water, and mules laden with baggage, fell into the hands of the grenadier and light companies of the Guards. These active-fingered gentry found that fishing for boxes and bodies out of the stream produced pieces of plate, and purses and belts full of gold money. Amid the scenes of death and desolation arose their shouts of the most noisy merriment [1].'

On the night of the 17th Soult's army poured into Montalegre, a dilapidated old town on the edge of the frontier, from which all the inhabitants had fled. Little or no food could be procured, and the houses did not suffice to shelter more than a part of the troops. Next morning the 2nd Corps took to its heels once more, and climbed the Serra de Gerez, which lies just above the town. On descending its northern slope they had at last entered Spain, and had reached safety. But the country was absolutely desolate : for twenty miles beyond Montalegre there was hardly a single village on this rugged by-path. Still dreading pursuit, the Marshal urged on his men as fast as they could be driven forward, and in two long marches at last reached Orense.

Wellesley, however, had given up any hope of catching the 2nd Corps, when once it had passed the Saltador and reached the Spanish frontier. He had halted the British infantry at Ruivaens, and only sent on in chase of the flying host the 14th Light Dragoons and the division of Silveira, which had at last appeared on the scene late in the evening of the seventeenth. What this corps had been doing during the last forty-eight hours it is impossible to discover. It had started from Amarante on the same day that Beresford marched for Chaves, and ought to have been at Ruivaens on the sixteenth, when it would have found itself just in time to intercept Soult's vanguard after it had passed the Ponte Nova. Apparently the same wild weather and constant rain which had delayed Beresford's column had checked his subordinate. At any rate it is certain that Silveira, though he had a shorter route than his chief, only got to Ruivaens late

[1] Lord Munster's *Campaign of 1809*, pp. 177–8.

on the seventeenth, while the other column had reached Chaves
more than twelve hours earlier.

The French had disappeared, and it was only next morning
that Silveira followed them up on the Montalegre road.   He
captured a few laggards by the way, but on reaching the little
town found that Soult's rearguard had quitted it two hours
before his arrival [1].   By Wellesley's orders he pushed on for one
day more in pursuit, but found that the enemy was now so far
ahead that he could do no more than pick up moribund
stragglers.   On the nineteenth, therefore, he turned back and
retraced his steps to Montalegre [2].

Much the same fortune had befallen Beresford's column.   By
Wellesley's orders Tilson's brigade and their Portuguese companions marched from Chaves by Monterey on the eighteenth, on
the chance that Soult, after passing the Serra de Gerez, might drop
into the Monterey-Orense road.   But the Marshal had not taken
this route : he had kept to by-paths, and marched by Porquera
and Allariz, to the left of the line on which Beresford's pursuit
was directed.   At Ginzo the cavalry of the pursuing column
picked up fifty stragglers, and came into contact with a small
party of Franceschi's *chasseurs*, which Soult had thrown out to
cover his flank.   Learning from the peasantry that the French
had gone off by a different route, Beresford halted and returned
to Chaves.   His men were so thoroughly worn out, and the
strength of the column was so much reduced, that he could have
done little more even if he had come upon the main body of the
enemy [3].

On May 19 Soult's dilapidated and starving host poured into
Orense, where they could at last take a day's rest and obtain
a decent meal.   The Marshal caused the troops to be numbered,
and found that he had brought back 19,713 men.   As he had
started from the Spanish frontier with 22,000 sabres and

---

[1] The French rearguard actually saw Silveira arriving.   Naylies, p. 90.

[2] For this part of the pursuit see the diary of Hawker [of the 14th
Light Dragoons], who returned to Montalegre with Silveira's men.

[3] These details are mainly from the letter of Gough of the 87th, which
I have already had occasion to quote, when dealing with Beresford's movements.   I cannot find any corroboration for Napier's account of Beresford's
and Silveira's pursuit in ii. pp. 112-3 of his history.

bayonets, and had received 3,500 more from Tuy, when Lamartinière's column joined him, it would appear that he had left in all some 5,700 men behind him. Of these, according to the French accounts [1], about 1,000 had fallen in the early fighting, or died of sickness, before Wellesley's appearance on the Vouga. About 700, mostly convalescents, had been captured at Chaves by Silveira [2]. After the storm of Oporto the British army found 1,500 sick in the hospitals of that city, of Braga and of Viana [3]. They also took some 400 unwounded prisoners at Oporto and at Grijon [4]. It results therefore that the losses of the actual retreat from Baltar to Orense, between the thirteenth and the nineteenth of May, must have been rather more than 2,000 men. But all these had been able-bodied fighting-men— the sick, as we have seen, were abandoned before the break-neck march over the mountains began : adding them and the prisoners of the eleventh–twelfth, to the actual casualties of the retreat, on the same principle which we used when calculating the losses of Moore's army in the Corunna campaign, we should get a total of 4,000 for the deficiency in the French ranks during the nine days which elapsed between Wellesley's passage of the Vouga and Soult's arrival at Orense. Thus it would seem that about one-sixth of the 2nd Corps had been destroyed in that short time—a proportion almost exactly corresponding to that which Moore's force left behind it in the retreat from Sahagun to Corunna, wherein 6,000 men out of 33,000 were lost.

In other respects these two famous retreats afford some interesting points of comparison. Moore had an infinitely longer distance to cover : in mere mileage his men marched more than twice as far as Soult's [5] : their journey occupied twenty days as against nine. On the other hand the French had to

---

[1] See mainly Le Noble's calculation on pp. 353–4 of his *Campagne de 1809*.

[2] The rest of Silveira's prisoners were Hispano-Portuguese ' legionaries,' see p. 266.

[3] Napier (ii. 113) says, ' 1,800 at Viana and Braga, 700 at Oporto,' figures that should be reversed,' for at the two last places only the sick of Heudelet's and Lorges' divisions were captured, while at Oporto the main central hospital fell into the hands of the British. Le Noble says that there were 2,150 men in hospital altogether on May 10.

[4] See p. 341.

[5] The respective distances seem to be about 255 and 120 miles.

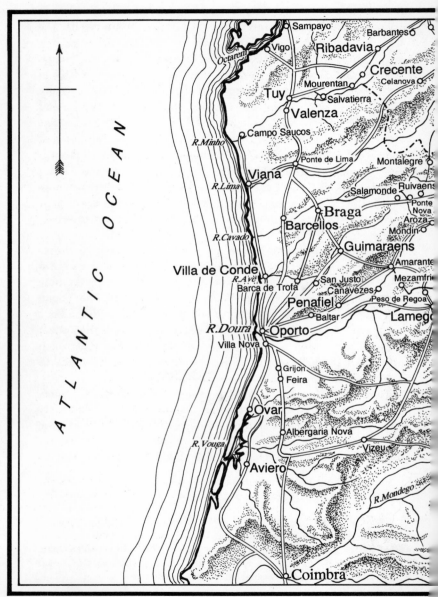

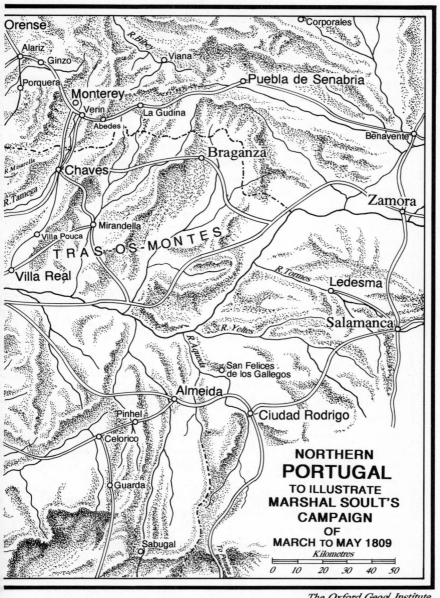

NORTHERN
PORTUGAL
TO ILLUSTRATE
**MARSHAL SOULT'S
CAMPAIGN**
OF
MARCH TO MAY 1809

Kilometres

0   10   20   30   40   50

The Oxford Geogl Institute.

use far worse roads.   From Benavente to Corunna there is a good *chaussée* for the whole distance : from Baltar to Orense the 2nd Corps had to follow impracticable mule-tracks for more than half the way.   As to the weather, there was perhaps little to choose between the two retreats : the nine days of perpetual rain, during which Soult effected his passage of four successive mountain chains, was almost as trying as the cold and snow through which the British had to trudge.   Moore's men were not so hardly pressed by starvation as the 2nd Corps, and they were moving through a country-side which was not actively hostile, if it could scarcely be described as friendly.   On the other hand they were pursued with far greater vigour than the French : their rearguard was beset every day, and had constantly to be fighting, while Soult's troops were hard pressed only on two days —the sixteenth and seventeenth of May.   This advantage the Marshal gained by choosing an unexpected line of retreat over obscure by-paths : if he had taken either of the high-roads by Braga and Chaves his fate would have been very different.   On this same choice of roads depends another contrast between the two retreats : to gain speed and safety Soult sacrificed the whole of his artillery and his transport.   When he arrived at Orense, as one of his officers wrote, 'the infantry had brought off their bayonets and their eagles, the cavalry their horses and saddles— everything else had been left behind—the guns, the stores, the treasure, the sick.'   Moore, in spite of all the miseries of his march, carried down to Corunna the whole of his artillery, part of his transport, and the greater number of his sick and wounded. If he lost his military chest, it was not from necessity but from the mismanagement of the subordinates who had charge of it. His army was in condition to fight a successful battle at the end of its retreat, and so to win for itself a safe and honourable departure.

Both generals, it will be observed, were driven into danger by causes for which they did not regard themselves as responsible. Soult was placed in peril by attempting to carry out his master's impracticable orders.   Moore thought himself bound to run the risk, because he had realized that there was a political necessity that the English army should do something for the cause of Spain, for it could not with honour retire to Portugal before it

had struck a blow.   In their management of their respective
campaigns both made mistakes.   Moore hurried his men too
much, and did not take full advantage of the many positions in
which he could have held' off the pursuer by judicious rearguard actions.   Soult's faults were even greater: nothing can
excuse his stay at Oporto during the days when he should have
been directing Loison's movements at Amarante.   That stay
was undoubtedly due to his vain intrigues with the Portuguese
malcontents; it was personal ambition, not any military necessity,
which detained him from his proper place.   Still more worthy
of blame was his disposition of his forces at the moment when
the British troops crossed the Vouga : they were scattered in
a dangerous fashion, which made concentration difficult and
uncertain.   But the weakest feature of his whole conduct was
that he allowed himself to be surprised in Oporto by Wellesley
on May 12.   When an army in close touch with the enemy
is taken unawares at broad midday, by an irruption of its
opponents into the middle of the cantonments, the general-in-
chief cannot shift the blame on to the shoulders of subordinates.
It was Soult's duty to see that his officers were taking all reasonable precautions to watch the British, and he most certainly did
not do so.   Indeed, we have seen that he turned all his attention
to the point of least danger—the lower reaches of the Douro—
and neglected that on which the British attack was really
delivered.   It was only when he found himself on the verge of
utter ruin, on May 13, that he rose to the occasion, and saved his
army, by the daring march upon Guimaraens which foiled
Wellesley's plans for intercepting his retreat.   To state that 'his
reputation as a general was nowise diminished by his Portuguese
campaign' is to do him more than justice [1].   It would be more
true to assert that he showed that if he could commit faults,
he could also do much towards repairing their consequences.

As to Wellesley, it is not too much to say that the Oporto
campaign is one of his strongest titles to fame.   He had, as we
have already seen, only 16,400 British and 11,400 Portuguese
troops [2], of whom the latter were either untried in the field or
demoralized by their previous experiences beyond the Douro.
His superiority in mere numbers to Soult's corps of 23,000 men

[1] Napier, ii. 113.   [2] See p. 321.

was therefore small, and he was lamentably destitute of cavalry and artillery.   It was no small feat to expel the enemy from Northern Portugal in nine days, and to cast him into Galicia, stripped of his guns and baggage, and with a gap of more than 4,000 men in his ranks.   This had been accomplished at the expense of no more than 500 casualties, even when the soldiers who fell by the way from sickness and fatigue are added to the 300 killed and wounded of the engagements of May 11, 12, and 17.   There is hardly a campaign in history in which so much was accomplished at so small a cost.   Wellesley had exactly carried out the programme which he had set before himself when he left Lisbon—the defeat of the enemy and the deliverance of the two provinces beyond the Douro.   He had expressly disclaimed any intention or expectation of destroying or capturing the 2nd Corps [1], which some foreign critics have ascribed to him in their anxiety to make out that he failed to execute the whole project that he had taken in hand.

There was, it is true, one short moment at which he had it in his power to deal Soult a heavier blow than he had contemplated.   On the night of May 12–13, when the Marshal in his bivouac at Baltar learnt of Loison's evacuation of Amarante, the main body of the 2nd Corps was in a deplorable situation, and must have been destroyed, had the British been close at hand.   If Wellesley had pursued the flying foe, on the afternoon of the victory of Oporto, with all his cavalry and the less fatigued regiments of his infantry, nothing could have saved the French.   But the opportunity was one which could not have been foreseen : no rational officer could have guessed that Loison would evacuate Amarante, and so surrender his chief's best line of retreat.   It was impossible that Wellesley should dream of such a chance being thrown into his hands.   He constructed his plans on the natural hypothesis that Soult had still open to him the route across the Tamega ; and he was therefore more concerned with the idea that Beresford might be in danger from the approach of Soult, than with that of taking measures to

---

[1] 'In respect to Soult, I shall omit nothing that I can do to destroy him—but I am afraid that with the force I have at my disposal, it is not in my power to prevent him retreating into Spain.'   Wellesley to Frere, May 9, 1809.

capture the Marshal. His men were fatigued with the long march of eighty miles in four days which had taken them from the Mondego to Oporto : his guns and stores had not yet passed the bridgeless Douro. It was natural, therefore, that he should allow himself and his army a night's rest before pressing on in pursuit of Soult. It will be remembered that he did push Murray's brigade along the Baltar road in the tracks of the Marshal, but that officer never came up with the French. If blame has to be allotted to any one for the failure to discover the unhappy situation of the 2nd Corps upon the morning of the thirteenth, it would seem that Murray must bear the burden rather than the Commander-in-chief. He should have kept touch, at all costs, with the retreating French, and if he had done so would have been able to give Wellesley news of their desperate plight.

As to the pursuit of Soult, between the fourteenth and the eighteenth, it is hard to see that more could have been done than was actually accomplished. 'It is obvious,' as Wellesley wrote to Castlereagh, 'that if an army throws away all its cannon, equipment, and baggage, and everything that can strengthen it and enable it to act together as a body ; and if it abandons all those who are entitled to its protection, but add to its weight and impede its progress [1], it must be able to march by roads on which it can not be followed, with any prospect of being overtaken, by an army which has not made the same sacrifices [2].' This puts the case in a nutshell : Soult, after he had abandoned his sick and destroyed his guns and wagons, could go much faster than his pursuers. The only chance of catching him was that Beresford or Silveira might be able to intercept him at the Misarella on the seventeenth. But the troops of the former were so exhausted by their long march in the rain from Amarante, that although they reached Chaves on the night of the sixteenth–seventeenth, they were not in a condition to march eighteen miles further on the following morning. Whether Silveira, who had taken a shorter but a more rugged route than Beresford, might not have reached Ruivaens ten or twelve hours earlier than he did is another matter. Had he

[1] From Montalegre, May 18, 1809.
[2] i. e. its sick and wounded.

done so, he might have held the cross-roads and blocked the
way to Montalegre. We have no details of his march, though
we know that he had a bad mountain-path to traverse in
abominable weather. All military critics have joined in con-
demning him [1], but without a more accurate knowledge of the
obstacles that he had to cross, and of the state of his troops, we
can not be sure of the exact amount of blame that should fall
upon him. It is at any rate clear that Wellesley was not
responsible for the late arrival of the Portuguese division at
Ruivaens and the consequent escape of the enemy.

Beyond Montalegre it would have been useless to follow the
flying French. An advance into Galicia would have taken the
British army too far from Lisbon, and have rendered it impossible to return in time to the Tagus if Victor should be on the
move. That marshal, as we shall see, was showing signs of
stirring from his long spell of torpidity, and it was a dispatch
from Mackenzie, containing the news that the 1st Corps was on
the move, that made Wellesley specially anxious to check the
pursuit, and to draw back to Central Portugal before matters
should come to a head in Estremadura. He could safely calculate that it would be months rather than weeks before Soult
would be in a condition to cause any trouble on the northern
frontier.

[1] Napier, Arteche, and Schepeler all agree in this, the former only
making the excuse that Silveira may not have fully understood Beresford's
orders, owing to the difficulty of language. But Beresford spoke and
wrote Portuguese fluently.

N.B.—There are admirable accounts of the horrors of Soult's retreat in
the works of Le Noble, St. Chamans, Fantin des Odoards, and Naylies.
The pursuit of the main body of the English army is well described by four
eye-witnesses—Lord Londonderry, Stothert, Hawker, and Lord Munster.
For the march of Beresford's corps I have only the details given by Lord
Gough's letter, cited heretofore.

SECTION XV

OPERATIONS IN NORTHERN SPAIN
(MARCH–JUNE 1809)

CHAPTER I

NEY AND LA ROMANA IN GALICIA AND THE ASTURIAS

WHILE following the fortunes of Soult and the 2nd Corps in Northern Portugal, we have been constrained to withdraw our attention from Galicia, where we left Marshal Ney busied in a vain attempt to beat down the insurrections which had sprung up in every corner of the kingdom, at the moment when the melting of the snows gave notice that spring was at hand. It was with no good will that the Duke of Elchingen had seen his colleague depart from Orense and plunge into the Portuguese mountains. Indeed he had done his best to induce Soult to disregard the Emperor's orders, and to join him in a strenuous effort to pacify Galicia before embarking on the march to Oporto[1]. When he found that his appeal had failed to influence the Duke of Dalmatia, and that the 2nd Corps had passed out of sight and left the whole of Galicia upon his hands, he was constrained to take stock of his position and to think out a plan of campaign.

Ney had at his disposal some 17,000 men, consisting of the twenty-four infantry battalions of his own corps, which formed the two divisions of Marchand and Maurice Mathieu, of the two regiments of his corps-cavalry, and of Fournier's brigade of Lorges' dragoons, which Soult, by the Emperor's orders, had transferred to him before crossing the Minho. Among his resources it would not be fair to count the two garrisons at

[1] See p. 192.

Vigo and Tuy which the 2nd Corps had left behind it. They numbered more than 4,000 men, but were so placed as to be more of a charge than a help to Ney. They failed to keep him in touch with Soult, and their necessities distracted some of his troops to their aid when he was requiring every man for other purposes.

On March 10, when he was left to his own resources, Ney had concentrated the greater part of his corps in the north-western corner of Galicia. He had placed one brigade at Lugo, a second with Fournier's dragoons at Mondonedo, in observation of the Asturias, a third at Santiago, the remainder at Corunna and Ferrol. The outlying posts had been called in, save a garrison at Villafranca, the important half-way stage between Lugo and Astorga, where the Marshal had left a battalion of the 26th regiment, to keep open his communication with the plains of Leon. The insurgents were already so active that touch with this detachment was soon lost, the peasants having cut the road both east and west of Villafranca.

The whole month of March was spent in a ceaseless endeavour to keep down the rising in Northern Galicia: the southern parts of the kingdom had been practically abandoned, and the French had no hold there save through the garrisons of Tuy and Vigo, both of which (as we have seen in an earlier chapter) were blockaded by the local levies the moment that Soult had passed on into Portugal.

Ney's object was to crush and cow the insurgents of Northern Galicia by the constant movement of flying columns, which marched out from the towns when his brigades were established, and made descents on every district where the peasantry had assembled in strength. This policy had little success: it was easy to rout the Galicians and to burn their villages, but the moment that the column had passed on the enemy returned to occupy his old positions. The campaign was endless and inconclusive: it was of little use to kill so many scores or hundreds of peasants, if no attempt was made to hold down the districts through which the expedition had passed. This could not be done for sheer want of numbers: 16,000 men were not sufficient to garrison the whole of the mountain valleys and coast villages of this rugged land. The French columns went far afield, even as far as Corcubion on the headland of Cape Finisterre, and Ribadeo on the borders of Asturias : but though they scathed the whole region with fire and sword, they made no impression. Moreover, they suffered serious losses : every expedition lost a certain number of stragglers cut off by the peasantry, and of foragers who had wandered too far from the main body in search of food. All were murdered : for the populace, mad at the burning of their homes and the lifting of their cattle— their only wealth—never gave quarter to the unfortunate soldiers who fell into their hands.

It is curious and interesting to compare Ney's actual operations with the orders which the Emperor had sent to him [1]. In these he was directed to establish his head quarters at Lugo, and to leave no more than a regiment at Ferrol and another regiment at Betanzos and Corunna. He was to keep a movable column of three battalions at work between Santiago and Tuy, to 'make examples' and prevent the English from landing munitions for the insurgents. With the rest of his corps, five regiments of infantry and a brigade of cavalry, he was to establish himself at Lugo, and from thence to send out punitive expeditions against rebellious villages, to seize hostages, to lend aid if necessary to Soult's operations in Portugal, and finally 'to utilize the months of March and April, when there is nothing to fear on the Galician coasts, for an expedition to conquer the Asturias.' Here we have all Napoleon's illusions concerning the character of the Peninsular War very clearly displayed. He supposes that a movable column of one regiment can hold down a rugged coast region one hundred miles long, where 20,000 insurgents are in arms. He thinks that punitive expeditions, and the taking of hostages, will keep a province quiet without there being any need to establish garrisons in it. 'Organize Galicia,' he writes, 'make examples, for severe examples well applied are much more effective than garrisons. . . . Leave the policing of the country to the Spanish authorities. If you cannot occupy every place, you can watch every place : if you cannot hold every shore-battery to prevent communication with the English, you can charge the natives with this duty. Your movable columns will punish any of the people of the coast who behave badly.'

[1] Napoleon to Ney, from Paris, Feb. 18, 1809.

To Ney, when he received this dispatch, many weeks after it had been written, all this elaborate advice must have appeared very futile. Considering the present attitude of the whole population of Galicia, he must have been much amused at the proposal that he should entrust them with the task of keeping off the British, should 'organize' them, and 'make them police themselves.' As to 'severe examples' he had now been burning villages and shooting monks and alcaldes for two months and more : but the only result was that the insurrection flared up more fiercely, and that his own stragglers and foragers were being hung and tortured every day. As to the idea of movable columns, he had (on his own inspiration) sent Maucune to carry out precisely the operations that the Emperor desired in the country between Santiago and Tuy. The column had to fight every day, and held down not one foot of territory beyond the outskirts of its own camp. And now, in the midst of all his troubles, he was ordered to attempt the conquest of the Asturias, no small undertaking in itself. The Emperor's letter ended with the disquieting note that 'no further reinforcements can be sent to Galicia. It is much more likely that it may be necessary to transfer to some other point one of the two divisions of the Sixth Corps[1].'

We have hitherto had little occasion to mention the two Spanish regular armies on which Ney, in addition to all his troubles with the insurgents, had to keep a watchful eye. The first was the force in the principality of Asturias, which had been lost to sight since the day on which it fled homeward after the battle of Espinosa. The second consisted of the much-tried troops of La Romana, who since their escape from Monterey had enjoyed some weeks of comparative rest, and were once more ready to move.

The Asturian force was far the larger in point of numbers, and ought to have made its influence felt long ere now. But even more than the other Spaniards, the Asturians were given over to particularism and provincial selfishness. In 1808 they had done nothing for the common cause save that they had lent the single division of Acevedo—comprising about half their

[1] 'Ne comptez sur aucun renfort: croyez plutôt qu'on pourrait être dans le cas de porter ailleurs une de vos divisions.'

provincial levy [1]—to the army which Blake led to defeat in Biscay. After Espinosa this corps had not retired with La Romana to Leon, but had fallen back within the frontier of its native principality, and had joined the large reserve which had never gone forward from Oviedo. During the three winter months, the Asturians had contented themselves with reorganizing and increasing the numbers of their battalions, and with guarding the passes of the Cantabrian chain. They had refused to send either men or money to La Romana, thereby provoking his righteous indignation, and furnishing him with a grudge which he repaid in due season. When he was driven away from their neighbourhood, and forced to retire towards Portugal, they still kept quiet behind their hills, and made but the weakest of attempts to distract the attention of the enemy. There were at first no French forces near them save Bonnet's single division at Santander, which was fully occupied in holding down the Montaña, and a provisional brigade at Leon consisting of some stray battalions of the dissolved Eighth Corps [2]. As neither of these forces had any considerable reserves behind them [3], when once Ney and Soult had passed on into Galicia, it is clear that a demonstration in force against Santander or Leon would have thrown dismay along the whole line of the French communications, and have disarranged all the Emperor's plans for further advance.

The only operation, however, which the Asturians undertook was a petty raid into Galicia with 3,000 or 4,000 men, who

---

[1] Acevedo's division, deducting the regular troops [Hibernia (two batts.), and Provincial of Oviedo], had some 6,000 men : while 5,200 remained behind in Asturias. See pp. 632 and 637 of vol. i.

[2] Apparently consisting in February of three battalions and a Spanish Legion which Napoleon had organized out of the prisoners of Blake's and La Romana's armies : 2,998 men in all. The Legion waited till it had received arms and clothing, and then deserted *en masse* and went to join the insurgents. For angry correspondence on this incident see Napoleon to King Joseph, Feb. 20, and King Joseph to Napoleon, March 7, 1809.

[3] The total of French troops in Old Castile, garrisoning Valladolid, Soria, Palencia, and Burgos, &c., was only 5,342 men. Nothing was disposable for field operations save Kellermann's division of dragoons. In Biscay, behind Bonnet, there were only 1,762 men, and in Alava 876. Practically nothing could have been sent to reinforce Leon or Santander, till Mortier's corps came up.

went to beat up Ney's detachment at Mondonedo on April 10, and were driven off with ease[1]. The Junta had fully 20,000 men under arms, but they contrived to be weak at every point by trying to guard every point. They had sent, to observe Bonnet, the largest body of their troops, nearly 10,000 men, under General Ballasteros: he had taken up the line of the Deba, and lay with his head quarters at Colombres, skirmishing occasionally with the French outposts. At the pass of Pajares, watching the main road that descends into the plain of Leon, were 3,000 men, and 2,000 more at La Mesa guarded a minor defile. Another division of 4,000 bayonets was at Castropol, facing Ney's detachment which had occupied Mondonedo: this was the column which had made the feeble advance in April to which we have already alluded. Finally, a Swiss Lieutenant-General named Worster lay at Oviedo, the capital of the principality, with a small reserve of 2,000 men. It does not seem that Cienfuegos, the Captain-General of Asturias, exercised any real authority, as the Junta took upon itself the settling of every detail of military affairs[3]. Thus a whole army was wasted

---

[1] For this fiasco see Toreno, i. pp. 400–1.

[2] These dispositions of the Asturian army, which have never before been published, are taken from a dispatch from the Junta at Oviedo, which Mr. Frere sent to Lord Castlereagh on March 24 [Record Office]. The regiments were :—

At Colombres, under Maj.-General F. Ballasteros :
 Luanco, Castropol, Navia, Luarca, Villaviciosa, Llanes, Cangas de Oñis, Cangas de Tineo, Don Carlos.

At Pajares and Farna, under Brigadier Don Christoval Lili :
 Siero, Provincial of Oviedo, Covadonga.

At La Mesa, under Brigadier Don F. Manglano :
 Riva de Sella, Pravia.

At Castropol, under Colonel T. Valdez :
 Lena, Grado, Salas, Ferdinando VII.

At Oviedo, under Lieut.-General Worster :
 Gijon, Infiesto.

The Junta report that they have over 20,000 men, the regiments being very strong, some of them reaching 1,200 bayonets, or even more.

[3] Carrol to La Romana, March 28, ' The Junta, in fact, command the armies in every respect. They have absolute power, and have rendered themselves highly obnoxious to the people of the province, and are at present entirely guided by the will and caprice of three or four individuals. . .'

by being distributed all along the narrow province, awaiting
an attack from an enemy who was far too weak to dream of
advancing, and who, as a matter of fact, did not move till May.
La Romana might well be indignant that the Asturians had
done practically nothing for the cause of Spain from December
to March, especially since they had obtained more than their
share of the British arms and money [1] which had been distributed
in the autumn of 1808.

Ney's new troubles in April did not spring from the activity
of the Asturian troops, but from that of the much-battered
army of Galicia, which was destined in this month to achieve
the first success that had cheered its depleted ranks since the
combat of Guenes. When La Romana, on March 8, had
found himself free from the pursuit of Franceschi's cavalry, he
had marched by leisurely stages to Puebla de Senabria on the
borders of Leon. He doubted for a moment whether he should
not turn southward and drop down, along the edge of Portugal,
to Ciudad Rodrigo, the nearest place of strength in Spanish
hands. But, after much consideration, he resolved to leave
behind him the weakest of his battalions and his numerous sick,
together with his small provision of artillery, and to strike back
into Galicia with the best of his men. It would seem that he
was inspired partly by the desire of cutting Ney's communications, partly by the wish to get into touch with the Asturians,
whose torpidity he was determined to stir up into action. Accordingly he left at Puebla de Senabria his guns and about 2,000
men, the skeletons of many ruined regiments, under General
Martin La Carrera, while with the 6,000 infantry that remained
he resolved to cross the Sierra Negra and throw himself into
the upper valley of the Sil. The road by Corporales and the
sources of the Cabrera torrent proved to be abominable; if the

---

[1] Such also was the opinion of Captain Carrol, the British representative
at Oviedo. He writes to Castlereagh on Feb. 10 in the following terms :
' I am sorry to have to represent that the supplies hitherto granted to
this province have not been applied (to use the mildest expressions) with
that judgment and œconomy that might have been expected, and that the
benefits resulting to this province and the common cause are by no means
proportionate to the liberality with which those supplies were granted by
the British Government' [Record Office]. Toreno, as a patriotic Asturian,
hushes up all these scandals.

army had possessed cannon or baggage it could not have reached its goal.   But after several hard marches La Romana descended to Ponferrada on March 16.   He learnt that the insurrection had compelled the French to concentrate all their small posts, and that there was no enemy nearer than Villafranca on the one hand and Astorga on the other.   Thus he found himself able to take possession of the high-road from Astorga to Lugo, and to make use of all the resources of the Vierzo, and of Eastern Galicia.   He might have passed on undisturbed, if he had chosen, to join the Asturians.   But learning that the French garrison at Villafranca was completely isolated, he resolved to risk a blow at it, in the hopes that he might reduce it before Ney could learn of his arrival and come down from Lugo to its aid.   He was ill prepared for a siege, for he had but one gun with him—a 12-pounder which he had abandoned in January when retreating from Ponferrada to Orense, and which he now picked up intact, with its store of ammunition, at a mountain hermitage, where it had been safely hidden for two months.

Marching on Villafranca next day he fell upon the French before they had any conception that there was a hostile force in their neighbourhood.   He beat them out of the town into the citadel after a sharp skirmish, and then surrounded them in their refuge, and began to batter its gates with his single gun. If the garrison could have held out for a few days they would probably have been relieved, for Ney was but three marches distant.   But the governor, regarding the old castle as untenable against artillery, surrendered at the first summons.   Thus La Romana captured a whole battalion of the 6th Léger, 600 strong[1], together with several hundreds more of convalescents and stragglers who had been halted at Villafranca, owing to the impossibility of sending small detachments through the mountains [2] when the insurgents were abroad [3].

Having accomplished this successful stroke La Romana was

[1] The number of unwounded prisoners was 574, that of killed and wounded nearly 700.

[2] The captives were sent off immediately into the Asturias.   Carrol saw them arrive at Oviedo.

[3] There is a long dispatch of Mendizabal to La Romana in the Record Office, giving details of the storm of Villafranca, which was all over in four hours.

desirous of pursuing his way to the Asturias, where he was determined to make his power felt[1]. He took with him only one
regiment (that of La Princesa, one of his old corps from the
Baltic), and handed over the temporary command of the army
to General Mahy, with orders to hold on to the Vierzo as long
as possible, but to retire on the Asturias if Ney came up against
him in force. The Marshal, however, did not move from Lugo ;
when he heard of the fall of the garrison of Villafranca, he was
already so much entangled with the insurrection that he could
spare no troops for an expedition to the Vierzo. In order to
reopen the communication with Astorga he would have had
to call in his outlying brigades, and at the present moment he
was more concerned about the fate of Tuy and Vigo than about
the operations of La Romana. Accordingly, Mahy was left
unmolested for the greater part of a month in his cantonments
along the banks of the Sil; it was a welcome respite for the
much-wandering army of Galicia.

Romana meanwhile betook himself to Oviedo with his escort,
and on arriving there on April 4 entered into a furious controversy with the Junta. Finding them obstinate, and not disposed
to carry out his plans without discussion, he finally executed
a petty *coup d'état*[2]. It bears an absurd resemblance to Crom-

---

[1] Captain Carrol had written to him a few days before to beg him to
hasten to Oviedo : ' I strongly advise your Excellency's repairing to this
city (Oviedo), and adopting such plans and measures for the better government of the province and the active operations of the army as your
Excellency shall think meet.' There were similar appeals from Spanish
officers discontented with the Junta.

[2] It may be worth while to quote the opening clauses of La Romana's
proclamation explaining his *coup d'état* ; it is dated the day after his
' purge ' of the Junta : a copy exists in the Record Office, forwarded to
Castlereagh by Carrol :—' Me es forzoso manifestar con mucho sentimiento
que la actual Junta de Asturias, aunque de las mas favorecidas por la
generosidad britannica en toda classe de subsidios, es la que menos ha
coadyuvado a la grande y heroyca empresa de arrojar a los enemigos de
nuestro patrio suelo. Formada esta Junta por intriga, y por la prepotencia
de algunos sugetos y familias conexionadas, se propuse arrogarse un poder
absoluto e indefinido : serven los individuos mutuamente en sus proyectos
y despiques, desechan con pretextos infundidos y aun calumniosos al que
no subscribiese a ellos, y contentan a los menesterosos con comisiones
o encargos de interes,' &c.

well's famous dissolution of the Long Parliament. Coming into
their council-room, with Colonel Joseph O'Donnell and fifty
grenadiers of the Princesa regiment, he delivered an harangue
to the members, accusing them of all manner of maladministra-
tion and provincial selfishness. Then he signed to his soldiers
and bade them clear the room [1].

La Romana then, on his own authority, nominated a new
Junta; but many of its members refused to act, doubting the
legality of his action, while the dispossessed delegates kept up
a paper controversy, and sent reams of objurgatory letters to the
Government at Seville. Ballasteros and his army, at the other
side of the Principality, seem to have paid little attention to
La Romana, but the Marquis so far got his way that he began
to send much-needed stores, medicines, munitions, and clothing
to his troops in the Vierzo. He even succeeded in procuring
a few field-pieces for them [2], which were dragged with difficulty
over the passes viâ Cangas de Tineo.

Thus strengthened Mahy, much to his chief's displeasure,
advanced from the Vierzo towards Lugo, with the intention of
beating up the French brigade there stationed. He took post
at Navia de Suarna, just outside the borders of the Asturias,
and called to his standards all the peasantry of the surrounding
region. La Romana wrote him urgent letters, directing him to
avoid a battle and to await his own return. 'He should
remember that it was the policy of Fabius Maximus that saved
Rome, and curb his warlike zeal [3].' It is satisfactory to find
that one Spanish general at least was free from that wild desire
for pitched battles that possessed most of his contemporaries.

Mahy, thus warned, halted in his march towards Lugo, and
remained in his cantonments in the valley of the Navia. His
chief should have returned to him, but lingered at Oviedo till
April was over, busy in the work of reorganization and in the

---

[1] Carrol, who was an eye-witness of the scene, thought that the Marquis
'had reformed the Junta in the most quiet, peaceable and masterly manner.'
The last epithet seems the most appropriate of the three. Carrol to
Castlereagh, April 10, 1809 [in Record Office].

[2] Letters of La Romana to Mahy in Appendix to Arteche, vol. vi.
p. 145.

[3] Ibid., p. 146.

forwarding of supplies. Meanwhile the French hold on Southern
Galicia had completely disappeared : Vigo had fallen in March,
Tuy had been evacuated. Maucune's column had cut its way
back to Santiago with some difficulty, bringing to Ney the news
of Soult's capture of Oporto, but also the assurance that the
whole valley of the Minho and the western coastland had passed
into the hands of the insurgents.

What the Duke of Elchingen's next move would have been,
if he had not received further intelligence from without, we
cannot say. But in the first week in May the long-lost communication with Madrid was at last reopened, and he was
ordered to take his part in a new and broad plan of operations
against La Romana's army and the Asturias.

Ever since La Romana had stormed Villafranca, and all news
from Galicia had been completely cut off, King Joseph and his
adviser Jourdan had been in a state of great fear and perplexity
as to the condition of affairs in the north-west. Soult had long
passed out of their ken, and now Ney also was lost to sight.
In default of accurate information they received all manner of
lugubrious rumours from Leon and Astorga, and imagined that
the Sixth Corps was in far more desperate straits than was
actually the case. Fearing the worst, they resolved to find out,
at all costs, what was going on in Galicia. To do so it was
necessary to fit out an expedition sufficiently strong to brush
aside the insurgents and communicate with Ney. Troops, however, were hard to find. Lapisse had already marched from
Salamanca to join Victor. In Old Castile and Leon there were
but Kellermann's dragoons and a few garrisons, none of which
could leave their posts. Marshal Bessières, to whom the general
charge of the northern provinces had been given by the Emperor,
could show conclusively that he was not able to equip a column
of even 5,000 men for service in Galicia.

The only quarter whence troops could be procured was Aragon,
where everything had remained quiet since the fall of Saragossa.
The Emperor had issued orders that of the two corps which had
taken part in the siege, the Third only should remain to hold
down the conquered kingdom : hence Mortier and the Fifth
should have been disposable to reinforce the troops in Old
Castile. But, with the Austrian war upon his hands, Napoleon

was thinking of withdrawing Mortier and his 15,000 men from Spain.   In a dispatch dated April 10, he announced that the Marshal was to retire from Aragon to Logroño in Navarre, from whence he might possibly be recalled to France if circumstances demanded it[1].   At the same moment King Joseph was writing to Mortier to summon him into Old Castile, and pointing out to him that the safety of the whole of Northern Spain depended upon his presence.   Much perplexed by these contradictory orders, the Duke of Treviso took a half-measure, and marched to Burgos, which was actually in Old Castile, but lay only three marches from Logroño and upon the direct route to France.   A few days later the Emperor, moved by his brother's incessant appeals, and seeing that it was all-important to reopen the communication between Ney and Soult, permitted Mortier to march to Valladolid, where he was in a good position for holding down the entire province of Old Castile.   He also gave leave to the King to employ for an expedition to Galicia the two regiments of the Third Corps, which had escorted the prisoners of Saragossa to Bayonne, and which were now on their homeward way to join their division in Aragon.

It was thus possible to get together enough troops to open the way to Galicia.   The charge of the expedition was handed over to Kellermann, who was given his own dragoons, the two regiments from Bayonne, a stray battalion of Leval's Germans from Segovia, a Polish battalion from Buitrago, and a provisional regiment organized from belated details of the Second and Sixth Corps, which had been lying in various garrisons of Castile and Leon[2].   He had altogether some 7,000 or 8,000 men, whom he concentrated at Astorga on April 27.   Marching on Villafranca he met no regular opposition, but was harassed by the way by the peasantry, who had abandoned their villages and retired into the hills.   Mahy had moved off the main road by making his advance to Navia de Suarna, and was not sighted by Kellermann, nor did the Spaniard think fit to meddle with such a powerful force as that which was now passing him.

On May 2 the column reached Lugo, where it fell in with

[1] Napoleon to Joseph, from Paris, April 10, 1809.

[2] For details concerning the composition of this expedition see Jourdan's *Mémoires*, p. 196.

Maurice Mathieu's division of the Sixth Corps, and obtained full information as to Ney's position. The Marshal was absent at Corunna, but sent his chief of the staff to meet Kellermann and concert with him a common plan of operations. It was settled that they should concentrate their attention on La Romana and the Asturians, leaving southern Galicia alone for the present, and taking no heed of Soult, of whom they had received no news for a full month.

For the destruction of the Spanish armies of the north a concentric movement was planned. Ney undertook to concentrate the main body of his corps at Lugo, and to fall on the Asturians from the west, crushing Mahy on the way. He stipulated, however, that he should be allowed to return to Galicia as quickly as possible, lest the insurgents should make havoc of his garrisons during his absence. Kellermann was to retrace his steps to Astorga and Leon, and from thence to march on the Asturias by the pass of Pajares, its great southern outlet. At the same moment Bonnet at Santander was to be requested to fall on from the east, and to attack Ballasteros and the division that lay behind the Deba.

When it was reported to Mahy and La Romana that Kellermann had turned back from Lugo, and was retreating upon Astorga, they failed to grasp the meaning of his movement, and came to the conclusion that his expedition had been sent out with no purpose save that of communicating with Ney. Unconscious that a simultaneous attack from all sides was being prepared against them, they failed to concentrate. By leaving small 'containing' detachments at the outlying posts, they could have massed 20,000 men against any one of the French columns: but they failed to see their opportunity and were caught in a state of complete dispersion. Ballasteros with 9,000 men still lay opposite Bonnet ; Worster at Castropol did not unite with Mahy's army at Navia de Suarna ; and La Romana remained at Oviedo with two regiments only.

Hence came hopeless disaster when the French attack was at last let loose upon the Asturias. On May 13 the Duke of Elchingen drew together at Lugo four of the eight infantry regiments which formed the Sixth Corps, with two of his four cavalry regiments, and eight mountain-guns carried by mules.

This formed a compact force of 6,500 bayonets and 900 sabres[1]. He left behind him four battalions and a cavalry regiment under Maucune at Santiago, the same force under the cavalry brigadier Fournier at Lugo, two battalions at Corunna, one at Betanzos, and one at Ferrol.

The obvious route by which the Marshal might have advanced on Oviedo was the coast-road by Mondonedo and Castropol, which Worster was guarding. But in order to save time and to fall upon the enemy on an unexpected line, he took a shorter but more rugged mountain road by Meyra and Ibias, which led him into the valley of the Navia. This brought him straight upon Mahy's army: but that general, when he learnt of the strength that was directed against him, retreated in haste after a skirmish at Pequin, and fled, not to the Asturias, but westward into the upper valley of the Minho. [May 14.] This move was vexatious to Ney, who would have preferred to drive him on to Oviedo, to share in the general rout that was being prepared for the Asturians. The Marshal refused to follow him, and pushed on to Cangas de Tineo in the valley of the Narcea, capturing there a large convoy of food and ammunition which was on its way from La Romana to Mahy. On May 17 he hurried on to Salas, on the 18th he was at the bridge of Gallegos on the Nora river, only ten miles from Oviedo. Here for the first time he met with serious opposition: hitherto he had suffered from nothing but casual 'sniping' on the part of the peasantry. His march had been so rapid that La Romana had only heard of his approach on the seventeenth[2], and had not been able to call in any of his out-

[1] The force that marched on the Asturias was composed of the 25th Léger, 27th and 59th of Maurice Mathieu's division, the 39th from Marchand's, the 3rd Hussars, and 25th Dragoons.

Maucune's detachment consisted of two battalions each of the 6th Léger and the 76th, with the 15th Chasseurs and one battery.

Fournier's detachment was composed of the 15th Dragoons, two battalions of the 69th, and one of the 76th.

[2] Carrol gives an excellent account of the French invasion in a long dispatch written from Vigo on June 3. He says that the Marquis only heard of Ney's approach by the peasants flying from Cangas de Tineo on the morning of May 17. He himself was sent out to verify the incredible information, and came on the French as they were crossing the Navia,

lying detachments. The Marquis was forced to attempt to defend the passage of the Nora with nothing more than his small central reserve—the one Galician regiment (La Princesa, only 600 bayonets) that he had brought with him from Villafranca, and one Asturian battalion—not more than 1,500 men. Naturally he was routed with great loss, though Ney allows that the Princesa regiment made a creditable defence at the bridge [1]. The Spanish troops therefore dispersed and fled eastward, while Romana rode down to the seaport of Gihon and took ship on a Spanish sloop of war along with the members of his Junta. The Marshal seized Oviedo on the nineteenth : the place was pillaged in the most thorough fashion by his troops. In his dispatch he makes the excuse that a few peasants had attempted to defend some barricades in the suburbs, and that they, not the soldiery, had begun the sack. *Credat Judaeus Apella!* The ways of the bands of Napoleon are too well known, and we shall not believe that it was Spaniards who stole the cathedral plate, or tore the bones of the early kings of Asturias from their resting-places in search of treasure [2]. On May 20 Ney marched with one regiment down to Gijon, where he found 250,000 lbs. of powder newly landed from England, and a quantity of military stores. An English merchantman was captured and another burnt [3]. A detached column occupied Aviles, the second seaport of the Asturias.

On the following day, May 21, a detachment sent inland from Oviedo up the valley of the Lena, with orders to search for the column coming from the south, got into touch with that

only thirty miles from Oviedo. He rode back in haste, and met one Asturian battalion coming up, and afterwards the regiment of La Princesa. Romana had no other troops, and only a few hundred half-armed peasantry joined in the defence of the bridge of Gallegos.

[1] 'Ce dernier pont de Gallegos fut assez bien défendu par le régiment de la Princesse, mais néanmoins il fut enlevé, ainsi qu'une pièce de douze.' Ney to King Joseph, Oviedo, May 21.

[2] 'Les magasins et les plus riches maisons de la ville furent pillés par les paysans et la populace. Ces malheureux, ivres d'eau-de-vie, entreprirent de défendre la ville et firent feu dans toutes les rues.' Ney to King Joseph, Oviedo, May 21.

[3] They were called the Pique and the Plutus. Carrol was nearly captured while burning the latter, and escaped in an open boat.

force. Kellermann had duly reached Leon, where he found orders directing him to send back to Aragon the two regiments of the Third Corps which had been lent him [1], and to take instead a division of Mortier's corps, which was now disposable for service in the north. Accordingly he picked up Girard's (late Suchet's) division, and leaving one of its brigades at Leon, marched with the other and the remainder of his original force, to storm the defiles of Pajares. He had with him between 6,000 and 7,000 troops, a force with which he easily routed the Asturian brigade of 3,000 men under Colonel Quixano, which had been set to guard the pass. At the end of two days of irregular fighting, Kellermann descended into the valley of the Lena and met Ney's outposts on May 21. The routed enemy dispersed among the hills.

It remains to speak of the third French column which started to invade the Asturias, that of Bonnet. This general marched from Santander on May 17 with 5,000 men, intending to attack Ballasteros, and force his way to Oviedo by the coast-road that passes by San Vincente de la Barquera and Villaviciosa. But he found no one to fight, for Ballasteros had been summoned by La Romana to defend Oviedo, and had started off by the inland road viâ Cangas de Oñis and Infiesto. The two armies therefore were marching parallel to each other, with rough mountains between them. On reaching Infiesto on May 21, Ballasteros heard of the fall of Oviedo and of the forcing of the pass of Pajares: seeing that it would be useless to run into the lion's mouth by proceeding any further, he fell back into the mountains, and took refuge in the upland valley of Covadonga, the site of King Pelayo's famous victory over the Moors in the year 718. Here he remained undiscovered, and was gradually joined by the wrecks of the force which Ney had routed at Oviedo, including O'Donnell and the Princesa regiment. Bonnet passed him without discovering his whereabouts, advanced as far as Infiesto and Villaviciosa, and got into touch with Kellermann.

Thus the three French columns had all won their way into the heart of the Asturias, but though they had seized its capital and its seaports, they had failed to catch its army, and only half their task had been performed. Of all the Asturian troops

[1] The 116th and 117th of Morlot's division.

only the two small forces at Oviedo and Pajares had been met
and routed. Worster had not been molested, Mahy had
doubled back into Galicia, Ballasteros had gone up into the
mountains. If the invasion was to have any definite results,
it was necessary to hunt down all these three divisions. But
there was no time to do so : Ney was anxious about his Galician
garrisons ; Bonnet remembered that he had left Santander in
charge of a weak detachment of no more than 1,200 men. Both
refused to remain in the Asturias, or to engage in a long stern
chase after the elusive Spaniards, among the peaks of the Peñas
de Europa and the Sierras Albas. They decided that Kellermann with his 7,000 men must finish the business. Accordingly
they departed each to his own province—and it was high time,
for their worst expectations had been fulfilled. Mahy in the
west and Ballasteros in the east had each played the correct
game, and had fallen upon the small garrisons left exposed in
their rear. Moreover, the insurgents of Southern Galicia had
crossed the Ulla and marched on Santiago. If Ney had remained ten days longer in the Asturias, it is probable that he
would have returned to find the half of the Sixth Corps which
he had left in Galicia absolutely exterminated.

The Marshal, however, was just in time to prevent this
disaster. Handing over the charge of the principality to
Kellermann, he marched off on May 22 by the coast-road which
leads to Galicia by the route of Navia, Castropol, and Ribadeo.
He hoped to deal with Worster by the way, having learnt that
the Swiss general had advanced from Castropol by La Romana's
orders, and was moving cautiously in the direction of Oviedo.
But Worster was fortunate enough to escape : he went up into
the mountains when he heard that Ney was near, and had the
satisfaction of learning that the Marshal had passed him by.
The rivers being in flood, and the bridges broken, the French
had a slow and tiresome march to Ribadeo, which they only
reached on May 26. Next day the Duke of Elchingen was at
Castropol, where he received the news that Lugo had been in
the gravest peril, and had only been relieved by the unexpected
appearance of Soult and the Second Corps from the direction
of Orense.

The sequence of events during the Marshal's absence had

been as follows. When Mahy found that he had escaped pursuit, he had immediately made up his mind to strike at the French garrisons. He tried to persuade Worster to join him, or to attack Ferrol, but could not induce him to quit the Asturias. So with his own 6,000 men Mahy marched on Lugo, beat General Fournier (who came out to meet him) in a skirmish outside the walls, and drove him into the town. Lugo had no fortification save a mediaeval wall, and the Spaniards were in great hopes of storming it, as they had stormed Villafranca. But when they had lain two days before the place, they were surprised to hear that a large French force was marching against them ; it was not Ney returning from the Asturias, but the dilapidated corps of Soult retreating from Orense. Wisely refusing to face an army of 19,000 men, Mahy raised the siege and retired to Villalba in the folds of the Sierra de Loba. On May 22 Soult entered Lugo, where he was at last able to give his men nine days' rest, and could begin to cast about him for means to refit them with the proper equipment of an army, for, as we have seen, they were in a condition of absolute destitution and wholly unable to take the field.

At Castropol Ney heard at one and the same moment that Lugo had been in danger and that it had been relieved. But he also received news of even greater importance from another quarter. Maucune and the detachment which he had left at Santiago had been defeated in the open field by the insurgents of Southern Galicia, and had been compelled to fall back on Corunna. This was now the point of danger, wherefore the Marshal neither moved to join Soult at Lugo, nor set himself to hunt Mahy in the mountains, but marched straight for Corunna to succour Maucune.

The force which had defeated that general consisted in the main of the insurgents who had beleaguered Tuy and Vigo in March and April. They were now under Morillo and Garcia del Barrio, who were beginning to reduce them to some sort of discipline, and were organizing them into battalions and companies. But the core of the 'Division of the Minho,' as this force was now called, was composed of the small body of regulars which La Romana had left at Puebla de Senabria, under Martin La Carrera. That officer, after giving his feeble detachment some weeks of rest, had marched via Monterey and Orense to join the insurrectionary army. He brought with him nine guns and 2,000 men. On May 22 Carrera and Morillo crossed the Ulla and advanced on Santiago with 10,000 men, of whom only 7,000 possessed firearms. Maucune came forth to meet them in the Campo de Estrella[1], outside the city, with his four battalions and a regiment of chasseurs, thinking to gain an easy success when the enemy offered him battle in the open. But he was outnumbered by three to one, and as the Galicians showed much spirit and stood steadily to their guns, he was repulsed with loss. Carrera then attacked in his turn, drove the French into Santiago, chased them through the town, and pursued them for a league beyond it. Maucune was wounded, and lost 600 men— a fifth of his whole force—and two guns. He fell back in disorder on Corunna. He had the audacity to write to Ney that he had retired after an indecisive combat : but the Marshal, reading between the lines of his dispatch, hastened to Corunna with all the troops which had returned from the Asturias, and did not consider the situation secure till he learnt that Carrera had not advanced from Santiago.

Leaving his main body opposite the 'Division of the Minho,' the Duke of Elchingen now betook himself to Lugo, to concert a joint plan of operation with Soult [May 30]. The results of their somewhat stormy conference must be told in another chapter.

Meanwhile the situation behind them was rapidly changing. On May 24 La Romana, who had landed at Ribadeo, rejoined Mahy and his army at Villalba. The Marquis, on surveying the situation, came to the conclusion that it was too dangerous to remain in the northern angle of Galicia, between the French army at Lugo and the sea. He resolved to return to the southern region of the province, and to get into touch with Carrera and the troops on the Minho. He therefore bade his army prepare for another forced march across the mountains. They murmured but obeyed, and, cautiously slipping past Soult's corps by a flank movement, crossed the high-road to Villafranca and reached Monforte de Lemos. From thence

[1] The plain from which Santiago gets its name of Santiago de Compostella.

they safely descended to Orense, where La Romana established his head quarters [June 6]. Thus the Spaniards were once more in line, and prepared to defend the whole of Southern Galicia.

We have still to deal with the state of affairs in the Asturias. After Ney's departure on May 22, Kellermann lay at Oviedo and Bonnet at Infiesto. But a few days later the latter general received the disquieting news that Ballasteros, whose movements had hitherto escaped him, was on the move towards the east, and might be intending either to make a raid into the plains of Castile, or to descend on Santander and its weak garrison.

Ballasteros, as a matter of fact, had resolved to stir up trouble in Bonnet's rear, with the object of drawing him off from the Asturias. Leaving his refuge at Covadonga on May 24 he marched by mule-tracks, unmarked on any map, to Potes in the upper valley of the Deba. There he remained a few days, and finding that he was unpursued, and that his exact situation was unknown to the French, resolved to make a dash for Santander. Starting on June 6 and keeping to the mountains, he successfully achieved his end, and arrived at his goal before the garrison of that place had any knowledge of his approach. On the morning of June 10 he stormed the city, driving out General Noirot, who escaped with 1,000 men, but capturing 200 of the garrison and 400 sick in hospital, as well as the whole of the stores and munitions of Bonnet's regiments. Among his other prizes was the sum of £10,000 in cash, in the military chest of the division. Some of the French tried to escape by sea, in three corvettes and two luggers which lay in the harbour, but the British frigates *Amelia* and *Statira*, which lay off the coast, captured them all. This was a splendid stroke, and if Ballasteros had been prudent he might have got away unharmed with all his plunder. But he lingered in Santander, though he knew that Bonnet must be in pursuit of him, and resolved to defend the town. The French general had started to protect his base and his dépôts, the moment that he ascertained the real direction of Ballasteros' march. On the night of June 10 he met the fugitive garrison and learnt that Santander had fallen. Late on the ensuing day he reached its suburbs, and sent in two battalions to make a dash at the place. They were beaten off; but next

morning Bonnet attacked with his whole force, the Asturians
were defeated, and Ballasteros' raid ended in a disaster. He
himself escaped by sea, but 3,000 of his men were captured, and
the rest dispersed. The French recovered their sick and prisoners,
and such of their stores as the Spaniards had not consumed [1].
The wrecks of Ballasteros' division drifted back over the hills to
their native principality, save one detachment, the regulars of
La Romana's old regiment of La Princesa. This small body of
300 men turned south, and by an astounding march across Old
Castile and Aragon reached Molina on the borders of Valencia,
where they joined the army of Blake. They had gone 250 miles
through territory of which the French were supposed to be in
military possession, but threaded their way between the garrisons
in perfect safety, because the peasantry never betrayed their position to the enemy.

Disastrous as was its end, Ballasteros' expedition had yet
served its purpose. Not only had it thrown the whole of the
French garrisons in Biscay and Guipuzcoa into confusion, but
even the Governor of Bayonne had been frightened and had sent
alarming dispatches to the Emperor. This was comparatively
unimportant, but it was a very different matter that Bonnet
had been forced to evacuate the Asturias, all of whose eastern
region was now free from the invaders.

More was to follow : Kellermann still lay at Oviedo, worried
but not seriously incommoded by Worster and the Asturians of
the west. But a few days after Bonnet's departure he received
a request from Mortier (backed by orders from King Joseph),
that the division of the 5th Corps which had been lent him
should instantly return to Castile. This was one of the results
of Wellesley's campaign on the Douro, for Mortier, hearing of
Soult's expulsion from Northern Portugal, imagined that the
British army, being now free for further action, would debouch
by Almeida and Ciudad Rodrigo and fall upon Salamanca.
He needed the aid of his second division, which Kellermann
was forced to send back. But it would have been not only
useless but extremely dangerous to linger at Oviedo with the
small remnant of the expeditionary force, when Girard's regiments

---

[1] All this may be studied in two dispatches of Bonnet to King Joseph,
dated Santander, June 12 and June 20.

had been withdrawn.   Therefore Kellermann wisely resolved to
evacuate the whole principality, and returned to Leon by the pass
of Pajares in the third week of June.

Thus ended in complete failure the great concentric attack on
the Asturias. The causes of the fiasco were two. (1) The French
generals chose as their objective, not the enemy's armies, but his
capital and base of operations.   Both Ney and Bonnet while
marching on Oviedo left what (adapting a naval phrase) we may
call an 'army-in-being' behind them, and in each case that army
fell upon the detachments left in the rear, and pressed them so
hard that the invading forces could not stay in the Asturias, but
were forced to turn back to protect their communications.
(2) In Spain conquest was useless unless a garrison could be left
behind to hold down the territory that was overrun.   But
neither Ney, Kellermann, nor Bonnet had any troops to devote
to such a purpose : they invaded the Asturias with regiments
borrowed from other regions, from which they could not long
be spared.   As later experience in 1811 and 1812 showed, it
required some 8,000 men merely to maintain a hold upon Oviedo
and the central parts of the principality.   The invaders had no
such force at their disposition—the troops from the 6th Corps
were wanted in Galicia, those of the 5th Corps in Castile, those
of Bonnet in the Montaña. If it were impossible to garrison
the Asturias, the invasion dwindled down into a raid, and a raid
which left untouched the larger part of the enemy's field army
was useless.   It would have been better policy to hunt Mahy,
Worster, and Ballasteros rather than to secure for a bare three
weeks military possession of Oviedo and Gihon.   If Soult had
not dropped from the clouds, as it were, to save Lugo : if
Ballasteros had been a little more prudent at Santander, the
Asturian expedition would have ended not merely in a failure,
but in an ignominious defeat. It should never have been undertaken while the Galician insurrection was still raging, and while
no troops were available for the permanent garrisoning of the
principality.

Searching a little deeper, may we not say that the ultimate
cause of the fiasco was Napoleon's misconception of the character
of the Spanish war ?   It was he who ordered the invasion of the
Asturias, and he issued his orders under the hypothesis that it

could be not only conquered but retained. But with the numbers then at the disposal of his generals this was impossible, because the insurrection absorbed so many of their troops, that no more could be detached without risking the loss of all that had been already gained. By grasping at the Asturias Napoleon nearly lost Galicia. Only Soult's appearance prevented that province from falling completely into the hands of Mahy and La Carrera: and that appearance was as involuntary as it was unexpected. If the Duke of Dalmatia had been able to carry out his original design he would have retreated from Oporto to Zamora and not to Orense. If Beresford had not foiled him at Amarante, he would have been resting on the Douro when Fournier was in such desperate straits at Lugo. In that case Ney might have returned from Oviedo to find that his detachments had been destroyed, and that Galicia was lost. It was not the Emperor's fault that this disaster failed to occur.

SECTION XV: CHAPTER II

THE FRENCH ABANDON GALICIA

WHEN, upon May 30, 1809, Ney arrived at Lugo, and met Soult in conference, it seemed that, now or never, the time had come when a serious endeavour might be made to subdue the Galician insurgents. The whole force of the 2nd and 6th Corps was concentrated in the narrow triangle between Ferrol, Corunna, and Lugo. The two marshals had still 33,000 men fit for service, after deducting the sick. If they set aside competent garrisons for the three towns that we have just named, they could still show some 25,000 men available for field operations, and with such a force Ney was of the opinion that the insurrection might be beaten down. It was true that the 2nd Corps was in a deplorable condition as regards equipment, but on the other hand Corunna and Ferrol were still full of the stores of arms and ammunition that had been captured when they surrendered. Clothing, no doubt, was lamentably deficient, and Ney could only supply hundreds where Soult asked for thousands of boots and *capotes*; but he refitted his colleague's troops with muskets and ammunition, and furnished him with eight mountain-guns—field-pieces the Duke of Dalmatia would not take, though a certain number were offered him; for after his experience of the way that his artillery had delayed him in February and March he refused to accept them. Horses and mules were unattainable—nearly half Soult's cavalry was dismounted, and he had lost most of his sumpter-beasts between Guimaraens and Montalegre. Nevertheless, the corps, after a week's rest at Lugo, was once more capable of service. Its weakly men had been left in hospital at Oporto, or had fallen by the way in the dreadful defiles of Ruivaens and Salamonde. All that remained were war-hardened veterans, and Soult, out of his 19,000 men, had no more than 800 sick and wounded.

He resolved to disembarrass himself of another hindrance, his
dismounted cavalry, and in each regiment made the 3rd and 4th
squadrons hand over their chargers to the 1st and 2nd.   The
1,100 troopers thus left without mounts were armed with
muskets, and formed into a column, to which were added the
cadres of certain infantry battalions belonging to the regiments
which had suffered most.   In these the 3rd, or the 3rd and 4th,
battalions turned over their effective rank and file to the others,
while the officers and non-commissioned officers were to be sent
home to their dépôts to organize new units.   The whole body
was placed under General Quesnel, who was directed to cut his way
to Astorga by the great high-road : it was hoped that he would
come safely through, now that La Romana had withdrawn his
army to Southern Galicia.   The expedient was a hazardous
one ; but the column was fortunate : it was forced to fight
with a large assembly of peasants at Doncos, halfway between
Lugo and Villafranca, but reached its goal with no great loss,
though for every mile of the march it was being 'sniped' and
harassed by the guerrillas.

Soult's available force, after he had sent his sick into the
hospitals of Lugo, and had dismissed Quesnel's detachment, was
about 16,500 or 17,000 sabres and bayonets.   Ney had about
15,000 men left.   The two marshals were bound, both by the
Emperor's orders and by the mere necessities of the situation, to
co-operate with each other.   But there was a fundamental diver-
gence between their aims and intentions.   Ney had been given
charge of Galicia, and he regarded it as his duty to conquer and
hold down the province.   He refused to look beyond his orders,
or to take into consideration the progress of operations in other
parts of the Peninsula.   Soult, on the other hand, always loved
to play his own game, and had no desire to stay in Galicia in
order to lighten his colleague's task.   He was disgusted with
the land, its mountains, and its insurgents, and was eager to
find some excuse for quitting it.   He had no difficulty in discovering many excellent reasons for retiring into the plains of Leon.
The first was the dilapidated state of his troops : in spite of the
resources which Ney had lent, the 2nd Corps still lacked clothing, pay, and transport.   Soult had written to King Joseph on
May 30 to ask that all these necessaries might be sent forward

to Zamora, where he intended to pick them up. A still more·
plausible plea might be found in the general state of affairs in
Northern Spain. The Emperor's main object was the expulsion
of the British army from the Peninsula. But if the 2nd Corps
joined the 6th in a long, and probably fruitless, hunt after the
evasive La Romana, Wellesley would be left free to march
whithersoever he might please. He might base himself on
Almeida and Ciudad Rodrigo, and make a sudden inroad into
Leon and Old Castile, where the small corps of Mortier would
certainly prove inadequate to hold him back. Or he might go
off to the south, and fall upon Victor in Estremadura, a move
which might very probably lead to the loss of Madrid. Soult
therefore was of opinion that his duty was to drop down into
Leon, and there join with Mortier in making such a demonstration against Portugal as would compel the British army to
stand upon the defensive, and to abandon any idea of invading
Spain either by the valley of the Douro or that of the Tagus.
' He could not keep his eye off Portugal,' as Jourdan and King
Joseph, no less than Ney, kept complaining [1]. There cannot
be the least doubt that Soult was quite right in turning his
main attention in this direction. It was the English army that
was the most dangerous enemy ; and it was the flanking position
of Portugal that rendered the French movements toward the
south of Spain hazardous or impracticable.

Nevertheless all the Duke of Dalmatia's arguments seemed to
his colleague mere excuses destined to cover a selfish determination to abandon the 6th Corps, and to shirk the duty of
co-operating in the conquest of Galicia. He insisted that Soult
must aid him in crushing La Romana before taking any other
task in hand. And he had a strong moral claim for pressing
his request, because it was from the resources which he had
furnished that the 2nd Corps had been re-equipped and rendered
capable of renewed service in the field. The marshals wrangled,
and their followers copied them, for a fierce feud, leading to a
copious exchange of recrimination and many duels, sprang up
during the few days that the staffs of the two corps lay together
at Lugo [2]. At last Soult yielded, or feigned to yield, to Ney's

---

[1] The phrase occurs in a dispatch of Jourdan's written in August.

[2] There is clear evidence of this quarrel in the diaries and memoirs

instances: he promised to lend his aid for the suppression of the Galician insurrection under certain conditions. A plan for combined action was accordingly drawn up.

According to this scheme Ney was to advance from Corunna to Santiago with the 6th Corps, and was to drive the main body of the insurgents southward in the direction of Vigo and Tuy, following the line of the great coast-road. Soult meanwhile was to operate in the inland, against the enemy's exposed flank. He was to march from Lugo down the valley of the upper Minho, pushing before him all that stood in his way, with the object of thrusting the enemy on to Orense, and then towards the sea. If all went right, La Romana's army as well as the insurgents of the coast, would finally be enclosed between the two marshals and the Atlantic cliffs, and, as it was hoped, would be exterminated or forced to surrender. The obviously weak point of the plan was that it did not allow sufficiently for the power which the enemy possessed of escaping, by dispersion, or by taking to the mountains. Even if the details of the two movements had been carried out with perfect accuracy, it is probable that the Galicians would have crept out of some gap,

---

of the officers of both corps. ' Nous fûmes d'abord bien reçus à Lugo'— writes Soult's aide-de-camp St. Chamans—'mais le Maréchal Ney étant arrivé, les choses changèrent de face, et on eût dit que nous n'étions plus un corps français : tout nous était refusé : même nos malades mouraient en foule dans les hôpitaux, faute d'aliments : car tout était réservé, par les ordres de Ney, pour son corps d'armée, et on peut bien dire qu'on nous traita de Turc en Maure' (p. 150). Des Odoards is equally precise : ' Une fâcheuse mésintelligence a éclaté entre les troupes de Ney et les nôtres : les duels sont survenus, et peu s'en est fallu qu'oubliant que nous sommes, les uns et les autres, enfants de la France, il n'y ait eu engagement général. Le non-succès de notre entreprise, l'état de délabrement de notre tenue, ont servi de texte aux mauvaises plaisanteries, aux propos outrageants, dont des scènes sanguinaires ont été la suite. Les soldats seuls ont d'abord pris part à ces rixes, puis elles ont gagné les officiers, et s'il faut croire certain bruits, les maréchaux ont eu eux-mêmes une entrevue fort orageuse' (p. 240). According to the common report this ' stormy interview' actually ended in Ney's drawing his sword upon Soult, and being only prevented by General Maurice Mathieu from assailing him. This tale was told to Captain Boothby (see his *Memoirs*, ii. p. 31) by a French officer who said that he had been an eye-witness of the scene.

or slipped away between the converging corps, or saved themselves by a headlong retreat into Portugal.   The Marshals might
have captured Vigo and Orense: it is extremely unlikely that
they could have done more, especially as they had to deal with
a general like La Romana, who had made up his mind that his
duty was to avoid pitched battles, and to preserve his army at
all costs.   If Cuesta or Blake had been in command the scheme
would have been much more feasible ; but La Romana was the
only Spanish commander then in the field who had resolved
never to fight if he could help it.

On June 1 Ney and Soult parted, starting the one upon the
road to Corunna, the other upon that which makes for Orense
by the valley of the upper Minho.   It would seem that neither
of them had any great confidence in the success of the plan
adopted, and that each was possessed by the strongest doubts
as to the loyalty with which his colleague would support him[1].
Soult was on the watch for any good excuse for throwing up the
scheme and retiring to Zamora.   Ney was determined not to
risk himself and his corps overmuch, lest he should find himself
left in the lurch by Soult at the critical moment[1].

Meanwhile the Spaniards had been straining every nerve to
reorganize the army of Galicia, employing the short time of
respite that they had gained in drafting back into the old corps
the numerous stragglers who began to return to their colours as
the summer drew on, and in raising new battalions of volunteers.
La Romana lay in person at Orense with the main body of the
original army, which had now risen to a force of about 7,000
properly equipped men, and nearly 3,000 unarmed recruits: he
had still only four guns[2].   The ' Division of the Minho ' was
no longer under Carrera and Morillo : they had been superseded
by the arrival of the Conde de Noroña to whom the Central Junta
had given over the command.   This officer found himself at the

---

[1] 'Il se sépara de Ney, avec lequel il eût l'air d'arrêter, pour la
conservation de la Galice, un plan de campagne auquel tous les deux
étaient, je crois, résolus d'avance de ne pas se conformer, car ils voulaient
le moins possible se trouver ensemble.' St. Chamans (p. 151). This represents the view of Soult's staff.

[2] La Romana (June 1, in the Record Office) gives present at Orense
9,633 men—of whom 7,094 were old soldiers, including 381 cavalry and
379 artillery.

head of about 10,000 men, of whom only about 2,500 were regulars, the rest were peasantry new to the career of arms, but so much exhilarated by their late successes at Vigo and the Campo de Estrella, that it was hard to hold them back from taking the offensive[1]. Fortunately Noroña was gifted not only with tact but with caution: he knew how to keep the horde together without allowing them to get out of hand, and utterly refused to risk them in the open field[2].

On June 5 Ney arrived before Santiago with the main body of the 6th Corps—eighteen battalions, three cavalry regiments and two batteries: he had again left Corunna, Ferrol, and Lugo in the charge of very small garrisons, and was by no means without misgivings as to their fate during his absence. But he thought that his first duty was to concentrate a field force sufficiently large to face and beat the whole army of Galicia, in case La Romana should join Noroña for a combined attack on the 6th Corps.

On the news of the Marshal's approach the Spanish general drew back all his forces behind the estuary known as the Octavem (or Oitaben), a broad tidal stretch of water where several small mountain torrents meet at the head of a long bay. Noroña might have disputed the lines of the Ulla and the Vedra, but neither of these rivers affords such a good defensive position as the Oitaben. Here the hills of the interior come down much nearer to the sea than they do at the mouths of the Ulla and the Vedra, so that there is a much shorter line to defend, between low-water mark and the foot of the inaccessible Sierra de Suido. There was no road inland by which the position could be turned, so that the Galicians had only to guard the six miles of river-bank between the sea and the mountain. There were two bridges to be watched: the more important was that of Sampayo, where the main *chaussée* to Vigo passes the Oitaben just where it narrows down and ceases to be tidal. The second was that of Caldelas, four miles further inland, where a side-road to the village of Sotomayor crosses the Verdugo, the most northern of the three torrents which unite to form the Oitaben. Noroña had broken down four arches of the great Sampayo bridge.

---

[1] Carrol to Castlereagh, from Vigo, June 11.

[2] For some notes concerning Noroña's character see Arteche, vi. 188.

That of Caldelas he had not destroyed, but had barricaded : he
had drawn a double line of trenches on the hillside that dominates it, and placed there a battery containing some of his small
provision of artillery—he had but nine field-guns and two
mortars taken from the walls of Vigo.   Morillo was given charge
of this part of the position, Noroña took post himself at
Sampayo.   He had neglected no minor precaution that was
possible—some gunboats, one of which was manned by English
sailors drawn from the two frigates in the bay, patrolled the tidal
part of the Oitaben, and flanked the broken bridge.   Winter, the
senior naval officer present, put his marines on shore: along with
sixty stragglers from Moore's army, who had been liberated by the
peasants from French captivity, they garrisoned Vigo, which lies
a few miles beyond the Oitaben.

On June 7 Ney reached the front of the position and ascertained that the bridge of Sampayo was broken.   His artillery
exchanged some objectless salvos with that of Noroña, while
his cavalry rode inland to look for possible points of passage.
They could find none save the fortified bridge of Caldelas, and
a very difficult ford just above it, commanded, like the bridge,
by the Spanish trenches on the hillside.   The Marshal was also
informed that at the Sampayo itself there was another ford,
passable only at low tide for three hours at a time.

These reports were by no means encouraging : the Spanish
position was almost impregnable, and there was no way of
turning it.   Indeed the only road by which the enemy could be
taken in flank or rear was that from Orense to Vigo, along the
Minho.   This Ney could not reach: but supposing that Soult had
carried out the plan of operations to which he had assented on
June 1, it was just possible that he might appear, sooner or
later, on that line, and so dislodge the enemy.   However it was
equally possible that he might be still far distant, and so Ney
resolved to make an attempt to force the passage of the Oitaben.
On the morning of June 8 therefore, after a long but fruitless
cannonade, one body of infantry endeavoured to pass at the ford
opposite the village of Sampayo [1], while another, with some cavalry,

---

[1] Carrol, writing from Vigo two days later, says that the French
infantry ' seemed determined *at any risk* to cross the water at low tide,' that
they came on very boldly, but could not face the fire, and finally gave back.

attempted to cross the other ford at Caldelas, and to storm its bridge. At both places the Galicians stood their ground, and the heads of the column were exposed to such a furious fire that they suffered heavily and failed to reach the further bank. The Marshal therefore drew them back, and refused to persist in an attack which would only have had a chance of success if the enemy had misbehaved and given way to panic. The French lost several hundred men [1], the Galicians, safe in their trenches, suffered far less.

That evening Ney received news which convinced him that Soult had left him in the lurch, and had no intention of prosecuting his march on Orense, to turn the enemy's flank. It was reported that the 2nd Corps, after making only two days' march from Lugo, had stopped short at Monforte de Lemos, and showed no signs of moving forward. Indeed the Duke of Dalmatia had put the regiments into cantonments and was evidently about to make a lengthy halt.

Since the Duke of Elchingen was now convinced that the enemy could not be dislodged from behind the Oitaben without his colleague's aid, and since that colleague showed no signs of appearing within any reasonable time, the game was up. On the morning of the ninth Ney gave orders for his troops to draw off, and to retire by the road to Santiago and Corunna. He made no secret of his belief that Soult had deliberately betrayed him, and had never intended to keep his promise [2]. Without the aid of the 2nd Corps he had no hopes of being able to suppress the Galician insurrection. But till he should learn precisely what his colleague was doing, he could not make up his mind to abandon the province. He therefore sent off on June 10 an aide-de-camp with a large escort, by the circuitous route via Lugo. This officer bore a dispatch, which explained the situation, reported the check at Sampayo, and demanded

---

[1] Carrol, in the letter just quoted, says that thirty-nine dead bodies were left before the bridge-head of Caldelas, which the French could not carry off because of the hot fire that played upon the spot. He estimates the French total loss at 300, while that of Noroña was only 111.

[2] 'I have been assured,' says Napier (ii. 127), ' by an officer of Ney's personal staff [Col. D'Esménard] that he rashly concluded that personal feelings had swayed Soult to betray the 6th Corps. In this error he returned in wrath to Corunna.' But was his conclusion rash, or wrong?

that the 2nd Corps should not move any further away, but should return to lend aid to the 6th in its time of need. It was more than ten days before an answer was received. But on the twenty-first Soult's reply came to hand : he had been found marching, not towards Orense, but eastward, in the direction of the frontiers of Leon. He refused to turn back, alleging that this was not in the bond signed at Lugo, and that his troops were in such a state of exhaustion that he was forced to lead them into the plains, to rest them and refit them. Such a reply seemed to justify Ney's worst suspicions; abandoned by his colleague, and with the care of the whole of Galicia thrown upon his hands, he refused to risk the safety of the 6th Corps in the unequal struggle. He evacuated Corunna and Ferrol on the twenty-second and concentrated his whole force at Lugo. There he picked up the sick and wounded of Soult's corps as well as his own, and in six forced marches retired along the high-road by Villafranca to Astorga, which place he reached on June 30. Every day he had been worried and molested by the local guerrillas, but neither Noroña nor La Romana had dared to meddle with him. In his anger at the constant attacks of the insurgents, he sacked every place that he passed, from Villafranca and Ponferrada down to the smallest hamlets. Twenty-seven Galician towns and villages are said to have been burned by the 6th Corps during its retreat. Such conduct was unworthy of a soldier of Ney's calibre : it can only be explained by the fact that he was almost beside himself with wrath at being foiled by Soult's breach of his plighted word, and vented his fury on the only victims that he could reach.

We must now turn back to trace the steps of the 2nd Corps in its devious march from Lugo to the plains of Leon. Soult had sent out Loison with one division by the road down the left bank of the Minho on June 1. He himself followed with the rest of the army on the next day. On the third the Marshal reached the little town of Monforte de Lemos, between the Minho and the Sil, which he found deserted by its inhabitants. In obedience to La Romana's orders they had all gone up into the mountains.

If Soult had been honestly desirous of carrying out his compact with Ney, his next step would have been to make a rapid march on Orense. He must have been able to calculate that his colleague would now be in touch with Noroña's forces somewhere to the south of Corunna, and it was his duty to co-operate by descending the Minho in the enemy's rear. The mere fact that he remained for the unconscionable space of eight days at Monforte, is a sufficient proof that he never intended to carry out his part of the compact. During this time [June 3–11], while Ney was fighting out to an unsuccessful end his campaign against Noroña, Soult was absolutely quiescent, at a place only thirty miles from his starting-point at Lugo. He was unmolested save by small bands of local guerrillas, who fled to the hills whenever they were faced. His official chronicler Le Noble pleads that there were no fords to be found either over the Minho or over the Sil [1]. But in eight days, unopposed by any serious enemy, the engineers of the 2nd Corps could certainly have built bridges if the Marshal had ordered them to do so. Meanwhile the troops rested, and rejoiced in the abundant supplies of food and wine which they gathered in from the neighbourhood, for Monforte lies in the centre of a fertile upland and its neighbourhood had never before suffered from the ills of war [2].

On the eleventh Soult at last moved on. But it was not in the direction of Orense. He had no news of Ney, and professed to be concerned that the 6th Corps had not yet been heard of on the Orense road. Finally he announced that he was compelled to believe that the Duke of Elchingen had not executed his part of the joint campaign [3], and that there was no longer any reason that the 2nd Corps should carry out its share of the plan. Accordingly he marched, not toward Ney, but in the opposite direction, up the valley of the Sil, with his face set towards the east. He pretended that he hoped to catch and disperse the corps of La Romana, to whom he attributed a design of marching on Puebla de Senabria—the same movement that the Marquis had executed once before in the first days of March. But as a matter of fact La Romana was at Orense, and far from

---

[1] Le Noble, p. 280.

[2] Fantin des Odoards, p. 242.

[3] ' Le Maréchal crut, *ou feignit de croire,* que Ney avait changé d'idée,' says his aide-de-camp St. Chamans, p. 151.

having any intention of retreating eastward, if he were attacked
by the 2nd Corps, he was looking on Portugal as his line of
retreat [1].

On the thirteenth Soult reached Montefurado, where the Sil
is bridged by masses of rocks which have fallen into its bed:
the river forces its way beneath them by a tunnel sixty feet
broad, which is supposed to have been cut by the Romans.
Crossing on this natural bridge, he turned southward to follow
the valley of the Bibey, which leads to Puebla de Senabria and
the plains of Leon. He met no resistance save from the local
insurgents, headed by the Abbot of Casoyo and a partisan
called El Salamanquino, who received little or no aid from the
regular army. Indeed the only Spanish troops in this remote
corner of Galicia were 200 men under an officer called Echevarria, a dépôt left behind at Puebla de Senabria by La Carrera,
when he had marched to Vigo in May. This handful of men
joined the local guerrillas, and the appearance of their uniforms
among the enemy's ranks served Soult as an excuse for stating
that he was contending with the army of La Romana. Any
reader of his dispatches would conclude that during the last
days of June he was opposed by a considerable body of that
force. As a matter of fact he was never anywhere near the
Galician army, which lay first at Orense, then at Celanova,
finally at Monterey on the Portuguese frontier, always moving
to the right, parallel with the Marshal's advance, so as to avoid
being outflanked on its southern wing. It was with the
peasants of the valley of the Bibey alone that Soult had to do.
Thrusting them to right and left, and cruelly ravaging the
country-side on both banks of the river, he reached Viana on
June 16. From thence Franceschi sent a flying expedition over
the hills to La Gudina, on the road from Monterey to Puebla de
Senabria. It brought back news that La Romana had come
down to Monterey when the 2nd Corps moved to Viana, but
that he was evidently not marching eastward. It had met and

---

[1] La Romana writes to Carrol from Orense, on June 9, to say that he
had been intending to march by cross-roads to fall on Ney's flank, and so
aid the division of Noroña. But Soult's appearance at Monforte with
12,000 men [an under-estimate] compels him to remain behind to observe
that marshal [Record Office].

routed a party of Spanish cavalry sent out from Monterey [1]; the prisoners taken from them said that the Marquis was returning to Orense now that he had seen the 2nd Corps committing itself to an advance up the valley of the Bibey, and passing away in the direction of the plains of Leon.

It was while halting at Larouco, during this march, that Soult received the dispatch which Ney had written to him from Santiago on June 10. His reply, as we have already seen, was a peremptory refusal to turn back to the aid of the 6th Corps. He asserted that he had fulfilled his part of the bargain made at Lugo (which he assuredly had not), and refused to undertake any further offensive operations with troops in a state of utter destitution and fatigue. He declared to his staff, and wrote to King Joseph, that he believed that Ney had deliberately mismanaged his expedition against Vigo, and had suffered himself to be checked, in order to have an excuse for detaining the 2nd Corps in Galicia [2]. Why, he asked, had not the Duke of Elchingen sent a turning column against Orense, instead of making a frontal attack against the line of the Oitaben? The plain answer to this query—viz. that Ney with a field-force of only 10,000 men, and having three weak garrisons behind him, could not afford either to divide his army or to go too far from Corunna and Lugo—he naturally did not give.

Accordingly, on June 23, Soult abandoned the valley of the Bibey, and crossed the watershed of the Sierra Segundera in two columns, one descending on to La Gudina, the other on to

---

[1] Carrol was with this party. He had come out from Vigo to join La Romana, was at La Gudina on June 16, and retreated to Monterey when Franceschi attacked that point. The Marquis turned back when he saw Franceschi move off eastward, and retired to his old head quarters at Orense. If Soult had pushed westward, the Spaniards had the choice between the road to Chaves and that back to Orense, and were in no danger.

[2] 'Il (Ney) m'engageait à rester en Galice, et me représentait qu'il pourrait résulter pour lui de fâcheuses conséquences si j'en sortais. Cette proposition m'étonna : il me parut que M. le Maréchal Ney se conduisait à m'obliger à rester en Galice : car certainement rien ne l'empêchait de manœuvrer sur Orense, tandis que moi-même j'agissais contre La Romana. . . . Je me crus encore plus obligé qu'auparavant de suivre mon premier projet.' Soult to Joseph, June 25.

Lobian. On the twenty-fourth and twenty-fifth the whole army was united at Puebla de Senabria. The town was taken without a shot being fired; and the French found there several cannon which La Carrera had not carried off when he marched to Vigo, and which Echevarria had spiked but neglected to destroy. The corps rested for five days in Puebla de Senabria, where it obtained abundance of food and comfortable lodging. But Franceschi and his light-horse, now reduced to not more than 700 sabres, were pushed on at once to Zamora, to bear news to King Joseph of the approach of the 2nd Corps, and to beg that the stores, money, artillery, and clothing, which Soult had demanded in his letter from Lugo, might be forwarded to him as soon as possible [1]. Although the authorities at Madrid had heard nothing of the doings of the Marshal since June 1, they had already prepared much of the material required, and sent it to Salamanca. From thence it was now transferred to Zamora and Benavente, where it was handed over to the war-worn 2nd Corps. Other stores were procured from Valladolid and even from Bayonne. But the artillery, the most important of all the necessaries, was long in coming.

Soult's main body had broken up from Puebla de Senabria on June 29: from thence Mermet's, Delaborde's, and Lorges' troops marched to Benavente, and those of Merle and Heudelet to Zamora. In these places they enjoyed a few days of rest and began to refit themselves. But it was not long before they were called upon to take part in another great campaign, and once more to face their old enemies the English.

[1] On reaching Zamora, Franceschi handed over the charge of his division to General Pierre Soult, the Marshal's brother, and rode on towards Madrid with no escort but two aides-de-camp. They were captured near Toro by the celebrated guerrilla chief El Capuchino (Fray Juan Delica), who sent the important dispatches which they were bearing to Seville: Frere instantly forwarded a copy to Wellesley (July 9), who thus got invaluable information as to Soult's situation and future intentions. In the Record Office there is a letter requesting that the news of Franceschi's captivity may be sent to his wife in Paris, which was duly done. The unfortunate general was imprisoned first at Granada and then at Cartagena: in both places, it is said, he was treated with unjustifiable rigour, and kept in close confinement within four walls— it was the same usage that Napoleon meted out to Palafox. He died of a fever in 1811, after two years' captivity.

The first care of the Duke of Dalmatia, after he had emerged from the Galician Sierras, had been to write long justificatory dispatches to the Emperor and King Joseph. They are most interesting documents, and explain with perfect clearness his reasons for abandoning Ney and returning to the valley of the Douro. His main thesis is that it was his duty to keep the English in check, since they were the one really dangerous enemy in the Peninsula. Since it was notorious that Wellesley had quitted Northern Portugal, it was practically certain that he must be intending to march southward, to fall upon Victor, and strike a blow at Madrid. It was necessary, therefore, that the 2nd Corps should follow him, and be ready to aid in the defence of the capital. The safety of Madrid was far more important than the subjection of Galicia, and the Marshal had no hesitation in sacrificing the lesser object in order to secure the greater. Ney, he thought, would be strong enough to make head against Noroña and La Romana united : but he could not hope to hold down the whole of Galicia, and he would have either to be reinforced, or to be permitted to evacuate the province.

As to the conquest of Galicia, it would take many men and many months. At present it would be impossible to find the forces necessary for its complete subjection. This could only be done by fortifying not merely Corunna, Ferrol, and Lugo, but also Tuy, Monterey, Viana, and Puebla de Senabria. Each of these places should be given a garrison of 5,000 or 6,000 men, and furnished with stores calculated to last for four months. In addition there would have to be blockhouses built along the high-road from Lugo to Villafranca, and on several other lines. Columns operating from each of the seven great garrisons should be continually moving about, keeping open the communication between stronghold and stronghold, and chastising the insurgents.

Thus Soult calculated that the subjection of Galicia would require from 35,000 to 42,000 men, continually on the move, and never liable to be called upon for any service outside the province. It was absurd, therefore, for him to suggest in a later paragraph that Ney might be left to hold his own. What was the use of setting 15,000 men to work on a task that would strain the energies of 35,000 ? And where was King Joseph

to find the additional 20,000 men, if the 2nd Corps were withdrawn into Leon to watch the British army? No such force
could be drawn from any other part of Spain, and it would be
useless to ask for reinforcements from France while the Austrian
War was calling every available man to the Danube. Soult's
view, clearly, was that Galicia would have to be abandoned for
the present, though he did not choose to say so. Till the
English had been destroyed, or driven into the sea, King Joseph
would never be able to find 35,000 men to lock up in the remote
and mountainous north-western corner of the Peninsula [1].

There is not the slightest doubt that Soult's views were
perfectly correct. Looking at the war in the Peninsula as
a whole, it was a strategical blunder to endeavour to hold
Galicia before Portugal had been conquered. And while the
force of the French armies in Spain remained at its present
figure, it was impossible to spare two whole army corps for this
secondary theatre of operations. The attempt to subdue the
province had only been made because Moore had drawn after
him to Corunna the armies of Soult and Ney: and, since they
were on the spot, the temptation to use them there was too
great to be withstood. This is but one more instance of the
way in which the famous march to Sahagun had disarranged all
the Emperor's original plans for the conquest of the Peninsula.

It has often been debated whether it would be truer to say
that Galicia was delivered by Wellesley's operations or by the
valour and obstinacy of its own inhabitants. After giving all
due credit to the gallant peasantry who checked Ney and
harassed Soult, to the prudence of the untiring La Romana,
and to Noroña's cautious courage, it is yet necessary to decide
that the real cause of the evacuation of the province by the
invaders was the presence of the victorious British army in
Portugal. The two Marshals might have maintained themselves
there for an indefinite time, if they could have shut their eyes to

---

[1] There is so much valuable information in these dispatches of Soult,
dated June 25, from Puebla de Senabria, that I have printed the most
important paragraphs as an Appendix—omitting the lengthy narrative of
the operations on the Sil and the Bibey in which the Marshal vainly
flattered himself that he had dispersed the armies of La Romana and
'Chavarria' (i. e. Echevarria).

what was going on elsewhere. But Soult was quite right in believing that it would be mad to persist in the attempt to subdue Galicia, while Wellesley was in the field, and nothing lay between him and Madrid but the 22,000 men of the 1st Corps. If he and Ney had lingered on in the north, engaged in fruitless hunting after La Romana, while July and August wore on, Madrid would have fallen into the hands of Wellesley and Cuesta, and King Joseph would once more have been forced to go upon his travels, to Burgos or elsewhere. The Talavera campaign only failed of success because the 2nd and the 6th Corps were withdrawn from the Galician hills just in time to concentrate at Salamanca and fall upon the rear of the victors. If they had been wandering around Monterey or Mondonedo at the end of July, instead of being cantoned in the plains of Leon, the capital of Spain would undoubtedly have been recovered by Wellesley and Cuesta—though whether those ill-assorted colleagues could have held it for long is another question. Into such possibilities it is useless to make inquiry.

N.B.—My best authority for this campaign is the set of dispatches by Carrol in the Record Office. He was at Vigo from June 3 to June 14; with La Romana from June 16 to July 11. Thus he was on the spot for the fight on the Oitaben, and also for the operations against Soult. Napier's narrative is more than usually faulty in dealing with the end of the Galician campaign. He writes as a partisan of Soult, and his whole tale is drawn from the Marshal's dispatches and from the book of the panegyrist, Le Noble. His whole picture of the desperate condition of La Romana is untrue: the Marquis had always open to him a safe retreat into Portugal, and his army was never engaged with Soult at all. Carrol's dispatches make this quite clear. The map (facing p. 125 of vol. ii.) is so hopelessly inaccurate both as to distances, and as to the relative positions of places to each other, that I can only compare it to those ingenious diagrams which a railway produces, in order to show that it possesses the shortest route from London to Edinburgh, or from Brussels to Berlin.

SECTION XV: CHAPTER III

OPERATIONS IN ARAGON : ALCAÑIZ AND BELCHITE
(MARCH–JUNE 1809)

WHEN, upon February 20, the plague-stricken remnant of the much-enduring garrison of Saragossa laid down their arms at the feet of Lannes, it seemed probable that the whole of North-Eastern Spain must fall a helpless prey to the invader. The time had come when the 3rd and the 5th Corps, freed from the long strain of the siege, were once more available for field-operations. For the last two months almost every dispatch that the Emperor or King Joseph wrote, had been filled with plans and projects that began with the words 'When Saragossa shall have fallen.' If only Palafox and his desperate bands were removed, it would be easy to trample down Aragon, to take Catalonia in the rear, and finally to march to the gates of Valencia, and end the struggle on the eastern coast.

Now at last the 30,000 men of Mortier and Junot could be turned to other tasks, and there seemed to be every reason to expect that they would suffice to carry out the Emperor's designs. There was no army which could be opposed to them, for, only a few days after the capitulation of Saragossa, Reding had risked and lost the battle of Valls, and the wrecks of his host had taken refuge within the walls of Tarragona.

The only surviving Spanish force which was under arms in the valley of the Ebro consisted of the single division, not more than 4,000 strong, under the Marquis of Lazan. After his vain attempt to come to the rescue of Saragossa in the early days of February, Lazan had drawn back to Fraga and Monzon, forced to look on from afar at the last stage of his brother's desperate resistance. In the rest of the kingdom of Aragon there were but two or three scattered battalions of new levies[1], and some guerrilla bands under Perena and other chiefs.

[1] See sect. xi. chap. i. pp. 101–2.

The mistaken policy which had led Joseph Palafox to shut up in Saragossa not only his own army but also the succours which he had procured from Valencia and Murcia, now bore its fruit. There was no force left which could take the field against the victorious army of Lannes. It seemed therefore that the war in Aragon must come to a speedy end: the French had but to advance and the whole kingdom must fall into their hands. The national cause, however, was not quite so desperate as might have been supposed. Here, as in other regions of Spain, it was ere long to be discovered that it was one thing to destroy a Spanish army, and another to hold down a Spanish province. A French corps that was irresistible when concentrated on the field of battle, became vulnerable when forced to divide itself into the number of small garrisons that were needed for the permanent retention of the territory that it had won. Though the capital of Aragon and its chief towns were to remain in the hands of the enemy for the next five years, yet there were always rugged corners of the land where the struggle was kept up and the invader baffled and held in check.

Yet immediately after the fall of Saragossa it seemed for a space that Aragon might settle down beneath the invader's heel. Lannes, whose health was still bad, returned to France, but Mortier and Junot, who now once more resumed that joint responsibility that they had shared in December, went forth conquering and to conquer. They so divided their efforts that the 5th Corps operated for the most part to the north, and the 3rd Corps to the south of the Ebro, though occasionally their lines of operations crossed each other.

The kingdom of Aragon consists of three well-marked divisions. On each side of the Ebro there is a wide and fertile plain, generally some thirty miles broad. But to the north and the south of this rich valley lie range on range of rugged hills. Those on the north are the lower spurs of the Pyrenees: those to the south form part of the great central ganglion of the Sierras of Central Spain, which lies just where Aragon, Valencia, and New Castile meet.

The valley of the Ebro gave the French little trouble: it was not a region that could easily offer resistance, for it was destitute of all natural defences. Moreover, the flower of its manhood

had been enrolled in the battalions which had perished at Saragossa, and few were left in the country-side who were capable
of bearing arms—still fewer who possessed them. The plain of
Central Aragon lay exhausted at the victor's feet. It was otherwise with the mountains of the north and the south, which
contain some of the most difficult ground in the whole of Spain.
There the rough and sturdy hill-folk found every opportunity
for resistance, and when once they had learnt by experience the
limitations of the invader's power, were able to keep up a petty
warfare without an end. Partisans like Villacampa in the
southern hills, and Mina in the Pyrenean valleys along the edge
of Navarre, succeeded in maintaining themselves against every
expedition that was sent against them. Always hunted, often
brought to bay, they yet were never crushed or destroyed.

But in March 1809 the Aragonese had not yet recognized
their own opportunities : the disaster of Saragossa had struck
such a deep blow that apathy and despair seemed to have spread
over the greater part of the kingdom. When Mortier and
Junot, after giving their corps a short rest, began to spread
movable columns abroad, there was at first no resistance. The
inaccessible fortress of Jaca in the foot-hills of the Pyrenees
surrendered at the first summons ; its garrison was only 500
strong, yet it should have made some sort of defence against
a force consisting of no more than a single regiment of Mortier's
corps, without artillery. [March 21 [1].] The fall of this place
was important, as it commands the only pass in the Central
Pyrenees which is anything better than mule-track. Though
barely practicable for artillery or light vehicles, it was useful
for communication between Saragossa and France, and gave the
French army of Aragon a line of communication of its own, independent of the long and circuitous route by Tudela and Pampeluna.

[1] Toreno gives some curious details about the surrender of Jaca, which
he says was largely due to the intrigues of a friar named José de
Consolation, who preached resignation and submission to God's will in
such moving terms that the greater part of the garrison deserted ! He
was afterwards found to have been an agent of the French. The central
Junta sent the Governor Campos, the Corregidor Arcón, and the officers
commanding the artillery and engineers before a court-martial, which
condemned them all to death. Only the engineer was caught (he had
openly joined the French) and shot. [Arteche, vi. p. 10.]

Other columns of Mortier's corps marched against Monzon and Fraga, the chief towns in the valley of the Cinca. On their approach the Marquis of Lazan retired down the Ebro to Tortosa, and both towns were occupied without offering resistance. Another column marched against Mequinenza, the fortress at the junction of the Ebro and Segre : here, however, they met with opposition ; the place was only protected by antiquated sixteenth-century fortifications, but it twice refused to surrender, though on the second occasion Mortier himself appeared before its walls with a whole brigade. The Marshal did not besiege it, deferring this task till he should have got all of Eastern Aragon well in hand. At this same time he made an attempt to open communications with St. Cyr in Catalonia, sending a regiment of cavalry under Colonel Briche to strike across the mountains beyond the Segre in search of the 7th Corps. Briche executed half his mission, for by great good fortune combined with very rapid movement, he slipped between Lerida and Mequinenza, got down into the coast-plain and met Chabot's division of St. Cyr's army at Montblanch. When, however, he tried to return to Aragon, in order to convey to the Duke of Treviso the information as to the distribution of the 7th Corps, he was beset by the *somatenes*, who were now on the alert. So vigorously was he assailed that he was forced to turn back and seek refuge with Chabot. Thus Mortier gained none of the news that he sought, and very naturally came to the conclusion that his flying column had been captured or cut to pieces.

Meanwhile Junot and the 3rd Corps were operating south of the Ebro. The Duke of Abrantes sent one of his three divisions (that of Grandjean) against Caspe, Alcañiz, and the valleys of the Guadalope and Martin, while another (that of Musnier) moved out against the highlands of the south, and the mountain-towns of Daroca and Molina. Most of the battalions of his third division, that of Morlot, were still engaged in guarding on their way to France the prisoners of Saragossa.

Of the two expeditions which Junot sent out, that which entered the mountains effected little. It lost several small detachments, cut off by the local insurgents, and though it ultimately penetrated as far as Molina, it was unable to hold the place. The whole population had fled, and after remaining there only six days, the French were forced to return to the plains by want of food. [March 22–April 10.] The Aragonese at once came back to their former position.

Grandjean, who had moved against Alcañiz, had at first more favourable fortune. He overran with great ease all the low-lying country south of the Ebro, and met with so little opposition that he resolved to push his advance even beyond the borders of Valencia. Accordingly he ascended the valley of the Bercantes, and appeared before Morella, the frontier town of that kingdom, on March 18. The place was strong, but there was only a very small garrison in charge of it [1], which retired after a slight skirmish, abandoning the fortress and a large store of food and equipment. If Grandjean could have held Morella, he would have secured for the French army a splendid base for further operations. But he had left many men behind him at Caspe and Alcañiz, and had but a few battalions in hand. He had gone too far forward to be safe, and when the Junta of Valencia sent against him the whole of the forces that they could collect—some 5,000 men under General Roca—he was compelled to evacuate Morella and to fall back on Alcañiz. [March 25.]

Mortier and Junot were concerting a joint movement for the completion of the conquest of Eastern Aragon, and an advance against Tortosa, when orders from Paris suddenly changed the whole face of affairs. The Emperor saw that war with Austria was inevitable and imminent: disquieted as to the strength of the new enemy, he resolved to draw troops from Spain to reinforce the army of the Danube. The only corps which seemed to him available was that of Mortier, and on April 5 he ordered that the Duke of Treviso should concentrate his troops and draw back to Tudela and Logroño. It might still prove to be unnecessary to remove the 5th Corps from the Peninsula; but at Logroño it would be within four marches of France if the Emperor discovered that he had need of its services in the north. On the same day Napoleon removed Junot from his command, probably

---

[1] Only the single regiment, America, whose cadre, sent back by Infantado from Cuenca, was being filled up with recruits from the Morella district. [Junot to King Joseph, from Saragossa, March 25.]

on account of the numerous complaints as to his conduct sent
in by King Joseph.   To replace him General Suchet, the commander of one of Mortier's divisions, was directed to take
charge of the 3rd Corps [1].

Ten days later the imperial mandate reached Saragossa, and
on receiving it Mortier massed his troops and marched away to
Tudela.   We have already seen [2] that his corps was never withdrawn from Spain, but merely moved from Aragon to Old
Castile.   But its departure completely changed the balance of
fortune on the Lower Ebro. The number of French troops in that
direction was suddenly reduced by one half, and the 3rd Corps
had to spread itself out to the north, in order to take over all
the positions evacuated by Mortier.   It was far too weak for
the duty committed to its charge, and at this moment it had
not even received back the brigade sent to guard the Saragossa
prisoners, which (it will be remembered) had been called off and
lent to Kellermann [3].   There were hardly 15,000 troops left in
the whole kingdom of Aragon, and these were dispersed in
small bodies, with the design of holding down as much ground
as possible.   The single division of Grandjean had to cover the
whole line from Barbastro to Alcañiz—places seventy miles
apart—with less than 5,000 bayonets.   The second division,
Musnier's, with its head quarters at Saragossa, had to watch the
mountains of Upper Aragon.   Of the 3rd division, that of
Morlot, the few battalions that were available were garrisoning
Jaca and Tudela, on the borders of Navarre.   No sooner had
Mortier's corps departed, than a series of small reverses occurred,
the inevitable results of the attempt to hold down large districts
with an inadequate force.   Junot, who was still retained in
command till his successor should arrive, seemed to lack the
courage to draw in his exposed detachments : probably his
heart was no longer in the business, since he was under sentence
of recall.   Yet he had six weeks of work before him, for by
some mischance the dispatch nominating Suchet to take his
place reached Saragossa after that general had marched off at
the head of his old division of Mortier's corps.   Cross-communi-

---

[1] See Joseph's letter of April 6, and the Emperor's orders, from Paris,
of April 5 and April 10.

[2] See p. 378.   [3] See p. 378.

cation being tardy and difficult, it failed to catch him up till he
had reached Valladolid. Returning from thence with a slow-
moving escort of infantry, Suchet did not succeed in joining his
corps till May 19. He found it in a desperate situation, for the
last four weeks had seen an almost unbroken series of petty
reverses, and it looked as if the whole of Aragon was about to
slip out of the hands of the French. It was fortunate for the
3rd Corps that its new commander, though hitherto he had
never been placed in a position of independent responsibility,
proved to be a man of courage and resource—perhaps indeed
the most capable of all the French generals who took part in
the Peninsular War. A timid or unskilful leader might have
lost Aragon, and imperilled the hold of King Joseph on Madrid.
It is hardly an exaggeration to say that the entire French
position in Spain would have been gravely compromised if
during the last weeks of May the 3rd Corps had been under the
charge of a less skilful and self-reliant commander.

In the month that elapsed before Suchet's arrival the consequences of the withdrawal of the 5th Corps from the Lower
Ebro were making themselves felt. The Aragonese were not
slow to discover the decrease in the numbers of the invaders,
and to note the long distances that now intervened between
post and post. The partisans who had retired into Catalonia,
or had taken refuge in the mountains of the south and the
north, began to descend into the plains and to fall upon the
outlying French detachments. On May 6 Colonel Perena came
out of Lerida, and beset the detachment of Grandjean's division
which held the town and fortress of Monzon, with a horde of
peasants and some Catalan *miqueletes.* The governor, Solnicki,
thereupon fell back to Barbastro, the head quarters of Habert's
brigade. That general considered that he was in duty bound
to retake Monzon, and marched against it with six battalions
and a regiment of cuirassiers. He tried to cross the Cinca, not
opposite the town, but much lower down the stream, at the
ferry of Pomar. [May 16.] But just as his vanguard[1] had

---

[1] It consisted of eight *compagnies d'élite*, viz. the *voltigeur* companies of
the 14th Line, and the 2nd of the Vistula, and the grenadier and voltigeur
companies of the 116th of the Line, with half a squadron of the 13th
Cuirassiers. [Von Brandt, p. 62.]

established itself on the other bank, a sudden storm caused such a rising of the waters that its communication with the main body was completely cut off. Thereupon Habert marched northward, and tried to force a passage at Monzon, so as to secure a line of retreat for his lost detachment. The bridge of that town however had been barricaded, and the castle garrisoned: Habert was held at bay, and the 1,000 men who had crossed at the ferry of Pomar were all cut off and forced to surrender. After marching for three days among the insurgents, and vainly endeavouring to force their way through the horde, they had to lay down their arms when their cartridges had all been exhausted. [May 19.] Only the cuirassiers escaped, by swimming the river when the flood had begun to abate, and found their way back to Barbastro.

In consequence of this disaster the French lost their grip on the valley of the Cinca, for the insurgents, under Perena and the Catalan chief Baget, moved forward into the Sierra de Alcuberre and raised the whole country-side in their aid. Habert, fearing to be cut off from Saragossa, thereupon retired to Villafranca on the Ebro, and abandoned all North-Eastern Aragon [1].

Meanwhile the other brigade of Grandjean's division, which still lay at Alcañiz, south of the Ebro, was also driven in by the Spaniards. Its commander Laval was attacked by a large force coming from Tortosa, and was forced to draw back to San Per and Hijar [May 18–19]. At the news of his retreat all the hill-country of Southern Aragon took arms, and the bands from Molina and the other mountain-cities extended their raids down the valley of the Huerta and almost to the gates of Saragossa.

The Spanish force which had seized Alcañiz was no mere body of armed peasants, but a small regular army. General

---

[1] This little campaign can be studied in detail in Von Brandt, pp. 60–8. He was serving as lieutenant in the 2nd of the Vistula, and gives many details which are not to be found in Suchet or Arteche. Toreno would seem (ii. 10) to be wrong in saying that Habert tried to storm Monzon, and got over the river there, but was beaten back by Baget. Von Brandt says that there was nothing but a hot fire across the water, and that the attack could not be pushed home.

Blake had just been given the post of commander-in-chief of all
the forces of the *Coronilla*—the old kingdom of Aragon and its
dependencies, Valencia and Catalonia. Burning to atone for
his defeats at Zornoza and Espinosa by some brilliant feat of
arms, he was doing his best to collect a new 'Army of the
Right.' From Catalonia he could draw little or nothing: the
troops which had fought under Reding at Valls were still cooped
up in Tarragona, and unfit for field-service. But Blake had
concentrated at Tortosa the division of the Marquis of Lazan—
the sole surviving fraction of the old Army of Aragon—and the
troops which he could draw from Valencia. These last consisted
at this moment of no more than the reorganized division of
Roca from the old 'Army of the Centre.' Its depleted *cadres*
had been sent back by Infantado from Cuenca, and the Junta had
shot into them a mass of recruits, who in a few weeks had raised
the strength of the division from 1,500 to 5,000 bayonets.
Other regiments were being raised in Valencia, but in the early
weeks of May they were not yet ready for the field, though by
June they gave Blake a reinforcement of nearly 12,000 men [1].

---

[1] It is necessary to enter a protest against Napier's statement (vol. ii.
p. 252), that Valencia did not do its fair share in defending the general
cause of Spain—that 'from the very commencement of the insurrection
its policy was characterized by a singular indifference to the calamities
that overwhelmed the other parts of the country.' The contribution of
Valencia to the national armies raised in 1808–9, compares well with that
of the other provinces. These troops, too, were not used for local defence,
but employed in other parts of Spain. Argüelles' answer to Napier on
this point seems conclusive : (see the appendix-volume of his *Observa-
ciones*, &c.). The troops sent out by Valencia were :—

	Men.
(1) To join the division of Llamas in the 'Army of the Centre' [Roca's later division], thirteen battalions, about .	6,000
(2) To join the division of O'Neille in Aragon, one regiment .	800
(3) To join the division of St. March in Aragon, nine battalions	6,000
(4) Joined Palafox at Saragossa between the date of Tudela and the commencement of the siege, one battalion .	500
(5) Sent to Catalonia in December, two battalions . .	800
(6) Raised to recruit Roca's division in January . . .	4,000
(7) Raised to join Blake between April and June 1809 . .	11,881
Total	29,981

These figures are exclusive of cavalry and artillery, and in some cases

Murcia could provide in May only one single battalion for Blake's assistance: all its field army had perished at Saragossa. The total force of the new 'Army of the Right' when it advanced against Alcañiz was less than 10,000 men—the Valencians in its ranks outnumbered the Aragonese by four to three.

When Suchet therefore arrived at Saragossa on May 19, and took over the command of the 3rd Corps from the hands of Junot, the prospect seemed a gloomy one for the French. Their outlying detachments had been forced back to the neighbourhood of Saragossa: the central reserve (Musnier's two brigades) was small: the third division (with the exception of one regiment) was still absent—one of its brigades was with Kellermann in Leon [1], and some detachments were scattered among the garrisons of Navarre. After the sick and the absent had been deducted, Suchet found that he had not much more than 10,000 men under arms, though the nominal force of the 3rd Corps was still about 20,000 sabres and bayonets. Nor was it only in numbers that the Army of Aragon was weak: its *morale* also left much to be desired. The newly-formed regiments which composed more than half of the infantry [2] were in a deplorable condition, a natural consequence of the haste with which they had been organized and sent into the field. Having been originally composed of companies drawn from many quarters, they still showed a mixture of uniforms of different cut and colour, which gave them a motley appearance and, according to their commander, degraded them in their own eyes and lowered their self-respect [3]. They had not yet fully recovered from the physical and moral strain of the siege of Saragossa. Their pay was in arrear, the military chest empty, the food procured from day to day by marauding. There was much grumbling among the officers, who complained that the

are under-estimated, as no morning-states of the troops survive for the earlier months of the campaign of 1808, and these totals are taken from returns made late in the year, when the regiments had begun to run low in numbers. For the enormous monetary contribution made by Valencia in 1808–9, see the tables in Argüelles.

[1] See p. 378.

[2] The 114th, 115th, 116th, 117th, and 121st of the line were all formed from the 'Provisional Regiments' of 1808.

[3] Suchet's *Mémoires*, i. p. 11.

promotions and rewards due for the capture of Saragossa had almost all been reserved for the 5th Corps. The guerrilla warfare of the last few weeks had disgusted the rank and file, who thought that Junot had been mismanaging them, and knew absolutely nothing of the successor who had just replaced him. The whole corps, says Suchet, was dejected and discontented [1].

Nevertheless there was no time to rest or reorganize these sullen battalions : the Spaniards were pressing in so close that it was necessary to attack them at all costs : the only other alternative would have been to abandon Saragossa. Such a step, though perhaps theoretically justifiable under the circumstances, would have ruined Suchet's military career, and was far from his thoughts. Only two days after he had assumed the command of the corps, he marched out with Musnier's division to join Laval's troops at Hijar. [May 21.] He had sent orders to Habert to cross the Ebro and follow him as fast as he was able : but that general, who was still on the march from Barbastro to Villafranca, did not receive the dispatch in time, and failed to join his chief before the oncoming battle [2].

[1] 'Le 3ᵐᵉ corps avait beaucoup souffert au siége de Saragosse. L'infanterie était considérablement affaiblie : les régiments de nouvelle formation surtout se trouvaient dans un état déplorable, par les vices inséparables d'une organisation récente et précipitée. . . . Des habits blancs bleus et de formes différentes, restes choquants de divers changements dans l'habillement, occasionnaient dans les rangs une bigarrure qui achevait d'enlever à des soldats déjà faibles et abattus toute idée de considération militaire. L'apparence de la misère les dégradait à leurs propres yeux . . . Dans un état voisin du découragement, cette armée était loin de compenser par sa force morale le danger de sa faiblesse numérique.' Suchet, p. 16.

Von Brandt speaks to much the same effect, and says that some of the troops gave a bad impression, and that he saw battalions which looked as if they would not stand firm against a sudden and fierce attack, such as that which Mina and his guerrillas used to deliver [p. 61].

[2] From a casual reading of Suchet, i. 17–21, it might be thought that the general had been joined by Habert before the battle. But he certainly was not, as the Memoirs of Von Brandt, who was with Habert, show that this brigade was at Villafranca, forty miles from Alcañiz, on the twenty-third, and only started (too late) to join its chief on the twenty-fourth. The mention of the 2nd of the Vistula on p. 21 of Suchet is a misprint for the 3rd of the Vistula of Musnier's division. Half the 13th Cuirassiers was also absent with Habert.

On May 23, however, Suchet, with Musnier's and Laval's men, presented himself in front of Blake's position at Alcañiz. He had fourteen battalions and five squadrons with him— a force in all of about 8,000 men, with eighteen guns [1]. He found the Spaniards ready and willing to fight. They were drawn up on a line of hills to the east of Alcañiz, covering that town and its bridge. Their position was good from a tactical point of view, but extremely dangerous when considered strategically : for Blake had been tempted by the strong ground into fighting with the river Guadalope at his back, and had no way of crossing it save by the single bridge of Alcañiz and a bad ford. It was an exact reproduction of the deplorable order of battle that the Russians had adopted at Friedland in 1807, though not destined to lead to any such disaster. The northern and highest of the three hills occupied by the Spaniards, that called the Cerro de los Pueyos, was held by the Aragonese troops. On the central height, called the hill of Las Horcas, was placed the whole of the Spanish artillery—nineteen guns—guarded by three Valencian battalions : this part of the line was immediately in front of the bridge of Alcañiz, the sole line of retreat. The southern and lowest hill, that of La Perdiguera, was held by Roca and the rest of the Valencians, and flanked by the small body of cavalry—only 400 sabres—which Blake possessed [2].

---

[1] According to Suchet's own figures from his May 15 return, the forces engaged must have been :—

Musnier's Division :		Laval's Brigade :	
114th Line (three batts.) .	1,627	14th Line (two batts.) .	1,080
115th Line (three batts.).	1,732	3rd of the Vistula (two batts.) . . .	964
1st of the Vistula (two batts.) . . .	1,039	Cavalry, 4th Hussars .	326
121st Line (one batt. only)	400	Half 13th Cuirassiers .	200
Detachment of the 64th and 40th of the Line [General's escort] .	450	Artillery . . .	320
	5,248		2,890

Total 8,138

[2] The Spanish line-of-battle was as follows :—

Left wing, General Areizaga :

    Daroca, Volunteers of Aragon, Tiradores de Doyle, Reserve of Aragon, 1st Tiradores de Murcia, Company of Tiradores de Cartagena—five and one-sixth batts.   2,669

The whole army, not quite 9,000 strong, outnumbered the enemy by less than 800 bayonets, though in French narratives it is often stated at 12,000 or 15,000 men [1].

Suchet seems to have found some difficulty at first in making out the Spanish position—the hills hid from him the bridge and town of Alcañiz, whose position in rear of Blake's centre was the dominant military fact of the situation. At any rate, he spent the whole morning in tentative movements, and only delivered his main stroke in the afternoon. He began by sending Laval's brigade against the dominating hill on the right flank of the Spanish position. Two assaults were made upon the Cerro de los Pueyos, which Suchet in his autobiography calls feints, but which Blake considered so serious that he sent off to this flank two battalions from his left wing and the whole of his cavalry. Whether intended as mere demonstrations or as a real attack, these movements had no success, and were repelled by General Areizaga, the commander of the Aragonese, without much difficulty. The Spanish cavalry, however, was badly mauled by Suchet's hussars when it tried to deliver a flank charge upon the enemy at the moment that he retired.

When all the fighting on the northern extremity of the line had died down, Suchet launched his main attack against Blake's centre, hoping (as he says) to break the line, seize the bridge of Alcañiz, which lay just behind the hill of Las Horcas, and thus to capture the greater part of the Spanish wings, which would have no line of retreat. The attack was delivered by two of

Centre, Marquis of Lazan :
  Volunteers of Valencia, Ferdinando VII, 3rd batt. of America,
    detachment of Traxler's Swiss—three and a half batts.   .   1,605
Right wing, General Roca :
  3rd batt. of Savoia, 2nd batt. of America, 1st of Valencia
    (three batts.), 2nd Cazadores of Valencia, 1st Volunteers
    of Saragossa—seven batts.   3,742
Cavalry (detachments of Santiago, Olivenza, and Husares
    Españoles)   445
Artillery   245

[1] Napier, for example, following French sources, gives Blake 12,000 men.

Musnier's regiments[1] formed in columns of battalions, and acting in a single mass—a force of over 2,600 men. A column of this strength often succeeded in bursting through a Spanish line during the Peninsular War. But on this day Suchet was unlucky, or his troops did not display the usual *élan* of French infantry. They advanced steadily enough across the flat ground, and began to climb the hill, in spite of the rapid and accurate fire of the artillery which crowned its summit. But when the fire of musketry from the Spanish left began to beat upon their flank, and the guns opened with grape, the attacking columns came to a standstill at the line of a ditch cut in the slope. Their officers made every effort to carry them forward for the few hundred yards that separated them from the Spanish guns, but the mass wavered, surged helplessly for a few minutes under the heavy fire, and then dispersed and fled in disorder. Suchet rallied them behind the five intact battalions which he still possessed, but refused to renew the attack, and drew off ere night. He himself had been wounded in the foot at the close of the action, and his troops had suffered heavily—their loss must have been at least 700 or 800 men[2]. Blake, who had lost no more than 300, did not attempt to pursue, fearing to expose his troops in the plain to the assaults of the French cavalry.

The morale of the 3rd Corps had been so much shaken by its unsuccessful début under its new commander, that a panic broke out after dark among Laval's troops, who fled in all directions, on a false alarm that the Spanish cavalry had attacked and captured the rearguard. Next morning the army poured into San Per and Hijar in complete disorder, and some hours had to be spent in restoring discipline. Suchet discovered the man who had started the cry of *sauve qui peut*, and had him shot before the day was over[3].

---

[1] Three battalions of the 114th of the Line, and two of the 1st of the Vistula.

[2] Suchet gives a very poor account of Alcañiz in his *Mémoires*. In spite of his many merits, he did not take a beating well, and slurs over this action, just as in 1812 he slurs over his defeat at Castalla. He does not even give an estimate of his killed and wounded, and has the assurance to say that he left the enemy only 'l'opinion de la victoire' (i. 20). Blake clearly makes too much of the French attack on his right in his dispatch.   [3] Suchet, *Mémoires*, p. 20.

The French had expected to be pursued, and many critics have blamed Blake for not making the most of his victory and following the defeated enemy at full speed. The Spanish general, however, had good reasons for his quiescence : he saw that Suchet's force was almost as large as his own ; he could not match the French in cavalry ; and having noted the orderly fashion in which they had left the battlefield, he could not have guessed that during the night they would disband in panic. Moreover—and this was the most important point—he was expecting to receive in a few days reinforcements from Valencia which would more than double his numbers. Till they had come up he would not move, but contented himself with sending the news of Alcañiz all over Aragon and stimulating the activity of the insurgents. As he had hoped, the results of his victory were important—the French had to evacuate every outlying post that they possessed, and the whole of the open country passed into the hands of the patriots. Perena and the insurgents of the north bank of the Ebro pressed close in to Saragossa : other bands threatened the high-road to Tudela : thousands of recruits flocked into Blake's camp, but he was unfortunately unable to arm or utilize them.

Within a few days, however, he began to receive the promised reinforcements from Valencia—a number of fresh regiments from the rear, and drafts for the corps that were already with him. He also used his authority as supreme commander in Catalonia to draw some reinforcements from that principality—three battalions of Reding's Granadan troops and one of *miqueletes*: no more could be spared from in front of the active St. Cyr. Within three weeks after his victory of Alcañiz he had collected an army of 25,000 men, and considered himself strong enough to commence the march upon Saragossa. It was in his power to advance directly upon the city by the high-road along the

---

[1] The drafts were so large that the troops of Lazan's division, which had numbered 3,979 in May, were 5,679 in June, those of Roca rose similarly from 3,449 to 5,525. The Valencian Junta claimed to have sent in all 11,881 men to reinforce Blake, and the returns bear them out. They also gave him 2,000,000 reals in cash—about £22,000—raised by a special contribution in fifteen days. Their report says that they had sent on every armed man in the province, and that the city was only guarded by peasants armed with pikes. (Argüelles.)

Ebro, and to challenge Suchet to a battle outside its southern
gates. He did not, however, make this move, but with a caution
that he did not often display, kept to the mountains and marched
by a side-road to Belchite [June 12]. Here he received news of
Napoleon's check at Essling, which had happened on the twenty-
second of the preceding month ; it was announced as a complete
and crushing defeat of the Emperor, and encouraged the
Spaniards in no small degree.

From Belchite Blake, still keeping to the mountains, pursued his march eastward to Villanueva in the valley of the
Huerba. This move revealed his design ; he was about to place
himself in a position from which he could threaten Suchet's lines
of communication with Tudela and Logroño, and so compel him
either to abandon Saragossa without fighting, or to come out
and attack the Spanish army among the hills. Blake, in short,
was trying to manœuvre his enemy out of Saragossa, or to induce
him to fight another offensive action such as that of Alcañiz
had been. After the experience of May 25 he thought that he
could trust his army to hold its ground, though he was not
willing to risk an advance in the open, across the level plain in
front of Saragossa.

Suchet meanwhile had concentrated his whole available force
in that city and its immediate neighbourhood ; he had drawn in
every man save a single column of two battalions, which was lying
at La Muela under General Fabre, with orders to keep back the
insurgents of the southern mountains from making a dash at
Alagon and cutting the high-road to Tudela. He had been
writing letters to Madrid, couched in the most urgent terms, to
beg for reinforcements. But just at this moment the Asturian
expedition had drawn away to the north all the troops in Old
Castile. King Joseph could do no more than promise that the
two regiments from the 3rd Corps which had been lent to
Kellermann should be summoned back, and directed to make
forced marches on Saragossa. He could spare nothing save
these six battalions, believing it impossible to deplete the
garrison of Madrid, or to draw from Valladolid the single
division of Mortier's corps, which was at this moment the only
solid force remaining in the valley of the Douro.

Suchet was inclined to believe that he might be attacked

before this small reinforcement of 3,000 men could arrive, and feared that, with little more than 10,000 sabres and bayonets, he would risk defeat if he attacked Blake in the mountains. The conduct of his troops in and after the battle of Alcañiz had not tended to make him hopeful of the result of another action of the same kind. Nevertheless, when Blake came down into the valley of the Huerba, and began to threaten his communications, he resolved that he must fight once again; the alternative course, the evacuation of Saragossa and a retreat up the Ebro, would have been too humiliating. Suchet devoted the three weeks of respite which the slow advance of the enemy allowed him to the reorganization of his corps. He made strenuous exertions to clothe it, and to provide it with its arrears of pay. He inspected every regiment in person, sought out and remedied grievances, displaced a number of unsatisfactory officers, and promoted many deserving individuals. He claims that the improvement in the morale of the troops during the three weeks when they lay encamped at Saragossa was enormous[1], and his statements may be verified in the narrative of one of his subordinates, who remarks that neither Moncey nor Junot had ever shown that keen personal interest in the corps which Suchet always displayed, and that the troops considered their new chief both more genial and more business-like than any general they had hitherto seen, and so resolved to do their best for him[2].

Forced to fight, but not by any means confident of victory, the French commander discharged on to Tudela and Pampeluna his sick, his heavy baggage, and his parks, before marching out to meet Blake upon June 14. The enemy, though still clinging to the skirts of the hills, had now moved so close to Saragossa that it was clear that he must be attacked at once, though Suchet would have preferred to wait a few days longer, till he should have rallied the brigade from Old Castile. These two regiments, under Colonel Robert, had now passed Tudela, and were expected to arrive on the fifteenth or sixteenth. But Blake had now descended the valley of the Huerba, and had pushed his outposts to within ten or twelve miles of Saragossa. He had reorganized his army

---

[1] Suchet, *Mémoires*, p. 23.
[2] Von Brandt, *Aus meinem Leben*, i. 67.

into three divisions, one of which (mainly composed of Aragonese troops) was placed under General Areizaga, while Roca and the Marquis of Lazan headed the two others, in which the Valencian levies predominated. Of the total of 25,000 men which the muster-rolls showed, 20,000 were in line: the rest were detached or in hospital. There were about 1,000 untrustworthy cavalry and twenty-five guns.

In his final advance down the Huerba, Blake moved in two columns. Areizaga's division kept to the right bank and halted at Botorita, some sixteen miles from Saragossa. The Commander-in-chief, with the other two divisions, marched on the left bank, and pushing further forward than his lieutenant, reached the village of Maria, twelve miles from the south-western front of the city. A distance of six or seven miles separated the two corps. Thus Blake had taken the strategical offensive, but was endeavouring to retain the tactical defensive, by placing himself in a position where the enemy must attack him. But he seems to have made a grave mistake in keeping his columns so far apart, on different roads and with a river between them. It should have been his object to make sure that every man was on the field when the critical moment should arrive.

Already on the morning of the fourteenth the two armies came into contact. Musnier's division met the Spanish vanguard, thrust it back some way, but then came upon Blake and the main body, and had to give ground. Suchet, on the same evening, established his head quarters at the Abbey of Santa Fé, and there dictated his orders for the battle of the following day. Having ascertained that Areizaga's division was the weaker of the two Spanish columns, he left opposite it, on the Monte Torrero, a mile and a half outside Saragossa, only a single brigade—five battalions—under General Laval, who had now become the commander of the 1st Division, for Grandjean had been sent back to France. Protected by the line of the canal of Aragon, these 2,000 men [1] were to do their best to beat off any attack which Areizaga might make against the city, while the main bodies of both armies were engaged elsewhere. The charge

[1] 44th of the Line, 1,069 bayonets, and 3rd of the Vistula, 964 bayonets, according to Suchet's figures.

of Saragossa itself was given over to Colonel Haxo, who had
but a single battalion of infantry[1] and the sapper-companies
of the army.

Having set aside these 3,000 men to guard his flank and rear,
Suchet could only bring forward Musnier's division, and the
remaining brigade of Laval's division (that of Habert), with
two other battalions, for the main attack. But he retained
with himself the whole of his cavalry and all his artillery, save
one single battery left with the troops on Monte Torrero. This
gave him fourteen battalions—about 7,500 infantry—800 horse,
and twelve guns—less than 9,000 men in all—to commence the
battle. But he was encouraged to risk an attack by the news
that the brigade from Tudela was now close at hand, and could
reach the field by noon with 3,000 bayonets more. It would
seem that Suchet (though he does not say so in his *Mémoires*)
held back during the morning hours, in order to allow this heavy
reserve time to reach the fighting-ground.

Blake was in order of battle along the line of a rolling hill
separated from the French lines by less than a mile. Behind
his front were two other similar spurs of the Sierra de la Muela,
each separated from the other by a steep ravine. On his right
flank was the river Huerba, with level fields half a mile broad
between the water's edge and the commencement of the rising
ground. The village of Maria lay to his right rear, some way
up the stream. The Spaniards were drawn out in two lines,
Roca's division on the northernmost ridge, Lazan's in its rear
on the second, while the cavalry filled the space between the hills
and the river. Two battalions and half a battery were in reserve,
in front of Maria. The rest of the artillery was placed in the
intervals of the first line.

The French occupied a minor line of heights facing Blake's
front: Habert's brigade held the left, near the river, having
the two cavalry regiments of Wathier in support. Musnier's
division formed the centre and right: a squadron of Polish
lancers was placed far out upon its flank. The only reserve
consisted of the two stray battalions which did not belong

---

[1] Apparently a battalion of the 121st of the Line, the rest of which
regiment was still in Navarre.

either to Musnier or Habert—one of the 5th Léger, another of
the 64th of the Line [1].

Blake's army was slow in taking up its ground, while Suchet
did not wish to move till the brigade from Tudela had got
within supporting distance.   Hence in the morning hours there
was no serious collision.   But at last the Spaniards took the
initiative, and pushed a cautious advance against Suchet's left,
apparently with the object of worrying him into assuming the
offensive rather than of delivering a serious attack.   But the
cloud of skirmishers sent against Habert's front grew so thick
and pushed so far forward, that at last the whole brigade was
seriously engaged, and the artillery was obliged to open upon
the swarm of Spanish *tirailleurs*.   They fell back when the
shells began to drop among them, and sought refuge by retiring
nearer to their main body [2].

About midday the bickering died down on the French left,
but shortly after the fire broke out with redoubled energy in
another direction.   Disappointed that he could not induce
Suchet to attack him, Blake had at last resolved to take the
offensive himself, and columns were seen descending from his
extreme left wing, evidently with the intention of turning the
French right.   Having thus made up his mind to strike, the
Spanish general should have sent prompt orders to his detached
division under Areizaga, to bid it cross the Huerba with all possible

---

[1] The battalion of the 5th Léger belonged to Morlot's division, the rest
of which was dispersed in Navarre or absent : that of the 64th was one
which Suchet had brought from Valladolid as his personal escort, and
which properly belonged to the 5th Corps.

[2] Suchet says the morning was occupied in mere ' tiraillement' of the
Spanish skirmishers and the 2nd of the Vistula.   This is not borne out
by the narrative of Von Brandt, of that corps.   He says that the enemy
came on ' sehr lebhaft,' that both battalions of his regiment were deeply
engaged, that a regiment of Spanish dragoons in yellow [he calls it
Numancia, but it was really Olivenza] charged into the skirmishing-line
and nearly broke it.   The 2nd of the Vistula used up all its cartridges,
and lost ground.   ' Die Kavalleriezüge wurden jedoch jedesmal zurück-
gewiesen, aber nichtsdestoweniger verloren wir allmählich Terrain.'   The
Spaniards were only driven off by a battery being drawn forward into the
fighting-line.   Then the fight stood still, but the regiment had suffered
very heavily, and was finally drawn back and put into the reserve.   (*Aus
meinem Leben*, pp. 71-2.)

speed, and hasten to join the main body before the engagement
had grown hot. It could certainly have arrived in two hours,
since it was but six or seven miles away. But Blake made no
attempt to call in this body of 6,000 men (the best troops in his
army) or to utilize it in any way. He only employed the two
divisions that were under his hand on the hillsides above Maria.

The attack on the French right, made between one and two
o'clock, precipitated matters. When Suchet saw the Spanish
battalions beginning to descend from the ridge, he ordered his
Polish lancers to charge them in flank, and attacked them in
front with part of the 114th regiment and some *voltigeur* companies. The enemy was thrown back, and retired to rejoin his
main body. Then, before they were fully rearranged in line of
battle, the French general bade the whole of Musnier's division
advance, and storm the Spanish position. He was emboldened
to press matters to an issue by the joyful news that the long-
expected brigade from Tudela had passed Saragossa, and would
be on the field in a couple of hours.

The eight battalions of the 114th, 115th, and the 1st of the
Vistula crossed the valley and fell upon the Spanish line
between two and three o'clock in the afternoon. Roca's men
met them with resolution, and the fighting was for some time
indecisive. Along part of the front the French gained ground,
but at other points they were beaten back, and to repair a
severe check suffered by the 115th, Suchet had to engage half
his reserve, the battalion of the 64th, and to draw into the
fight the 2nd of the Vistula from Habert's brigade upon the
left. This movement restored the line, but nothing appreciable
had been gained, when a violent hailstorm from the north
suddenly swept down upon both armies, and hid them for
half an hour from each other's sight.

Before it was over, Suchet learnt that Robert and his brigade
had arrived at the Abbey of Santa Fé, on his right rear. He
therefore resolved to throw into the battle the wing of his army
which he had hitherto held back,—Habert's battalions and the
cavalry. When the storm had passed over, they advanced
against the Spanish right, in the low ground near the river.
The three battalions [1] of infantry led the way, but when their

---

[1] The 2nd of the Vistula having been distracted to the centre, Habert

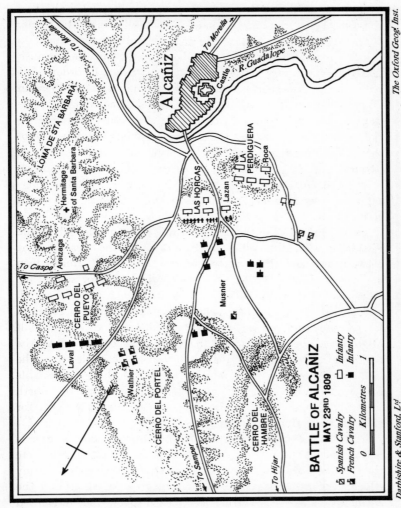

The Oxford Geog. Inst.

Darbishire & Stanford, Ltd

BATTLE OF ALCAÑIZ

MAY 23RD 1809

Spanish Cavalry   Infantry

French Cavalry   Infantry

0   Kilometres   1

Alcañiz

Castle

R. Guadalope

To Morella

To Morella

LOMA DE STA BARBARA

Hermitage of Santa Barbara

Areizaga

To Caspe

CERRO DEL PUEYO

Laval

Wathier

CERRO DEL PORTEL

CERRO DEL HAMBRE

To Samper

To Hijar

LAS HORCAS

Lazan

LA PERDIGUERA

Roca

Musnier

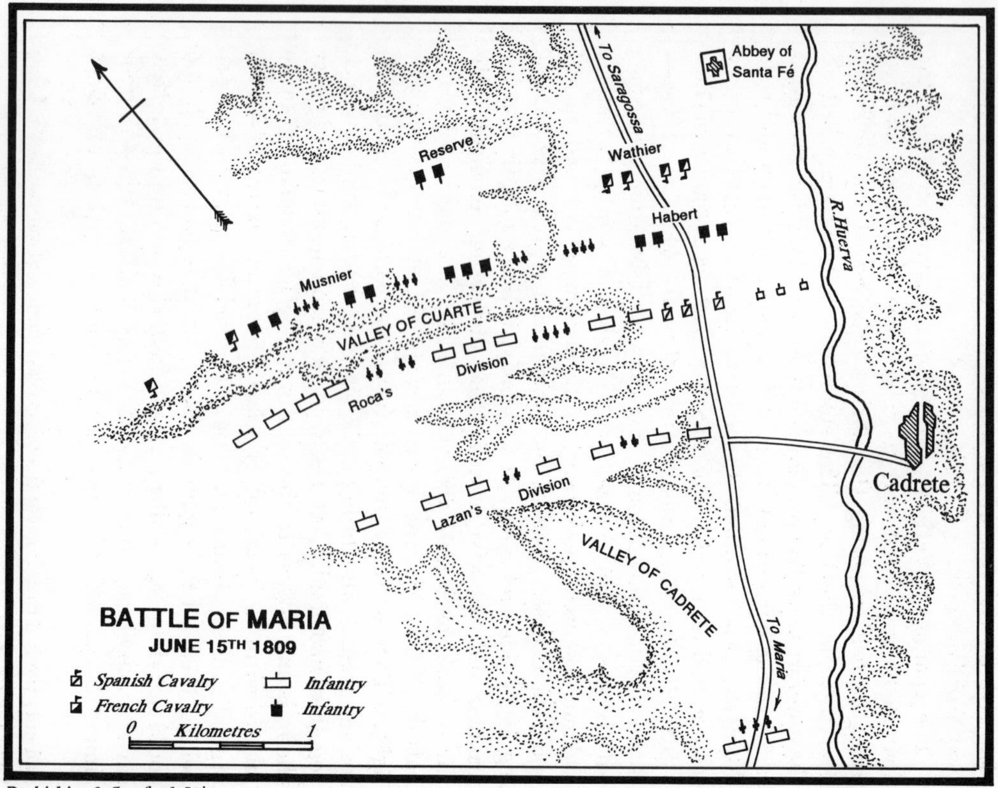

BATTLE OF MARIA
JUNE 15TH 1809

Spanish Cavalry — Infantry
French Cavalry — Infantry

0 Kilometres 1

Cadrete

R. Huerva

Abbey of Santa Fé

To Maria →

To Saragossa

Wathier

Habert

VALLEY OF CADRETE

Lazan's Division

Reserve

Musnier

VALLEY OF CUARTE

Division

Roa's

The Oxford Geog' Inst.

Darbishire & Stanford, Ltd

fire had begun to take effect, Suchet bade his hussars and cuirassiers charge through the intervals of the front line. The troops here opposed to them consisted of 600 cavalry under General O'Donoju—the whole of the horsemen that Blake possessed, for the rest of his squadrons were with Areizaga, far away from the field.

The charge of Wathier's two regiments proved decisive: the Spanish horse did not wait to cross sabres, but broke and fled from the field, exposing the flank of the battalions which lay next them in the line. The cuirassiers and hussars rolled up these unfortunate troops, and hunted them along the high-road as far as the outskirts of Maria; here they came upon and rode down the two battalions which Blake had left there as a last reserve, and captured the half-battery that accompanied them.

The Spanish right was annihilated, and—what was worse— Blake had lost possession of the only road by which he could withdraw and join Areizaga. Meanwhile Habert's battalions had not followed the cavalry in their charge, but had turned upon the exposed flank of the Spanish centre, and were attacking it in side and rear. It is greatly to Blake's credit that his firmness did not give way in this distressing moment. He threw back his right, and sent up into line such of Lazan's battalions from his rear line as had not yet been drawn into the fight. Thus he saved himself from utter disaster, and though losing ground all through the evening hours, kept his men together, and finally left the field in a solid mass, retiring over the hills and ravines to the southward. 'The Spaniards,' wrote an eye-witness, 'went off the field in perfect order and with a good military bearing[1].' But they had been forced to leave behind them all their guns save two, for they had no road, and could not drag the artillery up the rugged slopes by which they saved themselves. Blake also lost 1,000 killed, three or four times that number of wounded, and some hundreds of prisoners.

had only the two battalions of the 14th of the Line, and one of the 5th Léger from the reserve.

[1] 'Ihr Rückzug geschah in aller Ordnung und militärischer Haltung. Sie lagerten in der Nacht uns gegenüber, und hielten am anderen Morgen die Höhen von Botorita ganz in der Nähe des Schlachtfeldes.' [Von Brandt, i. 73.]

The steadiness of the retreat is vouched for by the small number
of flags captured by the French—only three out of the thirty-
four that had been upon the field. Suchet, according to his
own account, had lost no more than between 700 and 800 men.

When safe from pursuit the beaten army crossed the Huerba
far above Maria, and rejoined Areizaga's division at Botorita
on the right bank of that stream.

Next morning, to his surprise, Suchet learnt that the enemy
was still in position at Botorita and was showing a steady front.
The victor did not march directly against Blake, as might have
been expected, but ordered Laval, with the troops that had
been guarding Saragossa, to turn the Spaniards' right, while he
himself manœuvred to get round their left. These cautious
proceedings would seem to indicate that the French army had
been more exhausted by the battle of the previous day than
Suchet concedes. The turning movements failed, and Blake
drew off undisturbed at nightfall, and retired on that same road
to Belchite by which he had marched on Saragossa, in such
high hopes, only four days back.

The battle of Maria had been on the whole very creditable to
the Valencian troops. But the subsequent course of events was
lamentable. On the way to Belchite many of the raw levies
began to disband themselves: the weather was bad, the road
worse, and the consciousness of defeat had had time enough to
sink into the minds of the soldiery. When Blake halted at
Belchite, he found that he had only 12,000 men with him:
deducting the losses of the fifteenth, there should have been at
least 15,000 in line. Of artillery he possessed no more than
nine guns, seven that had been with Areizaga, and two saved
from Maria[1].

It can only be considered therefore a piece of mad presump-
tion on the part of the Spanish general that he halted at
Belchite and again offered battle to his pursuers. The position
in front of that town was strong—far stronger than the ground
at Maria. But the men were not the same; on June 15 they

---

[1] Suchet (i. 24) says that Blake had been reinforced by 4,000 Valencians,
when he fought at Belchite. This seems to have been an error, his
reinforcement being Areizaga's 6,000 men picked up at Botorita, who were
all Aragonese.

had fought with confidence, proud of their victory at Alcañiz and intending to enter Saragossa in triumph next day. On June 18 they were cowed and disheartened—they had already done their best and had failed: it seemed to them hopeless to try the fortunes of war again, and they were half beaten before a shot had been fired. The mere numerical odds, too, were no longer in their favour: at Maria, Blake had 13,000 men to Suchet's 9,000—if we count only the troops that fought, and neglect the 3,000 French who came up late in the day, and were never engaged. At Belchite, Blake had about 12,000 men, and Suchet rather more, for he had gathered in Laval's and Robert's brigades—full 5,000 bayonets, and could put into line 13,000 men, even if allowance be made for his losses in the late battle[1]. It is impossible to understand the temerity with which the Spanish general courted a disaster, by resolving to fight a second battle only three days after he had lost the first.

Blake's centre was in front of Belchite, in comparatively low-lying ground, much cut up by olive groves and enclosures. His wings were drawn up on two gentle hills, called the Calvary and El Pueyo : the left was the weaker flank, the ridge there being open and exposed. It was on this wing therefore that Suchet directed his main effort; he sent against it the whole of Musnier's division and a regiment of cavalry, while Habert's brigade marched to turn the right : the centre was left unattacked. The moment that Musnier's attack was well pronounced, the whole of the Spanish left wing gave way, and fell back on Belchite, to cover itself behind the walls and olive-groves. Before the French division could be reformed for a second attack, an even more disgraceful rout occurred on the right wing. Habert's brigade had just commenced to close in upon the Spaniards, when a chance shell exploded a caisson in rear of the battery in Blake's right-centre. The fire communicated itself to the other powder-wagons which were standing near, and the whole group blew up with a terrific report. 'This piece of luck threw the whole line into panic,' writes an eye-witness, 'the enemy thought that he was attacked in the

[1] He had twenty-two battalions and eight squadrons at Belchite (as he says himself, *Mémoires,* i. p. 34), while at Maria he had only fourteen battalions and seven squadrons.

rear. Every man shouted Treason! whole battalions threw
down their arms and bolted. The disorder spread along the
entire line, and we only had to run in upon them and seize
what we could. If they had not closed the town-gates, which
we found it difficult to batter in, I fancy that the whole
Spanish army would have been captured or cut to pieces. But
it took some time to break down the narrow grated door, and
then a battalion stood at bay in the Market Place, and had to
be ridden down by our Polish lancers before we could get on.
Lastly, we had to pass through another gate to make our exit,
and to cross the bridge over the Aguas in a narrow formation.
This gave the Spaniards time to show a clean pair of heels, and
they utilized the chance with their constitutional agility. We
took few prisoners, but got their nine guns, some twenty
munition wagons, and the whole of their very considerable
magazines. General Suchet wrote up a splendid account of
the elaborate manœuvres that he made. But I believe that my
tale is nearer to the facts, and that the order of battle which he
published was composed *après coup*. The whole affair did not
last long enough for him to carry out the various dispositions
which he details [1].'

The whole Spanish army was scattered to the winds. It was
some days before the Aragonese and Catalans began to rally at
Tortosa, and the Valencians at Morella. The total loss in the
battle had not been large—Suchet says that only one regiment
was actually surrounded and cut to pieces, and only one flag
taken [2]. But of the 25,000 men who had formed the 'Army of
the Right' on June 1, not 10,000 were available a month later,
and these were in a state of demoralization which would have
made it impossible to take them into action.

Suchet was therefore able to set himself at leisure to the task
of reducing the plains of Aragon, whose control had passed out
of his hands in May. He left Musnier's division at Alcañiz to
watch all that was left of Blake's army, while he marched with
the other two to overrun the central valley of the Ebro. On

---

[1] Certainly on reading Suchet's report one would not be inclined to
think that the whole matter was such a disgraceful rout as Von Brandt
(i. 74–5) describes in the above paragraphs.

[2] *Mémoires,* p. 36.

June 23 he seized Caspe and its long wooden bridge, and crossed the river. Next he occupied Fraga and Monzon, and left Habert[1] and the 3rd division to watch the valley of the Cinca. With the remaining division, that of Laval, he marched back to Saragossa [July 1], sweeping the open country clear of guerrilla bands. Then he sat down for a space in the Aragonese capital, to busy himself in administrative schemes for the governance of the kingdom, and in preparation for a systematic campaign against the numerous insurgents of the northern and southern mountains, who still remained under arms and seemed to have been little affected by the disasters of Maria and Belchite.

Thus ended Blake's invasion of Aragon, an undertaking which promised well from the day of Alcañiz down to the battle of June 15. It miscarried mainly through the gross tactical error which the general made in dividing his army, and fighting at Maria with only two-thirds of his available force. His strategy down to the actual moment of battle seems to have been well-considered and prudent. If he had put the Aragonese division of Areizaga in line between the river and the hill, instead of his handful of untrustworthy cavalry, it seems likely that a second Alcañiz might have been fought on the fatal fifteenth of June. For Suchet's infantry attack had miscarried, and it was only the onslaught of his cavalry that won the day. Had that charge failed, Saragossa must have been evacuated that night, and the 3rd Corps would have been forced back on Navarre—to the entire dislocation of all other French operations in Spain. If King Joseph had received the news of the loss of Aragon in the same week in which he learnt that Soult and Ney had evacuated Galicia, and Kellermann the Asturias, he would probably have called back Victor and Sebastiani and abandoned Madrid. For a disaster in the valley of the Douro or the Ebro, as Napoleon once observed, is the most fatal blow of all to an invader based on the north, and makes central Spain untenable. While wondering at Blake's errors, we must not forget to lay part of the blame at the door of his lieutenant Areizaga—the incapable man who afterwards lost the fatal fight of Ocaña.

---

[1] Morlot's division had been handed over to Habert, who resigned his brigade of Laval's division to the Polish colonel Chlopicki.

An officer of sound views, when left without orders, would have 'marched to the cannon' and appeared on the field of Maria in the afternoon. Areizaga sat quiescent, six miles from the battle-field, while the cannon were thundering in his ears from eleven in the morning till six in the afternoon!

As for Suchet, we see that he took a terrible risk, and came safely through the ordeal. There were many reasons for evacu-ating Saragossa, when Blake came down the valley of the Huerba to cut the communications of the 3rd Corps. But an enter-prising general just making his début in independent command, could not well take the responsibility of retreat without first trying the luck of battle. Fortune favoured the brave, and a splendid victory saved Saragossa and led to the reconquest of the lost plains of Aragon. Yet, with another cast of the dice, Maria might have proved a defeat, and Suchet have gone down to history as a rash officer who imperilled the whole fate of the French army in Spain by trying to face over-great odds.

SECTION XVI

THE TALAVERA CAMPAIGN

CHAPTER I

WELLESLEY AT ABRANTES: VICTOR EVACUATES
ESTREMADURA

WHEN Wellesley's columns, faint but pursuing, received the
orders which bade them halt at Ruivaens and Montalegre, their
commander was already planning out the details of their return-
march to the Tagus. From the first moment of his setting forth
from Lisbon, he had looked upon the expedition against Soult
as no more than a necessary preliminary to the more important
expedition against Victor. He would have preferred, as we
have already seen [1], to have directed his first blow against the
French army in Estremadura, and had only been induced to
begin his campaign by the attack upon Soult because he saw
the political necessity for delivering Oporto. His original intention had been no more than to manœuvre the 2nd Corps out
of Portugal. But, owing to the faulty dispositions of the
Duke of Dalmatia, he had been able to accomplish much more
than this—he had beaten the Marshal, stripped him of his
artillery and equipment, destroyed a sixth of his army, and flung
him back into Galicia by a rugged and impracticable road, which
took him far from his natural base of operations. He had done
much more than he had hoped or promised to do when he set
out from Lisbon. Yet these 'uncovenanted mercies' did not
distract him from his original plan: his main object was not the
destruction of Soult, but the clearing of the whole frontier of
Portugal from the danger of invasion, and this could not be
accomplished till Victor had been dealt with. The necessity
for a prompt movement against the 1st Corps was emphasized

[1] See p. 292.

F f

by the news, received on May 19 at Montalegre, that its commander was already astir, and apparently about to assume the offensive. Mackenzie reported from Abrantes, with some signs of dismay, that a strong French column had just fallen upon Alcantara, and driven from it the small Portuguese detachment which was covering his front.

Accordingly Wellesley turned the march of his whole army southward, the very moment that he discovered that the 2nd Corps had not fallen into the trap set for it at Chaves and Ruivaens. He had resolved to leave nothing but the local levies of Silveira and Botilho to watch Galicia, and to protect the provinces north of the Douro. 'Soult,' he wrote, 'will be very little formidable to any body of troops for some time to come.' He imagined—and quite correctly—that the Galician guerrillas and the army of La Romana would suffice to find him occupation. He did not, however, realize that it was possible that not only Soult but Ney also would be so much harassed by the insurgents, and would fall into such bitter strife with each other, that they might ere long evacuate Galicia altogether. This, indeed, could not have been foreseen at the moment when the British turned southwards from Montalegre. If Wellesley could have guessed that by July 1 the three French Corps in Northern Spain—the 2nd, 5th, and 6th—would all be clear of the mountains and concentrated in the triangle Astorga-Zamora-Valladolid, he would have had to recast his plan of operations. But on May 19 such a conjunction appeared most improbable, and the British general could not have deemed it likely that a French army of 55,000 men, available for field-operations, would be collected on the central Douro, at the moment when he had committed himself to operations on the Tagus. Indeed, for some weeks after he had departed from Oporto the information from the north made any such concentration appear improbable. While he was on his march to the south he began to hear of the details of Ney's and Kellermann's expedition against the Asturias, news which he received with complacency[1], as it showed that the French were entangling themselves in new and hazardous enterprises which would make it more difficult than ever for them to collect a force opposite

[1] See the letter to Colonel Bourke, *Wellington Dispatches*, iv. 390–400.

the frontier of Northern Portugal. Down to the very end of June
Wellesley had no reason to dread any concentration of French
troops upon his flank in the valley of the Douro. It was only
in the following month that Soult was heard of at Puebla
de Senabria and Ney at Astorga. By that time the British
army had already crossed the frontier of Spain and commenced
its operations against Victor.

At the moment when Wellesley turned back from Montalegre
and set his face southward, he had not yet settled the details
of his plan of campaign. There appeared to be two courses
open to him. The first was to base himself upon Almeida and
Ciudad Rodrigo, and advance upon Salamanca. This movement,
which he could have begun in the second week of June, would
undoubtedly have thrown into disorder all the French arrangements in Northern Spain. There would have been no force
ready to oppose him save a single division of Mortier's corps—
the rest of that marshal's troops were absent with Kellermann
in the Asturias. This could not have held the British army
back, and a bold march in advance would have placed Wellesley
in a position where he could have intercepted all communications
between the French troops in Galicia and those in and about
Madrid. The movement might appear tempting, but it would
have been too hazardous. The only force that could have been
used for it was the 20,000 troops of Wellesley's own army,
backed by the 12,000 or 15,000 Portuguese regulars whom
Beresford could collect between the Douro and the Tagus.
The Spaniards had no troops in this direction save the garrison
of Ciudad Rodrigo, and a battalion or two which Carlos d'España
had raised on the borders of Leon and Portugal. On the other
hand, the news that the British were at Salamanca or Toro
would certainly have forced Ney, Soult, and Kellermann to
evacuate Galicia and the Asturias and hasten to the aid of
Mortier. They would have been far too strong, when united,
for the 30,000 or 35,000 men of Wellesley and Beresford.
La Romana and the Asturians could have brought no corresponding reinforcements to assist the British army, and must
necessarily have arrived too late—long after the French corps
would have reached the Douro [1]. The idea of a movement on

---

[1] Napier (ii. 149) calls this alternative plan of campaign ' a movement

Salamanca, therefore, did not even for a moment enter into Wellesley's mind.

The other alternative open to the British general, and that which he had from the first determined to take in hand, was (as we have already seen) a march against Victor. Such a movement might be carried out in one of two ways. (1) It would be possible to advance against his flank and rear by keeping north of the Tagus, and striking, by Coria and Plasencia, at Almaraz and its great bridge of boats, across which ran the communication between the 1st Corps and Madrid. This operation would have to be carried out by the British army alone, while the Spanish army of Estremadura, acting from a separate base, kept in touch with Victor but avoided compromising itself by any rash attack upon him. The Marshal, placed in a central position between Wellesley's and Cuesta's forces, would certainly try to beat one of them before they got the chance of drawing together. (2) It was equally possible to operate against Victor not on separate lines, but by crossing the Tagus, joining the Spaniards somewhere in the neighbourhood of Badajoz, and falling upon the Marshal with the united strength of both armies. This movement would be less hazardous than the other, since it would secure the concentration of an army of a strength sufficient to crush the 25,000 men at which the 1st Corps might reasonably be rated. But it would only drive Victor back upon Madrid and King Joseph's reserves by a frontal attack, while the other plan—that of the march on Almaraz—would imperil his flank and rear, and threaten to cut him off from the King and the capital.

Before making any decision between the two plans, Wellesley wrote to Cuesta, from Oporto on May 22, a letter requesting him to state his views as to the way in which the operations of the British and Spanish armies could best be combined. He

in conjunction with Beresford, del Parque, and Romana by Salamanca. This is a most inappropriate description of it : about June 10, when operations might have commenced, Del Parque's army did not yet exist. There were only three or four of Carlos d'España's battalions at or near Rodrigo. La Romana, on the other hand, was at Orense facing Soult, and could not have reached Almeida or Rodrigo for weeks after the campaign would have begun.

informed him that the troops which had defeated Soult were
already on their way to the south, that the head of the column
would reach the Mondego on the twenty-sixth, and that the whole
would be concentrated near Abrantes early in June. It was
at that place that the choice would have to be made between
the two possible lines of attack on Victor—that which led to
Almaraz, and that which went on to Southern Estremadura.
A few days later Wellesley dispatched a confidential officer of
his staff—Colonel Bourke—to bear to the Spanish general
a definite request for his decision on the point whether the
allied armies should prepare for an actual junction, or should
manœuvre from separate bases, or should ' co-operate with communication,' i.e. combine their movements without adopting
a single base or a joint line of advance. Bourke was also
directed to obtain all the information that he could concerning
the strength, morale, and discipline of Cuesta's army, and to
discover what chance there was of securing the active assistance
of the second Spanish army in the south—that which, under
General Venegas, was defending the defiles in front of La
Carolina [1].

It was clear that some days must elapse before an answer
could arrive from the camp of the Estremaduran army, and
meanwhile Wellesley continued to urge the counter-march of his
troops from the various points at which they had halted between
Oporto and Montalegre.   All the scattered British brigades
were directed on Abrantes by different routes : those which had
the least distance to march began to arrive there on the eleventh
and the twelve of June.

The Commander-in-chief had resolved not to take on with
him the Portuguese regulars whom he had employed in the
campaign against Soult.   Both the brigades which had marched
on Amarante under Beresford, and the four battalions which
had fought along with Wellesley in the main column, were now
dropped behind. They were destined to form an army of observation, lest Mortier and his 5th Corps, or any other French
force, might chance to assail the front between the Douro and
the Tagus during the absence of the British in the south.

---

[1] See the ' Memorandum for Lieut.-Col. Bourke' in *Wellington Dispatches*,
iv. 372–3.

Beresford, who was left in command, was directed to arrange
his troops so as to be able to support Almeida, and resist any
raid from the direction of Salamanca or Zamora. The main
body of the army lay at Guarda, its reserves at Coimbra. The
Portuguese division which had been lying on the Zezere in
company with Mackenzie's troops, was also placed at Beresford's
disposition, so that he had about eighteen battalions, four regiments
of cavalry, and five or six batteries—a force of between 12,000
and 15,000 men. It was his duty to connect Wellesley's left wing
with Silveira's right, and to reinforce either of them if necessary.
The Commander-in-chief was inclined to believe, from his knowledge of the disposition of the French corps at the moment, that
no very serious attack was likely to be directed against Northern
Portugal during his absence—at the most Soult might threaten
Braganza or Mortier Almeida. But it was necessary to make
some provision against even unlikely contingencies.

The only Portuguese force which Wellesley had resolved to
utilize for the campaign in Estremadura was the battalion of
the Loyal Lusitanian Legion, under Colonel Mayne, which had
been stationed at Alcantara watching the movements of Victor.
Sir Robert Wilson, now recalled from Beresford's column and
placed once more with his own men, was to take up the command
of his old force, and to add to it the 5th Cazadores, a regiment
which had hitherto been lying with Mackenzie's division at
Abrantes. With these 1,500 men he was to serve as the northern
flank-guard of the British army when it should enter Spain.

When Wellesley first started upon his march, he was under
the impression that his plan of campaign might be settled for
him by the movements of Victor rather than by the devices of
Cuesta. The rapidity of his progress was partly caused by the
news of the Marshal's attack on Alcantara, an operation which
might, as it seemed, turn out to be the prelude of a raid in
force upon Central Portugal. That it portended an actual
invasion with serious designs Wellesley could not believe, being
convinced that Victor would have to leave so large a proportion
of his army to observe Cuesta, that he would not be able to set
aside more than 10,000 or 12,000 men for operations in the
valley of the Tagus [1]. But such a force would be enough to

---

[1] Wellesley to Mackenzie, from San Tyrso, May 21.

sweep the country about Castello Branco and Villa Velha, and to beat up Mackenzie's line of defence on the Zezere.

The actual course of events on the Tagus had been as follows. Victor, even after having received the division of Lapisse, considered himself too weak either to march on Cuesta and drive him over the mountains into Andalusia, or to fall upon Central Portugal by an advance along the Tagus[1]. He had received vague information of the formation of Mackenzie's corps of observation on the Zezere, though apparently he had not discovered that there was a strong British contingent in its ranks. But he was under the impression that if he crossed the Guadiana in force, to attack Cuesta, the Portuguese would advance into Estremadura and cut his communications; while if he marched against the Portuguese, Cuesta would move northward to attack his rear. Accordingly he maintained for some time a purely defensive attitude, keeping his three French infantry divisions concentrated in a central position, at Torremocha, Montanches, and Salvatierra (near Caceres), while he remained himself with Leval's Germans and Latour-Maubourg's dragoons in the neighbourhood of Merida, observing Cuesta and sending flying columns up and down the Guadiana to watch the garrison of Badajoz and the guerrillas of the Sierra de Guadalupe. He had not forgotten the Emperor's orders that he was to be prepared to execute a diversion in favour of Marshal Soult, when he should hear that the 2nd Corps was on its way to Lisbon. But, like all the other French generals, he was profoundly ignorant of the position and the fortunes of the Duke of Dalmatia. On April 22 the head-quarters staff at Madrid had received no more than a vague rumour that the 2nd Corps had entered Oporto a month before! They got no trustworthy information concerning its doings till May was far advanced[2]. Victor, therefore, depending on King Joseph for his news from Northern Portugal, was completely in the dark as to the moment when he might be called upon to execute his diversion on the Tagus. The Portuguese and Galician insur-

---

[1] Compare the two dispatches of Victor to Jourdan of April 25 (acknowledging the receipt of Lapisse's division) and of May 21.

[2] See King Joseph to Napoleon, of the dates April 22 and May 24, 1809.

gents had succeeded in maintaining a complete blockade of
Soult, and thus had foiled all Napoleon's plans for combining
the operations of the 1st and the 2nd Corps.

Victor was only stirred up into a spasmodic activity in the
second week in May, by the news that a Portuguese force had
crossed the frontier and occupied Alcantara, where the great
Roman bridge across the Tagus provided a line of communication between North-Western and Central Estremadura.   This
detachment—as we have already seen—consisted of no more
than Colonel Mayne's 1st battalion of the Loyal Lusitanian
Legion, brought down from the passes of the Sierra de Gata,
and of a single regiment of newly-raised militia—that of the
frontier district of Idanha.   They had with them the six guns
of the battery of the Legion and a solitary squadron of cavalry.
Wellesley had thrown forward this little force of 2,000 men to
serve as an outpost for Mackenzie's corps on the Zezere.   But
rumour magnified its strength, and Victor jumped to the conclusion that it formed the vanguard of a Portuguese army which
was intending to concert a combined operation with Cuesta, by
threatening the communication of the 1st Corps while the
Spaniards attacked its front.

Labouring under this delusion, Victor took the division of
Lapisse and a brigade of dragoons, and marched against Alcantara upon the eleventh of May.   As he approached the river he
was met at Brozas by Mayne's vedettes, whom he soon drove in
to the gates of the little town.   Alcantara being situated on
the south side of the Tagus, it was impossible to defend it: but
Mayne had barricaded and mined the bridge, planted his guns
so as to command the passage, and constructed trenches for his
infantry along the northern bank.   After seizing the town,
Victor opened a heavy fire of artillery and musketry against the
Portuguese detachment.   It was met by a vigorous return from
the further bank, which lasted for more than three hours before
the defence began to flag.   The Marshal very properly refused
to send forward his infantry to attempt the storm of the bridge
till his artillery should have silenced that of the defenders.   At
about midday the Idanha militia, who had already suffered not
inconsiderable losses, deserted their trenches and fled.   Thereupon Mayne fired his mine in the bridge, but unhappily for

him the tough Roman cement defied even the power of gun-
powder; only one side of the arch was shattered; the crown of
the vault held firm, and the passage was still possible. The
Legion still kept its ground, though it had lost many men, and
had seen one of his guns dismounted, and the rest silenced by
the French artillery. But when Victor hurled the leading
brigade of Lapisse's division at the bridge he succeeded in
forcing it[1]. Mayne drew off his legionaries in good order and
retreated to the pass of Salvaterra, leaving behind him a gun
and more than 250 killed and wounded[2] [May 14]—a heavy
loss from the 1,000 men of the single battalion which bore the
whole brunt of the fighting.

Victor went no further than Alcantara, having satisfied himself that the Portuguese force which had made such a creditable
resistance consisted of a single weak brigade, and did not form
the vanguard of an army bent on invading Estremadura. After
remaining for no more than three days at Alcantara, and trying
in vain to obtain news of the whereabouts of Soult—who was
at that moment being hunted past Guimaraens and Braga in the
far north—the Marshal drew back his troops to Torremocha
near Caceres.

His advance, though it had only lasted for six days, and had
not been pushed more than a few miles beyond Alcantara, had
much disturbed General Mackenzie, who dreaded to find himself
the next object of attack and to see the whole of the 1st Corps
debouching against him by the road through Castello Branco.
Wellesley wrote to him that he need not be alarmed, that
Victor could not spare more than 10,000 or 12,000 men for his
demonstration, and that the 8,000 British and Portuguese troops
behind the Zezere were amply sufficient to maintain defensive
operations till the main army from the north should come up.
He expressed his opinion that the French force at Alcantara
was 'a mere reconnoitring party, sent out for the purpose of

[1] Compare Victor to Jourdan of May 21, with the account of the combat
in Appendix I of Mayne and Lillie's *Lusitanian Legion*.

[2] The exact losses of the L. L. L. were—killed, three officers and 103
rank and file; wounded, five officers and 143 rank and file; missing, fifteen
rank and file. Of the Idanha militia, Mayne returned the whole as missing
next morning.

ascertaining what has become of Soult,' a conclusion in which he was perfectly right. Mackenzie [1], who betrayed an exaggerated want of confidence in his Portuguese troops, was profoundly relieved to see the enemy retire upon the seventeenth. He had advanced from Abrantes and taken up a defensive position along the Sobreira Formosa to resist the Marshal, but he had done so with many searchings of heart, and was glad to see the danger pass away. When Victor had retired into Central Estremadura, Mayne came back with all due caution, and re-occupied the bridge of Alcantara.

Wellesley, therefore, had been perfectly well justified in his confidence that nothing was to be feared in this direction. The French could not possibly have dared to undertake more than a demonstration in the direction of Castello Branco. King Joseph's orders to Victor had prescribed no more [2], and the Marshal had accomplished even less. In his letter of excuse to Jourdan he explained that he would gladly have left Lapisse's division at Alcantara, or even have moved it forward for some distance into Portugal [3], if he had not found it absolutely impossible to feed it in the bare and stony district north of the Tagus, where Junot's army had been wellnigh starved in November 1807. The peasantry of the villages for fifteen leagues round Alcantara had, as he declared, gone off into the mountains with their cattle, after burying their corn, and he had found it impossible to discover food for even three days' consumption of a single division.

During Victor's absence at Alcantara, Cuesta had sent down a part of his troops to make a raid on Merida, the Marshal's advanced post on the Guadiana. It failed entirely; the garrison, two battalions of Leval's German division, maintained themselves with ease in a large convent outside that town, which Victor had patched up and turned into a place of some little strength. On hearing that the Spaniards were descending

---

[1] See Wellesley to Mackenzie, May 21, and also Wellesley to Frere on the same day. *Wellington Dispatches,* iv. 350-1.

[2] See Jourdan's *Mémoires,* p. 190.

[3] A move by which he flattered himself that he would not only 'inquiéter les Anglais,' but also ' dégager le duc de Dalmatie,' an end which no raid with 8,000 or 10,000 men to Castello Branco could possibly have accomplished. Victor to Jourdan, May 29.

from the mountains, King Joseph ordered the Duke of Belluno
to attack them at once. But on the mere news of the Marshal's
approach Cuesta called back his detachment into the passes,
sweeping off at the same time the inhabitants of all the villages
along the Guadiana, together with their cattle and their stores
of provisions.

At the beginning of June Victor began to press the King and
Jourdan for leave to abandon his hold on Southern Estremadura,
and to fall back towards the Tagus. He urged that his position was very dangerous, now that Cuesta's army had been
recruited up to a force of 22,000 infantry and 6,000 horse,
especially since the Portuguese had once more got possession of
Alcantara. His main contention was that he must either be
reinforced up to a strength which would permit him to attack
Andalusia, or else be permitted to withdraw from the exhausted
district between the Guadiana and the Tagus, in order to seek
a region where his men would be able to live. The only district
in this neighbourhood where the country-side was still intact
was that north of the Tagus, around the towns of Plasencia
and Coria—the valleys of the Alagon and Tietar. To move
the army in this direction would involve the evacuation of
Central Estremadura—it would be necessary to abandon Merida,
Truxillo, and Caceres, with the sacrifice of a certain amount of
prestige. But unless the 1st Corps could be reinforced—and
this, as Victor must have known, was impossible[1]—there was
no other alternative. The internal condition of the army was
growing worse day by day. 'The troops are on half rations of
bread: they can get little meat—often none at all. The results
of starvation are making themselves felt in the most deplorable
way. The men are going into hospital at the rate of several
hundreds a day[2].' A few days later Victor adds, 'If I could
even get together enough biscuit to feed the army for merely
seven or eight days I should not feel so uncomfortable. But
we have no flour to issue for a bread ration, so cannot bake
biscuit[3].' And again he adds, 'The whole population of this

---

[1] He suggests in a letter of June 8, that Mortier's corps should be
brought up to Plasencia to help him. But this was wholly impracticable.

[2] Victor to Jourdan, from Torremocha, May 24.

[3] Victor to Jourdan, May 29.

region has retired within Cuesta's lines, after destroying the ovens and the mills, and removing every scrap of food. It seems that the enemy is resolved to starve us out, and to leave a desert in front of us if we advance. . . . Carefully estimating all my stores I find that I have barely enough to last for five days in hand. We are menaced with absolute famine, which we can only avoid by moving off, and there is no suitable cantonment to be found in the whole space between Tagus and Guadiana: the entire country is ruined.'

Joseph and Jourdan replied to the first of these dismal letters by promising to send the 1st Corps 300,000 rations of biscuit, and by urging its commander to renew his attack on Alcantara, in order to threaten Portugal and 'disengage the Duke of Dalmatia'—who, on the day when their dispatch was written, was at Lugo, in the north of Galicia, some 300 miles as the crow flies from Victor's head quarters [1]. They received the answer that such a move was impossible, as Mayne had just blown up the bridge of Alcantara, and it was now impossible to cross the Tagus [2].

A few days later the news arrived at Madrid that Soult had been defeated and flung out of Portugal [3]. It had taken three weeks for information of this transcendent importance to reach the king! Seriously alarmed, Joseph and Jourdan sent Victor his long-denied permission to retire from Estremadura and place himself behind the Tagus. They do not seem to have guessed that the victorious Wellesley would make his next move against the 1st Corps, but imagined that he would debouch into Old Castile by way of Rodrigo and Salamanca, wherefore their main idea was to strengthen Mortier and the army in the valley of the Douro [4]. Thus it fell in with their views that Victor should draw back to the line of the Tagus, a general concentration of all the French troops in the Peninsula seeming advisable, in face of the necessity for resisting the sup-

[1] Jourdan to Victor, June 1.

[2] Victor to Jourdan, June 8. Oddly enough he was wrong in his statement by two days, for Mayne blew up the bridge on the tenth only.

[3] June 10, Joseph to Napoleon.

[4] Cf. Joseph's letters of June 10 and June 16 to Napoleon : but there seems to be much vacillation in his decisions.

posed attack on Old Castile. Another reason for assuming
a defensive attitude was the gloomy news from Aragon, where
Suchet, after his defeat at Alcañiz, had retired on Saragossa
and was sending despairing appeals for reinforcements to
Madrid.

Accordingly, the 1st Corps evacuated Estremadura between
the fourteenth and the nineteenth of June, and, crossing the
Tagus, disposed itself in a position on the northern bank, with
its right wing at Almaraz and its left at Talavera. Here Victor
intended to make his stand, being confident that with the
broad river in front of him he could easily beat off any attack
on the part of the Spanish army.

But when Wellesley and Cuesta first began to correspond
concerning their joint movement against the French in Estremadura, Victor was still in his old cantonments, and their scheme
of operations had been sketched out on the hypothesis that he
lay at Merida, Torremocha, and Caceres. It was with the design
of assailing him while he still held this advanced position, that
Cuesta drew up his paper of answers to Wellesley's queries and
dispatched it to Abrantes to meet the British general on his
arrival [1].

If the old Captain-General's suggestions were by no means
marked with the stamp of genius, they had at least the merit of
variety. He offered Wellesley the choice between no less than
three plans of campaign. (1) His first proposal was that the
British army should descend into Southern Estremadura, and
join him in the neighbourhood of Badajoz. From thence the
united host was to advance against Victor and assail him in
front. But meanwhile Cuesta proposed to send out two subsidiary columns, to turn the Marshal's flanks and surround him.
One was to base itself on Alcantara and march along the
northern bank of the Tagus to seize Almaraz : the other was
to push by La Serena through the Guadalupe mountains to
threaten Talavera. By these operations, if Victor would be
good enough to remain quiet in his present cantonments,
he would be completely surrounded, his retreat would be cut

---

[1] Cuesta's replies, sent on by Bourke, are dated June 4 and June 6,
i. e. ten and eight days respectively before Victor began his retreat beyond
the Tagus on June 14.

off, and he would finally be compelled to surrender. The
scheme was of course preposterous. What rational man could
have supposed it likely that the Marshal would remain quiescent
while his flanks were being turned? He would certainly
have hastened to retire and to throw himself upon the detached
columns, one or both of which he could have annihilated before
the main armies of the allies could get within touch of him [1].
Wellesley refused to listen for a moment to this plan of campaign. (2) The second proposal of Cuesta was that the British
army should pass the Tagus at Alcantara and operate against
Victor's flank, while the Spanish army attacked him in front.
To this the same objection could be urged: it presupposed that
the Frenchman would remain fixed in his present cantonments:
but he certainly would not do so when he heard that he was to
be assailed on both flanks; he would retire behind the Tagus at
once, and the British army would have wasted its march, and be
obliged to return to the north bank of that river: moreover, it
would involve a very long movement to the south to get in
touch with Victor's flank. Probably it would be necessary to
descend as far into Estremadura as Caceres, and, when that
point was reached, the Marshal could make the whole manœuvre
futile by retiring at once behind the Tagus at Almaraz. To
follow him to the north bank the British would have to retrace
their steps to Alcantara.

The third proposal of Cuesta—the only one in which
Wellesley could find any prospect of success, was that the
British army, keeping north of the Tagus, should march by
Castello Branco on Plasencia. There it would be in the rear

---

[1] Wellesley writes in commenting on this plan [*Wellington Dispatches*,
iv. 402]: ' At all events these two detachments on the two flanks appear
to me to be too weak to produce any great effect upon the movements
of Victor. . . . I think it would be nearly certain that the Marshal would
be able to defend the passage [of the Tagus] with a part only of his force,
while with the other part he would beat one or both of the detachments
sent round his flank. Indeed the detachment which should have been
sent from La Serena toward Talavera, being between the corps of Victor
and Sebastiani, could hardly escape.' Wellesley also points out that it is
useless to expect that Victor would wait in his present cantonments: at
the first news of the approach of the British army he will retire to
Almaraz and Arzobispo.

of Victor's best line of retreat by the bridge of Almaraz.   If
the manœuvre could be kept very secret, and executed with
great speed, Almaraz, perhaps also the subsidiary passage at
Arzobispo, might be seized.   Should the Marshal get early news
of the movement, and hurry back across the Tagus to fend off
this stab in the rear, Wellesley was prepared to fight him in
the open with equal forces, conceiving that he was 'sufficiently
strong to defend himself against any attack which Victor might
make.'   He hoped that Cuesta was able to guarantee that he
also was competent to hold his own, supposing that the Marshal,
neglecting the British diversion, should concentrate his corps and
strike at the Spanish army.

On the whole, therefore, Wellesley was not disinclined to fall
in with this plan, which had the extra merit of remaining feasible
even if Victor withdrew north of the Tagus before either of the
allied armies had completed its march.   He made one counter-
suggestion, viz. that Cuesta might move eastward, with the
whole or part of his army, join the army of Venegas in La
Mancha, and attack Sebastiani, leaving the British alone to
deal with Victor.   But he did not wish to press this plan, thinking that an attack on the enemy's left was on first principles
less advisable than one on his right, because it did not offer
any chance of cutting him off from Madrid[1].

The answer to Cuesta's proposals was sent off from Abrantes,
which Wellesley, preceding his army by three or four days'
march, reached upon June 8.   He had now under his hand
Mackenzie's Anglo-Portuguese force, but the leading brigades
of the troops who had fought at Oporto could not arrive before
the eleventh or twelfth.   There was thus ample time to concert
the joint plan of campaign before the whole army would be
concentrated and ready to move.   But when Cuesta's reply to
the dispatch of June 8 came to hand upon June 13, Wellesley
was much vexed to find that the old Captain-General had
expressed a great dislike for the idea that the British army
should march upon Plasencia and Almaraz—though it had been
one of his own three suggestions.   He now pleaded urgently in
favour of the first of his original alternatives—that Wellesley

---

[1] I print as an Appendix this all-important letter to Bourke, regarding
Cuesta's three plans of campaign.

should come down to Badajoz and join him in a frontal attack upon Victor. With much reluctance the British general resolved to comply, apparently moved by his ally's openly expressed dislike to being left to face Victor alone. ' I must acknowledge,' he wrote to Colonel Bourke, ' that *I* entertain no apprehension that the French will attack General Cuesta : I am much more afraid that they are going away, and strengthening themselves upon the Tagus[1].' To the Spanish General he sent a dispatch to the same effect, in which he pledged himself to march to join the army of Estremadura, though he frankly stated that all his information led him to believe that Victor had no intention of taking the offensive, and that the junction was therefore unnecessary. He expressed his hope that Cuesta would avoid all fighting till they had met, the only possible danger to the allied cause being that one of the two armies should suffer a defeat before the other had started on the combined movement to which they were committed [2].

Fortunately for all parties concerned, the march on Badajoz which Wellesley so much disliked never had to be begun, for on the day after he had sent off his dispatch to Cuesta he received reliable information from several sources, to the effect that Victor had evacuated and blown up the fortified convent of Merida, and had sent off all his baggage and heavy artillery towards Almaraz. During the next four days the whole of the 1st Corps marched for that all-important bridge, and crossed it. On the nineteenth Victor had established his entire army north of the Tagus, at Almaraz, Arzobispo, and Talavera. Thus the whole face of affairs was changed, and the advance of the British army into Southern Estremadura was rendered unnecessary. It was fortunate that the news of the retreat of the 1st Corps was received at Abrantes just in time to allow of the countermanding of the march of Wellesley's army on Badajoz, for that fruitless movement would have begun if the Duke of Belluno had been able to retain his starving army in its positions for a few days longer.

[1] Wellesley to Bourke, from Abrantes, June 14.
[2] Wellesley to Cuesta, from Abrantes, June 14.

SECTION XVI: CHAPTER II

WELLESLEY ENTERS SPAIN

THE retreat of Victor beyond the Tagus forced Wellesley to concert yet another plan of operation with Cuesta, since the position of the French army, on which the whole of the recently adopted scheme depended, had just suffered a radical change. It was clear that every consideration now pointed to the necessity for adopting the combination which Wellesley had urged upon his colleague in his letter of June 8, viz. that the British army should move on Plasencia and Almaraz. It would now be striking at the flank instead of the rear of Victor's corps, but it was clear that under the new conditions it would still be in a position to roll up his whole army, if he should endeavour to defend the passages of the Tagus against the Spaniards, who were now approaching them from the front. For Cuesta had descended from the mountains when he heard of Victor's retreat, and was now approaching Almaraz.

It took some time, however, to induce the Captain-General to consent to this move. To the extreme vexation of his colleague he produced other plans, so gratuitously impracticable that Wellesley wrote to Castlereagh to say that he could conceive no explanation for the old man's conduct save a desire to refuse any scheme urged on him by others, and a resolve to invent and advocate alternative plans of his own out of mere pride and wrongheadedness. 'The best of the whole story,' he added [1], was that Cuesta was now refusing to accept a plan which he himself had suggested in one of his earlier letters, merely because that plan had been taken up and advocated by his ally. 'The obstinacy of this old gentleman,' he concluded, 'is

[1] Wellesley to Castlereagh, Abrantes, June 17. The real cause of Cuesta's angry and impracticable attitude will be shown in the next chapter.

throwing out of our hands the finest game that any armies ever had [1].'

The necessity for working out a new scheme for the combined operations of the British and Spanish armies, in view of Victor's retreat to Almaraz, entailed the loss of a few days. It would have been impossible to start on the advance to Plasencia till Cuesta had promised to accept that movement as part of the joint campaign. There was also some time to be allowed for concluding an agreement with Venegas, the General of the La Carolina army, whose connexion with the campaign must become much more intimate, now that the fighting was to take place not in Estremadura, but further north, in the valley of the Tagus. For while Victor lay at Merida and Sebastiani at Manzanares and Ciudad Real, the Spanish forces which faced them were very far apart. But when Victor retired to Talavera, and Sebastiani to Madridejos, in the end of June, Cuesta and Venegas—each following the corps opposed to him—could draw closer together. It was evident that the Andalusian army ought to be made to play an important part in the combined operations of July.

It would be unfair to the Spanish generals to let it be supposed that the necessity for settling on a common scheme of operations with them was the sole cause which detained Wellesley at Abrantes from the eighth to the twenty-seventh of June. The leading brigades of the British troops from Oporto had begun to reach Abrantes on the eleventh, and the more belated columns came up on the fourteenth and fifteenth. But it would have been impossible to have moved forward without some further delay, even if Wellesley had been in possession of a complete and satisfactory plan of operations on the day upon which his whole force was concentrated on the line of the Zezere. At the least he would have required another week for preparations.

His hindrances at this moment were manifold. The first was the distressed condition of those of his brigades which had seen most service during the Oporto campaign. Many regiments had been constantly on the march from May 9 to June 14, without obtaining more than two days' rest in the whole time. Their shoes were worn out, their jaded baggage-animals had dropped to the rear, and they were leaving so many stragglers

[1] Wellesley to Frere from the same place, June 14.

on the way that it was absolutely necessary to give them
a moderate rest at Abrantes, in order to allow the ranks to
grow full and the belated baggage to come up. The regiments
which had followed Beresford in the forced march from
Amarante to Chaves were worst off—they had never completely
recovered from the fatigues of those three days of constant rain
and storm spent on the stony roads of the Tras-os-Montes [1]. In
any case some delay must have occurred before all the troops
were ready to march. But many circumstances conspired to
detain the army at Abrantes for several days after the moment
at which Wellesley had determined to start for Plasencia. The
first was the non-arrival of convoys of shoes and clothing which
he had ordered up from Lisbon. The transport of the army
was not yet fully organized, its officers were lacking in experience,
if not in zeal, and orders were slowly executed. Many corps
had, in the end, to start for Spain without receiving the much-
needed stores, which were still trailing up from Santarem to
Abrantes when Wellesley gave the signal to advance. Another
hindrance was the lack of money : the army was obliged to pay
for its wants in coin, but hard cash was so difficult to procure both
in London and in Lisbon that arrears were already beginning to
grow up. At first they vexed the soul of Wellesley almost
beyond endurance, but as the war dragged on they only grew
worse, and the Commander-in-chief had to endure with resignation the fact that both the pay of the men and the wages of the
Portuguese muleteers and followers were overdue for many months.
In June 1809 he had not yet reached this state of comparative
callousness, and was endeavouring to scrape together money by
every possible device. He had borrowed £13,000 in Portuguese
silver from the merchants of the impoverished city of Oporto: he
was trying to exchange bills on England for dollars at Cadiz,
where the arrival of the American contribution had produced
a comparative plenty of the circulating medium. Yet after all

---

[1] With regard to these regiments [5/60th, 2/87th, 1/88th], Wellesley
writes in very bitter terms to Donkin on June 16, saying that the number
of their stragglers was scandalous, and that the laggards were committing
all manner of disorders in the rear of the army. It is fair to remember
that the battalions had suffered exceptional hardships, as may be seen
from the narratives of Gough of the 87th, and Grattan of the 88th.

he had to start from Abrantes with only a comparatively
moderate sum in his military chest [1], the rest had not reached
him on June 28, the treasure convoy having taken the unconscionable time of eleven days to crawl forward from Lisbon to
Abrantes—a distance of no more than ninety miles [2].

A third cause of delay was the time spent in waiting for
reinforcements from Lisbon. Eight or nine regiments had
landed, or were expected to arrive within the next few days.
It was in every way desirable to unite them to the army before
the campaign should begin. This was all the more necessary
because several corps had to be deducted from the force which
had been used in the Oporto campaign. Under stringent orders
from home, Wellesley had sent back two infantry battalions
and part of two cavalry regiments to Lisbon, to be embarked
for Gibraltar and Sicily [3]. In return he was to receive a much
larger body of troops. But while the deduction was immediate,
the addition took time. Of all the troops which were expected
to reinforce the army, only one battalion caught him up at
Abrantes, while a second and one regiment of Light Dragoons [4]
joined later, but yet in time for Talavera. Thus at the commencement of the actual campaign the force in the field was, if
anything, slightly less in numbers than that which had been
available in May. It was particularly vexatious that the
brigade of veteran light infantry, for which Wellesley had made
a special demand on Castlereagh as early as April, did not reach
Abrantes till long after the army had moved forward. These
three battalions, the nucleus of the famous Light Division [5],

[1] The main convoy only reached Abrantes when Wellesley had advanced
to Plasencia, in Spain. See letter to the officer commanding Artillery
at Castello Branco, dated July 8, from Plasencia.

[2] Cf. Wellesley to Frere, June 14, to Commissary-General Murray,
June 16, both from Abrantes, and to Castlereagh, June 27.

[3] The 2/9th and 2/30th were sent to Gibraltar in May. The two
squadrons of the 20th Light Dragoons and the one squadron of the 3rd
Hussars of the K. G. L. were sent to Sicily at the same time.

[4] The 1/48th, 1/61st, and 23rd Light Dragoons.

[5] 1/43rd, 1/52nd, 1/95th. Of these three units only 1/43rd had been
in Robert Craufurd's old brigade, during the march to Sahagun. The
other two had been in Anstruther's brigade of Paget's reserve ; they had
therefore fought at Corunna, while Craufurd and the 'flank brigade' which

had all gone through the experiences of Moore's campaign, and were once more under their old leader Robert Craufurd. Detained by baffling winds in the Downs, the transports that bore them only reached Lisbon at various dates between June 28 and July 2, though they had sailed on May 25. Their indefatigable brigadier hurried them forward with all speed to the front, but in spite of his exertions, they only came up with the main army after the day of battle was over. The same was the fate of two batteries of horse artillery [1]—an arm in which Wellesley was wholly deficient when he marched into Spain. They arrived late, and were still far to the rear when the march from Abrantes began.

It thus resulted that although there were over 33,000 British troops in the Peninsula at the commencement of July 1809, less than 21,000 could be collected for the advance on Plasencia which was now about to begin. More than 8,000 men lay at Lisbon, or were just starting from that city, while 4,500 were in hospital [2]. The sick seemed more numerous than might have been expected at the season of the year: though the fatigues of the Oporto campaign accounted for the majority of the invalids, yet Wellesley was of opinion that a contributory cause might be found in the slack discipline of certain regiments, where inefficient commanding officers had neglected sanitary precautions, and allowed their men to neglect personal cleanliness, or to indulge to excess in wine and unripe fruit and vegetables. It was his opinion that the number of men in hospital should never exceed ten per cent. of the total force. But all through the war he found that this proportion was exceeded.

includes the 1/43rd, had been detached from the main army and had embarked at Vigo.

[1] A and I troops. The first joined in company with Craufurd. The second only appeared much later.

[2] Writing to Castlereagh on June 30, Wellesley remarks that 'according to your account I have 35,000 men—according to my own I have only 18,000,' but this was before he had been joined by the 1/61st, the 23rd Dragoons, and certain details. It is certain, from the careful table of troops engaged at Talavera which is to be found in the Record Office, that somewhat over 22,000 men entered Spain, and that after deducting sick left at Plasencia and elsewhere, just 20,600 fought at Talavera.

With the internal condition of many of his regiments Wellesley was far from satisfied. His tendency to use the plainest,
indeed the harshest, terms concerning the rank and file, is so
well known that we are not surprised to find him writing that
'the army behave terribly ill : they are a rabble who cannot bear
success any more than Sir John Moore's army could bear
failure [1].' He complained most of all of the recruits sent him
from the Irish militia, who were, he said, capable of every sin,
moral or military. Though he was 'endeavouring to tame the
troops,' yet there were several regiments in such bad order that
he would gladly have sent them home in disgrace if he could
have spared a man. The main offence, of course, was robbery
of food from the Portuguese peasantry, often accompanied by
violence, and now and then by murder. The number of assist-
ant-provost-marshals was multiplied, some offenders were caught
and hanged, but marauding could not be suppressed, even while
the troops were receiving full rations in their cantonments at
Abrantes. When they were enduring real privation, in the
wilds of Estremadura, matters grew much worse. Though
many regiments were distinguished for their good behaviour,
yet there were always some whose excesses were a disgrace to
the British army. Their Commander never shrank from telling
them so in the most incisive language ; he was always complaining that he could not get a sufficient number of the criminals
flogged or hanged, and that regimental court-martials were far
too lenient in their dealings with offenders [2].

It was at Abrantes that Wellesley first arranged his army in
divisions, and gave it the organization which, with certain
modifications, it was to maintain during the rest of the war.
His six regiments of cavalry were to form a single division
consisting of one heavy and two light brigades, commanded
respectively by Fane, Cotton, and Anson. The twenty-five

[1] These topics occur in many dispatches to Castlereagh. Perhaps the
most notable is that of May 31, 1809, written at Coimbra.

[2] Wellesley's anxiety to make examples may be traced in the series
of letters concerning a private of the 29th which occur in his July
dispatches. The man had been acquitted by a court-martial on the
ground of insanity, but this did not satisfy the Commander-in-chief, who
sends repeated orders that the award must be revised, and the man, if
possible, executed.

battalions of infantry were distributed into four divisions of
unequal strength under Generals Sherbrooke, Hill, Mackenzie,
and A. Campbell. Of these the first was by far the largest,
counting four brigades of two battalions each : the first (Henry
Campbell's) was formed of the two battalions of Guards, the
second (Cameron's) of two line regiments, the third and fourth,
under Low and Langwerth, comprised the infantry of the King's
German Legion. The second and third divisions each consisted
of two brigades of three battalions each[1]. The fourth, and
weakest, showed only five battalions in line. Of artillery there
were only thirty guns, eighteen English and twelve German :
all were field-batteries, as none of the much-desired horse
artillery had yet reached the front[2]. They were all of very
light calibre, the heaviest being a brigade of heavy six-pounders
belonging to the German Legion.

On June 28 the army at last moved forward : that day the
head quarters were at Corticada, on the Sobreira Formosa.
On the thirtieth Castello Branco, the last Portuguese town, was
reached. On July 3 the leading brigades passed the Elga, the
frontier river, and bivouacked on the same night around Zarza-
la-Major, the first place in Spanish Estremadura. At the
same time Sir Robert Wilson's small column of 1,500 Portuguese crossed the border a little further north, and advanced in
a direction parallel to that of the main army, so as to serve as
a flank guard for it in the direction of the mountains.

King Joseph meanwhile was in a state of the most profound
ignorance concerning the impending storm. As late as July 9
he wrote to his brother that the British had not as yet made
any pronounced movement, and that it was quite uncertain
whether they would invade Galicia, or strike at Castile, or
remain in the neighbourhood of Lisbon[3]! On that day the
head of the British army had entered Plasencia, and was only
125 miles from Madrid. It is impossible to give any better
testimonial than this simple fact to the way in which the insurgents and the guerrillas served the cause of the allies. Wellesley

---

[1] Viz. 2nd, Tilson and Richard Stewart; 3rd, Mackenzie and Donkin ;
4th, A. Campbell and Kemmis.

[2] A and I batteries R. H. A. were both late for Talavera.

[3] Joseph to Napoleon, from Talavera, July 9, 1809.

had been able to march from Oporto to Abrantes, and from
Abrantes to Plasencia, without even a rumour of his advance
reaching Madrid.   All that Joseph had learnt was that there
was now an allied force of some sort behind Alcantara, in the
direction of Castello Branco.   He took it for granted that they
were Portuguese, but in one dispatch he broaches the theory
that there might be a few English with them—perhaps from
having heard a vague report of the composition of Mackenzie's
division on the Zezere in May.   He therefore wrote in a cheerful tone to the Emperor that 'if we have only got to deal with
Cuesta and the Portuguese they will be beaten by the 1st Corps.
If they have some English with them, they can be beaten
equally well by the 1st Corps, aided by troops which I can send
across the Tagus via Toledo' (i.e. the 5,000 or 6,000 men of
the Central Reserve which could be spared from Madrid).   'I am
not in the least disquieted,' he continued, 'concerning the
present condition of military affairs in this part of Spain [1].'   In
another epistle to his brother he added that 'if the English
should be at the back of Cuesta, it would be the happiest chance
in the world for the concluding of the whole war [2].'

It was lucky for the King that he was not induced to try the
experiment of falling upon Wellesley and Cuesta with the
28,000 men of Victor and the Central Reserve.   If he had done
so, he would have suffered a frightful disaster and have lost
Madrid.

In the end of June and the first days of July Joseph's main
attention had been drawn off to that part of his front where
there was least danger, so that he was paying comparatively
little heed to the movements of the allies on the lower Tagus.
He had been distracted by a rash and inexplicable movement of
the Spanish army of La Mancha.   When General Venegas had
heard of the retreat of Victor from Estremadura, and had been
informed that Cuesta was about to move forward in pursuit of
the 1st Corps, he had concluded that his own troops might also
advance.   He argued that Sebastiani and the 4th Corps must

[1] Joseph to Napoleon, from Almagro, July 2, 1809.

[2] Joseph to Napoleon, from Madridejos, July 3, 1809.   It is fair to the
King to say that in this letter he concludes that he had better call Mortier
down into New Castile if the English are really on the move.

beat a retreat, when their right flank was uncovered by Victor's
evacuation of the valley of the Guadiana. He was partly
justified in his idea, for Joseph had drawn back Sebastiani's
main body to Madridejos when Victor abandoned Merida. It
was safe therefore to advance from the Despeña Perros into the
southern skirts of La Mancha, as far as Manzanares and the line
of the Guadiana. But to go further forward was dangerous,
unless Venegas was prepared to risk a collision with Sebastiani.
This he was certainly not in a condition to do : his troops had
not yet recovered from the moral effects of the rout of Ciudad
Real, and his brigades were full of new battalions of untried
Andalusian reserves. He should have been cautious, and have
refused to move without concerting his operations with Cuesta :
to have had his corps put *hors de combat* at the very beginning
of the joint campaign of the allied armies would have been most
disastrous.

Nevertheless Venegas came down from the passes of the
Sierra Morena with 18,000 infantry, 3,000 horse, and twenty-
six guns, and proceeded to thrust back Sebastiani's cavalry
screen and to push in his outposts in front of Madridejos.
The French general had in hand at this moment only two
infantry divisions and Milhaud's dragoons ; his third division
and his light cavalry were still absent with Victor, to whom
they had been lent in March for the campaign of Medellin.
But with 13,000 foot and 2,000 horse [1] he ought not to have
feared Venegas, and could have given a good account of him
had he chosen to attack. But having received exaggerated
reports of the strength of the Spanish army, he wrote to the
King that he was beset by nearly 40,000 men and must be
reinforced at once, or he would have to fall back on Madrid [2].
Joseph, fully believing the news, sent orders to Victor to restore
to the 4th Corps the divisions of Leval and Merlin, and then,
doubting whether these troops could arrive in time, sallied out

[1] The July strength of Sebastiani's corps, *présents sous les armes,* was
1st division (French) 8,113, 2nd division (Valence's Poles) 4,784, Milhaud's
dragoons 2,249—total 15,151.

[2] Joseph to Napoleon, from Illescas, June 23 : ' Le général Sebastiani
a devant lui des forces triples des siennes.' Joseph to Napoleon, from
Moral, July 1 : ' L'armée de 36,000 à 40,000 hommes qui menaçait le
4me Corps s'est enfuie et a repassé la Sierre Morena.'

of Madrid on June 22 with his Guards and half the division of
Dessolles—about 5,500 men.

It was lucky for Venegas that Sebastiani had refused to fight
him, but still more lucky that the news of the King's approach
reached him promptly. On hearing that Joseph had joined the
4th Corps on June 25 he was wise enough to turn on his heel
and retreat in all haste towards his lair in the passes of the
Sierra Morena. If he had lingered any longer in the plains he
would have have been destroyed, for the King, on the arrival of
Leval's and Merlin's divisions, would have fallen upon him at the
head of 27,000 men. As it was, Venegas retired with such
promptitude to Santa Cruz de Mudela, at the foot of the passes,
that the French could never catch him. Joseph pursued him
as far as Almagro and El Moral, on the southern edge of La
Mancha, and there stopped short. He had received, on July 2,
a dispatch from Victor to the effect that Cuesta had repaired
the bridge of Almaraz and begun to cross the Tagus, while
a body of 10,000 allied troops, presumably Portuguese, had
been heard of in the direction of Plasencia[1]. (This was in
reality the whole army of Wellesley!) Rightly concluding that
he had pushed the pursuit of Venegas too far, the King turned
back in haste, left Sebastiani and the 4th Corps behind the
Guadiana, and returned with his reserve to Toledo, in order to
be in a position to support Victor. His excursion to Almagro
had been almost as reckless and wrongheaded as Venegas's advance
to Madridejos, for he had separated himself from Victor by a gap
of 200 miles, at the moment when the British army was just
appearing on the Marshal's flank, while Cuesta was in his front.
If the allied generals had concentrated their forces ten days
earlier—a thing that might well have happened but for the
vexatious delays at Abrantes caused by Cuesta's impracticability
—the 1st Corps might have been attacked at the moment when
Joseph lay at the foot of the Sierra Morena, in a position too
remote from Talavera to allow him to come up in time to
succour Victor.

While the King was absent on his expedition in pursuit of
Venegas the most important change in the situation of affairs

[1] For all this see Joseph to Napoleon, from Moral [July 1], and from
Almagro [July 2].

on the Tagus was that the Duke of Belluno had drawn back
his troops from the line of the Tagus, where they had been
lying since June 19, and had retired behind the Alberche.
His retreat was not caused by any apprehension as to the
appearance of Wellesley on his flank—a fact which was completely concealed from him—but by sheer want of provisions.
On June 25 he sent to the King to say that his army was again
starved out of its cantonments, and that he had eaten up in
a week the small remnant of food that could be squeezed out
of the country-side between the Tagus and the Tietar, and was
forced to transfer himself to another region. 'The position,'
he wrote, 'is desperate. The 1st Corps is on the eve of dissolution : the men are dropping down from mere starvation. I have
nothing, absolutely nothing, to give them. They are in a state
of despair. . . . I am forced to fall back on Talavera, where there
are no more resources than here. We must have prompt succour,
but where can it be found? If your Majesty abandons me in my
present wretched situation, I lose my honour, my military record
—everything. I shall not be to blame for the disaster which
menaces my troops, but I shall have to bear the blame. To-
morrow I shall be at Talavera, waiting your Majesty's orders.
The enemy [Cuesta] has a pontoon-train : if he wishes to cross
the Tagus he can do so, for the 1st Corps can no longer remain
opposite him. Never was there a more distressing situation
than ours[1].'

On June 26, therefore, Victor transferred himself to Talavera,
and adopted a position behind the Alberche, after burning the
materials of the late pontoon bridge at Almaraz, which he had
taken up and stored in case they might again be needed. His
movement was a lucky one for himself, as it took him further
away from Wellesley's army, which was just about to start from
Abrantes with the object of turning his flank. It puzzled Cuesta,
who sought for some other explanation of his departure than
mere starvation, and was very cautious in taking advantage
of it. However, on the day after the French had withdrawn,
he pushed troops across the Tagus, and prepared to construct

---

[1] Victor to King Joseph, from the head quarters of the 1st Corps,
Calzada, near Oropesa, June 25. Intercepted dispatch in the Record
Office.

another bridge at Almaraz to replace that which the French had destroyed. His cavalry pushed out to Navalmoral and Oropesa, and further to the east he passed some detachments of infantry across the bridge of Arzobispo, which Victor—most unaccountably—had left intact. Fortunately he did no more, and refrained from advancing against Talavera, a step which from his earlier record we should judge that he might well have taken into consideration.

On the part of the allies things were now in a state of suspense from which they were not to stir for a fortnight. Cuesta was waiting for Wellesley, Wellesley was pushing forward from Zarza-la-Major to join Cuesta. Venegas was recovering at Santa Cruz de Mudela from the fatigues of his fruitless expedition into La Mancha.

But on the French side matters suffered a sudden change in the last days of July—the hand of the Emperor was stretched out from the banks of the Danube to alter the general dispositions of the army of Spain. On June 12 he had dictated at Schönbrunn a new plan of campaign, based on information which was already many weeks old when it reached him. At this date the Emperor was barely aware that Soult was being pressed by Wellesley in Northern Portugal. He had no detailed knowledge of what was taking place in Galicia or the Asturias, and was profoundly ignorant of the intrigues at Oporto which afterwards roused his indignation. But he was convinced that the English army was the one hostile force in Spain which ought to engage the attention of his lieutenants. Acting on this belief he issued an order that the 2nd, 5th, and 6th Corps—those of Soult, Mortier, and Ney—were to be united into a single army, and to be told off to the task of evicting Wellesley from Portugal. They were to put aside for the present all such subsidiary enterprises as the subjection of Galicia and the Asturias, and to devote themselves solely to 'beating, hunting down, and casting into the sea the British army. If the three Corps join in good time the enemy ought to be crushed, and then the Spanish war will come to an end. But the troops must be moved in masses and not march in small detachments. . . . Putting aside all personal considerations, I give the command of the united army to the Duke of Dalmatia, as the senior marshal. His three

Corps ought to amount to something between 50,000 and
60,000 men [1].'

This dispatch reached King Joseph at El Moral in La Mancha
on July 1, and Soult at Zamora on July 2. It had been drawn
up in view of events that were taking place about May 15.
It presupposed that the British army was still in Northern
Portugal, in close touch with Soult, and that Victor was in
Estremadura [2]. As a matter of fact Soult was on this day
leading his dilapidated corps down the Esla, at the end of his
retreat from Galicia. Ney, furious at the way in which his colleague had deserted him, had descended to Astorga three days
before. Mortier was at Valladolid, just about to march for
Villa-Castin and Madrid, for the King had determined to draw
him down to aid in the defence of the capital. Finally, Cuesta,
instead of lying in the Sierra Morena, as he was when Napoleon
drew up his orders, was now on the Tagus, while Wellesley was
no longer in touch with Soult on the Douro, but preparing to
fall upon Victor in New Castile. The whole situation was
so changed that the commentary which the Emperor appended
to his orders was hopelessly out of date—as was always bound
to be the case so long as he persisted in endeavouring to direct
the course of affairs in Spain from the suburbs of Vienna.

Soult was overjoyed at receiving the splendid charge which
the Emperor's decree put into his hands, though he must have
felt secret qualms at the idea that ere long some account of his
doings at Oporto must reach the imperial head quarters and
provoke his master's wrath. There was a bad quarter of an hour
to come [3]. But meanwhile he was given a formidable army, and
might hope to retrieve the laurels that he had lost in Portugal,
being now in a position to attack the British with an overwhelming superiority of numbers. It must have been specially

---

[1] Napoleon to Clarke [Minister of War], from Schönbrunn, June 12,
1809.

[2] The Emperor's dispatch contained many rebukes to Victor for not
pushing towards the North, to join hands with Soult. Jourdan very truly
remarks that if the 1st Corps had been sent in that direction, King Joseph
must infallibly have lost Madrid.

[3] The Emperor's stormy dispatch came in due course, but only in
September, see pp. 276-7.

delightful to him to find that Ney had been put under his orders, so that he would be able to meet his angry colleague in the character of a superior officer dealing with an insubordinate lieutenant.

Soult's first action, on finding himself placed in command of the whole of the French forces in North-western Spain, was to issue orders to Mortier to march on Salamanca, and to Ney to bring the 6th Corps down to Benavente. These dispositions clearly indicate an intention of falling upon Ciudad Rodrigo and Almeida, and assailing Northern Portugal—the plan which the Duke of Dalmatia had broached to the King in his letter from Puebla de Senabria on June 25, before he had received the news that the 5th and 6th Corps had been added to his command.

It is clear that on July 2 Soult had no knowledge of Wellesley's movements, and thought that the British army was quite as likely to be aiming at Salamanca as at Madrid. It is also evident that he was aware that he would be unable to move for some weeks. Till the 2nd Corps should have received the clothing, munitions, and artillery which had been promised it, it could not possibly take the field for the invasion of Portugal.

Soult, therefore, was obliged to wait till his stores should be replenished, and till the two corps from Astorga and Valladolid should concentrate on his flanks. It was while he was remaining perforce in this posture of expectation that the news of the real condition of affairs in New Castile was at last brought to him.

SECTION XVI: CHAPTER III

WELLESLEY AND CUESTA

It was not till the third day of July that Wellesley had been able to cross the Spanish border. Since Victor had assumed his new position to the north of the Tagus as early as the nineteenth of the preceding month, there was a perilous fortnight during which Cuesta and his army were left alone to face the French. All through this time of waiting, the British Commander-in-chief was haunted by the dread that the old Captain-General might repeat his earlier errors, and once more—as at Rio Seco and Medellin—court a pitched battle. Wellesley had done his best to urge caution, by letters written not only to Cuesta himself, but to his Chief-of-the-staff O'Donoju and to Colonel Roche, who had now replaced Bourke as British representative at the head quarters of the Army of Estremadura. Fortunately they were not needed: the Spanish General was for once cautious: he followed Victor at a respectful distance, and when he had reached the Tagus and repaired the bridge of Almaraz, held back his army to the southern bank and only pushed a few small detachments beyond the stream to search for the enemy. Since the French had withdrawn to Talavera on June 26 there was no collision. The cavalry of the 1st Corps were discovered upon the upper Tietar and the Alberche, but they preserved a defensive attitude, and the Spaniards did not provoke them by any rash attempt to drive them back upon their main body. All remained quiet, as Wellesley had rather desired than expected.

Cuesta's strategical position, therefore, was perfectly secure, since he kept his main body to the south of the river, and showed no desire to meddle with Victor before the arrival of the British. At this moment military affairs were not the only things that were engaging the attention of the old Captain-General. He was watching with considerable anxiety the course of events at Seville, where he was aware that he had many enemies. Ever since his high-handed action against the deputies of Leon in the preceding autumn, he knew that the Central Junta, and especially its Liberal wing, viewed him with suspicion and dislike. It was with great reluctance that they had placed him in command of the Estremaduran army, and if he had not been popular with the Conservative and clerical party and with some of the military cliques, he would not have retained his post for long. At this moment there were many intrigues stirring in Andalusia, and if some of them were directed against the Junta, others had no other end than the changing of the commanders of the various armies. While the Junta were debating about forms of government, and especially about the summoning of a national Cortes in the autumn, there were a number of officers of damaged reputation whose main object was to recover the military rank of which they had been deprived after misfortunes in the field. Infantado, who thought that it was absurd that he should have been disgraced after Ucles, while Cuesta had been rewarded after Medellin, was at the head of one party of intriguers, which included Francisco Palafox and the Conde de Montijo, and had secured the aid of Colonel Doyle, late British agent in Aragon and Catalonia, an officer who showed a lamentable readiness to throw himself into the intestine quarrels of the Spanish factions [1]. Their actions went to the very edge of high treason, for Montijo stirred up a riot at Granada on April 16, attacked the provincial authorities, and almost succeeded in carrying out a *pronunciamiento* which must have led to civil war. The Junta did no more than banish him to San Lucar, from which place he continued his plots with Infantado, in spite of the warning that he had received.

In Seville, faction if not so openly displayed was equally violent. There was, as we have already said, a large section of the Junta whose dearest wish would have been to displace Cuesta: it was they who had obtained the nomination of Venegas

---

[1] Doyle, as his numerous letters in the Record Office show, was such a furious partisan of the family of Palafox, that he believed that all the Spanish authorities were in a conspiracy to keep them down. He especially hated Blake.

to take charge of the troops in La Mancha, merely because he was known to be an enemy of the elder general. Yet since the two armies would have to co-operate in any attempt to recover Madrid, it was clearly inexpedient that their commanders should be at enmity. Some of the politicians at Seville were set on giving high command to the Duke of Albuquerque, an energetic and ambitious officer, but one gifted with the talent of quarrelling with every superior under whom he served : he was now bickering with Cuesta just as in March he had bickered with Cartaojal. The Duke was a great admirer of all things English, and a personal friend of Frere, the British minister. The latter did his best to support his pretensions, often expressing in official correspondence with the Junta a desire that Albuquerque might be given an independent corps, and entrusted with the charge of the movement that was to be concerted in conjunction with Wellesley's army.

But it was not so much Albuquerque as Wellesley himself that Cuesta dreaded as a possible successor. For Frere was possessed with the notion that the time had now arrived at which it would be possible to press for the appointment of a single Commander-in-chief of all the Spanish armies. The obvious person to fill this post was the victor of Vimiero and Oporto, if only Spanish pride would consent to the appointment of a foreigner. Frere had sufficient sense to refrain from openly publishing his idea. But he was continually ventilating it to his private friends in the Junta, in season and out of season. There can be no doubt that both from the military and the political point of view the results of Wellesley's exaltation to the position of Generalissimo would have been excellent. If he had controlled the whole of the Spanish armies in the summer of 1809, the course of affairs in the Peninsula would have taken a very different turn, and the campaign of Talavera would not have been wrecked by the hopeless want of co-operation between the allied armies. But it was not yet the time to press for the appointment : great as Wellesley's reputation already was, when compared with that of any Spanish general, it was still not so splendid or so commanding as to compel assent to his promotion [1]. Legitimate national pride stood in the way, and

[1] On June 9, Frere writes to tell Wellesley that if he could only have

even after Espinosa, and Tudela, and Medellin the Spaniards could not believe that it was necessary for them to entrust the whole responsibility for the defence of their country to the foreigner. Only a few of the politicians of Seville showed any liking for the project. Wellesley himself would have desired nothing so much as this appointment, but being wiser and less hopeful than Frere, he thought it useless to press the point. When the sanguine diplomat wrote to him, early in June, to detail his attempts to bring home the advisability of the project to his Spanish friends, the general's reply was cautious in the extreme. 'I am much flattered,' he said, ' by the notion entertained by some of the persons in authority at Seville, of appointing me to the command of the Spanish armies. I have received no instruction from Government upon that subject: but I believe that it was considered an object of great importance in England that the Commander-in-chief of the British troops should have that situation. But it is one more likely to be attained by refraining from pressing it, and leaving it to the Spanish themselves to discover the expediency of the arrangement, than by any suggestion on our parts.' He concluded by informing Frere that he could not conceive that his insinuation was likely to have any effect, and that the opinion of the British Ministry was probably correct—viz. that at present national jealousy made the project hopeless [1].

Now it was impossible that Frere's well-meaning but mistaken endeavours should escape the notice of Cuesta's friends in Seville. The British Minister had spoken to so many politicians on the subject, that we cannot doubt that his colloquies were promptly reported to the Captain-General of Estremadura. This fact goes far to explain Cuesta's surly and impracticable behaviour towards Wellesley during the Talavera campaign. He disliked his destined colleague not only because he was a foreigner, and because he showed himself strong-willed and outspoken during

destroyed Soult at Oporto, instead of merely chasing him across the frontier, it would have been possible to secure him the post of Generalissimo at once. This chance had gone by, but ' your friends here (among whom you may count Mr. de Garay) are doing their best for you.' [Record Office, from Seville, June 9, 1809.]

[1] Wellington to Frere, from Abrantes, June 16, 1809.

their intercourse, but because he believed that the Englishman was intriguing behind his back to obtain the post of
Generalissimo. This belief made him determined to assert his
independence on the most trifling matters, loth to fall in with
even the most reasonable plans, and suspicious that every proposal made to him concealed some trap. He attributed to
Wellesley the design of getting rid of him, and was naturally
determined to do nothing to forward it.

The English officers who studied Cuesta's conduct from the
outside, during the Talavera campaign, attributed his irrational
movements and his hopeless impracticability to a mere mixture
of pride, stupidity, and obstinacy. They were wrong; the
dominant impulse was resentment, jealousy, and suspicion—a
combination far more deadly in its results than the other. He
awaited the approach of Wellesley with a predisposition to
quarrel and a well-developed personal enmity, whose existence
the British general had not yet realized.

We have dealt in the last chapter with the strength and
organization of the British army at the moment when Wellesley
crossed the frontier on July 3. It remains to speak of the two
Spanish armies which were to take part in the campaign. We
have already seen that Cuesta's host had been reinforced after
Medellin with a new brigade of Granadan levies, and a whole
division taken from the army of La Mancha[1]. Since that date
he had received large drafts both of infantry and cavalry from
Andalusia. Six more regiments of horse had reached him, besides
reinforcements for his old corps. All were now strong in numbers, and averaged between 400 and 500 sabres, so that by the
middle of June he had fully 7,000 mounted men under his orders.
Eight or nine additional regiments of infantry had also come to
hand since April—some of them new Andalusian levies, others
old corps whose *cadres* had been filled up since the disaster of
Ucles. His infantry counted about 35,000 bayonets, divided into

[1] I can nowhere find the date of the transference, but it took place
before July : the old regiments of Calatrava, Sagunto, Alcantara, and
Pavia, which were with Venegas's army in March, had been transferred to
Cuesta's by June, as also the new regiments of Sevilla, and Cazadores de
Madrid. My most valuable source of information is an unpublished
dispatch of Cuesta's in the Madrid War Office, which gives all the names
of regiments, but not their numbers.

five divisions and a 'vanguard': the latter under Zayas was about
4,000 strong, each of the others exceeded 5,000. The cavalry
formed two divisions, under Henestrosa and Albuquerque, one
composed of seven, one of six regiments. There were thirty guns—
some of heavy calibre, nine- and twelve-pounders—with about
800 artillerymen. The whole army, inclusive of sick and
detached, amounted to 42,000 men, of whom perhaps 36,000 were
efficients present with the colours [1].

The second Spanish army, that of La Mancha under Venegas,
was much weaker, having furnished heavy detachments to
reinforce Cuesta before it took the field in June. Its base was
the old 'Army of the Centre,' which had been commanded by
Castaños and Infantado. Some twenty battalions that had
seen service in the campaign of Tudela were still in its ranks:
they had been recruited up to an average of 500 or 600
bayonets. The rest of the force was composed of new Andalusian regiments, raised in the winter and spring, some of which
had taken part in the rout of Ciudad Real under Cartaojal,
while others had never before entered the field. The gross total
of the army on June 16 was 26,298 men, of whom 3,383 were
cavalry. Deducting the sick in hospital, Venegas could dispose
of some 23,000 sabres and bayonets, distributed into five
divisions. The horsemen in this army were not formed into
separate brigades, but allotted as divisional cavalry to the
infantry units. There was little to choose, in point of efficiency,
between the Estremaduran army and that of La Mancha; both
contained too many raw troops, and in both, as was soon to be
proved, the bulk of the cavalry was still as untrustworthy as it
had shown itself in previous engagements.

The Spaniards therefore could put into the field for the campaign of July on the Tagus some 60,000 men. But the fatal
want of unity in command was to prevent them from co-ordin-
ating their movements and acting as integral parts of a single
army guided by a single will. Venegas was to a certain degree
supposed to be under Cuesta's authority, but as he was continually receiving orders directly from the Junta, and was

[1] These totals may be regarded as certain, being drawn from the dispatch
of Cuesta's alluded to above, which I was fortunate enough to find at Madrid.
Unfortunately no regimental figures are given, only the gross total.

treated by them as an independent commander, he practically
was enabled to do much as he pleased. Being a personal enemy
of Cuesta, he had every inducement to play his own game, and
did not scruple to do so at the most important crisis of the
campaign,—covering his disregard of the directions of his senior
by the easy pretext of a desire to execute those of the central
government.

On July 15, the day when his share in the campaign commenced, the head quarters of Venegas were at Santa Cruz de Mudela, just outside the northern exit of the Despeña Perros. His
outposts lay in front, at El Moral, Valdepeñas, and Villanueva
de los Infantes. He was divided by a considerable distance—
some twenty-five miles—from the advanced cavalry of Sebastiani's
corps, whose nearest detachment was placed at Villaharta, where
the high-road to Madrid crosses the river Giguela.

Meanwhile we must return to Wellesley, who having crossed
the frontier on July 3, was now moving forward by short
marches to Plasencia. On the fourth the head quarters were
at Zarza la Mayor, on the sixth at Coria, on the seventh at
Galisteo ; on the eighth Plasencia was reached, and the general
halted the army, while he should ride over to Almaraz and
confer in person with Cuesta on the details of their plan of
campaign. In the valley of the Alagon, where the country was
almost untouched by the hand of war, provisions were obtainable in some quantity, but every Spanish informant agreed that
when the troops dropped down to the Tagus they would find
the land completely devastated. Wellesley was therefore most
anxious to organize a great dépôt of food before moving on :
the local authorities professed great readiness to supply him,
and he contracted with the Alcaldes of the fertile Vera de
Plasencia for 250,000 rations of flour to be delivered during the
next ten days [1]. Lozano de Torres, the Spanish commissary-
general sent by the Junta to the British head quarters, promised
his aid in collecting the food, but even before Wellesley departed to visit Cuesta, he had begun to conceive doubts whether
supplies would be easily procurable. The difficulty was want of
transport—the army had marched from Portugal with a light
equipment, and had no carts to spare for scouring the country-

---

[1] Wellesley to Frere, *Wellington Dispatches*, iv. 524.

side in search of flour. The General had relied on the assurances sent him from Seville to the effect that he would easily be able to find local transport in the intact regions about Coria and Plasencia: but he was disappointed: very few carts could be secured, and the store of food in the possession of the army seemed to shrink rather than to increase during every day that the army remained in the valley of the Alagon, though the region was fruitful and undevastated. It is certain that the British commissaries had not yet mastered the art of gathering in provisions from the country-side, and that the Spanish local authorities could not be made to understand the necessity for punctuality and dispatch in the delivery of the promised supplies.

On July 10 Wellesley started off with the head-quarters staff to visit Cuesta, at his camp beyond the bridge of Almaraz, there to concert the details of their joint advance. Owing to an error made by his guides he arrived after dusk at the hamlet below the Puerto de Mirabete, around which the main body of the Army of Estremadura was encamped. The Captain-General had drawn out his troops in the afternoon for the inspection of the British commander. When at last he appeared they had been four hours under arms in momentary expectation of the arrival of their distinguished visitor, and Cuesta himself, though still lame from the effect of his bruises at Medellin, had sat on horseback at their head during the greater part of that time.

Two admirable accounts of the review of the Estremaduran host in the darkness were written by members of Wellesley's staff. It is well worth while to quote one of them [1], for the narrative expresses with perfect clearness the effect which the sight of the Spanish troops made upon their allies:—

'Our arrival at the camp was announced by a general discharge of artillery, upon which an immense number of torches were made to blaze up, and we passed the entire Spanish line in review by their light. The effect produced by these arrangements was one of no ordinary character. The torches, held aloft at moderate intervals, threw a red and wavering light over the whole scene, permitting at the same time its minuter parts

---

[1] That of Charles Stewart (Lord Londonderry) on pp. 382-3 of the first volume of his *History of the Peninsular War*.

to be here and there cast into the shade, while the grim and swarthy visages of the soldiers, their bright arms and dark uniforms, appeared peculiarly picturesque as often as the flashes fell upon them. Nor was Cuesta himself an object to be passed by without notice: the old man preceded us, not so much sitting upon his horse as held upon it by two pages, at the imminent risk of being overthrown whenever a cannon was discharged, or a torch flamed out with peculiar brightness. His physical debility was so observable as clearly to mark his unfitness for the situation which he held. As to his mental powers, he gave us little opportunity of judging, inasmuch as he scarcely uttered five words during the continuance of our visit: but his corporal infirmities were ever at absolute variance with all a general's duties.

'In this way we passed by about 6,000 cavalry drawn up in rank entire, and not less than twenty battalions of infantry, each of 700 to 800 bayonets. They were all, without exception, remarkably fine men. Some indeed were very young—too young for service—particularly among the recruits who had lately joined. But to take them all in all, it would not have been easy to find a stouter or more hardy looking body of soldiers in any European service. Of their appointments it was not possible to speak in the same terms of commendation. There were battalions whose arms, accoutrements, and even clothing might be pronounced respectable[1]: but in general

---

[1] As to the equipment of the Spaniards, the following quotation from Leslie (p. 135) may be worth giving: 'Their uniforms were of every variety of colour, the equipment and appointments of the most inferior description. One could not but lament these defects, for the men were remarkably fine, possessing all the essential qualities to make good soldiers—courage, patience, and soberness. Their officers, in general, were the very reverse! The line infantry were in blue uniforms with red facings. The Provincial Corps, called "Volunteers," were mostly dressed in the brown Spanish cloth of the country, with green or yellow facings. Some had chakoes, others broad-brimmed hats with the rim turned up at one side : all had cap-plates of tin announcing their designation. Some had belts, others none. They had no pouches, but a broad belt of soft leather, in which were placed a row of tin tubes, each holding a cartridge, with a fold of leather to cover them, fastened round the waist. The cavalry were heavy and light dragoons, with some regiments of Hussars. Some were tolerably well dressed, in blue or yellow uniforms

they were deficient, particularly in shoes. It was easy to perceive, from the attitude in which they stood, and the manner in which they handled their arms, that little or no discipline prevailed among them : they could not but be regarded as raw levies. Speaking of them in the aggregate they were little better than bold peasantry, armed partially like soldiers, but completely unacquainted with a soldier's duty. This remark applied to the cavalry as much as to the infantry. Many of the horses were good, but the riders manifestly knew nothing of movement or of discipline : and they were on this account, as also on that of miserable equipment, quite unfit for service. The generals appeared to have been selected by one rule alone —that of seniority. They were almost all old men, and, except O'Donoju and Zayas, evidently incapable of bearing the fatigues or surmounting the difficulties of a campaign. It was not so with the colonels and battalion commanders, who appeared to be young and active, and some of whom were, we had reason to believe, learning to become skilful officers. . . . Cuesta seemed particularly unwilling that any of his generals should hold any serious conversation with us. It is true that he presented them one by one to Sir Arthur, but no words were exchanged on the occasion, and each retired after he had made his bow.' Albuquerque, of whom the Captain-General was particularly jealous, had been relegated with his division to Arzobispo, and did not appear on the scene.

The all-important plan of campaign was settled at a long conference—it lasted for four hours—on the morning of the following day. According to all accounts the scene at the interview must have been curious. Cuesta could not, or would not, speak French : Wellesley was not yet able to express himself fluently in Spanish. Accordingly, O'Donoju, the chief of the staff of the Army of Estremadura, acted as interpreter between them, rendering Wellesley's views into Spanish and Cuesta's into English. The greater part of the discussion consisted in the bringing forward of plans by the British commander and their rejection by the Captain-General. Cuesta was full of suspicion,

with red facings. Some had boots, but more long leather leggings, coming up above the knee. The horses were small, active, and hardy, of the Spanish Barbary breed.'

and saw a trap in every proposal that was made to him: he imagined that Wellesley's main object was to edge him out of the supreme command. He was almost silent throughout the interview, only opening his lips to give emphatic negatives, for which O'Donoju proceeded to find ingenious and elaborate explanations.

It was not the principles on which the campaign was to be conducted, but the details of the distribution of the troops on which the trouble arose. The enemy's position and force was fairly well known to both generals, except in one all-important particular. They were aware that Victor lay behind the Alberche with not much more than 22,000 men, that Sebastiani was at Madridejos with a somewhat smaller force[1], and that King Joseph with his central reserve, which they over-estimated at 12,000 men, was able at any moment to join the 1st Corps. Hence they expected to find some 34,000 French troops at Talavera, and rightly considered that with the 55,000 men of their two armies they ought to give a good account of them. Sebastiani, as they supposed, might be left out of the game, for occupation for him would be found by the army of La Mancha, which was to be told off for this purpose and directed to cling to the skirts of the 4th Corps and never to lose sight of it. As Venegas would have, according to their calculations, nearly double the numbers of Sebastiani, he would have no difficulty in keeping him in check.

But it was not only on the French troops in New Castile that watch had to be kept. It was necessary to take into account the enemy beyond the mountains, in the valley of the Douro. The allied generals were aware that Mortier and Soult must both be considered. The former they knew to be at Valladolid, and they had learnt that King Joseph was proposing to bring him down towards Madrid—as was indeed the fact. Accordingly they expected that he might turn up in a few days somewhere in the direction of Avila. Soult they knew to be at Zamora, and from the dispatches captured with General Franceschi ten days before, they had a good knowledge of his force and intentions. A study of these documents led them to conclude

[1] They estimated him at only 10,000 men, but he had really 20,000. Wellesley to Castlereagh, July 15, from Plasencia.

that he could not move for many weeks, owing to the dilapidated state of his corps—which he had painted in the most moving terms in his letters to King Joseph[1]. They also gathered that if he moved at all, he would be inclined to threaten Northern Portugal or Ciudad Rodrigo: in the dispatches captured with Franceschi he had named Braganza as a point at which he might strike. Accordingly they opined that he need not be taken very seriously into consideration, especially as he was wholly destitute of artillery[2]. Yet he might be drawn into the field by the news that Madrid was in danger. If he were induced to bring help to the King, he would almost certainly work by making a diversion against the communications of the British army, and not by directly joining himself to Joseph's army by the long and circuitous march from Zamora to Madrid. To carry out such a diversion he would be obliged to cross the lofty Sierra de Francia by one of the passes which lead from the Salamanca region into the valley of the

---

[1] Soult had written [from Puebla de Senabria, June 25]: 'Je me propose de reposer les troupes trois ou quatre jours : pendant ce temps elles se prépareront des subsistances, on raccommodera la chaussure, les chevaux seront ferrés, et je menacerai de nouveau le Portugal : peut-être même je ferai faire une incursion vers Bragance, afin d'opérer une diversion qui ne peut pas manquer de produire quelque effet. . . . Je me fais précéder à Zamora (où je compte être rendu le 2 juillet) par l'ordonnateur Le Noble, qui doit réclamer près l'intendant-général de l'armée des moyens en tout genre qui me manquent — tel que l'habillement, chaussure, ambulance, officiers de santé, administration, transport militaire, payeurs, argent pour solde et dépenses extraordinaires, postes etc. J'ai l'honneur de supplier Votre Majesté de daigner donner des ordres pour qu'il soit fait droit à ses demandes : mes besoins sont très grands. . . . Il y a plus de cinq mois que je n'ai reçu ni ordre, ni nouvelle, ni secours, par conséquent je dois manquer de beaucoup de choses.'

[2] Wellesley's views at this moment appear in his correspondence, e. g. to Mr. Villiers, July 8 : 'I defy Soult to do Beresford or Portugal any injury as long as his army is in its present situation—or any amelioration of that situation which can be produced in a short period of time.' To Beresford, July 9 : 'I have no apprehension that Soult will be able to do anything with his corps for some time, but I think that column ought to be watched.' To Beresford, July 14 : 'I do not believe that Ney has quitted Galicia, at least we have not heard that he has. Soult can do nothing against Portugal, for he is in a most miserable state, without arms, artillery or ammunition, stores, &c.'

Alagon—perhaps by the defile of Perales, but much more probably by the better known and more practicable pass of Baños. Wellesley took the possibility of this movement into serious consideration, but did not think that it would be likely to cause him much danger if it should occur, for he believed that Soult would bring with him no more than the 15,000 or 18,000 men of his own 2nd Corps. That he would appear not with such a small force, but with Ney and Mortier in his wake, leading an army of 50,000 bayonets, did not enter into the mind of the British commander. Mortier was thought to be moving in the direction of Avila: Ney was believed to be contending with the Galician insurgents in the remote regions about Lugo and Corunna. The news of his arrival at Astorga had not yet reached the allied camps, and he was neglected as a factor in the situation. Wellesley and Cuesta had no conception that any force save that of Soult was likely to menace their northern flank and their line of communications when they committed themselves to their advance on Madrid. To provide against a possible movement of the 2nd Corps into the valley of the Tagus, therefore, all that was necessary was to hold the defiles of Perales and Baños. The former had already been seen to, for even before the meeting of Wellesley and Cuesta, Carlos d'España had blocked it with two or three battalions drawn from the garrison of Ciudad Rodrigo. For the latter Wellesley hoped that Cuesta would provide a sufficient garrison[1]. The old Captain-General promised to do so, but only sent 600 men under the Marquis Del Reino, a wholly inadequate detachment[2].

Wellesley's first proposal to his Spanish colleague was that the main bodies of both armies should advance against Victor, while a detachment of 10,000 men should move out to the left, in the direction of Avila, to look for Mortier, if he were to be

[1] Wellesley to Beresford, July 9 : 'I have not forgotten either the Puerto de Baños or the Puerto de Perales, and have called upon Cuesta to occupy both. The former is already held, and the latter will be so in a day or two.' [This was unfortunately not to be the case.]

[2] I cannot discover the names of the two very weak battalions, the smallest in Cuesta's army, which were detached for this purpose under Del Reino. They are *not* the same as the two battalions which joined Wilson (Merida and 3rd of Seville).

found in that direction, and if not to turn the enemy's right and threaten Madrid. He hoped that Venegas and the army of La Mancha might at the same time move forward against Sebastiani, and keep him so fully employed that he would not be able to spare a man to aid Victor and King Joseph.

Cuesta at once refused to make any detachment in the direction of Avila from his own army, and suggested that Wellesley should find the 10,000 men required for this diversion. The English general objected that it would take exactly half his force, and that he could not split up such a small unit, while the Spaniards could easily spare such a number of troops from their total of 36,000 men. This argument failed to move Cuesta, and the project was dropped, Wellesley thinking that it was not strictly necessary, though very advisable [1].

The only flanking force which was finally set aside for operations on the left wing, for the observation of the French about Avila and the feint at Madrid, consisted of Sir Robert Wilson's 1,500 Portuguese, and a corresponding body of two battalions and one squadron from the Spanish army [2]—about 3,500 men in all. It played a part of some little importance in the campaign, but it is hard to see that it would have exercised any dominant influence even if it had been raised to the full strength that Wellesley had desired. Mortier, as a matter of fact, was not near Avila, and so the 10,000 men sent in this direction would not have served the end that the British general expected. The 5th Corps had been called off by Soult, contrary to the wishes of the King, and no body of troops was needed to contain it, on this part of the theatre of war. It was ultimately to appear at a very different point, where no provision had been made for its reception.

[1] Wellesley to Frere, July 13 : 'You will see, in the accompanying letter, an account of my endeavour to prevail on General Cuesta to make a detachment upon Avila. I agree with you that it would be a great advantage from a military point of view . . . but I must at the same time inform you that I do not consider the movement to be *necessary* as a military measure.' Frere and Wellesley had hoped that Albuquerque might be placed in command of this large detachment, and might distinguish himself at its head.

[2] Battalions of Merida (1,170 bayonets) and 3rd of Seville (810 bayonets).

Far more important were the arrangements which Wellesley and Cuesta made for the diversion on their other flank. It was from the miscarriage of this operation, owing to the wilful disobedience of the officer charged with it, that the failure of the whole campaign was to come about. They agreed that Venegas with the 23,000 men of the army of La Mancha, was to move up the high-road from his position at Santa Cruz de Mudela, and drive Sebastiani before him. Having pushed back the 4th Corps to the Tagus, Venegas was then to endeavour to force the passage of that river either at Aranjuez or at Fuente-dueñas, and to threaten Madrid. It was calculated that Sebastiani would be forced to keep between him and the capital, and would be unable to spare a man to reinforce Victor and King Joseph. Thus Wellesley and Cuesta with 56,000 men would close on the King and the Marshal, who could not have more than 35,000, and (as it was hoped) defeat them or at least manœuvre them out of Madrid. A glance at the map will show one peculiarity of this plan : it would have been more natural to bid Venegas march by the bridge of Toledo rather than by those of Aranjuez and Fuentedueñas ; to use the latter he would have to move towards his right, and to separate himself by a long gap from the main army of the allies. At Toledo he would be within thirty-five miles of them—at Aranjuez seventy, at Fuentedueñas 100 miles would lie between him and the troops of Wellesley and Cuesta. It would appear that the two generals at their colloquy came to the conclusion that by ordering Venegas to use the eastern passages of the Tagus they would compel Sebastiani to remove eastward also, so that he would be out of supporting distance of Victor. They recognized the bare possibility that Sebastiani might refuse to devote himself to the task of holding back the army of La Mancha, might leave Madrid to its fate, and then hurry off to join the King and the 1st Corps in an assault on the main Anglo-Spanish army. In this case they settled that Venegas should march on the capital and seize it, a move which (as they supposed) would force Joseph to turn back or to re-divide his army[1]. But it is clear that

---

[1] All these details as to the joint plan are better expressed in Cuesta's Apologetic *Manifesto,* published after his resignation, than in Wellesley's *Dispatches* to Castlereagh and Frere.

they did not expect to have to fight Victor, the King, and
Sebastiani combined, as they were ultimately forced to do at
Talavera on July 28.   They supposed that Venegas would find
occupation for the 4th Corps, and that they might count on
finding only the 1st Corps and Joseph's Madrid reserves in front
of them.

When armies are working in a joint operation from separate
bases it is all-important that they should time their movements
with the nicest exactitude. This Wellesley and Cuesta attempted
to secure, by sending to Venegas an elaborate time-table.   He
was ordered to be at Madridejos on July 19, at Tembleque on the
twentieth, at Santa Cruz de la Zarza on the twenty-first, and
at the bridge of Fuentedueñas on the twenty-second or twenty-
third.   All this was on the supposition that Sebastiani would
have about 12,000 men and would give ground whenever pressed.
If he turned out by some unlikely chance—presumably by having
rallied the King's reserves—to be much stronger, Venegas was
to manœuvre in the direction of Tarancon, to avoid a general
action, and if necessary to retreat towards the Passes from which
he had started.   It would be rather an advantage than otherwise if (contrary to all probability) the French had concentrated
their main force against the army of La Mancha, for this
would leave Victor helpless in front of the united hosts of
Wellesley and Cuesta, which would outnumber him by two
to one.

What the allied generals never expected was that Venegas
would let Sebastiani slip away from his front, without any
attempt to hold him, and would then (instead of marching on
Madrid) waste the critical days of the campaign (July 24-29)
in miserable delays between Toledo and Aranjuez, when there
was absolutely no French field-force between him and Madrid,
nor any hostile troops whatever in his neighbourhood save a weak
division of 3,000 men in garrison at Toledo.   The failure of the
Talavera campaign is due even more to this wretched indecision
and disobedience to orders on the part of Venegas than to the
eccentricities and errors of Cuesta.   If the army of La Mancha
had kept Sebastiani in check, and refused to allow him to
abscond, there would have been no battles on the Alberche on
July 27-28, for the French would never have dared to face the

4

Last Coinage of Charles IV.   Half-Dollar of 1807

1

Tarragona Siege-Dollar
of 1809

Gerona Siege-Dollar of 1808

2

Valencian
Quarter-Dollar
of 1809

With portrait of
Ferdinand VII and
patriotic inscription

5

3

6

Provisional
Dollar struck by the French at Barcelona, 1810

Provisional Piece for
30 Sueldos, struck at Palma,
1808

7

Madrid Dollar of Joseph Bonaparte, 1811

SPANISH COINS OF THE PERIOD OF THE PENINSULAR WAR

Anglo-Spaniards of the main host without the assistance of the 4th Corps.

But to return to the joint plan of Wellesley and Cuesta : on July 23, the day on which Venegas was to reach Fuentedueñas (or Aranjuez) the 56,000 men of the grand army were to be assailing Victor behind the Alberche. The British were to cross the Tietar at Bazagona on the eighteenth and follow the high-road Navalmoral-Oropesa. The Estremadurans, passing the Tagus at Almaraz and Arzobispo, were to move by the parallel route along the river bank by La Calzada and Calera, which is only five or six miles distant from the great *chaussée*. Thus the two armies would be in close touch with each other, and would not be caught apart by the enemy. On reaching Talavera they were to force the fords of the Alberche and fall upon Victor in his cantonments behind that stream. Sir Robert Wilson and the 3,500 men of his mixed Spanish and Portuguese detachment were to move up as the flank-guard of the allied host, and to push by the head waters of the Tietar for Escalona on the side-road to Madrid [1].

Criticisms of the most acrimonious kind have been brought to bear on this plan by English, French, and Spanish writers. Many of them are undeserved ; in particular the tritest objection of all, made *ex post facto* by those who only look at the actual course of the campaign, that Wellesley was exposing his communications to the united forces of Soult, Ney, and Mortier. There was on July 10, when Cuesta and Wellesley met, no reason whatever for apprehending the contingency of the march of the three marshals upon Plasencia. Soult, as his own letters of June 25 bore witness, was not in a condition to move—he had not a single piece of artillery, and his troops were in dire need of rest and re-equipment. Ney was believed to be at Corunna or Lugo—Soult's intercepted dispatches spoke of the 6th Corps as being destined to remain behind in Galicia, and he (as the allied generals supposed) ought best to have known what his colleague was about to do. How could they have guessed that, in wrath at his desertion by the Duke of Dalmatia, Ney would evacuate the whole kingdom, abandon fortresses like

[1] Cuesta's and Wellesley's accounts of their joint plan on the whole agree wonderfully well.

Ferrol and Corunna, and march for Astorga? Without Ney's
corps to aid him, Soult could not possibly have marched on
Plasencia—to have done so with the 2nd Corps alone would
have exposed him to being beset by Wellesley on one side and
by Beresford on the other. As to Mortier and the 5th Corps,
Cuesta and Wellesley undervalued their strength, being unaware
that Kellermann had sent back from the Asturias the division
that had been lent him for his expedition to Oviedo. They
thought that the Duke of Treviso's force was more like 7,000
than 17,000 bayonets, and—such as it was—they had the best
of reasons for believing that it was more likely to march on
Madrid by Avila than to join Soult, for they had before them
an intercepted dispatch from the King, bidding Mortier to move
down to Villacastin in order to be in supporting distance of the
capital and the 1st Corps.

On the whole, therefore, the two generals must be excused for
not foreseeing the descent of 50,000 men upon their communications, which took place three weeks after their meeting at the
bridge of Almaraz: the data in their possession on July 10 made
it appear most improbable.

A much more valid criticism is that which blames the method
of co-operation with Venegas which was employed. 'Double
external lines of operations' against an enemy placed in a
central position are notoriously perilous, and the particular
movement on Fuentedueñas, which the army of La Mancha was
ordered to execute, was one which took it as far as possible from
Wellesley's and Cuesta's main body. Yet it may be urged in
their defence that, if they had drawn in Venegas to join them,
they would have got little profit out of having 23,000 more
Spaniards on the Alberche. Sebastiani on the other hand, who
could join Victor at the same moment that the corps from La
Mancha joined the allies, would bring some 17,000 excellent
troops to Talavera. The benefit of drawing in Venegas would
be much less than the disadvantage of drawing in Sebastiani to
the main theatre of war. Hence came the idea that the army
from the Passes must be devoted to the sole purpose of keeping
the 4th Corps as far as possible from the Alberche. Even
knowing that Venegas was hostile to Cuesta, and that he was
a man of no mark or capacity, Wellesley could not have expected

that he would disobey orders, waste time, and fail utterly in keeping touch with Sebastiani or threatening Madrid.

The one irreparable fault in the drawing up of the whole plan of campaign was the fundamental one that Wellesley had undertaken to co-operate with Spanish armies before he had gauged the weak points of the generals and their men. If he had held the post of commander-in-chief of the allied forces, and could have issued orders that were obeyed without discussion, the case would have been different. But he had to act in conjunction with two colleagues, one of whom was suspicious of his intentions and jealous of his preponderant capacity, while the other deliberately neglected to carry out clear and cogent orders from his superior officer. Cuesta's impracticability and Venegas's disobedience could not have been foreseen by one who had no previous experience of Spanish armies. Still less had Wellesley realized all the defects of the Spanish rank and file when placed in line of battle. That he did not hold an exaggerated opinion of their merits when he started on the campaign is shown by letters which he wrote nine months before [1]. But he was still under the impression that, if cautiously handled, and not exposed to unnecessary dangers, they would do good service. He had yet to witness the gratuitous panic of Portago's division on the eve of Talavera, and the helplessness of the Spanish cavalry at the combats of Gamonal and Arzobispo. After a month's experience of Cuesta and his men, Wellesley vowed never again to take part in grand operations with a Spanish general as his equal and colleague. This was the teaching of experience—and on July 10 the experience was yet to come.

The interview at the bridge of Almaraz had not been very satisfactory to Wellesley, but it was far from having undeceived him as to the full extent of the difficulties that lay before him. He wrote to Frere at Seville that he had been on the whole well received, and that Cuesta had not displayed any jealousy of him. As that sentiment was at this moment the predominant feeling in the old man's breast, it is clear that he had succeeded in hiding it. But the obstinate silence of Wellesley's colleague had worried him. O'Donoju had done all the talking, and 'it was impossible to say what plans the general entertains.'

[1] See Wellington to Castlereagh, from Ramalhal, Sept. 1808.

He was moreover somewhat perturbed by the rumours which his staff had picked up from the Estremaduran officers, to the effect that Cuesta was so much the enemy of the Central Junta that he was plotting a *pronunciamiento* for its deposition [1]. As to the fighting powers of the Spanish army, Wellesley wrote to Castlereagh that 'the troops were ill clothed but well armed, and the officers appeared to take pains with their discipline. Some of the corps of infantry were certainly good, and the horses of the cavalry were in good condition.' Only ten days later he was to utter the very different opinion that 'owing to their miserable state of discipline and their want of officers properly qualified, these troops are entirely incapable of performing any manœuvre however simple [2],' and that 'whole corps, officers and men, run off on the first appearance of danger [3].'

The British Commander-in-chief had indeed many moral and mental experiences to go through between the interview at Mirabete on July 10, and the retreat from Talavera on August 2 !

[1] 'The general sentiment of the army appears to be contempt for the Junta and the present form of government, great confidence in Cuesta, and a belief that he is too powerful for the Junta, and will overturn that government. This sentiment appears to be so general that I conceive that the Duke of Albuquerque must entertain it equally with others : but I have not seen him.' Wellesley to Frere from Plasencia, July 13.

[2] Wellesley to Castlereagh, Talavera, Aug. 1.

[3] Wellesley to his brother the Marquis Wellesley, Deleytosa, Aug. 8.

SECTION XVI: CHAPTER IV

THE MARCH TO TALAVERA: QUARREL OF WELLESLEY AND CUESTA

HAVING returned to his army on July 12, Wellesley gave orders for the whole force to get ready for a general advance on the morning of the eighteenth, the day which had been chosen for the commencement of operations at the conference of Almaraz. It would have been in every way desirable to have moved out at once, and not to have waited for these six days. If the march against Victor had been fixed for the thirteenth or fourteenth, the French would have been caught unprepared, for as late as the seventeenth King Joseph and his adviser Jourdan were under the impression that the force at Plasencia consisted of nothing more than a Portuguese division of 10,000 men, and it was only on the twenty-second that they received the definite information that the whole British army was upon the Tietar [1]. It is clear that, by advancing five days earlier than he actually did, Wellesley might have caught the enemy in a state of complete dispersion—the 4th Corps being on July 20 still at Madridejos in La Mancha, and the King with his reserves at Madrid. If attacked on the seventeenth or the eighteenth, as he might well have been, Victor would have found it impossible to call up Sebastiani in time, and must have fallen back in haste to the capital. The allies could then have cut him off from the 4th Corps, which must have retreated by a circuitous route, and could not have rejoined the main body of the French army in time for a battle in front of Madrid.

It would appear that Wellesley had fixed the date of his

---

[1] See Jourdan's *Mémoires*, and his letter to Soult of July 17, in which no sign whatever appears of the knowledge of the advance of the British from Portugal.

advance so late as the eighteenth mainly because of the difficulty as to the collection of provisions, which was now looming before him in larger proportions than ever. But it is possible that the necessity for allowing some days for the transmission of the plan of campaign to Venegas also counted for something in the drawing up of the time-table. It would have been rash to start before the army of La Mancha was prepared to take its part in the joint plan of operations. So much depended upon the diversion which Venegas was to execute, that it would have been a mistake to move before he could break up from his distant cantonments at Santa Cruz de Mudela. No word, however, concerning this appears in Wellesley's correspondence. From July 13 to July 18 his dispatches show anxiety about nothing save his food and his transport. Every day that he stayed at Plasencia made him feel more uncomfortable concerning the all-important question of supplies. The corn which the Alcaldes of the Vera had promised to secure for him had begun to come in, though in driblets and small consignments, but there was no means of getting it forward: transport was absolutely unprocurable [1]. Wellesley sent officers to scour the country-side as far as Bejar and Ciudad Rodrigo, but they could procure him neither mules nor carts. He also pressed the Spanish commissary-general, Lozano de Torres, to hunt up every animal that could be procured, but to small effect. The fact was that Estremadura was not at any time rich in beasts or vehicles, and that the peasantry had sent away most of those they owned while the French lay at Almaraz, lest they should be carried off by the enemy. Wellesley, who did not understand the limited resources of this part of Spain, was inclined to believe that the authorities were hostile or even treacherous.

---

[1] That food was coming in, but no transport, is clearly proved by Wellesley's letter to the Junta of Plasencia on July 18 : ' Upon entering Spain I expected to derive that assistance in provisions and other means [i. e. transport] which an army invariably receives from the country in which it is stationed, more particularly when it has been sent to aid the people of that country. *I have not been disappointed in the expectation that I had formed of receiving supplies of provisions, and I am much obliged to the Junta for the pains they have taken.* I am convinced that they did everything in their power to procure us the other means we required [transport], although I am sorry to say that we have not received them.'

The Central Junta had promised him transport in order to
make sure of his starting on the campaign along the Tagus,
and when transport failed to appear, he attributed it to ill-will
rather than to poverty.   No doubt he was fully justified in his
view that an army operating in a friendly country may rationally expect to draw both food and the means to carry it from
the regions through which it is passing.   But sometimes the
provisions or the transport are not forthcoming merely because
the one or the other is not to be found.   It is certain that
both Estremadura and the valley of the central Tagus were at
this moment harried absolutely bare : Victor's despairing letters
from Caceres in May and from La Calzada in June are sufficient
proof of the fact.   In a district where the Marshal said that
' he could not collect five days' provisions by any manner of
exertion,' and that ' his men were dropping down dead from
actual starvation, so that he must retire or see his whole corps
crumble away [1],' it is clear that the Central Junta could not
have created food for the British army.   Cuesta's troops were
living from hand to mouth on supplies sent forward from Andalusia, or they could not have continued to exist in the land.
The only district which was intact was that between Coria and
Plasencia, and this was actually at the moment feeding the
British army, and had done so now for ten days or more.   But
unfortunately the Vera could give corn but no draught animals.
If Wellesley had known this, he must either have exerted himself
to procure more transport before leaving Abrantes—a difficult
task, for he had already drained Portugal of carts and mules—
or have refused to march till the Spaniards sent him wagon
trains from Andalusia.   It would have taken months for the
Junta to collect and send forward such trains : they had dispatched all that they could procure to Cuesta.   The campaign
on the Tagus, in short, would never have been fought if
Wellesley had understood the state of affairs that he was to
encounter.

The causes, therefore, of the deadlock that was about to
occur were partly the light-hearted incompetence of the Central
Junta in promising the British army the use of resources which
did not exist, partly Wellesley's natural ignorance of the

[1] See pp. 443 and 459.

miserable state of Central Spain. He had never entered the country before, and could not know of its poverty. He had trusted to the usual military theory that the country-side ought to provide for a friendly army on the march : but in Spain all military theories failed to act. Napoleon committed precisely similar errors, when he directed his army corps to move about in Castile as if they were in Germany or Lombardy, and found exactly the same hindrances as did the British general. In later years Wellesley never moved without a heavy train, and a vast provision of sumpter-beasts and camp-followers. In July 1809 he had still to learn the art of conducting a Spanish campaign.

Meanwhile he was beginning to feel most uncomfortable about the question of provisions. His anxiety is shown by his letters to Frere and Beresford ; ' it is impossible,' he wrote, ' to express the inconvenience and risk that we incur from the want of means of conveyance, which I cannot believe the country could not furnish, *if there existed any inclination to furnish them.* The officers complain, and I believe not without reason, that the country gives unwillingly the supplies of provisions that we have required . . . and we have not procured a cart or a mule for the service of the army [1].' But to O'Donoju, the chief of the staff of the Estremaduran army, he wrote in even more drastic terms, employing phrases that were certain to provoke resentment. He had, he said, scoured the whole region as far as Ciudad Rodrigo for transport, and to no effect. ' If the people of Spain are unable or unwilling to supply what the army requires, I am afraid that they must do without its services.' He had been forced to come to a painful decision, and ' in order to be fair and candid to General Cuesta' he must proceed to inform him that he would execute the plan for falling upon Victor behind the Alberche, but that when this had been done he would stir no step further, and ' begin no new operation till he had been supplied with the means of transport which the army requires [2].'

After dispatching this ultimatum, whose terms and tone leave something to be desired—for surely Cuesta was the last

[1] Wellesley to Frere, Plasencia, July 16.
[2] Wellesley to O'Donoju, Plasencia, July 16.

person to be saddled with the responsibility for the pledges made by his enemies of the Central Junta—Wellesley issued orders for the army to march. He had been joined at Plasencia by the last of the regiments from Lisbon, which reached him in time for Talavera [1], but had been forced to leave 400 sick behind him, for the army was still in a bad condition as regards health. It was therefore with little over 21,000 men that he began his advance to the Alberche. It was executed with punctual observance of the dates that had been settled at the interview at Almaraz. On July 18 the army crossed the Tietar on a flying bridge built at Bazagona, and lay at Miajadas. On the next night the head quarters were at Centinello ; on the twentieth the British entered Oropesa. Here Cuesta joined them with his whole army, save the two battalions lent to Wilson, and the two others under the Marquis Del Reino which had been sent to the Puerto de Baños. Deducting these 2,600 bayonets and his sick, he brought over 6,000 horse and 27,000 foot to the rendezvous. The junction having taken place on the twenty-first, the advance to Talavera was to begin next morning. Oropesa lies only nineteen miles from that town, and as Victor's cavalry vedettes were in sight, it was clear that contact with the enemy would be established during the course of the day. Accordingly the allied armies marched with caution, the Spaniards along the high-road, the British following a parallel path on the left, across the slopes of the hills which divide the valley of the Tietar from that of the Tagus.

About midday the Spaniards fell in with the whole of the cavalry division of Latour-Maubourg, which Victor had thrown out as a screen in front of Talavera. He had ascertained on the evening of the preceding day that Cuesta was about to move forward, and was anxious to compel him to display his entire force. Above all he desired to ascertain whether the rumours concerning the presence of British troops in his front were correct. Accordingly he had left two battalions of infantry in the town of Talavera, and thrown out the six regiments of dragoons in front of it, near the village of Gamonal. The Spaniards were advancing with Albuquerque's cavalry division as an advanced guard. But seeing Latour-Maubourg in his

[1] The 1/61st Foot and 23rd Light Dragoons.

front the Duke refused to attack, and sent back for infantry and guns. Cuesta pushed forward the division of Zayas to support him, but even when it arrived the Spaniards made no headway. They continued skirmishing for four hours [1] till the British light cavalry began to appear on their left. ' Though much more numerous than the enemy,' wrote an eye-witness, ' they made no attempt to drive him in, but contented themselves with deploying into several long lines, making a very formidable appearance. We had expected to see them closely and successfully engaged, having heard that they were peculiarly adapted for petty warfare, but we found them utterly incapable of coping with the enemy's *tirailleurs*, who were driving them almost into a circle.'

On the appearance, however, of Anson's cavalry upon their flank the French went hastily to the rear, skirted the suburbs of Talavera, and rode off along the great Madrid *chaussée* to the east, followed by the British light dragoons. As they passed the town two small columns of infantry came out of it and followed in their rear. Albuquerque sent one of his regiments against them, but could not get his men to charge home. On three separate occasions they came on, but, after receiving the fire of the French, pulled up and fell into confusion. The impression made by the Spanish cavalry on the numerous British observers was very bad. ' No men could have more carefully avoided coming to close quarters than did the Spaniards this day [2],' wrote one eye-witness. 'They showed a total lack not only of discipline but of resolution [3],' observes another.

After crossing the plain to the north of Talavera the French, both cavalry and infantry, forded the Alberche and halted on the further bank. On arriving at the line of underwood which masks the river the pursuers found the whole of Victor's corps in position. The thickets on the further side were swarming with *tirailleurs*, and two batteries opened on Anson's brigade as it drew near to the water, and sent balls whizzing among Wellesley's staff when he pushed forward to reconnoitre the position.

---

[1] ' And,' adds Lord Munster, from whom this quotation is taken (p. 199), ' it is my belief that they would have continued *till now* if we had not aided them.'

[2] Londonderry, i. 392.   [3] Lord Munster, p. 200.

It was soon seen that Victor had selected very favourable fighting-ground : indeed he had been staying at Talavera long enough to enable him to get a perfect knowledge of the military features of the neighbourhood. The 1st Corps was drawn up on a range of heights, about 800 yards behind the Alberche, with its left resting on the impassable Tagus, and its right on a wooded hill, behind which the smaller river makes a sharp turn to the east, so as to cover that flank. The position was formidable, but rather too long for the 22,000 men who formed the French army. Having learnt from the people of Talavera that the enemy had received no reinforcements up to that morning, from Madrid or any other quarter, Wellesley was anxious to close with them at once. The afternoon was too far spent for any attempt to force the passage on the twenty-second, but on the next day (July 23) the British general hoped to fight. The Alberche was crossed by a wooden bridge which the enemy had not destroyed, and was fordable in many places : there seemed to be no reason why the lines behind it might not be forced by a resolute attack delivered with numbers which were as two to one to those of the French.

Accordingly Wellesley left the 3rd division and Anson's light horse in front of the right wing of Victor's position, and encamped the rest of his army some miles to the rear, in the plain between Talavera and the Alberche. In the same way Albuquerque and Zayas halted for the night opposite the bridge on the French left, while the main body of the Spaniards occupied the town in their rear. In the evening hours Wellesley endeavoured to urge upon Cuesta the necessity for delivering an attack at dawn: he undertook to force the northern fords and to turn the enemy's right, if his colleague would attack the southern fords and the bridge. The Captain-General 'received the suggestion with dry civility,' and asked for time to think it over. After a conference with his subordinates, he at last sent word at midnight that he would accept the proposed plan of operations.

At 3 o'clock therefore on the morning of the twenty-third, Wellesley brought down Sherbrooke's and Mackenzie's divisions to the ground opposite the fords, and waited for the arrival of the Spanish columns on his right. They did not appear, and after long waiting the British general rode to seek his colleague. He found him opposite the bridge of the Alberche, 'seated on the cushions taken out of his carriage, for he had driven to the outposts in a coach drawn by nine mules, the picture of mental and physical inability.' The old man murmured that the enemy's position had not been sufficiently reconnoitred, that it would take time to get his army drawn out opposite the points which it was to attack, that he was not sure of the fords, that the bridge over which his right-hand column would have to advance looked too weak to bear artillery, and many other things to the same effect—finally urging that the forcing of the Alberche must be put off to the next day. As he had not got his troops into battle order, it was clear that the morning would be wasted, but Wellesley tried to bargain for an attack in the afternoon. The Captain-General asked for more time, and would listen to no arguments in favour of fighting on that day. After a heated discussion Wellesley had to yield : he could not venture to assail the French with his own army alone, and without any assistance from the Spaniards. Accordingly it was agreed that the advance should not be made till the dawn of the twenty-fourth.

In the afternoon the pickets sent back information that Victor seemed to be on the move, and that his line was growing thin. Cuesta was then persuaded to go forward to the outposts ; he was hoisted on to his horse by two grenadiers, while an aide-de-camp stood on the other side to conduct his right leg over the croup and place it in the stirrup. Then, hunched up on his saddle, he rode down to the river, observed that the greater part of the enemy were still in position, and refused to attack till next morning.

At dawn, therefore, on the twenty-fourth the allied army moved forward to the Alberche in three columns, and found, as might have been expected, that the French had disappeared. On seeing the masses of redcoats opposite his right upon the previous day, Victor had realized at last that he had before him the whole British army. He had sent his train to the rear in the afternoon, and drawn off his entire force after dusk. By dawn he was more than ten miles away, on the road to Santa Ollala and Madrid. It was useless to pursue him with any hope of forcing him to a battle. The chance of crushing him before he should receive any further reinforcements had disappeared. It is not at all to his credit as a general that he had held his ground so long ; if he had been attacked on the twenty-third, as Wellesley had desired, he must certainly have suffered a disaster. He had but 22,000 men ; and it is clear that, while the Spaniards were attacking his left and centre, he could not have set aside men enough to hold back the assault of the solid mass of 20,000 British troops upon his right. He should have vanished on the twenty-second, the moment that Latour-Maubourg reported that Wellesley's army was in the field. By staying for another day on the Alberche he risked the direst disaster.

The British general would have been more than human if he had not manifested his anger and disgust at the way in which his colleague had flinched from the agreement to attack, and sacrificed the certainty of victory. He showed his resentment by acting up to the terms of his letter written from Plasencia five days before, i.e. by announcing to Cuesta that, having carried out his pledge to drive the French from behind the Alberche, he should now refuse to move forward, unless he were furnished with transport sufficient to make it certain that the army could reach Madrid without any privations. He was able to state with perfect truth that he had already been forced to place his troops on half-rations that very morning : to the 10,000 men of Sherbrooke's and Mackenzie's divisions and of Anson's light cavalry, he had only been able to issue 5,000 rations of bread [1]. Nothing, of course, could be found at Talavera, where the French had been quartered for many days. Victor had only been maintaining his troops by the aid of biscuit sent down from Madrid, and by seizing and threshing for himself the small amount of corn which had been sown in the neighbourhood that spring. Wellesley was wrong in supposing that the 1st Corps had been supporting itself with ease from the country-side [2]. He was equally at fault when he asserted that the 'Spanish army has plenty to eat.' Cuesta was at this moment complaining to the Junta that he was short of provisions, and that the food which he had brought forward

[1] Wellesley to Sherbrooke, Talavera, July 24.
[2] Wellesley to Castlereagh, July 24.

from the Guadiana was almost exhausted. Meanwhile every
exertion was being made to collect flour and transport from the
rear : Wellesley wrote to O'Donoju that he had at last hopes
of securing some wagons from the Plasencia district within
three days, and that 'in the meantime he might get something
to eat.' He had some days before sent orders back even so far
as Abrantes, to order up 200 Portuguese carts which had been
collected there, and the Central Junta had informed him that
a train for his use had already started from Andalusia. But
'there was no very early prospect of relieving the present
distress [1].'

Cuesta was, as might have been expected, as angry with
Wellesley for refusing to move forward from Talavera, as
Wellesley was with Cuesta for missing the great opportunity of
July 23. When informed that the British army was not about
to advance any further, he announced that he for his part should
go on, that Victor was in full flight, and that he would pursue
him to Madrid. 'In that case' dryly observed Wellesley, 'Cuesta
will get himself into a scrape ; but any movement by me to his
assistance is quite out of the question. If the enemy discover
that we are not with him, he will be beaten, or must return.
The enemy will make this discovery to-day, if he should risk any
attempt upon their rearguard at Santa Ollala [2].' In reply to
the Captain-General's declaration that he should press Victor
hard, his colleague only warned him that he would be wiser 'to
secure the course of the Tagus and open communication with
Venegas, while the measures should be taken to supply the
British army with means of transport [3].' The Spaniard would not
listen to any such advice, and hurried forward ; though he had
been for many weeks refusing to fight the 1st Corps when it lay
in Estremadura, he was now determined to risk a second
Medellin. Apparently he was obsessed by the idea that Victor
was in full retreat for Madrid, and would not make a serious
stand. Underlying his sudden energy there was also some idea
that he would disconcert his masters of the Central Junta by
recovering the capital : he had discovered, it would seem, that

[1] Wellesley to Beresford, from Plasencia, July 14.
[2] Wellesley to Frere, Talavera, July 25.
[3] Ibid. ; and also Wellesley to O'Donoju, July 25.

the Junta had sent secret orders to Venegas, directing him to take charge of the city on its reconquest, and giving him authority to nominate the civil and military officers for its administration. If the Army of Estremadura seized Madrid, while the Army of La Mancha was still lingering on the way thither, all these plans would be frustrated [1].

Accordingly Cuesta pushed on very boldly on the afternoon of the twenty-fourth, dividing his army into two columns, of which one marched on Santa Ollala by the high-road to the capital, while the other moved by Cevolla and Torrijos on the side-road to Toledo. He was uncertain whether Victor had retired by one or by both of these routes : if all his corps had taken the former path, the natural deduction was that he was thinking only of Madrid : if the Toledo road had also been used, there was reason for concluding that the Marshal must be intending to join Sebastiani and the 4th Corps, who might be looked for in that direction. Late in the day the Spanish general ascertained that the main body of Victor's army had taken the latter route: he proceeded to follow it, placing his head quarters that night at Torrijos, only fifteen miles from Toledo. Next morning he learnt to his surprise and dismay that he had in front of him not only the 1st Corps, but also Sebastiani and the King's reserves from Madrid : for just at this moment the whole French force in New Castile had been successfully concentrated, and nearly 50,000 men were gathered in front of the 33,000 troops of the Army of Estremadura. Venegas's diversion had utterly failed to draw off the 4th Corps to the East ; the King had come down in haste from Madrid, and thus the whole plan of campaign which the allied generals had drawn up had been foiled—partly by the sloth of Venegas, partly by Cuesta's inexplicable and perverse refusal to fight on July 23 upon the line of the Alberche.

[1] Cf. Arteche, vi. 358, with Wellesley's remarks on the inexplicable eagerness of Cuesta to be in Madrid on an early day.

SECTION XVI: CHAPTER V

CONCENTRATION OF THE FRENCH ARMIES: THE KING TAKES THE OFFENSIVE: COMBATS OF TORRIJOS AND CASA DE SALINAS

It is now necessary to turn to the French camp, in order to realize the course of events which had led to the concentration of such a formidable force in the environs of Toledo. Down to the twenty-second of July Joseph and his adviser Jourdan had remained in complete ignorance of the advance of Wellesley upon Plasencia, and seem to have been perfectly free from any apprehension that Madrid was in danger. Since their return from their fruitless pursuit of the army of La Mancha, they had been spending most of their energy in a controversy with Soult. The Duke of Dalmatia, not content with the command of the three army corps which Napoleon had put at his disposal, had been penning elaborate dispatches to the King to demand that the greater part of the remaining French troops in Spain should be used to co-operate in his projected campaign against the English in Portugal. He wrote on July 13 to urge on Joseph the necessity (1) of drawing large detachments from the armies of Aragon and Catalonia, in order to form a corps of observation in the kingdom of Leon to support his own rear; (2) of placing another strong detachment at Plasencia to cover his flank; (3) of transferring every regiment that could be spared from Madrid and New Castile to Salvatierra on the Tormes, just south of Salamanca, in order to form a reserve close in his rear, which he might call up, if necessary, to strengthen the 60,000 men whom he already had in hand. He also demanded that Joseph should send him at once 200,000 francs to spend on the fortification of Zamora, Toro, and other places on the Douro, as also 500,000 francs more for the present expenses of the 2nd,

5th, and 6th Corps. If this were granted him, together with
2,000,000 rations of flour, and a battering-train of at least forty-
eight heavy guns for the sieges of Ciudad Rodrigo and Almeida,
he thought that he should be in a position to deliver a serious
attack on Northern Portugal, and ultimately to drive the British
army into the sea [1].

On the day upon which the Duke of Dalmatia made these
comprehensive demands upon King Joseph, the British army
had been for ten days in Spain, and was preparing to advance
from Plasencia on Madrid. It was therefore an exquisitely
inappropriate moment at which to demand that the greater part
of the King's central reserve should be sent off from the capital
to the neighbourhood of Salamanca. There were other parts
of Soult's lists of requisitions which were equally impracticable.
It is clear that Suchet could not have spared a man from
Aragon, and that St. Cyr, with the siege of Gerona on his
hands, would have found it absolutely impossible to make large
detachments from Catalonia. Even if he and Suchet had been
able to send off troops to Leon, they would have taken months
to reach the Galician frontier. The demand for 700,000 francs
in hard cash was also most unpalatable : King Joseph was at
this moment in the direst straits for money : his brother could
send him nothing while the Austrian war was in progress, and
as he was not in proper military possession of any large district
of Spain, he was at this moment in a condition of hopeless
bankruptcy. He confessed to Soult that he was living from hand
to mouth, by the pitiful expedient of melting down and coining
the silver plate in the royal palace at Madrid.

Jourdan therefore replied, in the King's behalf, to Soult that he
must do his best with the 60,000 men already at his disposition,
that no troops from Catalonia, Aragon, or Madrid could be spared,
and that money could not be found. All that could be given
was the battering-train that had been demanded, 600,000
rations of biscuit, and an authorization to raise forced contributions in Old Castile. For the protection of his flanks
and his communications the Marshal must utilize Kellermann's
dragoons and the other unattached troops in the valley of the

[1] Soult to Joseph, July 13. Compare with this Jourdan to Soult of
July 17, the reply to these modest demands.

Douro, a force which if raised to 12,000 men by detachments from the 5th or 6th Corps could keep La Romana and the Galicians in check [1].

It is curious to note how entirely ignorant both Soult and the King were as to the real dangers of the moment. Soult had drawn up, and Joseph acceded to [2], a plan for the siege of Ciudad Rodrigo, and an invasion of Northern Portugal— operations which would take long weeks of preparation—at the time when Madrid was in imminent danger from the combined armies of Wellesley, Cuesta, and Venegas. The Marshal's plan was perfectly correct from the point of view of the higher strategy—the main objective of the French was certainly the British army, and it would have been highly advisable to invade Northern Portugal with 60,000 men in the front line, and 40,000 in support, if the circumstances of the moment had permitted it. But these circumstances were hidden alike from Soult and the King, owing to the impossibility of obtaining accurate information of the movements of the allies. The fundamental difficulty of all French operations in the Peninsula was that the commanders could never discover the whereabouts of the enemy till he actually came in contact with their out-posts. Hence it chanced that Soult was planning, and Joseph approving, a campaign on the borders of Northern Portugal, at the precise moment when the British were on the march for Talavera.

It was actually not until July 22 that the King's eyes were at last unsealed. Victor having come into collision with the cavalry of Wellesley's advanced guard, sent news to Madrid that the British army had joined Cuesta, and had reached the Alberche. On the same day, by a fortunate chance, there also arrived in the capital another emissary of Soult, with a message much less impracticable than that which had last been sent. This was General Foy, whom the Duke of Dalmatia had dispatched on July 19, after receiving very definite rumours that the British were moving in the valley of the Tagus, and

---

[1] Jourdan to Soult, July 17, 1809, from Madrid.

[2] ' Le roi pense, comme vous, qu'il est important de s'emparer de Ciudad Rodrigo ; cette place servira de place d'armes aux troupes qui seront dans le cas d'entrer en Portugal.'—Ibid.

not approaching Old Castile [1]. The Marshal sent word that in this case he must of course concert a common plan of operations with the King, and abandon any immediate action against Portugal. He suggested that his best plan would be to concentrate his three corps at Salamanca, and to march against the flank and rear of the English by way of Bejar and the Puerto de Baños. If the King could cover Madrid for a time with the 1st and 4th Corps, he would undertake to present himself in force upon Wellesley's line of communications, a move which must infallibly stop the advance of the allies towards the capital. If they hesitated a moment after his arrival at Plasencia, they would be caught between two fires, and might be not merely checked but surrounded and destroyed. Soult added, however, that he could not move till the 2nd Corps had received the long-promised provision of artillery which was on its way from Madrid, and till he had rallied Ney's troops, who were still at Astorga, close to the foot of the Galician mountains.

Napoleon, at a later date, criticized this plan severely, declaring that Soult ought to have marched on Madrid to join the King, and not on Plasencia. He grounded his objections to the scheme on the strategical principle that combined operations on external lines should be avoided. 'The march of Marshal Soult,' he wrote, 'was both dangerous and useless—dangerous, because the other army might be beaten (as happened at Talavera) before he could succour it, so that the safety of all my armies in Spain was compromised: useless, because the English had nothing to fear; they could get behind the Tagus in three hours; and whether they crossed at Talavera or at Almaraz, or anywhere else, they could secure a safe line of retreat on Badajoz.' Against this criticism the defence made by both Soult and King Joseph was that it would have required a much longer time to bring the three corps from the Douro to Madrid than to Plasencia; that it would have taken them at least ten days to reach Madrid, and that during those days the King and his army might have been beaten and driven out of the capital by the united forces of Wellesley, Cuesta, and Venegas. It was, of course, impossible to foresee on

[1] Compare Le Noble's account of Soult's proposals (pp. 312–3) with Jourdan's *Mémoires*, and with the *Vie Militaire du Général Foy*, p. 83.

July 22 that Wellesley would refuse to pursue Victor beyond
Talavera, or that Venegas would let Sebastiani slip away from
him.   Accordingly King Joseph and Jourdan fell in with
Soult's suggestion, because they thought that he would come
sooner into the field if he marched on Plasencia, and would
remove the pressure of the British army from them at a
comparatively early date.   As a matter of fact, he took a much
longer time to reach Plasencia than they had expected : they
had hoped that he might be there on July 27, while his
vanguard only reached the place on August 1, and his main
body on the second and third [1].   But it seems clear that the
expectation that he would intervene on the earlier date was far
too sanguine.   Soult dared not move till his three corps were
well closed up, and since Ney had to come all the way from
Astorga, it would have been impossible in any case to mass
the army at Plasencia much earlier than was actually done.
Napoleon's remark that Soult could not hope to catch or
surround the British army seems more convincing than his
criticism of the march on Plasencia.   If the passes of the Sierra
de Gata had been properly held, and prompt news had been
transmitted to Talavera that the French were on the move from
the valley of the Douro, Wellesley would have had ample time
to cover himself, by crossing the Tagus and transferring his
army to the line of operations, Truxillo-Badajoz.   The British
general always defended himself by this plea : and complained
that those who spoke of him as being 'cut off from Portugal,'
by the arrival of Soult at Plasencia, forgot that he had as good
a base at Elvas and Badajoz as at Abrantes.

But we must not look too far forward into the later stages of
the campaign.   It is enough to say that Jourdan and Joseph
sent back Foy to rejoin Soult, on the same day that he had
reached Madrid, bearing the orders that the Marshal was to
collect his three corps with the greatest possible haste, and to
march by Salamanca on Plasencia, where they trusted that he
might present himself on the twenty-seventh or twenty-eighth
of the current month.   Meanwhile it was necessary to hold

---

[1] For the controversy about the expected date of Soult's arrival at
Plasencia, see Joseph's and Jourdan's letter to Napoleon, in Ducasse's
Mémoires du Roi Joseph, and on the other side Le Noble's *Campagne de 1809.*

back Cuesta and Wellesley till the Duke of Dalmatia's operations in their rear began to produce their effect. The only
possible way of doing this was to concentrate in all haste every
available man in New Castile, and to cover Madrid as long as
possible. This massing of the French forces turned out to be
perfectly feasible, since Venegas had neglected to press in upon
Sebastiani, so that it was possible to withdraw the whole 4th
Corps from in front of him, and to send it to reinforce Victor,
without any immediate danger. Accordingly, the 1st Corps was
directed to fall back from its perilous advanced position on
the Alberche, and to draw near to Toledo : Sebastiani was told
to abandon Madridejos and La Mancha, and to hasten by
forced marches toward the same point : while the King himself
resolved to leave Madrid with the slenderest of garrisons, and
to carry the rest of the central reserve to the general rendezvous.
Accordingly, he left only one brigade of Dessolles' division, with
a few of his untrustworthy Spanish levies, to hold the capital :
the total did not amount to much over 4,000 men, and General
Belliard, the governor of the city, was warned that he must be
prepared to retreat into the Retiro forts, with his troops and
the whole body of the *Afrancesados* and their families, if anything untoward should occur. For it was possible that an
insurrection might break out, or that Venegas might succeed in
slipping into Madrid by the roads from the east, or again, that
Wilson (whose column had been heard of at Escalona and was
believed to be much larger than was actually the case), might
attempt a *coup de main* from the west. Leaving Belliard in
this dangerous and responsible position, the King marched out
upon the twenty-third with the remaining brigade of Dessolles's
division, the infantry and cavalry of his French Guard, two
squadrons of chasseurs and fourteen guns, a force of some 5,800
men [1]. He had reached Naval Carnero, with the intention of
joining Victor on the Alberche, when he received the news that

---

[1] The whole consisted of :

Infantry of the Guard . .	1,800	Brought forward	5,400
Chevaux-Légers of the Guard	250	27th Chasseurs (two squad-	
Godinot's Brigade of Des-		rons)	250
solles's Division . . .	3,350	Artillery (two batteries) .	200
Carry forward	5,400	Total	5,850

the Marshal had retired towards Toledo, and was lying at Bargas
behind the Guadarama river.   Here Joseph joined him on the
morning of July 25.

On their concentration a force of 46,000 men was collected,
Victor having brought up 23,000, the King 5,800, and Sebastiani 17,500.   The latter had placed four of the six Polish
battalions of Valence's division in Toledo, and was therefore
short by 3,000 bayonets of the total force of his corps.   With
such a mass of good troops at their disposition, Joseph, Jourdan,
and Victor were all agreed that it was right to fall upon the
Spaniards without delay.   They were astonished to find that
the British army was not in their front, but only Cuesta's
troops.   They had expected to see the whole allied host before
them, and were overjoyed to discover that the Estremadurans
alone had pushed forward to Torrijos and Santa Ollala.
Instead, therefore, of being obliged to fight a defensive battle
behind the river Guadarama, it was in their power to take the
offensive.

This was done without delay : on the morning of July 26 the
French army advanced on Torrijos, with the 1st Corps at the
head of the column.   But Cuesta, when once he had discovered
the strength of the force in his front, had resolved to retreat.
Victor found opposed to him only the division of Zayas and
two cavalry regiments, which had been told off to cover the
withdrawal of the Estremaduran army.   The Marshal sent out
against this rearguard the chasseurs of Merlin and the dragoons
of Latour-Maubourg, who drove in the Spanish horse, almost
exterminating the unfortunate regiment of Villaviciosa, which,
in retiring, chanced to blunder against the high stone walls of
some enclosures from which exit was difficult[1].   Zayas then
went to the rear, and retired towards the cavalry division of
Albuquerque, which Cuesta hastily sent to his assistance.
The French cavalry took some time to re-form for a second
attack, and their infantry was still far off.   The Spanish rear-

---

[1] 'The cavalry regiment of Villaviciosa, drawn up in an enclosure with
but one exit, was penned in by the enemy and cut to pieces without
a possibility of escape.   A British officer of engineers, present with them,
saved himself by his English horse taking at a leap the barrier which the
Spanish horses were incapable of clearing.'   Lord Munster, p. 208.

guard therefore, covered by Albuquerque's horse, had time
enough to fall back on the main body, which was already in
full retreat. Their cavalry then followed, and being not very
strenuously pursued by Merlin and Latour-Maubourg, got off in
safety. The whole army, marching at the best of its speed, and
in considerable disorder, finally reached the Alberche without
being caught up by the enemy. Cuesta found the British
divisions of Sherbrooke and Mackenzie guarding the river:
Wellesley had sent them forward when he heard of the approach
of the French, and had placed the former on the hills above the
further side of the bridge, to cover the passage, and the latter
in reserve. He rode out himself to meet the Spanish general,
and begged him to carry his army beyond the Alberche, as it
would be extremely dangerous to be caught with such an
obstacle behind him, and no means of retreat save a long bridge
and three fords. But Cuesta tempted providence by declaring
that he should encamp on the further bank, as his troops were
too exhausted to risk the long defile across the bridge after
dark. His sullen anger against Wellesley for refusing to follow
him on the twenty-fourth was still smouldering in his breast,
and the English were convinced that he remained on the wrong
side of the river out of pure perversity, merely because his
colleague pressed him to put himself in safety. He consented,
however, to retreat next morning to the position which Wellesley
had selected in front of Talavera.

The French made no appearance that night, though they might
well have done so, and the Spanish army, bivouacing confusedly
in the narrow slip of flat ground between the heights and the
Alberche, enjoyed undisturbed rest during the hours of darkness. It is impossible not to marvel at the slackness with
which Victor conducted the pursuit: he had twelve regiments
of splendid cavalry to the front [1], and could undoubtedly have
pressed the Estremadurans hard if he had chosen to do so.
Cuesta's retreating columns were in such a state of confusion
and disorder that a vigorous assault on their rear might have
caused a general *débandade*. But after driving in Zayas in the

---

[1] He had six regiments of Latour-Maubourg's dragoons, 3,200 sabres, four
regiments of Merlin's Division, 1,007 sabres, two regiments of Beaumont's
(corps-cavalry of 1st Corps) 980—a total of over 5,000 men.

early morning, Victor moved very slowly, and did not even attempt to roll up Albuquerque's cavalry rearguard, though he could have assailed it with very superior numbers.   When taxed with sloth by Marshal Jourdan, he merely defended himself by saying that the horses were tired, and that the infantry was still too far to the rear to make it right for him to begin a combat which might develop into a general engagement.   But it is hard to see that he would have risked anything by pressing in upon Albuquerque, for if Cuesta had halted his whole army in order to support his rearguard, there was nothing to prevent the French cavalry from drawing off, and refusing to close till the main body of the 1st Corps should come up.

Thanks to Victor's slackness the Spaniards secured an un-molested retreat across the Alberche on the following morning. It is said that Cuesta, in sheer perversity and reluctance to listen to any advice proffered him by Wellesley, delayed for some hours before he would retreat, and that when at last he yielded to the pressing solicitations of his colleague he remarked to his staff 'that he had made the Englishman go down on his knees' before consenting.

All through the morning hours of the twenty-seventh the Army of Estremadura was pouring across the bridge and the fords, not in the best order.   They had almost all passed, when about noon the French cavalry began to appear in their front. When the enemy at last began to press forward in strength, Wellesley directed Sherbrooke's and Mackenzie's divisions to prepare to evacuate their positions on the eastern bank, which they did as soon as the last of the Spaniards had got into safety. The first division passed at the bridge, the third at the fords near the village of Cazalegas : then Sherbrooke marched by the high-road towards Talavera, while Mackenzie, who had been told off as the rearguard, remained with Anson's light horse near the ruined Casa de Salinas, a mile to the west of the Alberche.

It may seem strange that Wellesley made no attempt to dispute the passage of the river, but the ground was hopelessly indefensible.   The left bank (Victor's old position of July 22) completely commands the right, the one being high, the other both low and entirely destitute of artillery positions.   Moreover, a great part of the *terrain*.was thickly strewn with woods and olive plantations, which made it impossible to obtain any general view of the country-side. They would have given splendid cover for an army advancing to storm the heights on the French bank, but were anything but an advantage to an army on the defensive. For, unable to hold the actual river bank because of the commanding hills on the further side, such an army would have been forced to form its line some way from the water, and the tangled cover down by the brink of the stream would have given the enemy every facility for pushing troops across, and for pressing them into the midst of the defender's position without exposing them to his fire. Wellington had examined the line of the Alberche upon the twenty-fourth and twenty-fifth, and had pronounced it absolutely untenable; 'no position could be worse,' he wrote to O'Donoju [1], but he had discovered one of a very different kind a little to the rear, and had already settled the way in which it was to be occupied. It presented so many advantages that even Cuesta had consented to accept it as a good fighting-ground, and the Estremaduran army was at this very moment occupied in arraying itself along that part of the line which had been allotted to it. Sherbrooke's division was retiring across the plain to fall into the section which Wellesley had chosen for it, and Hill's and Campbell's troops were moving to their designated ground. Only Mackenzie and the light cavalry had yet to be established in their post.

In the act of withdrawing, this division became involved in an unfortunate combat, which bid fair for a moment to develop into a disaster. Its two brigades had been halted close to the ruined house called the Casa de Salinas, in ground covered partly with underwood and partly with olive groves. The cavalry had been withdrawn to the rear, as it was impossible to use it for vedettes in such a locality. The infantry was supposed to have a chain of pickets thrown out in its front, but it would appear that they must have been badly placed: as one eye-witness confesses, 'we were by no means such good soldiers in those days as succeeding campaigns made us, and sufficient precautions had not been taken to ascertain what was passing in the wood [2],' and

---

[1] Wellesley to O'Donoju, from Cazalegas, July 25.
[2] Lord Munster, p. 210.

between it and the ford below Cazalegas. French cavalry alone
had hitherto been seen, and from cavalry Mackenzie's troops were
certainly safe in the tangled ground where they were now lying.

But already Victor's infantry had reached the front, and its
leading division, that of Lapisse, had forded the Alberche far
to the north, and had entered the woods without being observed
by the outlying pickets of Mackenzie's left brigade [1]. It had
even escaped the notice of Wellesley himself, who had just
mounted the roof of the ruined Casa de Salinas, the only point
in the neighbourhood from which anything like a general view
of the country-side could be secured. While he was intent on
watching the heights above the Alberche in his front, and the
cavalry vedettes descending from them, the enemy's infantry was
stealing in upon his left.

Lapisse had promptly discovered the line of British outposts,
and had succeeded in drawing out his division in battle order
before it was observed. He had deployed one regiment, the
16th Léger, as a front line, while the rest of his twelve battalions
were coming on in support.

While, therefore, Wellesley was still unconscious that the
enemy was close upon him, a brisk fire of musketry broke out
upon his left front. It was the French advance driving in the
pickets of Donkin's brigade. The division had barely time to
stand to its arms—some men are said to have been killed before
they had risen from the ground—and the Commander-in-chief
had hardly descended from the roof and mounted his charger,
when the enemy was upon them. The assault fell upon the whole
front of Donkin's brigade, and on the left regiment (the 2/31st)
of that of Mackenzie himself. So furious and unexpected was
it, that the 87th, 88th, and 31st were all broken, and driven
some way to the rear, losing about eighty prisoners. It was

---

[1] Several eye-witnesses declare that Lapisse's division escaped notice
owing to a curious chance. Before abandoning the further bank of the
Alberche, Mackenzie's troops had set fire to the huts which Victor's corps
had constructed on the Cazalegas heights, during their long stay in that
position. The smoke from the burning was driven along the slopes and
the river bottom by the wind, and screened one of the fords from the
British observers in the woods ; over this ford came Lapisse's unsuspected
advance.

fortunate that the French advance did not strike the whole line, but only its left and centre. The 1/45th, which was just outside the limit of Lapisse's attack, stood firm, and on it Wellesley reformed the 31st, while, a little further to the north, the half-battalion of the 5/60th also held its ground and served as a rallying-point for the 87th and 88th. The steadiness of the 1/45th and 5/60th saved the situation; covered by them the division retired from the woods and formed up in the plain, where Anson's light horsemen came to their aid and guarded their flanks. The French still pressed furiously forward, sending out two batteries of horse artillery to gall the retreating columns, but they had done their worst, and during the hours of the late afternoon Mackenzie's infantry fell back slowly and in order to the points of the position which had been assigned to them. Donkin's brigade took post in the second line behind the German Legion, while Mackenzie's own three regiments passed through the Guards and formed up in their rear. Their total loss in the combat of Casa de Salinas had been 440 men—the French casualties must have been comparatively insignificant—probably not 100 in all [1].

From the moment when the fray had begun in the woods till dusk, the noise of battle never stopped, for on arriving in front of the allied position, the French artillery drew up and commenced a hot, but not very effective, fire against those of the troops who held the most advanced stations. As the cannonade continued, the different regiments were seen hurrying to their battle-posts, for, although the arrangements had all been made, some brigades, not expecting a fight till the morrow, had still to take up their allotted ground.

'The men, as they formed and faced the enemy, looked pale, but the officers riding along their line, only two deep, on which all our hopes depended, observed that they appeared not less tranquil than determined. In the meanwhile the departing sun showed by his rays the immense masses moving towards us, and the last glimmering of the light proved their direction to be across our front, toward the left. The darkness, only broken

---

[1] Unfortunately the French returns do not separate the losses of the twenty-seventh from those of the twenty-eighth of July. Only the 16th Léger can have suffered any appreciable damage.

in upon by the bursting shells and the flashes of the French
guns, closed quickly upon us, and it was the opinion of many
that the enemy would rest till the morning [1].'

Such, however, was not to be the case : there was to be hard
fighting in front of Talavera before the hour of midnight had
arrived.

[1] Lord Munster, p. 212.

SECTION XVI: CHAPTER VI

THE BATTLE OF TALAVERA: THE PRELIMINARY COMBATS
(JULY 27-28)

THE position which Wellesley had selected as offering far better ground for a defensive battle than any which could be found on the banks of the Alberche, extends for nearly three miles to the north of the town of Talavera. It was not a very obvious line to take up, since only at its northern end does it present any well marked features. Two-thirds of the position lie in the plain, and are only marked out by the stony bed of the Portiña, a brook almost dried up in the summer, which runs from north to south and falls into the Tagus at Talavera. In the northern part of its course this stream flows at the bottom of a well-marked ravine, but as it descends towards the town its bed grows broad and shallow, and ceases to be of any tactical or topographical importance. Indeed, in this part of the field the fighting-line of the allies lay across it, and their extreme right wing was posted upon its further bank.

The town of Talavera, a place of 10,000 souls, which had been a flourishing industrial centre in the sixteenth century, but had long sunk into decay, lies in a compact situation on the north bank of the Tagus. It possesses a dilapidated bridge of forty-five arches, the only passage across the river between Arzobispo and Toledo. Its site is perfectly flat, save for a low knoll crowned by the chapel of Nuestra Señora del Prado, just outside the eastern, or Madrid, gate, and overlooking the *Alameda* (public promenade) and the neighbouring gardens. The place had no suburbs, but was surrounded by a broad belt of olive groves and enclosures, which extend for a full mile to the north and east, and hide the houses and walls from the traveller approaching from either of those directions. When the allies entered Talavera they found it deserted by most of its inhabitants,

who had fled up into the villages of the Sierra de Toledo
during the French occupation. Many, however, descended to
reoccupy their homes when the enemy departed. Victor's men
had plundered most of the houses, and turned many of the
churches into barracks or stables: hence the town presented
a picture of abject desolation [1].

For a mile and a half beyond the northern wall of Talavera
the ground covered by gardens and olive groves is perfectly flat;
it then commences to rise, and swells up into a long hill, the
Cerro de Medellin. This height runs from east to west, so that
its front, and not the full length of its side, overhangs the
Portiña ravine. Its loftiest point and its steepest face are
presented to that declivity, while to the west and south it has
gentle and easily accessible slopes, sinking gradually down into
the plain. This hill, the most commanding ground in the
neighbourhood of Talavera, had been chosen by Wellesley as
the position of his left wing. It formed, including its lower
slopes, about one-third of the line which he had determined
to occupy, the rest of the front lying in the low ground among
the olives and gardens. North of the Cerro de Medellin is
a narrow lateral valley, only half a mile broad, separating this
hill from the main chain of the Sierra de Segurilla, the mountains
which form the watershed between the basin of the Tagus and
that of the Tietar. The British general had intended at first
that his position should extend no further north than the hill,
but in the course of the action he was compelled to lengthen his
front, and to post troops both in the valley and on the mountain
spurs beyond it.

By the agreement made with Cuesta, at the conference near
the bridge of the Alberche on the evening of the twenty-sixth,
it was settled that the Spanish army should hold the town of

---

[1] 'The French troops during their stay had been guilty of great excesses:
a number of houses were completely destroyed, and the furniture burnt
for fuel. In every quarter were to be seen marks of the devastation they
had committed. The Cathedral, a handsome modern building, was
uninjured, the enemy having contented himself with carrying off all
the splendid ornaments used in the ceremonies of religion. But in the
church of San Antonio the French had destroyed everything, and converted it into a barrack,' &c. Stothert's *Narrative of the Campaigns of
1809-11*, pp. 81-2.

Talavera and the wooded and enclosed ground for a mile beyond it. The British had their right among the olive groves, but their centre and left on the open slopes of the Cerro de Medellin. This order of battle was the only one which it was possible to adopt. Wellesley had already discovered that the army of Estremadura could not manœuvre, and would be much safer behind walls and enclosures than in the open, and Cuesta had gladly accepted the proposal that he should occupy this part of the position. Having only a little more than a mile of front to defend, he was able to provide a double and triple line with his 32,000 men [1]. His Vanguard and 1st division, under Zayas, occupied the eastern outskirts of the town, with a battery placed upon the knoll crowned by the chapel of Nuestra Señora del Prado. A brigade of cavalry (four regiments) was deployed in the open ground of the Prado, close to the bank of the Tagus. The 2nd division, that of Iglesias, held Talavera, whose ancient walls, though imperfect in many places, were still quite defensible. The 3rd and 4th divisions (Manglano and Portago) were ranged in a double line among the gardens and enclosures to the north of the town, as far as a low hillock called the Pajar de Vergara, where they touched Wellesley's left. Behind them were the rest of Cuesta's cavalry (ten regiments) and the 5th division (Bassecourt) forming the reserves.

The Spanish position was immensely strong. The front was completely screened by groves and enclosures occupied by skirmishers: the first line was drawn up along the slightly sunken road leading from Talavera to the north, which provided the men with an excellent parapet and good cover [2]. The second line was equally well placed behind the Portiña rivulet, which was bordered by trees along its whole front. The only good artillery position was that outside the Madrid gate, in front of Zayas' division, but three other batteries were planted in the least defective emplacements that could be found in the front line. The rest of the Spanish guns were in reserve, in line with Bassecourt and the cavalry.

The northern half of the position had its strong points, but

---

[1] The Spaniards had lost 1,000 men, mainly by dispersion, in the retreat from Torrijos on the twenty-sixth.

[2] Cf. Londonderry, i. 403; and Arteche, vi. 293.

also its defects. For the first half mile beyond the Spanish left it was still covered by groves and gardens, and had on its right front the little eminence of the Pajar de Vergara. On this knoll a redoubt had been commenced, but no more had been done than to level a space, eighty yards long and twenty feet broad, on its summit, and to throw up the excavated earth in front, thus forming a bank three or four feet high. In this work, indifferently well protected, lay Lawson's battery of 3-pounders, the lightest guns of Wellesley's artillery. Beside and behind them were the five battalions of the 4th division, Campbell's brigade in the front line, Kemmis's in the second, to the rear of the Portiña.

On the left of the 4th division the enclosed ground ended, and cover ceased. Here, forming the British centre, were drawn up the eight battalions of Sherbrooke's division, in a single line. The Guards' brigade, under Henry Campbell, was in perfectly flat level ground, without shade or cover. Next to them, where there is a gentle ascent towards the foot of the Cerro de Medellin, were Cameron's two battalions; while the two weak brigades of the King's German Legion, under Langwerth and Low, continued the front on to the actual hill, with the Portiña, now flowing in a well-marked ravine, at their feet [1]. The whole of this part of the British line was bare rolling ground covered with long dry grass and scattered shrubs of thyme. There was no cover, and before the Guards' and Cameron's brigades the front was not defined by any strong natural feature. On the other hand, the *terrain* on the opposite side of the Portiña was equally bare, and gave no advantage to an enemy about to attack.

It was otherwise in the portion of the front where the four German battalions of Langwerth and Low were placed. They had a steep ravine in front of them, but on the opposite side, as a compensating disadvantage, the rolling upland swells into a hill called the Cerro de Cascajal, which, though much less lofty than the Cerro de Medellin, yet afforded good artillery positions from which the English slopes could be battered.

---

[1] Thus, counting from right to left, the front of Sherbrooke's brigade was composed as follows : 1st Coldstream Guards, 1st Scots Fusilier Guards, 61st, 83rd, 1st Line K. G. L., 2nd ditto, 5th ditto, 7th ditto.

Behind Sherbrooke's troops, as the second line of his centre, Wellesley had drawn up his 3rd division and all his cavalry. Cotton's light dragoons were in the rear of Kemmis's brigade of the 4th division. Mackenzie's three battalions supported the Guards: then came Anson's light and Fane's heavy cavalry, massed on the rising slope in the rear of Cameron. Lastly Donkin's brigade, which had suffered so severely in the combat of Casa de Salinas, lay high up the hill, directly in the rear of Low's brigade of the King's German Legion.

It only remains to speak of the British left, on the highest part of the Cerro de Medellin. This section of the front was entrusted to Hill's division, which was already encamped upon its reverse slope. Here lay the strongest point of the position, for the hill is steep, and well covered in its front by the Portiña, which now flows in a deep stony ravine. But it was also the part of the British fighting-ground which was most likely to be assailed, since a quick-eyed enemy could not help noting that it was the key of the whole—that if the upper levels of the Cerro de Medellin were lost, the rest of the allied line could not possibly be maintained. It was therefore the part of the position which would require the most careful watching, and Wellesley had told off to it his most capable and experienced divisional general. But by some miscalculation, on the evening of the twenty-seventh Hill's two brigades were not lying on their destined battle-line, but had halted half a mile behind it— Richard Stewart's battalions on the left, Tilson's on the right flank of the reverse slope. It is difficult to see with whom the responsibility lay, for Wellesley was far to the right, engaged in planting Mackenzie's troops in their new position behind the centre, while Hill had ridden over towards Talavera to search for his Commander-in-chief and question him about details, and returned rather late to give his brigadiers the exact instruction as to the line they were to take up at nightfall [1]. There

---

[1] It would seem, on the whole, that the responsibility for the absence of the division from its destined fighting-ground lay with Hill, generally the most cautious and reliable of subordinates. He says, in a memorandum drawn up in 1827, in answer to an inquiry about Talavera, that he had gone to dine in Talavera, and then saw Mackenzie's division come back into the line. Returning to his own troops, he found them moving out of

were piquets on the crest, and the greater part of the front slopes were covered by Low's two battalions of the King's German Legion, but the actual summit of the Cerro was not occupied by any solid force, though the brigades that were intended to hold it lay only 800 yards to the rear. It was supposed that they would have ample time to take up their ground in the morning, and no one dreamt of the possibility of a night attack.

Of the very small force of artillery which accompanied the British army, we have already seen that Lawson's light 3-pounder battery had been placed in the Pajar de Vergara entrenchment. Elliott's and Heyse's were in the centre of the line ; the former placed in front of the Guards, the latter before Langwerth's brigade of the German Legion. Rettberg's heavy 6-pounders were on the Cerro de Medellin, with Hill's division : at dusk they had been brought back to its rear slope and were parked near Richard Stewart's brigade. Finally Sillery's battery was in reserve, between the two lines, somewhere behind Cameron's brigade of Sherbrooke's division [1]. This single unit was the only artillery reserve of which Wellesley could dispose.

The precise number of British troops in line was 20,194, after deducting the losses at Casa de Salinas ; that of the Spaniards was within a few hundreds of 32,000. The French, as we have already seen, had brought a little more than 46,000 men to the field, so that the allies had a superiority of some 6,000 in mere numbers. If Wellesley could have exchanged the Army of Estremadura for half their strength of British bayonets, he might have felt quite comfortable in his strong position. But his confidence in the value of his allies, even when firmly planted among walls and groves, was just about to receive a rude shock.

It was about seven o'clock when the heads of Victor's columns,

their bivouac, but not on their fighting-ground. He was getting them into line, when the firing suddenly began in his front.

These details I give from the valuable (unpublished) map by Lieut. Unger of the K. G. L. artillery, which Colonel Whinyates has been good enough to place at my disposition. It carefully marks the emplacement of every British battery. Elliott was at this moment in command of the battery which had been under Baynes during the Oporto campaign, while Sillery had that which had been under Lane.

following in the wake of the horse artillery which had been galling Mackenzie's retreat, emerged from the woods on to the rolling plateau facing the allied position. Ruffin appeared on the right, and occupied the Cascajal hill, opposite the Cerro de Medellin. Villatte followed, and halted in its rear. More to the left Lapisse, adopting the same line that had been taken by Mackenzie, halted in front of the British centre: the corps-cavalry, under Beaumont, was drawn up in support of him. Latour-Maubourg's six regiments of dragoons, further to the south, took ground in front of the Spaniards. The King and Sebastiani were still far to the rear: their infantry was only just passing the Alberche, though their advanced cavalry under Merlin was already pushing forward in the direction of Talavera down the high-road from Madrid [1].

If Napoleon, or any other general who knew how to make himself obeyed, had been present with the French army, there would have been no fighting on the evening of July 27. But King Joseph counted for little in the eyes of his nominal subordinates, and hence it came to pass that the impetuous Victor took upon himself the responsibility of attacking the allies when only half the King's army had come upon the field. With no more object, as it would seem, than that of harassing the enemy, he sent to the front the batteries belonging to Ruffin, Lapisse, and Latour-Maubourg, to join in the cannonade which his horse artillery had already begun. At the same time Merlin's light horse pressed forward in the direction of Talavera, to feel for the front of the Spaniards, whose exact position was hidden by the olive groves. The British artillery replied, but no great harm was done to either side. Yet in the Spanish part of the line a dreadful disaster was on the point of occurring. When the artillery fire began, and the French light horse were seen advancing, the Estremaduran troops between Talavera and the Pajar de Vergara delivered a tremendous salvo of infantry fire along the whole line, though the enemy was too far off to take any damage. But, immediately after, four battalions of Portago's division, which formed part of the left of Cuesta's line and touched Campbell's right, suddenly shouted 'treason!'

[1] All these details are from the report drawn up by Sémélé, the chief of the staff of the 1st Corps, at Talavera on Aug. 10.

broke, and went off to the rear in complete disorder. Wellesley, who, as it chanced, was behind Campbell's troops, and witnessed the whole rout, declared that he could conceive no reason for their behaviour except that they must have been frightened by the crash of their own tremendous volley [1]. Two of these four battalions were troops who had never been in action before : the other two had been badly cut up at Medellin, and brought up to strength by the incorporation of a great mass of recruits [2]. This might have excused a momentary misconduct, but not a prolonged rush to the rear when the enemy was still half a mile off, still less the casting away of their arms and the plundering of the British camp, through which the multitude fled. Cuesta sent cavalry to hunt them up, and succeeded in hounding back the majority to their ranks, but many hundreds were still missing on the following morning. They fled in small bands all down the valley of the Tagus, dispersing dismal information on all sides. It is sad to have to acknowledge that in their rush through the British camp they carried away with them some commissaries and a few of the baggage guard, who did not halt till they got to Oropesa, twenty miles from the field [3]. Strange to say, this panic had no appreciable ill effects : the

[1] Wellesley to Castlereagh, Aug. 25 : 'Two thousand of them ran off on the evening of the twenty-seventh, not 100 yards from where I was standing, who were neither attacked, nor threatened with an attack, and who were only frightened by the noise of their own fire. They left their arms and accoutrements on the ground, their officers went with them, and they plundered the baggage of the British army, which had been sent to the rear. Many others went, whom I did not see.'

[2] The panic-stricken regiments were Leales de Fernando VII, which had been garrisoning Badajoz when Medellin was fought, Badajoz (two batts.) which had been in the battle, and Toledo.

[3] 'I wish I could assert with truth that this retrogression was confined to our Spanish allies. But the truth must be told, and I regret to say that stragglers from the British army were among them, taking a similar direction to the rear. As they passed, they circulated reports of a most disheartening nature.' Col. Leach's *Rough Sketches*, p. 81. He was with Craufurd's brigade, then coming up by forced marches from Plasencia, which met the fugitives near Oropesa on the morning of the twenty-eighth. 'The road was crowded with fugitives, Spaniards innumerable, and lots of English commissary clerks, paymasters and sutlers, to say nothing of a few soldiers who said they were *sick*.' *Autobiography* of Sir George Napier, p. 108.

French were not in a position to take advantage of it, having no troops, save a few light horse, in front of the spot where it occurred. The Spaniards to the right and rear of the absconding regiments did not flinch, and as the second line held firm, there was no actual gap produced in the allied position. But Wellesley noted the scene, and never forgot it : of all that he had witnessed during the campaign, this was the sight that struck him most, and most influenced his future conduct. Cuesta also took account of it in his own fashion, and at the end of the battle of the next day proposed to decimate in the old Roman fashion, the battalions that had fled ! He actually chose by lot some 200 men from the fugitives, and after trying them by court-martial prepared to shoot them. His British colleague begged off the majority, but the old Captain-General insisted on executing some twenty-five or thirty who were duly put to death on the morning of the twenty-ninth [1].

After the panic had died down, Victor gradually withdrew his batteries [2], but it was with no intention of bringing the combat to a real termination. He had resolved to deliver a night attack on the key of the British position, when the whole of his corps should have reached the front. Having reconnoitred the allied lines, and noted the distribution of their defenders, he had determined to storm the Cerro de Medellin in the dark. During his long stay at Talavera he had acquired a very thorough knowledge of its environs, and understood the dominating importance of that height. If he could seize and hold it during the night, he saw that the battle of the next day would be already half won. Accordingly, still without obtaining King

---

[1] ' Early in the morning some twenty-five Spanish soldiers, dressed in white, attended by several Popish priests, were marched up to the front of our regiment and shot. One, a young lad of nineteen or twenty years, dropped before the party fired, but to no use. For after the volley at ten paces, the firing party ran forward and shooting them in the head or breast completed their horrid work. These unfortunates belonged to regiments that had given way in the late battle.' *Diary* of Cooper (of the 7th Fusiliers), pp. 25–6.

[2] That the panic took place at dusk, and not during the night attack, is completely proved by the *Journal* of General Sémélé, where it is noted as occurring in consequence of Victor's earliest demonstration ; as also by Wellesley's note.

Joseph's leave, he determined to assail the Cerro. He told off for the storm his choicest division, that of Ruffin, whose nine battalions were already ranged on the front of the Cascajal heights. At the same time Lapisse's division was to distract the attention of the British centre by a noisy demonstration against its front.

Night attacks are proverbially hazardous and hard to conduct, and it cannot be disputed that Victor showed an excessive temerity in endeavouring to deliver such a blow at the steady British troops, at an hour when it was impossible to guarantee proper co-operation among the attacking columns. But for an initial stroke of luck he ought not to have secured even the small measure of success that fell to his lot.

At about nine o'clock, however, Ruffin moved down to the attack. Each of his three regiments was formed in battalion columns, the 9th Léger in the centre, the 96th on its left, the 24th on its right. The first-named regiment was to deliver a frontal attack, the other two to turn the flanks of the hill and attack over its side-slopes. At the appointed moment the three regiments descended simultaneously into the ravine of the Portiña, and endeavoured to carry out their respective sections of the programme. The 9th, chancing on the place where the ravine was most easily negotiable, crossed it without much difficulty, and began to climb the opposite slope. On mounting half way to the crest, it suddenly came on Low's brigade of the German Legion, lying down in line, with its pickets only a very small distance in advance of the main body. It is said that the brigadier was labouring under the delusion that some of Hill's outposts were in his front, and that he was screened by them. It is at any rate clear that he was taken wholly unprepared by the midnight attack of the French. His sentries were trampled down in a moment, and the 9th Léger ran in upon the Germans, firing into them point blank and seizing many of them as prisoners almost ere they were awake. The 7th K. G. L. was completely broken, and lost 150 men—half of them prisoners—in five minutes. The 5th, the right-hand battalion of Low's brigade, came off better, as it was not in the direct path of the French; but it was flung sideways along the southern slope of the hill, and could not be re-formed for

some time. Meanwhile the three French columns, somewhat
separated from each other in this first clash of arms, went
straight on up the Cerro, and in a few minutes were nearing its
crest. The two leading battalions actually reached and crowned
it, without meeting with any opposition save from the outlying
picket of Richard Stewart's brigade. The third was not far
behind, and it seemed almost certain that the position might be
won. At this moment General Hill, who was occupied in drawing out his division on the rear slope, but had not yet conducted it to its fighting-ground, interfered in the fight. He had
seen and heard the sudden outbreak of musketry on the frontal
slopes, as the French broke through Low's brigade. But when
it died down, he was far from imagining that the cause was the
complete success of the enemy. Nevertheless, he directed his
nearest brigade, that of Richard Stewart, to prepare to support
the Germans if necessary. He was issuing his orders to the
colonel of the 48th, when he observed some men on the hill top
fire a few shots in his direction. 'Not having an idea,' he
writes, 'that the enemy were so near, I said to myself that
I was sure it was the old Buffs, as usual, making some blunder.'
Accordingly he galloped up the hill, with his brigade-major
Fordyce, shouting to the men to cease firing. He rode right in
among the French before he realized his mistake, and a voltigeur
seized him by the arm and bade him surrender. Hill spurred
his horse, which sprang forward and got clear of the Frenchman,
who lost his hold but immediately raised his musket and fired
at three paces' distance, missing the General but hitting his
charger. Hill escaped in the midst of a scattering volley, which
killed his companion Fordyce, and got back as fast as he could
to Richard Stewart's brigade. Without delaying for a moment,
even to change his wounded horse, he led on the nearest regiments to recover the hill top. So great was the confusion,
owing to the sudden attack in the dark, that Stewart's men
moved forward, not in their proper order, but with the 1st
Battalion of Detachments on the right, the 29th in the centre,
and the 1/48 on the left. This arrangement brought the first-
named unit first into touch with the enemy. The Detachments
came into immediate collision with the leading battalions of the
French, who were now somewhat in disorder, and trying to

re-form on the ground they had won. The two forces opened a furious fire upon each other, and both came to a standstill [1]. But Hill, coming up a moment later at the head of his centre regiment, cleared the hill top by a desperate charge: passing through the Detachments, the 29th delivered a volley at point-blank range and closed. The enemy broke and fled down the slope that they had ascended. The 29th wheeled into line and followed them, pouring in regular volleys at short intervals. But before they had gone far, they became dimly conscious of another column to their left, pushing up the hill in the darkness. This was the rear battalion of the 9th Léger, which had fallen somewhat behind its fellows. It was moving up diagonally across the front of the British regiment, with drums beating and loud shouts of *vive l'Empereur*. Taken in flank by the fire of the right companies of the 29th, it could make no effective resistance, and ere long broke and rolled back in disorder into the bed of the Portiña, where it met with the wrecks of the rest of the regiment, and retired in company with them up the slopes of the Cerro de Cascajal.

The remainder of Ruffin's division took little or no part in the fighting. The three battalions of the 24th, which ought to have mounted the hill on the right, lost their way in the darkness and wandered up the valley between the Cerro de Medellin and the northern mountains: they never came into action. The 96th, on the left of the attack, chanced upon a part of the Portiña ravine which was very precipitous: they found it difficult to descend, were very late in reaching the other side, and then fell into a futile bickering fight with the 5th and 2nd battalions of the King's German Legion, which terminated —with small damage to either party—when the main attack in the centre was seen to have failed.

The loss of the French in this night battle was about 300 men, almost all in the 9th Léger. It included sixty-five prisoners, among whom was the colonel of the regiment, who

---

[1] The Battalion of Detachments was decidedly checked. They got somewhat into confusion, and halted. 'The soldiers seemed much vexed,' writes Leslie of the 29th, 'we could hear them bravely calling out " There is nobody to command us! Only tell us what to do, and we are ready to dare anything." There was a fault somewhere.' Leslie, p. 144.

was left on the ground desperately wounded. The British casualties were somewhat heavier, entirely owing to the disaster to the 5th and 7th battalions of the K. G. L., which suffered when surprised, a loss of 188 men, eighty-seven of whom were made captives. Richard Stewart's brigade, which bore the brunt of the fighting and decided the affair, had only 125 killed and wounded [1].

Thus ended, in well-deserved failure, Victor's night attack, of which it may suffice to say that even its initial success was only due to the gross carelessness of Low's brigade in failing to cover their front with a proper screen of outlying pickets. To attack in the dark across rugged and difficult ground was to court disaster. The wonder is not that two-thirds of the division went astray, but that the other third almost succeeded in the hazardous enterprise to which it was committed. Great credit is due to the 9th Léger for all that it did, and no blame whatever rests upon the regiment for its ultimate failure. The Marshal must take all the responsibility.

The wrecks of the French attacking columns having rolled back beyond the ravine, and the flanking regiments having abandoned their futile demonstrations, the Cerro de Medellin was once more safe. The troops occupying it were rearranged, as far as was possible, in the dark. The front line on its left and highest part was now formed by Richard Stewart's brigade, ranged, not in its proper order of seniority, but with the 29th on the left, the 1st Battalion of Detachments in the centre, and the 1/48 on the right. Tilson's brigade, the other half of Hill's division, was to the south of Stewart, continuing his line along the crest. Low's battalions of the King's German Legion were drawn off somewhat to the right, closing in towards Langwerth's brigade, so as to leave the central slopes of the Cerro de Medellin entirely to Hill's men. Donkin's brigade of Mackenzie's division lay close behind them. After the warning that had been given by Victor's first assault, the greatest care was

[1] Though the French official reports of casualties do not give any officers of the 9th Léger as prisoners, it is certain that Colonel Meunier was taken. See Leslie, p. 143. Being recovered, along with the other wounded prisoners, when Talavera was evacuated, his name did not get down among the list of missing, which was only drawn up on Aug. 10.

taken to make a second surprise impossible. Stewart's and
Low's brigades threw forward their pickets to the brink of
the Portiña ravine, so close to the enemy that all night they
could hear the *Qui vive* of the sentries challenging the visiting
rounds, only two or three hundred yards above them. On
several occasions the outposts opened fire on each other, and the
word 'stand to your arms,' ran along the whole line. In front
of Sherbrooke's division, about midnight, there was a false
alarm, which led to a whole brigade delivering a volley at an
imaginary column of assault, while their own pickets were still
out in front, with the result that two officers and several men
were killed or wounded [1]. A similar outbreak of fire, lasting for
several minutes, ran along the front of the Spanish lines an hour
later. It seems to have been caused by French foragers, in
search of fuel, blundering against the Estremaduran pickets on
the edge of the olive groves.

Altogether the night was not a peaceful one, and the troops
were much harassed by the perpetual and unnecessary calls to
stand to their arms. Many of them got little sleep, and several
British diarists have left interesting impressions on record of
their long vigil. There was much to keep them awake: not
only the repeated blaze of fire running along parts of the allied
line, but the constant signs of movement on the French side of
the Portiña. Some time after midnight long lines of torches
were seen advancing across and to the right of the Cerro de
Cascajal; these were markers with flambeaux, sent out to fix
the points on which Victor's artillery were to take up their
positions, as was soon shown by the rattling of gun-carriages,
the noise of wheels, and the cracking of whips, which were plainly
heard in the intervals of stillness, when the hostile pickets
ceased their bickering musketry fire. The French were pushing
up their guns into the very front of their line, and when the
dawn began to break they were visible only 600 or 800 yards
away from the British lines. A few deserters came over during
the night, mainly from Leval's German division; all agreed that
the enemy was about to deliver a second attack in the early
morning.

[1] See the Diary of Boothby of the R. E., one of the victims of this
unhappy fusilade, p. 5.

The dawn was an anxious moment : with the growing light it was possible to make out broad black patches dotting the whole of the rolling ground in front of the British army. Every instant rendered them more visible, and soon they took shape as French regiments in battalion columns, ranged on a front of nearly two miles, from the right end of the Cerro de Cascajal to the edge of the woods facing the Pajar de Vergara. The object which drew most attention was an immense solid column at the extreme right of the hostile line, on the lower slopes above the Portiña, with a thick screen of *tirailleurs* already thrown out in its front, and evidently ready to advance at the word of command. The other divisions lay further back : in front of them artillery was everywhere visible : there were four batteries on the mid-slope of the Cascajal hill, and six more on the rolling ground to the south. In the far distance, behind the infantry, were long lines of cavalry dressed in all the colours of the rainbow— fifteen or sixteen regiments could be counted—and far to the rear of them more black masses were slowly rolling into view. It was easily to be seen that little or nothing lay in front of the Spaniards, and that at least five-sixths of the French army was disposed for an attack on the British front. There were 40,000 men visible, ready for the advance against the 20,000 sabres and bayonets of Wellesley's long red line [1].

An attack was imminent, yet there were many things which might have induced the French generals to hold back. Was it worth while to assail the allies in the admirable position which they now held, when it was possible to drive them out of it without risking a battle? Orders had been sent to Soult, six days before, to bid him fall on Wellesley's communications by way of Plasencia. It was believed that he must have started ere now, and that the news of his approach would reach the enemy within the next forty-eight hours. This intelligence would compel them to go behind the Tagus, and to abandon the Talavera position. Both Jourdan and King Joseph were doubt-ful of the policy of risking a general action. But the initiative was taken out of their hands by Victor. He had already placed his corps so close to the British lines that it would have been

[1] There are admirable narratives of the night-vigil and the dawn of Talavera, in the narratives of Leslie, Leith-Hay, and Lord Munster.

hard to withdraw it without an engagement. He had also, during the night, sent a dispatch to the King, stating that he should storm the Cerro de Medellin at dawn unless he received counter-orders. He appeared so confident of success that Joseph and his adviser Jourdan did not venture to bid him desist. They were, as the latter confessed, largely influenced by the knowledge that if they refused, Victor would delate them to the Emperor for culpable timidity in letting the British army escape [1].

The Duke of Belluno was still persisting in his idea that it might be possible to seize the key of Wellesley's position by a partial attack, without engaging the rest of his corps till it had already been won. Accordingly he gave orders to his subordinates Lapisse and Villatte that they were not to move till Ruffin, with the first division, should have gained the Cerro de Medellin. In a similar way the King made the advance of the 4th Corps conditional on the preliminary success of Victor's right. This seems to have been bad policy, as it left Wellesley free to devote the whole of his attention to the point where the first attack was to be delivered. It was clear that the threatening column on the lower slopes of the Cerro de Cascajal would start the game. Victor had drawn up his troops in the following order. Ruffin on the extreme left, and considerably in advance, was to attack the Cerro on its north-eastern and eastern fronts. Behind him on the summit of the Cascajal Hill, were Villatte's twelve battalions, and in rear of all the two regiments of Beaumont, the Marshal's corps-cavalry. To Villatte's left, but on lower ground opposite Sherbrooke's line, lay Lapisse's division, with Latour-Maubourg's six regiments of dragoons in support. This completed the array of the 1st Corps: on their left stood Sebastiani and his 4th Corps, facing the Guards, Campbell, and the northernmost battalions of the Spanish army, opposite

[1] ' Le duc de Bellune rendit compte au roi du résultat de sa première attaque, et le prévint qu'il la renouvellerait au point du jour. Peut-être aurait on dû lui donner l'ordre d'attendre. . . . Mais ce maréchal, étant resté longtemps aux environs de Talavera, devait connaître parfaitement son terrain, et il paraissait si sûr du succès, que le roi le laissait libre d'agir comme il le désirait. . . . Il sentait que s'il adopterait l'avis du Maréchal Jourdan le duc de Bellune ne manquerait pas d'écrire à l'empereur " qu'on lui avait fait perdre l'occasion d'une brillante victoire sur les Anglais ".' Jourdan's *Mémoires*, pp. 256 and 259.

the Pajar de Vergara. Sebastiani's French division was on his right, his German division on his left, while the stray Polish brigade (the only part of Valence's division that was on the field) supported the Germans. In second line was Merlin's light horse, while Milhaud's six regiments of dragoons lay out on the extreme left, observing the town of Talavera. King Joseph and his reserve — the Guards and the brigade of Dessolles—were far to the rear, just outside the woods round the Casa de Salinas.

At about five in the morning the watchers on the Cerro de Medellin saw the smoke of a gun curl up into the air from the central battery in front of Villatte's division. The ensuing report was the signal for the whole of Victor's artillery to open, and twenty-four guns spoke at once from the Cascajal heights, and thirty more from the lower ground to their right. The cannonade was tremendous, and the reply wholly inadequate, as Wellesley could only put four batteries in line, Rettberg's on the summit of the Cerro, Sillery's from the lower slope near Donkin's position, and those of Heyse and Elliott from the front of Sherbrooke's division. The French fire was both accurate and effective, 'they served their guns in an infinitely better style than at Vimeiro : their shells were thrown with precision, and did considerable execution [1].' Wellesley, who stood in rear of Hill's line on the commanding height, at once ordered Richard Stewart's and Tilson's brigades to go back from the sky-line, and to lie down. But no such device was practicable in Sherbrooke's division, where the formation of the ground presented no possibility of cover, and here much damage was done. After a few minutes the English position was obscured, for the damp of the morning air prevented the smoke from rising, and a strong east wind blew it across the Portiña, and drove it along the slopes of the Cerro [2]. So thick was the atmosphere that the defenders heard rather than saw the start of Ruffin's division on its advance, and only realized its near approach when they saw their own skirmishers retiring up the slope towards the main line. The light companies of Hill's division came in so slowly and unwillingly, turning back often

---

[1] Eliott's Narrative, in his *Defence of Portugal*, p. 238.
[2] Lord Munster, p. 226.

to fire, and keeping their order with the regularity of a field-day. The general, wishing to get his front clear, bade the bugles sound to bring them in more quickly, and as they filed to the rear in a leisurely way was heard to shout (it was one of the only two occasions on which he was known to swear), 'D—n their filing, let them come in anyhow[1].'

When the light companies had fallen back, the French were at last visible through the smoke. They had mounted the lower slopes of the Cerro without any loss, covered by their artillery, which only ceased firing at this moment. They showed nine battalions, in three solid columns : Victor had arranged the divisions with the 24th in the centre, the 96th on the left, and the 9th Léger, which had suffered so severely in the night-battle, upon the right. This arrangement brought the last-named regiment opposite their old enemies of the 29th, and the Battalion of Detachments, while the 1/48th and 2/48th had to deal with the French centre, and the Buffs and 66th with their left. When Ruffin's columns had got within a hundred yards of the sky-line, Hill bade his six battalions stand to their feet and advance. As they lined the crest they delivered a splendid volley, whose report was as sharp and precise as that of a field-day. The effect was of course murderous, as was always the case when line met column. The French had a marked superiority in numbers ; they were nearly 5,000 strong, Hill's two brigades had less than 4,000[2]. But there was the usual advantage that every British soldier could use his weapon, while the French, in column of divisions, had the normal mass of useless muskets in the rear ranks. The first volley brought them to a standstill—their whole front had gone down at the discharge—they lost the impetus of advance, halted, and kept up a furious fire for some minutes. But when it came to a standing fight of musketry, there was never a doubt in any Peninsular battle how the game would end. The French fire began ere long to slacken, the front of the columns shook and

---

[1] Leslie, p. 147. The other occasion on which Hill used strong language was at the battle of St. Pierre in 1814, when Wellington remarked: ' If Hill is beginning to swear we had better get out of the way.'

[2] Ruffin had 5,200 men, minus about 300 lost on the previous night, while Hill had 3,853, minus 138 lost in that same battle in the dark.

wavered. Just at this moment Sherbrooke, who had noted that the divisions in his own front showed no signs of closing, took the 5th battalion of the King's German Legion out of his left brigade[1], and sent it against the flank and rear of Ruffin's nearest regiment—the 96th of the line. When the noise of battle broke out in this new quarter, the French lost heart and began to give ground. Richard Stewart, at the northern end of the British line, gave the signal to his brigade to charge, and —as a participator in this fray writes, ' on we went, a wall of stout hearts and bristling steel. The enemy did not fancy such close quarters, and the moment our rush began they went to the right-about. The principal portion broke and fled, though some brave fellows occasionally faced about and gave us an irregular fire.' Nothing, however, could stop Hill's division, and the whole six battalions rushed like a torrent down the slope, bayonetting and sweeping back the enemy to the line of black and muddy pools that marked the course of the Portiña. Many of the pursuers even crossed the ravine and chased the flying French divisions right into the arms of Villatte's troops, on the Cascajal Hill. When these reserves opened fire, Hill's men re-formed on the lower slope of the Cerro, and retired to their old position without being seriously molested, for Victor made no counter-attack.

Ruffin's three regiments had been terribly punished: they had lost, in forty minutes' fighting, 1,300 killed and wounded, much more than a fourth of their strength. Hill's brigades had about 750 casualties[2], including their gallant leader, who received a wound in the head, and had to go to the rear, leaving the command of his division to Tilson. The loss of the German battalion which had struck in upon the French rear was insignificant, as the enemy never stood to meet it.

[1] This operation is described in the narrative of the K. G. L. officer, printed by Beamish (p. 212). The narrator, however, mistakes the French regiment's number, and says twenty-six for ninety-six.

[2] These losses can be accurately ascertained. Ruffin's whole loss in the two days of fighting was 1,632, of whom 300 of the 9th Léger had fallen on the night of July 27. He was not seriously engaged during the rest of the day, so must have lost 1,300 in this fight. Hill's total loss on July 28 was 835, but much of it was suffered in the afternoon, when (though not attacked by infantry) his division was under a heavy shell fire.

Thus was Victor's second attempt to storm the Cerro de Medellin rebuked. It was a rash and unscientific operation, and received a merited chastisement. The Marshal should have sent in all his corps, and attacked the whole British line, if he wished to give his men a fair chance. He obviously underrated the troops with which he had to deal—he had never seen them before the combat of Casa de Salinas on the previous day—and had no conception of the power of the line against the column. Even now baffled rage seems to have been his main feeling, and his only desire was to make the attempt again with larger forces.

The whole engagement had taken about an hour and a half, and the morning was still young when the Marshal re-formed his line, and reported his ill-success to the King. After the cannonade died down he bade his men take their morning meal, and the British on the Cerro could see the whole 1st Corps turn to cooking, behind their strong line of pickets. A sort of informal armistice was established in a short time ; both parties wished to use the stagnant water of the Portiña, and after a little signalling hundreds of men came down with their canteens from either side, and filled them with the muddy fluid. In spite of the heavy fighting which had just ended, all parties agree that a very friendly spirit was shown. The men conversed as best they could, and were even seen to shake hands across the pools. Many of the officers came down a little later, and after a short colloquy agreed that either party might take off its wounded without molestation. As there were hundreds of French lying on the west bank of the Portiña, and a good many English on its further side, there was a complete confusion of uniforms as the bearers passed and repassed each other at the bottom of the ravine. But no difficulties of any sort arose, and for more than two hours the two parties were completely mixed. This was the first example of that amicable spirit which reigned between the hostile armies all through the war, and which in its later years developed into that curious code of signals (often described by contemporaries), by which French and English gave each other notice whenever serious work was intended, refraining on all other occasions from unnecessary outpost bickering or sentry-shooting.

SECTION XVI: CHAPTER VII

THE BATTLE OF TALAVERA: THE MAIN ENGAGEMENT
(JULY 28)

THE informal armistice which had followed the combat of
the early morning had drawn to an end, when at about 10 o'clock
the British observers on the Cerro de Medellin saw a large and
brilliant staff riding along the French line from right to left.
It finally halted, and took post on the most commanding point
of the Cascajal heights. This was the entourage of King Joseph
and Marshal Jourdan, who had determined to make a careful
examination of the allied lines before committing themselves to
any further action. When they halted on the summit of the
hill, from which the best general view was obtainable, Victor
came to meet them, and a council of war was held.

It soon developed into a lengthy and animated dispute;
lasting for more than an hour. Jourdan was of opinion that,
considering the strength of the hostile position, and the decisive
way in which the 1st Corps had been repulsed, it would be
unwise to proceed with another attack. He pointed out that
Wellesley would now be perfectly aware that his left was the
point which must be assailed, and that movements visible behind
the British line showed that it was already being reinforced.
The only good move now available was to endeavour to turn
the Cerro by the little valley to its north-east, which separates
it from the Sierra de Segurilla: but it was clear that the enemy
realized this as well as themselves. A considerable body of
cavalry was already appearing at its southern end. If the Duke
of Belluno, instead of delivering two frontal assaults, had been
prudent enough to push men down this valley under cover of
the darkness, so as to have a lateral attack ready at dawn,
something might have been done. But now the imperial troops
would have to win the valley by hard fighting, before they could

use it as a starting-point for the assault on the hill. If a general attack were delivered, and the army were once more repulsed, it risked its line of communication and its retreat on Madrid. For the whole Spanish host might come out of the woods and fall upon its flank, while it was engaged with the British, and in that case the Madrid road would be cut, and the King would have to retreat on Avila, sacrificing his capital and his arsenals. On the whole Jourdan held that it would be wise and prudent to assume a defensive posture, and either to hold the present position or to retire to the more favourable ground behind the Alberche, four miles to the rear. In a few days the enemy would hear of Soult's operations upon their line of communication, and would be forced to break up and retire.

Very different, as might have been expected, were Victor's views. He declared that the British position was far from impregnable, and that the prestige of the French army would be destroyed if it retired, after two partial checks, from in front of an enemy who had not been seriously attacked. The only fault in the preceding operations had been that the whole army had not joined in, at the moment when the Cerro had been stormed. If the King would undertake to use the 4th Corps against the allied centre, he pledged himself to break their right with his own three divisions of infantry. He would not only assail the Cerro from in front, but would turn it from both flanks. If such an attack did not succeed *il faudrait renoncer à faire la guerre.* This phrase he dinned into Joseph's and Jourdan's ears so repeatedly that they both saved it up for future use, and taunted him with it in the acrimonious correspondence which followed the battle.

King Joseph would have preferred to follow Jourdan's cautious plan, and to hold back. Sebastiani, whose opinion he asked, agreed with him. But both seem to have been terrorized by the Marshal's stormy tirades, and still more by the thought of what the Emperor would say, if he heard that battle had been refused, contrary to Victor's advice. The ultimate decision was still in the balance, when two pieces of news were received : the first was a dispatch from General Valence, the Governor of Toledo, to effect that the army of Venegas, whose position had hitherto been unknown—for nothing had been heard of him since Sebastiani had escaped from his front—had at last come on the scene. His advanced guard had presented itself before the bridges of Toledo, and was already skirmishing there. The second item of intelligence was a dispatch from Soult, acknowledging the receipt of the orders which had been sent to him upon the twenty-second, and stating his intention of carrying them out at the earliest possible moment. But he complained that the promised train of artillery had not yet reached the 2nd Corps, and declared that he could not move till it had come to hand, and till he had brought down the 6th Corps from Astorga. He was therefore of opinion that he could not possibly reach Plasencia till August 3, perhaps not till two days later.

This news was decisive : it was now clear that the Duke of Dalmatia would not be able to bring pressure to bear upon the rear of the allies for some six or seven days. Meanwhile Venegas was within two marches of Madrid, and had nothing in front of him save the four Polish battalions at Toledo. If the King refused to fight, and took up a defensive position on the Alberche, he would have to detach 15,000 men to hold back the army of La Mancha from the capital. This would leave him with only 30,000 men to resist Wellesley and Cuesta, and it was clear that such a force would be overmatched by the allies. If he kept a larger number in their front, Venegas would be able to capture Madrid, the thing of all others which Joseph was resolved to prevent. Accordingly the King and Jourdan reluctantly fell in with Victor's plans, and consented to fight in the afternoon. If they defeated the British and the Estremadurans on the twenty-eighth, the army of La Mancha could easily be disposed of upon the twenty-ninth or thirtieth.

This decision once made, it only remained to settle the details of the attack. The King determined to assail the British centre and right with the infantry of Sebastiani's corps—twenty-three battalions in all, or some 14,000 men. Victor with the three infantry divisions of the 1st Corps—thirty-three battalions, still over 16,000 strong in spite of their losses—undertook to fall upon the English left, to storm the Cerro de Medellin and also to turn it on its northern side, so as to envelop Wellesley's flank. The Spaniards were to be left alone behind their walls and orchards—only Milhaud's dragoons were told off to watch

the exits from Talavera. Of the rest of the cavalry a few could
be utilized in Victor's turning movement in the valley below the
Sierra de Segurilla: but the main body—all Beaumont's and
Latour-Maubourg's eight regiments—were ranged in a second
line, to act as a reserve for the frontal attack of the infantry, and
to aid it if it were checked. The King's Guards and the brigade
of Dessolles were to be kept back, and only utilized to clinch the
victory or to retrieve a repulse.

The 30,000 men who were to deliver the grand assault on the
allied position were drawn up as follows. Leval's Germans
advanced on the left, taking as their objective the battery on
the Pajar de Vergara. They faced Campbell's British division,
and slightly overlapped it, so as to cover the three or four
battalions on the extreme northern wing of Cuesta's line. In
their rear as supports followed the two Polish battalions from
Valence's division. On Leval's right, Sebastiani's four French
regiments continued the line: this was the strongest division on
the field and counted over 8,000 bayonets. It faced the Guards
and the right battalion of Cameron's brigade. Here ended the
troops of the 4th Corps: beyond them Victor's 2nd division,
that of Lapisse, was about to assail the German Legion and
Cameron's left-hand regiment, the 83rd. Still further north
Villatte's division lay opposite the steepest slopes of the Cerro
de Medellin. This position looked more formidable in the eyes
of the Duke of Belluno since he had seen his first two assaults
upon it fail. It was now heavily manned: Tilson's, Richard
Stewart's, and Donkin's brigades were all visible upon its crest.
After some hesitation the Marshal resolved to leave it alone for
the present, and not to attack it till some impression should
have been made upon other parts of Wellesley's line. Accordingly he left in front of it only Villatte's second brigade—the six
battalions of the 94th and 95th regiments. The other brigade
—the 27th and 63rd—was directed to join in the flanking
movement to the north of the Cerro, which was to encompass
Wellesley's extreme left. But the main force told off for this
advance consisted of the much-tried remnants of Ruffin's division,
now not more than 3,700 strong. The employment of these
troops for such a critical operation seems to have been a
mistake—they had already received two bloody checks, and had

lost more than a third of their officers and 1,500 men in the late fighting. Though good regiments, they could now be considered as little more than 'a spent force.' This fact sufficiently explains the feebleness of the French advance upon this part of the field during the afternoon hours.

Behind the French infantry of the 4th and 1st Corps were deployed no less than twelve regiments of horse : Latour-Maubourg's three brigades of dragoons were drawn up in the rear of Lapisse and Sebastiani : Beaumont supported Villatte, and lastly the four regiments of Merlin's (late Lasalle's) division followed Ruffin in his turning movement. Far to the rear Dessolles and Joseph's Guards took up a position facing the British centre, from which they could support the right or the left of their own front line as might be necessary.

The drawing up of this line of battle took time, and while the French were shifting their positions and establishing their new front, Wellesley had ample leisure to provide against the oncoming storm. He had established himself upon the crest of the Cerro, and from thence could overlook every movement of the enemy. Of the new dispositions the only one which struck him as likely to cause trouble was the extension of Ruffin and Villatte to the northward. It was clear that they were intending to advance up the valley that separates the Sierra de Segurilla from the Cerro de Medellin, in order to take the hill in the flank, and assail the 2nd Division from the side. It was therefore necessary to make arrangements for checking this manœuvre. Wellesley's first order was that Fane's and Anson's cavalry should move round the back of the Cerro, and take up new ground at the head of the valley. From this position they would be able to charge in the flank any force that might push up the trough of the depression, in order to get behind Hill's line. He also withdrew half Rettberg's battery from the front of the height, and placed it on a projecting lateral spur from which it could enfilade the valley. Nor were these his only precautions ; he sent a hasty message to Cuesta, pointing out that the greater part of the Spanish line was not threatened, and asking if he could spare reinforcements for the left wing. The Spanish general behaved in a more liberal fashion than might have been expected from his previous conduct. He consented to lend Wellesley his reserve division, that of Bassecourt, about 5,000 strong, and also put at his disposition a battery of twelve-pounders, heavier guns than any which the British army possessed. The French were so slow in moving that there was ample time, before the battle grew hot, to send Bassecourt's division round the rear of the British line, and to place it on the lower slopes of the Sierra de Segurilla, so as to continue to the northward the front formed by the British cavalry. Of the Spanish guns placed at Wellesley's disposition, four were put into the Pajar de Vergara redoubt, by the side of Lawson's battery : the other two accompanied Bassecourt's infantry, and were placed on the northern spur of the Cerro de Medellin, near Rettberg's six-pounders. Somewhat later the Duke of Albuquerque brought round the whole of his cavalry division —six regiments and a horse-artillery battery—to the same quarter, and drew them up in two lines to the rear of Anson's and Fane's brigades. But before he arrived the battle had already begun.

When the whole of the French infantry was ready, at about two o'clock in the afternoon, the King gave orders for the artillery to open, and eighty guns of the 1st and 4th Corps began to play upon the British line. In some places the troops were only some 600 yards from the enemy's batteries, and the loss in many regiments was very appreciable before a single musket had been fired. Only thirty British and six Spanish pieces could reply : they were overwhelmed from the first by the superior number of the French guns. It was therefore with joy that Wellesley's infantry saw that the artillery engagement was not to last for long. All along the hostile line the battalion-columns of Ruffin, Lapisse, Sebastiani, and Leval were moving up to the attack, and when they reached the front, and threw out their screen of tirailleurs, the guns grew silent. Only from the Cerro de Cascajal, where Villatte was hanging back in obedience to Victor's orders, did the cannonade against Hill's brigades continue.

The first troops to come into collision with the allies were Leval's Germans, upon the extreme left of the French line. This, it is said, was contrary to the King's orders; he had intended to hold this division somewhat back, as it was in danger of being outflanked by the Spaniards if it made a premature advance[1]. But Leval had a tangled terrain of vines and olive groves in his front: when once he had entered it he lost sight of the troops on his right, and fearing to be late on account of the obstacles in his front, committed the opposite fault. He came rushing in upon Campbell's outpost line half an hour before the other divisions had closed with the British centre, the time being then 2.30 in the afternoon.

The nine battalions of the German division were arrayed in a single line of battalion columns[2], with a thick screen of tirailleurs in their front. But their order had been so much broken up by the walls and thickets that the 4,500 bayonets appeared to the British like one confused mass of skirmishers. They came on fast and furiously, chasing the pickets of the 7th and 53rd before them, till they emerged into the comparatively open ground in front of the Pajar de Vergara[3]. Here the

---

[1] See Jourdan's *Mémoires*, p. 260.

[2] Their order from left to right was as follows: Frankfort—Hesse (two batts.), Baden (two batts.), Holland (two batts.), Nassau (two batts.).

[3] There is a legend which occurs in all French narratives of Talavera—starting with the contemporary accounts, and including Desprez's and Jourdan's *Mémoires*. It is to the effect that Leval's division, in its first advance, came upon an English battalion, which several writers call the 45th, lying in front of the rest of the allied line. It is alleged that the Nassau regiment surrounded and almost captured it—that they would have taken it prisoner indeed *en masse*, if the troops on their left (Holland and Baden) had held firm. But at least 'on lui prit une centaine d'hommes, le major, le lieutenant-colonel, et le colonel—ce dernier mourut de ses blessures' (Jourdan). No such incident can have occurred, for (1) no English regiment lost more than twenty-one 'missing' on this side of the field. (2) No English officer of higher rank than a captain was taken prisoner in the battle. (3) Only one officer was killed in the whole of Campbell's division, and he was a lieutenant of the 7th Fusiliers. (4) The 45th was not engaged with Leval's men, but lay to the left and supported the Guards in resisting Sebastiani: it lost one officer (a captain) and twelve men missing, but this was in the great *mêlée* in the centre, at the end of the day's fighting: it had no officer killed. I am driven to conclude that the whole is some gross exaggeration of the surprise of Campbell's pickets in the vineyards, and that instead of a 'battalion' we should read the light companies of the division.' Cooper of the 7th Fusiliers, who was in the skirmishing line, says that the Germans got close among them by calling out 'Españoles' and pretending to be Spaniards. A few prisoners (twenty-six in all) were lost in this way.

defence was standing ready for them: Campbell had brought
up one battalion of his rear brigade into his front line, so that
the 40th, as well as the 53rd and 7th, were facing the attack.
On his right lay the redoubt with its ten guns: further to the
south the two left-hand units of the French division were
opposed to troops of Cuesta's army.   Hence it came that
while the Nassau and Dutch regiments faced the British
infantry, the Baden regiment was in front of the guns, while
the Hessians and the Frankfort battalion had to do with
the Spaniards.

When the Germans surged out from among the olive groves
into the comparatively open ground in front of the Pajar de
Vergara, the musketry opened along both lines at a distance
of about 200 yards, the assailants delivering a rolling fire, while
the defenders of the position answered with regular battalion
volleys.   Several times Leval's men advanced a few score
paces, and the distance between the two divisions was growing
gradually less.   But the attacking force was evidently suffering
more than the allies: in the centre especially, where the ten
guns of the redoubt were firing canister into the disordered
mass, the casualties of the Baden battalions were terrible:
they could not bear up against the blasts of *mitraille*, and
after their colonel, von Porbeck, had fallen, they broke and
began to recoil.   Seeing part of the enemy's line falling into
disorder, General Campbell ordered his front line to charge.
Then Colonel Myers of the 7th, seizing the King's colour of
his regiment, ran out in front of the line and calling ' Come on,
Fusiliers,' led the advance [1].   His own battalion, the 40th and
the 53rd, at once closed with the Nassau and Dutch regiments,
who shrank back into the thickets and melted away from the
front.   The victors pursued them for some distance, capturing
in their onward career a whole battery of six guns, which was
being brought forward to reply to the artillery of the redoubt,
but had failed to reach the clearing before the line in front of
them gave way.   The three battalions on Leval's extreme left,
which had the Spaniards in front of them, had been exchanging
volleys with their opponents without notable advantage on

---

[1] This was the Myers who fell in storming the famous hill of Albuera in
1811.   See Cooper (of the 7th), p. 22.

either side, when the rest of the division broke. When their
companions retired they also were forced to draw back, in
order to prevent themselves from being turned on both flanks.
Campbell was cautious enough to stop his men before they had
gone far forward among the thickets, and brought them back
to their old position: he spiked the guns that he had taken,
and left them in the clearing in front of the redoubt. His
losses had been very small, owing to his admirable self-restraint
in calling back his charging regiments before they got out of hand.

Leval therefore was able to rally his division at leisure, upon
the two Polish battalions which formed its supports. He had
lost in the three-quarters of an hour during which he was
engaged some six or seven hundred men. The battle was
raging by now all down the line, and when the Germans were
re-formed, they received orders to advance for a second time, to
cover the flank of Sebastiani's division, now hotly engaged with
Sherbrooke's right brigades. Neglecting chronological considerations, in order to finish the narrative of the action in this
quarter, it may suffice to say that Leval's second attack was
made at about 4 o'clock in the afternoon: it was not delivered
with so much energy as had been shown in his first. It
encountered the same obstacles, and could not surmount them.
Once more the advance rolled up through the olive groves, and
reached the clearing in front of the battery. Again the head
of the attacking masses withered away under the musketry fire
and the salvos from the English and Spanish guns, and the
whole finally went to the rear in disorder. Campbell, in
repelling this attack, used his second brigade as well as his
first, and pushed the enemy further back than he had done
during the earlier fighting: the Spaniards also came out of
their line and continued to flank the retreating enemy with two
or three battalions and a half-battery [1]. As the Hessians and
Frankforters in their front began to give way, they were assailed

---

[1] 'Another lull in the storm, and fresh formation. "Here they come
again" said many voices: so they did, but we were ready and gave them
such a warm reception that they speedily went to the right-about. As in
their first attack they now left behind several pieces of cannon, which we
secured as before. After these two attacks and sharp repulses we were not
troubled with their company any more.' Cooper, p. 23.

by one of Henestrosa's cavalry regiments, the *Regimiento del Rey*, which charged with great spirit, and cut up many men before they could form square. The bulk of the two battalions, however, clubbed together in a mass and retired into the woods, defending themselves as best they could. The victorious Spanish horsemen while following them, came upon a second French battery which (like that captured by the British brigade on their left) was being brought forward by a narrow lane between two olive groves. They cut down the gunners and took four pieces, which were dragged back into the redoubt. This was by far the best piece of work done by Spanish cavalry during the whole of the first years of the war, and did much to atone for the panic of the previous night in the eyes of the British observers upon the right wing.

The repulse of Leval's division was complete, and its wrecks, once more rallied upon the two Polish battalions in their rear, drew back into the plain, and were completely put out of action. In this attack they lost not only the four guns taken by the Spaniards, but seven more pieces of artillery. Convinced that he could not carry the Pajar de Vergara position unless he could bring guns to bear upon the redoubt, and check the ravages of its salvos of canister, Leval had tried to push his remaining two batteries into the firing line. Again, as in the first attack, they were left helpless when the infantry broke, and became the prey of the pursuers. It would seem that he lost on this day seventeen guns in all [1]. The total of the

---

[1] There can be no rational doubt that the total number of guns taken was seventeen, as set forth in Charles Stewart's report to Wellesley, as Adjutant-general, viz. ' four eight-pounders, four six-pounders, one four-pounder, one six-inch howitzer, taken by Brigadier-general A. Campbell's brigade, with one six-inch howitzer and six other guns left by the enemy and found in the woods' of which four were in the hands of the Spaniards. Wellesley, in his dispatch, made the error of stating that twenty guns had been taken, being under the impression that the Spaniards had captured seven pieces, while they themselves only claim four—a Captain Piñero was mentioned in Eguia's dispatch for causing them to be brought back to the Spanish line. The British took thirteen guns : three days after the battle Wellesley made them over to his allies. He writes to O'Donoju [Talavera, Aug. 1] : ' We have got thirteen pieces of French artillery, which I wish to give over to the Spanish army—the other seven [four] you have already

casualties in his division were 1,007, nearly a quarter of its force: the colonels of the Baden and Frankfort regiments and the major commanding the Dutch battery had been left on the got. I shall be obliged if you will urge General Cuesta to desire the commanding officer of his artillery to receive charge of them from the officer commanding the British artillery.' This is surely conclusive as to the numbers.

Jourdan in his *Mémoires* acknowledges the loss of apparently *all* Leval's guns — three batteries. ' L'artillerie du général Leval, qu'on avait imprudemment engagée au milieu des bois, des vignes et des fosses, ayant eu la plupart de ses chevaux tués, ne put pas être retirée ; événement fàcheux qu'on eut le tort impardonnable de cacher au roi' [p. 261]. Desprez says that *six* pieces only were lost : Thiers allows *eight*.

But the most interesting point of the controversy comes out in Napoleon's correspondence with his brother Joseph. On Aug. 25, the Emperor writes in hot anger to say that he sees from the English newspapers that Joseph had lost twenty guns, a fact concealed in the King's dispatch. He desires to be told at once the names of the batteries that were captured and the divisions to which they belonged. Jourdan replies in the King's behalf on Sept. 15, that *no* guns have been lost—four pieces of Leval's artillery had been for a moment in the hands of the British, but they were recaptured. Joseph himself writes to the same effect next day : ' Wellesley n'a pris aucune aigle, il n'en montrera pas plus que de canons.' On the nineteenth, Jourdan writes to Clarke, the Minister of War, to say that he has just found out that *two* guns had been lost by Leval. Sénarmont, the artillery chief of the 4th Corps, explains to Jourdan, in a letter of September 27, that *ten* pieces had been lost in the olive groves, but that all were recovered save *two*, one Dutch six-pounder, and one French eight-pounder. The truth comes out in Desprez's narrative. He says that the King, hearing that Leval had left guns abandoned in front of the Pajar de Vergara, ordered Sebastiani to have them brought in : ' Le général assura que déjà elles avaient été reprises. Cette assertion était inexacte. Le général Sebastiani était-il lui-même en erreur ? Ou les ordres donnés lui paraissaient-ils inexécutables ? Je n'ai jamais eu le mot de l'énigme : quoi qu'il en soit, les pièces tombèrent le lendemain au pouvoir de l'ennemi. Le Général Sénarmont, qui commandait l'artillerie, ne rendit pas compte de cette perte. Le général Sebastiani l'avait prié avec instance de la cacher. Aussi dans son rapport sur la bataille Joseph déclara-t-il positivement qu'on n'avait pas perdu un canon. Plus tard les journaux anglais firent connaître la vérité. L'Empereur, qui savait apprécier leur exactitude, reprocha à son frère de l'avoir trompé. Joseph eut assez de délicatesse pour accepter ces reproches et ne point déclarer de quelle manière les choses s'étaient passées' [p. 491].

In short, Sebastiani and Sénarmont conspired to hide the truth, and Joseph, who liked them both (see his letters in Ducasse, especially vi. 456,

field [1]. Campbell had suffered on a very different scale—he had only lost 236 men, and it is improbable that the Spaniards on his right had more than 150 or 180 casualties, since they only fought with one wing of the attacking force. Wellesley, not without reason, gave the highest praise in his dispatch to Campbell, for the admirable and cautious defence which he had made. The management of the 4th Division, indeed, contrasted strongly with that of the troops to its left, where Sherbrooke's brigades—as we shall see—risked the loss of the battle by their rash pursuit of the enemy, far beyond the limits of the position which had been given them to defend.

We must now turn to their doings—the most desperate fighting that occurred during the day. Sherbrooke's eight battalions had to endure the preliminary cannonade for more than half an hour after Campbell's men were closely engaged with the enemy. It was not till three o'clock that the two French divisions opposed to them began to descend towards the Portiña, in an orderly and imposing array. Each of the French generals had drawn up his twelve battalions in two lines—the front line deployed in column of divisions, the supporting line in solid column of battalions. But there was this difference in their arrangements, that Lapisse had placed his brigades one behind the other, while Sebastiani had preferred to work his brigades side by side, each with one regiment in first and one in second line. The former therefore had Laplannes' brigade (16th Léger and 45th Line) opposed to Low's and Langwerth's regiments of

where on Sept. 30 he sends Sénarmont a gold box as a sort of 'consolation prize'), hushed the matter up in their interests. The most curious part of the matter is that on Sept. 27, Sénarmont was able to say with literal exactness that only two pieces were missing, for fifteen of the lost guns had been retaken on August 5, behind the bridge of Arzobispo, during the retreat of Cuesta's army. They had been given back to their owners long before September, so were no longer missing. But this can hardly be called 'the whole truth and nothing but the truth.'

[1] The losses were killed: officers six, men ninety-seven: wounded, officers twenty-four, men 803: prisoners, seventy-seven men. Campbell lost killed: officers one, men thirty-two: wounded, officers six, men 171: missing, officers one, men twenty-five—a total of 236. The Spaniards may have had 150 casualties—it is difficult to see that they can have suffered much more, as they had only two hostile regiments in front of them.

the German Legion and Cameron's 2/83rd. The latter had the
28th of Rey's and the 58th of Liger-Bellair's brigades ranged
over against the 1/61st and the British Foot-Guards. When
the cannonade of the French batteries ceased, the twelve
battalions of their first line, preceded by the usual swarm of
tirailleurs, moved down toward the Portiña. They crossed the
brook and pressed on towards the red line that stood awaiting
their approach, driving before them with ease the comparatively
insignificant screen of light troops that lay in front of the British
centre. Sherbrooke, who was responsible for the whole line of
the defence, since his division exactly covered the ground on
which the French attack was delivered, had issued orders that
the troops were not to fire till the enemy came within fifty
yards of them, and that they were then to deliver a single
volley and charge. This programme was executed with precise
obedience : though suffering severely from the enemy's musketry,
the division held in its fire till the hostile columns were close
upon them, and then opened with one tremendous discharge
which crashed out simultaneously along the whole eight battalions. The leading ranks of Lapisse's and Sebastiani's front
line went down in swathes,—one French witness says that the
infantry of the regiments of the 4th Corps lost a third of
their numbers in less than ten minutes. When the charge
which Sherbrooke had ordered followed close upon the blasting
musketry fire, the enemy retired in disorder and fell back
beyond the Portiña.

The divisional general had apparently forgotten to caution
his colonels against the danger of carrying their advance too
far. Instead of contenting themselves with chasing the broken
enemy as far as the brook, and then returning to their positions,
the four brigades of the 1st division all crossed the water and
pursued the French into their own ground ; the German Legion
on the left actually began to push them up the lower slopes
of the Cerro de Cascajal, while the Guards on the right went
forward far into the rolling plain in front of them. Cameron
halted his two battalions not far beyond the Portiña ; but on
each side of him the pursuit was pressed with reckless energy,
and without any remembrance of the fact that the enemy had
strong reserves.

Thus it came to pass that a disaster followed the first success of Sherbrooke's division. Both the Germans on the left and the Guards on the right found themselves in face of intact troops, behind whom the broken front line of the enemy took refuge. They were in no condition to begin a new combat, for they were in complete disorder, and there was a broad gap on the inner flank of each brigade, owing to the fact that Cameron had halted and refused to push forward into danger. Hence came a perilous crisis: the French reserves moved forward, the guns on the Cascajal height enfiladed the German Legion, while two regiments of Latour-Maubourg's dragoons moved in upon the right flank of the Guards. The whole of the six battalions that had joined in the reckless advance were forced to recoil, fighting desperately but losing ground every moment, and pressed into clumps and masses that presented no trace of their former line of battle. When they fell back to the point where Cameron had stopped, the 61st and 83rd became involved in their retreat, and were forced to repass the Portiña in their company. The French followed with shouts of victory, pushing their advantage to the utmost and slaughtering the disordered battalions by hundreds. The disaster was worst on the left, where half the strength of the 2nd Line Battalion of the German Legion—387 men—was destroyed in twenty minutes, and the 5th battalion of that same corps lost over 100 prisoners. The Guards suffered almost as heavily: out of their 2,000 men 611 went down killed or wounded: but they left no prisoners behind.

It seemed that the day might well be lost, for Wellesley's reserves were small. Such as they were, however, they were at once put into action. Mackenzie brought forward his brigade to the ground which the Guards had originally covered, and drew them up to withstand the rush of Sebastiani's division—the 2/24th on the right, the 2/31st on the left, with the 1/45th between them. The disordered household troops passed through their intervals, and rallied behind them with splendid promptness: 'their good humour and determination after such dreadful losses' says an eye-witness, 'was shown by their giving a loud hurrah as they took up their new ground[1].' At the same time Cotton brought up the single brigade of light cavalry which

[1] Lord Munster, p. 231.

was in reserve, and drew them up on Mackenzie's right, so as to cover his flank. Sebastiani came up with great boldness against the fresh front thus presented to him, and for twenty minutes there was a furious musketry battle in the British right centre. Mackenzie himself fell, and his three battalions lost 632 men out of about 2,000 : but they held their own, and finally the enemy recoiled. They were helped somewhat in their inclination to retreat by a charge of the Light Dragoons upon the flank of their left-hand regiment, the 75th, which had about 150 men sabred [1]. Thus on this point the battle was saved : the main credit must go to Mackenzie's brigade, which has never received the praise that was its due, for its general was killed, and thus no report from the 3rd division was sent in to Wellesley, who omitted all mention of its doings in his Talavera dispatch [2]. It is never too late to do homage to forgotten valour, and to call attention to a neglected feat of arms. The services of the 24th, 31st, and 45th saved the day for Britain [3].

Sebastiani therefore drew back terribly mauled : his division had lost *all* its four colonels, seven of its twelve battalion-chiefs, seventy other officers and 2,100 rank and file—including some sixty prisoners. There was no more fight left in them. They recoiled into the plain, and drew up at last not far from the wrecks of Leval's division, a full mile beyond the Portiña.

Meanwhile, however great may have been the danger in the British right-centre, that in the left-centre was even greater. Cameron's, Low's, and Langwerth's brigades were all in the most desperate position : the former, not having pushed so far to the front as the four German battalions, had suffered least of the three—though it had lost 500 men out of 1,400.

---

[1] General Desprez, relating the doings of Sebastiani's division, says that the 75th were cut up by *Spanish* light horse : but there were no cavalry of that nation in this part of the field, and it would seem that the French were misled by the blue uniforms of the Light Dragoons.

[2] Except that he mentioned the colonels of the 31st and 45th among the officers who had done well in the battle.

[3] The only place where a good account of the doings of Mackenzie's brigade is to be found is in the excellent regimental history of the 24th. I fully share the indignation expressed by its author at the unmerited oblivion in which its splendid doings have been lying for so many years. [See Paton's *Annals of the 24th Regiment.*]

But the Legionary troops were in far worse case—Langwerth had been killed, and his brigade was reduced from 1,300 to 650 bayonets—just fifty per cent. of the men had been lost. Low had gone into action with only 950 rank and file, owing to the heavy casualty-list of the preceding night. Of these he now lost 350, including 150 made prisoners in the disorderly retreat down the slope of the Cerro de Cascajal. That these troops ever rallied and made head at all, when they had recrossed the Portiña, is much to their credit.

The situation was saved by Wellesley's own prescience. The moment that he saw the rash attack on the French line to which Sherbrooke had committed himself, he looked round for supports which might be utilized to stay the inevitable reaction that must follow. Mackenzie's brigade was available on the right-centre, and was used as we have seen. But there were no infantry reserves behind the left-centre : it was necessary to send down troops from the Cerro de Medellin. Villatte was then threatening its front, Ruffin was marching to turn its northern flank, and Wellesley did not dare to detach a whole brigade from the key of the position. He took, however, Richard Stewart's strongest battalion, the 1/48th under Colonel Donnellan (which had still over 700 bayonets in line even after its losses in the morning) and sent it at full speed down the southern slope of the Cerro. It arrived in time to take position on the old ground of the British line, at the moment that the retreating masses came rolling back across the Portiña. If the 48th had been carried away in the general backward movement, the day would have been lost : but the regiment stood firm, and allowed Cameron's and Langwerth's troops to pass by its flanks and form up in its rear. While it was holding back Lapisse's central advance, the defeated brigades rallied and re-formed with admirable celerity, and the battle was restored. Here, as further to the right, the fighting now resolved itself into a furious musketry-combat between enemies both of whom were now spent and weakened by their previous exertions [1]. In such

---

[1] In most modern English narratives of Talavera it is stated that the 1/48th supported the Guards. This must be a mistake, caused by a mis-reading of Wellesley's dispatch. It is certain that the Guards fell back on Mackenzie's brigade. Contemporary accounts by officers of the 2/24th

a duel the line had always the advantage over the column in the end. The French, when once brought to a standstill by the 1/48th, lost their *élan*, and stood heaped together in disorderly masses, keeping up a rolling fire but gaining no ground. Howorth turned upon them the batteries on the Cerro de Medellin, which enfiladed their flank and added to their confusion. General Lapisse himself was killed at this moment, as he was trying to urge on his men to a final advance. It was probably, however, not his death—on which all the French accounts lay great stress—but rather the defeat of Sebastiani's division on their immediate right which finally shook the *morale* of the French regiments, and induced them to move back, first at a slow pace, then in undisguised retreat. The shattered remnants of the German Legion and of the 1/48th, 1/61st, and 2/83rd were in no condition to follow. Seldom have two combatants so thoroughly mauled each other as had the twelve French and the seven allied battalions which fought in this part of the field. Of the 6,800 men of Lapisse's division, the general, sixty-nine other officers, and 1,700 men were *hors de combat*. Of 4,300[1] British and German troops opposed to them almost exactly the same number had been lost—a general (Langwerth), seventy-seven officers, and 1,616 men. That the smaller force should ever have held its ground after losing more than a third of its number is almost miraculous. There was no such a victory as this during the whole war, save Albuera.

While the main stress of the battle had been rolling across the lower slopes, above the middle course of the Portiña, matters

speak of the Coldstreams passing through them to re-form : the Scots Fusiliers therefore must have had the 2/31st and 1/45th behind them. Donnellan and the 1/48th really supported Langwerth's German battalions, as Lord Londonderry (the only historian who has got the facts right) clearly shows (i. p. 410). It is curious that the historians of the battle have not seen that the Germans, in their dreadfully mauled condition, could not have been rallied without external aid : this aid was given by Donnellan, while Mackenzie was saving the Guards.

[1] The figures are (after deducting the losses of the earlier combats) : Low's brigade 964, Langwerth's 1,315, Cameron's 1,306, 1/48th 700, a total of 4,285. The losses were : Low 326, Langwerth 721, Cameron 547, 1/48th *about* 100, a total of 1,694, including officers. (See tables in Appendix.)

had been comparatively quiet on the Cerro de Medellin. Victor, it will be remembered, had ordered that Villatte was to make no serious attack on the height until the divisions to his left had made some impression upon the British centre. But Lapisse and Sebastiani, in spite of their temporary successes, had never broken into Wellesley's position. The assault on the Cerro therefore was never made, though a furious artillery fire was kept up against its garrison throughout the afternoon. The handful of British guns upon the crest could make no adequate reply : hence the three brigades of Tilson, Richard Stewart, and Donkin were suffering very serious losses from the long cannonade. Wellesley had made them shelter themselves, as far as was possible, behind the sky-line. Nevertheless the storm of shot and shell that beat upon the position was not without effect. In Donkin's brigade no one, save the light companies skirmishing along the lower slopes, discharged a musket that afternoon, yet the casualties in its ranks were no less than 195 [1]. Hill's two brigades, though better covered, had still many killed and wounded. That the return-fire of the British artillery and skirmishers was not altogether ineffective is shown by the fact that the two regiments of Villatte's second brigade, which held the opposite slope, lost 185 men, and even the squadrons of Beaumont in its rear had a few troopers disabled [2]. Nevertheless the fighting in this part of the field was not only indecisive but comparatively innocuous to both sides, when compared with the awful slaughter that was going on to their right.

It only remains to tell of the combat to the north of the Cerro, in the narrow valley that separated the British position from the Sierra de Segurilla. Here the engagement began at a much later hour than in the centre. All the observers on the hill speak of the first contest of Campbell and Leval as being concluded, and of that of Sherbrooke and Sebastiani as being at its height, before the French right wing began to move.

The French troops in this direction, it will be remembered,

---

[1] For a description of the sufferings of the 88th, whose battalion companies did not fire a single shot, during the cannonade of the afternoon, see Grattan's *Connaught Rangers*, vol. iii. p. 91.

[2] For these losses, see the Talavera Appendix.

were the three regiments of Ruffin, now mere wrecks of their former selves, and the first brigade of Villatte's division, that of Cassagne. The six battalions of the latter force were near the Cerro de Medellin, while Ruffin's men stood further to the north, under the Sierra de Segurilla. In support of them both lay Merlin's division of light cavalry.

At the moment when Victor had received permission to turn the flank of the Cerro, it had appeared that he would meet little opposition. But long ere the French were ready to advance, they had seen allied troops arriving in haste and taking up their position at the southern end of the valley. First Fane's and Anson's cavalry had drawn up on the level ground, then Bassecourt's Spanish infantry had appeared on the rocky slopes of the Sierra, and had thrown out a long skirmishing line opposite Ruffin's right. Lastly Albuquerque's whole cavalry division had ridden round from the rear of the centre, and taken post behind Anson and Fane. There were now over 5,000 bayonets and 5,000 sabres in face of the French brigades.

It was clear that any attempt to storm the northern face of the Cerro would expose the troops that attempted it to a flank attack from the allied troops in the valley. It was this that made Ruffin and Villatte (who was present in person with Cassagne's brigade) very chary of molesting Hill's position. On the other hand if the French advanced up the valley to attack the cavalry at its southern end, they would expose themselves to a flanking fire from the guns on the Cerro and from Hill's right-hand infantry brigade.

Nevertheless, when the roar of the invisible battle on the other side of the Cascajal height was at its loudest, the two French generals began a cautious advance towards the front. They at once came under a tiresome flanking artillery fire from the Cerro : half Rettberg's battery of the German Legion had been placed on a spur from which it enfiladed Villatte's nearest regiment. Two heavy Spanish twelve-pounders opened from another part of the slope [1], and Albuquerque had also placed

---

[1] Hartmann of the K.G.L. artillery has a note on these pieces : they were useful because of their heavy calibre, none of the British guns being heavier than six-pounders. They were bright new brass cannon from the arsenal at Seville : their machinery for sighting and elevation was of

his horse-artillery guns in a position from which they bore up the valley. The pieces that accompanied the French advance, being in the trough of the depression, could do little harm in return.

After advancing as far as the path which leads from Talavera to Segurilla, Ruffin deployed his right regiment, the much depleted 9th Léger, and sent it up the Sierra to form a screen opposite Bassecourt's infantry. The other six battalions, the 24th and 96th, advanced in column along the valley, with the 27th from Cassagne's brigade on their left ; presently the whole came level with the northern slope of the Cerro, just reaching the farm of Valdefuentes at its foot.

At this moment Lapisse's attack had already been beaten off, and Wellesley was able to turn his attention from the centre to the flank of his line [1]. Crossing the crest of the Cerro, he studied for a moment the situation of the French regiments, and then sent down orders for Anson's brigade of light dragoons to charge them, with Fane's heavy cavalry in support. The moment that the British horsemen were seen to be advancing the enemy hastily formed squares—the 24th and 96th slightly to the west of the Segurilla road, the 27th in a more advanced position just under the walls of the farm of Valdefuentes. A battalion of *grenadiers réunis*, and the 63rd of the Line, which formed Villatte's supports, also fell into square far to the rear. The concentration of the French regiments in vast masses of

a most primitive type—a century out of date. The lieutenant in command seemed unable to hit anything with them, whereupon Hartmann got off his horse, himself laid a gun, and had the luck to dismount a French piece in the valley. After this the Spaniards fired better and did very good service.

[1] That the charge of Anson's light dragoons came after victory had been secured in the centre is clear from several eye-witnesses, e. g. Leith-Hay of the 29th, who was on top of the Cerro, and close to Wellesley, writes : 'The favourable termination of the battle in the centre created great excitement : the cheer, which had been re-echoed from the height had hardly died away, when a scene of another character was in preparation. The movements of the divisions Ruffin and Villatte had during the late contest been vacillating and uncertain. Formed to all appearance to attack the height, they had even advanced some distance towards its base. Sir Arthur crossed with rapid steps from the right of the 29th to the part of the hill looking down on Anson's brigade. It was immediately known that a charge would take place' (i. p. 158).

three battalions each gave a great opportunity to the allied artillery, which found easy targets in the square blocks of men at their feet.

As Anson's brigade advanced, the right regiment, the 23rd Light Dragoons, found itself opposite the large square of the 27th Léger, while the 1st Light Dragoons of the German Legion faced the smaller masses of the 24th and 96th. The ground seemed favourable for a charge, and though an attack on unbroken infantry is always hazardous, the squadrons came on with great confidence and were soon closing in at headlong speed upon the hostile line.

An unforeseen chance of war, however, wrecked the whole plan. The long dry waving grass of the valley seemed to show a level surface, but the appearance was deceitful. About a hundred and fifty yards in front of the French squares was a narrow but deep ravine, the bed of a small winter-torrent which discharges its waters into the Portiña during the rainy season. It was about fifteen feet broad and ten feet deep in the northern part of the field, a little narrower in its southern course. There were many places at which it could be crossed with ease by a horseman moving alone and at a moderate pace. But for squadrons riding knee to knee at headlong speed it was a dangerous obstacle, and indeed a trap of the most deadly sort. It was wholly invisible to the horsemen till they came upon it. Colonel Elley, the second in command of the 23rd, who rode two lengths ahead of the front line of his regiment, mounted on a grey horse, and conspicuous to every observer on the Cerro de Medellin, was the first man to discover the peril[1]. His charger cleared it at a bound; but knowing that the inferior mounts of the rank and file would certainly come to grief, he wheeled round on the further bank, threw up his hand and tried to wave back his followers. It was too late: the two squadrons of the front line were on the brink of the ravine before they could understand his action. Some of the troopers cleared the obstacle in their stride; some swerved in time and refused to take the leap; others scrambled into and over the less difficult points of the ditch: but many fell horse and man into the trap, and were then crushed by the rear rank falling in on top of them. There

---

[1] Leith-Hay, p. 159.

were several broken necks, and scores of broken arms and legs in the leading squadrons. The second line got warning of the obstacle by seeing the inexplicable disorder into which their fellows had fallen. They slackened their pace, but were borne into the confused mass at the ravine before they could entirely bring themselves to a stand. Meanwhile the front face of the square formed by the 27th Léger opened fire on the unhappy regiment.

The German light dragoons, on the northern side of the valley, came upon the fatal cutting at a point where it was somewhat shallower and broader than in front of the 23rd—one of their officers estimates it in his narrative at eighteen feet in width and six or eight in depth [1]. Their disaster therefore was not so complete as that of their British comrades. But many troopers of the first line were unhorsed, and others, though keeping their saddles, could not manage to scramble up the further side of the ravine. The rear squadrons came up in time to add to the confusion, and reined up among the survivors of the front [1].

The two regiments were now in utter confusion, and had already suffered severe loss both by the fall into the ravine and by the French musketry which had opened upon them. Their colonels would have been wise to give up the attempt to advance and to fall back in their old position. How could squadrons in such a disordered state hope to break into French squares? But both Seymour of the 23rd and Arentschildt were officers of high mettle, and throwing prudence to the winds they collected such of their men as had leaped or scrambled over the ravine, and led them against the hostile infantry. Probably little more than half of either corps took part in the final charge.

[1] Napier, ii. 176, has a story that Col. Arentschildt of the German dragoons discovered the ravine in time, and checked his line, crying, ' I will not kill my young mans'—thereby saving his regiment and taking no part in the charge. This is entirely disproved by the narratives of the officers of the 1st K.G.L. Dragoons, quoted in Beamish's *History of the King's German Legion*. The evidence of Colonel von der Decken alone suffices to show that the regiment fell into the trap, suffered severe losses therein, and then executed a disorderly and ineffective charge on Ruffin's squares, after which it returned to its old position, with a loss of nearly forty men. Napier seems to have been misled by the statement of Major Ponsonby of the 23rd, to the effect that the Germans turned back at the ravine. He also says that Seymour, Colonel of the 23rd, was wounded, but that officer's name does not appear in the casualty list.

Be this as it may, both the 23rd and the Legionary dragoons made an attempt to gallop in upon the squares in their front. The Germans rode at that of the 24th regiment, received its fire, and were repulsed, though a few men fell close in upon the bayonets. They then galloped off and fell back up the valley. Far more disastrous was the fate of the English regiment. The survivors of the two left squadrons charged the square of the 27th Léger, were repulsed with heavy loss, recrossed the ravine, and struggled back to the British lines. But Colonel Elley and the right squadrons, having no enemy immediately in their front, rode furiously between the French square and the farm of Valdefuentes, and charged a line of cavalry which was visible a few hundred yards to the rear [1]. This was the leading brigade [10th and 26th Chasseurs] of Merlin's division, which was acting in support of Villatte and Ruffin. The squadrons in front of the 23rd swerved to the side when charged [2], but on passing them the British dragoons found another regiment of Merlin's second line opposed to them [3]. They dashed at it, whereupon the regiment that had evaded them swung round and fell upon their rear. Encircled by fivefold numbers the remnant of Drake's and Allen's squadrons of the 23rd were annihilated. Only a few well-mounted officers [4], including their leader Elley,

[1] In this charge they carried away with them, and almost captured, Generals Villatte and Cassagne, who had failed to take refuge in the square of the 27th, and were caught outside it. [Séméle's Report.]

[2] In the French official reports it is said that General Strolz, the brigadier, drew aside the 10th Chasseurs, in order to fall upon the British dragoons from the flank. Rocca (p. 104) says that the regiment was charged and broke, but rallied again. *Victoires et Conquêtes* has : ‘le 10me de chasseurs ne pouvait soutenir cette charge, ouvrit ses rangs, mais bientôt rallié il chargea ses adversaires en queue.’ As the regiment only lost five killed it does not seem likely that it was broken. The French records do not give the number of its wounded.

[3] This was the Westphalian *chevaux-légers* regiment.

[4] Among the other officers who cut their way through was Lord George William Russell, desperately wounded by a cut on the shoulder. Only three officers (two wounded) were taken prisoners from these two squadrons : two others were killed : it would seem therefore that out of twelve present with the two right squadrons, several succeeded in getting out of the trap. Elley says that the whole body that followed him did not exceed 170 sabres, and that seven or eight only cut their way through the enemy.

and two or three troopers cut their way through the enemy, rode off to the northward, and ultimately escaped to Bassecourt's Spanish line on the Sierra de Segurilla. The total loss of the regiment was 207 killed, wounded and missing out of 450 sabres who took the field in the morning. Of these, three officers and 105 men were prisoners—most of them wounded.

It was late in the afternoon when the survivors of the 23rd found their way back to the western end of the valley, and the battle in the centre had long died down to a cannonade. Ruffin and Villatte now had it in their power to advance again, but did not do so. If they had gone further forward they would have lent their flank still more to Hill's troops upon the Cerro, and would have had to deploy, a movement which would have exposed them, when no longer protected by formation in square, to charges from the mass of allied cavalry still visible in their front—Fane's brigade and Albuquerque's strong division. Bassecourt's Spaniards were holding their ground against the flank-guard which had been sent up on to the Sierra de Segurilla, and to drive them back Ruffin would have had to detach more battalions from his main column. News had been received that the central attack had completely failed. It was natural, therefore, that after some hesitation the French right wing retired, and fell back up the valley of the Portiña. Villatte's two regiments had lost about 200 men while standing in square under the fire of the guns on the Cerro. They could no longer be regarded as fresh troops fit for a prolonged advance, while the wrecks of Ruffin's battalions, having now been under fire three separate times in eighteen hours, were utterly exhausted. It is clear that Victor could not have dared to risk a serious attack upon the British left with these forces.

The battle had now come to a standstill : of the five French infantry divisions in the front line those of Leval, Sebastiani, and Lapisse were reforming their diminished ranks in the plain, far to the east of the Portiña, while Villatte and Ruffin had fallen back on to the slopes of the Cerro de Cascajal. The only intact infantry still remaining at the disposition of the King were his own 1,800 Guards, and the 3,300 bayonets of Dessolles. With these and with Villatte's two brigades, which had only lost 400 men, it would have been possible to prepare one more assault upon the British position. Victor, raging with anger at his third repulse, was anxious to continue the action, though he had lost nearly one man in four of his infantry, and had not won an inch of ground. The King was less hopeful : the frightful slaughter had subdued his spirits, and he asked himself whether the 5,000 men of his reserve would suffice to break the thin red line against which the whole of the 1st and 4th Corps had hurled themselves in vain. For a moment he seemed inclined to risk his last stake, and the Guards and Dessolles were ordered to move forward. But they had not gone far when a counter-order was sent to check them : Milhaud, whose dragoons had spent the whole day in observing the Spanish lines, had sent in a message to the effect that Cuesta was at last showing signs of life, and that he could see numerous troops pushing to the front among the olive groves in front of the town. The news was not true, for nothing more than vedettes and small exploring parties had been sent out by the Spanish general. But the very suspicion that the Army of Estremadura might at last be preparing to take the initiative was enough to damp the very moderate ardour of King Joseph. If he committed himself to one final dash at the English, and engaged both his reserve and the rallied divisions of his front line, in an attack upon their allied centre and left, what could he do in the event of the sudden appearance of the whole Spanish army in the act of turning his southern flank ? Twenty-five thousand men, or more, might suddenly sally out from the screen of groves, and fling themselves upon the left flank of Sebastiani's corps. To hold them back nothing would be available but the 5,000 sabres of Milhaud and Latour-Maubourg ; of infantry not one man would be left to parry such a stroke. The King could not flatter himself that anything but a disaster could ensue. Even if it were not true that the Spaniards were already in motion, there was every reason to believe that they might deliver an attack when they saw the last French reserves put into action against the British. Few generals would have resisted such a tempting opportunity. It was to be remembered also that some of the Spaniards had actually come out of their lines, and fallen upon Leval's flank, when the last assault had been pressed against the Pajar de Vergara. A third advance in this quarter

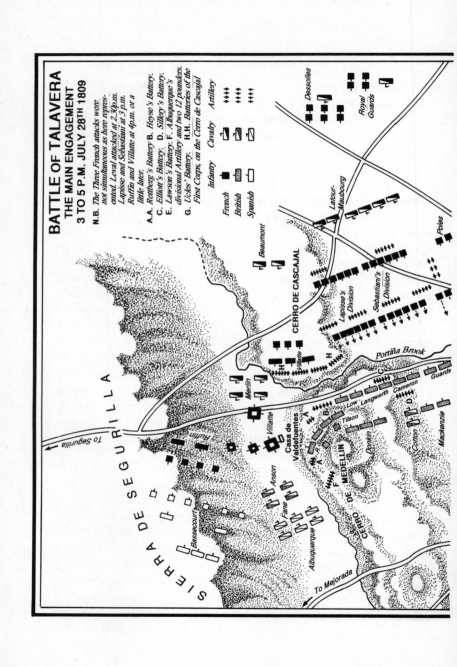

BATTLE OF TALAVERA
THE MAIN ENGAGEMENT
3 TO 5 P.M. JULY 28TH 1809

N.B. *The Three French attacks were not simultaneous as here represented. Leval attacked at 2.30p.m. Lapisse and Sebastiani at 3 p.m. Ruffin and Villatte at 4p.m. or a little later.*

A.A. *Retlberg's Battery.* B. *Heyse's Battery.*
C. *Elliot's Battery.* D. *Silley's Battery.*
E. *Lawson's Battery.* F. *Albuquerque's divisional Artillery and two 12 pounders.*
G. *Ucles' Battery.* H.H. *Batteries of the First Corps, on the Cerro de Cascajal*

	Infantry	Cavalry	Artillery
French			
British			
Spanish			

SIERRA DE SEGURILLA

To Segurilla ←

Bassecourt

Albuquerque

To Mejorada

CERRO DE MEDELLIN

Casa de Valdefuentes

Villatte

Ruffin

Anson

Fane

Merlin

Villatte

Mackenzie

Cotton

Donkin

Tilson

Low Langwerth Cameron

Guards

Portiña Brook

CERRO DE CASCAJAL

Beaumont

Lapisse's Division

Sebastiani's Division

Latour-Maubourg

Poles

Dessolles

Royal Guards

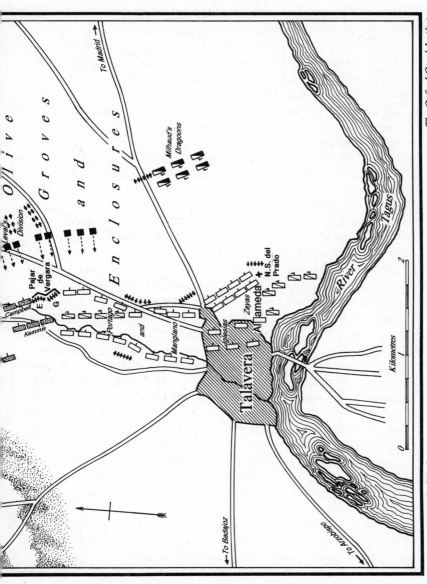

To Madrid

Milhaud's
Dragoons

Olive Groves and Enclosures

Leval's
Division

Pajar
de
Vergara

Campbell

E
G

Kemmis

Portago
and
Manglano

Iglesias

Talavera

Zayas

Alameda

N.S. del
Prado

River Tagus

Kilometres

0   1   2

To Badajoz

To Arzobispo

The Oxford Geog? Institute.

Darbishire & Stanford, Ltd.

might yet rouse the whole Estremaduran army out of its apathy, and induce it to charge home upon Sebastiani's left wing.

Jourdan and most of the members of Joseph's staff were convinced that it would be mad to deliver a last attack on the British line, in face of the possible consequences of an advance by the Spaniards. The Marshal declared that [1] it was impossible to proceed with any further scheme of advance, and that the only safe course was to draw back the whole army towards the Alberche. His master was relieved to find a good reason for ending a battle which had been begun without his permission, and continued under his very reluctant sanction. Orders were sent along the whole line, directing both the 1st and the 4th Corps to abandon their fighting-ground and fall back to their old position of the twenty-seventh. The cavalry divisions of Merlin, Latour-Maubourg, and Milhaud were to cover the retreat.

Victor was furious at receiving these directions. He averred to the officer who bore the King's dispatch that from his point of vantage on the Cascajal he could command a view of the whole Spanish army, and that he was positive that not a Spaniard had moved. He even pretended to observe signs of a retreat in Wellesley's lines, and persisted that the mere demonstration of a fourth attack would induce the allies to abandon their position. How he came to form any such conclusion it is hard to see, for the whole British army was still preserving its old ground, and no one from the Commander-in-chief down to the youngest private was dreaming of a movement to the rear. It would indeed have been insane to desert a strong position, in order to retreat across the open in face of an army possessing 7,000 excellent cavalry! But Victor, still loth to withdraw and to own himself beaten, sent word to the King that he took it upon himself to remain on the slopes of the Cascajal till he should receive further orders, and that he yet hoped that the reserve might be sent forward and the battle renewed.

When Victor's message reached the King, it had already been discovered that all the rumours concerning the advance of the Spaniards were false. But the hour was now late, and (as

[1] The best account of all this comes from the *Mémoire* of General Desprez, who was riding with the head-quarters staff at this moment.

Jourdan observed) if the army were to gain a final success— a most problematical occurrence—there would be no daylight left in which to push it to its legitimate end. He thought it better to take the prudent course, to refuse to risk the reserve, whose defeat would have the most fatal consequences, and to prepare for a retreat. The orders were accordingly issued that the army should fall back to its old camping-ground of the morning, deferring the passage of the Alberche till the next day [1].

While the French commanders were in controversy concerning their movements, the battle had died down into a cannonade, kept up with great vehemence by the batteries on the Cerro de Cascajal. The British and German guns never ceased their reply, but—as had been the case during the whole day—they were far too few to subdue the enemy's fire: considering how they were overmatched, it is wonderful that there was but one piece disabled, and that only sixty-six gunners were put *hors de combat*. The opposing batteries were hit almost as hard, for the artillery of the 1st Corps had sixty-four casualties.

A distressing accident took place during this final strife between the hostile batteries: a large area of dry grass on the lower slopes of the Cerro de Medellin took fire, from smouldering wadding fanned by the wind. Many of the severely wounded of both sides were scorched, and some burnt to death, by the short but devouring conflagration that ran along the hillside [2].

By dusk the whole of the 4th Corps was rolling to the rear, and the last rays of daylight showed Wellesley the welcome view of a general retreat opposite his right and centre. Victor clung obstinately to the Cerro de Cascajal till far into the hours of darkness. But at last the cold fit supervened, his spirits sank, and he withdrew at 3 A.M. full of resentment, and well stocked with grievances for the acrimonious correspondence with Joseph and Jourdan in which he indulged for the next six weeks.

There can be little doubt that Jourdan was right in refusing

---

[1] All this is again derived from Desprez, who both carried the King's orders to Victor, and bore back Victor's remonstrances to the King.

[2] Lord Munster, p. 235 ; Leith-Hay, p. 162.

to fall in with the younger marshal's plans for a fourth assault on the British. Wellesley was well settled into his fighting-ground : at the southern end of his line Campbell was perfectly safe at the Pajar de Vergara redoubt. He had lost no more than 236 men, so that his whole division was practically intact. Hill's brigades on the Cerro were also in perfectly good order— they had not been attacked since the morning, and would have been quite competent to defend themselves at five o'clock in the afternoon. The cannonade which they had been enduring had done some harm, but there were still 3,000 men in line, to hold a most formidable position. The only point of the British front on which the French could have hoped to make any impression was the centre. Here the Guards and Cameron's brigade had suffered heavily, and the four battalions of the German Legion even worse—they had lost a full fifty per cent. of their numbers. But Mackenzie's division was now in line with Sherbrooke's, its first brigade supporting the Guards, its second (Donkin's) linked to the Germans. Considering the way in which the British centre had dealt with the 15,000 bayonets of Sebastiani and Lapisse during the main engagement, the French critics who hold that they would have given way before the 5,000 men of Dessolles and the Royal Guard, even when backed by the rallied divisions, show a very optimistic spirit. Moreover when the battle had waxed hot in this quarter, the French would have had no certainty that Campbell and the Spaniards might not have fallen upon their flank. For Leval's much depleted division was no longer in front of the British right—it had been withdrawn behind Sebastiani [1], and there was nothing to prevent the reserve-brigade of the 4th division from going to the aid of Sherbrooke's men. The chances of war are incalculable, but there seems no reason to believe that Victor's judgement as to the probability of success was any better at five o'clock in the afternoon than it had been at five o'clock in the morning. Jourdan was the wiser man.

Thus ended the battle of Talavera, in which 16,000 British supported and repulsed the attack of 26,000 French infantry— omitting from the total of the assailants the division of Villatte,

[1] See Jourdan's *Mémoires*, p. 262.

which was only slightly engaged. The Cerro de Medellin was strong ground, but not so strong as to counterbalance a superiority of 10,000 men. The real fighting power of Wellesley's foot-soldiery was shown in the lower parts of the field, where Sherbrooke's and Mackenzie's 8,000 bayonets achieved their marvellous success over the 15,000 men of Lapisse and Sebastiani. Doomed to apparent ruin by their own rash valour in pursuing the enemy across the Portiña, they yet recovered their line, re-established the battle, and finally won an almost incredible victory. The 'First Division' of the Peninsular army,—the Guards and the German Legion who fought side by side throughout the whole war,—had many proud days between 1809 and 1814, but surely Talavera was the most honourable of them all. Yet probably Mackenzie's brigade and Donnelan's 48th must claim an even higher merit— it was their prompt and steady help which gave their comrades time to reform, and warded off the possibility of disaster at the critical moment.

The Spaniards had little to do upon July 28, but what little they had to do was well done. The charge of the cavalry regiment Rey was well timed and gallantly delivered. The few battalions engaged near the Pajar de Vergara and in Bassecourt's division behaved steadily. The artillery sent to aid the British was manfully worked and did good service. But if only the Spanish army had been able to manœuvre, what a difference there must have been in the battle! When Leval, Sebastiani, and Lapisse fell back in disorder at 4 P.M., what would have been the fate of the French if Cuesta could have led out 25,000 men upon their flank and rear? He did not attempt to do so, and probably he was right. Yet it was hard for a British army to have to fight in line with allies who were perfectly useless for any large offensive movement.

The losses of Talavera, as we have already shown, were tremendous on both sides. Adding together the casualties of the twenty-seventh and the twenty-eighth, the British lost 5,365 men, 801 killed, 3915 wounded, and 649 missing. Of the last-named 108 belonged to the unfortunate 23rd Dragoons, and nearly 300 to the German Legion. Two generals, Mackenzie and Langwerth, had been killed, and three colonels, Ross of the Coldstream Guards, Donnelan of the 48th, and Gordon of the 83rd.

The French losses were decidedly heavier, though the percentage in the regiments was in most cases far lower than that in the victorious British force. The total was 7,268, of whom 761 were killed, 6,301 wounded, and 206 missing [1]. General Lapisse and von Porbeck of the Baden regiment, one of Leval's brigadiers, were the only officers of distinction slain. But the number of field-officers wounded was enormous—in Sebastiani's division *all* the colonels, and seven out of twelve of the battalion commanders were disabled.

Cuesta never issued any proper return of his casualties. He stated in one of his dispatches that they amounted to 1,201 men. This figure cannot possibly represent killed and wounded alone. Only one cavalry regiment, five or six battalions, and three batteries were engaged, none of them heavily. The British troops which fought in their neighbourhood had very modest losses, which made it incredible that the comrades in line with them should have suffered to the extent of more than 400 or 500 men. The balance must represent the missing from the stampede of Portago's division upon the night of the twenty-seventh. Major-General Manglano, who commanded one of the divisions near the Pajar de Vergara, and de Lastra, the gallant colonel of the *regimiento del Rey*, were wounded.

The only trophies taken on either side were the seventeen guns of Leval's division captured by Campbell and the Spanish cavalry.

[1] These 'missing' do not include the French wounded taken on the field, and recovered when Victor came back to Talavera on Aug. 6 and captured the British hospitals. The French return was drawn up only after Aug. 18, when these men had been released.

N.B.—I have used of British sources mainly Lord Londonderry, Lord Munster, Leslie and Leith-Hay of the 29th, Stothert of the Guards, Cooper of the 2/7th, Hawker of the 14th Light Dragoons, and letters of Elley and Ponsonby of the 23rd Light Dragoons. Of French sources I have found Jourdan's *Mémoires*, Victor's dispatches and controversial letters with King Joseph, Sémélé's journal of the 1st Corps, and Desprez's narrative the most useful. From Colonel Whinyates I have received an unpublished map, drawn on the spot by Unger of the K.G.L., which fixes all the artillery position with admirable accuracy.

NOTES ON THE TOPOGRAPHY OF TALAVERA

I LOOKED over the proofs of the last three chapters, seated on the small square stone that marks the highest point of the Cerro de Medellin, after having carefully walked over the whole field from end to end, on April 9, 1903. The ground is little changed in aspect, but the lower slopes of the Cerro, and the whole of its opposite neighbour the Cascajal hill, are now under cultivation. The former was covered with barley nine inches high, and the rough vegetation of thyme and dry grass, which the narratives of 1809 describe, was only to be seen upon the higher and steeper parts of the hill, and on the sides of the ravine below. The latter is steep but neither very broad nor particularly difficult to negotiate. Even in April the Portiña had shrunk to a chain of pools of uninviting black water. The ditch fatal to the 23rd Light Dragoons, in the northern valley, is still visible. In its upper part, where the German regiment met it, the obstacle is practically unchanged. But nearer to the farm of Valdefuentes it has almost disappeared, owing to the extension of cultivation. There is only a four-foot drop from a field into a piece of rough ground full of reeds and bent-grass, where the soil is a little marshy in April. I presume that when the field was made, the hollow was partly filled up, and the watercourse, instead of flowing in a well-defined narrow ditch, has diffused itself over the whole trough of the ground.

In the central parts of the field the Portiña forms a boundary, but not an obstacle. Where Cameron and the Guards fought Sebastiani's 8,000 men, the ground is almost an exact level on both sides of the little stream. There is no ' position ' whatever on the English bank, which is, if anything, a little lower than the French. The Pajar de Vergara is a low knoll twenty feet high, now crowned by a large farmhouse, which occupies the site of the old battery. The ground in front of it is still covered with olive groves, and troops placed here could see nothing of an advancing enemy till he emerges from the trees a hundred yards or so to the front. On the other hand an observer on the summit of the Cerro de Medellin gets a perfect bird's-eye view of this part of the ground, and could make out the enemy all through his progress among the olives. Wellesley must have been able to mark exactly every movement of Leval's division, though Campbell could certainly not have done so. In the Spanish part of the line the groves have evidently been thinned, as there are now many houses, forming a straggling suburb, pushed up to and along the railway, which now crosses this section of the line. In 1809 Talavera was still self-contained within its walls, which it has now overstepped. The Cascajal is practically of the same height as the main eastern level of the Cerro de Medellin : but the triple summit of the latter is much loftier ground ; and standing on it one commands the whole of the Cascajal—every one of

Villatte's battalions must have been counted by Wellesley, who could also mark every man along the whole French front, even into and among the olive groves occupied by Leval's Germans. Victor on the Cascajal could get no such a general view of the British position, but could see very well into Sherbrooke's line. Hill's troops, behind the first crest of the Cerro de Medellin, and Campbell's in the groves must have been much less visible to him. There is a ruined house, apparently a mill, in the ravine between the two Cerros. As it is not mentioned in any report of the battle, I conclude that it was not in existence in 1809. The Pajar de Vergara farm is also modern, and the only building on the actual fighting-ground which existed on the battle-day was evidently the farm of Valdefuentes, which is alluded to by several narrators, French and English.

SECTION XVI: CHAPTER VIII

THE RETREAT FROM TALAVERA

WHEN the dawn of July 29 had arrived, the plain and the rolling hills in front of the allied position were seen to be absolutely deserted. No trace of the French army was visible save the heaps of dead upon the further side of the Portiña: the wounded had been carried off, with the exception of those who had fallen within the British lines, and so become prisoners of war. It was soon discovered that the enemy had left a screen of cavalry along the western bank of the Alberche: but whether his main body lay close behind the stream, or had retired towards Madrid, could not be ascertained without making a reconnaissance in force. Such an operation was beyond Wellesley's power on the morning after the battle. He was neither able nor willing to send out a large detachment to beat up the enemy's camps, with the object of ascertaining his situation and intentions. The British army was utterly exhausted: on the preceding day the men had fought upon half-rations: when the contest was over they had found that only a third of a ration had been issued: this scanty pittance was sent up to the regiments in the evening, as they still lay in battle-order on the ground that they had held during the day. Water was almost equally deficient: it was difficult to procure: nothing but the wells of the few houses in the rear of the position being available. Only on the morning of the twenty-ninth, when the departure of the enemy had become certain, were the troops allowed to return to their old bivouacs in the rear, and there to seek repose. Even then it was only a minority of the men who could be spared from duty. The gathering in of the vast numbers wounded—French as well as English—and their removal into Talavera demanded such enormous fatigue-parties that the larger number of the survivors had to be told off to this work and were denied the rest that they had so well earned.

It is certain that the British army could have done nothing upon the twenty-ninth even if their commander had desired to push forward against the enemy. The men were not only tired out by two days of battle, but half-starved in addition. But Wellesley was far from feeling any wish to pursue the French. His infantry had suffered so dreadfully that he could not dream of exposing them to the ordeal of another engagement till they had been granted a respite for the refreshment of body and spirit. Of his divisions only that of A. Campbell—the smallest of the four—was practically intact. The others had suffered paralysing losses—in Hill's ranks one man out of every four had been stricken down, in Mackenzie's one man in every three, while Sherbrooke's frightful casualty-list showed that nearly two men out of five were missing from the ranks. Never, save at Albuera, was such slaughter on the side of the victors seen again during the whole course of the Peninsular War. 'The extreme fatigue of the troops,' wrote Wellesley, 'the want of provisions, and the number of wounded to be taken care of, have prevented me from moving from my position [1].'

On the morning of the twenty-ninth the depleted strength of the army was partly compensated by the arrival of the first of those reinforcements from Lisbon which Wellesley had been anxiously expecting. At about six o'clock Robert Craufurd came upon the scene with the three regiments of his Light Brigade—all old battalions who had shared in Moore's Corunna campaign. He was accompanied by a battery of horse artillery (A troop), the first unit of that arm which came under Wellesley's command. But the Light Brigade were almost as weary as their comrades who had fought in the battle : they had only reached Talavera by a forced march of unexampled severity. Hearing at Naval Moral that the two armies were in presence, Robert Craufurd had hurried forward with almost incredible swiftness. Dropping his baggage and a few weakly men at Oropesa he had marched forty-three miles in twenty-two hours, though the day was hot and every soldier carried some fifty pounds' weight upon his back. All day long the cannon was heard growling in the distance,

---

[1] Wellesley to Castlereagh, Aug. 1, *Wellington Dispatches*, iv. p. 553.

and at short intervals the brigade kept meeting parties of Spanish fugitives, interspersed with British sutlers and commissaries, who gave the most dismal accounts of the progress of the fight. In spite of his desperate efforts to get up in time Craufurd reached the field thirteen hours too late, and heard to his intense chagrin that the battle had been won without his aid [1]. Weary though his men were, they were at once hurried to the front, to relieve A. Campbell's division on the line of advanced posts. There they found plenty of employment in burying the dead, and in gathering up the French wounded, whom it was necessary to protect from the fury of the Spanish peasantry.

The arrival of Craufurd's brigade did something towards filling up the terrible gap in the ranks of the British infantry, but was far from enabling Wellesley to assume the offensive. Indeed the advent of fresh troops only accentuated the difficulty of feeding the army. Corn was still almost unobtainable; the supplies from the Vera de Plasencia showed no signs of appearing, and even oxen for the meat-ration, which had hitherto been obtainable in fair quantities, were beginning to run short. Nothing was to be had from Talavera itself, where Victor had exhausted all the available food many weeks before, nor could any assistance be got from the Spanish army, who were themselves commencing to feel the pinch of starvation.

All Wellesley's hopes at this juncture were founded on the idea that the diversion of Venegas upon the Upper Tagus would force the French host in his front to break up, in order to save Madrid from an attack in the rear. The army of La Mancha had failed to keep Sebastiani in check, and to prevent him from appearing on the field of Talavera. But since the enemy had concentrated every available man for the battle, it was certain that Venegas had now no hostile force in his front, and that the way to the capital was open to him. If he had

---

[1] For excellent accounts of this forced march see Col. Leach (95th), *Rough Sketches of the Life of an Old Soldier* (pp. 81-2), and Sir George Napier's *Autobiography*, pp. 108-10. The distance was forty-three miles, not as W. Napier states sixty-two. That all the stragglers met on the way were not Spaniards is unfortunately evident from both narratives. Nor were all the British stragglers non-combatants.

pushed on either by Aranjuez or by Toledo, he must now be
close to the capital, and King Joseph would be obliged to
detach a large force against him.   That detachment once made,
the army behind the Alberche would be so much weakened that
it would be unable to face the British and Cuesta.   If it offered
fight, it must be beaten : if it retired, the allies would follow it
up and drive it away in a direction which would prevent it from
rejoining the troops that had been sent against Venegas.   On the
twenty-ninth Wellesley was under the impression that the army
of La Mancha had already brought pressure to bear upon the
French, for a false report had reached him that on the previous
day it had captured Toledo.   His dispatches written after the
arrival of this rumour indicate an intention of moving forward
on the thirtieth or thirty-first.   The King, he says, must now
detach troops against Venegas.   This being so, it will be necessary to
induce Cuesta to advance, supporting him with the British army
' as soon as it shall be a little rested and refreshed after two
days of the hardest fighting that I have ever been a party to.
We shall certainly move towards Madrid, if not interrupted by
some accident on our flank [1].'

The last words of this sentence are of great importance, since
they show that already upon the day after Talavera Wellesley
was beginning to be uneasy about his left flank.   Some time before
the battle he had received news from the north, to the effect
that both Ney and Kellermann had returned to the valley of
the Douro, after evacuating Galicia and the Asturias [2].   He
had therefore to take into consideration the chance that the
enemy might move southward, and fall upon his line of communication with Portugal, not only with the corps of Soult, but
with a large additional force.   Unfortunately the information
that had reached him from the plains of Leon had been to the

---

[1] Wellington to Beresford, Talavera, July 29, 1809.

[2] On July 14 Wellesley writes to Beresford that he does not believe
that Ney has quitted Galicia [*Wellington Dispatches*, iv. 510], because
of the tenour of the captured dispatches of Soult to King Joseph.   These,
of course, had been written under the idea that the 6th Corps was still
holding on to Corunna and Lugo : it was not till some days later that
Soult learned of his colleagues' unexpected move.   But Wellesley knew
of Ney's move before the battle of Talavera, as is shown by *Wellington
Dispatches*, iv. 545.

effect that Ney's and Kellermann's troops were much reduced in numbers and efficiency, so that even when they had joined Soult the total of the French field army upon the Douro would not much exceed 20,000 men [1]. This misconception affected all his plans: for if the hostile force about Salamanca, Zamora, and Benavente was no greater than was reported, it followed that any expedition sent against his own communications could not be more than 12,000 or 15,000 strong, since Soult would be forced to leave a containing force in front of Beresford and Del Parque, who now lay in the direction of Almeida and Ciudad Rodrigo. Any French advance against Bejar and Plasencia, therefore, would, as Wellesley supposed, be a mere raid, executed by a comparatively small force. He doubted whether Soult dared undertake such an operation: 'the enemy,' he wrote, 'would not like to venture through the passes into Estremadura, having me on one side of him, and you [Beresford] and Romana upon the other [2].' He was therefore not much disturbed in mind about the movements of the French in the valley of the Douro. If he had but known that not 20,000 men but 50,000 men were now concentrating at Salamanca, his feelings would have been far different. But it was not till some days later that it began to dawn upon him that Soult was far stronger than he had supposed, and that there might be serious danger to be feared from this quarter. Meanwhile he hoped to prevent any advance of the French in the direction of Plasencia, by causing a strong demonstration to be made in the valley of the Douro. He wrote to Beresford that he must contrive to arrange for joint action with La Romana and the Army of Galicia. If they appeared in strength in the direction of Ciudad Rodrigo, the Duke of Dalmatia might be deterred from making any movement to the south. If, however, the Spaniards proved helpless or impracticable, the Portuguese army would have to confine itself to the defence of its own frontier.

On the morning of July 30 Wellesley received the first

---

[1] 'The enemy have on the Douro and in the neighbourhood not less than 20,000 men, being the remains of the Corps of Soult, Ney, and Kellerman.' To Frere, July 30.

[2] To Beresford, from Talavera, July 29, 1809.

definite information which led him to conclude that the French
forces from the north were actually contemplating the raid
upon his communications which on the preceding day he had
regarded as doubtful. The Marquis Del Reino, whom, as it
will be remembered, Cuesta had sent to the Puerto de Baños
with two weak battalions, reported that troops from the Douro
valley were threatening his front. At the same time messages
were received from the Alcaldes of Fuente Roble and Los Santos,
places on the road between Salamanca and Bejar, to the effect
that they had received orders from Soult to prepare 12,000 and
24,000 rations respectively, for troops due to arrive on July 28.
The numbers given counted for little in Wellesley's estimation,
since it is the commonest thing in the world for generals to
requisition food for a far larger force than they actually bring
with them. But at least it seemed clear that some considerable
detachment from Salamanca was on its way towards the Puerto
de Baños. In consequence of this fact Wellesley wrote to the
Spanish government, and also informed Cuesta, that in the
event of a serious attempt of the enemy to cut his communications, he should 'move so as to take care of himself,' and do
his best to preserve Portugal [1]—in other words, that he should
abandon the projected march on Madrid which had been his
main purpose on the preceding day. He was still, however,
under the impression that Soult had no very large force with
him, as is sufficiently shown by the fact that on the thirty-first
he suggested to Cuesta that it would be well to detach one of
his divisions—say 5,000 men—to strengthen the insignificant
force which was already in position at the Puerto de Baños.
'I still think,' he wrote, 'that the movements of General
Beresford with the Portuguese army on the frontier, and that
of the Duque del Parque from Ciudad Rodrigo, combined
with the natural difficulties of the country, and the defence
by the Marquis Del Reino, may delay the enemy's advance
till the arrival of your division [2].' It is clear that when he

[1] Wellesley to Frere, July 30. 'My first duty is to attend to the
safety of Portugal: at all events if my flank and communication with
Portugal are not secured for me, while I am operating in the general cause,
I must move to take care of myself, and then the general cause will suffer.'

[2] Wellesley to O'Donoju, July 31, 1809.

wrote in these terms Wellesley was still labouring under the delusion that Soult's advance was a mere raid executed by one or two divisions, and not a serious operation carried out by a large army.

While Wellesley was spending the three days which followed the battle of the twenty-eighth in resting his men and pondering over his next move, the enemies whom he had defeated at Talavera were in a state of even greater uncertainty and indecision. By daylight on July 29, as we have already seen, the whole French army had retired behind the Alberche, leaving only a screen of cavalry upon its western bank. The King was under the impression that Wellesley and Cuesta would probably follow him up ere the day had passed, and drew up his whole force along that same line of heights which Victor had occupied upon the twenty-second and twenty-third of the month. But when nothing appeared in his front during the morning hours save a few vedettes, he realized that he might count upon a short respite, and took new measures. After sending off to his brother the Emperor a most flagrantly mendacious account of the battle of Talavera [1], he proceeded to divide up his army. As Wellington had foreseen, he detached a large force to hold back Venegas and the army of La Mancha, who were at last coming into the field upon his flank. He was bound to do so, under pain of imperilling the safety of Madrid.

It is time to cast a glance at the operations of the incompetent general whose sloth and disobedience had wrecked the plan that Wellesley and Cuesta had drawn out at their con-

---

[1] A few lines of this astounding document may be worth quoting— 'Sire, hier l'armée anglaise a été forcée dans ses positions. Outre les 25 à 30 mille Anglais de Wellesley, nous avons eu affaire à l'armée de Cuesta, qui s'élevait de 35 à 40 mille hommes. Le champ de bataille *sur lequel nous sommes établis* (!) est jonché de leurs morts. . . . Je me mets en marche pour secourir Madrid, qui est menacé par un corps de Portugais arrivés à Navalcarnero, et par l'armée de Venegas, qui tente de pénétrer par Aranjuez. . . . J'ai un regret, sire, c'est celui de n'avoir pas fait prisonnière toute l'armée anglaise.' *Mémoires de Joseph*, vi. 284. Napoleon, not deceived for a moment by this rhodomontade, sent back a scathing rebuke to his brother for endeavouring to hide the truth from him. (Napoleon to Jourdan, Aug. 21.)

ference near Almaraz. On July 16 Venegas had begun to move forward from El Moral, Valdepeñas, and Santa Cruz de Mudela, in accordance with the directions that had been sent him. He occupied Manzanares and Daimiel, and then came into collision with Sebastiani's cavalry at Villaharta and Herencia, for the 4th Corps had not yet begun to withdraw towards Madrid. Owing to the profound ignorance in which the enemy still lay as to the advance of Wellesley and Cuesta, Sebastiani had not, on the nineteenth, received any order to fall back or to join Victor and the King. Thus, when pressed by the advanced troops of Venegas, he did not retire, but held his ground, and showed every intention of accepting battle. Learning from the peasantry that he had the whole of the 4th Corps in front of him, and might have to deal with nearly 20,000 men, the Spanish general halted, and refused to advance further. In so doing he was fulfilling the spirit of the instructions that had been sent him, for Cuesta and Wellesley had wished him to detain Sebastiani and keep in touch with him—not to attack him or to fight a pitched battle. They had taken it for granted that the Frenchman would receive early news of their own advance, and would already be in retreat before Venegas came up with him. But it was not till July 22, as we have already seen, that Victor and King Joseph obtained certain intelligence of the march of the allies upon Talavera. Until the orders for a retreat arrived from Madrid, the 4th Corps was kept in its old position at Madridejos, and courted rather than avoided an engagement with the army of La Mancha[1].

Venegas, after summoning his divisional generals to a council of war, refused to attack Sebastiani, and wisely, for his 23,000 men would certainly have been beaten by the 20,000 Frenchmen who still lay in front of him. From the nineteenth to the twenty-second the two armies faced each other across the upper Guadiana, each waiting for the other to move. Late on the twenty-third, however, Sebastiani received his orders to evacuate La Mancha, and to hasten to Toledo in order to join Victor

---

[1] For these operations I am relying on General Arteche's excerpts from the *Vindicacion de los Agravios,* published by Venegas in his own defence.

and the King, in a combined assault upon Wellesley and
Cuesta.

It was on the next day that Venegas committed the ruinous
error which was to wreck the fate of the whole campaign. On
the morning of the twenty-fourth the 4th Corps had disappeared
from his front: instead of following closely in the rear of
Sebastiani with all speed, and molesting his retreat, as his orders
prescribed, he made no attempt to prevent the 4th Corps
from moving off, nor did he execute that rapid flanking march
on Aranjuez or Fuenteduéñas which his instructions prescribed.
He moved forward at a snail's pace, having first sent off to
Cuesta an argumentative letter, in which he begged for leave
to direct his advance on Toledo instead of on the points which
had been named in his orders. On the twenty-sixth he received
an answer, in which his Commander-in-chief authorized him to
make his own choice between the route by Aranjuez and that
by Toledo.

Venegas had already committed the fatal error of letting
Sebastiani slip away unmolested: he now hesitated between
the idea of carrying out his own plan, and that of obeying
Cuesta's original orders, and after much hesitation sent his
first division under General Lacy towards Toledo, while he
himself, with the other four, marched by Tembleque upon
Aranjuez. So slow and cautious was their advance that Lacy
only arrived in front of Toledo on July 28—the day that the
battle of Talavera was fought, while Venegas himself occupied
Aranjuez twenty-four hours later, on the morning of the twenty-
ninth. He had taken six days to cross the sixty miles of open
rolling plain which lie between the Guadiana and the Tagus,
though he had been absolutely unopposed by the enemy whom
he had allowed to slip away from his front. Sebastiani had
marched at the rate of twenty miles a day when he retired
from Madridejos to Toledo, Venegas and Lacy followed at
the rate of ten and twelve miles a day respectively. Yet the
special duty imposed on the army of La Mancha had been
to keep in touch with the 4th Corps. Further comment is
hardly necessary.

On the morning of the day when Wellesley was assailed by
the forces of Victor and King Joseph, General Lacy appeared

in front of Toledo. The town was held by 3,000 men of
Valence's Polish division: it is practically impregnable against
any attack from the south, presenting to that side a front of
sheer cliff, overhanging the river, and accessible only by two
fortified bridges. To make any impression on the place Lacy
would have had to cross the Tagus at some other point, and
then might have beset the comparatively weak northern front
with considerable chances of success. But he contented himself
with demonstrating against the bridges, and discharging some
fruitless cannon-shot across the river. General Valence, the
Governor of Toledo, reported to Jourdan that he was attacked,
and his message, reaching the battlefield of Talavera after
Victor's second repulse, had a certain amount of influence on
the action of King Joseph. The place was never for a moment
in danger, as Lacy made no attempt to pass the Tagus in order
to press his attack home.

On the following morning (July 29) Venegas reached the
other great passage of the Tagus, at Aranjuez, with two of his
divisions, and occupied the place after driving out a few French
vedettes. He pressed his cavalry forward to the line of the
Tajuna, and ere nightfall some of them had penetrated almost
as far as Valdemoro, the village half way between Aranjuez
and Madrid. No signs of any serious hostile force could be
discovered, and secret friends in the capital sent notice that
they were being held down by a very weak garrison, consisting
of no more than a single French brigade and a handful of the
King's Spanish levies. There was everything to tempt Venegas
to execute that rapid march upon the capital which had been
prescribed in his original orders, but instead of doing so this
wretched officer halted for eight whole days at Aranjuez [July
29 to August 5].

On the day after Talavera Jourdan and Joseph had not yet
discovered the whereabouts of the main body of the army of La
Mancha: but Lacy had made such a noisy demonstration in
front of Toledo that they were inclined to believe that his
chief must be close behind him. Accordingly the garrison of
Toledo was reinforced by the missing brigade of Valence's
Polish division, and raised to the strength of 4,700 men. The
King, with the rest of Sebastiani's corps and his own Guards and

reserves, marched to Santa Ollala, and on the next day [July 30] placed himself at Bargas, a few miles in rear of Toledo. In this position he would have been wholly unable to protect Madrid, if Venegas had pressed forward on that same morning from Aranjuez, for that place is actually nearer to the capital than the village at which Joseph had fixed his head quarters. The sloth displayed by the Spanish general was the only thing which preserved Madrid from capture. On August 1, apprised of the fact that the main body of the army of La Mancha was at Aranjuez and not before Toledo, Joseph transferred his army to Illescas, a point from which he would be able to attack Venegas in flank, if the latter should move forward. Only Milhaud's division of dragoons was thrown forward to Valdemoro, on the direct road from Aranjuez to Madrid : it drove out of the village a regiment of Spanish horse, which reported to Venegas that there was now a heavy force in his front. For the next four days the King's troops and the army of Venegas retained their respective positions, each waiting for the other to move. The Spaniard had realized that his chance of capturing Madrid had gone by, and remained in a state of indecision at Aranjuez. Joseph was waiting for definite news of the movements of Wellesley and Cuesta, before risking an attack on the army of La Mancha. He saw that it had abandoned the offensive, and did not wish to move off from his central position at Illescas till he was sure that Victor was not in need of any help. Yet he was so disturbed as to the general state of affairs that he sent orders to General Belliard at Madrid to evacuate all non-combatants and civilians on to Valladolid, and to prepare to shut himself up in the Retiro.

The doings of Victor, during the five days after he had separated from the King, require a more lengthy consideration. Left behind upon the Alberche with the 1st Corps, which the casualties of the battle had reduced to no more than 18,000 men, he felt himself in a perilous position : if the allies should advance, he could do no more than endeavour to retard their march on Madrid. Whether he could count on any further aid from the King and Sebastiani would depend on the wholly problematical movements of Venegas. Somewhat to his surprise Wellesley and Cuesta remained quiescent not only on the twenty-ninth but on the thirtieth of July. But an alarm now came from another quarter: it will be remembered that the enterprising Sir Robert Wilson with 4,000 men, partly Spaniards, partly Portuguese of the Lusitanian Legion, had moved parallel with Wellesley's northern flank during the advance to Talavera. On the day of the battle he had 'marched to the cannon' as a good officer should, and had actually approached Cazalegas, at the back of the French army, in the course of the afternoon. Learning of the results of the fight, he had turned back to his old path upon the twenty-ninth, and had entered Escalona on the upper Alberche. At this place he was behind Victor's flank, and lay only thirty-eight miles from Madrid. There was no French force between him and the capital, and if only his division had been a little stronger he would have been justified in making a raid upon the city, relying for aid upon the insurrection that would indubitably have broken out the moment that he presented himself before its gates.

It was reported to Victor on the thirtieth not only that Wilson was at Escalona, but also that he was at the head of a strong Portuguese division, estimated at 8,000 or 10,000 men. The Marshal determined that he could not venture to leave such a force upon his rear while the armies of Wellesley and Cuesta were in his front, and fell back ten miles to Maqueda on the high road to Madrid. On the following day, still uneasy as to his position, he retired still further, to Santa Cruz, and wrote to King Joseph that he might be forced to continue his retreat as far as Mostoles, almost in the suburbs of Madrid [Aug. 2]. He was so badly informed as to the movements of the allies, that he not only warned the King that Wilson was threatening Madrid, but assured him that the British army from Talavera had broken up from its cantonments and was advancing along the Alberche towards the capital[1]. Joseph, better instructed as to the actual situation of affairs, replied by assuring him that Wellesley and Cuesta were far more likely to be retreating on Almaraz than marching on Madrid, as they must have heard ere now of Soult's advance on Plasencia. He ordered the

---

[1] Jourdan to Belliard, Aug. 3, from Illescas : ' Le duc de Belluno dit que toute l'armée anglaise marche sur la rive droite de l'Alberche, et qu'hier elle était à une lieue d'Escalona.'

Marshal to fall back no further, and to send a division to feel
for Wilson at Escalona. On detaching Villatte to execute this
reconnaissance [Aug. 5] Victor was surprised to find that Sir
Robert's little force had already evacuated its advanced position,
and had retreated into the mountains. For the last four days
indeed Victor had been fighting with shadows—for the British
and Estremaduran armies had never passed the Alberche, while
Wilson had absconded from Escalona on receiving from
Wellesley the news that Soult had been heard of at the Puerto
de Baños. In consequence of the needless march of the 1st
Corps to Maqueda and Santa Cruz, the allied generals were
able to withdraw unmolested, and even unobserved, from
Talavera, and were far upon their way down the Tagus before
their absence was suspected. The erratic movements of Victor
may be excused in part by the uniform difficulty in obtaining
accurate information which the French always experienced in
Spain. But even when this allowance is made, it must be confessed that his operations do not tend to give us any very high
idea of his strategical ability. He was clearly one of those
generals, of the class denounced by Napoleon, *qui se font des
tableaux*, who argue on insufficient data, and take a long time
to be convinced of the error of their original hypothesis.

Neither Victor nor King Joseph, therefore, exercised any
influence over the doings of Wellesley and Cuesta at Talavera
between the 29th of July and the 3rd of August. The allies
worked out their plans undisturbed by any interference on the
part of the old enemies whom they had beaten on the battle
day. Down to August 1 the British general had been unconvinced by the rumours of Soult's approach, at the head of
a large army, which were persistently arriving from the secret
agents in the direction of Salamanca[1]. It was only on the
evening of that day that he received news so precise, and so
threatening, that he found himself forced to abandon for the
moment any intention of pushing on towards Madrid, in consequence of the impending attack on the line of his communications

---

[1] There are two letters of Wellington to Castlereagh, written on Aug. 1 ;
both indicate that Wellesley was still unconvinced as to Soult's intention,
and the second states that he does not believe that the French will pass
the Puerto de Baños. The definite news came at night.

with Portugal. It was announced to him that the vanguard of
the French army from the north had actually entered Bejar on
the twenty-ninth and was driving in the trifling force under the
Marquis Del Reino, which Cuesta had sent to the Puerto de Baños.

Whatever might be the force at Soult's disposal—and
Wellesley was still under the delusion that it amounted at
most to a single corps of 12,000 or 15,000 men—it was impossible to allow the French to establish themselves between
the British army and Portugal. If they were at Bejar on the
twenty-ninth they might easily reach Plasencia on the thirty-first.
On receiving the news Cuesta, who had hitherto shown the greatest
reluctance to divide his army, detached his 5th division under
Bassecourt, with orders to set out at the greatest possible speed,
and join the Marquis Del Reino. This move was tardy and
useless, for it is four long marches from Talavera to Plasencia,
so that Bassecourt must arrive too late to hold the defiles. If
he found the French already established on the river Alagon,
his 5,000 men would be utterly inadequate to 'contain' double
or triple that number of Soult's troops. As a matter of fact
the enemy had entered Plasencia on the afternoon of August 1,
before the Spanish division had even commenced its movement
to the west [1].

On the morning of August 2 Wellesley and Cuesta held
a long and stormy conference. The Captain-General proposed
that Wellesley should detach half his force to assist Bassecourt,
and stay with the remainder at Talavera, in order to support
the Army of Estremadura against any renewed attack by Victor
and King Joseph [2]. The English commander refused to divide

[1] Napier seems to have the dates wrong here : he says that the 5th Corps
seized Plasencia on July 31 [vol. ii. p. 184]. But Soult's official report to
the Minister of War, dated Aug. 13, says that his vanguard forced the
Puerto de Baños on the twenty-ninth, but only captured Plasencia on
Aug. 1. If Plasencia had fallen on the thirty-first, Wellesley and Cuesta
would have known the fact on the second : but as it was captured on the
first only, they were still in ignorance when their conference took place.

[2] Wellesley's letters in these critical days are full of complaints as
to his colleague's impracticability : ' I certainly should get the better
of everything,' he writes to Castlereagh, 'if I could manage General Cuesta :
but his temper and disposition are so bad that this is impossible.' *Wellington
Dispatches*, iv. p. 553.

his force—he had only 18,000 effectives even after Craufurd had joined him, and such a small body would not bear division. But he offered either to march against Soult with his entire host, or to remain at Talavera if his colleague preferred to set out for Plasencia with his main body. Cuesta chose the former alternative, and on the morning of the third Wellesley moved out with every available man, intending to attack the enemy at the earliest opportunity. He was still under the impression that he would have to deal with no more than a single French corps, and was confident of the result. His only fear was that Victor might descend upon Talavera in his absence, and that Cuesta might evacuate the place on being attacked. If this should happen, the English hospitals, in which there lay nearly 5,000 wounded, might fall into the hands of the enemy. On halting at Oropesa he sent back a note to O'Donoju, the chief of the staff of the Estremaduran army, begging him to send off westward all the British wounded who were in a condition to travel. He asked that country carts might be requisitioned for their assistance, if no transport could be spared by the Spanish troops [1].

Wellesley was setting out with 18,000 men to attack not the mere 15,000 men that he believed to be in his front, but three whole *corps d'armée*, with a strength of 50,000 sabres and bayonets. In his long career there were many dangerous crises, but this was perhaps the most perilous of all. If he had remained for a little longer in ignorance of the real situation, he might have found himself involved in a contest in which defeat was certain and destruction highly probable.

The real situation in his front was as follows. On receiving the dispatch from Madrid which permitted him to execute his projected march upon Plasencia, Soult had begun to concentrate his army [July 24]. Mortier and the 5th Corps were already in march for Salamanca in pursuance of earlier orders: they arrived in its neighbourhood the same day on which Foy brought the King's orders to his chief. The 2nd Corps was already massed upon the Tormes, and ready to move the moment that it should receive the supply of artillery which had been so long upon its way from Madrid. Ney and the

---

[1] Wellesley to O'Donoju, from Oropesa, afternoon of Aug. 3.

6th Corps from Benavente and Astorga had far to come: they only reached Salamanca on July 31; if we remember that the distance from Astorga to the concentration point was no less than ninety miles we cease to wonder at their tardy arrival.

Soult had strict orders from the Emperor to march with his troops well closed up, and not to risk the danger of being caught with his corps strung out at distances which would permit of their being met and defeated in detail[1]. He was therefore entirely justified in refusing to move until the 6th Corps should be in supporting distance of the rest of his army, and the 2nd Corps should have received the cannon which were needed to replace the pieces that they had lost in Portugal. For this reason we must regard as unfounded all the vehement reproaches heaped upon him by Joseph and Jourdan during the acrimonious correspondence that followed upon the end of the campaign. It would have been wrong to start the 5th Corps upon its way to Plasencia till the 2nd Corps was ready to follow, and the much needed guns only came into Salamanca on the twenty-ninth, though their approach had been reported on the preceding day.

We cannot therefore blame Soult for sloth or slackness when we find that he started Mortier upon his way on July 27, and followed him with his own corps upon July 30, the day after the guns arrived, and the day before Ney and his troops were due to reach Salamanca from the north.

The order of march was as follows: the vanguard was composed of the whole corps of Mortier, nearly 17,000 strong[2], reinforced by three brigades of dragoons under Lahoussaye and Lorges with a strength of 2,000 sabres. The 2nd Corps followed; though it started three days later than the 5th it was gradually gaining ground on the vanguard all through the march, as it had no fighting to do or reconnaissances to execute.

---

[1] Orders of Napoleon from Schönbrunn, June 12 : ' Les trois corps doivent fournir 50 à 60 mille hommes. Si cette réunion a lieu promptement les Anglais doivent être détruits ; mais il faut se réunir, *et ne pas marcher par petits paquets.* Cela est le principe général pour tous les guerres, mais surtout pour un pays où l'on ne peut pas avoir de communication.'

[2] By the return of July 15, the 5th Corps had 16,916 men, the attached brigades of dragoons, 1,853 : the 2nd Corps had 18,740 (deducting Lorges

Hence it was only twenty-four hours behind Mortiér in arriving at Plasencia. Its strength was 18,000 men, even after it had detached the brigades of dragoons to strengthen the vanguard, and placed five battalions at the disposal of General Kellermann [1]. During its stay at Zamora and Toro it had picked up a mass of convalescents and details, who had not taken part in its Galician campaign. The rear was formed by Ney's troops, which started from Salamanca only one day behind the 2nd Corps. The infantry was not complete, as a brigade of 3,000 men was left behind on the Douro, to assist Kellermann in holding down the kingdom of Leon. Hence, even including a brigade of Lorges' dragoons, the 6th Corps had only some 12,500 men on the march. The whole army, therefore, as it will be seen, was about 50,000 strong.

Just before he marched from Salamanca Soult had heard that Beresford's Portuguese were commencing to show themselves in force in the direction of Almeida, while Del Parque's small division at Ciudad Rodrigo was beginning to be reinforced by troops descending from the mountains of Galicia. Trusting that the danger from this quarter might not prove imminent, the Marshal left in observation of the allies only the remains of the force that Kellermann had brought back from the Asturias —the 5th division of dragoons and a few battalions of infantry, strengthened by the five battalions from the 2nd Corps and the one brigade detached from Ney. The whole did not amount to more than 9,000 or 10,000 men, scattered along the whole front from Astorga to Salamanca. It was clear that much was risked in this direction, for Beresford and Del Parque could concentrate over 20,000 troops for an attack on any point that they might select. But Soult was prepared to accept the chances of war in the Douro valley, rightly thinking that if he could crush Wellesley's army on the Tagus any losses in the north could easily be repaired. It would matter little if the

and Lahoussaye) : the 6th Corps 15,700, of whom one brigade of infantry (3,200 bayonets) was left behind. The total then was 50,009.

[1] The Marshal had dissolved one of his four divisions, that of Mermet, making over the 122nd of the line, reduced to two battalions, and the Swiss units to Kellermann, and distributing the other regiments between Merle, Delaborde, and Heudelet.

Spaniards and Portuguese occupied Salamanca, or even Valladolid, after the British had been destroyed.

Mortier, starting on July 27, on the road by Fuente Roble and Los Santos, made two marches without coming in touch with any enemy. It was only on the third day that he met at La Calzada the vedettes of the trifling force under the Marquis Del Reino which Cuesta had sent to hold the Puerto de Baños. After chasing them through Bejar, the Marshal came upon their supports drawn up in the pass [July 30]. Del Reino thought himself obliged to fight, though he had but four battalions with a total of 2,500 or 3,000 bayonets [1]. He was of course dislodged with ease by the overwhelming numbers which Mortier turned against him—the first division of the 5th Corps alone sufficed to drive him through the pass. Thereupon he retired down the Alagon, and after sending news of his defeat to Cuesta fell back to Almaraz, where he took up the bridge of boats and removed it to the southern bank of the Tagus.

Having cleared the passes upon the thirtieth, the 5th Corps advanced to Candelaria and Baños de Bejar upon the thirty-first, and entered Plasencia on the first of August. Here Mortier captured 334 of Wellesley's sick, who had been left behind as being incapable of removal. On the preceding day the town had been full of British detachments: the place was the half-way house between Portugal and Talavera, and many commissaries, isolated officers going to or from the front, and details marching to join their corps, had been collected there. Captain Pattison, the senior officer present, withdrew to Zarza, with every man that could march, when he heard of Mortier's

[1] Cuesta, in a dispatch in the *Deposito de la Guerra,* which seems unpublished, says that Del Reino fought with four battalions. He had started with no more than two, so must have rallied two others. I can find no trace of what they were, but conclude that they must have been some of those battalions of the Army of Estremadura which are not named in the *Ordre de Bataille* of the divisions present at Talavera. As I have shown in my Talavera Appendix, there were eight regiments which had belonged to Cuesta's army in March but do not appear in the divisional return of July. Most of these were in garrison at Badajoz: but two or three may well have been sent to guard the passes when the army advanced from the Guadiana in the end of June.

approach, taking with him a convoy which had recently arrived from Abrantes. But he was obliged to leave behind him a considerable amount of corn, just collected from the Vera, which had been destined for Wellesley's army. The whole civil population of Plasencia fled to the hills, in obedience to an order of the local Junta, and the British soldiers in the hospital were the only living beings whom the French vanguard found in the city. The men of the 5th Corps plundered the deserted houses, as was but natural, but behaved with much humanity to the captured invalids [1].

After seizing Plasencia Mortier halted for a day, in obedience to Soult's orders, that he might allow the 2nd Corps to close up before he pressed in any further towards Wellesley. The Duke of Dalmatia was determined to run no risks, when dealing with an adversary so enterprising as his old enemy of Oporto. On August 2 he himself and the leading divisions of his corps reached Plasencia: the rest were close behind. On the same afternoon, therefore, the advance could be resumed, and Mortier set out on the high road towards Almaraz and Talavera, having eight regiments of horse—3,000 men—in his front. He slept that night at Malpartida, seven miles in advance of Plasencia, and moved on next morning to the line of the Tietar and the village of Toril. One of his reconnoitring parties approached the bridge of Almaraz and found it broken: another reached Naval Moral. He was now drawing very close to Wellesley, who had encamped that day at Oropesa, and was only thirty miles away: indeed the British and the French cavalry came in contact that evening in front of Naval Moral.

On August 3, by a curious coincidence, each Commander-in-chief was at last informed of his adversary's strength and intentions by a captured dispatch. A Spanish messenger was arrested by Soult's cavalry, while bearing a letter from Wellesley to General Erskine dated August 1. In this document there was an account of the battle of Talavera, which had

---

[1] For details of Mortier's march see the memoir of Naylies, of Lahoussaye's Dragoons, who was with the vanguard. According to the *Diary* of Fantin des Odoards, Soult pushed his kindness to the British invalids so far as to leave with them a small supply of muskets, with which to defend themselves against guerrillas.

hitherto been unknown to Soult. But the most important
clause of it was a request to Erskine to find out whether the
rumours reporting the advance of 12,000 French towards the
Puerto de Baños were correct. The Duke of Dalmatia thus
discovered that his adversary, only two days before, was grossly
underrating the numbers of the army that was marching against
his rear. He was led on to hope that Wellesley would presently
advance against him with inferior numbers, and court destruction by attacking the united 2nd and 5th Corps [1].

This indeed might have come to pass had not the allies on
the same day become possessed of a French dispatch which
revealed to them the real situation of affairs. Some guerrillas
in the neighbourhood of Avila intercepted a friar, who was an
agent of King Joseph, and was bearing a letter from him to
Soult. They brought the paper to Cuesta on August 3: it
contained not only an account of the King's plans and projects,
but orders for the Marshal, which mentioned Ney and the 6th
Corps, and showed that the force marching on Plasencia was at
least double the strength that Wellesley had expected [2]. This
letter Cuesta sent on to his colleague with laudable promptness;
it reached the British commander in time to save him from
taking the irreparable step of marching from Oropesa to Naval
Moral, where the vanguard of Mortier's cavalry had just been
met by the vedettes of Cotton's light horse. Wellesley had
actually written to Bassecourt to bid him halt at Centinello till
he himself should arrive, and then to join him in an attack on
the French [3], when he was handed the intercepted letter which
showed that Soult had at least 30,000 men in hand.

[1] See Le Noble, p. 320.

[2] See Arteche, vi. 342, and *Wellington Dispatches*, iv. 561; the letter
itself is not published by Gurwood, but Lord Londonderry, then on
Wellesley's staff, gives an analysis of it. It contained, according to him,
orders to Soult to hasten his march, and to bring up Ney's corps with all
speed, while the king himself undertook to threaten Talavera again with
Victor's forces [Londonderry, i. p. 416].

[3] Wellesley to Bassecourt, from Oropesa, August 3. So confident was
the British commander at this moment, that he wrote to Beresford on the
same morning, telling him that Soult when assailed would probably retire
at once, either by the pass of Perales or that of Baños. He wished his
lieutenant to send Portuguese troops to the outlets of those defiles, to
intercept the retreating enemy.

This unpalatable news changed the whole prospect of affairs : it would be mad to assail such an enemy with a force consisting of no more than 18,000 British troops and Bassecourt's 5,000 Spaniards. Wellesley had therefore to reconsider the whole situation, and to dictate a new plan of campaign at very short notice, since his cavalry were actually in touch with the enemy at the distance of a single day's march from Oropesa. On the morrow he must either fight or fly. The situation was made more complicated by the fact that Cuesta, when forwarding the French dispatch, had sent information to the effect that he considered his own situation at Talavera so much compromised that he was about to retreat at once, with the design of crossing the Tagus at Almaraz, and of taking up once more his old line of communications, which ran by Truxillo to Badajoz. It may be asked why the Captain-General did not adopt the simpler course of crossing the Tagus at Talavera, and moving under cover of the river, instead of executing the long flank march by Oropesa to Almaraz on the exposed bank, where the French were known to be in movement. The answer, however, is simple and conclusive : the paths which lead southward from Talavera are impracticable for artillery and wheeled vehicles. Infantry alone could have retreated by the route which climbs up to the Puerto de San Vincente, the main pass of this section of the Sierra de Guadalupe : nor was the track along the edge of the river from Talavera to Arzobispo any better fitted for the transport of a large army. It is this want of any adequate communication with the south which makes Talavera such a dangerous position : no retreat from it is possible save that by the road to Oropesa, unless the retiring army is prepared to sacrifice all its impedimenta.

Cuesta has been criticized in the most savage style by many English writers, from Lord Londonderry and Napier downwards, for his hasty departure from Talavera. It is fair to state in his defence the fact that if he had tarried any longer in his present position he might have been cut off not merely from Almaraz—that passage was already impracticable—but also from the bridge of Arzobispo, the only other crossing of the Tagus by which artillery and heavy wagons can pass southward. If he had started on the fourth instead of the third he might have found Mortier and Soult interposed between him and this last line of retreat. He would then have been forced to abandon all his *matériel*, and to hurry back to Talavera, in order to take the breakneck track to the Puerto de San Vincente. But there was every reason to believe that Victor might arrive in front of Talavera on the evening of the fourth or the morning of the fifth, so that this last road to safety might have been already blocked. Thus the Spanish army, if it had started on the fourth for Oropesa, might have found itself caught between the two French corps, and vowed to inevitable destruction. As a matter of fact Victor moved slowly and cautiously, and only reached Talavera on the sixth—but this could not possibly have been foreseen. We cannot therefore blame Cuesta's precipitate departure upon the night of August 3.

His main body marched under cover of the darkness to Oropesa, where they arrived, much wearied and in some disorder, on the following morning. He left Zayas's division and Albuquerque's horse as a rearguard, to hold Talavera till midday on the fourth, with orders to make a semblance of resistance and to detain Victor for a few hours if he should appear. But no hostile force showed itself : by his unwise retreat to Santa Cruz the Marshal had drawn back so far from the enemy that he could not take advantage of their retrograde movement when it became known to him. Villatte's division and Beaumont's cavalry only reached Talavera on the morning of the sixth.

The departure of the Estremaduran army had one deplorable result. It exposed the English hospitals at Talavera, with their 4,000 wounded, to capture by the enemy. Wellesley, before he had marched off, had given orders that all the men capable of being moved should be sent off towards Plasencia and Portugal as soon as possible. But he had no transport that could cope with the task of transferring such a mass of invalids towards his base. He wrote from Oropesa begging Cuesta to requisition carts from the country-side for this purpose[1]. But it was notorious that carts were not to be had—all Wellesley's letters for the last three weeks were full of complaints to the effect that he could not procure them by money

[1] Wellesley to O'Donoju, Aug. 3, 1809.

or by force. When the Spaniards were themselves departing, bag and baggage, it was an inopportune moment at which to ask them to provide transport: yet since the British wounded had been left to their care they were bound in honour to do all that could be done to save them. It is said that Cuesta made over [1] no more than seven ox-carts and a few mules to Colonel Mackinnon, the officer charged with the task of evacuating the hospitals. These and about forty vehicles of various kinds belonging to the British themselves were all that could be procured for the use of the wounded. They could only accommodate a tithe of the serious cases: the men with hurts of less consequence were forced to set out upon their feet. 'The road to Oropesa,' writes one of their fellow sufferers, 'was covered with our poor limping bloodless soldiers. On crutches or sticks, with blankets thrown over them, they hobbled wofully along. For the moment panic terror lent them a force inconsistent with their debility and their fresh wounds. Some died by the road, others, unable to get further than Oropesa, afterwards fell into the hands of the enemy [2].' The rest trailed onward to the bridge of Arzobispo, where Wellesley provided transport for many of them by unloading baggage-wagons, and ultimately reached Truxillo, at which place the new hospitals were established. Of the whole 4,000 about 1,500 had been left at Talavera as hopeless or dangerous cases, and these became the captives of the French: 2,000 drifted in, at various times, to Truxillo: the remaining 500 expired by the wayside or were taken by the French in the villages where they had dropped down [3].

Long before Cuesta and his host had arrived at Oropesa,

[1] I am bound to say that after reading the Spanish narratives, I doubt whether Cuesta had at his disposal the large amount of spare vehicles of which Londonderry and Napier speak.

[2] Boothby, *A Prisoner of France*, p. 40. For the adventures of two wounded officers on their weary way to Truxillo see the *Diary* of Hawker, and the narrative of Colonel Leslie. The latter made a personal appeal to Cuesta, whose carriage he had met by the roadside. The old general sent for the Alcalde, and made him provide a mule—though it turned out to be a very bad one—for the wounded officer. This small fact to his credit needs recording, after the copious abuse heaped on him.

[3] The invalids were admirably cared for by the enemy. See Boothby.

Wellesley had made up his mind that the only course open to him was to abandon the march towards Naval Moral and Almaraz, and to turn aside to the bridge of Arzobispo. As the French were known to be at Naval Moral, it would have been impossible to force a passage to Almaraz without a battle. If the enemy were to be estimated at two corps, or 30,000 men, according to the indications of the intercepted letter, they would probably be able to detain the Anglo-Spanish army till Victor should arrive from the rear. For, without accepting a pitched battle, they would be strong enough to harass and check the allies, and to prevent them from reaching Almaraz till the 1st Corps should come upon the scene. 'I was not certain,' wrote Wellesley to Beresford two days later, 'that Ney was not with Soult: and I *was* certain that, if not with him, he was at no great distance. We should therefore have had a battle to fight in order to gain the road to Almaraz—Plasencia was then out of the question—and if Victor had followed Cuesta, as he ought to have done, another battle, probably, before the bridge could be re-established [1]. Then it was to be considered that, Cuesta having left Talavera, the bridge of Arzobispo would have been open to the enemy's enterprise: if they had destroyed it, while we had failed in forcing Soult at Naval Moral, we were gone.'

It is impossible not to bow before Wellesley's reasoning. The French critics object that only Mortier was at Naval Moral on August 4, Soult being twenty miles behind him at Bazagona on the Tietar, so that it would have been possible for the British army to have driven back the 19,000 men of the Duke of Treviso, and to have forced its way to Almaraz [2]. But even if Wellesley had fought a successful action with Mortier on August 4, Soult would certainly have joined his colleague on the fifth, before the bridge could have been repaired, or at any rate before the whole Anglo-Spanish army and all its impedimenta could have crossed the Tagus. If attacked during their passage by the 37,000 men of the 2nd and 5th Corps they

---

[1] The Marquis del Reino (it will be remembered) had broken the boat-bridge of Almaraz on August 2, after abandoning the Puerto de Baños.

[2] See for example, Le Noble, pp. 339–40.

would have fared badly. Wellesley was perfectly correct in his decision ; indeed the only point in which he was deceived was that he believed the enemy in his front to be Soult's and Ney's Corps, whereas they were in reality those of Soult and Mortier. Ney only reached Plasencia on August 4, and did not join the main body of the army till two days later.

When Wellesley and Cuesta met at Oropesa, early on the morning of August 4, they found themselves as usual engaged in a heated controversy. The British general had directed his divisions to hold themselves ready to march on the bridge of Arzobispo without further delay. Cuesta on the other hand had been attacked by a recrudescence of his old disease, the mania for fighting pitched battles [1]. He proposed that the allied armies should remain on the north bank of the Tagus, adopt a good defensive position, and defy Soult to attack them. Wellesley would not listen for a moment to this project, and finally declared that in spite of all arguments to the contrary, he should cross the Tagus that day at the head of his army. The two generals parted in wrath, and at six o'clock the British commenced their march to Arzobispo, only nine miles distant ; the whole force crossed its bridge before evening, and established itself in bivouac on the south side of the river.

Cuesta remained at Oropesa for the whole day of August 4, and was there joined both by Bassecourt, who had fallen back from Centinello, and by Zayas and Albuquerque, who had evacuated Talavera at noon and made a forced march to join their chief. He appeared disposed to fight even though his ally had abandoned him. In the afternoon Mortier's cavalry pressed in against him. He turned fiercely upon them, deployed a whole division of infantry and 1,200 horse in their front, and drove them back towards their supports. This vigorous action had a result that could not have been foreseen : Mortier jumped to the conclusion that he was himself about to be attacked by the whole Spanish army—perhaps by Wellesley also [2]. He

---

[1] 'As usual, General Cuesta wanted to fight general actions,' writes Wellesley to Beresford, from Arzobispo, on the afternoon of this same day.

[2] 'M. le Maréchal duc de Trévise crut qu'il serait attaqué,' says Soult in his report of August 13. He therefore held back, and sent for the 2nd Corps. Hence came Cuesta's salvation.

halted the 5th Corps in advance of Naval Moral, and wrote to
implore Soult to come up to his aid without delay. The Duke
of Dalmatia hurried up with all speed, and on August 5 brought
the 2nd Corps to Casatejada, only six miles in the rear of his
colleague. Ney, following with a like promptness, advanced
that day to Malpartida, a march behind the position of Soult.

On the sixth, therefore, the whole army from the Douro was
practically concentrated, and Soult and Mortier advanced against
Cuesta with Ney close in their rear. They found that they were
too late : after remaining in battle order in front of the bridge
of Arzobispo during the whole of the fifth, courting the attack
which Mortier had been too cautious to deliver, the Captain-
General had crossed the Tagus that night, and had occupied its
further bank. He had left in front of the bridge only a small
rearguard, which retired after a skirmish with the advanced
cavalry of the 5th Corps. For once Cuesta had found luck
upon his side; if Mortier had ventured to assail him on the
fifth, and had forced him to an engagement, in a position from
which retreat was difficult, and with the Tagus at his back, his
situation would have been most perilous. For even if he had
kept the 5th Corps at bay, he could not easily have withdrawn
in face of it, and Soult would have been upon him on the next
morning. In escaping across the narrow bridge of Arzobispo
his losses must have been terrible : indeed the greater part of
his army might have been destroyed.

Finding, on the evening of August 6, that both the British
and the Estremaduran armies were now covered by the Tagus,
whose line they appeared determined to defend, Soult was forced
to think out a new plan of campaign. His original design of
taking the allies in the rear and cutting off their retreat had
miscarried : he must now either halt and recognize that his march
had failed in its main purpose, or else deliver a frontal attack
upon the line of the Tagus. The bridge of Almaraz was broken,
and troops (the detachment of the Marquis Del Reino) were
visible behind it. The bridge of Arzobispo was not destroyed,
but the Spaniards were obviously ready to defend it. It was
barricaded, the mediaeval towers in its midst were manned by
a detachment of infantry, and a battery for twelve guns had
been placed in an earthwork erected on a knoll thirty yards in

its rear, so as to sweep all the approaches. Considerable forces both of cavalry and of infantry were visible on the hillsides and in the villages of the southern bank. Cuesta, in fact, while proposing to fall back with his main body to Meza de Ibor and Deleytosa, in order to recover his communication with his base at Badajoz, had left behind a strong rearguard, consisting of Basse-court's infantry division and Albuquerque's six regiments of cavalry, a force of 5,000 bayonets and nearly 3,000 sabres. They were ordered to defend the bridge and the neighbouring ford of Azutan till further orders should reach them. The ground was very strong; indeed the ford was the one perilous point, and as that passage was narrow and hard to find, Cuesta trusted that it might be maintained even against very superior numbers. So formidable did the defence appear that Soult halted during the whole day of August 7, while he took stock of the Spanish positions, and sought up-stream and down-stream for means of passage other than the bridge. He was not at first aware of the existence of the ford: it was only revealed to him by the imprudence of the Spanish cavalry, who rode their horses far into the stream when watering them, thus showing that there were long shallows projecting from the southern bank. By a careful search at night the French intelligence-officers discovered that the river was only deep for a few yards under their own bank [1]: for the rest of its breadth there were only two or three feet of water. Having found the point, not far from the bridge, where the more dangerous part of the channel was fordable, they advised the Marshal that the passage of the river would present no insurmountable diffi-culties. Soult resolved to deliver an assault both on the bridge and on the ford upon the morning of August 8. Nor was it only at Arzobispo that he determined to force the line of the Tagus. He directed Ney, who was bringing up his rear at the head of the 6th Corps, to turn aside to the broken bridge of

---

[1] General Arteche, who has examined the ford, notes that the main channel, narrow but with a rocky bottom, is close under the northern, i. e. the French, bank. The remaining two-thirds of the breadth of the river has a hard sandy bottom and is in August extremely shallow. If once, therefore, the deep water under the nearer bank was crossed, the French had no difficulties before them.

Almaraz, and to endeavour to cross the river by aid of a ford which was said to exist in that neighbourhood. Sketch-maps were sent to the Marshal in order to enable him to locate the exact point of passage—it would seem that they must have been very faulty.

Meanwhile Wellesley had passed the Tagus four days and Cuesta three days before the Marshal's attack was ready, and both had been granted time to proceed far upon their way. It was fortunate that they were not hurried, for the road from Arzobispo to Meza de Ibor and thence to Deleytosa and Jaraicejo, though passable for guns and wheeled vehicles, was steep and in a deplorable condition of disrepair. It took Wellesley two days to march from the bridge to Meza de Ibor, a distance of only seventeen miles, because of the endless trouble caused by his artillery. There were places where he had practically to remake the roadway, and others where whole companies of infantry had to be turned on to haul the cannon up slopes where the half-starved horses could make no headway. These exertions were all the more exhausting because the men were falling into a state of great bodily weakness from insufficient supplies. Even at Talavera they had on many days received no more than half rations: but after passing Oropesa regular distributions of food ceased altogether for some time: there were still a few slaughter-oxen with the army, but bread or biscuit was unobtainable, and the troops had to maintain themselves on what they could scrape up from the thinly peopled and rugged country-side. A diet of overripe *garbanzos*, parched to the hardness of bullets, was all that many could obtain. Better foragers eked them out with honey-comb stolen from the peasants' hives, and pork got by shooting the half-wild pigs which roam in troops among the woods on the mountain side. · Many, in the ravenous eagerness of hunger, ate the meat warm and raw, and contracted choleraic complaints from their unwholesome feeding [1].

Divining that Soult would probably make a dash at Almaraz as well as at Arzobispo, Wellesley sent on ahead of his main body the brigade of Robert Craufurd, to which he attached Donkin's

[1] For details of these privations see the diary of Leach of the 95th, p. 92.

much depleted regiments, in order to make up a small division.
As they were unhampered by guns or baggage this detachment
reached Almaraz on the sixth, after a fifteen hours' forced
march on the preceding day. They took over charge of the
broken bridge and the ford from the Spanish troops of
the Marquis Del Reino, and proceeded to entrench themselves
in the excellent positions overlooking the point where the river
was passable. Thus Ney, when he reached Almaraz on the
following day, found the enemy already established opposite
him, and ready to dispute the crossing. About 4,000 British
troops and 1,500 Spanish troops were holding the river bank :
immediately at their backs was the narrow and eminently
defensible defile of Mirabete, which completely commands the
road to Truxillo : it was an even stronger position than that
which covered the ford and the ruined bridge.

On August 7 therefore Wellesley considered himself in a
comparatively satisfactory situation. The passage at Almaraz
was held by a vanguard consisting of the best troops in the
army. Two divisions, the cavalry, and all the guns had
traversed the worst part of the road, and had reached Deleytosa,
only nine miles behind Craufurd's position. If the French
should attack on the following day, the main body could reinforce the light brigade in a few hours. One division, in the
rear, was holding the position of Meza de Ibor, which Wellesley
did not wish to evacuate until the Spanish army was ready to
occupy it. He had discovered that there were points between
Arzobispo and Almaraz where the passage of the Tagus was not
wholly impracticable for small bodies of infantry [1], and dreaded
that the enemy might throw a detachment across the stream to
make a dash for the Meza. If this position had been lost
the communication between the two armies would have been
broken.

Cuesta, meanwhile, was engaged in the steep and stony
mountain road over which Wellesley had toiled on the 5th and
the 6th of August. His vanguard was now close to Meza de Ibor :
the rest of the army was strung out between that point and Val
de la Casa : the Captain-General himself had his head quarters
on the night of the seventh at Peraleda de Garbin, ten miles

[1] Wellesley to O'Donoju, from Deleytosa, Aug. 7.

west of Arzobispo. Bassecourt and Albuquerque were still
covering the rear, with Mortier's corps now plainly visible in
their front. On their steadiness depended the safety of the
whole army, for Cuesta had more baggage and more guns [1] than
Wellesley, and therefore the road over the hills was even more
trying to him than to his colleague. There was a congestion
of wheeled transport at certain spots on the road which created
hopeless confusion, and barred the march of the cavalry and
even of the infantry divisions. It was only removed by setting
whole battalions to work to drag the wagons out of the way.
Cuesta's ultimate destination was the Meza de Ibor, a position of
unparalleled strength, which could be held even after the enemy
had crossed the Tagus. That they would ultimately win their
way over the river was certain, for already news had arrived
that Victor, after reaching Talavera on Aug. 6, had pushed
infantry over its bridge on the road to Herencia and Aldea
Nueva. Troops coming from this direction would outflank the
Arzobispo position, and compel Albuquerque to abandon it.
Even without cavalry or guns this detachment of the 1st Corps
would be strong enough to dislodge the guard of the bridge, by
falling upon its rear, while Mortier was attacking it in front.
As the cavalry of Victor and Soult had met, half way between
Oropesa and Talavera, upon the afternoon of the seventh, the
two marshals were now in full communication, and able to
concert any plans that they might please for joint operations.

The Duke of Dalmatia, however, preferred to win all the
credit for himself, and attacked without allowing his colleague's
troops time to approach the Spanish position. It was fortunate
for Albuquerque that the rivalry of the two hostile commanders
saved him from the joint assault, which would have been far
more ruinous to him than the actual combat of Aug. 8 was
destined to prove.

Having full knowledge of the existence and the locality of
the ford of Azutan, Soult had resolved to launch his main
attack upon this point, while directing only a subsidiary attack
upon the fortified bridge. This last was only to be pushed

---

[1] Beside his own thirty guns he had the seventeen captured French pieces
which had been won at Talavera. Wellesley, it will be remembered (p. 543),
had handed them over to him.

home in case the troops sent against the ford should succeed in making good their footing upon the further bank. A careful observation of the Spanish lines showed that both Albuquerque and Bassecourt were holding back the main body of their divisions at some distance from the water's edge, in the groves around the three villages of Pedrosa, Burgillo, and Azutan. There was only a single regiment of cavalry watching the river bank, and two or three battalions of infantry manning the towers of the bridge of Arzobispo and the redoubt in its rear. The Spaniards showed every sign of a blind confidence in the strength of their position behind the broad but shallow Tagus.

Knowing their habits, Soult selected for the moment of his attack the hour of the *siesta*. It was between one and two o'clock in the afternoon when he bade his columns, which had been drawn up under cover, and at some distance from the water's edge, to advance to force the passage. For the assault upon the ford he had collected the whole of his cavalry, no less than twelve regiments. Lahoussaye's dragoons formed the van, then came Lorges' brigade, then the division of light horse belonging to the 2nd Corps, in the rear the corps-cavalry of Mortier. This mass of 4,000 horsemen was to be followed by the first brigade of Girard's infantry division of the 5th Corps, while its second brigade was to assault the bridge, when Lahoussaye and Lorges should have won the passage of the ford and have established themselves on the flank of the Spanish defences. Gazan's division, the second of the 5th Corps, was to support Girard, while the masses of the infantry of the 2nd Corps remained in reserve. All the light artillery of the army was to gallop down to the water's edge at various selected points, when the attacking columns were first put in movement, and to distract the attention of the enemy's guns so far as lay in their power.

At about 1.30 p.m. Caulaincourt's brigade of Lahoussaye's dragoons, a force of about 600 sabres, sallied out from its cover behind the village of Arzobispo, and moved down to the ford at a sharp trot. It plunged into the water, had passed the deeper part of the channel almost before the Spaniards had guessed its intention, and soon reached the shallows on the opposite bank. The only hostile force ready to meet it was a single regiment (the 1st Estremaduran Hussars) which was watching the ford, and a battalion of infantry which Bassecourt sent down in haste from the redoubt behind the bridge. A fierce charge of Caulaincourt's dragoons dispersed and routed the Spanish horse; after they had been driven off the victors turned upon the battalion, which tried to form square on their approach, but was late in finishing its manœuvre. It was assailed before the rear side had been formed, broken up, and cut to pieces.

Soult had thus gained a precious half-hour, during which the remainder of his cavalry, squadron after squadron, came pouring over the ford, and began to form up on the southern bank. When several regiments had passed he also let loose the infantry brigade which was to attack the bridge. So narrow was the approach that only a single battalion (the 1st of the 40th of the line) could deliver the assault. But the *tirailleur* companies of several other battalions, and two batteries of horse artillery, opened a lateral fire from various points of the northern bank, to distract the Spaniards from the frontal attack. The fraction of Bassecourt's division which was in position at the bridge and the redoubt had already been com- pletely cowed by seeing Lahoussaye's cavalry forming up in their flank and rear. If they waited to resist the infantry attack, it was clear that they would be cut off from their sole line of retreat by the dragoons. They abandoned their positions after firing a couple of scattering volleys, and fled eastward along the river bank towards the village of Azutan. The heavy guns in the redoubt were left behind, and fell into the hands of Caulaincourt. Girard's infantry was therefore able to cross the river almost without loss, two regiments at the bridge, two at the ford which the cavalry had already utilized. A few men were drowned in the second column, having strayed into deep water by swerving to the right or left of the proper route.

Meanwhile Albuquerque's horse and Bassecourt's second brigade, roused from their ill-timed siesta, were pouring out of the villages which had sheltered them from the noontide heat. The infantry—four battalions apparently—drew up beside a wood, on the slope a mile above the bridge, and waited to be attacked. The cavalry, however, came on in one great mass, and charged down upon Lahoussaye's division, which was covering the deployment of the rest of the French horse. Albuquerque's only thought was to engage the enemy before he had succeeded in passing the whole of his squadrons over the ford. Vainly hoping to atone for his previous slackness by haste that came too late, he had hurried his five regiments forward as soon as the men could saddle and bridle their horses. Fractions of the different corps were mixed together, and no proper first or second line had been formed. The whole mass —some 2,500 sabres—in great disorder, galloped down upon the two brigades of Lahoussaye, and engaged them for a short time. But Lorges' dragoons and part of Soult's light horse were now at hand to aid the leading division; the Spaniards were beset in flank as well as in front, and broke after the first shock. Albuquerque, who showed plenty of useless personal courage, tried in vain to rally them on the 2nd Estremaduran Hussars, the only regiment which remained intact. It was borne away by the backrush of the rest, and scattering over the hillsides the whole body fled westward and northward, some towards Peraleda de Garbin, others towards Pedrosa. Basse-court's infantry went off to the rear as soon as they saw their comrades routed, and took to the hills. By keeping to rocky ground they suffered comparatively little loss.

The French urged the pursuit of Albuquerque's fugitive horsemen for many miles, chasing them as far as the defile of La Estrella in the Sierra de Guadalupe in one direction, and beyond Val de la Casa in the other. On the latter road the chase only ceased when the dragoons came upon the divisions of Henestrosa and Zayas, from Cuesta's main army, drawn up across their path. The losses of the Spaniards were very considerable—600 men and 400 horses were captured, and over 800 killed and wounded. One flag was taken, that of the regiment cut to pieces by Lahoussaye's dragoons at the commencement of the fighting. The pieces in the redoubt, and the divisional battery of Albuquerque, 16 guns in all, were lost. By an additional mischance the French also recovered fourteen of their own seventeen guns that had been taken at Talavera. Cuesta had not been able to utilize these pieces for want of gunners: they were trailing along in the rear of his army, very indifferently horsed, when the French dragoons swept along the road to Peraleda. On the approach of the pursuers they were abandoned by the wayside. This capture enabled Soult to assert that he had taken in all 30 cannon, and emboldened Sebastiani, a few weeks later, to declare that he had never lost his guns at Talavera[1]. Having recovered them he could exhibit them—all save two or three—in evidence of his mendacious statement.

Soult declared in his official report that his cavalry had lost only 28 killed and 83 wounded, his artillery 4 wounded, his infantry hardly a man, save some few drowned at the ford.

The rout of the Spanish rearguard and the capture of the bridge of Arzobispo gave Soult a foothold on the southern bank of the Tagus, but little more. The road by which he could now advance against the allies was detestable—we have already seen how its cliffs and ravines had tried the British and the Estremaduran armies. To reach Cuesta's new position on the Meza de Ibor the Duke of Dalmatia would have had to make a two days' march through these defiles, dragging his guns with him. His cavalry he would have been forced to leave behind him, as there would have been no means of employing it in the mountains. Meanwhile Wellesley had established himself in the ground which he had selected behind the broken bridge of Almaraz, and Cuesta had got the whole of his infantry and half his artillery over the Ibor stream and arrayed them on the Meza, where the rocky slopes are impregnable against a frontal attack, if the defending army shows ordinary determination[2].

[1] The fact that these guns were actually French explains Le Noble's statement that the captured pieces were largely ' de modèle français.' Napier has a strange statement, whose source I cannot discover, to the effect that 'Cuesta on his march to Meza d'Ibor left fifteen guns upon the road, which Albuquerque's flight uncovered. A trumpeter attending an English flag of truce treacherously or foolishly made known the fact to the French, who immediately sent cavalry to fetch them off.' Napier, ii. 189.

[2] It will be remembered that on March 17, Victor turned Del Parque's division out of the Meza de Ibor position. But the latter had only 5,000 men, not enough to man the whole line, while the Duke of Belluno had two divisions for the frontal attack, and turned the Meza with another,

All through the ninth and the morning of the tenth the Spaniards were dragging the rest of their guns and their baggage up the steep zigzag path between the river and the summit of the plateau, and it was not till the end of the latter day that everything was in position. It is probable therefore that if Soult had pressed his pursuit with all possible speed, he might have captured some of the Spanish *impedimenta* on the morning of the tenth. But there were defiles between Peraleda and the Ibor river where Cuesta's rearguard might possibly have detained him till the guns and baggage were in safety [1].

The Duke of Dalmatia, however, paused at the bridge of Arzobispo before committing himself to a second advance against the allies. He was averse to making an isolated attack upon the admirable position now occupied by the Estremaduran army, and wished to combine it with a simultaneous assault upon the British. It will be remembered that he had detached Ney's corps from the rear of his line of march, and ordered it to attempt the passage of the Tagus at Almaraz, by the ford which he knew to exist close to the ruined bridge. He also wrote to Victor to desire him to push forward the two infantry divisions which had crossed the river at Talavera, and to direct them on Mohedas and Alia, so as to turn Cuesta's flank by a long circuitous march among the rugged summits of the Sierra de Guadalupe.

Neither of these subsidiary movements was carried out. One division of Ney's corps, and Fournier's brigade of dragoons reached Almaraz on Aug. 8 : the other division and the light cavalry had followed the 2nd Corps so closely that it had passed Naval Moral on its way eastward, and had to make a long countermarch. It was not till the ninth or tenth therefore that

that of Villatte. Cuesta had 30,000 men and more, quite sufficient to hold the entire position.

[1] Wellesley went to visit his allies on the Meza upon the morning of Aug. 10, and found that half the guns and baggage had been dragged up on the ninth, but that there was still a great accumulation at the foot of the steep slope, between the Ibor river and the lower edge of the plateau. He was in great distress at the notion that the French might come up at any moment, drive in the rearguard, and capture the rear sections of the Spanish train ; see *Wellington Dispatches*, v. 22, to Lord Wellesley, from Deleytosa, Aug. 10.

the Duke of Elchingen would have been in a position to attempt the passage of the Tagus. Craufurd's detachment had been established at Mirabete, behind the broken bridge, since Aug. 6, and two days later the main body of the British army had reached Deleytosa, where it was within a few hours' march of the vanguard, and perfectly ready to support it. If Ney had endeavoured to pass the Tagus on the ninth or tenth with his 12,500 men, it is clear that the head of his column must have been destroyed, for the ford was narrow and difficult, and indeed barely passable for infantry even in the middle of August [1]. But the Marshal did not even attempt the passage, for the simple reason that his intelligence officers failed to discover the ford, and reported to him that none existed. He sent word to Soult that the scheme was impracticable, and drawing back from the water's edge concentrated his whole corps at Naval Moral [Aug. 9].

Victor, at the other end of the French line, showed no desire to adventure his infantry among the defiles of the Sierra de Guadalupe, without guns or cavalry, and refused to move up into the mountains in order to turn Cuesta's right flank. Thus the whole plan concerted by the Duke of Dalmatia for a general attack on the allies came to an ignominious conclusion.

It would appear, indeed, that his chance of inflicting a serious blow on the enemy had passed away long ere he brought the 2nd and 5th Corps down to the bridge of Arzobispo. It was on the fifth, when Mortier refused to close with Cuesta and allowed him to withdraw across the Tagus, that Soult had lost his best opportunity. On that day the Spaniards were still on the

---

[1] From Soult's dispatch of Aug. 13, it appears that a Colonel Ornano, with a regiment of dragoons, was detailed to examine the banks of the Tagus in search of the ford, but failed to find it. The cause is not hard to seek, for it crosses the river diagonally on a narrow shelf of rock with deep water on either side. It is not less than four feet deep, and Leach of the 95th, who was on guard at its southern end, describes it as 'not exactly practicable for infantry even at the driest season of the year' (p. 94). The English, knowing its exact course, were established in positions from which they could concentrate upon it in a few minutes. We may rationally suppose, therefore, that Ney would have found the Tagus not less difficult to pass on Aug. 9, than the Oitaben had been on June 8.

wrong side of the river, and the British vanguard had not yet reached the broken bridge of Almaraz. If Mortier had engaged the army of Cuesta, and Ney had found and attacked the ford at Almaraz before Craufurd's arrival, the position of the allies would have been forlorn indeed. But on the fifth Soult had not yet discovered the real position of affairs ; and the head of Ney's corps was only just debouching from Plasencia, two long marches from Almaraz. In short 'the fog of war,' as a modern writer has happily called it, was still lying thick about the combatants, and Soult's best chance was gone before he was even aware of it.

On August 9, matters looked far less promising, even though the bridge of Arzobispo had been won. Since Ney sent word that he could not cross at Almaraz, while Victor declined to commit himself to any schemes for an advance into the eastern mountains, Soult saw that he must construct another scheme of operations. His own preference was for a march into Portugal by way of Coria and Castello Branco. Such an attack upon Wellesley's base, made by the 50,000 men of the 2nd, 5th, and 6th Corps, would compel the British to abandon Almaraz, to give up their connexion with Cuesta, and to march in haste by Truxillo, Caçeres, and Portalegre on Abrantes, in order to cover Lisbon. It was even possible that, if the invading army made great haste, it might reach Abrantes before the British : in that case Wellesley would be forced to keep to the southern bank of the Tagus and cross it at Santarem, comparatively close to the capital. Thus all Central Portugal might be won without a battle, and Lisbon itself might fall ere the campaign ended, since the 20,000 men of the British general, even when aided by the local levies, could not (as Soult supposed) hold back three French *corps d'armée*[1]. There was another alternative

---

[1] Soult to Joseph, Aug. 9, from Arzobispo : ' Je serai disposé soit à marcher sur Lisbonne pour détruire les établissements anglais avant que leur armée ne puisse y arriver, et à lui rendre son embarquement difficile, soit à marcher sur Ciudad Rodrigo pour en faire le siège. . . . Dans le cas du premier mouvement (qui produira infailliblement de grands résultats) j'aurai l'honneur de prier V. M. d'avoir la bonté de faire connaître à MM. les maréchaux ducs de Trévise et d'Elchingen que telle est son intention, afin que toute observation soit ainsi prévenue, et qu'on ne puisse m'attribuer aucun sentiment d'amour-propre.'

possible—to march not on Lisbon but on Ciudad Rodrigo and Almeida, and to invade Portugal by the northern road. But this plan would take a longer time to execute, and promised less decisive results.

But even before the combat of Arzobispo had taken place, Joseph and Jourdan had determined that they would not permit Soult to carry out any schemes of advance against Portugal. They could show very good grounds for their decision. If the Duke of Dalmatia marched off to attack Lisbon, he would leave the 1st and 4th Corps and the King's reserve,—less than 50,000 men in all, after the losses of Talavera,—opposed to Cuesta, Wellesley, and Venegas, who between them would have at least 75,000 [1]. If the British army should refuse to be drawn away towards Portugal, and should recross the Tagus at Almaraz with Cuesta in its wake, the situation would be deplorable. Victor would be exposed, just as he had been on July 22 and 23, to a joint attack from the two armies. And on this occasion Sebastiani and the King would not be able to bring him help, for they were now closely engaged with Venegas near Aranjuez. If they moved away from the front of the army of La Mancha, Madrid would be lost in two days. If they did not so move, Wellesley and Cuesta might crush Victor, or drive him away on some eccentric line of retreat which would uncover the capital. Jourdan therefore, writing in the name of Joseph, had informed Soult in a dispatch dated Aug. 8, that it was impossible to permit him to march on Portugal, as his departure would uncover Madrid and probably bring about a fatal disaster. He also urged that the exhaustion of the troops rendered a halt necessary, and that it would be impossible to feed them, if they advanced into the stony wilderness on the borders of Portugal before they had collected magazines. For the present the King would be contented to keep the allies in check, without seeking to attack or disperse them, until the weather began to grow cooler and the troops had rested from their fatigues.

As if intending to put it out of Soult's power to undertake his projected expedition into Portugal, Jourdan and Joseph

---

[1] Joseph, exaggerating the enemy's force, was under the impression that they had fully 100,000 men : see his letter to Napoleon of July 31.

now proceeded to deprive him of the control of one of his three
army corps. They authorized Ney to recross the mountains
and to return to Salamanca, in order to protect the plains of
Leon from the incursions of the Spaniards of Galicia. Deprived
of such a large section of his army, Soult would be unable to
march against Abrantes, as he so much desired to do. There
were good military reasons, too, for sending off Ney in this
direction : Kellermann kept reporting that La Romana was on
the move, and that unless promptly succoured he should find
himself obliged to abandon Benavente and Zamora and to fall
back on Valladolid. The Spaniards from Ciudad Rodrigo had
already taken the offensive, and Del Parque's advanced guard
had even seized Salamanca.

Ney accepted with alacrity the chance of withdrawing himself
from the immediate control of his old enemy Soult ; he received
his permission to return to Leon on Aug. 9 : on the tenth his
whole corps was on the move, and on the eleventh he had
retired to Plasencia. On the following day he plunged into
the passes and made for Salamanca with all possible speed [1].

While the 6th Corps was dispatched to the north, the King
directed Soult to take up, with the rest of his troops, a defensive position opposite the allied armies on the central Tagus.
The 2nd Corps was to occupy Plasencia, the 5th to watch the
passages at Almaraz and Arzobispo, while keeping a detachment at Talavera. Thus all Soult's plans for an active campaign were shattered, and he was told off to act as a ' containing
force.' Meanwhile Joseph drew Victor and the 1st Corps away
from Talavera, towards Toledo and La Mancha, with the intention of bringing them into play against Venegas. For just as

---

[1] Ney has been accused of deserting Soult, and retiring from Almaraz
and Naval Moral on his own responsibility, and contrary to the orders
of his immediate superior. But Jourdan's dispatch of Aug. 9 to the
Minister of War shows that the Duke of Elchingen was obeying directions
sent to him from the royal head quarters. ' Le roi a pensé,' he writes,
'qu'on ne devait pas, quant à présent, chercher à pénétrer ni en Andalousie
ni en Portugal. . . . Le duc de Dalmatie renverra promptement le
6me corps sur Salamanque pour en chasser les ennemis, et couvrir la
Vieille Castille conjointement avec le Général Kellermann.' Ney then
was strictly correct in stating in his dispatch of Aug. 18, that he had acted
in obedience to his orders.

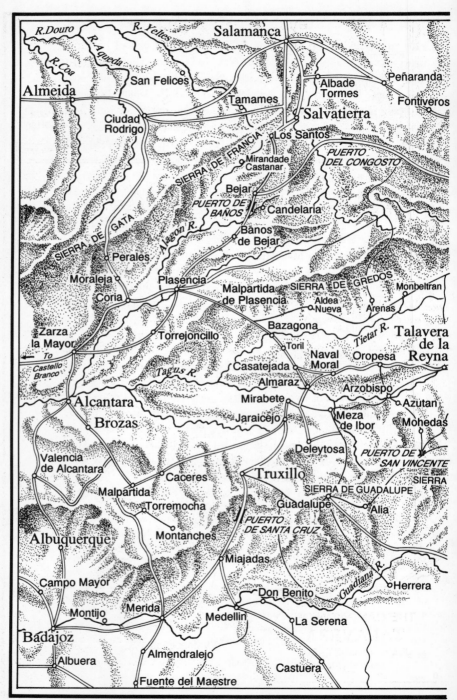

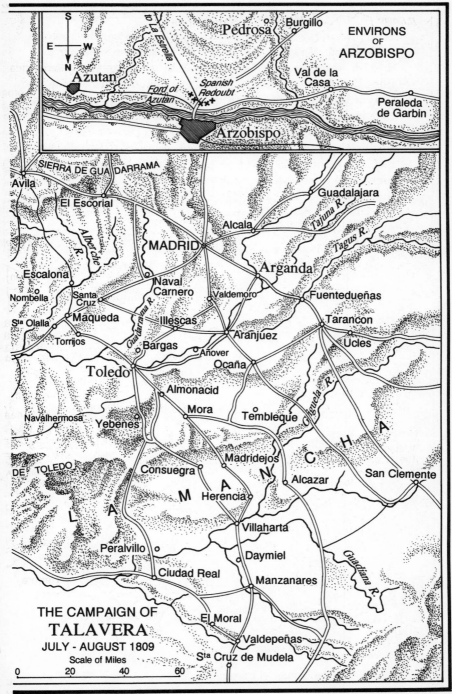

ENVIRONS
OF
ARZOBISPO

Pedrosa
Burgillo

Val de la
Casa

Azutan

Spanish
Redoubt

Ford of
Azutan

Peraleda
de Garbin

Arzobispo

S
E — W
N

SIERRA DE GUADARRAMA

Avila

El Escorial

Guadalajara

Alcala

Tajuna R.

Tagus R.

MADRID

Arganda

Alberche R.

Escalona

Naval
Carnero

Valdemoro

Fuentedueñas

Nombella

Santa
Cruz

Tarancon

Sta Olalla

Maqueda

Illescas

Aranjuez

Ucles

Torrijos

Bargas

Guadarrama R.

Añover

Ocaña

Toledo

Almonacid

Navalhermosa

Mora

Tembleque

Cigüela R.

Yebenes

DE TOLEDO

Madridejos

C   H   A

San Clemente

Consuegra

Alcazar

L   A

M   Herencia

N

Villaharta

Peralvillo

Daymiel

Guadiana R.

Ciudad Real

Manzanares

THE CAMPAIGN OF
TALAVERA
JULY – AUGUST 1809

Scale of Miles

0   20   40   60

El Moral

Valdepeñas

Sta Cruz de Mudela

The Oxford Geog[l] Institute.

Soult had always 'an. eye on Portugal,' so Joseph had always 'an eye on Madrid.' He could not feel secure so long as a Spanish army lay near Toledo or Aranjuez, only two marches from the gates of his capital, and was determined to dislodge it from this threatening position before taking any other operation in hand. He had accepted as true rumours to the effect that part of Cuesta's troops had retired in the direction of Ocaña[1] to join the army of La Mancha, and even that 6,000 British[2] had been detached in this same direction. Thus he had persuaded himself that Venegas had 40,000 men, and was desirous of drawing in Victor to his head quarters before delivering his attack, thinking that Sebastiani and the central reserve would be too weak for the task.

[1] Joseph to Napoleon, from Valdemoro, August 7.
[2] Jourdan to Belliard, from Bargas, August 8.

SECTION XVI: CHAPTER IX

THE END OF THE TALAVERA CAMPAIGN

While King Joseph's orders were being carried out, Wellesley and Cuesta found themselves, to their great surprise, unmolested by any hostile force. The army which had been in their front at Almaraz and Arzobispo disappeared on August 10, leaving only small detachments to watch the northern bank of the Tagus. It was soon reported to Wellesley that Victor had passed away towards Toledo, and that another corps—or perhaps two [1]—had retired to Plasencia. The object of this move however had to be determined, before the British general could take corresponding measures. Was Soult about to invade Portugal by way of Coria and Castello Branco, or was he merely taking up cantonments, from which he could observe the British and Estremaduran armies, while the King and Victor moved off against Venegas? On the whole Wellesley was inclined to believe that the latter hypothesis was the correct one, and that the enemy was about to 'refuse' his right wing, and to use his left for offensive action against the army of La Mancha. As was generally the case, his prescience was not at fault, and he had exactly divined the King's intentions [2]. He had nevertheless to guard against the possibility that the other alternative might

[1] See Wellesley's letter of Aug. 14 to Beresford, concerning the departure of the French. Robert Craufurd estimated the force that had marched on Plasencia at 15,000 men, Donkin at 25,000. If the latter had judged the numbers correctly, Wellesley supposed that both Ney and Soult must have gone by this road : this was actually the case.

[2] Wellesley to Villiers, Aug. 12 : 'The French having been moving since the ninth towards Plasencia . . . I can form no decided opinion respecting their intentions. I think, however, that if they meditated a serious attack on Portugal they would not have moved off in daylight, in full sight of our troops. I suspect these movements are intended only as a feint, to induce us to separate ourselves from the Spaniards, in order to cover Portugal.'

prove to be correct, and that Central Portugal was in danger—
as indeed it would have been if Joseph had allowed Soult to
carry out his original plan.

Wellesley resolved therefore to maintain his present position
at Jaraicejo and Mirabete till he should be certain as to the
intentions of the French. If they were really about to invade
Portugal, he would march at once for Abrantes. If not, he
would keep his ground, for by holding the passage at Almaraz
he was threatening the French centre, and detaining in his front
troops who would otherwise be free to attack the Spaniards
either in La Mancha or in Leon.

Meanwhile measures had to be taken to provide a detaining
force in front of Soult, lest an attack on Portugal should turn
out to be in progress. This force was provided by bringing
down Beresford and the Portuguese field army to Zarza and
Alcantara, and sending up to their aid the British reinforcements which had landed at Lisbon during the month of July.
Beresford, it will be remembered, had received orders at the
commencement of the campaign directing him to concentrate
his army behind Almeida, to link his operations with those of
Del Parque and the Spanish force at Ciudad Rodrigo, but at
the same time to be ready to transfer himself either northward
or southward if his presence should be required on the Douro or
the Tagus. In accordance with these instructions Beresford had
collected thirty-two battalions of regular infantry, with one
more from the Lusitanian Legion, and the University Volunteers
of Coimbra, as also five squadrons from various cavalry regiments, and four batteries of artillery—a force of 18,000 men in
all [1]. On July 31 he had crossed the Spanish frontier, and lay
at San Felices and Villa de Cervo, near Ciudad Rodrigo. There
he heard of Soult's march from Salamanca towards Plasencia,
and very properly made up his mind to bring his army down to
Estremadura by a line parallel to that which the French had
taken. He crossed the Sierra de Gata by the rough pass of
Perales, and on August 12 fixed his head quarters at Moraleja,

[1] These regiments were, Line infantry, nos. 2, 3, 4, 6, 7, 9, 10, 11, 13,
14, 15, 18, 19, 23, all (save no. 15) two battalions strong, and the 1st, 2nd,
3rd, 4th and 6th Cazadores, with no. 2 of the Lusitanian Legion, and
the 'Voluntarios Académicos' of Coimbra.

near Coria, on the southern slope of the mountains. His cavalry held Coria, while his right wing was in touch with the English brigades from Lisbon, which had just reached Zarza-la-Major. These were the seven battalions of Lightburne and Catlin Craufurd [1], which Wellesley had vainly hoped to receive in time for Talavera. They numbered 4,500 bayonets, and had with them one battery of British artillery.

Thus even before Soult reached Plasencia, there was an army of 18,000 Portuguese and 4,500 British on the lower Tietar, ready to act as a detaining force and to retard the Marshal's advance, if he should make a serious attempt to invade Portugal. On Aug. 15, by Wellesley's orders, Beresford left Moraleja and transferred his whole army to Zarza, in order to be able to fall back with perfect security on Castello Branco should circumstances so require. If he had remained at Moraleja he might have been cut off from the high-road to Abrantes by a sudden movement of the enemy on Coria [2].

Wellesley now felt comparatively safe, so far as matters strategical were concerned. If the enemy, contrary to his expectation, should march into Portugal, he could join Beresford at Abrantes, and stand at bay with some 24,000 British and 18,000 Portuguese regulars, a force sufficient to check the 30,000 men who was the utmost force that Soult could bring against him after Ney's departure. Meanwhile, till the Marshal should move, he retained his old position at Mirabete and Jaraicejo. Though the French showed no signs of activity in his front, the weary fortnight during which the British army lay in position behind the Tagus were perhaps the most trying time that Wellesley spent during his first campaign in Spain. It was a period of absolute starvation for man and beast, and the army was going to pieces under his eyes. Ever since the British had arrived in front of Talavera on July 22, rations as we have already seen had been scanty and irregular. But the fourteen days spent at Deleytosa and Jaraicejo were even worse than those which had preceded them. The stores collected at Plasencia had been captured by the French: those gathered at Abrantes were so far distant that they could not be

---

[1] Viz. 2/5th, 2/11th, 2/28th, 2/34th, 2/42nd, 2/39th, 2/88th.

[2] See Wellesley to Beresford, Aug. 14.

drawn upon, now that the high-road north of the Tagus had been cut by the enemy. The army had to live miserably on what it could wring out of the country-side, which Victor two months before had stripped to the very bones. Wellesley had hoped to be fed by the Spanish Government, when he threw up his line of communication with Abrantes, and took up that with Badajos. But the Spanish Government was a broken reed on which to lean : if it fed its own armies most imperfectly, it was hardly to be expected that it would deal more liberally with its allies. The trifling stores brought from Talavera had long been exhausted : the country-side had been eaten bare : from the South very little could be procured. The Spanish Commissary-General Lozano de Torres[1] occasionally sent up a small consignment of flour from Caçeres and Truxillo, but it did not suffice to give the army even half-rations. It was to no purpose that at Abrantes provisions abounded at this moment, for there was no means of getting them forward from Portugal [2]. The enemy lay between the army and its base dépôt, and there was no transport available to bring up the food by the circuitous route of Villa Velha and Portalegre. Even so early as August 8 Wellesley began to write that 'a starving army is actually worse than none. The soldiers lose their discipline and their spirit. They plunder in the very presence of their officers. The officers are discontented, and almost as bad as the men. With the army that a fortnight ago beat double their numbers, I should now hesitate to meet a French corps of half that strength.' On the eleventh he wrote to warn Cuesta that unless he was provided with food of some sort he should remain no longer in his advanced position, but fall back towards Badajoz, whatever might be the consequences. 'It is impossible,' he

---

[1] That this official did something, if not so much as Wellesley required, is shown by the letter to Cuesta of Aug. 11, in which it is said that ' the British army has received no provisions since it was at Deleytosa, excepting some sent from Truxillo by Señor Lozano de Torres,' while again on Aug. 8, Wellesley says that ' we have had nothing since the third, save 4,000 lbs. of biscuit, and that was divided among 30,000 [say 23,000] mouths.'

[2] On Aug. 12, Wellesley writes from Jaraicejo to say that the dépôt at Abrantes is much too large, and that some of the flour ought to be sent back to Santarem, or even to Lisbon, till only 300,000 rations should be left.

stated, ' for me to remain any longer in a country in which no
arrangement has been made for the supply of provisions to the
troops, and in which all the provisions that are either found in
the country or are sent from Seville (as I have been informed
for the use of the British army) are applied solely and exclusively
to the use of the Spanish troops [1].'

The Junta sent Wellesley a letter of high-flown praise for his
doings at Talavera, a present of horses, and a commission as
Captain-General in their army. But food they did not send in
any sufficient quantities. All the convoys that came up from
Andalusia were made over to Cuesta's army, and the Estremaduran districts which were supposed to be allotted for the
sustenance of the British had little or nothing to give. When
we remember that in June Victor had described this same region
as absolutely exhausted and incapable of furnishing the 1st
Corps with even five days' supplies, we shall not wonder that
Wellesley's troops starved there in August. It was impossible
however to convince the British general that the suffering of
his men were the result of Spanish penury rather than of
Spanish negligence and bad faith. There was much just foundation for his complaints, for the Junta, after so many promises,
had sent him no train from Andalusia. Moreover detachments
and marauding bands from Cuesta's army frequently intercepted
the small supplies of food which British foraging parties were
able to procure [2]. When taxed with their misdoings, Cuesta
replied that Wellesley's men had not unfrequently seized and
plundered his own convoys, which was undoubtedly true [3], and that
the British soldiers were enjoying such abundance that he had
been told that some of them were actually selling their bread-
ration to the Spaniards because they had no need of it—which
was most certainly false [4].

That Wellesley was using no exaggerated terms, when he

[1] Wellesley to his brother Lord Wellesley, at Seville, Aug. 8.

[2] See Wellesley to Cuesta from Jaraicejo, Aug. 11.

[3] Lord Munster (p. 251) confesses that ' so pressing were our wants that
one of our commissaries took from them (the Spaniards) by force a hundred
bullocks and a hundred mule loads of bread.' Cuesta needs no further
justification. But it is clear that his own men were doing things precisely
similar.

[4] See the above-quoted dispatch to Cuesta of Aug. 11.

declared that his army was literally perishing for want of food, is proved by the narratives of a score of British officers who were present in the Talavera campaign [1]. That his ultimate retreat was caused by nothing but the necessity of saving his men is perfectly clear. The strategical advantage of maintaining the position behind the Almaraz passage was so evident, and the political disadvantages of withdrawing were so obvious, that a man of Wellesley's keen insight into the facts of war must have desired to hold on as long as was possible. Unless Soult were actually attacking Portugal, Mirabete and Jaraicejo afforded the best ground that could be selected for 'containing' and imposing upon the enemy. So long as the British army lay there it was practically unassailable from the front, while it was admirably placed for the purpose of making an irruption into the midst of the enemy's lines, if he should disperse his corps in search of food, or detach large forces towards La Mancha or Leon. 'If I could only have fed,' wrote Wellesley, 'I could, after some time, have struck a brilliant blow either upon Soult at Plasencia, or upon Mortier in the centre [2]. It is clear that by a dash across the Almaraz passage he could have fallen upon either of these forces, and assailed it with good hope of success before it could be succoured by the other. But such a venture was impossible to an army which had lost one-third of its cavalry horses from starvation within three weeks, and whose battalions were brought so low by physical exhaustion that few of them could be relied upon to march ten miles in a day.

Wellesley declared that, having once linked his fortunes to those of the Spanish army of Estremadura, he had considered himself bound to co-operate with it as long as was humanly speaking possible, and implicit credit may be given to his assertion [3]. The limit of physical endurance, however, was reached

[1] See especially the remarks of Leach, George Napier, Leith-Hay, Stothert, and Cooper.

[2] Wellesley to Castlereagh, from Truxillo, Aug. 21, 1809.

[3] In his dispatch to the Marquis Wellesley, from Merida, Aug. 24, he observes that he had considered himself in honour bound to continue his co-operation unless (1) Soult should invade Portugal, or (2) the Spaniards should move off towards another theatre of war, i. e. La Mancha, or (3) he should himself be starved out, as actually happened.

on August 20, the day on which he was finally compelled
to commence his retreat in the direction of Truxillo and
Badajoz.

Before that day arrived one event occurred which seemed to
make useful co-operation between the two allied armies more
feasible than it had been at any date since the campaign began.
On the night of August 12–13 Cuesta, whose health had been
steadily growing worse since the injuries that he had received at
Medellin, was disabled by a paralytic stroke which deprived him
of the use of one of his legs. He resigned on the following day,
and was succeeded by his second-in-command Eguia, an officer
whose conciliatory manners and mild disposition promised to
make communication between the head quarters of the two
allied armies comparatively friendly. Cuesta, after receiving
from the Central Junta a letter of recall couched in the most
flattering terms, retired to the baths of Alhama. When he had
somewhat recovered his strength, he turned his energies to writing a long vindication of his whole conduct in 1809, and then
engaged in a furious controversy with Venegas, concerning the
latter's disobedience of orders in July. Engaged in these harm-
less pursuits he ceased to be a source of danger to his country.
Unfortunately his removal from the theatre of war was not of
such benefit to the common cause as might have been hoped.
The Junta found ere long a general just as rash and incapable,
if not quite so old, to whom to entrust the command of its
largest army. Juan Carlos Areizaga, the vanquished of Ocaña,
was entirely worthy to be the spiritual heir of Cuesta's policy.

But for the present General Eguia was for some weeks in
charge of the Army of Estremadura. His first idea was to
persuade Wellesley to postpone his departure, and to retain his
advanced position. He urged this request upon his colleague
with more zeal than tact, and to no good effect. By using in
one of his dispatches the phrase that other considerations besides
the want of food must be determining the movements of the
British army [1], he roused Wellesley's wrath. The famine was

---

[1] Eguia's unhappy phrase was ' If notwithstanding this answer [to the
effect that the Truxillo magazines should be placed in charge of a British
commissary] your Excellency should persist in marching your troops into
Portugal, I shall be convinced that other causes, and not only the want of

so real that any insinuation that it was a mere pretext for retreat was certainly calculated to wound the general whose troops
were perishing before his eyes. Expressing deep indignation [1]
Wellesley refused to listen to a proposal that he should divide
with the Estremadurans the stores of food at Truxillo—which
indeed were hopelessly inadequate for the sustenance of two
armies. Nor would he even accept an offer made him on
August 20 by Lorenzo Calvo de Rozas, who came in haste from
the Central Junta, to the effect that he might appropriate the
whole of the magazine at Truxillo, leaving the Spanish army
to provide for itself from other resources. The proposal was
probably honest and genuine, but Wellesley knew the dilatory
habits of the Junta so well that he was convinced that the
dépôt made over to him would never be properly replenished,
and would soon run dry [2].

Marching therefore by short stages, for the exhaustion of his
troops made rapid progress impossible [3], he started from Jaraicejo
on August 20, and moved by Truxillo and Miajadas to the
valley of the Guadiana, where he cantoned the army about

subsistence, have induced your Excellency to decide on taking such a step.'
[From Deleytosa, Aug. 19.]

[1] ' I have had the honour of receiving your Excellency's letter of this
day's date, and I feel much concerned that anything should have occurred
to induce your Excellency to express a doubt of the truth of what I have
written to you. As however your Excellency entertains that doubt, any
further correspondence between us appears unnecessary, and accordingly
this is the last letter which I shall have the honour of addressing to you.'
Wellesley to Eguia, Aug. 19.

[2] ' It is said that Don L. de Calvo promised and engaged to supply the
British army, upon which I have only to observe that I had already trusted
too long to the promises of Spanish agents, and I had particular reason for
want of confidence in Don L. de Calvo. At the moment when he was
assuring me that the British army should have all the food the country
could afford, I had in my possession an order from him directing the
magistrates of Guadalupe to send to the Spanish head quarters provisions
which a British commissary had prepared for the magazine at Truxillo.'
Oct. 30, to Marquis Wellesley.

[3] ' I have no provisions, no horses, no means of transport, I am overloaded
with sick ; the horses of the cavalry are scarcely able to march, or those
of the artillery to draw their guns. The officers and soldiers alike are
worn down by want of food and privations of every description.' Wellesley
to Marquis Wellesley, Miajadas, Aug. 22.

Merida, Montijo, and Badajoz. The British head quarters were fixed at the last-named place from September 3 till December 27, 1809, and, excepting for some small changes in detail, the army retained the position which it had now taken up for nearly four months. In the fertile region along the Guadiana the troops were fed without much trouble: but they did not recover the health that they had lost in the time of starvation among the barren hills behind Arzobispo and Mirabete. In spite of the junction of reinforcements and the return of convalescents to the ranks, the army could never show more than from 23,000 to 25,000 men under arms during the autumn months. When the rainy season began, the intermittent ague which was known to the British as 'Guadiana fever' was never absent: it did not often kill, but it disabled men by the thousand, and it was not till Wellesley moved back into Portugal at midwinter that the regiments recovered their normal health.

If he had been free to follow his personal inclination, it is probable that Wellesley would have moved back into Portugal in September. But strategical and political reasons made this impossible. While based on Badajoz he still threatened the French hold on the valley of the Tagus, and compelled the King to keep two army corps at least in his front. Since it was always possible that he might return to Almaraz and threaten Madrid, a containing force had to be told off against him. He was also in a position from which he could easily sally out to check raids upon Portugal: from Badajoz he could either join Beresford in a few marches, or fall by Alcantara upon the flank of any detachment that Soult might lead forward in the direction of Castello Branco and Abrantes. He was convinced that no such raids would be made, but their possibility had to be taken into consideration, and while lying in his present cantonments he was well placed for frustrating them. But political considerations were even more powerful than military considerations in chaining him to Badajoz. The Junta at Seville were most anxious to keep the British army in their front: they were convinced that, if it retired on Portugal, Joseph and Soult would at once organize an invasion of Andalusia, and they were well aware that Eguia and Venegas would not suffice to hold back the 70,000 men who might then be directed against them. In the dispatches which the Marquis Wellesley (who had superseded Frere at Seville on August 11) kept sending to his brother, the main fact conveyed was the absolute despair with which the Spanish Government viewed the prospect of the removal of their allies towards Portugal. 'Don Martin de Garay [the secretary to the Junta] declared to me with expressions of the deepest sorrow and terror'—wrote the Marquis on August 22—'that if your army should quit Spain, at this critical moment, inevitable and immediate ruin must ensue to his government, to whatever provinces remain under its authority, to the cause of Spain itself, and to every interest connected with the alliance so happily established between Great Britain and the Spanish nation. . . . No argument produced the effect of diminishing the urgency of his entreaties, and I have ascertained that his sensations are in no degree more powerful than those of the Government and of every description of people within this city and its vicinity. . . . Viewing the painful consequences that would follow your retreat into Portugal, I feel it my duty to submit to your consideration the possibility of adopting some intermediate plan, which may have some of the advantages of retreat into Portugal, without occasioning alarm in Spain, and so endangering the foundations of the alliance between that country and Great Britain [1].'

A stay at Badajoz was obviously the only 'intermediate plan' that was worth taking into consideration ; and considering the urgency of his brother's representations Wellesley could not refuse to halt within the Spanish border. The military advantages of the position that he had now taken up were not inconsiderable, and no profit that could have been got by returning into Portugal could have counterbalanced the loss of the Spanish alliance. In the valley of the Central Guadiana, therefore, the British army remained cantoned. But no arguments that the Junta could produce availed to persuade Wellesley to engage in another campaign with a Spanish colleague at his side. Not even when the tempting offer was made that Albuquerque should be given command of half of the Estremaduran army, and placed under his orders, would he consent to pledge himself to offensive operations.

[1] Lord Wellesley to Sir Arthur Wellesley, Seville, Aug. 22.

Meanwhile, dispatches had arrived from England, containing the official news that the Austrian War was at an end: rumours to that effect had already reached the British camps from French sources before Wellesley left Oropesa [1]. The whole character of the continental struggle was changed by the fact that the Emperor had once more the power to send reinforcements to Spain, or even to go there himself. The situation required further consideration, and the British Government resolved to place upon Wellesley's shoulders the all-important task of deciding whether the struggle in the Peninsula could still be maintained, and how (in the event of his giving an affirmative answer) it could best be carried on [2]. He replied that in the existing state of affairs, and considering the bad state of the Spanish armies, neither 30,000 nor even 40,000 British troops would suffice to maintain Andalusia against the unlimited numbers of French whom the Emperor could now send across the Pyrenees. But he held that Portugal might be defended with success, if the Portuguese army and militia could be com-

---

[1] The Armistice of Znaim was signed July 12. The Falmouth packet with the news reached Lisbon only on Aug. 9. Yet Wellesley had heard rumours of peace as early as Aug. 4 [*Well. Disp.* iv. 560].

[2] Canning to Lord Wellesley, London, Aug. 12 : ' The question which first arises is whether the state of things in Spain be such as that a British army of 30,000 men, acting in co-operation with the Spanish armies, could be reasonably expected either to effect the deliverance of the whole Peninsula, or to make head against the augmented force which Bonaparte may now be enabled to direct against that country. Upon this question your Excellency will receive the opinion of Sir A. Wellesley, to whom a copy of this dispatch is transmitted. If the opinion of Sir A. Wellesley shall be that, with so limited a force as 30,000 men, offensive operations in Spain could not prudently be attempted, and if he shall conceive that the utmost object to which such an army would be adequate is the defence of Portugal, your Excellency will then only have to state to the Spanish Government the nature of the instructions under which Sir A. Wellesley now acts. . . . If on the other hand Sir A. Wellesley shall entertain the opinion that with an effective British army of 30,000, combined with the Spanish and Portuguese armies, it might be possible either to expel the French from Spain, or to resist even their augmented force with a reasonable prospect of success . . . your Excellency will then also receive the opinion of Sir A. Wellesley as to the conditions necessary to be obtained from the Spanish Government, as a preliminary to entering on any concerted system of joint military operations.'

R r

pleted to their full strength, and the country well organized for resistance. It was probable that the borders of Portugal could not be maintained ; 'the whole country is frontier, and it would be difficult to prevent the enemy from penetrating by some point or other.' He would have therefore 'to confine himself to preserving what is most important,—the capital.' But this he was prepared to undertake, and strongly advised the ministry to make no attempt to defend both Andalusia and Portugal, but to leave the Junta to their own vain devices, and to make sure of Lisbon [1].

Thus, in September 1809 Wellesley enunciated with great clearness the policy that he was about to employ in the next year. The lines of Torres Vedras are already hovering before his imagination, and after a flying visit to Lisbon in October they took definite shape in his 'Memorandum for Colonel Fletcher' of the twentieth of that month. In that document the whole project for defending the Portuguese capital by a series of concentric fortifications is set forth, and the modifications which it afterwards suffered were only in matters of detail. In short the Lines which were to check Masséna had been thought out in the British general's provident mind exactly twelve months before the French army appeared in front of them.

In following the fortunes of Wellesley we have now got far beyond the point to which we have conducted the general history of the Talavera campaign. It is time to turn back to the movements of Soult and King Joseph, and to explain the reasons which made it possible for the British army to remain unmolested at Jaraicejo and Mirabete till August 20, and then to retire to Merida and Badajoz without imperilling the safety of their Estremaduran allies.

The King, as we have already seen, had made up his mind that the all-important point, at this stage of the campaign, was to make an end of the army of Venegas, and to relieve Madrid

---

[1] For Wellesley's answer to Canning see his reply to his brother on Sept. 5, containing his ' Observation on Mr. Secretary Canning's Dispatch of Aug. 12,' combined with the reference to his own dispatch of Aug. 24, which (as he writes to Castlereagh on Sept. 4) 'gives the government my opinion upon all the points referred to in Mr. Canning's dispatches.' The quotation above comes from this last-named document of Aug. 24.

from danger. He had therefore called Victor towards Toledo, and directed Mortier to relieve the divisions of the 1st Corps which lay at Talavera with troops from the 5th Corps. The result of this movement was to leave Soult too weak to undertake any important operations against Portugal. For Mortier's men, being strung out on the long line from Talavera to Naval Moral, with both Wellesley's and Cuesta's armies in their front, could not be relied upon to lend aid for an advance on Castello Branco or Abrantes. The Duke of Dalmatia therefore, when he had reached Plasencia, could dispose of nothing but his own 2nd Corps and Lahoussaye's four regiments of dragoons. He dared not march on Portugal with no more than 20,000 men, when the allies had it in their power to fall upon Mortier the moment that his back was turned. Accordingly he waited at Plasencia, sending out cavalry to Coria and Torejoncillo, but did nothing more. Meanwhile Beresford and the two British brigades from Lisbon were drawing near him, and on August 16 the Portuguese cavalry, advancing from the pass of Perales and Moraleja, drove out the two French squadrons which were occupying Coria, and thus warned Soult that a new army was coming into play against him. Two days later Beresford had transferred himself to the Castello Branco road, and a force of 23,000 men had been thrown between the 2nd Corps and the Portuguese frontier.

Meanwhile the King had met with unexpected good fortune in his attack on Venegas. On August 5 he had set out from Valdemoro with the intention of attacking the army of La Mancha in its position at Aranjuez. It seemed unlikely that he would find it there, for Venegas had displayed such excessive caution in his advance from the Sierra Morena to the Tagus, and had so tamely refused to take his opportunity of pouncing upon Madrid, that it seemed probable that he would retreat at the first sign of the King's approach. But rushing to the opposite extreme of conduct, the Spanish general was now ready to court destruction. He had received on the preceding night, that of August 4, Cuesta's dispatch of the third, informing him that Soult had crossed the mountains and that both the British and the Estremaduran armies were quitting Talavera. The Captain-General warned him that he might expect an attack from the King's army, and ordered him to avoid an action, and to fall back

towards the Despeña Perros if he were pressed. Serenely putting
aside the orders of Cuesta, Venegas refused to retreat, and announced that he should not copy the conduct of a superior who
had fled even before the enemy was in sight. He announced
his intention of fighting, and directed his army to concentrate
in the neighbourhood of Aranjuez. Of his five divisions, three
were holding that town when the French came in sight; the
other two were écheloned between Aranjuez and Tembleque,
apparently in order to watch the roads from Toledo and Añover.
The enemy might, as Venegas saw, turn his flank either by
crossing the bridges of the former place, or by passing the easy
ford at the latter. A detachment of 800 men had been left to
watch the debouches from Toledo, and a couple of battalions
observed the ford of Añover.

King Joseph meanwhile, marching with a force composed of
Sebastiani's corps, the Central Reserve, and Milhaud's division
of dragoons, arrived in front of Aranjuez on August 5. Sebastiani, whose troops led the advance, drove in the Spanish outposts, who retired across the Tagus and broke the town bridge
behind them. But beyond the river the greater part of the
army of La Mancha was visible in battle order, prepared to
receive the attack: Venegas himself, however, chanced to be
absent at the moment, as he had ridden over that morning
to visit his left wing, and General Giron was in temporary
charge of the defence. Sebastiani risked an attack on the
Spanish position, which was accessible by means of two fords.
But finding that the enemy was in great force and stood firm,
he drew off his men after a sharp skirmish.

King Joseph now determined not to press the attack on
Aranjuez and its fords, but to cross the Tagus at points where
he could secure a less difficult passage. He countermarched
Sebastiani's corps to the bridge of Toledo, and gave Milhaud
orders to force the ford of Añover. This manœuvre cost him
three days; it was only on the evening of August 8 that he
succeeded in concentrating his main body at Toledo. On the
following morning Sebastiani passed the bridges and drove off
the Spanish detachment that was observing them: it fell back
on a larger force, and the 4th Corps pressing its advance, came
into contact with a whole hostile division.

Venegas had not failed to guess the plan which the King would adopt, and had moved off from Aranjuez towards Toledo, by roads parallel to those which the French had employed. His 5th division, 4,000 bayonets, under Major-General Zerain, was in front, and thus was the first to meet Sebastiani's attack. It was driven in after a sharp skirmish, and retired a few miles to the small town of Almonacid, on the high-road to Mora and Madridejos. On the same evening Milhaud's dragoons assailed the ford of Añover, drove off the small force that was guarding it, and fell into line on Sebastiani's left flank. On the next morning Venegas came up with his remaining four divisions, those of Lacy, Vigodet, Giron, and Castejon, and joined Zerain at Almonacid. Thus both sides were concentrated for battle, save that Joseph and his reserves, owing to the delay caused by a defile over the narrow bridge of Toledo, were some ten miles to the rear of Sebastiani. The Spanish army, after the deduction of men in hospital or detached, amounted to about 23,000 men, of whom nearly 3,000 were horse: it had forty guns. The King and Sebastiani had some 21,000 sabres and bayonets, but of these nearly 4,000 were cavalry, so that the French army enjoyed its usual preponderance in that arm, in numbers no less than in efficiency. Two of its infantry divisions, those of Leval and Sebastiani, had suffered heavily at Talavera: the rest of the infantry—Valence's Poles and the King's guards and reserves—had not been engaged in that battle; all the cavalry was equally intact [1].

Both armies were prepared to fight : King Joseph had resolved that Madrid would never be safe till the army of La Mancha had been beaten. Venegas was eager to meet him : he had persuaded himself that the French troops which had passed the bridge of Toledo did not amount to more than 14,000 men, and hoped for an easy victory. He held a council of war on the night of the tenth, and found his subordinates as ready to fight as himself. They determined to attack Sebastiani on the dawn

---

[1] The French force at Almonacid stood as follows:—4th Corps; Sebastiani's division 6,000 men, Valence's 4,000, Leval's 3,000, and corps-cavalry (Merlin) 1,000. Milhaud's dragoons had 2,200 men present; the King had brought up 600 horse and about 4,800 foot of his guards and of Dessolles' division. The total therefore was about 3,800 cavalry and 17,800 foot.

of August 12, and the Commander-in-chief exclaimed with
exultation that, whatever other Spanish officers might do, he at
least would never earn the nickname of *El General Retiradas* [1].

The French, however, anticipated Venegas, for on the morning of August 11, at half-past five o'clock, Sebastiani presented
himself in front of the Spanish position and opened a furious
attack, without waiting for the arrival of King Joseph and the
reserve. The army of La Mancha had therefore to fight
a defensive engagement, and never got the chance of carrying
out the ambitious designs of its chief.

The battlefield of Almonacid bears a strong resemblance to
that of Ucles, where Venegas six months before had made such
a deplorable début in the character of a 'fighting general.' As
at Ucles, the Spanish army was arrayed on a series of eminences
on each side of a small town, with a long array of infantry and
guns in its centre, and the cavalry on the wings. As if to
emphasize the resemblance, Venegas committed his old fault of
keeping no adequate reserve in hand, and distributed his whole
force in one thin line, with no more than four battalions and
two cavalry regiments drawn up in support to the rear of the
centre! The only points in which there was a marked difference
between Ucles and Almonacid was that on the latter field the
eminence on the Spanish left—a hill called Los Cerrojones—
was so much higher than the rest of the ground that it formed
the key of the position, just as the Cerro de Medellin had done
at Talavera. Moreover, there was a long hill behind Almonacid
—the Cerro del Castillo—which gave an admirable rallying-
point for the army if it should be forced out of its first fighting-
ground.

The main line of the Spanish order of battle was formed,
counting from right to left, by the divisions of Vigodet (no. 2),
Castejon (no. 4), Zerain (no. 5), and Lacy (no. 1), with a brigade
of the division of Giron (no. 3) continuing the array on to the
Cerrojones. The second brigade of Giron formed the sole

---

[1] This remark I find in the narrative of General Bouligni, the commanding
officer of engineers in the Army of La Mancha [Arteche, vi. 370]. Venegas
was aiming his sneer at Castaños and at La Romana, who had got the
nickname of 'Marquis de la Romeria' from his perpetual strategical
movements to the rear.

reserve; it was drawn up on the Cerro del Castillo, where the
ruins of the mediaeval fort that gave the hill its name were
turned to account as a place of strength. It had two cavalry
regiments in its rear: the rest of the troops of that arm were
distributed between the two flanks.

When Sebastiani came upon the field he fell upon the Spanish
line without a moment's hesitation. Apparently he thought
that delay would only give the enemy time to rearrange his
troops and strengthen his weak points. At any rate he did not
wait for the arrival of the King and the reserve, but attacked at
once. It was the same fault that Victor had committed at
Talavera, but Sebastiani was not destined to receive the condign
punishment that befell the Duke of Belluno. Noting that the
steep hill on the Spanish left was the key of the position, he resolved
to storm it before attacking the rest of the hostile line. Accordingly he threw out Milhaud's dragoons and his own French
division to 'contain' the Spanish centre and right, while Leval's
Germans and Valence's Poles were directed to assail the
Cerrojones. The former division turned the flank of the hill,
while the latter attacked it in front.

The Spanish brigade on the hill made a stubborn resistance,
and even held back the Poles till its flank was turned by the
Germans. Venegas sent to its aid his miserably inadequate
reserve under Giron, and some battalions drawn from the first
division. But these troops came too late, the Cerrojones were
lost, and the reinforcements only succeeded in checking the
French advance behind the hill, on the slopes between it and
Almonacid. The key of the position was thus in Sebastiani's
hands, and, seeing the Spanish centre outflanked, he let loose
upon it his French division, which drove in Lacy and Zerain,
and captured the town of Almonacid and three guns. Venegas
was thus forced to draw back his whole line, and re-formed it
on the Cerro del Castillo, which lay behind his original position.
The troops were much disordered by this retrograde movement,
yet made a very creditable effort to maintain their new ground.
But King Joseph and the reserve had now come on the field,
and Dessolles' troops were thrown into the front line to aid the
infantry of the 4th Corps. After a stubborn fight the Spanish
left and centre again broke, and Venegas was only able to save

them from complete destruction by bringing up Vigodet's division, which was almost intact, and throwing it in the way of the advancing enemy. It held out long enough to allow the main body to escape, and then followed its comrades in retreat down the high-road to Mora and Madridejos. The French cavalry was let loose in pursuit, but does not seem to have been so successful in its work as had been the case at Ucles and Medellin. At any rate the bulk of the Spaniards escaped in more or less order, and only the stragglers were cut up.

The losses of Venegas's army would appear to have been about 800 killed and 2,500 wounded [1], besides a considerable number of prisoners—perhaps 2,000 in all, for Sebastiani's dispatch giving the figure of 4,000 cannot be trusted. The army of La Mancha had also lost twenty-one of its forty guns, all its baggage and several standards. Still the defeat was far less crushing than Medellin had been, and the whole army was rallied at the passes with no great difficulty. It had fought very creditably, as is sufficiently vouched for by the fact that Sebastiani acknowledged a loss of 319 killed and 2,075 wounded. The Polish division in especial had suffered very severely while storming the Cerrojones at the opening of the combat.

Thus ended the part taken by the Army of La Mancha in the Talavera campaign. No words are too strong to use in condemnation of Venegas's conduct. After wrecking the plan of campaign drawn up by Wellesley and Cuesta by his criminal slackness and timidity in July, he then proceeded to the extreme of culpable rashness. He had ample time to retire to the South, when his position was compromised by the departure of the British and Estremaduran armies from Talavera. Instead of doing so he remained behind, and courted an unnecessary battle, in which his unskilful dispositions secured the defeat of an army which tried to do its duty and defended itself far better than could have been expected. He should have been court-martialled and shot for his repeated and impudent disobedience of Cuesta's orders. But the Junta, conscious that they were themselves to blame for giving him secret directions which clashed with those of the Commander-in-chief, spared him, and only removed him

[1] But see General Arteche's calculation in vi. 392 of his *Guerra de la Independencia.*

from command some weeks later, in order to replace him by Areizaga, an officer of exactly the same level of merit and intelligence.

After his—or rather Sebastiani's—victory at Almonacid King Joseph established the 4th Corps in cantonments around Toledo and Aranjuez, and sent Victor and the 1st Corps into La Mancha to observe the passes and to contain the wrecks of Venegas's army. He returned himself with his guards and the reserve to Madrid on August 15, celebrated a *Te Deum*, and published an extravagant account of his own achievements, in which he claimed to have discomfited the attempt of 120,000 enemies (there were but 80,000 at the most liberal estimate) with the aid of 40,000 invincible French troops. The co-operation of Soult's 50,000 men was consigned to oblivion in this extraordinary document.

The moment that he heard of the defeat of Venegas, Soult wrote to the King, renewing the demand which he had made ten days before for permission to invade Portugal. Now that the army of La Mancha had been disposed of, he considered that Victor might come back to Talavera and Almaraz, so as to set free Mortier and the 5th Corps for the attack on Portugal. He also suggested that Ney, having put things right at Salamanca, might now be recalled to the valley of the Tagus, and rejoin the 2nd and 5th Corps. He supported his demands by an unfounded assertion that Wellesley was on his march to unite with Beresford by way of Alcantara, and asked for leave to attack the latter before the main British army should have joined him. In a few days more, he said, it would be too late to move, for Beresford and Wellesley would have concentrated their forces, so that he would have 45,000 Anglo-Portuguese in his front [1].

Joseph refused to listen to these arguments, and had fair reasons to show for his negative reply to the Marshal's requests. Wellesley, as he truly remarked, was not marching for Alcantara to join Beresford : he was still at Jaraicejo in close touch with the Estremaduran army. If Mortier were removed to the Portuguese border, Wellesley and Eguia might descend upon Victor and crush him. It was impossible to leave less than two corps to defend the Middle Tagus. As for Ney, he could not

[1] Soult to Joseph, Aug. 18, from Plasencia.

quit Leon, for Del Parque and the Galicians were concentrating in great force upon his front. Indeed, he had just written to request that the 2nd Corps might be moved up to Salamanca to support him [1]. It was not now the time to engage in further offensive operations either against Portugal or against Andalusia. The troops were exhausted; the hospital of Madrid contained at the moment 12,000 sick and wounded, the cavalry was so distressed by incessant work that few regiments could put 250 men in line. The transport was worn out, and new horses and mules were impossible to procure, for the King had no money with which to purchase them. Finally, and this was the most conclusive point of all, orders had been received from the Emperor countermanding all active operations till the hot season should be over [2]. It was impossible to say what his intentions might be, now that he was freed from the Austrian War. He might come himself to Spain, or he might send large reinforcements to the King. In any case it would be impossible to move till his will was known and his mind made up [3].

These arguments were conclusive, and Soult was forced to remain quiescent: all that he could do was to push small parties to Zarza and Coria when Beresford had evacuated those places.

Thus the Talavera campaign came to an end. There was now a long pause in the movements both of the allies and of the French. The subsequent fighting in October belongs to a totally independent series of operations. The combatants who had been engaged in July and August rested in September: Soult was left at Plasencia, Mortier at Talavera and Naval Moral, Ney at Salamanca; Victor's head quarters were at Daymiel in La Mancha, Sebastiani lay along the Tagus from Aranjuez to Toledo. Of the allied troops Wellesley's army was cantoned about Badajoz and Merida. The Estremadurans under Eguia covered the passages of the Tagus from Deleytosa, Jaraicejo, and Truxillo: Venegas was reorganizing his depleted corps at his old quarters in the passes by La Carolina. Beresford was observing Soult from Castello Branco, and lastly, the Galicians were moving down by divisions to join Del Parque's

---

[1] Ney to Jourdan, from Salamanca, Aug. 22.

[2] See Joseph to Clarke, Aug. 22, and Napoleon to Clarke, Sept. 7.

[2] For a presentment of Joseph's case see Chapter xii. of Jourdan's *Mémoires*.

forces at Ciudad Rodrigo, where a formidable army was now beginning to be collected.

The Talavera campaign, in short, had settled nothing. The attempt of the allies to capture Madrid had failed, but the attempt of the French to surround Wellesley and Cuesta by Soult's flank march had failed also. Looking to the net results of all the fighting since May, it could be said that the balance of loss stood against the French. They had abandoned Galicia and the Asturias, as well as their precarious hold on Northern Portugal. They had gained nothing, save that their forces were concentrated in a good central position, instead of being scattered from Corunna and Oporto as far as Merida and Manzanares. The next move was in the hands of the Emperor : it remained to be seen how he would deal with the situation in the Peninsula, now that he, at last, had time to study it in detail.

Before passing on to the new series of operations which took place in the late autumn, one minor side-issue of the Talavera campaign remains to be narrated—the fate of the small roving column of 4,000 Spaniards and Portuguese under Sir Robert Wilson, which had been threatening Madrid in the King's absence, and which had caused so many misgivings in the mind of Marshal Victor. Wilson's doings were to give one more proof of his extraordinary resourcefulness and vigour, if any further evidence were needed after his masterly handling of Lapisse in the spring. It will be remembered that on August 4 he had slipped away from Escalona, on hearing from Wellesley that Soult had descended upon Plasencia. He intended to join the main army at Talavera, but on nearing that place discovered that it had already been evacuated, and that both the British and the Estremaduran armies had disappeared in the direction of Oropesa. Accordingly he directed his steps to the westward, hoping to overtake Wellesley on his march. On his way, however, he was caught up by Villatte's division of Victor's corps, which had been vainly hunting for him at Nombella and Escalona since the fifth. Thrown out of his path by this force, Wilson turned up into the mountains, intending to escape by the northern bank of the Tietar. He soon learnt, however, from the peasantry that Soult had sent a brigade under Foy to look for him in the Vera of Plasencia, and that Hugo, the governor of Avila, had come down to hold against him the passes of Arenas and Monbeltran. Thus ringed around with foes, he did not lose his nerve, but turning up into the Sierra de Gredos, by a mule-path that leads from Aldea Nueva to the upper valley of the Alagon, escaped in the direction of Bejar. From thence he intended to strike across towards Portugal. But a new enemy now came upon him : he had evaded Villatte and Foy only to run into the arms of Ney, who on this day [August 12] was preparing to cross the Puerto de Baños on his way to Salamanca. There was still time to escape from the Marshal's front and to retire to Ciudad Rodrigo unmolested. But Wilson saw the rocky defile of the Puerto in front of him, and could not resist the temptation of holding it against the enemy, though he was well aware that with a force of less than 4,000 men, destitute of artillery, he could not seriously hope to repulse a whole army corps. Nevertheless he offered battle in the pass, and fought a running fight for nine hours against Ney's vanguard, defending three successive positions, from each of which he had to be expelled. In his last stand he held on too long, and allowed the enemy to close. His four battalions were all broken, and fled over the hills to Miranda de Castanar, where they rallied on the next day. The Marshal acknowledged in his dispatch to King Joseph a loss of five officers and thirty men killed, and ten officers and 140 men wounded, which shows that he had been forced to fight hard to clear the pass. He claimed to have 'destroyed' Wilson's detachment, and declared that 1,200 Spaniards and Portuguese had fallen. But Wilson's returns show that his total loss, killed, wounded, and missing, was under 400, among whom there was not a single field officer or captain. Having assuaged his thirst for a fight by this gallant, if unnecessary, engagement, Wilson escaped to the Pass of Perales, and finally reached Castello Branco on August 24, where he fell in with Beresford, and was at last in safety, after his many wanderings among the summits of the Sierra de Gredos and the Sierra de Gata. This hazardous march was his last achievement in the Peninsula ; after a bitter quarrel with Beresford concerning the status of his Lusitanian Legion in the Portuguese army, he sailed for England in October, and never returned to Portugal.

APPENDICES

I

THE 'ARMY OF THE CENTRE,' JAN. 11, 1809

[N.B.—From the Tables in Arteche, vol. v.]

The Battalions which fought at Ucles are indicated by a star *.

Vanguard Division, Major-General Duke of Albuquerque :
Corona (1st and 3rd batts.) 415, *Murcia 652, *Cantabria (1st
batt.) 315, *Provincial of Jaen 342, *Provincial of Chinchilla
354, *Voluntarios Catalanes 499, *Cazadores de Barbastro 221,
*Campo Mayor 465, Tiradores de Castilla 666 . . = 3,929

1st Division, Lieut.-General Marquis de Coupigny :
Reyna (1st and 3rd batts.) 494, *Africa (1st and 3rd batts.) 771,
*Burgos (1st and 3rd batts.) 519, 1st of Seville 193, *3rd of
Seville 106, Provincial of Granada 176, Provincial of Bujalance
101, *Provincial of Cuenca 626, Provincial of Ciudad Real 268,
Provincial of Plasencia 180, Voluntarios de Valencia 327,
*Navas de Tolosa 542, *Tiradores de Cadiz 818 . . = 5,121

2nd Division, Major-General Conde de Orgaz :
*Ordenes Militares (1st, 2nd, and 3rd batts.) 848, *4th of Seville
224, 5th of Seville 304, 1st Voluntarios de Madrid 688, Provincial de Leon 484, Provincial de Logroño 265, *Provincial de
Toro 265, Provincial de Valladolid 378, *Baylen 472, Tiradores
de España 407, *Voluntarios de Carmona 456, Voluntarios de
Ledesma 497 . . . . = 5,288

Reserve, Lieut.-General La Peña :
Spanish Guards (1st and 2nd batts.) 1,217, *Walloon Guards (1st
batt.) 425, *Granaderos Provinciales de Andalucia 522, *Irlanda
(1st batt.) 377, Granaderos del General 324, Provincial de
Cordova 622, Provincial de Guadix 391, Provincial de
Lorca 417 . . . . = 4,295

CAVALRY.

*Reyna 276, *Principe 141, *Borbon 119, *España 342, *Santiago
74, *Tejas 131, *Pavia 428, *Lusitania 158, *Dragones de

Castilla 125, Farnesio ?, Montesa ?, Calatrava ?, Sagunto ?,
Alcantara ? . . . . = 1,814
Estimating the 5 regiments without returns at 1,000 sabres, we get
2,814 in all.

ARTILLERY 386.   *SAPPERS 383.

Total of the Army, 21,216.

Of these the following, with a strength of 11,500 men, were present at
Ucles,

Of the Vanguard	. . 2,848		Brought forward	.	9,203
,, 1st Division	. . 2,804		Cavalry . . .	.	1,814
,, 2nd ,,	. . 1,917		Sappers . . .	.	383
,, Reserve	. . 1,634		Artillery . .	.	100
Carry forward	. 9,203		Total	.	11,500

There is a discrepancy between this total and the numbers borne in the
battalions above. It is caused by the fact that Irlanda, Ordenes Militares,
and Tiradores de Cadiz were not complete on the battle-morning, but had
companies detached.

II

THE GARRISON OF SARAGOSSA

[From the return of Jan. 1, 1809, given by Ibieca, corrected by reference
to Arteche iv. 550-1, and the Conde de Clonard, ii. 284-93.]

INFANTRY.

1st Division, Brigadier-General F. Butron :

	Gross Total.	Present under arms.		Gross Total.	Present under arms.
Walloon Guards.	530	450	Brought forward	6,335	4,672
Estremadura. .	610	390	Batallon de Torrero	720	485
Granaderos de Palafox. . .	1,005	752	,, de Calatayud	967	881
Fusileros del Reyno . . .	1,571	1,291	1st Ligero de Zaragoza.	680	566
Don Carlos . .	1,014	534	2nd Ligero de Zaragoza.	666	546
Batallon del Carmen. . . .	771	661	1st Cazadores Catalanes	625	465
Batallon del Portillo. . .	834	594	2nd Voluntarios de Aragon. . . .	1,200	1,060
Carry forward	6,335	4,672	Divisional Total	11,193	8,675

2nd Division, Brigadier-General D. Fiballer :

Spanish Guards .	898	676	Brought forward .	3,035	2,372
2nd of Valencia .	954	726	Cazadores de Fernando		
1st Volunteers of			VII (Aragonese). .	545	345
Aragon . . .	1,183	970			
Carry forward .	3,035	2,372			
			Divisional Total	3,580	2,717

3rd Division, Brigadier-General José Manso :

Peñas de San Pedro	594	241	Brought forward .	2,970	1,786
1st of Huesca . .	1,274	973	1st of Murcia . .	1,272	631
Florida Blanca .	352	229	2nd ,, . .	1,159	477
1st Tiradores de			3rd ,, . .	1,098	438
Murcia . . .	750	343	Suizos de Aragon .	496	361
Carry forward .	2,970	1,786			
			Divisional Total	6,995	3,693

4th Division, Major-General F. St. March :

Voluntarios de			Brought forward .	2,670	1,621
Borbon . . .	436	317	Cazadores de Fern-		
Voluntarios de			ando VII (Valen-		
Castilla . . .	542	292	cians)	304	190
Voluntarios de			Segorbe	412	313
Chelva . . .	789	529	Soria [Militia] . .	172	130
Voluntarios de			1st of Alicante . .	730	309
Turia . . .	903	483	5th of Murcia . .	1,040	423
			2nd Tiradores de		
Carry forward .	2,670	1,621	Murcia	131	91
			Divisional Total	5,459	3,077

Roca's Division of the ' Army of the Centre':

1st of Savoia . .	347	105	Brought forward .	1,583	695
Orihuela . . .	731	315	Murcia [Militia] .	633	426
1st Cazadores de			America	?	148
Valencia . . .	505	275	Avila [Militia] . .	?	277
Carry forward .	1,583	695			
			Total	2,216	1,546

Details from Regiments of the 1st, 2nd, 3rd, and 4th Divisions of the ' Army of the Centre': viz. :—

Carmona, Guadix [Militia], Voluntarios de Madrid, Ordenes
Militares, Toro (Militia) Africa, Burgos [Militia] Navas de
Tolosa, Baylen, 5th of Seville, Campo Mayor, Cadiz, Cuenca,
Tiradores de Cartagena, 1st of Valencia—all small fragments
of regiments which had fought at Tudela in the left wing, but
had taken refuge in Saragossa : the numbers vary from 200
to ten men . . . . Total, perhaps   1,200

CAVALRY.

Rey, Numancia, Fuensanta, Husares de Palafox, Cazadores de Fernando VII, Husares de Aragon. With fragments of the following regiments of the 'Army of the Centre': Borbon, Lusitania, Olivenza, Pavia, Reyna, Santiago, Tejas .   .

. . . . Gross Total sabres, about   2,000

ARTILLERY   . . . .   about   1,800

ENGINEERS.

Zapadores de Aragon, ditto de Valencia, ditto de Calatayud .   800

TOTALS.

	Gross.	Effectives Present.
Infantry of the four Aragonese Divisions . .	27,227	18,162
Cavalry	2,000	1,600
Artillery	1,800	1,600
Engineers	800	700
Details of the Army of the Centre . . .	4,191	2,746
	36,018	24,808

All these are regularly organized corps. It is impossible to state the figures of the irregulars with any certainty.

N.B.—Ibieca errs in including Doyle, La Reunion, Fieles Zaragozanos and 3rd of Valencia in the Garrison, they were detached in Aragon, the first at Jaca, the two next with the Marquis of Lazan. See the tables on pp. 284–293 of vol. vi. of the Conde de Clonard's great work.

III

STATE OF THE FRENCH ARMY IN SPAIN,

FEBRUARY 1, 1809

N.B.—This return includes effective men, *présents sous les armes,* only, not sick or detached.

1st Corps, Marshal VICTOR :

1st Division, Ruffin [9th Léger, 24th and 96th Line (three batts. each)]	5,429
2nd Division, Lapisse [16th Léger, 8th, 45th, and 54th Line (three batts. each)]	7,692
3rd Division, Villatte [27th Léger, 63rd, 94th, and 95th Line (three batts. each)]	6,376
Corps-Cavalry, Beaumont [2nd Hussars, 5th Chasseurs] . .	1,386
Westphalian Chevaux-Légers	487
Artillery [with 48 guns]	1,523
État Major	33
	Total 22,926

2nd Corps, Marshal Soult :

1st Division, Merle [2nd and 4th Léger, 15th (four batts. each)
and 36th Line (three batts.)] 6,498

2nd Division, Mermet [31st Léger (four batts.), 47th Line (four
batts.), 122nd (four batts.), 2nd, 3rd, 4th Swiss (one batt.
each)] 5,459

3rd Division, Delaborde [17th, 70th, 86th Line (three batts.
each)] 4,954

4th Division, Heudelet [26th Line (two batts.), 66th Line (two
batts.), 15th Léger (one batt.), 32nd Léger (one batt.), 82nd
Line (one batt.), *Légion du Midi* (one batt.), Hanoverian
Legion (one batt.), *Garde de Paris* (one batt.)] . . . 3,158

Corps-Cavalry, Franceschi [1st Hussars, 8th Dragoons, 22nd
Chasseurs, Hanoverian Chevaux-Légers] 1,340

Artillery (the men included under divisional totals), 54 guns .

État Major 43
                                                    ―――――
                                        Total   21,452

N.B.—Lahoussaye's Dragoons, and one brigade of Lorges' Dragoons,
were also present with the corps, with a strength of 2,000 sabres.

3rd Corps, General Junot :

1st Division, Grandjean [14th Line (three batts.), 44th Line
(three batts.), 2nd and 3rd of the Vistula (two batts. each)] . 5,866

2nd Division, Musnier [114th and 115th Line (three batts. each),
1st of the Vistula (two batts.), 2nd Legion of Reserve] . 3,544

3rd Division, Morlot [5th Léger (one batt.), 116th and 117th
Line (four batts. each), 121st Line (four batts.)] . . . 2,637

Corps-Cavalry, Wathier [13th Cuirassiers, 4th Hussars, Polish
Lancers, Provisional regiments] 1,652

Engineers and Sappers (for siege of Saragossa) . . . 2,336

Artillery (the men included under divisional totals), 40 guns.

État Major 36
                                                    ―――――
                                        Total   16,071

4th Corps, General Sebastiani :

1st Division, Sebastiani [28th, 32nd, 58th, 75th Line (three
batts. each)] 5,660

2nd Division, Leval [Holland, Nassau, Baden, Hesse (two batts.
each), Frankfort (one batt.)] 3,127

3rd Division, Valence [4th, 7th, 9th Polish (two batts. each)] . 3,915

Corps-Cavalry [5th Dragoons, 3rd Dutch Hussars, Polish
Lancers] 1,781

Artillery (with 30 guns) 894

État Major 22
                                                    ―――――
                                        Total   15,399

5th Corps, Marshal MORTIER :

1st Division, Suchet [17th Léger, 40th, 64th, 88th Line (three batts. each), 34th Line (four batts.)] 8,477

2nd Division, Gazan [21st, 28th, 100th, 103rd Line (three batts. each)]. 7,110

Corps-Cavalry, Delaage [10th Hussars, 21st Chasseurs] . . 926

Artillery (with 30 guns) 1,420

État Major 26

Total 17,959

6th Corps, Marshal NEY :

1st Division, Marchand [6th, 39th, 69th, 76th Line (three batts. each)]. 6,853

2nd Division, Maurice Mathieu [25th Léger, 27th, 50th, 59th (three batts. each)] 6,917

Corps-Cavalry, Lorcet [3rd Hussars, 15th Chasseurs] . . 840

Artillery (with 30 guns) 1,534

État Major 32

Total 16,176

N.B.—One brigade of Lorges' Dragoons was also present with the corps.

7th Corps, General GOUVION ST. CYR :

1st Division, Souham [1st Léger (three batts.), 3rd Léger (one batt.), 7th Line (two batts.), 42nd Line (three batts.), 67th Line (one batt.)] 6,220

2nd Division, Chabran [2nd, 10th, 37th, 56th, 93rd Line, and 2nd Swiss (one batt. each)] 4,037

3rd Division, Chabot [Chasseurs des Montagnes (one batt.), 2nd Neapolitans (two batts.)] 1,633

4th Division, Reille [2nd Line (one batt.), 32nd Léger (one batt.), 113th Line (two batts.), 16th and 56th Line (one batt. each), Valais (one batt.)] 3,980

5th Division, Pino [Italian 1st and 2nd Léger, 4th and 6th Line (three batts. each), 7th Line (one batt.)] 8,008

6th Division, Lecchi [Italian 2nd, 4th, 5th Line, Velites (one batt. each), 1st Neapolitans (two batts.)] 3,941

German Division, Morio [2nd, 3rd, 4th, and 1st Light of West-phalia] 5,321

Cavalry, French [24th Dragoons, 3rd Provisional Cuirassiers, 3rd ditto Chasseurs] 1,730

,, Italian [Dragoons of Napoleon, Royal Chasseurs, Chasseurs of the Prince Royal, Neapolitan Chasseurs] . . 1,862

Artillery, French 2,050

,, Italian 585

,, German 48

Total 39,415

RESERVE CAVALRY.

1st Division of Dragoons, Latour-Maubourg:
   1st, 2nd, 4th, 9th, 14th, 26th Dragoons   2,527
2nd Division of Dragoons, Milhaud:
   12th, 16th, 20th, 21st Dragoons   2,125
3rd Division of Dragoons, Lahoussaye:
   17th, 18th, 19th, 27th Dragoons   1,335
4th Division of Dragoons, Lorges:
   13th, 15th, 22nd, 25th Dragoons.   .   .   .   .   .   1,228¡
5th Division of Dragoons, Millet:
   3rd, 6th, 10th, 11th Dragoons   1,470
Light-Cavalry Division of Lasalle:
   10th, 26th Chasseurs, 8th Dragoons ,   .   .   .   1,495
Artillery, batteries attached to the Cavalry Divisions: .   .   712

                                                   Total   10,892

RESERVE AT MADRID:

   Division Dessolles [12th Léger, 43rd, 51st, 55th Line (each
   three batts.), 8,507 ; Royal Guards, 2,200 ; 27th Chasseurs,
   500]   11,207

GARRISONS OF THE NORTH (Marshal BESSIÈRES):
   In Biscay, Alava, Guipuzcoa, Santander, Old Castile, and Leon   19,902

GRAND PARK OF ARTILLERY   2,579

GRAND TOTAL OF '*Présents sous les armes,*' 193,978.

At the same time there were Sick 56,404, Detached 36,326, Prisoners 1,843.

GROSS TOTAL of the whole army in Spain, 288,551.

IV

THE SPANISH ARMY AT MEDELLIN

    Cuesta's army at Medellin was composed of the following regiments.   It is, unfortunately, impossible to say how they were brigaded at the moment, as the only return available is that of April 4, when the original distribution of the army had been broken up, and the Andalusian division distributed among the other four.   The Estremaduran battalions were very strong, some few of them ranging up to 1,100 and even 1,400 bayonets, though others had but 500 or 700.

(1) Troops of Belvedere's old army of Estremadura :
    * Spanish Guards (4th batt.);   * Walloon Guards (4th batt.);   * 2nd
    of Majorca ;   * 2nd Light of Catalonia ;   † Provincial of Badajoz ;

†Provincial Grenadiers ; ‡Badajoz (two batts.) ; ‡Zafra; ‡Truxillo; ‡Merida; ‡Plasencia; ‡La Serena; ‡Leales de Ferdinando VII (two batts.) . . . Total. Fifteen batts.

(2) Troops of San Juan's old 'Army of Reserve of Madrid' :

Walloon Guards (2nd batt.) ; *Jaen (two batts.) ; *Irlanda (two batts.) ; †Provincial of Toledo ; †Provincial of Burgos ; ‡2nd Volunteers of Madrid ; ‡3rd of Seville . . Total. Nine batts.

(3) Troops under Albuquerque, from the Army of the Centre :

*Campo Mayor; †Provincial of Guadix; †Provincial of Cordova ; ‡Osuna (two batts.) ; ‡Granaderos del General ; ‡Tiradores de Cadiz . . . . Total. Seven batts.

N.B.—Of these troops, Plasencia, Zafra, Truxillo, and the 'Leales de Ferdinando VII' (two batts.) were in garrison at Badajoz and not present in the field.

The probable strength of the infantry engaged at Medellin was about 20,000 bayonets.

CAVALRY.

(1) Old troops of the Army of Estremadura :

*4th Hussars ('Volunteers of Spain') ; *1st Hussars of Estremadura [late Maria Luisa].

(2) Old troops of La Romana's army, from Denmark :

*Rey ; *Infante ; *Almanza.

(3) New Levies :

‡Cazadores de Llerena ; ‡Imperial de Toledo.

There was also present one regiment from Andalusia, which had joined with Albuquerque, apparently *Reyna.

Eight regiments in all, with an odd squadron of Carabineros Reales in addition. Effectives very low. Total about 3,000 or 3,200 sabres. Several regiments had a squadron detached in Andalusia, in search of remounts.

ARTILLERY.

Thirty guns, about 650 men ; Sappers, two companies, about 200 men. Total, about 24,000 men.

V

ORGANIZATION OF THE PORTUGUESE ARMY
IN 1809

The numbers are from the first complete return available, that of Sept. 15 in the Record Office

INFANTRY OF THE LINE.

N.B.—Each regiment consisted of two battalions of seven companies each, which should have numbered 770 officers and men, the regiment totalling 1,550, with staff.

	Strength.		*Strength.*
1st Regt. (1st of Lisbon or La Lippe) . . .	1,330	13th Regt. (Peniche) . .	1,361
		14th Regt. (Tavira) . .	1,239
2nd Regt. (Lagos or Algarve)	1,301	15th Regt. (2nd of Olivenza*)	577
3rd Regt. (1st of Olivenza *)	679	16th Regt. (Viera Telles) .	696
4th Regt. (Freire) . .	1,477	17th Regt. (2nd of Elvas) .	1,218
5th Regt. (1st of Elvas) .	759	18th Regt. (2nd of Oporto)	1,371
6th Regt. (1st of Oporto) .	1,082	19th Regt. (Cascaes) . .	1,519
7th Regt. (Setubal) . .	1,312	20th Regt. (Campomayor) .	1,218
8th Regt. (Evora) . .	369	21st Regt. (Valenza) . .	193
9th Regt. (Viana) . .	1,511	22nd Regt. (Serpa) . .	1,479
10th Regt. (2nd of Lisbon).	1,370	23rd Regt. (2nd of Almeida)	1,521
11th Regt. (1st of Almeida)	1,498	24th Regt. (Braganza) .	505
12th Regt. (Chaves) . .	1,491		
		Total	27,076

* Though named from Olivenza these regiments were actually raised in Northern Beira, with head quarters at Lamego, Olivenza having been ceded to Spain in 1801 at the treaty of Badajoz.

CAZADORES.

N.B.—These were single-battalion corps with a proper effective of 770 men.

	Strength.		*Strength.*
1st (Castello de Vide) . .	620	4th (Vizeu)	619
2nd (Moura). . . .	425	5th (Campomayor) . .	321
3rd (Villa Real) . . .	607	6th (Oporto) . . .	560
		Total	3,152

The 7th, 8th, and 9th Cazadores were formed later, out of the three battalions of the Lusitanian Legion. The 10th, 11th, and 12th were raised in the year 1811.

The brigading of the Portuguese regular infantry was practically permanent, very few changes having been made after 1810, when the greater part of the regiments were attached in pairs to the British divisions. The arrangement was as follows, 1811-14 :—

1st Brigade 1st (Lisbon) and 16th (Viera Telles) [attached to 1st Division].

2nd   ,,   2nd (Lagos) and 14th (Tavira).

3rd   ,,   3rd (1st of Olivenza) and 15th (2nd of Olivenza) [attached to 5th Division].

4th   ,,   4th (Freire) and 10th (2nd of Lisbon) [attached to 2nd Division].

5th   ,,   5th (1st of Elvas) and 17th (2nd of Elvas).

6th   ,,   6th (Oporto) and 18th (2nd of Oporto).

7th   ,,   7th (Setubal) and 19th (Cascaes) [attached to 7th Division].

8th   ,,   8th (Evora) and 12th (Chaves) [attached to 6th Division].

9th   ,,   9th (Viana) and 21st (Valenza) [attached to 3rd Division].

10th   ,,   11th (1st of Almeida) and 23rd (2nd of Almeida) [attached to 4th Division].

11th   ,,   13th (Peniche) and 24th (Braganza).

The 20th (Campomayor) and 22nd (Serpa) were never brigaded.

The 1st and 3rd Cazadores were attached to the Light Division.

The 2nd was attached to the 7th Portuguese Brigade, in the 7th Division.

The 4th was attached to the 1st Portuguese Brigade, in the 1st Division.

The 6th was attached to the 6th Portuguese Brigade.

CAVALRY.

N.B.—Each regiment should have had 594 men, in four strong squadrons.

	Strength.		*Strength.*
1st (Alcantara Dragoons) .	559	7th (Lisbon)	564
2nd (Moura)	400	8th (Elvas)	287
3rd (Olivenza) . . .	394	9th (Chaves)	572
4th (Duke of Mecklenburg,		10th (Santarem) . . .	475
Lisbon) . . .	559	11th (Almeida) . . .	482
5th (Evora)	581	12th (Miranda) . . .	589
6th (Braganza) . . .	578		
		Total	6,040

ARTILLERY.

Four regiments with head quarters respectively at (1) Lisbon, (2) Faro in Algarve, (3) Estremos in Alemtejo, (4) Oporto. The total strength was 4,472 officers and men.

There were also a few garrison companies, largely composed of invalids, which were mainly stationed in the forts round Lisbon. Their force is not given in Beresford's *General State* of the Regular Army.

THE LUSITANIAN LEGION.

This abnormal force, under Sir Robert Wilson, comprehended in 1809–10 three battalions of infantry, with an establishment of ten companies and 1,000 men each, one regiment of cavalry of three squadrons, which never seems to have been complete, and one battery of field artillery. Its total force was about 3,500 men. In 1811 the three battalions were taken into the regular army as the 7th, 8th, and 9th Cazadores.

ENGINEERS.

There were a few officers of the old army, who were engaged in raising new companies of sappers, which were not yet ready when Beresford's report was drawn up. No figures are there given.

It would appear then that the total Regular force of Portugal in 1809 amounted to about 33,000 foot, 6,300 horse, and 5,000 artillery.

MILITIA.

The Portuguese Militia was raised by conscription, on a local basis, the kingdom being divided into forty-eight regions, each of which was to supply a regiment. These districts were combined into three divisions, called the North, South, and Centre, each of which gave sixteen regiments. The unit was a two-battalion corps, with nominally 1,500 men in twelve companies : this number was in practice seldom reached. It was usual to keep the battalions under arms alternately, for periods of two, three, or six months : it was seldom that the whole regiment was embodied at once. In 1809 the whole force was but in process of organization, many corps had not even been officered or armed, and the majority had not commenced to raise their second battalion. The local distribution was as follows :—

1st Division : 'The South.' Comprising Algarve, Alemtejo, and Beira Alta.
Regiments of Lagos, Tavira, Beja, Evora, Villaviciosa, Portalegre, Castello Branco, Idanha, Vizeu, Guarda, Trancoso, Arouca, Tondella, Arganil, Covilhão, Lamego.

2nd Division : 'The Centre.' Comprising Estremadura and Beira Baixa.
Four Lisbon regiments, and one each from Torres Vedras, Santarem, Thomar, Leyria, Soure, Lousão, Alcazar do Sul, Setubal, Coimbra, Figueira, Aveiro, and Oliveira de Azemis.

3rd Division : 'The North.' Comprising Tras-os-Montes and Entre-Douro-e-Minho.
Regiments of Oporto, Villa de Conde, Braga, Viana, Barcellos, Guimaraens, Penafiel, Arcos, Feira, Barca, Baltar, Mayo, Chaves, Villa Real, Miranda and Braganza.

VI

THE INTRIGUES AT OPORTO

I. GENERAL RICARD'S CIRCULAR.

Le général Ricard, chef d'état-major du 2ᵉ corps d'armée en Espagne, à
M. le général de division Quesnel.

Oporto, le 19 avril 1809.

Mon général,

Son Excellence M. le maréchal duc de Dalmatie m'a chargé de vous écrire pour vous faire connaître les dispositions que la grande majorité des habitants de la province du Minho manifestent.

La ville de Braga, qui une des premières s'était portée à l'insurrection, a été aussi la première à se prononcer pour un changement de système, qui assurât à l'avenir le repos et la tranquillité des familles, et l'indépendance du Portugal. Le corrégidor que son Excellence avait nommé s'était retiré à Oporto lors du départ des troupes françaises, dans la crainte que les nombreux émissaires que Sylveira envoyait n'excitassent de nouveaux troubles, et n'attentassent à sa vie. Les habitants ont alors manifesté le vœu que ce digne magistrat leur fût renvoyé, et une députation de douze membres a été à cet effet envoyée près de Son Excellence. Pendant ce temps les émissaires de Sylveira étaient arrêtés et emprisonnés.

A Oporto, et à Barcelos, les habitants ont aussi manifesté les mêmes sentiments, et tous sentent la nécessité d'avoir un appui auquel les citoyens bien intentionnés puissent se rallier pour la défense et le salut de la patrie, et pour la conservation des propriétés. A ce sujet de nouvelles députations se sont présentées à Son Excellence, pour la supplier d'approuver que le peuple de la province du Minho manifestât authentiquement le vœu de déchéance du trône de la maison de Bragance, et qu'en même temps S. M. l'Empereur et roi fût suppliée de désigner un prince de sa maison, ou de son choix, pour régner en Portugal, mais qu'en attendant que l'Empereur ait pu faire connaître à ce sujet ses intentions, Son Excellence le duc de Dalmatie serait prié de prendre les rênes du gouvernement, de représenter le souverain, et de se revêtir de toutes les attributions de l'autorité suprême : le peuple promettant et jurant de lui être fidèle, de le soutenir et de le défendre aux dépens de la vie et de la fortune contre tout opposant, et envers même les insurgés des autres provinces, jusqu'à l'entière soumission du royaume.

Le maréchal a accueilli ces propositions, et il a autorisé les corrégidors des Comargues à faire assembler les Chambres, à y appeler des députés de tous les ordres, des corporations, et du peuple dans les campagnes, pour dresser l'acte qui doit être fait, et y apposer les signatures de l'universalité des citoyens. Il m'a ordonné de vous faire part de ces dispositions, pour que, dans l'arrondissement où vous commandez, vous en favorisiez l'exécution, et qu'ensuite vous en propagiez l'effet sur tous les points du royaume, où vous pourrez en faire parvenir la nouvelle.

M. le Maréchal ne s'est pas dissimulé qu'un évènement d'aussi grande importance étonnera beaucoup de monde et doit produire des impressions diverses ; mais il n'a pas cru devoir s'arrêter à ces considérations : son âme est trop pure pour qu'il puisse penser qu'on lui attribue aucun projet ambitieux. Dans tout ce qu'il fait il ne voit que la gloire des armes de Sa Majesté, le succès de l'expédition qui lui est confiée, et le bien-être d'une nation intéressante, qui, malgré ses égarements, est toujours digne de notre estime. Il se sent fort de l'affection de l'armée, et il brûle du désir de la présenter à l'Empereur, glorieuse et triomphante, ayant rempli l'engagement que Sa Majesté a elle-même pris, de planter l'aigle impériale sur les forts de Lisbonne, après une expédition aussi difficile que périlleuse, où tous les jours nous avons été dans la nécessité de vaincre.

Son Excellence ne s'est pas dissimulé non plus que depuis Burgos l'armée a eu des combats continuels à soutenir ; elle a réfléchi sur les moyens d'éviter à l'avenir les maux que cet état de guerre occasionne, et elle n'en a pas trouvé de plus propre que celui qui lui est offert par la grande majorité des habitants des principales villes du Minho, d'autant plus qu'elle a l'espoir de voir propager dans les autres provinces cet exemple, et qu'ainsi ce beau pays sera préservé de nouvelles calamités. Les intentions de Sa Majesté seront plus tôt et plus glorieusement remplie, et notre présence en Portugal, qui d'abord avait été un sujet d'effroi pour les habitants, y sera vue avec plaisir, en même temps qu'elle contribuera à neutraliser les efforts des ennemis de l'Empereur sur cette partie du continent.

La tâche que M. le Maréchal s'impose dans cette circonstance est immense, mais il a le courage de l'embrasser, et il croit la remplir même avec succès, si vous voulez bien l'aider dans son exécution. Il désire que vous propagiez les idées que je viens de vous communiquer, que vous fassiez protéger d'une manière particulière les autorités ou citoyens quelconques qui embrasseront le nouveau système, en mettant les uns et les autres dans le cas de se prononcer et d'agir à l'avenir en conséquence. Vous veillerez plus soigneusement que jamais à la conduite de votre troupe, l'empêcherez de commettre aucun dégât ou insulte qui pourrait irriter les habitants, et vous aurez la bonté, monsieur le général, d'instruire fréquemment Son Excellence de l'esprit des habitants et du résultat que vous aurez obtenu.

J'ai l'honneur de vous prier d'agréer l'hommage de mon respect et de mon sincère attachement.

Le général chef de l'état-major général
Signé : RICARD.

Pour copie conforme à l'original resté dans les mains du général de division Quesnel.

Paris, le 11 juillet 1809.

Le ministre de la guerre
Comte d'Hunebourg.

II. WELLESLEY'S ACCOUNT OF ARGENTON'S PLOT.

' To Viscount Castlereagh, Secretary of State.

' Villa Nova, 15th May, 1809.

' My Lord,

' In my secret dispatch, of the 27th ultimo, I apprised your Lordship that I had had certain communications with an Officer of the French army, in respect to the discontent which prevailed against Marshal Soult. I have since had further communications with the same Officer, with the details of which I proceed to acquaint your Lordship.

' Captain Argenton met me within the posts of the British army, between Coimbra and Aveiro on the night of the 6th instant, accompanied by Mons. Viana, in the presence of Lieut.-Colonel Bathurst. He informed me that the discontent had increased, and that there were a larger number of Officers who were determined to seize their General than when he had last seen me. He said, however, that they were divided into two parties, one discontented with Buonaparte himself, and determined to carry matters to extremities against him : the other, consisting of Loison, Laborde, and others (whom he had before mentioned as attached to the cause of the Emperor,) were dissatisfied with Soult's conduct, particularly with an intention which he was supposed to entertain to declare himself King of Portugal ; and that they were determined, if he should take that step, to seize him and to lead the army back into France, where it was understood the Emperor wished to see it.

' Captain Argenton then urged me again to lose no time in pressing upon Soult, as the mode most likely to induce the more violent of the two parties to endeavour to accomplish their purpose. But he said that if my attack was likely to be delayed, it was desirable that I should endeavour to prevail upon some of the towns over which I was supposed to have influence, such as Coimbra, Aveiro, &c., to follow the example of Oporto, and petition Soult to take upon himself the government of the kingdom, as King ; and that I even should write to him to urge the adoption of this measure.

' In answer to this, I told him, that I certainly should make my attack as soon as it was in my power, but that I could not fix any day, nor state to him the plan of my operations ; and that in respect to his propositions, regarding the measures to be adopted by me to induce Soult to declare himself King of Portugal, they were quite out of the question ; that I could not risk the loss of the confidence of the people of Portugal by doing what he desired in respect to the people of Coimbra, Aveiro, &c., nor my own character by writing the letter which he proposed I should. I told him at the same time that I considered that, notwithstanding all that had passed between him and me, I had a full right to take what steps I pleased, even if the Officers of the French army should seize their General.

' He then went away, and Mons. Viana returned with me to Coimbra, and confirmed all the statements which Captain Argenton had made of the discontent of the Officers of the army.

'I heard no more of Captain Argenton till the 13th, the day after the capture of Oporto, on which day the original orders for the arrest and secret detention of Captain Argenton, Colonel Lafitte of the 18th dragoons, and Colonel Donadieu of the 47th regiment of infantry, were found among some papers sent to me by the police of the town ; the order for the arrest of the first bearing date the 9th, and of the last two the 10th instant.

'In a few hours afterwards, on the same day, Captain Argenton came into Oporto, and informed me that, on the night of the day he had returned from his last interview with me, he had been arrested, and his papers had been seized, among which had been found the three passports which I had given him. He said that he attributed his arrest to the General of Division Lefevre, a man of weak intellect, to whom he had formerly been aide de camp, and on whom he had endeavored to prevail, as he thought successfully, to join the party. General Lefevre had, however, informed Soult of all the circumstances, requiring only his promise that Argenton should not be injured, and should retain his commission and his military pretensions.

'Soult examined him in presence of General Lefevre respecting his accomplices, but he declined to name any, and he was sent back to prison in charge of a Captain of Gendarmerie. This person prevailed upon him, with promises of pardon and indemnity to all concerned, to consent to tell Soult the names of his accomplices, which he did on the following night, notwithstanding, as he says himself, similar promises in his own favor, made to General Lefevre, had not been performed, and that as soon as he had named Colonels Lafitte and Donadieu, immediate orders were sent for their arrest and secret detention. They marched, in confinement, with the army from Oporto on the 12th, and on the 13th, at five o'clock in the morning, Captain Argenton made his escape, at the desire of Colonel Lafitte, from the party of Gendarmes in whose charge he was detained. He now declares that the conspiracy still exists, and that sooner or later it must burst forth and fall heavily upon the head of the usurper ; and he talked of the war in Spain as being odious to the army and to the whole nation.

'Captain Argenton expressed a desire to return secretly to France, and to bring to England his wife and family, she having, as he says, some property, to enable him to live in England till the arrival of better times in France.

'I told him that I would send him to England when an opportunity should offer to apply for permission to go to France ; and I shall have the honor of addressing him to your Lordship when the opportunity shall occur of sending him.

'I have the honor to be, &c.,

'ARTHUR WELLESLEY.

'VISCOUNT CASTLEREAGH.'

III. RÉSUMÉ DE L'AFFAIRE ARGENTON.

(This analysis of the documents in the French archives relating to the Oporto conspiracy has been placed at my disposal by the great kindness of Commandant Balagny.)

Le 8 mai 1809, dans la nuit, le capitaine Argenton était arrêté à Oporto par ordre du maréchal Soult. Son arrestation avait été provoquée par les déclarations que, dans cette même nuit du 8, le général Lefebvre et son aide de camp Favre étaient venus faire au maréchal. Argenton leur avait, disent-ils, fait à l'un et à l'autre, dans la journée du 8, des confidences sur l'objet de deux voyages successifs à Lisbonne et à Coïmbre, près des généraux anglais, et leur avait développé le plan d'une vaste conspiration militaire, dont les ramifications s'étendaient dans toutes les armées impériales et dans plusieurs départements de la France. Malgré la promesse formelle qu'ils avaient faite à Argenton de garder un secret absolu, après s'être concertés à Richuza, ils vinrent, dans la nuit, à Oporto, et, après avoir obtenu du maréchal une audience secrète (à 10 heures et demie du soir), lui dévoilèrent ce que leur avait confié Argenton. Aux termes de leurs déclarations, il aurait dit, à l'un et à l'autre séparément, qu'il était l'agent d'un comité, composé des généraux Laborde, Loison, Merle, Lorges, Lahoussaye, Debelle, et des colonels Donadieu, Mejean, Lafitte, Girardin, Corsin, et dont le but était de renverser l'Empereur pour mettre fin au régime de guerres continuelles et de perpétuelles conscriptions, que la France était lasse de supporter pour servir l'ambition de Napoléon. Pour réaliser ce projet, le comité devait par son intermédiaire passer une convention avec l'armée anglaise en Portugal. Aux termes de cette convention, l'armée française évacuerait le Portugal, suivie de l'armée anglaise, qui l'escorterait jusqu'aux Pyrénées, où cette dernière resterait en observation pour l'appuyer et pour déterminer les départements du Midi à se déclarer pour le nouvel état de choses. A la faveur de trois passeports, délivrés par les généraux anglais, trois officiers français [1], dont, lui, Argenton, devaient se rendre, l'un aux armées d'Espagne, l'autre à l'armée d'Autriche, un troisième en France, pour rallier à la cause de l'entreprise les mécontents de l'intérieur et des armées. L'Angleterre promettait d'appuyer de son argent le succès de l'entreprise, et Wellesley aurait promis à Argenton 60,000 fr. pour les débuts. Le général Moreau devait être ramené d'Amérique par un navire anglais, et prendre, sous un titre non encore désigné, la place de Napoléon déchu. Le maréchal Soult serait invité à se mettre à la tête du mouvement. Si le maréchal refusait, on devait s'emparer de sa personne, de façon à ce que son opposition ne nuisît en rien à la réussite de l'entreprise.

[1] Ces passe-ports devaient être délivrés aux noms supposés de *Dupont* et *Garis*, d'après les déclarations d'Argenton lui-même, du m^{al} Soult, du g^{al} Ricard, &c. L'un de ces passe-ports devait être utilisé par le cap^e Favre, aide de camp du g^{al} Lefebvre, qui voulait rentrer en France pour démissionner. L'autre devait servir à un officier supérieur *qu'Argenton ne nomme pas*, qui devait aller rendre compte de la situation à l'Empereur.

En présence de pareilles révélations, le maréchal Soult fit arrêter sur-le-champ et conduire chez lui le capitaine Argenton, qui, devant le général Lefebvre et Favre, refit, dans les mêmes termes, la narration du plan du Comité, insistant, paraît-il, à diverses reprises, pour tenter de décider le maréchal à entrer dans ses vues, en lui dépeignant, sous des couleurs séduisantes, la grandeur et la noblesse de l'entreprise, dont le but principal était de rendre à la France et à l'Europe entière une paix que tout le monde souhaitait ardemment, et que la folle ambition de l'Empereur rendait seule impossible. Mais ne pouvant obtenir du maréchal la promesse formelle qu'aucun des officiers dont il citerait les noms ne serait inquiété, il se refusa à désigner les membres du Comité qui l'avait fait agir. Plus tard, dans ses interrogatoires en France, il déclara que devant ce refus de sa part le maréchal s'emporta violemment, le menaça de le faire fusiller sur-le-champ, et qu'il ne dut son salut qu'à l'intervention généreuse du général Lefebvre, qui rappela durement au Duc de Dalmatie la promesse solennelle qu'il lui avait faite (à lui, Lefebvre), sur l'honneur, qu'Argenton ne serait point inquiété. Il fut réintégré dans sa prison, à son grand étonnement, dit-il. Furieux de se voir sous les verrous, malgré la promesse formelle que lui aurait faite le maréchal, prétend-il, il s'obstina d'abord dans un mutisme absolu, refusant, pendant toute la matinée du 9, de se prêter à aucun nouvel interrogatoire. Cependant, sur les instances réitérées et pressantes du lieutenant de gendarmerie Bernon, que le maréchal envoya, à plusieurs reprises, le voir dans sa prison, et sous la foi de la promesse solennelle que lui apporta ce dernier, de la part du Duc, que lui et tous les officiers compromis auraient l'honneur et la vie saufs, et qu'un voile épais serait jeté à jamais sur cette affaire, il se décida dans la soirée à écrire au maréchal qu'il consentait à lui faire des aveux complets. Mais se ravisant, il lui écrivit une deuxième lettre où il mettait comme condition à ses aveux qu'il n'y aurait *qu'un seul témoin* présent à ses déclarations, et qu'il désirait que ce témoin fût le général Lefebvre. Pour des raisons qui sont demeurées inconnues, le maréchal substitua, comme témoin, au général Lefebvre, le général Ricard et le lieutenant Bernon. Argenton accepta cependant de faire ses aveux et fut introduit à 10 heures du soir dans le salon du maréchal. Le lieutenant Bernon et le général Ricard firent, dès le 10 mai, une déclaration écrite des révélations faites devant eux au maréchal par Argenton dans l'entrevue du 9 mai. Leurs déclarations concordent entièrement avec celles du général Lefebvre et du capitaine Favre, et ce serait toujours le fameux projet de renversement de l'Empire qu'Argenton aurait indiqué comme but du Comité.

A la suite de ces aveux, Argenton est reconduit dans sa prison et le maréchal, faussant sa promesse, fait arrêter le colonel Lafitte, qui commandait le régiment où servait Argenton.

Mais cependant l'armée anglaise se portait en avant et, à la suite de circonstances demeurées bien obscures, le maréchal Soult était surpris dans Oporto et sur le point de ne pouvoir s'en échapper. Argenton, confié à la garde du lieutenant Bernon et d'un détachement d'infanterie, est emmené dans la retraite. Le second jour il s'évade subitement, dans des circonstances tellement romanesques que, malgré le rapport du lieutenant Bernon au Duc de Conégliano, on est quelque peu porté à croire que sa fuite fut facilitée par le commandement.

Le 14 mai, au soir, Argenton fugitif gagnait Oporto, et de là se rendait à Lisbonne d'où l'amiral anglais le faisait conduire à Londres sur un vaisseau anglais, avec des lettres de recommandation pour le ministre de la marine. Bien accueilli par ce dernier, qui lui proposa même, dit-il, de le pensionner, il séjourna quelque temps à Londres. Mais pris bientôt de la nostalgie du pays natal et dévoré du désir de venir rejoindre sa femme pour vivre en France ' ignoré dans quelque coin perdu,' il avise aux moyens de passer la Manche. Il fabrique un faux cartel d'échange au nom de ' Dessort,' sous la signature du général Ricard, chef d'état-major du maréchal Soult, et sur les recommandations de l'Amirauté anglaise il s'embarque à Deal et atterrit à Sangatte le 28 juin 1809. Malgré son faux nom, Argenton ne tarde pas en effet à être arrêté.

Dès son premier interrogatoire, il s'était décidé à reconnaître son identité et, avouant son faux de cartel d'échange, il abandonne le pseudonyme de ' Dessort' et redevient Argenton. Mais ici la scène change : se prêtant volontiers aux interrogatoires, il ne fait aucune difficulté pour expliquer ses voyages près des généraux anglais ; mais il leur donne un but tout autre et il assigne au Comité, dont il se dit toujours avoir été l'agent, des intentions totalement différentes de celles que, selon Lefebvre, Ricard, Favre, et Bernon, il aurait indiquées à Oporto. Il n'est plus question de conspiration contre l'Empereur, de projets de renversement dynastique. Bien au contraire, le Comité, entièrement dévoué à Napoléon et à sa cause, voulait lui ramener une armée dont le sort était gravement compromis par la maladresse du maréchal Soult, qui ne rêvait rien moins que de faire de cette armée la sienne propre, et de s'en servir pour la réalisation de ses projets ambitieux. Devant ses projets ouvertement affichés de se faire décerner la couronne de Portugal, un parti de mécontents s'était formé pour déjouer des vues et le mettre dans l'impossibilité de commettre le crime de lèse-majesté qu'il méditait. A la tête de ce parti, se trouvait, dit Argenton, un comité composé des généraux Laborde et Loison, des colonels Lafitte et St. Géniéz et d'un colonel aide-de-camp du général Loison. Le Comité devait, dès que le maréchal aurait mis en exécution son projet, nullement déguisé, de s'emparer de la couronne, se saisir de sa personne, et, à la suite d'une convention passée avec les généraux anglais, ramener en France l'armée restée fidèle à Napoléon, et sauvée par cette intervention d'une perte infaillible. Mais pour mener à bonne fin l'exécution de ce projet, il fallait obtenir des généraux anglais qu'ils consentissent à retarder leur attaque, qui était imminente, et se faire délivrer par eux des passe-ports pour les officiers qui devaient aller rendre compte à l'Empereur de ce qui se passait en Portugal. Argenton accepta la mission d'aller à l'armée anglaise soumettre les propositions du Comité. On l'adressa, dit-il, au nommé Viana, à qui il fut présenté par le colonel Donadieu qui logeait chez lui, et ce fut ce Viana qui lui servit de guide et d'escorte jusqu'à l'armée anglaise. Il se rendit à Lisbonne, où il obtint du général Wellesley trois passe-ports et la promesse d'une suspension d'armes de quelques jours. Revenu à Oporto, il y resta quatre jours chez Viana, qui lui remit, à destination du Comité, un dialogue intitulé ' Le Moineau et le Perroquet,' qui n'était, paraît-il, que le sommaire d'une longue conversation entre Viana et le maréchal, où ce dernier aurait développé ses projets ambitieux et exposé en détail la ligne de conduite qu'il comptait suivre. Porteur de ce document, il va rendre compte de sa mission au Comité. Le général Laborde étant malade, il rendit compte au colonel Lafitte et, le général Loison survenant à ce moment, il y eut chez Laborde une conférence entre ces deux généraux et Lafitte. Lui, Argenton, n'y assista pas ; mais à l'issue de cette conférence son colonel lui déclara qu'il fallait retourner près des Anglais, et lui fit tenir une lettre écrite par le général Loison au général Wellesley. Toujours accompagné de Viana, il partit d'Oporto le 1er mai, et se rendit à Coïmbre, où il eut, en présence de Viana, une conférence avec Wellesley et finit, après quelques difficultés, par obtenir une nouvelle suspension d'hostilités pendant quatre jours, à la condition que le Comité tiendrait le général anglais au courant des faits et gestes du Duc de Dalmatie. De retour à Oporto, le 8 mai, il était arrêté au moment où il s'apprêtait à partir pour se rendre près du Comité.—Telle est la thèse qu'Argenton ne cesse de soutenir avec la dernière énergie, depuis son retour en France jusque devant le peloton d'exécution qui va le fusiller. Il subit trois interrogatoires à Boulogne, trois autres au Ministère de la Police, quatre devant la Commission militaire chargée d'instruire sa cause. Toujours avec la même impassibilité et le calme le plus absolu, il répète la même chose, ne variant que sur quelques questions de détails. Quand on lui donne lecture des dépositions accablantes des généraux Lefebvre et Ricard, du capitaine Favre et du lieutenant Bernon, il leur oppose froidement les dénégations les plus formelles. Il est confronté avec les colonels Donadieu et Lafitte, qui, arrêtés par ordre du Ministre de la Guerre, prétendent n'avoir jamais eu connaissance de l'existence d'un comité dans l'armée, et n'avoir jamais servi d'intermédiaire entre Argenton et ce comité. Vis-à-vis d'eux, le capitaine garde toujours la même attitude. Lui seul dit la vérité, assure-t-il, et il s'étonne du peu de mémoire des colonels.

Traduit devant un conseil de guerre le 21 décembre 1809, le capitaine Argenton se retranche toujours derrière les mêmes moyens de défense et produit les mêmes arguments. Il a agi par ordre (verbal, il est vrai), et il a cru servir à la fois les intérêts de l'armée qu'il a sauvée et ceux de l'Empereur. Malgré une plaidoirie très éloquente et très habile de son défenseur Falconnet, qui, pour défendre son client, n'épargne pas le duc de Dalmatie, Argenton est condamné à mort. Jusqu'à la dernière heure, il proteste de la pureté de ses intentions, et maintient qu'il a toujours dit la vérité et qu'il est victime de l'égoïsme de ceux qui l'ont fait agir. Avec une calme résignation, il commande lui-même son peloton d'exécution et tombe sous les balles avec ce courage romanesque qui caractérisait en lui l'homme extraordinaire qui, à Tarvis, fit *seul* toute une compagnie prisonnière.

VII

MORNING STATE OF THE BRITISH FORCES IN PORTUGAL,

UNDER SIR ARTHUR WELLESLEY, K.B.

HEAD QUARTERS, COIMBRA, MAY 6, 1809.

		Sergeants, Drummers, Rank and File, &c.				Total Efficients Present, Officers and Men.
	Officers.	Present.	Sick.	On Command.	Total.	
CAVALRY.						
1st Brigade [Stapleton Cotton]						
14th Light Dragoons . .	27	628	21	73	749	655
16th ,, ,, . . .	37	673	20	35	765	710
20th ,, ,, [two squadrons]	6	237	6	63	312	243
3rd Light Dragoons K.G.L. [one squadron] . . .	3	57	2	77	139	60 ——1,668
2nd Brigade [Fane]						
3rd Dragoon Guards . .	25	698	10	—	733	723
4th Dragoons	27	716	13	—	756	743 ——1,466
Total Cavalry	125	3,009	72	248	3,454	3,134
INFANTRY.						
Brigade of Guards [H. Campbell]						
Coldstream Guards, 1st batt.	33	1,194	75	3	1,305	1,227
3rd Foot Guards, 1st batt.	34	1,228	79	8	1,349	1,262
1 company 5/60th Foot .	2	61	4	—	67	63 ——2,552
1st Brigade [Hill]						
3rd Foot, 1st batt. . .	28	719	104	50	901	747
48th ,, 2nd ,, . .	32	721	52	—	805	753
66th ,, 2nd ,, . .	34	667	38	10	749	701
1 company 5/60th Foot .	2	61	4	—	67	63 ——2,264
2nd Brigade [Mackenzie]						
27th Foot, 3rd batt. . .	28	726	134	2	890	754
31st ,, 2nd ,, . .	27	765	99	6	897	792
45th ,, 1st ,, . .	22	671	125	27	845	693 ——2,239

	Offi-cers.	Sergeants, Drummers, Rank and File, &c.				Total.	Total Efficients Present, Officers and Men.
		Pre-sent.	Sick.	On Com-mand.			
3rd Brigade [Tilson]							
5/60th Foot [5 companies]	14	306	32	2		354	320
87th ,, 2nd batt. .	32	669	88	1		790	701
88th ,, 1st batt. .	30	608	143	28		809	638
1st Portuguese, 1st batt.	—	—	—	—		—	—
							——1,659
4th Brigade [Sontag]							
97th Foot	22	572	74	20		688	594
2nd batt. of Detachments	35	787	221	16		1,059	822
1 company 5/60th Foot .	2	61	6	—		69	63
16th Portuguese, 2nd batt.	—	—	—	—		—	—
							——1,479
5th Brigade [A. Campbell]							
7th Foot, 2nd batt. . .	26	559	50	3		638	585
53rd ,, ,, . .	23	691	59	3		776	714
1 company 5/60th Foot .	4	64	11	1		80	68
10th Portuguese, 1st batt.	—	—	—	—		—	—
							——1,367
6th Brigade [R. Stewart]							
29th Foot	26	596	85	7		714	622
1st batt. of Detachments	27	803	169	24		1,023	830
16th Portuguese, 1st batt.	—	—	—	—		—	—
							——1,452
7th Brigade [Cameron]							
9th Foot, 2nd batt. . .	27	545	227	22		821	572
83rd ,, ,, . .	39	833	73	23		968	872
1 company 5/60th Foot .	2	60	3	1		66	62
10th Portuguese, 2nd batt.	—	—	—	—		—	—
							——1,506
King's German Legion Brigade [Murray]							
1st Line batt. K.G.L. .	34	767	125	9		935	801
2nd ,, ,, ,, . .	32	804	52	9		897	836
5th ,, ,, ,, . .	28	720	101	12		861	748
7th ,, ,, ,, . .	22	688	83	10		803	710
							——3,095
Unattached Troops (Lisbon)							
24th Foot, 2nd batt. . .	18	750	26	3		797	768
30th ,, ,, ,, . .	15	447	49	197		708	462
Independent Light Co. K.G.L.	3	35	14	4		56	38
							——1,268
Total Infantry	703	18,178	2,405	501		21,787	18,881

	Offi- cers.	Sergeants, Drum- mers, Rank and File, &c.			Total.	Total Effi- cients Pre- sent, Officers and Men.
		Pre- sent.	Sick.	On Com- mand.		
ARTILLERY						
British	31	550	83	499	1,163	581
King's German Legion .	18	331	34	134	517	349
Wagon Train attached .	3	61	18	83	165	64
Total Artillery	52	942	135	716	1,845	994
ENGINEERS.	12	27	1	—	40	39
WAGON TRAIN . . .	2	65	21	17	105	67

General Total 894 22,221 2,634 1,482 27,231 23,115

VIII
SOULT'S REPORT ON GALICIA,
JUNE 25, 1809.

N.B.—The first half of this report, a lengthy narrative of the Marshal's march from Lugo to Puebla de Senabria, is omitted.

. . . .

Je me permettrai, avant de terminer ce rapport, de présenter à Votre Majesté quelques observations sur la situation actuelle de Galice. Cette province est toujours en état de fermentation. Les menaces de mort et d'incendie qu'employe La Romana ; les nombreux agents qui agissent en son nom ; les exécutions qu'il fait ; les dévastations qui ont inévitablement lieu par les fréquents mouvements des troupes ; la ruine de la plupart des habitants ; l'absence de toute autorité qui représente Votre Majesté ; l'influence des prêtres, qui sont très-nombreux, et la grande majorité opposante ; l'argent que les Anglais répandent ; la détresse des généraux français, qui, faute des moyens, ne peuvent souvent payer les émissaires qu'ils employent : toutes ces causes contribuent à augmenter de jour en jour le nombre des ennemis, et à rendre la guerre qu'on fait dans ce pays très-meurtrière, infiniment désagréable, et d'un résultat fort éloigné. On s'y battra encore longtemps avant que Votre Majesté en retire quelque avantage, à moins qu'elle n'adopte le système de faire fortifier sept à huit postes importants, susceptibles de contenir chacun 5,000 à 6,000 hommes de garnison, un hôpital, et des vivres pour quatre mois, pour maintenir la population, fermer et garder les principaux débouchés dont l'ennemi ne pourrait plus profiter, et aussi pour offrir aux colonnes qui agiraient dans la province des appuis, quelque direction qu'elles suivissent. Ainsi elles pourraient recevoir des secours et déposer leurs malades. Cette dernière considération est très-puissante, et je ne dois pas dissimuler à Votre Majesté qu'elle fait beaucoup sur le moral des soldats, qui, dans l'état actuel des choses, sont exposés à périr de misère, ou sous les coups des paysans, s'ils ont le malheur d'être blessés, ou atteints de la fièvre, et de se trouver éloignés d'un lieu sûr pour y chercher des secours.

Je crois qu'avec une dépense d'un million on parviendrait à mettre en état de défense la Galice, et certes jamais argent n'aurait été mieux employé, d'autant plus que par la suite on pourrait diminuer le nombre des troupes qui pour le moment y sont nécessaires ; dans cette persuasion j'ai engagé M. le Maréchal Ney à faire fortifier Lugo, et à ordonner la construction de trois blocus sur la ligne de Villa Franca ; les places de Tuy, de Monterey, de Viana et de Puebla de Sanabria, qui toutes peuvent contenir des canons, ont une enceinte et un reste de fortification, pourraient aisément être rétablies et rempliraient parfaitement cet objet ; et, s'il le fallait, il est encore d'autres postes qui par leur situation seraient à même de concourir à la défense, sans que les frais fussent considérablement augmentés.   Si cette mesure, que je considère comme urgente et d'un résultat assuré, n'est point adoptée, il deviendra nécessaire que des renforts soient envoyés à M. le Maréchal Ney, ne fusse que pour remplacer ses pertes et maintenir libres les communications, quoique aujourd'hui il puisse être assez fort pour tenir tête au corps de La Romana et de Carrera réunis, s'ils se présentaient en ligne.   Mais leur système étant d'harceler sans cesse et d'éviter une affaire générale, avec le temps ils auraient l'avance la plus forte, et ils finiraient, même sans combattre, par le détruire s'il n'était soutenu, et on ferait une perte d'hommes incalculable sans obtenir le résultat qu'on se propose.

Il est probable que je ne serai plus dans le cas d'entretenir Votre Majesté au sujet de la Galice ; ainsi, pour cette dernière fois, j'ai cru de mon devoir de lui rendre compte des observations que mon séjour dans cette partie de ses états et la connaissance que j'ai acquise du caractère de ses habitants m'ont mis à même de faire.   J'ai donc l'honneur de supplier Votre Majesté de daigner excuser cette digression en faveur et en considération des motifs qui l'ont dictée.

J'ai l'honneur d'être, &c.,

MARÉCHAL DUC DE DALMATIE.

Puebla de Senabria, 25 juin 1809.

IX A

SUCHET'S ARMY OF ARAGON [3RD CORPS],

MAY 15, 1809.

Total *présents sous les armes.*

1st Division, General LAVAL :
    14th Line (two batts.), 1,080; 44th Line (two batts.), 1,069;
    2nd of the Vistula (two batts.), 880 ; 3rd ditto, 964 .   .   3,993

2nd Division, General Musnier :

114th Line (three batts.),1,627; 115th Line (three batts.),1,732; 1st of the Vistula (two batts.), 1,039 4,398

3rd Division, General Morlot :

116th and 117th Line (each three batts.), *absent in Castile* ; 121st Line,*three batts. absent in Navarre,* one present in Aragon, 400 ; 5th Léger (one batt.), 490 890

Troops detached from 5th Corps :

64th Line (one batt.), one voltigeur company of 40th Line . 450

Cavalry Brigade, General Wathier :

4th Hussars, 326 ; 13th Cuirassiers, 390 ; Polish Lancers (one squadron), 80 796

Artillery. 450

General Total . 10,977

N.B.—Of the nine absent battalions the 116th and 117th with a strength of somewhat over 3,000 men rejoined Suchet on the day of Maria (June 15), thus raising this available force to about 13,000 men. The 121st never came up from Navarre.

IX b

BLAKE'S ARMY OF ARAGON,

JUNE 15, 1809.

Total present under arms at Maria.

Vanguard Brigade, Colonel J. Creagh :

Almeria (two batts.), Cazadores de Valencia (one batt.) . . 2,298

1st Division, Major-General P. Roca :

1st of Savoia (three batts.), Granada (one batt.), Avila Militia, Tiradores de Cariñena (one batt.), Tercio of Tortosa . . 4,888

2nd Division, Lieut.-General Marquis of Lazan :

1st Volunteers of Saragossa (one batt.), 3rd Cazadores de Valencia (one batt.), 1st of Valencia (three batts.), America (two batts.). 5,837

Cavalry Brigade, Colonel J. O'Donnell :

Olivenza (four squadrons), Santiago (one squadron) . . 698

Artillery (seventeen guns) 200

Sappers (three companies) 309

Total present . 14,230

3rd Division, Lieut.-General C. Areizaga (absent at Botorrita) :

Fernando 7th (one batt.), Grenadiers (four companies), 1st Volunteers of Aragon (one batt.), 2nd ditto (one batt.), Volunteers of Valencia (one batt.), Cazadores de Palafox (one batt.), Daroca (one batt.), Tiradores de Doyle (one batt.), Tiradores de Murcia (one batt.) 5,842

Cavalry : Husares Españoles, Santiago (one squadron each) . 368

Artillery (eight guns). 120

Sappers 103

Total absent at Botorrita . 6,433

X

APPENDICES RELATING TO THE TALAVERA CAMPAIGN

1

THE BRITISH FORCE AT TALAVERA

FROM THE MORNING STATE OF JULY 25, 1809

Present and fit for Duty.

CAVALRY DIVISION (Lieut.-Gen. PAYNE).

Fane's Brigade :			Anson's Brigade :		
3rd Dragoon Guards . .	525		23rd Light Dragoons . .	459	
4th Dragoons	545		1st ,, ,, K.G.L.	451	
Cotton's Brigade :					
14th Light Dragoons . .	464				
16th ,, ,, . .	525		Total Cavalry	2,969	

INFANTRY.

1st (SHERBROOKE'S) DIVISION.

H. Campbell's Brigade :		Langwerth's Brigade :	
1st batt. Coldstream		1st Line batt. K.G.L. .	604
Guards	970	2nd ,, ,, ,, .	678
1st batt. 3rd Guards . .	1,019	Light Companies K.G.L.	106
One company 5/60th Foot	56		
	2,045		1,388
Cameron's Brigade :		Low's Brigade :	
1/61st Foot	778	5th Line batt. K.G.L. .	610
2/83rd ,, ...	535	7th ,, ,, ,, .	557
One company 5/60th Foot	51		
	1,364		1,167
		Total of the 1st Division	5,964

2nd (HILL'S) DIVISION.

Tilson's Brigade :		R. Stewart's Brigade :	
1/3rd Foot	746	29th Foot	598
2/48th Foot	567	1/48th Foot	807
2/66th ,, ...	526	1st batt. of Detachments	609
One company 5/60th . .	52		
	1,891		2,014
		Total of the 2nd Division	3,905

3rd (MACKENZIE's) DIVISION.

Mackenzie's Brigade :		Donkin's Brigade :	
2/24th Foot	787	2/87th	599
2/31st ,, ...	733	1/88th	599
1/45th ,, ...	756	Five companies 5/60th .	273
	2,276		1,471

Total of the 3rd Division   3,747

4th (CAMPBELL's) DIVISION.

A. Campbell's Brigade :		Kemmis's Brigade :	
2/7th Foot	431	1/40th Foot	745
2/53rd Foot	537	97th ,, ...	502
One company 5/60th . .	64	2nd batt. of Detachments	625
		One company 5/60th Foot	56
	1,032		1,928

Total of the 4th Division   2,960

ARTILLERY.

British :		German :	
Three batteries, Lawson, Sillery, Elliot	681	Two batteries, Rettberg and Heyse	330

Total of Artillery   1,011

ENGINEERS, 22.   STAFF CORPS, 63.

Total Present   20,641

The Army had also sick left in Portugal, about 3,246 : sick at Plasencia and Talavera about 1,149 : on detachment in Portugal about 1,396 : on detachment in Spain about 107.   Total absent or non-effective 5,898. The newly arrived regiments at Lisbon, and the troops on their way to the front under R. Craufurd are, of course, left out of this return.

2

THE ARMY OF ESTREMADURA AT TALAVERA

[From an unpublished document in the Deposito de la Guerra, Madrid.]

General-in-Chief, Lieut.-Gen. Gregorio de la Cuesta.
Second in Command, Lieut.-Gen. Francisco de Eguia.
Major-General of Infantry, Major-Gen. J. M. de Alos.
,, , ,, of Cavalry, Major-Gen. R. de Villalba, Marques de Malaspina.
Officer Commanding Artillery, Brigadier-Gen. G. Rodriguez.
,, ,, Engineers, Brigadier-Gen. M. Zappino.

INFANTRY.

Vanguard—Brigadier-Gen. José Zayas :
  2nd Voluntarios of Catalonia, Cazadores de Barbastro (2nd batt.),
    Cazadores de Campo-Mayor, Cazadores de Valencia y Albu-
    querque, Cazadores Voluntarios de Valencia (2nd batt.)   five batts.

1st Division—Major-General Marques de Zayas :
  Cantabria (three batts.), Granaderos Provinciales, Canarias,
    Tiradores de Merida, Provincial de Truxillo . . seven batts.

2nd Division—Major-General Vincente Iglesias :
  2nd of Majorca, Velez-Malaga (three batts.), Osuna (two batts.),
    Voluntarios Estrangeros, Provincial de Burgos . . eight batts.

3rd Division—Major-General Marques de Portago :
  Badajoz (two batts.), 2nd of Antequera, Imperial de Toledo, Pro-
    vincial de Badajoz, Provincial de Guadix . . . six batts.

4th Division—Major-General R. Manglano :
  Irlanda (two batts.), Jaen (two batts.), 3rd of Seville, Leales de
    Fernando VII (1st batt.), 2nd Voluntarios de Madrid, Volun-
    tarios de la Corona . . . . eight batts.

5th Division—Major-General L. A. Bassecourt :
  Real Marina, 1st Regiment (two batts.), Africa (3rd batt.), Murcia
    (two batts.), Reyna (1st batt.), Provincial de Sigüenza   seven batts.

CAVALRY.

1st Division, Lieut.-General J. de Henestrosa :
  Rey, Calatrava, Voluntarios de España, Imperial de Toledo, Caza-
    dores de Sevilla, Reyna, Villaviciosa, Cazadores de Madrid.

2nd Division, Lieut.-Gen. Duque de Albuquerque :
  Carabineros Reales (one squadron), Infante, Alcantara, Pavia,
    Almanza, 1st and 2nd Hussars of Estremadura.

Totals, inclusive of sick, and troops on detachment :
  35,000 Infantry, 7,000 Cavalry, 30 guns.

It is most unfortunate that no regimental or divisional totals are given,
but only the gross total of the whole army.

N.B.—There were *at least* four battalions detached, viz. Merida and
3rd of Seville, with Sir R. Wilson, and two others (names not to be
ascertained, Cuesta does not give them) under Del Reino at the Puerto
de Baños. Another was apparently dropped at Almaraz to guard the
bridge. Allowing 3,000 for these troops, and 5,000 for sick and men
' on command,' the Army of Estremadura marched to Talavera with about
28,000 foot, more than 6,000 horse, and 800 artillery.

The following troops which had all been with the Army of Estremadura
in April are not named in the above return. Most of them were in garrison
at Badajoz, but some were in the Northern Passes—Spanish Guards (one
batt.), Walloon Guards (one batt.), Zafra, Plasencia, La Serena, Leales
de Fernando VII (2nd batt.), Provincial de Cordova, Tiradores de Cadiz.

3

STRENGTH OF THE FRENCH ARMY AT TALAVERA

(Figures of July 15, excluding sick and men detached.)

	Strength.
1st Corps, Marshal Victor :	
État-Major	47
1st Division (Ruffin), 9th Léger, 24th and 96th of the Line, three batts. each	5,286
2nd Division (Lapisse), 16th Léger, 8th, 45th, 54th of the Line, three batts. each	6,862
3rd Division (Villatte), 27th Léger, 63rd, 94th, 95th of the Line, three batts. each	6,135
Corps-Cavalry (Beaumont), 2nd Hussars, 5th Chasseurs .	980
	19,310
4th Corps, General Sebastiani :	
État-Major	13
1st Division (Sebastiani), 28th, 32nd, 58th, 75th of the Line, three batts. each	8,118
2nd Division (Valence), one regiment only, 4th Polish, two batts.	1,600
3rd Division (Leval), Nassau, Baden, Hesse-Darmstadt, Holland, two batts. each : Frankfort, one batt. . .	4,537
Merlin's Light Cavalry, 10th and 26th Chasseurs, Polish Lancers, Westphalian *Chevaux-Légers*	1,188
	15,456
Reserve Cavalry :	
1st Dragoon Division (Latour-Maubourg), 1st, 2nd, 4th, 9th, 14th, 26th Dragoons	3,279
2nd Dragoon Division (Milhaud), 5th, 12th, 16th, 20th, 21st Dragoons, and 3rd Dutch Hussars	2,356
	5,635
From Madrid :	
One Brigade of Dessolles' Division, 12th Léger, 51st Line, three batts. each	3,337
King's Guards, infantry	1,800
„ „ cavalry	350
27th Chasseurs (two squadrons)	250
	5,737

The artillerymen are included in the divisional totals.

	Total	46,138

TALAVERA.—BRITISH LOSSES ON JULY 27

(1) In the Combat of Casa de Salinas.

Regiments.	Killed.		Wounded.		Missing.		Total.
	Officers.	Men.	Officers.	Men.	Officers.	Men.	
Cavalry :							
14th Light Dragoons . . .	—	—	—	1	—	—	1
1st ,, ,, K.G.L.	—	2	1	1	—	—	4
3rd Division							
Mackenzie's Brigade :							
2/24th Foot	—	1	1	6	—	1	9
2/31st ,, ...	1	23	5	88	—	2	119
1/45th ,, ...	—	4	1	13	—	7	25
Donkin's Brigade :							
5/60th Foot	—	3	1	4	—	19	27
2/87th ,, ...	1	26	10	127	—	34	198
1/88th ,, ...	2	7	—	25	—	30	64
Total	4	66	19	265	—	93	447

(2) In the Combat in front of Talavera at 9 p.m.

Regiments.	Killed.		Wounded.		Missing.		Total.
	Officers.	Men.	Officers.	Men.	Officers.	Men.	
Staff	1	—	—	—	—	—	1
1st Division							
H. Campbell's Brigade :							
1st Coldstream Guards .	1	—	—	2	—	—	3
Cameron's Brigade :							
1/61st Foot	—	3	1	3	—	—	7
Langwerth's Brigade :							
1st Line batt. K.G.L. . .	—	2	—	7	—	—	9
2nd ,, ,, ,, . .	—	—	—	3	—	—	3
Light Companies, K.G.L.	—	4	2	25	—	5	36
Low's Brigade :							
5th Line batt. K.G.L. .	—	6	—	34	—	11	41
7th ,, ,, ,, .	—	19	1	49	—	77	146
2nd Division							
Tilson's Brigade :							
2/48th Foot	—	—	—	3	—	—	3
R. Stewart's Brigade :							
29th Foot	—	10	1	43	—	1	55
1/48th Foot	—	—	—	8	—	—	8
1st batt. Detachments .	1	14	—	40	2 [1]	13	70
Artillery	—	—	—	2	—	—	2
Engineers	—	—	1	—	—	—	1
Total	3	58	6	219	2	107	385

[1] The official report gives *three* missing officers here. But one of them was not a prisoner but turned up at Oropesa next morning, nominally sick. For this distressing story, see Leslie, pp. 155–6.

5

BRITISH LOSSES AT TALAVERA

SECOND DAY. JULY 28, 1809.

Regiments.	Killed. Offi-cers.	Men.	Wounded. Offi-cers.	Men.	Missing. Offi-cers.	Men.	Total.
Staff	4	—	9	—	—	—	13
CAVALRY.							
Fane's Brigade :							
3rd Dragoon Guards .	—	—	1	1	—	1	3
4th Dragoons . . .	—	3	—	9	—	—	12
							15
Cotton's Brigade :							
14th Light Dragoons .	—	3	6	6	—	—	15
16th ,, ,, .	—	6	1	5	—	2	14
							29
Anson's Brigade :							
1st Light Dragoons K. G. L.	—	1	2	32	—	2	37
23rd Light Dragoons .	2	47	4	46	3	105	207
							244
INFANTRY.							
1st Division (General Sherbrooke) :							
H. Campbell's Brigade :							
1st Coldstream Guards	1	33	8	251	—	—	293
1st 3rd Guards . . .	5	49	6	261	—	1	322
							615
Cameron's Brigade :							
1/61st Foot	3	43	10	193	—	16	265
2/83rd ,, . . .	4	38	11	202	—	28	283
							548
Langwerth's Brigade :							
1st Line batt. K. G. L.	2	37	10	241	—	1	291
2nd ,, ,, ,, .	—	61	14	288	—	24	387
Light Companies, K. G. L.	—	6	—	37	—	—	43
							721
Low's Brigade :							
5th Line batt. K. G. L.	3	27	6	118	—	101	255
7th ,, ,, ,, .	—	17	4	35	—	54	110
							365
2nd Division (General Hill) :							
Tilson's Brigade :							
1/3rd Foot	—	26	2	107	—	7	142
2/48th ,, ...	—	12	2	53	1	—	68
2/66th ,, ...	—	16	11	88	—	11	126
							336

Regiments.	Killed. Offi-cers.	Men.	Wounded. Offi-cers.	Men.	Missing. Offi-cers.	Men.	Total.
R. Stewart's Brigade :							
29th Foot	—	26	6	98	—	2	132
1st batt. Detachments	—	26	9	166	—	2	203
1/48th Foot . . .	—	22	10	135	—	1	168
							— 503
3rd Division (General Mackenzie):							
Mackenzie's Brigade:							
2/24th Foot . . .	—	44	10	268	—	21	343
2/31st ,, . . .	—	21	3	102	—	5	131
1/45th ,, . . .	—	9	2	134	1	12	158
							— 632
Donkin's Brigade:							
5/60th Foot . . .	—	7	6	25	—	12	50[1]
2/87th ,, . . .	—	9	3	43	—	5	60
1/88th ,, . . .	1	12	3	69	—	—	85
							— 195
4th Division (General A. Campbell):							
Campbell's Brigade:							
2/7th Foot	1	6	3	54	—	1	65
2/53rd ,, ...	—	6	2	30	—	1	39
							— 104
Kemmis's Brigade:							
1/40th Foot . . .	—	7	1	49	—	1	58
97th ,, . . .	—	6	—	25	1	21	53
2nd batt. Detachments	—	7	—	13	—	1	21
							— 132
ARTILLERY.							
British	1	7	3	21	—	—	32
German	—	3	—	30	—	1	34
ENGINEERS . . .	—	—	1	—	—	—	1
STAFF CORPS . . .	—	—	2	—	—	—	2
Total	27	643	171	3,235	6	439	4,521

Total of the two days:—killed: 34 officers, 767 men ; wounded: 196 officers, 3,719 men ; missing : 8 officers, 639 men.   Grand Total, 5,363.

[1] Many of the casualties of the 5/60th were in the companies detached from the head quarters of the regiment, and not serving in Donkin's brigade. It is unfortunately impossible to distinguish them, as all the regimental losses are given *en bloc* in the return.

6

TALAVERA.—THE FRENCH LOSSES

N.B.—I owe these figures to the kindness of Commandant Balagny, who has caused them to be copied in detail from the French Archives.

Regiments.	Killed.		Wounded.		Prisoners.		Total.
	Offi-cers.	Men.	Offi-cers.	Men.	Offi-cers.	Men.	
1st Corps (Marshal Victor):							
État-Major Général .	—	—	1	—	—	—	1
1st Division (Ruffin):							
9th Léger	3	35	14	340	—	65	457
24th Line . . .	1	92	17	456	1	—	567
96th Line	3	36	19	548	—	—	606
État-Major	—	—	2	—	—	—	2
							—1,632
2nd Division (Lapisse):							
16th Léger	8	49	8	342	—	—	407
8th Line	3	41	17	376	—	—	437
45th Line . . .	3	43	12	328	—	2	388
54th Line	2	54	14	462	—	—	532
État-Major	—	—	3	—	—	—	3
							—1,767
3rd Division (Villatte):							
27th Léger	1	25	4	159	—	—	189
63rd Line	—	2	2	36	—	—	40
94th Line . . .	1	20	1	123	—	—	145
95th Line	—	—	—	27	—	—	27
							— 401
Corps-Cavalry (Beaumont):							
2nd Hussars . . .	—	3	2	11	—	—	16
5th Chasseurs . . .	—	1	3	19	—	—	23
							— 39
Artillery and Engineers	1	9	1	53	—	—	64
Total of 1st Corps. .	26	410	120	3,280	1	67	3,904
4th Corps (General Sebastiani):							
1st Division (Sebastiani): 28th, 32nd, 58th, 75th Line . . .	13	187	67	1,852	—	61	2,180
2nd Division (Leval): Baden, Hesse, Nassau, Holland, Frankfort	6	97	24	803	—	77	1,007
3rd Division (Valence): 4th Polish Regiment .	—	3	—	37	—	—	40
Total of 4th Corps .	19	287	91	2,692	—	138	3,227

Regiments.	Killed.		Wounded.		Prisoners.		Total.
	Officers.	Men.	Officers.	Men.	Officers.	Men.	
CAVALRY DIVISIONS—							
1st DIVISION of Dragoons (Latour-Maubourg): 1st, 2nd, 4th, 9th, 14th, 26th Dragoons	—	13	9	61	—	—	83
2nd DIVISION of Dragoons (Milhaud): 5th, 12th, 16th, 20th, 21st Dragoons . .	—	—	—	3	—	—	3
Milhaud's Artillery .	—	—	—	3	—	—	3
Merlin's Light Cavalry DIVISION: 10th, 26th Chasseurs, Polish Lancers, Westphalian Chevaux-Légers	—	6	—	42	—	—	48
Total of Cavalry Divisions	—	19	9	109	—	—	137

GENERAL TOTALS :—45 officers, 716 rank and file *killed* ;
220 officers, 6,081 rank and file *wounded* ;
1 officer, 205 rank and file *missing* = 7,268.

NOTE.—No distinction is made in the French returns between losses on July 27 and July 28, which cannot therefore be ascertained separately.

These 'Missing' do not include the French wounded who were left within the British lines on the night of July 28, and became prisoners, but were freed again on Aug. 6 when Victor reoccupied Talavera and captured the British hospitals. They must have been numerous in the divisions of Ruffin, Lapisse, and Sebastiani. The French returns are those made up for the Emperor's use, some weeks after the battle—those of the 4th Corps as late as Sept. 19. The men in question therefore appear as 'wounded,' but not as 'prisoners.'

XI

THE ROYAL ARTILLERY IN THE PENINSULA IN 1809

N.B.—I owe this Appendix to Colonel F. A. Whinyates, R.A., who has been good enough to compile it for the volume.

STAFF.

Brigadier-General E. HOWORTH arrived at Lisbon in April 1809, and took over the command of the R.A. from Lieut.-Colonel W. Robe.

Brigade-Major R.A., Captain A. Dickson until appointed to the Portuguese Artillery in June, when Captain J. May took over that position.

FIELD-OFFICERS IN PORTUGAL.

Lieut.-Col. H. Framingham, Lieut.-Col. W. Robe, Lieut.-Col. G. B. Fisher, Major Julius von Hartmann, K.G.L.

Troops R.H.A. and Companies R.A. in Portugal in 1809 :—
(a) Horse Artillery :   *Strength.*
    1. Captain H. Ross's 'A' Troop, landed at Lisbon, July 2,
       or 3, 1809 162
    2. Captain R. Bull's 'I' Troop, landed at Lisbon,
       August 21, 1809 162
(b) Foot Artillery :
    3. Captain C. D. Sillery's[1] No. 6 company, 7th batt.,
       landed at Lisbon, March 7, 1809 120
    4. Captain A. Bredin's No. 1 company, 8th batt., landed
       at Lisbon, August 1808 125
    5. Captain J. May's No. 2 company, 1st batt., landed
       at Lisbon, March 1809 127
    6. Captain F. Glubb's No. 10 company, 5th batt., landed
       at Lisbon, March 1809 93
    7. Captain R. Lawson's No. 7 company, 8th batt., landed
       at Lisbon, August 1808 66
(c) K.G.L. Artillery :
    1. Captain Tieling's Company (No. 2).
    2. Captain Heise's Company (No. 4).

On taking up the command, General Howorth, with Colonel Robe's assistance, equipped five brigades of guns to take the field with the army,

---

[1] On arrival in Portugal, No. 6 company, 7th batt., was under 2nd Captain H. B. Lane ; Captain C. D. Sillery joined shortly after the occupation of Oporto.

viz. one brigade of heavy six-pounders, three brigades of light six-pounders, and one brigade of three-pounders. Captain Glubb's company was stationed in Fort St. Julian, Lisbon, and Captain Bredin's in the Forts at Cascaes. The other companies were with the field army.

BRIGADES R.A. AT OPORTO.

Captain C. D. Sillery's No. 6 company, 7th batt., under 2nd Captain H. B. Lane. Light six-pounder guns.

Captain R. Lawson's No. 7 company, 8th batt. Three-pounder guns.

Captain Tieling's No. 2 company, K.G.L., under 2nd Captain de Rettberg. Heavy six-pounder guns.

Captain Heise's No. 4 company, K.G.L. Light six-pounder guns.

[Captain May's brigade was detached with Mackenzie's force at Abrantes.]

BRIGADES R.A. AT TALAVERA.

Captain C. D. Sillery's No. 6 company, 7th batt. Light six-pounder guns.

Captain J. May's No. 2 company, 1st batt., under 2nd Captain W. G. Elliott. Light six-pounder guns.

Captain R. Lawson's No. 7 company, 8th batt. Three-pounder guns.

Captain Tieling's No. 2 company, K.G.L., under 2nd Captain de Rettberg. Heavy six-pounder guns.

Captain Heise's No. 4 company, K.G.L. Light six-pounder guns.

CASUALTIES AT TALAVERA.

Killed : Lieut. H. Wyatt and seven men ; wounded : Lieut.-Colonel H. Framingham, 2nd Captain H. Baynes and J. Taylor and twenty-one men, R.A.

K.G.L., killed : three men ; wounded : thirty men.

In December 1809 the strength of the Royal Artillery under General Howorth was as follows, viz. :
R.H.A., 187 of all ranks, with 106 drivers attached.
Foot Artillery, 627 of all ranks, with 545 drivers attached.
K.G.L. 332 of all ranks with 160 drivers.
There were 951 horses, and 132 mules with the Artillery.

XII

VENEGAS'S ARMY OF LA MANCHA

FROM A RETURN OF JUNE 16, 1809.

1st Division, Brigadier-General PEDRO GIRON [afterwards Brigadier-General T. LACY]:
Burgos (two batts.), 1,085, Cuenca, 869, 1st of Loxa, 703, Alcala, 629, 1st of España, 548, 1st of Seville, 593 . . Total 4,427

2nd Division, Brigadier-General GASPAR VIGODET:

Corona (two batts.), 1,130, Ronda, 1,096, Ordenes Militares (two batts.), 836, Alcazar, 825, 1st of Guadix, 522, Ciudad Real, 258 . . . . Total 4,667

3rd Division, Major-General PEDRO GRIMAREST [afterwards Brigadier-General P. GIRON]:

2nd of Jaen, 985, Ecija, 902, 2nd of Cordova, 849, Bailen (two batts.), 1,121, 1st Walloon Guards, 663, Alpujarras, 579, Velez-Malaga, 445 . . . . Total 5,544

4th Division, Brigadier-General FRANCISCO CASTEJON:

5th of Seville, 535, 1st of Malaga, 743, 2nd Spanish Guards, 953, Jerez, 650, 2nd of Loxa, 510, Bujalance, 469, 3rd of Cordova, 422 . . . . Total 4,282

5th Division, Major-General T. ZERAIN:

2nd of España (two batts.), 1,064, 1st of Cordova (three batts.), 2,044, Provincial of Seville, 887 . . . . Total 3,995

CAVALRY:

Montesa, 349, Reina, 183, Granada, 322, España, 287, Farnesio, 404, Santiago, 295, Alcantara, 343, Principe, 324, Granaderos de Fernando VII, 527, Dragones de la Reina, 180, Cazadores de Cordova, 169 . . . . Total 3,384

ARTILLERY : 35 guns ; sappers, five companies, about 1,100 in all.

Total, 27,399, including sick and men on detachment.

INDEX

Albergaria Nova, combat of, 325
Albuquerque, Duke of, attacks Digeon at Mora, 145; his quarrel with Cartaojal, 145; sent to join Cuesta's army, 145, 157; at the battle of Medellin, 159–63; his intrigues against Cuesta, 465; at Talavera, 532, 545; at Oropesa, 583; routed by Soult at Arzobispo, 589–91.
Alcañiz, battle of, 418–20.
Alcantara, sacked by Lapisse, 261; combat of, 440, 441.
Almonacid, battle of, 614–6.
Alorna, Marquis of, raises an 'experimental legion' in the Portuguese army, 210.
Alvarez, Julian, Governor of Gerona, his attempt to relieve Rosas, 51.
Amarante, defended by Silveira, 267–71; captured by Loison, 271; Loison defeated at, 344, 345.
Aranjuez, Venegas at, 568; combat of, 612.
Areizaga, Juan Carlos, general, at Alcañiz, 418; his error at Maria, 431; commands army of Andalusia, 605.
Argenton, captain, his conspiracy against Soult, 279; makes overtures to the English, 284; his first interview with Wellesley, 315; his second visit to Wellesley, 321; his arrest and confession, 322–3; his escape and death, 323.
Arzobispo, combat of, 591.
Astorga, Marquis of, elected President of the Central Junta, 21.
Asturias, Junta and army of, their selfish policy, 370–1; dissolution of the Junta by La Romana, 375, 376; invaded by Ney and Kellermann, 379; evacuated by the French, 387.
Avé, passage of, by Soult, 239.

Badajoz, summoned to surrender by Victor, 168; Wellington retires to, 607.
Ballasteros, Francisco, general, in command at Colombres, 372; escapes from the advancing French, 382; his descent on Santander, 386; driven out by Bonnet, 387.
Barcelona, held by Duhesme against Vives, 41
Barrio, Manuel Garcia, Del, colonel sent by the Central Junta to lead Galician insurgents against Vigo, 263.
Bennett, captain, R. N. at the siege of Rosas, 50, 55, 56.
Beresford, William Carr, general, appointed Commander-in-chief of the Portuguese army, 216; his reorganization of the army, 217, 218; joins Wellesley with ten line regiments, 314; commands flanking column at the advance on Oporto, 318; at Amarante, 344, 345; pursues Soult, 351, 360; his march to Perales and Coria, 599; retires to Castello Branco, 611.
Blake, Joaquin, general, commands in Aragon, 414; wins battle of Alcañiz, 418–20; defeated at Maria, 423–7; at Belchite, 429, 430.
Blanca, Florida, Marquis, President of the Junta, death of, 21.
Bogiero, Padre Basilio, chaplain of Palafox, shot by the French, 139.
Bonnet, general, his advance into Asturias, 382; his pursuit of Ballasteros, 386–7.
Botilho, general, commands Portuguese force on the Minho, 223; opposes Soult's advance, 237.
Bouchard, captain, French engineer officer, his ingenious scheme for crossing the Tamega at Amarante, 270–1.

THE
NAPOLEONIC LIBRARY
Published by Greenhill Books

Sir Charles Oman:
Studies in the Napoleonic Wars

Wellington's Army

F. Loraine Petre:
Napoleon's Campaign in Poland, 1806–1807

Napoleon's Conquest of Prussia, 1806

Napoleon and the Archduke Charles: A History of the Franco-Austrian Campaign in the Valley of the Danube in 1809

Napoleon's Last Campaign in Germany, 1813

Napoleon at Bay, 1814

Jac Weller:
Wellington in India

Wellington in the Peninsula

Wellington at Waterloo

Adventures with the Connaught Rangers, 1809–1814
by William Grattan

A Boy in the Peninsular War
by Robert Blakeney

A British Rifleman:
Journal and Correspondence during the Peninsular War
by Major George Simmons

The Notebooks of Captain Coignet
by Captain Jean-Roche Coignet

The Peninsular Journal, 1808–1817
by Major-General Sir Benjamin D'Urban

Waterloo Letters
Edited by Major-General H. T. Siborne

With the Guns in the Peninsula: The Peninsular War Journal of Captain William Webber
Edited by Richard Henry Wollocombe

OTHER
NAPOLEONIC BOOKS
Published by Greenhill Books

Dictionary of the Napoleonic wars
by David G. Chandler

The Eagle's Last Triumph:
Napoleon's Victory at Ligny, June 1815
by Andrew Uffindell

1812: The March on Moscow
by Paul Britten Austin
Introduction by David G. Chandler

1812: Napoleon in Moscow
by Paul Britten Austin

The Illustrated Napoleon
by David G. Chandler

Military Maxims of Napoleon
Edited and with Introduction and Commentary
by David G. Chandler

On the Napoleonic Wars: Collected Essays
by David G. Chandler

With Eagles to Glory:
Napoleon and his German Allies in the 1809 Campaign
by John H. Gill